EUROPEAN HISTORICAL DICTIONARIES
Edited by Jon Woronoff

Historical Dictionary of Albania

New Edition

Robert Elsie

European Historical Dictionaries, No. 42

The Scarecrow Press, Inc.
Lanham, Maryland, and Oxford
2004

SCARECROW PRESS, INC.

Published in the United States of America
by Scarecrow Press, Inc.
A wholly owned subsidary of
The Rowman & Littlefield Publishing Group, Inc.
4501 Forbes Boulevard, Suite 200, Lanham, Maryland 20706
www.scarecrowpress.com

PO Box 317
Oxford
OX2 9RU, UK

British Library Cataloguing in Publication Information Available

Library of Congress Cataloging-in-Publication Data

Elsie, Robert, 1950–
  Historical dictionary of Albania new edition / Robert Elsie.
    p. cm. — (European historical dictionaries ; no. 42)
  Includes bibliographical references.
  ISBN 0-8108-4872-4 (alk. paper)
  1. Albania—History—Dictionaries. I. Title. II. Series.
DR927 .E44 2004
949.65'003—dc21

                                        2003012238

Contents

Editor's Foreword

Historical dictionaries are useful books for all countries, but they are more essential for some than others. Albania is a case in point. Never particularly well known by outsiders under earlier regimes, it was deliberately closed to the outside world during the communist era. Now, despite increased efforts to enter the international community, Albania remains remote and our knowledge of it is faint. Worse, some of the things we think we know are wrong. For these reasons, this new *Historical Dictionary of Albania* should be particularly welcome.

This volume takes a long view, presenting the various peoples, regimes and rulers who shaped its earlier development and the leaders who now tentatively seek other, more promising directions. It also takes a broad view, covering not only history and politics, but culture and religion, foreign relations, language, economics and social customs. And it adds a further dimension: the Albanians living outside of the country, whether part of an earlier diaspora or cut off by artificial and sometimes contested borders. The introduction, chronology and dictionary entries already give readers a solid grounding on Albania and the Albanians. Those who want to learn more on specific aspects can consult the helpful bibliography.

Not surprisingly, the number of foreigners who know Albania is quite limited, and the number of those who have mustered any "expertise" is even more so. We were, thus, fortunate that this new edition could be written by one of that tiny circle, Robert Elsie. Dr. Elsie, along with extensive studies, has traveled widely in Albania and other places inhabited by Albanians. Over recent decades he has published numerous articles and books on a wide variety of related topics. He has also served as a translator and interpreter of Albanian. Few have gained as much insight into the region and its inhabitants, and even fewer can convey their accumulated knowledge so easily and effectively.

Jon Woronoff
Series Editor

Preface

Compiling a historical dictionary for a whole country, even for a small one like Albania, is a major undertaking. Compiling a historical dictionary for a country as traditionally reclusive as Albania presents even more of a daunting task, in particular since there is still no objective and reliable historiography in Albania upon which such a work can be based. Decades of politically motivated censorship and self-censorship, combined with generations of nationalist thinking, have given rise to many myths and misconceptions. It has been difficult for Albanian historians and scholars to set aside the standard fare of hero glorification and to turn their backs on pompous assertions of national grandeur. Albanian history abounds with myths, which have served to disguise the inferiority complexes of a small and underdeveloped people, but, on the other hand, have also helped to hold the nation together in times of crisis. Poet Dritëro Agolli described Albania as a country which has produced more heroism than grain.

The few foreign historians who have dealt in depth with Albanian history and have published in this field have proven to be more trustworthy, working as they do from an objective distance. Nonetheless, some erroneous claims and naive views still pass from hand to hand. A full-length, comprehensive and reliable history of Albania has yet to be written. The present work does not endeavor to fill the void, but only to offer the reader basic, factual information on the country, its historical development, its current situation and the culture of its people.

The majority of the over 700 entries in this *Historical Dictionary of Albania* are person entries. They comprise not only figures of Albanian history, but also contemporary public figures and political leaders in Albania, as well as individuals, Albanian and foreign, who have made notable contributions to Albanian studies and Albanian culture. Since a large proportion of the material in this dictionary has never appeared in English, it is to be hoped that most readers will discover new information to make the elusive Albanian nation more accessible to them.

The *Historical Dictionary of Albania* thus endeavors to provide a comprehensive overview, not only of Albanian history, but also of contemporary Albania as it enters the 21st century, focusing as it does both on the past and on a modern European nation struggling to put its formidable Stalinist past behind it. It must not be forgotten that, for half a century, Albania was a planet of its own, isolated from the rest of Mother Earth. Since the fall of the communist regime, the Albanians have been striving, not without difficulty, to find their place among the nations of Europe.

A few technical remarks must be made. Users of this volume should note that cross-references in each dictionary entry are printed in boldface type. The dates given at the start of person entries for births and deaths are provided here in the year/month/day system, which is used, for instance, by the Canadian government to avoid confusion between the international day/month/year system and the month/day/year system widely followed in the United States. The entries are listed according to the English alphabet, not the Albanian alphabet, which treats *ç, dh, ë, gj, ll, nj, rr, sh, th, xh* and *zh* as separate letters. Albanian nouns and place names often cause confusion because they can be written with or without the postpositive definite article, e.g., Tirana vs Tiranë and Elbasani vs Elbasan. In line with recommended international usage for Albanian toponyms, feminine place names appear here in the definite form, and masculine place names in the indefinite form, thus: Tirana, Vlora, Prishtina and Shkodra rather than Tiranë, Vlorë, Prishtinë and Shkodër; and Elbasan, Durrës and Prizren rather than Elbasani, Durrësi and Prizreni. Exceptions are made for tribal designations and regions for which English forms such as Hoti, Kelmendi and Shkreli are better known. In this connection, reference is made to political leader Ahmet Zogu, but when he became king of Albania, to King Zog, in line with common usage. Finally, preference has been given here to the Albanian form Kosova over the traditional Kosovo. English usage of eastern European toponyms is in flux at the moment, and now that Byelorussia has become Belarus and Moldavia has become Moldova, there is no reason why the traditional Serb form Kosovo should not be replaced by Kosova, as a sign of respect for the long-suffering majority population there.

There are many people to be thanked for their assistance in the compilation of this book. I would like to express my particular gratitude to Peter Bartl of Munich and Michael Schmidt-Neke of Kiel in Germany, upon whose works I have relied extensively for the early twentieth century period. Bejtullah Destani and David Smiley of London put much useful material at my disposal and Maksim Gjinaj of the National Library in Tirana assisted me, as ever, with dates and details. Other sources are given in the bibliography. My thanks go, in particular, to Janice Mathie-Heck of Calgary, Alberta, for her kind revision of the manuscript.

Robert Elsie
Olzheim / Eifel, Germany

Abbreviations and Acronyms

AACL	Albanian-American Civic League
AANO	Albanian-American National Organization
AD	Aleanca Demokratike (Democratic Alliance)
APC	Albanian Communist Party
AVC	American Vocational School
BBC	British Broadcasting Corporation
BF	Bashkimi për Fitore (Union for Victory)
CSCE	Conference for Security and Cooperation in Europe
DBSH	E Djathta e Bashkuar Shqiptare (United Albanian Right)
EU	European Union
FAC	Free Albania Committee
FRESSH	Forumi i Rinisë Eurosocialiste Shqiptare (Forum of Albanian Euro-Socialist Youth)
FYROM	Former Yugoslav Republic of Macedonia
KESH	Korporata Elektroenergjetike Shqiptare (Albanian Electrical Energy Corporation)
KLA	Kosova Liberation Army
KONARE	Komiteti Nacional Revolucionar (National Revolutionary Committee)
kV	kilovolt
kWh	kilowatt-hours
LDK	Lidhja Demokratike e Kosovës (Democratic League of Kosova)
MW	megawatt
NAAC	National Albanian American Council
NATO	North Atlantic Treaty Organization
OSCE	Organization for Security and Cooperation in Europe
PAD	Partia Aleanca Demokratike (Democratic Alliance Party)
PALSH	Partia Alternativa Liberale Shqiptare (Albanian Liberal Alternative Party)
PASH	Partia Agrare Shqiptare (Albanian Agrarian Party)
PBD	Partia Bashkimi Demokratik (Democratic Union Party)
PBDKSH	Partia Bashkimi Demokristian Shqiptar (Albanian Christian Democratic Union Party)

PBDNJ	Partia Bashkimi për të Drejtat e Njeriut (Union for Human Rights Party)
PBK	Partia Balli Kombëtar (National Front Party)
PBKD	Partia Balli Kombetar Demokrat (Democratic National Front Party)
PBKSH	Partia Bashkësia Kombëtare Shqiptare (Albanian National Unity Party)
PBKSH	Partia e Bashkuar Komuniste Shqiptare (United Albanian Communist Party)
PBL	Partia Bashkimi Liberal (Liberal Union Party)
PBRSH	Partia Bashkimi Republikan Shqiptar (Albanian Republican Union Party)
PBSD	Partia Bashkimi Socialdemokrat (Social Democratic Union Party)
PBSH	Partia e Biznesit Shqiptar (Albanian Business Party)
PD	Partia Demokratike (Democratic Party)
PDD	Partia e Djathtë Demokrate (Democratic Right Party)
PDK	Partia Demokristiane e Shqipërisë (Christian Democratic Party of Albania)
PDR	Partia Demokratike e Re (New Democratic Party)
PDSH	Partia Demokratike e Shqipërisë (Democratic Party of Albania)
PESH	Partia e Emigracionit Shqiptar (Albanian Emigration Party)
PFA	Partia Forca Albania (Forca Albania Party)
PKONS	Partia Konservatore (Conservative Party)
PKSH	Partia Komuniste Shqiptare (Albanian Communist Party)
PLD	Partia Lëvizja për Demokraci (Movement for Democracy Party)
PLFSH	Partia Lidhja Fshatare Shqiptare (Albanian Rural League Party)
PLL	Partia Lëvizja e Legalitetit (Movement for Legality Party)
PL Mona.	Partia Lëvizja Monarkiste Demokrate Shqiptare (Albanian Democratic Monarchist Movement Party)
PLPSH	Partia Lëvizja Punëtore Shqiptare (Albanian Labor Movement Party)
PMP	Partia e Mirëqenies Popullore (People's Welfare Party)
PPD	Partia Progresi Demokratik (Democratic Progress Party)
PPK	Partia e Pajtimit Kombëtar Shqiptar (Albanian National Reconciliation Party)

PPSH	Partia e Punës e Shqipërisë (Party of Labor of Albania)
PRDSH	Partia Reformatore Demokratike Shqiptare (Albanian Democratic Reform Party)
PRSH	Partia Republikane Shqiptare (Albanian Republican Party)
PSDSH	Partia Socialdemokrate e Shqipërisë (Social Democratic Party of Albania)
PSHA	Partia Shqiptare Ambientaliste (Albanian Environmentalist Party)
PSKSH	Partia Socialkristiane Shqiptare (Albanian Social Christian Party)
PSSH	Partia Socialiste e Shqiperisë (Socialist Party of Albania)
PUKSH	Partia e Unitetit Kombëtar Shqiptar (Albanian National Unity Party)
SHIK	Shërbimi Informativ Kombetar (National Information Service)
SHISH	Shërbimi Informativ Shtetëror (State Information Service)
SOE	Special Operations Executive
TOB	Teatri i Operas dhe Baletit (Opera and Ballet Theater)
UÇK	Ushtria Çlirimtare e Kosovës (Kosova Liberation Army)
UÇK	Ushtria Çlirimtare Kombëtare (National Liberation Army) in Macedonia
UCLA	University of California in Los Angeles
UÇPMB	Ushtria Çlirimtare e Preshevës, Medvegjës e Bujanovcit (Liberation Army of Presheva, Medvegja and Bujanovc)
UNDP	United Nations Development Program
UNESCO	United Nations Education, Scientific, and Cultural Organization
UNRRA	United Nations Relief and Rehabilitation Administration
VOA	Voice of America

List of Albanian Heads of State and Government

Heads of State

1912-1914	Ismail Qemal bey Vlora, acting head of state
1914	Prince Wilhelm zu Wied
1914-1916	Essad bey Toptani, president of the provisional government
1918-1924	Turgut Pasha
1925-1928	Ahmet bey Zogu, president
1929-1939	King Zog I
1939-1943	King Vittorio Emanuele III (Albania under Italian occupation)
1946-1953	Omer Nishani, chairman of the Presidium of the People's Assembly
1953-1982	Haxhi Lleshi, chairman of the Presidium of the People's Assembly
1982-1991	Ramiz Alia, chairman of the Presidium of the People's Assembly
1991-1992	Ramiz Alia, president
1992-1997	Sali Berisha, president
1997-2002	Rexhep Meidani, president
2002	Alfred Moisiu, president

Heads of Government

1912-1914	Ismail Qemal bey Vlora, chairman of the provisional government and acting head of state
1914	Turhan Pasha Përmeti, prime minister
1914-1916	Essad bey Toptani, president of the provisional Albanian government
1918-1920	Turhan Pasha Përmeti, prime minister (2nd time)
1920	Sulejman bey Delvina, prime minister
1920-1921	Iljaz bey Vrioni, prime minister
1921	Pandeli Evangjeli, prime minister
1921	Qazim Koculi, prime minister
1921	Hasan bey Prishtina, prime minister
1921	Idhomene Kosturi, prime minister

1921-1922   Xhafer bey Ypi, prime minister
1922-1924   Ahmet bey Zogolli (Ahmet bey Zogu), prime minister
1924   Shefqet bey Vërlaci, prime minister
1924   Iljaz bey Vrioni, prime minister (2nd time)
1924   Fan S. Noli, prime minister
1924-1925   Iljaz bey Vrioni, prime minister (3rd time)
1925   Ahmet bey Zogu, styled savior of the nation
1925-1928   Ahmet bey Zogu, president and head of government
1928-1930   Kostaq Kota, prime minister
1930-1935   Pandeli Evangjeli, prime minister (2nd time)
1935-1936   Mehdi bey Frashëri, prime minister
1936-1939   Kostaq Kota, prime minister (2nd time)
1939-1941   Shefqet bey Vërlaci, prime minister (2nd time)
1941-1943   Mustafa Merlika-Kruja, prime minister
1943   Eqrem bey Libohova, prime minister
1943   Maliq bey Bushati, prime minister
1943   Eqrem bey Libohova, prime minister (2nd time)
1943-1944   Rexhep bey Mitrovica, prime minister
1944   Fiqri bey Dine, prime minister
1944   Ibrahim bey Biçaku, prime minister
1944-1954   Enver Hoxha, chairman of the Council of Ministers
1954-1981   Mehmet Shehu, chairman of the Council of Ministers
1982-1991   Adil Çarçani, chairman of the Council of Ministers
1991   Fatos Nano, chairman of the Council of Ministers
            (2 times)
1991   Ylli Bufi, chairman of the Council of Ministers
1991-1992   Vilson Ahmeti, chairman of the Council of Ministers
1992-1997   Aleksandër Meksi, prime minister (2 times)
1997   Bashkim Fino, prime minister
1997-1998   Fatos Nano, prime minister (3rd time)
1998-1999   Pandeli Majko, prime minister
1999-2002   Ilir Meta, prime minister (2 times)
2002   Pandeli Majko, prime minister (2nd time)
2002   Fatos Nano, prime minister (4th time)

List of Albanian Political Parties and Organizations

Akademia e Shkencave e Republikës së Shqipërisë: *Academy of Sciences of the Republic of Albania*
Aleanca për Shtetin: *Alliance for the State*
Bashkimi për Demokraci: *Union for Democracy*
Bashkimi për Fitore (BF): *Union for Victory*
E Djathta e Bashkuar Shiqptare (DBSH): *United Albanian Right*
Fronti Demokratik i Shqipërisë: *Democratic Front of Albania*
Lëvizja për Demokraci: *Movement for Democracy*
Lidhja Demokratike e Kosovë (LDK): *Democratic League of Kosova*
Lidhja e Shkrimtarëve dhe e Artistëve të Shqipërisë: *Union of Writers and Artists of Albania*
Partia Agrare Shqiptare (PASH): *Albanian Agrarian Party*
Partia Aleanca Demokratike (PAD): *Democratic Alliance Party*
Partia Alternativa Liberale Shqiptare (PALSH): *Albanian Liberal Alternative Party*
Partia Balli Kombëtar (PBK): *National Front Party*
Partia Balli Kombetar Demokrat (PBKD): *Democratic National Front Party*
Partia Bashkësia Kombëtare Shqiptare (PBKSH): *Albanian National Unity Party*
Partia Bashkimi Demokratik (PBD): *Democratic Union Party*
Partia Bashkimi Demokristian Shqiptar (PBDKSH): *Albanian Christian Democratic Union Party*
Partia Bashkimi për të Drejtat e Njeriut (PBDNJ): *Union for Human Rights Party*
Partia Bashkimi Liberal (PBL): *Liberal Union Party*
Partia Bashkimi Republikan Shqiptar (PBRSH): *Albanian Republican Union Party*
Partia Bashkimi Socialdemokrat (PBSD): *Social Democratic Union Party*
Partia e Bashkuar Komuniste Shqiptare (PBKSH): *United Albanian Communist Party*
Partia e Biznesit Shqiptar (PBSH): *Albanian Business Party*
Partia Demokrate (PD): *Democrat Party*
Partia Demokratike e Re (PDR): *New Democratic Party*

Partia Demokratike e Shqipërisë (PDSH): *Democratic Party of Albania*
Partia Demokristiane e Shqipërisë (PDK): *Christian Democratic Party of Albania*
Partia e Djathtë Demokrate (PDD): *Democratic Right Party*
Partia e Emigracionit Shqiptar (PESH): *Albanian Emigration Party*
Partia Forca Albania (PFA): *Forca Albania Party*
Partia Komuniste Shqiptare (PKSH): *Albanian Communist Party*
Partia Konservatore (PKONS): *Conservative Party*
Partia Lëvizja për Demokraci (PLD): *Movement for Democracy Party*
Partia Lëvizja e Legalitetit (PLL): *Movement for Legality Party*
Partia Lëvizja Monarkiste Demokrate Shqiptare (PL Mona.): *Albanian Democratic Monarchist Party*
Partia Lëvizja Punëtore Shqiptare (PLPSH): *Albanian Labor Movement Party*
Partia Lidhja Fshatare Shqiptare (PLFSH): *Albanian Peasant League Party*
Partia e Mirëqenies Popullore (PMP): *People's Welfare Party*
Partia e Pajtimit Kombëtar Shqiptar (PPK): *Albanian National Reconciliation Party*
Partia Progresi Demokratik (PPD): *Democratic Progress Party*
Partia e Punës e Shqipërisë (PPSH): *Party of Labor of Albania*
Partia Reformatore Demokratike Shqiptare (PRDSH): *Albanian Democratic Reform Party*
Partia Republikane Shqiptare (PRSH): *Albanian Republican Party*
Partia Shqiptare Ambientaliste (PSHA): *Albanian Environmentalist Party*
Partia Socialdemokrate e Shqipërisë (PSDSH): *Social Democratic Party of Albania*
Partia Socialiste e Shqipërisë (PSSH): *Socialist Party of Albania*
Partia Socialkristiane Shqiptare (PSKSH): *Albanian Social Christian Party*
Partia e Unitetit Kombëtar Shqiptar (PUKSH): *Albanian National Unity Party*

Chronology

Early Albania (to 1416)

7th cent. B.C.	Greek colonization of Epidamnos (Durrës) and Apollonia.
272 B.C	Death of Pyrrhus, king of the Molossi, in Epirus.
229 B.C.	Rome declares war on Illyria and sends military forces to the Balkans for the first time. Durrës comes under Roman protection.
227 B.C.	Illyrian queen Teuta of Lezha surrenders to Roman forces.
168 B.C.	Roman forces vanquish Genthius, the last Illyrian king of Shkodra.
48 B.C.	Naval battle between Julius Caesar and Pompey off the coast of Durrës during the first Roman civil war.
395 A.D.	Illyricum is divided between east and west. The provinces of Moesia, Dardania and Epirus become part of the Byzantine Empire.
ca. 600 A.D.	Slavic invasion and settlement of Albania.
851	Bulgarian invasion of Albania.
1018	Expulsion of the Bulgarians and restoration of Byzantine rule.
1038	First reference to the existence of the Albanians by Byzantine historian Michael Attaleiates.
1043	Shkodra is conquered by the Slavic rulers of Montenegrin Zeta.
1054	Albanian territory is divided by the great schism between western Roman Catholicism and eastern Byzantine Orthodoxy.
1081-1085	Norman reign in Albania. Robert Guiscard de Hauteville, Duke of Apulia (r. 1057-1085), lays siege to Durrës in 1081 and defeats the Byzantine emperor there.
1096	Armies of the First Crusade pass through and devastate Albania.
1180	Shkodra is taken over by the Serb dynasty of Stephen Nemanja.

1190	Founding of the medieval state of Arbanon with its capital in Kruja.
1204	Arbanon attains full, though temporary, political independence after the pillage of Constantinople during the Fourth Crusade.
1205	Venetian forces take possession of Durrës.
1248	Monks of the Franciscan Order arrive in Albania.
1257	Reference by Byzantine historian George Acropolites to an Albanian uprising.
1267	Severe earthquake in Durrës recorded by Byzantine historian George Pachymeres.
1272	Charles of Anjou (1226-1285), having landed in Vlora in 1269, proclaims the kingdom of Albania (*regnum Albaniae*).
1285	Earliest reference to the Albanian language, in Dubrovnik.
1308	"Anonymous Description of Eastern Europe," containing an account of Albania.
1322	Irish monk Simon Fitzsimmons visits Albania.
1332	*Directorium ad passagium faciendum* (Directive for Making the Passage), containing a detailed description of Albania.
1343-1355	Serb reign in Albania under Stephan Dushan.
1359-1388	Reign of Charles Thopia as prince of Albania (*princeps Albaniae*).
1385	18 September: the Battle of Savra marks the beginning of Turkish involvement in Albania.
1389	28 June: the Turks defeat a coalition of Balkan forces under Serbian leadership at the Battle of Kosovo Polje and establish themselves as masters of the Balkans.
1392	Durrës is conquered by the Venetians.
1393	Shkodra is overrun by the Turks.
1396	Shkodra is reconquered by the Venetians.
1405	Birth of Scanderbeg.

Albania in the Ottoman Empire (1415-1912)

1415	Fortress of Kruja is conquered by the Turks.
1417	Vlora, Kanina and Berat are conquered by the Turks.
1419	Gjirokastra is conquered by the Turks.

1431	Founding of the Ottoman sandjak of Albania (*Sancak-i Arnavid*).
1432	George Arianiti begins his uprising against the Turks.
1438	Scanderbeg is appointed military commander of the fortress of Kruja.
1443-1468	Uprising of Scanderbeg.
1448	Albanian refugees begin settling in southern Italy.
1462	Baptismal formula is recorded in Albanian.
1466	Sultan Mehmet reconstructs the fortress of Elbasan.
1468	17 January: death of Scanderbeg.
1478	Kruja falls to the Turks.
1479	January: Shkodra falls to the Turks after a long siege.
1492	Construction of the Sultan Mosque of Berat.
1495	Construction of the Mirahor Mosque of Korça.
1497	Pilgrimage of Arnold von Harff, with a description of Durrës and a recording of the Albanian language.
1501	Durrës falls to the Turks.
1504	Shkodra historian Marinus Barletius publishes his *De obsidione Scodrensi* (On the Siege of Shkodra).
1515	Chronicle of John Musachi.
1531	Sultan Suleyman the Magnificent constructs a fortress in Vlora.
1532-1533	Albanians in the Morea (Peloponnese) flee to Italy after Turkish encroachments.
1537-1542	Construction of the Murad Mosque of Vlora.
1555	The missal of Gjon Buzuku, the first Albanian-language book.
1591	Journey of Venetian ambassador Lorenzo Bernardo through Albania.
1592	Albanian-language "Christian Doctrine" written by Italo-Albanian priest Leke Matrënga.
1610	Visit to northern Albania by Marino Bizzi, Catholic archbishop of Bar.
1614	Description of the Sandjak of Shkodra, including Kelmendi territory, by Italian diplomat Mariano Bolizza.
1618	Albanian-language "Christian Doctrine" written by Pjetër Budi.
1621	Pjetër Budi, Catholic bishop of Sapa and Sarda in northern Albania, calls for an uprising against the Turks.

1635	Latin-Albanian dictionary is published by Frang Bardhi.
1670	Turkish traveler Evliya Çelebi visits southern Albania.
1685	Albanian-language *Cuneus Prophetarum* is published by Pjeter Bogdani.
1703	14-15 January: Albanian Council (*Kuvendi i Arbënit*) is held near Lezha.
1716	Francesco Maria da Lecce publishes the first Albanian grammar.
1725	The earliest Albanian-language poem written in Arabic script, by Muçi Zade.
1731	Nezim Frakulla prepares his Albanian-language divan of poems.
1732	Founding of the Corsini Seminary in San Benedetto Ullano in Calabria.
1740	Gjon Nikollë Kazazi discovers Buzuku's *Meshari* in Rome.
1744	Founding of the Orthodox New Academy or *Hellênikon Frontistêrion* as a center of learning in Voskopoja.
1744-1746	Albanian settlement in Villa Badessa near Pescara in Italy.
1757-1775	Dynasty of Mehmed Bushatlliu, Pasha of Shkodra.
1762	Giulio Variboba from Calabria publishes his Albanian-language "Life of the Virgin Mary."
1773-1774	Construction of the Lead Mosque of Shkodra.
1774	Albanian settlement in Brindisi di Montagna near Potenza in Italy.
1777	Nicola Chetta of Palermo in Sicily composes the first Albanian sonnet.
1778-1796	Reign of Kara Mahmud, Pasha of Shkodra, in northern Albania.
1787-1822	Reign of Ali Pasha Tepelena, the Lion of Janina, in southern Albania and Epirus.
1793-1794	Construction of the Et'hem Bey Mosque in Tirana.
1811-1832	Reign of Mustafa Pasha Bushatlliu of Shkodra.
1822	5 February: death of Ali Pasha Tepelena in Janina.
1827	Publication of a bilingual Albanian-Greek edition of the New Testament in Corfu.
1836	Girolamo De Rada publishes the first edition of his best-known Albanian-language poem, the "Songs of Milosao."

1839	3 November: beginning of Tanzimat reform in the Ottoman Empire. Resistance in Albania to compulsory military service.
1845	Publication of Naum Veqilharxhi's "Very New Albanian Spelling Book for Elementary Schoolboys."
1848	Publication in Naples of *l'Albanese d'Italia*, the first Albanian newspaper.
1854	Publication of *Albanesische Studien* (Albanian Studies) by Johann Georg von Hahn, father of Albanian studies.
1855	Founding of the Franciscan school in Shkodra, the first school in which Albanian was taught.
1859	Opening by the Jesuits of the Albanian Pontifical Seminary (*Kolegjia Papnore Shqyptare*) in Shkodra.
1861	Founding of a Franciscan seminary in Shkodra.
1872	Kostandin Kristoforidhi translates the New Testament into Gheg dialect.
1876	2 July: Serbia and Montenegro declare war on Turkey.
1877	Founding of the College of St. Francis Xavier, also known as the Saverian College (*Kolegja Saveriane*), in Shkodra.
	December: founding of the *Komitet qendror për mbrojtjen e të drejtave të kombësisë shqiptare* (Central Committee for the Defense of the Rights of the Albanian People) in Constantinople.
1878	Pashko Vasa writes his stirring nationalist poem *O moj Shqypni* (Oh Albania, poor Albania).
	3 March: Treaty of San Stefano.
	10 June: founding of the League of Prizren.
	13 June - 13 July: Congress of Berlin.
1881	Turkish forces occupy Prizren and disperse the League of Prizren.
1883	Girolamo De Rada founds the bilingual monthly journal *Fiàmuri Arbërit—La bandiera dell'Albania* (The Albanian Flag).
1884	August: Albanian-language periodical *Drita* (The Light) published in Istanbul.
1886	Naim bey Frashëri publishes his verse collection, *Bagëti e bujqësija* (Bucolics and Georgics).
1887	7 March: opening of the first Albanian-language school, in Korça.
1891	First Albanian girls' school founded in Korça.

1899	Sami bey Frashëri publishes his manifesto, *Shqipëria—ç'ka qënë, ç'është e ç'do të bëhetë?* (Albania—what it was, what it is and what will become of it?).
1899-1900	League of Peja.
1901	Founding of the *Agimi* (The Dawn) cultural society by Ndre and Lazar Mjeda.
1908	February: founding by Fan Noli of the Albanian Autocephalic Orthodox Church in Boston. July: Young Turk revolution. 14-22 November: Congress of Monastir sets forth a common Albanian alphabet.
1909-1912	Uprisings in northern Albania and Kosova.
1909	Founding of the Boston weekly *Dielli* (The Sun) by Fan Noli and Faik bey Konitza. 1 December: opening of the Normal School (*Shkolla Normale*) in Elbasan, Albania's first teacher-training college.
1912	28 April: founding in Boston of the Pan-Albanian *Vatra* (The Hearth) federation. 8 October: beginning of the first Balkan War.

Independent Albania (1912-1944)

1912	28 November: Ismail Qemal bey Vlora declares Albanian independence in Vlora.
1913	22 April: the citadel of Shkodra, the last Turkish stronghold in the Balkans, is abandoned by Ottoman forces. 30 May: end of the first Balkan war and peace treaty in London. 5 July: formation of a provisional government with Ismail Qemal bey Vlora as prime minister. 29 July: Albanian independence is recognized at the Conference of Ambassadors in London. 16 October: Essad Pasha Toptani forms a government in Durrës. 1 November: German Prince Wilhelm zu Wied agrees to accept the Albanian throne.
1914	7 March: arrival of Prince Wilhelm zu Wied in Durrës to take the throne.

1914-1918	World War I. Albania invaded and occupied by seven foreign armies: Austrian, Italian, Greek, Serbian, Montenegrin, French and Bulgarian.
1914	3 September: departure of Prince Wilhelm zu Wied from Albania.
	30 October: Italian troops occupy the island of Sazan.
	26 December: Italian troops occupy Vlora.
1916	Austro-Hungarian troops occupy northern and central Albania.
	The Albanian Literary Commission (*Komisija Letrare Shqype*) set up in Shkodra by the Austro-Hungarian administration.
	10 December: French forces proclaim the autonomous Republic of Korça.
1918	February: end of the autonomous Republic of Korça.
1919	Formation of the Bogdani Theater Company in Shkodra.
	18 January: beginning of the Paris Peace Conference.
	29 July: Tittoni-Venizelos agreement for the partitioning of Albania.
1920	28-31 January: Congress of Lushnja and first genuinely independent Albanian government with its seat in Tirana.
	8 February: Tirana becomes capital of Albania.
	15 May: Kapshtica agreement, by which Greece renounces possession of Korça.
	5 June: beginning of the battle for Vlora.
	13 June: assassination of Essad Pasha Toptani in Paris.
	17 December: Albania, represented by Fan Noli, joins the League of Nations.
1921	Growing conflict between Fan Noli and Ahmet Zogu.
1922	Founding of the Albanian Publishing Society (*Shoqeria botonjesé shqipetaré*) in Cairo, headed by Milo Duçi.
	2 December: Ahmet Zogu becomes prime minister for the first time.
1923	Population census shows 817,460 people in Albania.

	21 November: Fan Noli is consecrated Bishop of Korça and Metropolitan of Durrës.
1924	23 February: Ahmet Zogu is shot and wounded in Tirana.
	20 April: revolutionary Avni Rustemi is shot and killed in Tirana.
	30 April: funeral of Avni Rustemi in Vlora marks the beginning of the Democratic Revolution.
	16 June: Bishop Fan Noli as prime minister officially forms a government.
	24 December: Ahmet Zogu takes over power in Albania in a coup d'état, thus putting an end to the Democratic Revolution.
1925-1939	Albania under Ahmet Zogu, alias King Zog.
1925	21 January: Albania is declared a republic.
	31 January: Ahmet Zogu becomes president of Albania.
	7 March: new Albanian constitution.
	15 March: Albanian national bank founded, with its headquarters in Rome.
	18 July: parliament authorizes territorial concessions to Yugoslavia.
1926	27 November: first Pact of Tirana ensures Italian predominance in Albanian affairs.
1927	22 November: second Pact of Tirana ensures Italian military influence in Albania.
1928	1 September: Ahmet Zogu is proclaimed King of the Albanians.
	1 December: constitution of the Kingdom of Albania (*Mbretnija Shqiptare*).
1930	13 April: law on agrarian reform.
1934	23 June: the Italian fleet pays a visit to Durrës in a show of strength.
1935	14-15 August: anti-Zogist demonstrations in Fier.
1936	19 March: twelve economic and financial agreements and a secret military agreement are signed with Italy.
1937	Gjergj Fishta publishes the definitive edition of his *Lahuta e malcis* (The Highland Lute), a 15,613-line historical verse epic.
	27 April: King Zog marries the Hungarian-American countess Geraldine Apponyi.
1938	28 November: first transmission of Radio Tirana.

1939-1945	World War II.
1939	5 April: Queen Geraldine gives birth to a son, Leka, in Tirana, before the royal family flees to Greece.
	7 April: Italian invasion of Albania.
	12 April: the Albanian parliament offers the crown of Scanderbeg to King Victor Emmanuel III of Italy, thus making the latter King of Albania in "personal union."
	16 April: the Italian ambassador, Francesco Jacomoni di San Savino, is appointed viceroy (Ital. *luogotenente generale*) of Albania.
	23 April: the Albanian Fascist Party (*Partia Fashiste Shqiptare*) is founded as the only legal political organization.
1940	28 October: beginning of the Italian invasion of Greece.
1941	6 April: German troops invade Yugoslavia and Greece.
	12 April: reunification of Kosova with Albania.
	17 May: an assassination attempt is made in Tirana on the life of King Victor Emmanuel III by the young revolutionary, Vasil Llaçi (1922-1941).
	29 June: Greater Albania is proclaimed by Benito Mussolini.
	8 November: creation of the Albanian Communist Party.
1942	16 September: Conference of Peza which proclaims the national liberation struggle.
	November: founding of the *Balli Kombëtar* resistance movement.
1943	1-3 August: communist and nationalist resistance movements agree in Mukja to cooperate.
	8 September: Italy capitulates. Albania is occupied by German troops.
	5 November: the government of Rexhep bey Mitrovica, under German occupation, declares Albania's neutrality in the war.
	21 November: founding of the Legality movement.
1944	24-28 May: antifascist congress of national liberation meets in Përmet.
	2 October - 29 November: German troops evacuate Albania.

Communist Albania (1944-1990)

1944	28 November: communist forces under Enver Hoxha take control of Tirana.
	29 November: last German troops leave Albania.
1945	March: beginning of the open persecution of the Catholic Church.

1944   28 November: communist forces under Enver Hoxha take control of Tirana.
29 November: last German troops leave Albania.
1945   March: beginning of the open persecution of the Catholic Church.
22 March: a special tax of 7,250,000,000 lek, which is imposed on businessmen for supposed war profits, liquidates the middle class in Albania.
29 April: Yugoslavia becomes the first country to recognize the new communist regime.
August: beginning of the agrarian reform.
7 October: first writers' conference and founding under Sejfulla Malëshova of the Albanian Writers' Union.
10 November: establishment of diplomatic relations with the United Kingdom, the United States and the Soviet Union.
2 December: first parliamentary elections under communist rule.
1946   5 January: compulsory military service.
11 January: the People's Republic of Albania is formally established.
17 January: the government closes down all Catholic cultural institutions and begins with the mass arrest of priests.
15 February: nationalization of all Italian companies.
19 February: expulsion from Albania of all non-Albanian priests.
23 June - 2 July: Enver Hoxha pays an official visit to Belgrade.
9 July: treaty on friendship, cooperation and mutual assistance with Yugoslavia.
22 October: Corfu Channel incident.
15 November: the United States mission withdraws from Albania because the new government refuses to recognize prewar agreements between the two countries.
27 November: treaty on a customs union with Yugoslavia.

1947 Implementation of the agrarian reform and state planning for the economy.

10 February: peace treaty with Italy and the return of the island of Sazan.

10 July: Albanian government rejects the Marshall Plan.

14-26 July: Enver Hoxha meets Joseph Stalin in Moscow for the first time. Loan agreement with the Soviet Union.

9 August: introduction of forced labor throughout the country.

28 September: sixteen persons sentenced to death, accused of spying for the United Kingdom and the United States with the intention of overthrowing the regime. Others are sentenced to prison.

7 November: railway line from Durrës to Peqin is inaugurated.

1948-1961 Alliance with the Soviet Union.

1948 28 June: Yugoslavia is expelled from the Cominform after Warsaw conference of communist parties.

30 June: Albania renounces all economic agreements with Yugoslavia.

27 September: a trade and loan agreement is signed with the Soviet Union.

3 October: Koçi Xoxe is fired as deputy prime minister and later denounced as an anti-Marxist, a Trotskyite and Titoist.

8-22 November: first congress of the Albanian communist party, which is renamed the Party of Labor. The pro-Yugoslav faction in the party is eliminated.

1949 1 January: introduction of rationing.

23 February: railway line from Durrës to Tirana is inaugurated.

21 March - 11 April: second meeting between Enver Hoxha and Stalin. A trade and loan agreement is signed with the Soviet Union.

3 May: diplomatic relations with Italy.

11 May: beginning of the trial of Koçi Xoxe and conclusion of the political witch hunts in Albania.

2 June: national assembly approves a two-year plan for 1949-1950.

11 June: Koçi Xoxe is executed.

2 August: anticommunist forces attempt to infiltrate Albania from Greece.

26 August: anticommunist parties in Paris form a National Committee for a Free Albania, headed by Mid'hat bey Frashëri.

October: the third conference of the Albanian Writers' Union introduces Zhdanovism and Soviet literary models.

12 November: Yugoslavia renounces the pact of friendship, cooperation and mutual assistance.

26 November: third meeting between Enver Hoxha and Stalin, in Sukhumi on the Black Sea.

26 November: law on religious communities obliging them to show allegiance to the "people's power."

15 December: the International Court of Justice rules that Albania must pay £843,947 in damages to the United Kingdom as a result of the Corfu Channel incident.

1950   5 January: fourth meeting between Enver Hoxha and Stalin, in Moscow.

11 October: Yugoslavia breaks diplomatic ties with Albania.

21 December: railway line from Peqin to Elbasan is inaugurated.

1951   19 February: a bomb explodes outside the Soviet legation in Tirana. A wave of arrests ensues, and purges in the Party of Labor.

2 April: fifth and last meeting between Enver Hoxha and Stalin, in Moscow.

30 July: law on the statute of the Catholic Church, forcing it to sever all ties with the Vatican.

2 November: three institutes of higher education are established in Tirana: the pedagogical institute, the polytechnic and the agricultural institute.

1952   April: second party congress. Adoption of the first five-year plan (1951-1955).

10 July: New Albania Film Studios open.

1953   5 March: the death of Stalin is commemorated in Albania.

22 December: resumption of diplomatic relations with Yugoslavia.

1954   20 July: Mehmet Shehu becomes prime minister.

1955   Purge of Tuk Jakova and Bedri Spahiu on charges of
                revisionism.
                March: Albania rejects an offer from President
                Eisenhower for US$850,000 in food aid.
                14 May: Albania becomes a founding member of
                the Warsaw Pact.
                18 July: unofficial meeting between Enver Hoxha
                and Nikita Khrushchev.
                14 December: Albania joins the United Nations.
1956-1960   Second five-year plan.
1956   October: Enver Hoxha and Mehmet Shehu travel to
                China.
1957   16 September: founding of the University of Tirana.
1958   8 February: agreement reached with Greece to clear
                mines in the Corfu Channel.
1959   24 April: trial against Catholic priests and laymen in
                Shkodra ends in death sentences.
                25 May-4 June: Nikita Khrushchev visits Albania.
1960   5-8 September: Koço Tashko is expelled from the
                party and Liri Belishova is expelled from the
                Central Committee. Ramiz Alia is appointed
                secretary to the Central Committee.
                10 November-1 December: conference of eighty-
                one communist and workers' parties in Moscow,
                during which Enver Hoxha denounces Khrushchev's
                policies in a speech on 16 November.
1961-1965   Third five-year plan.
1961-1978   Alliance with the People's Republic of China.
1961   2 February: economic, loan and trade agreement
                with China.
                March: the Soviet Union breaks off food aid to
                Albania.
                15-27 May: a number of high-ranking officers are
                tried for plotting against the government.
                9 April: death of King Zog in Suresnes near Paris.
                3 December: rupture of diplomatic relations with the
                Soviet Union, and the beginning of a blockade by
                the Comecon countries.
1962   2 June: the Democratic Front wins 99.99 percent of
                votes in parliamentary elections, with 99.99 percent
                participation.
1964   10-17 January: visit to Albania by Chinese prime
                minister Chou En-lai.

| 1965 | 24 December: party campaign against "bureaucracy." |

1966-1970   Fourth five-year plan.

1966   March: "revolutionization" of Albanian culture in the wake of the Chinese Cultural Revolution which had begun in November 1965. The highest wages are reduced and military ranks are eliminated. Thousands of white-collar workers, including many writers and artists, volunteer to be sent to the countryside to work the land with the peasants.

November: the fifth party congress sets about to intensify class struggle by making manual labor in the production sectors of the economy obligatory for everyone.

1967   6 February: speech by Enver Hoxha in Tirana to revolutionize the country. Beginning of the campaign against religion. All churches and mosques are closed down.

29 April: private gardens are forbidden.

19 July: personal income tax is abolished.

30 November: earthquake in Dibra and Librazhd.

1968   13 September: Albania withdraws from the Warsaw Pact after the Soviet invasion of Czechoslovakia.

1969   April: end of the "revolutionization" campaign in Albania.

1970   25 October: electricity supply is made available to the whole country.

1970   27 October: cooperation agreement between the universities of Tirana and Prishtina.

1971-1975   Fifth five-year plan.

1971   February: the establishment of diplomatic relations between Albania and Yugoslavia brings about a thaw in cultural relations with Kosova.

6 May: diplomatic relations with Greece.

1972   25-26 February: speech by Enver Hoxha in Mat about the leading role of the party.

10 October: founding of the Albanian Academy of Sciences.

19 November: Albania refuses to take part in the Conference for Security and Cooperation in Europe (CSCE) in Helsinki.

20-25 November: Tirana orthography congress approves standard Albanian (*gjuha letrare*) as the unified literary language of Albania and of Albanian speakers in Yugoslavia.

25 December: the eleventh Song Festival is held, which was used as a pretext of the purge of June 1973.

1973   26-28 June: fourth Plenary Session of the Central Committee crushes the "liberal movement." Fadil Paçrami and Todi Lubonja are condemned as deviationists and enemies of the people.

8 December: all villages in the country are linked by telephone.

1974   July-August: purge of Beqir Balluku, Petrit Dume and Hito Çako for allegedly organizing a military coup d'état.

27 November: inauguration of regular flights between Tirana and Beijing.

1975   26-29 May: purge of Abdyl Këlliçi, Koço Theodhosi and Kiço Ngjela at the seventh Congress of the Central Committee for alleged grave "revisionist" mistakes and sabotage of the economy.

23 September: decree on the Albanization of all personal and place names which are not in line with political, ideological and moral guidelines.

1976-1980   Sixth five-year plan.

1976   November: seventh party congress. Enver Hoxha criticizes China.

28 December: constitution of the Socialist People's Republic of Albania.

1977   7 July: article in newspaper *Zëri i Popullit* (The People's Voice) denounces the Chinese "theory of the three worlds" as anti-revolutionary.

18 July: inauguration of regular flights between Tirana and Athens.

1978   7 July: China withdraws its experts and blocks all further economic and military assistance to Albania.

29 July: rupture of the Sino-Albanian alliance.

1979   15 April: severe earthquake in northern Albania causes thirty-five deaths.

1981-1985   Seventh five-year plan.

1981   March-April: uprising in Kosova.

22 November: railway line from Lezha to Shkodra is inaugurated.

18 December: mysterious death of Enver Hoxha's rival Mehmet Shehu.

1982   4 January: Adil Çarçani is appointed prime minister to succeed Mehmet Shehu.

24 February: the Politburo decrees the collectivization of privately owned farm animals.

29 May: purge of the followers of Mehmet Shehu.

22 November: Ramiz Alia takes over as de facto head of state.

1983   24 June: a bomb explodes at the Albanian embassy in Athens.

1985   11 January: railway line from Shkodra to the Montenegrin border crossing Hani i Hotit is inaugurated.

11 April: death of Enver Hoxha, who is succeeded on 13 April by Ramiz Alia.

26 November: railway line between Shkodra and Titograd (Podgorica) is opened for international freight traffic.

1986-1990   Eighth five-year plan.

1987   11 September: diplomatic relations with Canada.

2 October: diplomatic relations with the Federal Republic of Germany.

1990   26 March: anticommunist demonstrations in Kavaja.

9 May: restoration of religious freedom.

11-12 May: United Nations Secretary General Perez de Cuellar visits Albania.

28-31 May: American politicians Tom Lantosh and Joseph DioGuardi visit Albania and are received by Ramiz Alia.

2-3 July: over 5,000 Albanians take refuge in foreign embassies in Tirana and are allowed to leave the country on 13 July.

31 July: resumption of diplomatic relations with the Soviet Union.

15 September: Albania applies for full membership in the CSCE.

24 September: Ramiz Alia visits the United States as part of an Albanian delegation to the United Nations. UN speech on 28 September.

25 October: writer Ismail Kadare seeks and obtains political asylum in France.

1-5 December: Mother Teresa visits Albania and is received by Nexhmije Hoxha.
7 December: beginning of student demonstrations at the University of Tirana.

Modern Albania (from 1990-)

1990	11 December: introduction of political pluralism in Albania. Unrest in Kavaja, then in Shkodra, Elbasan and Durrës. 12 December: founding of the Democratic Party under Sali Berisha.
1991	1 January: the first 3,000 Albanians flee to Greece. 3 January: the Democratic Party holds mass protest meetings in Shkodra and Durrës. 5 January: 202 political prisoners are granted amnesty. The first issue of the opposition newspaper *Rilindja Demokratike* (Democratic Rebirth) appears. 18 January: public prayer at the Et'hem Bey Mosque in Tirana. 6 February: students go on strike, demanding that the name Enver Hoxha be removed from the University of Tirana. 8 February: thousands of young people storm the ferries in Durrës and are driven back by the police. 20 February: the statue of Enver Hoxha is toppled in Tirana during a large demonstration. 22 February: Fatos Nano is appointed prime minister in a short-lived administration. March: some 20,000 Albanians flee by sea to Brindisi in southern Italy. 15 March: diplomatic relations with the United States. 17 March: release of 175 political prisoners. 31 March: first pluralist elections in Albania, in which the communist Party of Labor wins 55.8 percent of the popular vote. 2 April: opposition demonstrations in Shkodra result in deaths and injuries. 25 April: boats and ships in Shkodra, Lezha and Shëngjin are seized by Albanians wanting to get to Italy.

30 April: Ramiz Alia is elected president of the Republic of Albania.

29 May: diplomatic relations with the United Kingdom.

5 June: coalition "stability" government under prime minister Ylli Bufi.

10-13 June: founding of the Socialist Party of Albania from the ranks of the former Party of Labor.

19 June: Albania joins the CSCE.

22 June: U.S. Secretary of State James Baker is given an enthusiastic reception in Tirana.

19 July: the privatization of land and property is legalized.

6-8 August: some 12,500 Albanians flee by boat to Bari in southern Italy (and are deported from 9-12 August).

2 September: the statue of Enver Hoxha is removed from the Enver Hoxha museum, which is now transformed into an international cultural center.

7 September: diplomatic relations with the Vatican.

16 September: Albania signs the CSCE Final Act of Helsinki.

27-29 September: first congress of the Democratic Party confirms Sali Berisha's election as party leader, despite growing opposition within the party.

16 October: Albania joins the International Monetary Fund and the World Bank.

3-7 December: food stocks and shops are plundered, resulting in deaths and injuries when Prime Minister Bufi admits that food supplies are low.

5 December: Nexhmije Hoxha, widow of the communist dictator, is arrested.

1992

25-29 February: food stocks and shops are plundered in Pogradec, Lushnja and Tirana, resulting in several deaths.

22 March: victory of the Democratic Party under Sali Berisha in the general elections.

3 April: Ramiz Alia announces his resignation as president of Albania.

9 April: Sali Berisha becomes president of Albania.

12 April: Aleksandër Meksi becomes prime minister.

6 June: Albania joins the NATO Cooperation Council.

13-20 June: President Berisha visits the United States.

July: thousands of people try to flee the country.

16 July: the communist party is banned.

26 July: local government elections result in heavy losses for the Democratic Party.

12 September: Ramiz Alia is placed under house arrest.

19 September: Democratic Alliance Party is founded from the ranks of the Democratic Party.

1993

8-27 January: trial of Nexhmije Hoxha, who is sentenced to nine years in prison.

25-26 April: Pope John Paul II visits Tirana and Shkodra.

20 July: the Bektashi community holds its sixth congress in Tirana.

30 July: opposition leader Fatos Nano is arrested.

26 December: diplomatic relations with the Republic of Macedonia.

1994

21 March: the editors of opposition newspaper *Koha jonë* (Our Time) are tried and jailed for revealing state secrets.

April-July: tension with Greece.

3 April: opposition leader Fatos Nano is sentenced to twelve years in prison.

10 April: a group of mercenaries from Greece attack an Albanian military post four kilometers inside Albanian territory, killing two soldiers.

20 April: police raid the offices of the Greek minority Omonia organization in connection with the attack on 10 April.

21 May - 2 July: trial of Ramiz Alia and six other members of the communist politburo.

15 August: the trial of five members of Greek minority Omonia organization causes outrage in Greece and a substantial degradation of political relations between the two countries.

6 November: referendum for a new constitution is rejected. Rise of further anti-Berisha sentiment.

1995

29 June: Albania joins the Council of Europe.

12 September: President Berisha visits the White House in Washington.

1996   26 May: the Democratic Party under Sali Berisha wins the parliamentary elections under questionable circumstances.

20 October: local government elections in which the Democratic Party wins 52.5 percent of the popular vote.

28 October: writer Ismail Kadare elected to the Académie Française in Paris.

December: demonstrations demanding the resignation of the government.

3 December: U.S. State Department criticizes the Berisha regime for human rights violations.

17 December: the Sudja pyramid investment company ceases payments to investors, causing violent demonstrations in Tirana.

1997   January: aggravation of the pyramid finance scandal and massive anti-government demonstrations.

21 January: the Xhaferri pyramid investment company announces bankruptcy.

February: political tension throughout the country.

11 February: police lose control of public order in Vlora and withdraw from the town.

1 March: protesters in Vlora burn down the headquarters of Berisha's secret service, the National Information Service.

2 March: parliament imposes martial law.

3 March: Sali Berisha is reelected president to an "orchestra of kalashnikovs," with the country on the brink of civil war.

4 March: press censorship is introduced.

9 March: political parties meet in Tirana in an attempt to solve the crisis.

12 March: rebel forces in Gjirokastra form a National Committee of Public Salvation.

13 March: government of national reconciliation under Bashkim Fino.

14 March: foreign governments begin evacuating their citizens from Albania.

28 March: about 100 Albanian clandestine emigrants die in the Straits of Otranto when their boat is rammed by an Italian corvette and capsizes.

15 April: 6,000 United Nations troops under Italian command land in Durrës to restore order in Operation Alba.

29 June: parliamentary elections result in a victory for the Socialist Party under Fatos Nano, in coalition with two other parties.

23 July: Sali Berisha resigns as president and is replaced by Rexhep Meidani.

25 July: government under Fatos Nano, replacing the administration of Bashkim Fino.

8 August: Kosova Liberation Army publicly assumes responsibility for armed attacks against Serb forces and Albanian collaborators in Kosova.

11 August: Operation Alba is completed with the withdrawal of the last Italian units from Albania.

19 September: controversial political figure Azem Hajdari is shot and wounded, giving rise to demonstrations in Shkodra.

25-28 November: fighting around Skenderaj in Kosova causes several deaths.

1998

22-24 February: public disorder in Shkodra, during which a number of public buildings are burnt down and several dangerous criminals escape from prison. The Tirana government sends in special troops.

1 March: Serb troops begin a major offensive in the Drenica region of Kosova.

9 March: over 200,000 Kosova Albanians demonstrate in Prishtina and are beaten back by the Serb police.

June: thousands of Kosova Albanian refugees flee to Albania.

4 August: massacre of Kosova Albanian civilians in Rahovec. Llausha in the Drenica region is burnt to the ground by Serb forces.

6 August: the Albanian parliament demands immediate NATO intervention in Kosova.

16 August: Serb troops occupy Junik in western Kosova after weeks of combat with the Kosova Liberation Army (KLA).

17-21 August: NATO maneuvers in Albania.

23 August: several politicians of the Democratic Party are placed under arrest for their military involvement in combating rebel forces in March 1997.

This leads to unrest in the following week in Tirana and in the north.

12 September: assassination of Azem Hajdari, leading figure of the Democratic Party.

13 September: severe unrest in Tirana following the Hajdari assassination. Supporters of the Democratic Party make an armed attack on the office of the prime minister after Berisha accuses Nano of personal responsibility for the assassination.

14 September: funeral of Azem Hajdari. His supporters attack government buildings and take over parliament and Albanian radio and television. Government troops take control of the buildings and expel protesters. Albania is once more on the brink of civil war.

16 September: state prosecutor accused Berisha of armed uprising, requesting that his immunity as a member of parliament be rescinded.

18 September: parliament rescinds Berisha's immunity to make him liable for arrest. Large and angry pro-Berisha demonstrations in Tirana.

28 September: Fatos Nano resigns as prime minister and is replaced by Pandeli Majko, also of the Socialist Party.

10 November: unrest in Shkodra following the arrest of several members of the Democratic Party.

22 November: a new constitution is approved by ninety percent of the voting electorate.

15 December: Sali Berisha is charged with armed insurrection as a result of the events of 13-14 September.

24-27 December: Serb offensive in Podujeva. KLA offers a cease-fire.

1999

15 January: massacre by the Serb police of forty-five Kosova Albanian civilians in Reçak causes international outrage.

6 February: beginning of the Rambouillet conference to avoid full-scale war in Kosova.

24 March - 9 June: NATO military campaign in Yugoslavia. Half a million Kosova Albanians seek refuge in Albania after being expelled by Serb forces.

27 May: Serb leader Slobodan Milošević is accused of genocide and war crimes by International Court of Justice in The Hague.

12 June: NATO forces enter and liberate Kosova.

13 August: Prime Minister Pandeli Majko visits Kosova in a private capacity.

29 October: Pandeli Majko resigns as prime minister and is replaced by Ilir Meta.

22 December: Prime Minister Ilir Meta visits Greece to discuss the legalization of Albanian emigrants and to bring up the issue of Çamëria.

2000   24 February: the border crossing to Montenegro at Hani i Hotit is reopened after two years.

4 April: Albania signs the European Human Rights Convention against capital punishment.

24 May: President Rexhep Meidani visits Kosova.

17 July: Albania joins the World Trade Organization.

2 August: the chief of police in Shkodra, Arben Zylyftari, is shot dead.

1 October: local government elections result in a victory for the Socialist Party, with 42.9 percent of the popular vote. Edi Rama is elected mayor of Tirana.

2001   2 February: the New Democratic Party under Genc Pollo is created from the ranks of the Democratic Party of Sali Berisha.

17 January: Albania and Yugoslavia resume diplomatic relations.

20 February: fighting in Macedonia between Albanian guerrillas and Macedonian government forces.

14 March: fighting in Macedonia spreads to the center of Tetova.

17 March: the National Liberation Army of Macedonia calls on all Albanians there to join its struggle.

15 May: serious fighting flares up in the Presheva valley between Yugoslav forces and the Liberation Army of Presheva, Medvegja and Bujanovc.

24 June: parliamentary elections in Albania give the lead to the Socialist Party coalition over the opposition Union for Victory. The elections were subsequently criticized in an OSCE report on 11 October.

13 August: the Ohrid Peace Agreement is signed, putting an official end to the armed conflict in Macedonia.

27 August: beginning of the Essential Harvest operation in Macedonia to collect weapon from Albanian rebels.

16 November: the Macedonian parliament approves a constitutional reform making Albanian the second official language of Macedonia.

17 November: the Democratic League of Kosova (LDK) wins the first parliamentary elections in Kosova.

2002

29 January: Prime Minister Ilir Meta resigns to give way to pressure from Socialist Party leader Fatos Nano.

31 January: the opposition alliance Union for Victory abandons its boycott and returns to parliament.

7 February: Pandeli Majko once again becomes prime minister of Albania.

20 March: controversial state prosecutor, Albert Rakipi, is relieved of his duties by parliament.

6 April: Prime Minister Majko pays an official visit to Kosova.

29 April: a Tirana court sentences Jaho Mulosmani (Salihi) to life in prison for the murder of Azem Hajdari on 12 September 1998.

24 June: Alfred Moisiu becomes president of Albania.

28 June: the former royal family, including pretender Leka Zogu and his mother Queen Geraldine, widow of King Zog, return to Albania to take up permanent residence.

24 July: President Rexhep Meidani retires from office, making way for new President Alfred Moisiu.

24 July: Pandeli Majko resigns as prime minister and is replaced by Fatos Nano.

29 July: fourth government cabinet under Fatos Nano, with Ilir Meta as foreign minister and deputy prime minister, Pandeli Majko as minister of defense, and Kastriot Islami as minister of finance.

7 August: Fatos Klosi resigns as head of the secret service and is accused of corruption.

2 September: Prime Minister Fatos Nano meets Yugoslav President Vojeslav Koštunica in Johannesburg and the two agree to exchange ambassadors.
20 September: trade agreement with Yugoslavia.
21 October: agreement with European Union foreign ministers for the start of negotiations on an Albania-EU association agreement.
22 October: former Queen Geraldine dies in Tirana.
26 November: Foreign Minister Ilir Meta signs several agreements in Belgrade on travel and trade relations with Yugoslavia.
28 November: commemoration of the ninetieth anniversary of Albanian independence.

Introduction

Albania is a small country in southeastern Europe. It is situated on the coast of the Mediterranean Sea in the southwestern part of the Balkan Peninsula and borders on Montenegro to the north, Kosova to the northeast, Macedonia (FYROM) to the east, and Greece to the south. To the west of Albania, across the sea, is the southeastern coast of Italy. Albania is a primarily mountainous country with a Mediterranean climate—hot, dry summers and temperate winters, although it can be cold in the winter months in inland regions and at upper altitudes.

Albania has a population of about three million people, all of whom speak Albanian, an Indo-European language. There are also several, mostly bilingual ethnic minorities, notably of Greeks in the south of the country, but also small groups of Slavs, Roma and Vlachs. As to traditional religious identification, about seventy percent of the population is Muslim, about twenty percent is Albanian Orthodox and about ten percent, in the north, is Roman Catholic. There is also a sizable community of Bektashi, a liberal Islamic sect.

With regard to the territory traditionally settled by the Albanian people, only about half of the Albanians live within the borders of the Republic of Albania itself. The other half live in the surrounding countries, primarily in Kosova, which has about two million Albanians, and in Macedonia, which has about half a million Albanians. Aside from small Albanian-speaking minorities in southern Italy and Greece who settled there centuries ago, there are now also large emigrant communities who left Albania in the 1990s in search of jobs and a better life. Most of these Albanian emigrants have settled in Greece and Italy, legally or illegally, though Albanian emigrants are now to be found throughout Europe and in many other parts of the globe.

The Republic of Albania is by far the poorest and most underdeveloped country in Europe. Although situated on a prosperous continent and very near to countries like Italy and Greece, which have vastly higher standards of living, Albania is, in fact, a third-world country and suffers from all the problems which the poor and underdeveloped countries of Africa, Latin America and Asia suffer.

Historical Development

The southwestern Balkans, along the Adriatic coast, were known in ancient times as Illyria and were inhabited by Balkan tribes such as the Illyrians. Whether the Albanians are direct descendants of the ancient Illyrians is difficult to ascertain because too little is known about the Illyrian language. It can, however, be assumed that the ancestors of the Albanians were living in the southern part of the Balkan peninsula long before the Slavic invasions of the sixth and seventh centuries A.D., and an affiliation with the Illyrians would seem logical.

Geographically, Albania has always been at the crossroads of empires and civilizations, even though it has often been isolated from the mainstream of European history. For centuries in ancient times, it formed the political, military and cultural border between East and West, i.e., between the Roman Empire of the western Mediterranean including much of the northern Balkans, and the Greek Empire of the eastern Mediterranean including the southern Balkans. In the Middle Ages, Albania was once again a buffer zone, this time between Catholic Italy and the Byzantine Greek Empire. Later, after its definitive conquest by the Ottoman Empire in the fifteenth century, it formed a bridgehead between Christian Europe and the Islamic Orient.

As a people, the Albanians first emerged from the mist of history in the early years of the second millennium A.D. Their traditional designation, based on a root *alban- and its rhotacized variants *arban-, *albar- and *arbar-, first appears from the eleventh century onwards in Byzantine chronicles as Albanoi, Arbanitai and Arbanites), and from the fourteenth century onwards in Latin and other Western documents as Albanenses and Arbanenses. Originally a small herding community in the most inaccessible reaches of the Balkans, they grew and spread their settlements throughout the southwest of the peninsula. With time, as well as with innate vigor, unconscious persistence and much luck, they came to take their place among the nation states of Europe.

At the end of the tenth century, the great Bulgarian empire fell to the Byzantine Greeks, and it was no doubt the political void in the region which allowed the pastoral Albanians room for expansion. They began migrating from their mountain homeland in the eleventh and twelfth centuries, initially taking full possession of the northern and central Albanian coastline, and by the thirteenth century spreading southwards towards what is now southern Albania and western Macedonia. In the mid-fourteenth century they migrated even farther south into Greece. By the mid-fifteenth century, which marks the end of this process of migration and colonization, the Albanians had settled in over half of Greece and indeed in such great numbers that in many regions they constituted the majority of the population.

By the middle of the eleventh century, the Byzantine Empire, to which Albania belonged, was increasingly on the defensive. The Normans under Robert Guiscard de Hauteville (1016-1085) took possession of the last Byzantine territories in southern Italy and in 1081 crossed the Adriatic to occupy Durrës and central Albania. Although Byzantine forces managed to regain Durrës the following year, East and West were to continue to vie for Albania during the following centuries. The Venetians took possession of Durrës (1205) after the pillage of Constantinople during the Fourth Crusade in 1204. To the east and northeast of Venetian territory in Albania arose the first autonomous Albanian state under Prince Progon, that of *Arbanon*, which lasted from 1190 to 1216. In 1269, Charles of Anjou (1226-1285) landed in Vlora and three years later proclaimed himself king of Albania (*rex Albaniae*).

In the early fourteenth century, from 1343-1347, almost all of Albania, with the exception of Durrës, was conquered by the Serbs, under whose dominion it remained until the death of the great Stephan Dushan in 1355. Thereafter, the country was divided up by a number of feudal dynasties: the Thopias, Ballshas and Dukagjinis in the north, and the Muzakas (Musachi) and Shpatas in the center and south of the country.

From the arrival of the Slavs in Albania until the Turkish conquest in the fifteenth century, the Albanians lived in close contact with their Slavic neighbors, both peoples coming under the strong influence of Byzantine culture. One may indeed speak of a Slavic-Albanian symbiosis throughout much of the country, in which the rural and no doubt largely nomadic Albanians were under a constant threat of ethnic assimilation. There were no noticeable Albanian-speaking communities in the cities of the Albanian coast throughout the Middle Ages. Durrës was inhabited by the Venetians, Greeks, Jews and Slavs, Shkodra by the Venetians and Slavs, and Vlora by the Byzantine Greeks. Names of towns and rivers in Albania, always a good indicator of settlement patterns, are to a surprising extent Slavic. It is thought that a considerable proportion of the Albanians had already been assimilated by the eve of the Turkish invasion. Like the indigenous people of North America after European colonization, the Albanians had been largely marginalized in their own country.

On 28 June 1389, the Turks defeated a coalition of Balkan forces under Serbian leadership at Kosovo Polje, the Plain of the Blackbirds, and established themselves as masters of the Balkans. By 1393 they had overrun Shkodra, although the Venetians were soon able to recover the town and its imposing citadel. The conquest of Albania continued into the early years of the fifteenth century. The mountain fortress of Kruja was taken in 1415 and the equally strategic towns of Vlora, Berat and Kanina in southern Albania fell in 1417. By 1431, the Turks had incorporated all of southern Albania into the Ottoman Empire and set up a sandjak administration with its capital in Gjirokastra, captured in 1419. Feudal northern Albania remained under the control of its autonomous tribal leaders, though now under the suzerain authority of the sultan.

The Turkish conquest met with resistance on the part of the Albanians, notably under George Castriotta, known as Scanderbeg (1405-1468), prince and now national hero of Albania. Scanderbeg successfully repulsed thirteen Ottoman incursions, including three major Ottoman sieges of the citadel of Kruja led by the sultans themselves (Murad II in 1450 and Mehmet II in 1466 and 1467). He was widely admired in the Christian world for his resistance to the Turks and was given the title *Athleta Christi* by Pope Calixtus III (r. 1455-1458). Albanian resistance held out until Scanderbeg's death at Lezha on 17 January 1468. In 1478, the fortress at Kruja was finally taken by Turkish troops, Shkodra fell in 1479, and Durrës at last in 1501. By the end of the sixteenth century, the Ottoman Empire had reached its political zenith and Albania was to be subjected, in all, to over four centuries of Turkish colonization, which changed the country and its culture radically. A new, Muslim culture developed and contributed substantially to make the Albanians what they are today.

It has been argued that the Turkish invasion and occupation of the southern Balkans had the positive consequence for the Albanians of saving them from ethnic assimilation by the Slavs. It was in the Ottoman period, at any rate, that Albania became truly Albanian in an ethnic sense. Aside from their military garrisons and civilian administrators, the Turks do not seem to have settled the unruly country in any great numbers.

The Albanians adapted to the new culture and their new rulers over the coming centuries but, at the same time, strove to maintain as much local autonomy as possible. Local warlords, beys and pashas created their own largely autonomous regions, making of themselves noble families under the suzerain authority of the sultan. The isolated tribes of the northern mountains had little contact with the empire anyway.

The gradual political and economic decay of the Ottoman Empire in the eighteenth century, accompanied by slow but certain territorial disintegration, created a power vacuum in Albania which resulted in the formation of two semi-autonomous pashaliks: that of Shkodra in the north ruled by the Bushatlliu dynasty and that of Janina in the south, which, in 1787, came under the formidable sway of Ali Pasha Tepelena (1741-1822), known as the Lion of Janina. Though the autonomy of the pashalik of Shkodra ceased with the death of Kara Mahmud Pasha in 1796, Ali Pasha, by using a skillful blend of diplomacy and terror, kept his region virtually independent until 1822.

The restoration of power to the hands of the sultan left Albania a backwater of poverty and provincial corruption. The centralist Tanzimat reforms decreed on 3 November 1839, which were intended to modernize the whole of the Ottoman Empire, met with the firm opposition of local beys in Albania, intent on retaining their privileges. Nor were the wild tribes of the north, always skeptical of and recusant to anything the Turks might do, to be lured by promises of universal equality or of administrative and taxation reform. In this rugged mountainous region in particular, the Tanzimat reforms led directly to a series of uprisings against the Sublime Porte during which the seeds of Albanian nationalism were sown.

Though the European Romantic movement initially had no direct echo among the Albanians, the struggle against Turkish rule had now taken on a definite nationalist dimension, in particular in view of progress made by Albania's Christian neighbors. Serbia had attained limited autonomy as a tributary state of the Ottoman Empire in 1817; Walachia and Moldavia, in what is now Romania, formed self-governing principalities in 1829; and Greece won independence in 1830 after a long and bloody war which had begun in 1821. The Albanians became increasingly aware of their own ethnicity and the need to run their own affairs. The struggle for autonomy and cultural sovereignty in Albania was, however, to evolve at a much slower pace, due among other things to the higher degree of Islamization and, in particular, to the lack of unity within the country itself. But the long-dormant seeds of an Albanian national awakening finally sprouted, not only in Albania itself, but also in the thriving Albanian colonies abroad, in Constantinople, in Greece, Romania, Bulgaria and Egypt, and among the Arbëresh in southern Italy.

The second half of the nineteenth century thus marked the rise of the Albanian national movement known as *Rilindja* (rebirth). It can be asserted without any hesitation that the *Rilindja* period was one of inestimable significance for Albania's political and cultural survival. The country evolved from an obscure and primitive backwater of the Ottoman Empire to take its place among the nation states of Europe. Through its literature and cultural history, the *Rilindja* age created an awareness of national identity and made the Albanian language the matter-of-course vehicle of literary and cultural expression for the Albanian people.

It was by no means evident from the start that the impassioned endeavors of the Albanian writers, publicists and intellectuals of the period towards cultural consolidation and statehood would be crowned with success. The League of Prizren, which came into being in 1878 as a reaction to the Congress of Berlin, was in actual fact a failure. While it did prevent the annexation of much Albanian territory by Serbia and Montenegro, it did not succeed in its objective of uniting the whole country into one vilayet, i.e., into one administrative unit of the Ottoman Empire, which had been regarded as a major prerequisite for a certain degree of autonomy. The League of Prizren was crushed by the Porte in 1881, and many of its leaders were killed, imprisoned or exiled. Nonetheless, most of the uprisings in the years to follow, and there were many of them, were less concerned with lofty national goals than they were with venting practical grievances, for instance, to resisting Turkish government attempts to disarm the tribes of the north, to collect taxes, or to conscript the male population.

The thought of political autonomy or indeed of independence placed Albanian intellectuals in a dilemma. They were well aware of the possible boomerang effect that independence for the little Balkan country might have. As part of the Ottoman Empire, flagging though it was, the Albanians were at least protected from the expansionist designs of the neighboring Christian states. Despite the sorry level of corruption and incompetence of the Ottoman administration under which Albanians suffered in the last decades of the empire, many *Rilindja* leaders appreciated the tactical advantage of being ruled from the distant Bosporus rather than from Cetinje, the nearby mountain capital of the rising Kingdom of Montenegro, or by the Serbs and Greeks, and confined themselves to strengthening national awareness and identity rather than inciting direct political confrontation with the Porte. In a memorandum sent by the Albanians of Monastir (Bitola) to the Great Powers in October 1896, Muslim and Christian Albanians alike rightly protested that the Serbs, Bulgarians and Greeks enjoyed the support and protection of the Great Powers, whereas the Albanians had no support at all. They were not looking for privileges nor did they desire full independence from Turkey. All they wanted was to be able to live their lives as Albanians. To this end, they demanded the unification of their five vilayets (Kosova, Monastir, Thessalonika, Janina and Shkodra) into one administrative unit with its capital at Monastir, a bilingual (Turkish/Albanian) government administration, an assembly of representatives, Albanian-language schools, full religious and linguistic freedoms, and the restriction of compulsory military service to duties in the European part of the empire. But the Porte showed no willingness to compromise on the issue of Albanian autonomy. As a result, popular uprisings against Turkish rule continued in this period with an almost predictable regularity, in particular in northern Albania and Kosova. Guerrilla bands throughout the country added to the general confusion and insecurity, destroying what remnants of economic order existed and poisoning inter-communal relations.

Many Albanian nationalists initially held great faith in the movement of the Young Turks, which was to lead to revolution in July 1908 and to the overthrow of Sultan Abdul Hamid II (r. 1876-1909) the following year. Mid'hat bey Frashëri (1880-1949) called upon Albanian leaders to give their full support to the Young Turks, who had their headquarters in his hometown of Thessalonika. There can be no doubt that the Albanians themselves also played a major role in the Young Turk revolution, which precipitated the demise of this age of stagnation, and which gave the empire a constitution and a semblance of equality among citizens regardless of faith. But the hopes which the Albanians had stored with the Young Turks were soon dashed when it became apparent that the new administration was just as centralistic as the old one, or even more so.

As the survival of the Ottoman Empire became more and more questionable, the Albanian uprisings continued: 1910 in Kosova and the northern Albanian highlands, 1911 in the Catholic Mirdita region and the northern highlands, and 1912 in Skopje, Dibra and Vlora. In October 1912, the final demise of Turkey-in-Europe was signaled by the outbreak of the first Balkan War in which the Greeks, Serbs, Montenegrins and Bulgarians united to drive the Turks back to the Bosporus. Within two months, virtually all of Albania was occupied by the neighboring Balkan states, which, in their anti-Turkish and to an extent anti-Muslim campaign, had no intentions of recognizing the legitimate aspirations of the Albanian people. In the midst of the chaos and confusion created by the swift defeat of the Turks, the presageful Albanian politician, Ismail Qemal bey Vlora (1844-1919), assured of Austro-Hungarian support, convoked a national congress of Albanian intellectuals at Vlora on the southern coast, which was attended by thirty-seven delegates from southern and central Albania. At this meeting on 28 November 1912, Albania was finally declared independent, thus bringing centuries of Turkish occupation to an end. The "long night" of Ottoman rule was over.

After the Conference of Ambassadors in London (1912-1913) at which the Great Powers de facto recognized the existence of the fledgling Albanian state, an international border commission was set up, charged with the awesome and thankless task of delineating the frontiers of the new country. Though independence had been declared and at least temporarily secured at an international level, enthusiasm among the Albanians was soon dampened. More than half of the Albanian-speaking territory and about forty percent of the Albanian population were excluded from the new state. Most tragic of all, Kosova, which had been "liberated" by the Serbian army, was given to the Kingdom of Serbia, an error which haunted the Balkans right to the end of the twentieth century.

The new provisional government of Albania, whose sphere of influence hardly extended beyond the town of Vlora, was formed with Ismail Qemal bey Vlora as prime minister and with a senate composed of eighteen members. Durrës and Tirana remained under the sway of landowner Essad Pasha Toptani (1863-1920), and it was not until 22 April 1913 that the citadel of Shkodra, the last Turkish stronghold in the Balkans, was abandoned by Ottoman forces to the Montenegrins and given over to the International Control Commission. In addition to domestic chaos and intrigue created by the conflicts of interest amongst the various feudal landowners, tribes and religious groups within the country, neighboring Greece, Serbia and Montenegro all strove to exert as much influence in Albania as possible. Though Albanian independence had been recognized de facto on 17 December 1912 at the Conference of Ambassadors, it was not until 29 July 1913, after the second Balkan War and the solving of the delicate problem of Shkodra, that the international community agreed to support Albania as a neutral, sovereign and hereditary principality. The choice of a head of state for the new Balkan nation fell on Prince Wilhelm zu Wied (1876-1945). The well-meaning German prince, a compromise solution, arrived in the port of Durrës on 7 March 1914 and was welcomed to the booming of cannons, but in the months to follow he was unable to gain control of much more than the port city itself.

With the outbreak of World War I, Prince Wilhelm lost all semblance of international support and left Albania on 3 September 1914 after a mere six months of inglorious reign. Though Essad Pasha Toptani was able to maintain his power base in central Albania for a time, much of the country was occupied by a succession of Italian, Greek, Serbian, Bulgarian, Montenegrin, Austrian and French troops.

This chaotic period was brought to an end at the Congress of Lushnja on 28-31 January 1920, at which Tirana was declared the country's new capital and a new regency government was formed under Sulejman bey Delvina (1884-1932) as prime minister and the twenty-four-year-old Ahmet Zogu (1895-1961) as minister of the interior. By September 1920, virtually all of Albania was under the control of the new government and, on 17 December of that year, Albania was admitted to the League of Nations as a sovereign state.

The following years saw the gradual rise of the authoritarian Ahmet Zogu (Zog), initially as minister of the interior, and on 2 December 1922 to the position of prime minister. Zogu, supported primarily by the landed aristocracy and conservative circles, was obliged to flee the country in the so-called Democratic Revolution of 1924 during which Bishop Fan Noli (1882-1965) led the country for a brief period of six months as head of a first more or less progressive government. The American-educated Noli set out to introduce sweeping changes, including a desperately needed land reform in Albania, but his idealism was soon crushed by the weight of tradition. With help from Belgrade and from the remnants of General Piotr Nikolayevich Wrangel's White Russian Army, the power-hungry Zogu returned to Albania and took possession of the country in a coup d'état on 24 December 1924. On 22 January 1925, Albania, still formally a principality, was declared a republic with Ahmet Zogu as its first president. By stifling all opposition within the country and by playing Italy and Yugoslavia off against one another, Zogu created a certain degree of political stability and authority in the coming years, but by the second half of the 1920s, Albania's increasing economic dependence on neighboring fascist Italy had transformed the little Balkan country into an Italian protectorate, in particular after the conclusion of the first Pact of Tirana on 27 November 1926. On 1 September 1928, Ahmet Zogu proclaimed himself Zog I, King of the Albanians, by the grace of Benito Mussolini. Italy's expansionist designs on Albania culminated in its invasion of the country on 7 April, Good Friday, 1939. King Zog, his Hungarian-American wife Geraldine and their three-day-old son Leka fled to Greece and, within four days, the whole country was under Italian control. The national assembly met in Tirana on 12 April and, in the presence of Italian Foreign Minister Count Ciano (1903-1944), it proclaimed Victor Emmanuel III (1869-1947) as King of Albania. The Albanian state had ceased to exist.

In October 1940, fascist Italy attacked Greece but, despite initial success, it was soon pushed back by a resolute Greek counter-offensive. Italian rule was secured once again in the spring of 1941 by the collapse of Yugoslavia and Greece at the hands of Nazi Germany. In these years of foreign occupation and civil war, Kosova was reunited with Albania. Albania itself was, however, deeply divided by the presence of three rival resistance groups: the communists under Enver Hoxha (1908-1985) and Mehmet Shehu (1913-1981), the anticommunist *Balli Kombëtar* (National Front) under Mid'hat bey Frashëri, and the smaller royalist *Legaliteti* (Legality) movement under Abaz Kupi (1892-1976). After the capitulation of fascist Italy on 8 September 1943, the German foreign office endeavored to create a neutral and independent Albanian state to safeguard German strategic interests in the Balkans. A new administration was formed in Tirana, but it was not able to exert much authority over the country, which was now enmeshed in a bloody civil war. When German troops withdrew from Albania at the end of November 1944, the communists under Enver Hoxha took power and subsequently set up the People's Republic of Albania.

Once in office, the new government took immediate measures to consolidate its power. In January 1945, a special people's court was set up in Tirana under Koçi Xoxe (1917-1949), the new minister of the interior from Korça, for the purpose of trying "major war criminals." This tribunal conducted a series of show trials which went on for months, during which hundreds of actual or suspected opponents of the regime were sentenced to death or to long years of imprisonment. In March, private property and wealth were confiscated by means of a special profit tax, thus eliminating the middle class, and industry was nationalized. In August 1945, a radical agrarian reform was introduced, virtually wiping out the landowning class which had ruled the country since independence in 1912. At the same time, initial efforts were undertaken to combat illiteracy, which cast its shadow over about eighty percent of the population. Apart from a shattered economy and anticommunist uprisings in the north of the country, the new regime had a number of major foreign policy problems to deal with. Greece still considered itself in a state of war with Albania, relations with the United States had declined dramatically, and ties with the United Kingdom were severely strained after the so-called Corfu Channel incident, in which two British destroyers hit mines off the Albanian coast.

Relations with neighboring Yugoslavia also entered a precarious phase over Kosova. When the Germans withdrew from northern Albania in November 1944, Kosova, which had been reunited with Albania several years earlier, was taken over by Yugoslav partisans. Hideous massacres were committed against the Albanian population there, which was accused of collaboration with the Germans. The problem of Kosova was originally to be decided by the principle of self-determination, i.e., by a plebiscite, but Tito, realizing that he would never win the support of Serb nationalists, persuaded the Albanian communist leaders in 1943 to abandon hope of implementing a "Marxist solution." One idea raised as a solution to the thorny Kosova issue was that of uniting Yugoslavia and Albania into one state.

The communist leadership in Albania, always plagued by factional division, had split into two camps shortly after it took power. One side, represented by poet Sejfulla Malëshova (1901-1971), in charge of cultural affairs, contended that Albania should conduct an independent foreign policy, maintaining relations with both East and West, and more moderate domestic policies to encourage national reconciliation. The pro-Yugoslav faction, led by minister of the interior Koçi Xoxe, advocated closer ties with Yugoslavia and the Soviet Union, and insisted that more radical social and economic policies be introduced and coordinated with those being implemented by Belgrade. Xoxe and his Yugoslav advisors won out, and in February 1946, Malëshova was expelled from the Politburo and condemned as a "right-wing opportunist." Enver Hoxha himself seems to have maintained a tactically vague position, lying low and waiting for a chance to eliminate his opponents for good. Relations with the United Kingdom and the United States worsened, and in July 1946, Enver Hoxha signed a treaty of friendship, cooperation and mutual assistance with Yugoslavia following a visit to Belgrade. This was envisaged as the first step towards the union of the two countries. Serbo-Croatian was introduced as a compulsory subject in all Albanian schools, and Yugoslav advisors took over key positions in government and economic affairs. Albania was to remain a virtual Yugoslav colony until June 1948. During this period, Koçi Xoxe, as minister of the interior, had made ample use of his powers over the security apparatus and police to eliminate all potential rivals and enemies. These witch hunts, known euphemistically in official party history as the period of Koçi-Xoxism, resulted in the execution or imprisonment not only of political figures but also of a great many talented writers and intellectuals.

The rift between Tito and Stalin in 1948 gave Enver Hoxha a Soviet ally with whose support he could now act to preserve his own position, and he soon managed to eliminate his rivals. Albania became the first Eastern European country to denounce Yugoslavia after the latter's expulsion from the Cominform, i.e., the Soviet bloc, on 17 June 1948, and all Yugoslav advisors were expelled from the country without delay. Albania had entered the Soviet fold.

The series of show trials and purges which ensued were similar to those that took place elsewhere in Eastern Europe in the late 1940s and early 1950s. At its first congress of 8-22 November 1948, the purged Albanian Communist Party was renamed the Albanian Party of Labor. Koçi Xoxe's own reign of terror came to an end when he was convicted of treason in May 1949 and executed on 11 June of that year.

Albania's alliance with the Soviet Union had several advantages. The Soviets offered much food and economic assistance to replace the losses caused by the interruption of Yugoslav aid. They also gave the Hoxha regime military protection both from neighboring Yugoslavia and from the West at a time when the Cold War was at its height. As Albania had no common border with the Soviet Union, there was no immediate risk of direct political absorption, and the Albanian leadership was in many ways very mindful of preserving the country's formal independence.

Integrated into the Soviet sphere, Albania entered a period of profound isolation from the rest of the world. *"Ndërtojmë socializmin duke mbajtur në njërën dorë kazmën dhe në tjetrën pushkën"* (We are building socialism with a pickaxe in one hand and a rifle in the other) was the slogan spread by the party to create a state-of-siege mentality that would stifle all opposition. By 1955, Albania had become the epitome of a Stalinist state, with Soviet models being copied or adapted for virtually every sphere of Albanian life.

When Nikita Khrushchev (1894-1971) denounced Joseph Stalin's crimes and personality cult in a secret report to the twentieth congress of the Soviet Communist Party in February 1956, Enver Hoxha decried revisionism. After some shrewd and ruthless political maneuvering, he managed to overcome criticism of his own Stalinist policies and maintain power. Events in Hungary and Poland now convinced him that Khrushchev represented the greatest threat to Albania's sovereignty and to his own power. The ideological divergence between the two parties and Khrushchev's attempts to come to an agreement with the renegade Tito led to an initial political rift in relations with the Soviet Union, a rift which increased substantially in the years to come despite Albania's extreme dependence on Soviet aid and food shipments. At a conference of eighty-one communist and workers' parties held in Moscow in November 1960, Enver Hoxha stubbornly refused to condemn the Chinese communists under Mao Tse-tung (1893-1976), and in an unusually open speech before delegates on 16 November, he attacked Khrushchev for his deviation from Marxism-Leninism. Relations between the two parties deteriorated rapidly, to the point that in March 1961 Khrushchev suspended food shipments to Albania, which the population desperately needed. By December 1961, the Soviet Union broke off diplomatic ties with Albania, and Enver Hoxha, in search of a new patron, turned his attention to the Far East.

The Sino-Albanian alliance, which was to last from 1961 until July 1978, radicalized political, economic and social life in Albania and isolated the country even more from Europe and the rest of the world. The People's Republic of China provided Albania with much development assistance, including goods and low-interest loans, but this aid did not prove to be enough to promote economic growth. In order to stem the tide of popular dissatisfaction with his rule, Enver Hoxha employed his usual tactic of counterattack, launching a Chinese-style campaign at the end of 1965 for the "revolutionizing of all aspects of life in the country," a campaign which coincided with the Cultural Revolution in China. A new revolutionary cultural policy, presented to the public by the chief ideologist on cultural affairs, Ramiz Alia (b. 1925), insisted on a break with all foreign influence in Albanian culture. The role of literature and the arts was now to immunize the population against all bourgeois and revisionist trends wherever they occurred. Writers were to concentrate their energies on national themes such as the partisan movement and the construction of socialism. In practice, this policy led to the banning of foreign books and films and to the stifling of the modicum of intellectual freedom which had survived in the country. In response to Enver Hoxha's open letter of 4 March 1966, thousands of white-collar workers, including many writers and artists, "volunteered" to be sent to the countryside to work the land with the peasants. Confident after the 99.99 percent victory in the general elections of July 1966, the fifth party congress, held in November of that year, set about to intensify "class struggle" even further by making manual labor in the production sectors of the economy obligatory for everyone. The slogan of the day was "Think, work and live as a revolutionary."

In a speech on 6 February 1967, Enver Hoxha instigated a campaign against one of the last bastions of tradition, religion. Within months, almost all mosques, churches and Bektashi *tekkes* in the country had been closed down, most of them being demolished or renovated for use as cinemas, gymnasiums (like the Catholic cathedral in Shkodra) and warehouses. Albania was proclaimed the "first atheist state on earth." This so-called spontaneous wish of the youth not only stripped Albania of many of its cultural traditions but also of the vast majority of its architectural monuments. The campaign for the eradication of religion, conducted with the religious fervor of a crusade, constituted an unprecedented act of cultural suicide. Monuments of culture were razed to the ground, icons and valuable books burnt, and old manuscripts left to rot. Everything vaguely associated with religion became taboo for the next two decades. At the same time, the education system was radically reformed to purge it of Soviet influence. Political commissars also took control of the military, which was purged of its ranks.

The revolutionary period, which began in 1965 and lasted up to mid-1969, was brought to an end by a cooling of relations with China. After the Soviet invasion of Czechoslovakia in 1968, which resulted in Albania's definitive withdrawal from the Warsaw Pact, the Chinese leadership endeavored to improve relations with Yugoslavia and Romania in order to undermine Soviet control in the Balkans. Enver Hoxha, for his part, came to realize that his alliance with China was insufficient to protect his country from a Soviet military threat. By 1971, he was extending discrete feelers to the West and normalized diplomatic ties with neighboring Yugoslavia and Greece. Chinese foreign policy also changed in the early 1970s when isolationism was abandoned. Ideological differences with the Albanian leadership reached an all-time high when American president Richard Nixon visited Beijing in February 1972. Enver Hoxha decried revisionism once again. In spite of Albania's turbulent foreign relations, a brief period of calm, however deceptive, took hold on the home front in the wake of the Albanian cultural revolution. After years of sacrifice and turmoil, the population had grown sullen and resentful, and the intellectual community was more restless than ever.

Despite constant party harping about the dangers of bourgeois influence, Western dress styles appeared on the streets of Tirana, a pale reflection of the social revolution taking place in the West. Bell-bottom trousers, long hair and the occasional mini-skirt were to be seen, and Western pop music on Italian radio stations began to be listened to more openly. At the Fourth Plenary Session of the Central Committee on 26-28 June 1973, Enver Hoxha took the offensive once again and presented a report, which must now be regarded as a classic in the annals of European obscurantism: *Të thellojmë luftën ideologjike kundër shfaqjeve të huaja e qëndrimeve liberale ndaj tyre* (Let us strengthen the ideological struggle against foreign manifestations and liberal attitudes towards them). It was the quite harmless eleventh Song Festival of 25 December 1972, which served as a pretext in Hoxha's struggle to maintain power. Protagonists of the so-called liberal movement, if indeed there had been one, were dramatist Fadil Paçrami (b. 1922), party secretary for ideological affairs in Tirana, and Todi Lubonja (b. 1923), director of radio and television broadcasting, who served as scapegoats to keep writers and artists, and, consequently, the whole country, in line. The two were said to have encouraged liberal trends and permitted decadent Western ideas and influence to penetrate Albanian culture. The liberal movement was swiftly crushed and its two figureheads mercilessly condemned for their sins as deviationists and enemies of the people.

What followed from 1973 to at least 1975 was a reign of terror against Albanian writers and intellectuals, comparable, in spirit at least, to the Stalinist purges of the 1930s. These years constituted the major setback for the development of Albanian culture. In the spring of 1973, 130 writers and artists announced that they were leaving the city to work in the fields and on construction sites to strengthen their contacts with the working masses. Poets and prose writers began vying with one another in the proclamation of their revolutionary fervor and in their rejection of foreign and liberal influences. Those who were less convincing or whose publications were found to be tainted with liberality were banned to the provinces or were thrown into prison. The more fortunate simply lost their rights to publish. Almost all major authors had a work withdrawn from circulation and "turned into cardboard." Learning foreign languages was effectively banned, and those who had the misfortune of knowing French or Italian found themselves in dangerously embarrassing positions.

In the following years, a series of purges kept other sectors of society, indeed the whole population, in a state of confusion and insecurity. In 1974, Beqir Balluku (1917-1975), minister of defense from 1953, was purged together with Petrit Dume, chief of staff, and Hito Çako, head of the army's political directorate, and in May of the following year, Abdyl Këllezi (1919-1977), chairman of the State Planning Commission, Koço Theodhosi (1913-1977), minister of industry and mining, and Kiço Ngjela (1917-2002), minister of trade, were relieved of their offices and mercilessly condemned.

The ideological differences which had arisen with the Chinese leadership led to the end of the Sino-Albanian alliance in 1978. Albania was now isolated from the whole world, an island of revolution in a sea of revisionism.

The mysterious death on 18 December 1981 of Hoxha's rival Mehmet Shehu who, as head of the military and of the awesome security apparatus *Sigurimi*, was responsible for much of the terror, brought about another sweeping purge of government and party officials. In November 1982, the aging Hoxha, in one of the most amusing public declarations ever made by an experienced tyrant,

announced to a stunned world that his one-time closest ally, Mehmet
Shehu, had been working for three decades as a foreign agent simul-
taneously for the Americans, the British, the Soviets and the Yugoslavs and, confronted with his wicked deeds, had chosen to commit
suicide. Needless to say, no deviation from the ideological course set
by the party was attempted until well after Hoxha's death.

With the demise of Enver Hoxha on 11 April 1985, political
power fell to his successor Ramiz Alia of Shkodra, who ruled the
country with a slightly gentler hand, although with no fundamental
change of policy. With the fall of communism in Eastern Europe in
the late 1980s, and in particular with the death of Romanian dictator
Nicolae Ceausescu on 25 December 1989, the party leadership
realized that it was only a matter of time until communism would be
overthrown in Albania, too. The foundations of the system were
shaken in early July 1990 when thousands of young Albanians risked
their lives to seek political asylum in the German, Italian and French
embassies in Tirana. Within half a year, the one-party dictatorship
which had dominated all aspects of Albanian life for almost half a
century had imploded. Political pluralism was introduced in December 1990, and the country's first multiparty elections were held on
31 March 1991.

Incredible as it now seems in retrospect, even to the Albanians
themselves, orthodox Stalinism survived unscathed and unabated in
Albania for a whole thirty-seven years after Stalin's death in 1953.
Though a definitive judgment on the "socialist" period in Albania
will have to be left to historians and political scientists of the future,
the legacy of forty-six years of "splendid isolation" under Marxist-
Leninist rule seems to have bequeathed the country with little more
than universal misery and a backward economy. When one-party rule
was finally done away with, there was virtually no intellectual leadership left to fill the void. Albania's tiny socialist economy and its
society lay in ruins. The beginning of the 1990s thus found the
Albanian nation in a state of political, economic and social catastrophe.

**Modern Albania—Europe's Youngest and Most Dynamic Nation
or the Basket Case of the Continent?**

The 1990s were cataclysmic years in recent Albanian history. No
other nation of Eastern Europe was so harshly treated by freedom
and democracy. The great bronze statue of Enver Hoxha looming
over the central Scanderbeg square in Tirana was toppled during a

large demonstration on 20 February 1991, but the first pluralist elections in the country, on 31 March of that year, were won by the communist Party of Labor. There were, however, few people in the country who wanted a return to one-party communist rule. Most Albanians were frightened and unnerved by the country's economic collapse and simply wanted to get away. In March 1991, 20,000 Albanians fled by boat to Brindisi in southern Italy, and in August of that year, another 12,500 landed in Bari, much to the distress of the Italian government. At the same time, crossing the land border into Greece, was a more discreet but even more massive exodus of impoverished Albanians fleeing in search of jobs and a better life. Albania had become an international problem.

In June 1991, a depoliticized "stability" administration under Ylli Bufi (b. 1948) ensured a modicum of governance, and the communist Party of Labor transformed itself into the new Socialist Party of Albania. In the following winter, food stocks and shops were plundered when it was announced that the country no longer had enough food to feed itself. New elections were held in March 1992, which resulted in a massive victory for the opposition Democratic Party under Sali Berisha (b. 1944). A new era had begun.

Sali Berisha turned an important page in Albanian history. He rid the country of its communist heritage and anchored parliamentary democracy and a free market economy. In these historic endeavors, he received much support from western Europe and the United States, in particular from his protege, the American ambassador in Tirana, William Ryerson, and set Albania on the right path, initially at least. Despite general agreement on the need for western democracy and a free market, the Albanians became highly politically polarized during the early years of the Berisha regime. The underprivileged, who had now acquired jobs and risen to power, supported Berisha, but the traditional class of intellectuals, many of whom had lost their positions because of real or alleged ties with the *ancien régime,* became his bitter opponents. From the start, political dialogue, or, rather, confrontation in Albania, was not concerned with ideology or with platforms of left and right but with influence, connections and jobs in the public sector, and with lucrative kickbacks.

By 1994, Albania's frail democracy was in jeopardy. The ruling Democratic Party, and Sali Berisha in particular, had lost the support of the majority of the population in central and southern Albania. Opposition leader Fatos Nano (b. 1952) had been arrested in July 1993 and was sentenced to twelve years in prison in April 1994. The editors of the only major opposition newspaper *Koha jonë* (Our

Time) were tried and jailed in March for revealing state secrets. Albania had once again become a one-party state, ruled by an increasingly authoritarian president who now had total control over the media. By May 1996, when the Democratic Party won parliamentary elections, which were widely criticized as a farce, the country was on the verge of a new dictatorship. The new secret police, SHIK, was out of control, and the justice system functioned only for card-carrying members of the Democratic Party. The intimidated population reverted to the mute silence of the previous age.

In mid-1996, another even more tragic event eclipsed the extreme political tension and confrontation in the country. Pyramid investment companies had risen in Tirana and elsewhere and were offering huge interest on savings deposits. By the end of the year, almost everyone in the country with cash or assets had invested in them. Such scams had already hit Bulgaria and Russia hard, but in Albania, they were to rock the very foundations of the state.

In January 1997, the bubble burst. The first pyramid investment companies ceased payments to investors and later declared bankruptcy. Violent demonstrations ensued, which in view of the general dislike of the Berisha regime, took on an increasingly anti-government character. By February, police and government forces had lost control over Vlora and southern Albania. With the south in rebel hands and under the influence of the Socialist Party, the government declared martial law on 2 March and introduced severe press censorship two days later. On 12 March, rebel forces in Gjirokastra formed the National Committee of Public Salvation and began marching on Tirana to throw Berisha and his government out of office. Northern Albania, which had suffered less from the pyramid investment scams and had profited under the Democratic Party, threw its support behind Berisha. Albania was on the brink of civil war. Anarchy broke out in March and the structures of the Albanian police and army disintegrated. Public order was replaced by chaos. Military installations and arms depots were plundered, and weapons (kalashnikovs) became available to anyone and everyone who wanted them. Foreign governments began evacuating their citizens from Albania on 14 March. With law and order having broken down, the population took its anger and frustration out on public property and institutions, wreaking great destruction. For several weeks in 1997, the Albanian state ceased to exist.

On 15 April 1997, 6,000 United Nations troops under Italian command landed in Durrës to restore order to the country and, after tense political negotiations under international supervision, the political parties agreed on elections in late June. These were won by the Socialist Party under Berisha's arch-rival Fatos Nano. On 23 July 1997, President Berisha resigned, giving way to a Socialist administration.

The pyramid investment scandal and the 1997 uprising not only shook the pillars of the Albanian state, they also threw the country back to square one in economic terms. Albania had lost five years of development. In addition to financial losses, Albania was also suffering tremendously from a "brain drain." Most of the intellectuals and people of talent had emigrated for good, either to neighboring Greece and Italy, or farther afield to the United States and Canada. This made reconstruction all the more difficult.

Though the worst was over by the end of 1997, political tensions between the two sides did not subside. Berisha and the Democratic Party withdrew from parliament, a step which paved the way once again for a one-party state, this time under the Socialist Party. September 1998 saw severe unrest in Tirana after the assassination of Azem Hajdari (1963-1998), a controversial leader of the Democratic Party. The Socialists denounced the unrest as an attempted coup d'état and threatened to arrest Berisha, leader of the opposition. An eye for an eye.

As if the Albanian people had not gone through enough chaos and suffering, yet another calamity of international proportion loomed on the horizon, the war in neighboring Kosova.

Civil war had been raging in Kosova since mid-1998 between the majority Albanian population on the one hand, and the Milosevic regime and Serb forces on the other, the latter incited and supported fanatically by the Serbian minority. Albania, though supportive of the demands of the people of Kosova, was no match for Yugoslavia and did its best not to get involved in the conflict. With the beginning of NATO bombing on 24 March 1999, however, Serb forces began a well-orchestrated campaign to expel the whole population of Kosova from the country. By the end of the war in June 1999, there were almost half a million Kosovar refugees in Albania, people who had to be fed and cared for in a state which could scarcely feed itself. The total population of Albania had increased by almost one-sixth within the space of two months.

The people of Albania did the best they could. Their achievements in coming to terms with this unprecedented humanitarian catastrophe were all the more impressive given the extremely limited resources and primitive infrastructure in the country. Traditional solidarity and the unwritten law of Albanian hospitality prevailed, despite the desperate circumstances.

The Kosova War and the opening of the border with the "other half" of the Albanian nation, i.e., the people of Kosova, have since changed the Albanian people. For the first time, the Albanians are getting to know one another. They are in the process of reuniting, perhaps not politically, but certainly culturally, into one large nation. The two sides have much to learn from one another, both from their positive and from their negative experience. Kosova is now free, and, as the new century dawns, mother Albania is herself progressing, slowly but surely, along the bumpy road towards Europe.

The Dictionary

- A -

ACADEMY OF SCIENCES *(AKADEMIA E SHKENCAVE).* The Albanian Academy of Sciences was founded in **Tirana** on 10 October 1972 as the highest and most important scholarly institution in Albania. It is still the center of most academic research in the country, although it has suffered from the brain drain of recent years and the lack of younger scholars. Its current president is Ylli Popa, who replaced linguist **Shaban Demiraj** in 1997. The Academy of Sciences now comprises nine scientific research institutes and four research centers. The institutes in question are: the Institute of History *(Instituti i Historisë)* headed by Ana Lalaj; the Institute of Linguistics and Literature *(Instituti i Gjuhësisë dhe i Letërsisë)* headed by **Jorgo Bulo**; the Institute of Folk Culture *(Instituti i Kulturës Popullore)* headed by Afërdita Onuzi; the Institute of Archeology *(Instituti Arkeologjik)* headed by **Muzafer Korkuti**; the Institute of Nuclear Physics *(Instituti i Fizikës Bërthamore)* headed by Fatos Ylli; the Institute of Hydro-meteorology *(Instituti i Hidrometeorologjisë)* headed by Mitat Sanxhaku; the Institute of Biological Research *(Instituti i Kërkimeve Biologjike),* headed by Efigjeni Kongjika; the Institute of Seismology *(Instituti i Sizmologjisë)* headed by Shyqyri Aliaj; and the Institute of Informatics and Applied Mathematics *(Instituti i Informatikës dhe Matematikës së Aplikuar)* headed by Gudar Beqiraj. The four research centers are: the Center for Geographic Studies *(Qendra e Studimeve Gjeografike),* headed by Arqile Bërxholi; the Center for Arts Studies *(Qendra e Studimeve të Artit)* headed by Josif Papagjoni; the Center for Hydraulic Research *(Qendra e Kërkimeve Hidraulike)* headed by Stavri Lami; and the Center for the Albanian Encyclopedic Dictionary *(Qendra e Enciklopedisë Shqiptare)* headed by Emil Lafe. The academy publishes numerous books and scholarly periodicals and maintains international contacts with other academies and such institutions. *See* www.academyofsciences.net.

ACCURSED MOUNTAINS. Mountain range extending along the Albanian-Montenegrin border approximately from **Kelmendi** territory in the west, to the border region of Albania, Kosova and Montenegro in the east. The highest peaks of this range are Mount Jezerca, 2694 meters, in Albania, and Mount Gjerovica, 2656 meters, in Kosova. The range is known in Albanian as *Bjeshkët e Namuna,* and in Serbian as *Prokletije,* both meaning "accursed, damned."

AGOLLI, DRITËRO (1931.10.13-). Poet and prose writer. Dritëro Agolli has had a far from negligible influence on the course of contemporary Albanian **literature.** He was born to a peasant family in Menkulas in the **Devoll** region near **Korça** and went to secondary school in **Gjirokastra** from 1948 to 1952. His first verse was published in newspapers in 1947. Agolli had originally wanted to become a veterinarian but was chosen by the party for a literary career and sent off to Leningrad in 1952 to study language and literature. On his return to Albania in 1957, he worked as a journalist for the newspaper *Zëri i popullit* (The People's Voice) for fifteen years. He visited the People's Republic of **China** in 1967 and the Congo in 1971 on official government delegations. Agolli was head of the **Union of Writers and Artists** from the purge of **Fadil Paçrami** and **Todi Lubonja** at the fourth party congress in 1973 until his retirement on 31 January 1992, and was a member of **parliament** from 1974 to 1998.

Dritëro Agolli turned increasingly to prose in the 1970s after attaining success as a poet of the soil. He first made a name for himself with the novel *Komisari Memo* (Commissar Memo), Tirana 1970, originally conceived as a short story. His second novel, *Njeriu me top* (The Man with a Cannon), Tirana 1975, was also a rather conformist novel of partisan heroism, the standard fare encouraged by the party. Agolli then produced a far more interesting work, his satirical *Shkëlqimi dhe rënja e shokut Zylo* (The Splendor and Fall of Comrade Zylo), Tirana 1973, which has proved to be his claim to fame. Comrade Zylo was the epitome of the well-meaning but incompetent *apparatchik,* director of an obscure government cultural affairs department. His pathetic vanity, his quixotic fervor, his grotesque public behavior, in short, his splendor and fall, are all recorded in ironic detail.

Though Agolli was a leading figure in the **communist** nomenclature, he remained a highly respected figure of public and literary life after the fall of the dictatorship and is still one the most widely read authors in Albania. In the early 1990s, he was active for several years as a member of parliament for the **Socialist Party of Albania.** He also founded his own *Dritëro* Publishing Company by which means he has been able to publish many new volumes of prose and poetry and make a further impact on literary and intellectual life in the country.

AGRICULTURE. Despite the generally mountainous terrain, agriculture and animal husbandry are and always have been the mainstays of the Albanian economy. In the 1930s, over eighty percent of the Albanian **population** was occupied in primitive forms of agriculture, the best of the land being held by large, privately owned estates. In 1938, forest land accounted for thirty-six percent of the country, grassland and pastures for thirty-one percent, and farmland and orchards for eleven percent.

Even after half a century of **communist** dictatorship, which, on the one hand, endeavored to promote the industrialization of the country with huge projects and, on the other, thoroughly transformed agriculture by nationalizing land and collectivizing all agricultural endeavors, Albania remains a primarily agricultural country.

With the collapse of the communist system, socialist agriculture collapsed, too. In the early 1990s, Albania found itself on the brink of starvation and had to be supported from abroad, primarily by the European Union, with massive food aid.

On 19 July 2001, the Albanian **parliament** passed a bill to divide farmland up among the members of the former agricultural cooperatives according to the number of employees and members thereof. Farmland was thus reprivatized, mostly into tiny family plots, and the rural population soon attained a subsistence level, i.e., farmers produced enough to feed their families, but had very little left over to sell in the towns for profit. Things improved in the second half of the 1990s such that Albanian agriculture and animal husbandry are regarded as one of the more successful aspects of Albanian transition—successful, however, only in relative terms.

A General Agricultural Census was carried out in June 1998, which gave a clearer picture of the situation. As to land utilization, fifty-four percent of available land is considered forest land, twenty-three percent grassland and pastures, ten percent arable land for agriculture, and two percent land for permanent crops, i.e., orchards and vineyards, etc.

There are currently 466,659 agricultural holdings, the vast majority of which are small privately owned family plots. The total surface area for arable crops is 345,258 hectares.

The major farm crops produced in Albania are: cereals (fifty-four percent), forage (thirty percent), white beans (six percent), other vegetables (six percent), potatoes (two percent) and industrial crops (two percent). According to production surface, the major vegetables, excluding white beans, are: melons (thirty-four percent), tomatoes (seventeen percent) and dried vegetables (sixteen percent).

Animal husbandry has revived substantially since the years of forced collectivization, in particular since the disastrous collectivization campaign of 1981. In 1998, there were 1,482,275 sheep, 808,063 goats, 635,435 head of cattle, 180,540 horses and other equidae, 61,904 pigs, 3,595,600 head of poultry (primarily chickens, but also turkeys, geese and ducks), and 28,736 beehives in Albania. It should be noted that pigs are generally restricted to the traditionally **Catholic** areas of northwestern Albania, i.e., they are rare in traditionally Muslim areas.

AGRON. Illyrian ruler and king of **Shkodra** from ca. 250 to 231 B.C. Son of Pleuratus, Agron financed his **Illyrian** kingdom centered around Shkodra on piracy. His ships plundered Greek and Roman vessels in the Adriatic as far south as Epirus and Greece. In alliance with Demetrius II of Macedonia, he defeated the Aetolians in Acarnania in 231 and died after the battle of a heavy bout of drinking. He was succeeded by his wife, Queen **Teuta**. Many of today's Albanian men bear the name Agron in honor of this ancient Illyrian king.

AHMETI, MIMOZA (1963-). Poet and prose writer. Mimoza Ahmeti from **Kruja** is one of the literary "enfants terribles" of the 1990s. She has managed in recent years to provoke Albania's impoverished and weary society into much-needed reflection, which, with time, may lead to new and more sincerely human values. After two volumes of verse in the late 1980s, it was the fifty-three poems of the collection *Delirium* (Delirium), Tirana 1994, which caught the public's attention. Mimoza Ahmeti's poetry has been well received by the new generation of readers, in tune for the first time, with Western culture. Her candid expressions of wide-eyed feminine desire and indulgence in sensual pleasures, and the crystalline fluidity of her language have already made of her a modern classic. Ahmeti's works have been translated into Italian, Spanish and French.

AIR TRANSPORTATION. Civil air transportation is provided at only one airport, Rinas, which is situated fifteen kilometers northwest of **Tirana**. There are currently twelve airlines providing service to and from Albania: ten foreign companies and two Albanian joint ventures. Daily connections exist to Rome, Bari, Zurich and Vienna, and there are also regular direct flights to Bologna, Milan, Athens, Salonika, Istanbul, Skopje, Prishtina, Sofia, Budapest, Frankfurt and Ljubljana.

Air transportation was at an all-time low for years during the isolationist **communist** dictatorship. From 1944 to 1948, there was a service to Belgrade, but after the break of relations with Yugoslavia until 1953, there was only a Soviet-Hungarian Maszovlet connection to Budapest twice a month. From 1953 to 1955, there was no air service to Albania at all. In February 1955, a service was instituted between Tirana and Moscow and thereafter to other eastern European capitals. In the late 1980s, there were still only six airlines flying to Tirana, with a total of nine round-trips per week. Traffic increased dramatically in the early 1990s with the country's opening. In 1999, there were 8,249 flights and 356,823 passengers, seven times more people flying in and out of Albania than in 1991.

Domestic aviation dates from March 1926 when the German airline Adria-Aero-Lloyd, having obtained a monopoly for all air routes in the country on 2 November 1924, began service between Tirana and **Shkodra, Korça** and **Vlora**. The undertaking proved unprofitable and Adria-Aero-Lloyd sold its concession to the Italian company Ala Littoria, which instituted air service in 1935 between Tirana, Shkodra, **Kukës**, Peshkopia, **Kuçova**, Vlora, **Gjirokastra** and Vlora. It also later provided connections to Rome, Brindisi, Salonika and Sofia. There were no domestic flights in the communist period. Services between Tirana and a number of regional airfields were resumed partially in the mid-1990s with a small Cessna belonging to an American missionary group but were disrupted by the **uprising of 1997**.

AITOLOS, COSMAS. *See* COSMAS AITOLOS.

AKADEMIA E SHKENCAVE. *See* ACADEMY OF SCIENCES.

ALARUPI, VASIL (1908-1977). Journalist and writer. Vasil Alarupi, together with **Vangjel Koça**, was one of the few genuine proponents of fascism in Albania during the late 1930s. Under Giovanni Giro, head of the fascist *Dopolavoro* program, he led the so-called action committees, or *Lupi di Roma* (wolves of Rome), fascist gangs who provoked street fights with political adversaries. He was also apparently involved in a plot to assassinate **King Zog** in 1938 and was interned in **Kruja** at the end of that year.

ALBA. *See* OPERATION ALBA.

ALBANIAN-AMERICAN CIVIC LEAGUE, AACL (*LIGA QYTETARE SHQIPTARO-AMERIKANE***) (1989-).** Organization. The American-Albanian Civic League was founded in 1989 by Joseph DioGuardi, a Republican congressman from New York who is of **Arbëresh** origin. The following year, it successfully lobbied for the first congressional hearings on Kosova, with testimony from Ibrahim Rugova. Though it was not always successful, its rallies and lobbying on behalf of human rights in Kosova were essential in pushing through economic sanctions against **Yugoslavia** in the early 1990s. *See* www.aacl.com.

ALBANIAN-AMERICAN NATIONAL ORGANIZATION, AANO (1946-). Organization. The Albanian-American National Organization is a nonreligious and nonpolitical organization established in 1946. Among its priorities is to support the academic endeavors of Albanian-American college students through annual scholarships. It has nine chapters located throughout the United States and Canada. Its current national president in Philip Christe of Albany, New York. *See* www.aano.org.

ALBANIAN COUNCIL (*KUVENDI I ARBËNIT***) (1703).** Council of the **Catholic Church** held in Mërqia, three kilometers north of **Lezha**, on 14-15 January 1703 to affirm the po ition of the Catholic Church in Albania and to stem the tide of conversions to **Islam**. The conference was organized during the reign of Pope Clement XI Albani (r. 1700-1721), himself of Albanian origin, and was held under the direction and in the presence of the Croatian archbishop Vincentius Zmajevich (1670-1745) of Bar, who was "apostolic visitor" of Albania, Serbia and Macedonia. The council was attended by about 200 Catholic dignitaries to discuss the state of the Church, to prevent further conversions to Islam and to settle serious property disputes between the various parishes. Both the opening speech by Zmajevich himself and the resolutions taken by the council were made in Albanian. The records of the meeting, which are of historical, linguistic and ecclesiastical significance, were sent to Rome for papal inspection and published in Albanian and Latin by the Propaganda Fide in 1706 with the assistance of Francesco Maria Da Lecce O.F.M. They constitute an important source of our knowledge of the **language** of northern Albania in the early eighteenth century.

ALBANIAN LANGUAGE. *See* LANGUAGE, ALBANIAN.

ALBANIAN LITERARY COMMISSION (*KOMISIJA LETRA-RE SHQYPE*) (1916). Commission set up in **Shkodra** on 1 September 1916 by the Austro-Hungarian authorities at the instigation of Consul General August Ritter von Kral (1859-1918). Its aim was to create a literary norm and a standard orthography for Albanian for official use, and in particular for school teaching. It also encouraged the publication of Albanian school texts. Among the members of the commission were **Gjergj Fishta, Luigj Gurakuqi, Maximilian Lambertz, Mati Logoreci, Ndre Mjeda, Hilë Mosi, Sotir Peci, Gjergj Pekmezi** and **Aleksandër Xhuvani.** After some deliberation, the commission decided to use the central dialect of **Elbasan** as a neutral compromise for a standard literary **language**.

ALBANIAN REPUBLICAN PARTY. *See* REPUBLICAN PARTY.

ALBANIAN SOCIETY (1957-1991). The Albanian Society of **Britain** was founded in 1957 as a "non-party organization to spread information about the People's Republic of Albania and to foster friendship and understanding between the British and Albanian peoples." It was the most important of the so-called "friendship societies" in the English-speaking world during the **communist** period. The society was administered by a committee elected by its members, and issued a little quarterly journal called *Albanian Life.*

The moving figure of the Albanian Society throughout its history was **Bill Bland**, a British Marxist-Leninist from Ilford in Essex, who served as its secretary and leader from 1960 almost without interruption until July 1990. Although officially a non-political organization open to anyone interested in Albania, it was, in fact, a very Stalinist-oriented movement promoting the political objectives of the Albanian **Party of Labor**, as opposed to the more anticommunist Anglo-Albanian Association. The Albanian Society was denied official recognition from Albania during the period 1968-1978 when it rejected the pro-Chinese, Maoist stance of the Albanian party leadership. During this period, the pro-Maoist elements withdrew from the group and formed their own New Albanian Society, which received strong support from Albania and **China** until its dissolution in 1978. By the 1980s, the Albanian Society had several hundred members. It was disbanded with the advent of pluralist democracy in Albania in 1991.

ALEANCA DEMOKRATIKE. *See* DEMOCRATIC ALLIANCE PARTY.

ALESSIO. *See* LEZHA.

ALI PASHA TEPELENA (1744-1822.02.05). Ruler and pasha of Janina and southern Albania. Ali Pasha, once known in Europe as the "Lion of Janina," was born of a Turkish family from Asia Minor. He served in the Ottoman administration before managing to acquire the stronghold of Janina, now in northern Greece, from where he expanded his reign to take over Epirus, Thessaly and all of southern and central Albania. Here, ca. 1788, he set up a quasi-autonomous principality within the Ottoman Empire, had an army of his own and maintained diplomatic relations with England, France and Russia, all with a view to creating an independent Albania and Epirus. He was visited among others by **Lord Byron**, who recorded his meetings with the aging and brutal tyrant. Ali's relations with the Sublime Porte were tenuous but he managed to avoid an open breach for a long time. In 1820, when Sultan Mahmud II relieved him of all his positions and dispatched an army against him, Ali Pasha allied himself with the Greeks who were already in revolt against Ottoman rule. He was eventually captured on an island in Lake Janina and beheaded. Although he was not Albanian himself, Ali Pasha is regarded by many Albanians as a nationalist figure who led the country in the direction of autonomy and independence.

ALIA, RAMIZ (1925.10.18-). Political figure of the **communist** period and last head of state of communist Albania. Ramiz Alia was born in **Shkodra** and graduated from secondary school in

Tirana in 1943. In 1939-1940, he was a member of a fascist youth organization, but soon changed allegiance to the communist party, of which he became a member in 1943. Alia took part in the partisan movement as a political commissar and fought with Albanian troops in Yugoslavia in 1944. In 1949, he became the first secretary of the Union of Albanian Antifascist Youth, and served as minister of **education** and culture from 1954 to 1958.

Within the communist party hierarchy, Ramiz Alia was a member of the Central Committee from 1948 to 1991, and a full member of the Politburo from 1961 to 1991. From 22 November 1982 to 1991, as **parliamentary** president, he was de facto head of state, and on 13 April 1985, after the death of **Enver Hoxha**, he became first secretary of the Albanian **Party of Labor**, i.e., the political leader of Albania, and ruled the country until the end of the communist dictatorship in 1991.

During the period of transition to democracy, Alia remained president of Albania for one year from 30 April 1991 to 3 April 1992, having resigned from all communist party functions on 4 May 1991 according to the provisions of constitutional law. In July 1992, he gave a number of candid interviews to Kosova journalist Blerim Shala (1963-), which were published and widely read in the volume *Unë, Ramiz Alia dëshmoj për historinë* (I, Ramiz Alia Testify before History), Prishtina 1992.

In September 1992, Alia was placed under house arrest, on 19 August 1993 he was arrested and, on 21 May - 2 July 1994, he was tried and sentenced to eight years in prison, a sentence he served until the **uprising of 1997**. He is the author of three volumes of memoirs and reflections: *Shpresa dhe zhgënjime* (Expectations and Disappointments), Tirana 1993; *Ditari i burgut* (Prison Diary), Athens 1998; and *Duke biseduar për Shqipërinë* (Talking about Albania), Athens 2000, and now lives in retirement in Tirana.

ALIZOTI, FEJZI BEY (1874.09.22-1945.04.14). Political figure. Fejzi bey Alizoti was born in **Gjirokastra** and attended school in Istanbul. He began his political carrier with the Ottoman administration, serving in 1911 as *mutessarif* of Prizren and of Al-Khums in western Libya. When Italian troops invaded, he was arrested and interned in **Italy**. There, he turned into a loyal supporter of the Italian cause, in particular with regard to relations with his native Albania. From 28 January to 15 March 1914, he headed a "central administration" in Albania under the auspices of the

International Control Commission. Under **Prince Wilhelm zu Wied**, he was secretary-general in the ministry of the interior and governor of **Shkodra**, heading investigations into the conduct of Albanian officers who were suspected of having taken part in uprisings. He later worked with the Austrian occupation forces as a finance director on the civilian administration council set up by August Ritter von Kral (1859-1918), Austro-Hungarian consul general in Shkodra between 1905 and 1910. In December 1918, he headed the Congress of Durrës and became minister of finance in the government of the time. He attempted to impede the work of the **Congress of Lushnja** and was described as a "traitor" by Ahmet Zogu, then minister of the interior. In the 1924-1925 coup d'état against the **Noli** government, he joined forces with Zogu, who made use of him because of his good contacts with the Italians. Alizoti took part in various negotiations between Albania and Italy, always siding with Italy to the detriment of Albanian interest, to the extent that he was called the "kavass of the Italians." From February to October 1927, he was minister of finance and substituted for a short time as minister of foreign affairs for the ailing **Iljaz bey Vrioni**. Alizoti played a major role in the proclamation of the monarchy in September 1928, but because of his extreme italophile sympathies, he received no further cabinet appointments until the Italian occupation. He is reported to have lived off Italian subsidies that he received from time to time and to have been corrupt. In 1939, he was made minister of finance by the Italians and given the rank of an Italian minister of state. **Sir Andrew Ryan**, British minister in Albania from 1936 to 1939, describes him as "a gross creature physically and morally, with a certain amount of low cunning." After Yugoslavia's defeat at the hands of the German Reich, which enabled the reunification of **Kosova** and Albania for a couple of years, Alizoti served as high commissioner for Kosova and **Dibra**. He was arrested by the **communist** authorities in 1944, put on trial in March 1945 and shot as a collaborator on 14 April of that year.

ALTIMARI, FRANCESCO (1955-). Arbëresh scholar, linguist and poet. Altimari was born in San Demetrio Corone (Alb. *Shën Mitri*) in the southern Italian province of Cosenza. He studied at the University of Calabria in Rende, where he currently holds the chair of Albanian **language** and **literature**. His interests focus in particular upon Albanian literature and Arbëresh dialectology. Among his major publications, primarily in Italian and Albanian, are: *Studi sulla letteratura albanese della Rilindja* (Studies on the

Albanian Literature of the Rilindja Period), Cosenza 1984; *Studi linguistici arbëreshë* (Arbëresh Linguistic Studies), Cosenza 1988; *Per una storia della dialettologia arbëreshe* (Towards a History of Arbëresh Dialectology), San Demetrio Corone 1992; *Scripta minora albanica* (Minor Albanian Writings), Cosenza 1994; and *Vëzhgime gjuhësore dhe letrare arbëreshe* (Observations on Arbëresh Language and Literature), Prishtina 2002. He has edited the works of **Girolamo De Rada** and **Naim bey Frashëri** and is co-editor of *L'Esilio della parola: la minoranza linguistica albanese in Italia* (Exile of the Word: The Albanian-Language Minority in Italy), Pisa 1986; *I dialetti italo-albanese* (Italo-Albanian Dialects), Rome 1994; and *Testi folclorici di Falconara Albanese* (Folklore Texts from Falconara Albanese), Rende 1995.

AMANTIA. Archeological site near the present-day villages of Ploça and Vajza in the District of **Vlora**. The ancient town, no doubt originally an **Illyrian** settlement, was the fortified capital of the Amantians and is known to have existed in 350 B.C. Preserved are walls, an unfortified acropolis, a sports stadium with seating for about 4,000 spectators, the remains of a temple and an early Christian basilica.

AMERICAN VOCATIONAL SCHOOL, AVC (1921-1933). The American Vocational School, Alb. *Shkolla Teknike e Tiranës*, was set up in **Tirana** in 1921 by the American Junior Red Cross, which was aware that the lack of vocational training in Albania would inhibit the country's economic growth. Indeed, there were only two secondary schools in the whole country at the time. The AVS provided the (male) students with a solid basic **education** and gave them a five-year course of vocational training in fields such as masonry, carpentry, metalwork, plumbing, **agriculture**, printing, machine shop, electrical work and mechanical drawing. The language of instruction was English. The school, under the direction of Harry T. Fultz, had its own printing press, ice plant and its own engine for generating **electricity**, a phenomenon in Tirana in the 1920s. **Stuart Mann**, who taught at the school from 1929 to 1931, reports that, after a visit from **King Zog**, they were forced to put in a power line from the school to the palace. By 1933, the educational staff had been expanded from seven to thirty-five, and student enrollment had increased from sixty to something in excess of 600. The vocational school was managed by the American Junior Red Cross until it was nationalized in

1933. Thereafter, it was rebaptized the Technical Institute (*Institut Teknik*) and the languages of instruction became Albanian and Italian. Among noted figures who attended the American Vocational School were **Beqir Balluku**, **Dervish Duma**, **Sadik Kaceli**, Qazim Kastrati (1905-1974), **Ibrahim Kodra**, **Anton Logoreci**, **Mehmet Shehu** and **Nexhmedin Zajmi**.

AMERY, JULIAN (1919.03.27-1996.09.03). British military officer and writer. Harold Julian Amery was educated at Eton and Balliol College, Oxford. He was press attaché at the British Embassy in Belgrade in 1939 and was recruited during **World War II** by the **Special Operations Executive** to foment anti-Italian resistance in Albania.

Amery was dropped into central Albania in April 1944 and spent seven months in the mountains, where he maintained close contacts with **Abaz Kupi** and the **Legality** movement. After the war, he was involved in Western attempts to overthrow the **communist** regime in Albania, in particular by the training of secret agents in Malta in 1949-1953, and embarked on a political career: Conservative member of parliament for Preston North in 1950, minister of aviation in 1962-1964, minister of state at public buildings and works in 1970 and at housing in 1970-1972. Amery was particularly influential during the administration of Sir Harold Macmillan, who was his father-in-law. In 1992, he was made a life peer as Lord Amery of Lustleigh. His memoirs of the period have appeared in *Sons of the Eagle: A Study in Guerilla War,* London 1948; and *Approach March: A Venture in Autobiography,* London 1973.

ANAGNOSTI, DHIMITËR (1936.01.23-). **Film** director and script writer. Anagnosti was born in Vuno on the coast of **Himara** and studied at the Institute of Cinematography in Moscow. His 1961 film, *Njeriu kurrë nuk vdes* (Man Never Dies), based on a tale by Ernest Hemingway, won first prize at a film festival in Holland. He later went on to write and direct numerous Albanian films, the most successful of which were *Plagë të vjetra* (Old Wounds), 1969; *Lulëkuqet mbi mure* (Red Poppies on Walls), 1976; and *Përrallë nga e kaluara* (Tale from the Past), 1987. After the fall of the dictatorship, he became a member of the **Democratic Party of Albania** and in March 1991 was appointed minister of culture, youth and sports in the first post-communist government, a position he held until 4 December

1994. He now heads the **Fan Noli** Foundation for culture and the arts.

ANGLO-ALBANIAN ASSOCIATION (1912-). A group of friends in London set up a committee at the end of 1912, which was to develop into the Anglo-Albanian Association. Prominent founding members of the association were writer **Edith Durham**, who served as its honorary secretary, and member of parliament **Aubrey Herbert**, who served as its president. The objective of the association was to support the Albanian cause in Britain and to promote recognition for the newly independent Albanian state. The association was at the height of its activities in 1918-1923. According to contemporary writer Joseph Swire, it was largely as a result of the efforts of the association that the League of Nations accepted Albania as a member state. The Anglo-Albanian Association declined somewhat after the death of Herbert in 1923 but enjoyed a new lease on life, in particular after **World War II** when it became a forum for the anticommunist Albanian diaspora and their like-minded English friends, as opposed to the more Stalinist-oriented **Albanian Society**. Nonetheless, it was only officially active after 1962. Among the executive officials of the Anglo-Albanian Association have been Lord Lamington, Mary Herbert (the widow of Aubrey Herbert), **Julian Amery,** Col. **David Smiley**, **Dayrell Oakley-Hill**, **Harry Hodgkinson** and **Dervish Duma**. Its current president is **Noel Malcolm**.

ANTIGONEIA. Archeological site near the present-day village of Jerma in the District of **Gjirokastra**. The ancient town was founded between 295 and 190 B.C. by **Pyrrhus**, King of the Molossi, on the site of an earlier **Illyrian** fortification and was named after his wife. Excavations have revealed houses, a market square and two early Christian churches.

APOLLONIA. Archeological site near the present-day village of Pojan in the District of **Fier**. After **Durrës** and **Butrint**, Apollonia, west of the town of Fier, is the most important ancient site in Albania. It was founded by Greek colonists from Corinth and Corfu in 588 B.C. Cicero called the city a *magna urbs et gravis* (great and important city) and Strabo referred to it as a *pólis eunomôtatê* (a city of good laws). The remains of the site are situated on a hill six kilometers from the coastline, though the ancient town was originally 500 meters from the sea. It had a harbor which could hold 120 ships.

In 229 B.C., Apollonia came under the protection of Rome, and in 148 B.C. it became part of the Roman province of Macedonia. Apollonia was one of the two Balkan points of departure of the **Via Egnatia**. Julius Caesar had his stronghold here during the Roman civil war, and Octavian, later the Emperor Augustus, studied at the famed school of rhetoric here for six months in 45-44 B.C. Apollonia seems to have reached its zenith in the third century A.D. It declined thereafter when the river **Vjosa** (ancient Aoos) changed its course and deprived the town of its harbor. The town was abandoned in the sixth century. The present Byzantine church of Saint Mary's was built in the ancient ruins in the early thirteenth century, using ancient stonework.

Initial excavations at Apollonia were carried out by Austrian archeologists Camillo Praschniker (1884-1949) and Arnold Schober (1886-1959) during **World War I**, and by French archeologists under Léon Rey from 1924 to 1938. Italian and, in particular since **World War II**, Albanian archeologists such as **Hasan Ceka** and Skënder Anamali (1921-1996), have also investigated the site. The objects uncovered are on exhibit in **Tirana** and at the museum of Apollonia. Of the ruins on-site, mention may be made of the bouleuterion, also known as the Agonothetes monument, with its six restored Corinthian columns, an odeon for about 600 spectators, a Roman bath, two stoas, a badly preserved Hellenistic theater for about 8,000 spectators, a temple to Apollo or Artemis, vestiges of about twenty-two Roman houses, a nymphaeum, an acropolis and the walls. Much of the site remains to be excavated.

APPONYI, GERALDINE (1915.08.06-2002.10.22). Queen of Albania. Geraldine Apponyi was born in Budapest as a countess. Her father was a Hungarian aristocrat, Count Gyula Apponyi de Nagy-Appony, and her mother was an American, Gladys Stewart Girault, of an old family from Virginia. Though her father died in 1924 and her mother married a French army officer, the father's family insisted that Geraldine and her two sisters be educated in Hungary. While she was attending a ball at the age of seventeen, a photographer took her picture, and it was this picture which eventually reached the hands of **King Zog** of Albania, who was in search of a bride. King Zog invited Geraldine to **Tirana** and she arrived shortly after Christmas in 1937. She accepted the king's proposal on New Year's Day 1938, and was married to him on 27 April 1938.

A year later, on 5 April 1939, Geraldine gave birth to a son called **Leka**. It was also in April 1939, however, that the Italians invaded Albania. The royal family was forced to flee overland to Greece and went into exile in London. From 1946 to 1955, they lived in Egypt with King Farouk (1920-1965), who was himself of Albanian origin. After the deposition of King Farouk in 1952, the Albanian royal family moved to Cannes on the French Riviera and to Paris. After the death of her husband in Paris in April 1961, Geraldine moved to Spain and later to Bryanston, South Africa, where she lived in exile with her son and his family. She returned to Albania on 28 June 2002 to spend the final months of her life where she had once reigned.

ARAPI, FATOS (1930.07.19-). Poet and prose writer. Fatos Arapi is among the best-known contemporary poets of Albania and is author of philosophical verse, love lyrics and poignant elegies on death. He was born in Zvërnec near the port city of **Vlora** and, after studies in economics in Sofia from 1949 to 1954, worked in **Tirana** as a journalist and lecturer in modern Albanian **literature**. In his first two collections, *Shtigje poetike* (Poetic Paths), Tirana 1962, and *Poema dhe vjersha* (Poems and Verse), Tirana 1966, he made use of more modern verse forms than his contemporaries and set the course for a renewal of Albanian poetry after years of stagnation. Criticized in the 1973 purge for the volume *Më jepni një emër* (Give Me a Name), Tirana 1973, which was "turned into cardboard" along with many other works of literature, he fell silent for a time as the poet he is and published little of significance until 1989.

Child of the Ionian coast, Arapi has never lost his fascination for the sparkling waters of the sea, the tang of the salt air and the intensity of Mediterranean light, all of which flood his verse. Indeed, beyond the echoing pathos of much of his revolutionary verse production on industrial and political themes in numerous publications during the dictatorship, his true poetic vocation can be seen in the creation of an equilibrium between the harmony of the waves and the rhythmic impulses of his being. Among his recent volumes of verse are: *Gloria victis* (Glory to the Vanquished), Tirana 1997; *Më duhet një gjysëm ëndrre* (I Need Half a Dream), Tirana 1999; and *Eklipsi i ëndrrës* (Eclipse of the Dream), Tirana 2002. Arapi has also written much prose in recent years. His short stories have appeared in the volumes *Cipa e dëborës* (The Tip of the Snow),Tirana 2000; *Gjeniu, një kokë të prerë* (Genius, a Severed Head), Peja 2000; and *Nuk shitet shpirti në tetor* (Souls Are Not Sold in October), Tirana 2002.

ARBANA, RESHAT (1940.09.15-). Stage and **film** actor. Reshat Arbana, born in **Tirana,** has been one of the most successful film actors in Albania, playing in thirty-five roles from 1963 to 1995. He has also appeared in numerous stage productions at the **National Theater** in Tirana. Arbana is remembered in particular for his roles in *Fijet që priten* (Broken Threads), 1976; *Gjeneral gramafoni* (General Gramophone), 1978; and *Kur hapen dyert e jetës* (When the Gates of Life Open), 1986.

ARBËRESH. *See* ITALY, ALBANIANS IN.

ARBNORI, PJETËR (1935.01.18-). Writer, political figure and high-ranking member of the **Democratic Party of Albania.** Pjetër Arbnori was born of a poor family in **Durrës.** Despite early anticommunist activities, he managed to finish secondary school and complete a five-year correspondence course with the University of **Tirana** in 1960. He was affiliated in these early years of the **communist** dictatorship with the **Social Democratic Party of Albania,** for which he drafted the program. He was arrested in the spring of 1961 and sentenced to death. His sentence was subsequently commuted to twenty-five years in prison. While serving his term, he was sentenced to a further ten years for secretly writing a novel and some short stories.

Pjetër Arbnori was released from prison in August 1989, having served over twenty-eight years of his sentence. He joined the burgeoning democratic movement and took part in the first anticommunist demonstration in **Shkodra** on 14 January 1990. In December 1990, he was elected head of the Democratic Party for Shkodra and, in 1991, was a member of **parliament.** From 6 April 1992 to March 1997, he served as speaker of the Albanian parliament.

In addition to his political activities, Pjetër Arbnori has published numerous works of **literature,** among which are: the short story *Kur dynden Vikinget* (When Vikings Migrate), Tirana 1992; and the novels *Mugujt e mesjetës* (The Twilight of the Middle Ages), Tirana 1993; *E bardha dhe e zeza* (The White and the Black), Tirana 1996; *Shtëpia e mbetur përgjysëm* (The Half-Built House), Lezha 1997; *Vorbulla* (The Whirlpool), Tirana 1997; and *Brajtoni një vetëtimë e largët* (Brighton, a Distant Bolt of Lightning), Tirana 2000.

ARDENICA. Orthodox monastery on a hilltop between **Fier** and **Lushnja**. Ardenica, Gk. *Αρδεύουσα*, is one of the most important monasteries and pilgrimage sites of Central Albania. It was visited by pilgrims, Christian and Muslim alike, because of a miracle-working spring. The pilgrims, mostly **women**, would drink the holy water in the hope of being cured of their illnesses. Surrounded by lofty cypress trees, the monastery of Ardenica was originally founded in the thirteenth or fourteenth century. It received many precious gifts from pilgrims over the years and developed into one of the most splendid monasteries in all of Albania. The well-preserved church in the inner courtyard of the monastery, completed in 1743, is devoted to the Virgin Mary. It was here in the fifteenth century that **Scanderbeg** and Andronica Arianiti are said to have been married.

ARIANITI, GEORGE (ca. 1400-1463). Historical figure. George Arianiti stemmed from an important and noble family who owned much territory in central and southern Albania (Çermenika, Shpat, Mokra, **Elbasan**, etc.). He made a name for himself during the years of Albanian resistance to the **Ottoman** invasion, defeating Turkish forces in important battles in 1433, 1434 and 1438-1439. Arianiti was known abroad for his deeds and received the support and protection of the pope, the Holy Roman Emperor and the king of Naples. He was the father-in-law of the more famous **Scanderbeg**, who married his daughter Andronica. Arianiti died, having the title of a captain, on Venetian territory, probably in **Durrës**. His son Constantine Arianiti (1456-1530) was a soldier and diplomat at the court of the Emperor Maximilian I. The Arianiti dynasty ended in 1551 when the last male heir died.

ARMENIAN MINORITY IN ALBANIA. There is a dwindling minority of Armenians in Albania, probably numbering several hundred people. A large portion of them left the country after the end of the dictatorship. They lived primarily in **Tirana, Vlora** and **Elbasan**, and were descendants both of government officials from the time of the **Ottoman Empire** and of refugees who survived the genocide in Anatolia in 1914-1915. As an urban minority, those who remain are now quite assimilated, comparatively well-educated and successful in their professions. Among them is a notable number of doctors and dentists. Very few speak their original western Armenian dialect. The remaining members of the Armenian community have formed their own organization called the "Armenians of Albania Association."

AROMANIAN MINORITY IN ALBANIA. *See* VLACH MINORITY IN ALBANIA.

ASDRENI (1872.04.11-1947.12.11). Poet. Asdreni, pseudonym of Aleks Stavre Drenova, was born in the village of Drenova near **Korça** in southeastern Albania. He attended a Greek-language elementary school, and in the autumn of 1885, he emigrated to Bucharest to join his two elder brothers. It was here in the culturally active Albanian colony that he first came into contact with the ideas and ideals of the nationalist movement in exile.

In 1905, Asdreni taught at an Albanian school in the port city of Constanza and the following year became president of the new Bucharest chapter of the *Dija* (Knowledge) society, originally founded in Vienna. Inspired by the creation of an independent Albanian state, he set out for **Durrës** in the spring of 1914 to welcome the country's newly chosen head of state, **Prince Wilhelm zu Wied**, from whom he hoped to obtain an appointment as an archivist in the new royal administration. It soon became apparent, however, that there would be little to administer and no need for his services at all.

After a short visit to **Shkodra**, Asdreni returned to Bucharest in July 1914. In the following years, Asdreni continued to take an active interest in the Albanian national movement, but chose to remain in Romania, serving as secretary at the Albanian consulate in Romania, which opened in March 1922. He made another visit to Albania in November 1937 on the twenty-fifth anniversary of independence, hoping after many years of service to the Albanian state to receive a government pension. He spent some time in **Tirana** before visiting Shkodra where he met **Gjergj Fishta** in February 1938. The chaos caused by the Italian invasion of Albania on Easter 1939 made it bitterly obvious to him that his hopes for a pension were in vain, and he returned to Bucharest again in July of that year, where he lived until his death.

It was in the early years of the twentieth century that Asdreni had begun writing poetry and publishing articles in the local press. He is remembered for four collections of verse: *Rézé djélli* (Sunbeams), Bucharest 1904; *Endra e lote* (Dreams and Tears), Bucharest 1912; *Psallme murgu* (Psalms of a Monk), Bucharest 1930, which marks the zenith of his poetic creativity; and *Kambana e Krujës* (The Bell of Kruja), which remained unpublished during his lifetime. All in all, Asdreni played a decisive role in setting Albanian verse on the path towards modernity. His collection *Psallme murgu* with its classical refinement is still considered by many to be one of the best volumes of Albanian verse published in the twentieth century.

ATHEISM. The Albanians have never been described as a people particularly devoted to organized **religion**, although beliefs and religions in one form or another have always been part of their lives. The great religions, **Orthodoxy**, **Catholicism** and **Islam**, which penetrated the country over the centuries, were long regarded as foreign imports. As opposed to their Serbian, Bulgarian and Greek neighbors who were early in making their own national churches out of Byzantine Orthodoxy, the Albanians did not come to identify with these religions as easily, primarily because, at least over the last 150 years, ethnic and national identity took priority over religious identity.

With the **communist** takeover in 1944, so-called scientific atheism was spread throughout the country as part of the Marxist revolution which changed the face of the nation so completely. It was propagated by the Albanian **Party of Labor,** hand in hand with universal **education,** as an element of what was viewed as "progress." Militant atheism was also spread as a means of overcoming the rival power of the religious communities in the country, especially that of the Catholic Church. General **Mehmet Shehu**, in a public address in **Shkodra** on 28 January 1945, called the Catholic Church a "nest of reaction" and warned that church leaders would receive their "just" rewards before the people's court. Most native priests and Italian missionaries were imprisoned and some were put to death.

The result of this wave of persecution was that the structures of the Catholic and Orthodox churches in Albania as well as of Islam and **Bektashism** were wiped out in the late 1940s and early 1950s. For reasons more political than theological, atheism was propagated with "religious fervor" in the mid-1960s and turned into a militant and extremist movement culminating in the banning of religion in the country entirely. At the time of the ban in 1967, there were about 1,050 mosques, 200 Bektashi *tekkes* and about 400 Catholic and Orthodox churches in the country, most of which were subsequently destroyed. Albania became the first atheist country in the world, as the people were proudly told by their leaders. Article thirty-seven of the Albanian constitution of 1976 stipulated, "The State recognizes no religion, and supports and carries out atheistic propaganda in order to implant a scientific materialistic world outlook in people." The ban was maintained until the end of the dictatorship. The law against the public practice of religion was rescinded in December 1990.

- B -

BACKER, BERIT (1947.08.03-1993.03.07). Norwegian anthropologist. Berit Backer was born in Oslo. She attended the Nansen School in Lillehammer in 1965-1966 and, later, in the spring of 1968 registered as a student at the University of Bergen. During the following years she studied statistics, social anthropology, philosophy and sociology. She visited Albania in 1969 and was intrigued by the culture and political system of the country. She, therefore, decided to dedicate her research in social anthropology to the Albanians. Unable to carry on research in Albania itself, Backer went to **Kosova,** where in 1974-1975 she was one of the first foreigners to conduct anthropological field work. She spent one year in the village of Isniq in western Kosova. Her work, which was submitted as a masters thesis for the Institute of Social Anthropology of the University of Oslo in April 1979, was published posthumously as *Behind Stone Walls: Changing Household Organization among the Albanians of Kosova* (Peja 2003). Berit Backer was a great friend of the Albanian people and, during the 1980s became a leading human rights activist, in particular in defense of the cause and rights of the Kosova Albanians. She was active on behalf of the Helsinki Watch Committee and in support of Kosova Albanian refugees in Norway. She was stabbed to death in Oslo by a Kosova Albanian suffering from a severe mental disorder.

BAHA'I. Religion. The Baha'i faith was introduced to Albania in the 1930s by Refo Çapari. Çapari was born in 1900 in the southern **Camëria** region and studied in Istanbul. He emigrated to the United States, where he became a Baha'i in 1928. In 1931, he returned to **Korça** and began translating Baha'i texts into Albanian. In May 1938, Çapari started editing a forty-four-page periodical in Albanian and occasionally in English called *Penda siprore* (The Supreme Plume). The Baha'i community returned to Albania in 1992 following the repeal of the ban on **religion** and now maintains a center in **Tirana**.

BAJRAKTARI, MUHARREM (1896.05.15-1989.01.21). Political figure and guerrilla fighter. Colonel Muharrem Bajraktari, a tribal leader from Ujmisht in the northeastern district of **Kukës**, joined the forces of **Ahmet Zogu** in 1919. In June 1924, he was expelled as commander of Kukës by **Bajram Curri**, and in December of that year took part in the successful coup d'état of Zogu. He subsequently sentenced members of the **Democratic Revolution** who had not fled the country to prison. He was then made commander of the police force in the northeast of the country. In 1926, he led a punitive expedition against the rebels of **Dukagjini**, and in 1929, was made supreme commander of the Gendarmerie. In 1931, he was appointed aide-de-camp to King Zog. In December 1934, Bajraktari rose in revolt against increasing Italian encroachments and fled to Yugoslavia and, in 1936, to France. He returned to Albania in 1939 and organized a band of approximately 1,000 guerrillas in his native **Luma** region, where, as an independent northern tribal chieftain, he took part in the **Legality** resistance movement until the end of the German occupation. A report in the British Foreign Office archives by **Billy McLean** describes him as having a persecution complex that sometimes verged on insanity. Bajtraktari took to the hills after the **communist** takeover in 1944 and then fled to Italy, where he became an independent nonparty member of the **Free Albania Committee** in Rome. He subsequently lived in Athens, and in 1957 moved to Brussels, where he died.

BALDACCI, ANTONIO (1867-1950). Italian scholar, botanist and geographer. Baldacci carried out field research in the southern Balkans from the end of the nineteenth century onwards. Aside from many articles on Albanian and Balkan flora, he is remembered for the following monographs: *Itinerari albanesi, 1892-1902, con uno sguardo generale all' Albania e alle sue communicazioni stradali* (Albanian Wanderings, 1892-1902, with Special Attention to Albania and Its Road Network), Rome 1917; *L'Albania* (Albania), Rome 1929; and the three-volume *Studi speciali albanesi* (Special Albanian Studies), Rome 1932, 1933, 1937.

BALKAN WARS (1912-1913). Albania did not play a prominent role in the Balkans Wars, though as a de facto part of the **Otto-**

man Empire it was to be caught up in the fighting. During the first Balkan War from October 1912 to May 1913, the Albanians found themselves in an extremely awkward position, between the devil and the deep blue sea. There had been numerous major uprisings against the Turks in the period 1909-1912, but Albanian leaders were now more concerned about the coalition of neighboring Christian forces (Montenegro, Serbia and Greece) than they were about the weakened Ottoman military presence in their country. What they wanted was to preserve the territorial integrity of Albania. Within two months, Ottoman forces had all but capitulated, and it was only in **Shkodra** and Janina that Turkish garrisons were able to maintain position. The very existence of the country was threatened.

It was at this time that **Ismail Qemal bey Vlora** returned to Albania with Austro-Hungarian support and declared Albanian independence in the town of **Vlora** on 28 November 1912. The declaration was more theoretical than practical because Vlora was the only town in the whole country not occupied by coalition forces—yet it proved to be effective in the vacuum of power. The Montenegrins had taken **Lezha** and Shëngjin and were besieging Shkodra; the Serbs had seized not only **Kosova** and western Macedonia, but also **Dibra**, **Elbasan**, **Tirana** and **Durrës**; and the Greeks had invaded **Saranda** and stationed their forces on the island of Sazan outside the Bay of Vlora. Fighting continued in and around Shkodra from March until May 1913, by which time both Turkish and Serb troops began to withdraw from the country. On 29 July 1913, the **Conference of Ambassadors** in London resolved that Albania should become a sovereign state ruled by a European prince. Albanian independence had thus been recognized and the country was only superficially affected by the second Balkan War from July to August 1913.

BALLI KOMBËTAR (1943-). Anticommunist resistance movement and political organization. The *Balli Kombëtar* (National Front) was founded by **Mid'hat bey Frashëri** in November 1942 as an alliance of Albanian resistance fighters and patriots. It promoted the goals of an ethnic Albania, i.e., a state including all Albanian territory, and a republican system, i.e., anti-Zog. Its social and economic platform was initially more radical than that of its rival, the **communist** National Liberation Front. *Balli Kombëtar* held its first conference in **Berat** in 1943 and elected an eight-man presidium under Mid'hat bey Frashëri. Its partisan units took to the fight against Italian forces, which capitulated in

September 1943. Initially, attempts were made, in particular by the Special Operations Executive (SOE), to get the *Balli Kombëtar* and the communists to work together in the fight against the occupiers, but they soon became bitter rivals and Albania descended into civil war. With the victory of the communists in the autumn of 1944, *Balli Kombëtar* was accused of having collaborated with the Germans, and its leaders fled abroad or were killed.

The *Balli Kombëtar* organization was revived in Albania as a political party in the early 1990s after the fall of the dictatorship under the leadership of Abaz Ermenji, and in 1996 won five percent of the popular vote and two seats in **parliament**.

BALLUKU, BEQIR (1917.02.14-1975.11.05). Political and military figure of the **communist** period. Beqir Balluku was born in **Tirana** and attended the **American Vocational School** for a time, though he did not finish his formal education. From 1935 to 1939 he made his living as a metalworker. In 1940, he joined the resistance movement and helped form the communist party in 1941. During **World War II**, he was chief of staff of various military brigades and political commissar of the first army corps. He was later member of a special court set up to try "war criminals and enemies of the people." In February 1948, Balluku was promoted to the rank of major-general. From 1948 to 1953, he was chief of staff of the Albanian army and, after training at the Voroshilov military academy in Moscow from August 1952 to August 1953, he served as minister of defense from July 1953 to July 1974. He was also chairman of the people's assembly from 1957 to 1974.

Beqir Balluku was a member of the communist party's Central Committee and the Politburo from 1948 to 1974. In August 1974, he was arrested and accused of organizing a military coup d'état with two other military figures, Petrit Dume and Hito Çako. He was found guilty of high treason and executed on 5 November 1975. The bodily remains of the three were discovered in 2000 and were reburied with military honors on 29 July of that year.

BARDHI, FRANG (1606-1643.06.09). Early Albanian writer. Frang Bardhi, known in Latin as Franciscus Blancus or Blanchus, is author of the first Albanian dictionary, published in Rome on 30 May 1635, which at the same time constitutes the first work in Albanian not of direct religious content. He was born in Kallmet (north of **Lezha**) in the **Zadrima** region of northern Albania to a family who had a tradition of furnishing its sons as bishops for the church and as soldiers and officials for the Republic of Venice. His uncle was bishop of Sapa and **Sarda**. Bardhi was sent to Italy, where he studied theology at the Illyrian College of Loretto, and later at the College of the Propaganda Fide in Rome. On 30 March 1636, no doubt with family influence, he was appointed bishop of Sapa and **Sarda** himself, replacing his uncle, who became archbishop of Antivari (Bar). From 1637 onwards, Bardhi submitted reports in Italian and Latin to the Congregation of the Propaganda Fide, which contained a wealth of information about his diocese, about political developments, Albanian customs, and the structure and position of the church. Nineteen of these letters and reports are preserved in the archives of the Propaganda Fide. In 1641, two years before his death, he is known to have traveled back to Rome to submit one report personally. After a short but intense life as a writer and ecclesiastical figure, Frang Bardhi died at the age of thirty-seven.

It was during his last year at the College of the Propaganda Fide when he was twenty-nine years old that Bardhi published the 238-page Latin-Albanian dictionary for which he is remembered. The work, bearing the title *Dictionarium latino-epiroticum, una cum nonnullis usitatioribus loquendi formulis* (Latin-Epirotic Dictionary with Several Common Expressions), Rome 1635, comprises 5,640 Latin entries translated into Albanian and is supplemented by an appendix of parts of speech, proverbs and dialogues. In one of his reports, dated 8 February 1637, Bardhi noted that he had translated other ecclesiastical works into Albanian. Whether his other translations were ever circulated or published is not known.

Bardhi also published a seventy-six-page treatise in Latin on **Scanderbeg** entitled *Georgius Castriottus Epirensis vulgo Scanderbegh, Epirotarum Princeps fortissimus ac invictissimus suis et Patriae restitutus* (George Castriotta of Epirus, Commonly called Scanderbeg, the very Mighty and Invincible Prince of Epirus, Restored to His People and His Country), Venice 1636, in which he refuted the assertion of the Bosnian bishop, Tomeus Marnavitius, that the Albanian national hero was of Bosnian origin. It is a work of erudition and patriotic sentiment, not dissimilar to polemics still conducted and appreciated in the Balkans today.

BARDHI, RESHAT Haxhi Dede (1935.03.04-). Bektashi religious figure. Reshat Bardhi was born in **Kukës** and acquired his religious training privately. In 1950, he became a *muhib*, a spiritual member of the Bektashi community, and, in 1954, he became a dervish. Bardhi kept a low profile during the years when **religion** in Albania was banned (1967-1991). On 22 March 1991, he was chosen as *kryegjysh* (head grandfather), i.e., spiritual leader of the Bektashis in Albania, and indeed in the world, and has led the Bektashi community since that time.

BARIĆ, HENRIK (1888.01.28-1957.04.03). Croatian scholar and historical linguist. Barić was born in Dubrovnik and studied Indo-European and Romance linguistics in Graz and Vienna. He moved to Belgrade at the end of **World War I,** where from 1920 he lectured in Indo-European linguistics. He was later appointed professor of Indo-European at the University of Belgrade, a post which he held until 1944. From 1954 to his death in 1957, he was professor of General and Comparative Linguistics at the University of Sarajevo, where he founded the Balkanological Institute.

Although an Indo-Europeanist and Romance scholar by training, Barić very soon devoted his energies to tracing the history and development of the Albanian **language** and, in particular, elucidating its position in the Indo-European family of languages. As opposed to many scholars of the period who favored an **Illyrian** connection, Barić viewed Albanian as having descended from Thracian and, at the Indo-European level, as being more closely related to Phrygian and Armenian than to the western centum languages. He also realized the significance of Romanian for the historical development of Albanian.

Henrik Barić was not a prolific author, but he left his mark on Albanian linguistic studies. Among his major publications, primarily in Serbo-Croatian and German, are: *Albanorumänische Studien* (Albano-Romanian Studies), Sarajevo 1919; *Ilirske jezične studije* (Illyrian Linguistic Studies), Zagreb 1948; *Lingvističke studije* (Linguistic Studies), Sarajevo 1954; *Hŷmje në historín e gjuhës shqipe* (Introduction to the History of the Albanian Language), Prishtina 1955; *Istorija arbanaškog jezika* (History of the Albanian Language), Sarajevo 1959; and a *Rečnik srpskoga ili hrvatskoga i arbanaskoga jezika* (Dictionary of the Serbian or Croatian and Albanian Languages), Zagreb 1950. He is also remembered as editor-in-chief of the noted though short-lived Albanological journal *Arhiv za arbanasku starinu, jezik i etnologiju* (Archive for Albanian History, Language and Ethnology), Belgrade 1923-1925. In later years, Barić founded the

periodical *Godišnjak* (Yearbook) of the Balkanological Institute
of Sarajevo, although he did not live to see the first edition.

BARLETI, MARIN. *See* BARLETIUS, MARINUS.

BARLETIUS, MARINUS (ca. 1450-1512). Italian historian of
early Albania. Marinus Barletius, known in Albanian as Marin
Barleti, is thought to have been born in **Shkodra,** where he viv-
idly experienced and survived the second siege of the city by the
Turks in 1478. When Shkodra was finally taken, Barletius, like
many of his compatriots, fled to **Italy** and settled in Padua, where
he became rector of the parish church of St. Stephan. His experience inspired him to document Albania's turbulent history during
the Turkish invasion and its national resistance under
Scanderbeg. Barletius is the author of three Latin works: *De
obsidione Scodrensi* (On the Siege of Shkodra), Venice 1504;
Historia de vita et gestis Scanderbegi, Epirotarum Principis
(History of the Life and Deeds of Scanderbeg, Prince of Epirus),
Rome, ca. 1508-1510; and *Compendium vitarum summorum
pontificium et imperatorum romanorum usque ad Marcellum II*
(Compendium of the Lives of the Popes and Roman Emperors up
to Marcellus II), Rome 1555.

Barletius' history of Scanderbeg was widely read and translated in the sixteenth and seventeenth centuries and constitutes a
basic source of our information on fifteenth-century Albania. The
English-language version of the work, published in London in
1596, was entitled *The Historie of George Castriot, Surnamed
Scanderbeg, King of Albinie, Containing his Famous Actes, his
Noble Deedes of Armes and Memorable Victories again the
Turkes for the Faith of Christ.* Strongly influenced in style and
outlook by the Roman historians, in particular by Livy (59 B.C.-
17 A.D.), Barletius captured the imagination of the sixteenth-
century reader who, with the Turks at the gates of Vienna in
1529, was becoming increasingly obsessed by the prospect of a
Turkish conquest of Western Europe. Barletius also laid the
foundations for what can only be called the cult of Scanderbeg
among the Albanians at home and in the diaspora, an almost
saintly veneration of the Albanian national hero as the symbol
and quintessence of resistance to foreign domination.

BARTL, PETER (1938-). German scholar and historian. Peter
Bartl was born in Cottbus and studied eastern European history,
Slavic and Turkish in Göttingen and Munich. He is currently

professor for the history of eastern and southeastern Europe at the University of Munich and is also head of the Albanien-Institut (Albania Institute) there. Bartl is a specialist in Albanian history. Among his major publications are: *Die albanischen Muslime zur Zeit des nationalen Unabhängigkeitsbewegung, 1878-1912* (The Albanian Muslims at the Time of the National Independence Movement, 1878-1912), Wiesbaden 1968; *Der Westbalkan zwischen spanischer Monarchie und osmanischem Reich: zur Türkenproblematik an der Wende vom 16. zum 17. Jahrhundert* (The Western Balkans between the Spanish Monarchy and the Ottoman Empire: On the Turkish Problem at the Turn of the Sixteenth to Seventeenth Century), Wiesbaden 1974; *Quellen und Materialien zur albanischen Geschichte im 17. und 18. Jahrhundert* (Sources and Material on Albanian History in the Seventeenth and Eighteenth Centuries), Wiesbaden 1975, Munich 1979; *Grundzüge der jugoslawischen Geschichte* (Outline of Yugoslav History), Darmstadt 1985; and *Albanien: vom Mittelalter bis zur Gegenwart* (Albania: From the Middle Ages to the Present), Regensburg 1995.

BASHKIMI PËR FITOREN. *See* UNION FOR VICTORY.

BASHKIMI PËR TË DREJTAT E NJERIUT. *See* UNION FOR HUMAN RIGHTS PARTY.

BASILIAN ORDER. Order of Christian monks. The order of Saint Basil, based on the monastic rules of Byzantine rite and inspired by the teachings of Saint Basil the Great, was widely diffused in the Balkans at an early date and is said to have spread **Christianity** throughout Albania in the sixth and seventh centuries prior to the arrival of the **Benedictines**. Among its protagonists in **Italy** was Saint Nilus of Rossano (910-1004). Nilus was a Calabrian Greek, who, after the death of his wife and child, joined a Byzantine monastery at Palma in Campania. In 955, he founded the Basilian monastery of Saint Adrian in the Italo-Albanian village of San Demetrio Corone (Alb. *Shën Mitri*), in the mountains of Calabria. In about 981, he took refuge from the Saracens at Monte Cassino and finally settled, just before his death, at Grottaferrata in the Alban hills south of Rome, where he founded a monastery. His third successor, Saint Bartholomew of Grottaferrata (d. 1055), established the Abbey of Grottaferrata there on a permanent basis. The Basilian monks of Grottaferrata, with their dependencies in Mezzojuso (Alb. *Munxifsi*) in Sicily and San Basile (Alb. *Shën Vasili*) in Calabria, were instrumental in preserving the **Uniate Church of Byzantine Rite** among the Italo-Albanians. From 1693, they sent missionaries to the **Himara** district of southern Albania and maintained close relations with the **Orthodox** community there. Even today, the Abbey of Grottaferrata has strong links with Albanian and Italo-Albanian culture.

BECI, BAHRI (1936.03.06-). Scholar and linguist. Bahri Beci studied at the University of **Tirana** from 1954 to 1958 and was thereafter appointed to the Institute of Linguistics and Literature. In 1966, he was relieved of his job for political reasons and sent to the north to teach school. In 1969, he returned to the institute of which he was to become director from 1993 to 1997 in the years of the regime of **Sali Berisha**. He also studied in France from 1975 to 1977. In 1997, he emigrated to Paris, where he now lives, and taught Albanian at the Institute for Oriental Languages and Cultures (INALCO).

Bahri Beci is the author of numerous books on the Albanian **language** and its dialects. He has also been a major figure in the movement to revalue **Gheg** literary dialect. Among his book publications are: *Të folmet veriperëndimore të shqipës dhe sistemi fonetik i së folmës së Shkodrës* (The Northwestern Dialects of Albanian and the Phonetic System of the Dialect of Shkodra), Tirana 1995; *Gramatika e gjuhës shqipe* (Grammar of the Albanian Language), Tirana 1997; *Gramatika e gjuhës shqipe për të gjithë* (Grammar of the Albanian Language for Everyone). Shkodra 2000; *Probleme të politikës gjuhësore dhe të planifikimit gjuhësor në Shqipëri* (Problems of Language Policy and Language Planning in Albania), Peja 2000; *Dialektet e shqipes dhe historia e formimit të tyre* (The Dialects of Albanian and the History of Their Formation), Tirana 2002; and *Probleme të lidhjeve të shqipes me gjuhët e tjera ballkanike* (Problems of the Links between Albanian and the Other Balkan Languages), Peja 2002.

BEGEJA, LIRIA (1955.02.16-). Franco-Albanian **film** director. Liria Begeja was born in Paris of an Albanian father and French mother. She graduated with a degree in history from the University of Paris in 1977, and from film school in 1978. She began her film debut in the 1980s, working with directors such as Patrice Chéreau (1944-) and Chantal Akerman. The first film she made on her own was *Paris Paparazzi*. Her *Avril brisé* (Broken April), based on a novel by **Ismail Kadare**, received awards in Locarno and in Italy. Her *Loin des Barbares* (Far from the Barbarians), made in 1993, is a film about Albanian emigration with **Timo Flloko**. She has most recently completed the film *Change moi ma vie* (Change My Life), 2000, with Fanny Ardant.

BEJTEXHINJ LITERATURE. Period of Albanian **literature**. The *Bejtexhinj*, from Alb. *bejtexhi*, pl. *bejtexhinj*, deriving from the Turkish word *beyit* "couplet," were popular poets in the Muslim tradition, literally "couplet makers." The first attempts in the early eighteenth century by Albanian writers who had been raised in an **Islamic** culture to express themselves not in the languages of the Orient but in their own native tongue, resulted in the creation of *Bejtexhinj* literature. This period of Albanian writing consists almost exclusively of verse composed in Arabic script. The Arabic writing system had already been adapted, albeit rather awkwardly, to the needs of Ottoman Turkish and was then molded to fit the more elaborate phonetic system of Albanian, or more precisely, of the Albanian dialects in question. It proved to be just as unsatisfactory for Albanian as it had been for Turkish. But not only was the script oriental, the language of the *Bejtexhinj* was an Albanian so laden with Turkish, Arabic and Persian vocabulary that it is quite tedious for Albanians today to read without a lexicon. Indeed it is likely that the reader of classical Turkish not knowing Albanian would understand more of many poems than the reader of Albanian not knowing any oriental languages.

BEKTASHI ORDER OF DERVISHES. Islamic Sufi order or *tariqa* and major religious community of Albania. The Bektashi order is said to have been founded in Anatolia by Haji Bektash Veli (Turk. *Haci Bektaş Veli*) who lived in the thirteenth century. With the expansion of the **Ottoman Empire**, it spread from central Anatolia notably to the Balkans, Greece, Crete and elsewhere, where the Bektashi served as missionaries of **Islam** and chaplains to the janissaries.

Little is known of the early history of the Bektashi in Albania, though it can be assumed that they were well established by the late sixteenth to mid-seventeenth centuries. The Bektashi themselves trace their entry into Albania to the legendary figure **Sari Salltëk**. The Turkish traveler **Evliya Çelebi**, who visited southern Albania in the summer of 1670, noted a Bektashi monastery or *tekke,* Alb. *teqe*, in Kanina near **Vlora**, describing the site as follows: "There is in addition a *tekke* of Haji Bektash Veli here, which was also endowed by Sinan Pasha. This *tekke* is famous throughout Turkey, Arabia and Persia. Here one finds many devotees of the mystical sciences and the dervish life of poverty. Among them are some lovely young boys. Visitors and pilgrims are fed copious meals from the kitchen and pantry of the *tekke* because all the surrounding mountains, vineyards and gardens belong to it. Near the *tekke*, the benefactor of the endowment, Ghazi Sinan Pasha, lies buried along with all his household and retainers in a mausoleum with a lofty dome—may God have mercy on their souls. In short, it is a rich and famous *tekke*, beyond my powers to describe (*Seyahatname* VIII, 361a)." The mausoleum referred to by Evliya, which has now since disappeared, was still an object of veneration during the visit of Austrian consul **Johann Georg von Hahn** in the mid-nineteenth century. Hahn reports: "[The owners of the fortress] are descendants of the first Turkish conqueror of this region, the famous Sinan Pasha of Konya, whose grave can be seen in a small *tekke* at the base of the castle. People come here on pilgrimage from far and wide, as the Turks consider Sinan to be a saint (1854)." When the Porte ordered the closure of all Bektashi *tekkes* in 1826, the Bektashi *tekke* of Kanina was conferred upon the **Halveti order**.

Among other early Bektashi monasteries was the *tekke* in Tetova (Tetovo) in Macedonia, founded at the end of the sixteenth century. According to legend, Sersem Ali Dede, a vizier under Sultan Suleyman (r. 1520-1566), saw Bâlim Sultân, second *pîr* "patron, founder" of the Bektashi order, in a dream and abandoned his post as vizier to live the life of a simple dervish in the village of Haci Bektaş, where the Bektashi movement arose. Before his death in 1569, he ordered that all his possessions be sold and the money be used to purchase land for a monastery in Tetova. The monastery was constructed accordingly by one Harâbâtî (Harabti) Baba, after whom the *tekke* is named. This *tekke* was expanded in the late eighteenth and early nineteenth centuries to include a group of buildings and a beautiful garden, which still exist today as a hotel complex. From the early eighteenth century onwards, the *tekke* in Tetova served as the mother house (*âsitâne*) for many other *tekkes* in **Kosova** and Macedonia. In 1780, there followed the building of a Bektashi *tekke* in **Gjirokastra** under Asim Baba. This *tekke* laid the foundations for the Bektashi movement in Albania itself and was of particular significance in the late nineteenth century.

The Albanians were especially receptive to certain features of Bektashism, namely, its traditional tolerance and regard for different **religions**, and the related open-minded attitude to practices and beliefs. Indeed some see Christian and pre-Christian practices continuing under the liberal umbrella of Bektashism. Furthermore, the Bektashis were receptive to local concerns and language, in contrast to Sunni Islam, which identified itself primarily with the Ottoman capital and the Arabic language.

Much of southern Albania and Epirus converted to Bektashism initially under the influence of **Ali Pasha Tepelena**, the awesome "Lion of Janina," who was himself a follower of the order. In 1826, four years after Ali Pasha's death, the order suffered a setback in Albania when Sultan Mahmud II (r. 1808-1839) suppressed the janissary corps and ordered the closure of all Bektashi *tekkes* in the Ottoman Empire. The Bektashi were, nonetheless, prominent once again during the years of the Albanian nationalist movement, **Rilindja**, in the late nineteenth century and it is this link, no doubt, which gave rise to their surprising popularity. Such was the level of conversion to Bektashism that it grew into a religious community of its own and became the fourth religion of Albania.

It is estimated that at the beginning of the twentieth century, fifteen percent of the **population** of Albania were Bektashi, equivalent to one-quarter of all Muslims in the country. Their *tekke*s served as centers for the nationalist movement, in particular for the underground propagation of Albanian-language books and education. Despite this, the sect did not succeed in becoming the Albanian national religion, as many Bektashi intellectuals had hoped. One reason for this was their disproportionate concentration in the south of the country. About seventy percent of all Bektashi *tekkes* were to be found south of **Berat** and only three percent in the north.

Bektashism also suffered a major setback with the revolt, during independence, of many Muslims demanding the country's return to the Ottoman Empire and, in particular, with the burning and looting of the Albanian *tekkes* by Greek extremists during the **Balkan War** and **World War I**. At that time, about eighty percent of the *tekkes* were damaged or completely destroyed, an immeasurable loss from which this Islamic culture never really recovered.

During their first national congress, held in Prishta in **Skrapar** in January 1922, the Bektashi declared themselves independent of the Turkish Bektashi and, after the ban of all **dervish orders** in Turkey in the autumn of 1925, it was to **Tirana** that the Turkish Bektashi transferred their world headquarters. In Albania, they set up a recognized and independent religious community, which existed there until 1967. The Bektashi community was divided into six districts: **Kruja** with its headquarters at the *tekke* of Fushë Kruja, **Elbasan** with its headquarters at the *tekke* of Krasta, **Korça** with its headquarters at the *tekke* of Melçan, Gjirokastra with its headquarters at the *tekke* of Asim Baba in Gjirokastra, Prishta representing Berat and part of Përmet, and Vlora with its headquarters at the *tekke* of Frashër. In 1928, the publicist Teki Selenica recorded the presence in Albania of sixty-five *babas,* meaning theoretically that there were at least sixty-five *tekkes* in the country at the time. There were also about a dozen Bektashi *tekkes* in Kosova. By the mid-1940s, there were an estimated 280 *babas* and dervishes in Albania, and in the 1960s it is known that there were still about fifty Bektashi *tekkes* in the country and about eighty dervishes—fifteen in Fushë Kruja alone. By 1993, however, after the collapse of the dictatorship, there were only five *babas* and one dervish left alive, and only six *tekkes* remained standing in any recognizable state.

The Bektashi community, like the other religious communities in Albania, was persecuted by the **communist** authorities from the start and many of its rulers soon met their death. Baba Murteza of Kruja died in 1946 after being tortured and thrown out of a prison window. Baba Kamil Glava of **Tepelena** was executed in 1946 in Gjirokastra. The writer Baba Ali Tomori (1900-1947) and Baba Shefket Koshtani of Tepelena were executed the following year. The American anthropologist **Frances Trix** has published a more or less complete list of Bektashi *babas* who suffered during the early years of communist rule.

In 1967, the Bektashi community was dissolved entirely when a communist government edict banned all religious activity in Albania. During the dictatorship, there were only two Albanian *tekkes* which strove to carry on the tradition: one in Gjakova in Kosova under the direction of Baba Qazim Bakalli, who died in the late 1980s, and the other in Taylor, near Detroit, Michigan, founded in 1954 and long under the direction of the eminent **Baba Rexhebi**. It is now led by Baba Flamur Shkalla. The beautiful *tekke* of Gjakova was razed to the ground by Serb extremists in the spring of 1999 along with the rest of the old town.

After almost a quarter of a century of silence in Albania, a provisional committee for the revival of the Bektashi community was founded in Tirana on 27 January 1991. Since that time, the new community, under Baba **Reshat Bardhi**, has been active in reviving Bektashi traditions in Albania. The *tekke* and, at the same time, world headquarters in Tirana was reopened on 22 March 1991 on the occasion of *Nevruz*, and the sixth Bektashi national congress was held in July 1993. There are now six functioning Bektashi *tekkes* in Albania: Turan under Baba Edmond Ibrahimi (ca. 1957-), Gjirokastra under Baba Haxhi, Elbasan under Baba Sadik Ibro (1972-), Fushë Kruja under the learned Baba Selim Kaliçani (1922-2001), Tomorica under Baba Shaban, and Martanesh under Baba Halil Curri. Others are in the process of being set up: Berat, Shëmbërdhenj, Bllaca and Vlora, where the mausoleum of Kusum Baba was reopened in April 1998 at an inspiring site overlooking the city. Outside of Albania proper, there are Albanian Bektashi *tekkes* in Tetova under Baba Tahiri and—until its destruction by Serb forces in the spring of 1999—in Gjakova under Baba Mumin Lama.

The Bektashi religious order has a hierarchical structure as well as specific beliefs, rites and practices. The main categories in the hierarchy of this faith are as follows. The *ashik*, Turk. *aşik*, literally "lover," is the simple Bektashi believer or faithful who has not been initiated in any way. He is often an individual who has been drawn to a particular *baba* and has become devoted to him. The *muhib*, also meaning "one who loves, sympathizer," is a spiritual member of the Bektashi community, i.e., an individual who has received some initiation involving a ritual purification and a profession of faith during a ceremony held at a *tekke*. After a trial period, a *muhib* can become a *varf* "dervish." The dervish receives a white headdress called a *taj*, Alb. *taxh* from Turk. *tac,* as well as other garments, lives full-time at a *tekke*, and is in a sense the equivalent of a Christian monk. The *myxher,* from Turk. *mücerred* "person tried by experience, pure, unmarried" is the member of a special category of dervishes, that of the celibate dervishes, who wear a ring in their right ear. There has been much controversy in the history of modern Bektashism about the adherence to celibacy. The *baba*, also Alb. *atë* "father," is a spiritual master, equivalent to a sheikh in other dervish orders. Each *tekke* is normally headed by a *baba.* The *gjysh*, literally "grandfather," equivalent to Turk. *dede* or *halife*, is the superior of the *babas* and is responsible for all the *tekkes* in a certain region. The *gjysh* has passed through the final level of ceremony and wears his white *taj* with a green cloth band wrapped around it. Finally, the *kryegjysh* "head grandfather," known in Turk. as *dede baba*, is the leader of the Bektashi order as a whole, chosen from among all the *gjysh.*

As in Sufism in general, the emphasis in Bektashism is on inner meaning rather than on the following of outer convention. Bektashi practices and rites are thus characterized, as has been noted above, by a good degree of liberality. Sunni religious leaders have often been scandalized at the indifference which the Bektashi often seem to show towards some of the tenets of mainstream Islam. The Bektashi pray only twice a day and are not obliged to do so in the direction of Mecca, in contrast to Sunni Muslims who pray five times a day. Bektashi prayers do not necessarily involve prostration. As with other Muslims, most Bektashi refuse to eat pork, nor will they touch turtles, dogs, snakes and, the most abhorrent of all, hares. Some Bektashis drink alcohol and, indeed, in a number of Albanian *tekkes* they make their own *raki*. Their **women** participate on an equal footing with the men in ceremonies and gatherings, something which again scandalizes some mainstream Muslims and which, in the past, led to wild speculation and rumors about the goings-on in Bektashi *tekkes.* The Bektashi are not expected to fast during *Ramadan*, but they do fast or at least abstain from drinking during *matem*, the first ten days of the month of Muharrem during which the suffering and death of Imam Husein is commemorated. Indeed, during the period of *matem,* they will drink only bitter yogurt and lentil soup. The feast of *ashura* then follows during which a dish is eaten made of cracked wheat, dried fruit, crushed nuts and cinnamon all cooked together. *Nevruz*, the Persian new year and birthday of Imam Ali, is also commemorated by the Albanian Bektashi.

Bektashism has a long history and has absorbed influences from various sources. Among the earliest components of Bektashi doctrines and beliefs in the Middle East are Turkmen heterodoxy, the ascetic Kalenderi (Qalandari) movement of the thirteenth-fourteenth centuries inspired by Persian and Indian mysticism, otherworldly Sufic Melametism (Malamatiyya), the Futuwwa order in the Middle East, and the gnostic and cabbalistic doctrines of Persian Hurufism. It subsequently evolved in close contact with Shi'ite and Alevite Islam and, in the Balkans at least, took on many Christian elements.

As to their pantheistic core beliefs, about which the Bektashi can be rather secretive, they believe in Allah, in Mohammed and in Imam Ali, to whom a special position is accorded. Indeed, Ali, his wife Fatima and their two sons Hasan and Husein are the central figures of the Bektashi and Shi'ite creed. Many Bektashi homes have pictures of Ali, considering him to be the manifestation of God on earth. He is invoked on a variety of occasions by believers with a *"ya, Ali!"* or *"Muhammed-Ali!"* The figures of Allah, Muhammed and Ali have thus come to constitute a sort of Bektashi trinity. The Bektashi, like other Shi'ites, revere the twelve imams, particularly Ali of course, and consider themselves descendants of the sixth imam, Jafer Sadik. Naturally, they also revere Haji Bektash as the founder of the order. As to ethics, the Bektashi adhere to the Turkish formula, *eline, diline, beline sahip ol* (Be master of your hands, your tongue and your loins), used during initiation ceremonies. Essentially, this means not to steal, not to lie or talk idly and not to commit adultery.

A major source of information on Albanian Bektashi beliefs is *Fletore e Bektashinjet* "Bektashi Notebook," written by one of the best-known writers of Albanian **literature**, **Naim bey Frashëri**. Frashëri had hoped that the liberal Bektashi beliefs to which he had been attached since his childhood would one day take hold as a new religion for all of Albania. Since they had their roots both in the Muslim Koran and in the Christian Bible, the Bektashi could promote unity among their religiously divided people. Naim Frashëri supported the confessional independence of the Albanian Bektashi movement from the central *pîr evi* in the village of Haci Bektaş Köy in Anatolia and proposed an Albanian *baba* or *dede* as its leader. He also introduced Albanian terms which replaced the Turkish ones in order to give his Bektashi religion a national character and unite all Albanians.

BEKTESHI, BESNIK (1941.08.11-). Political figure of the **communist** period. Bekteshi was born in **Shkodra** and studied construction engineering at the University of **Tirana**, later participating in the construction of the "Light of the Party" (*Drita e Partisë*) hydroelectric dam and power plant in Fierza on the river **Drin**. He became a member of the **Party of Labor** in 1973 and, promoted by **Ramiz Alia**, was elected to the Central Committee in 1981. He served as a member of **parliament** from Shkodra in November 1982 and was deputy prime minister from 23 November 1982 to 2 February 1989. He was a full member of the Politburo from 1986 to the end of the dictatorship. Bekteshi was tried together with nine other members of the Politburo and sentenced on 30 December 1993 to six years in prison for the misappropriation of public funds.

BELISHOVA, LIRI (1923-). Political figure of the **communist** period. Liri Belishova was born in the village of Belishova in the

District of **Mallakastra.** She attended the Queen Mother Pedagogical Institute (*Instituti Nanë Mbretneshë*) in **Tirana** in the late
1930s and studied nursing. During **World War II,** she joined the
communist resistance movement and lost one eye. From 1946 to
1947, she was president of the People's Youth (*Rinia Popullore*).
When her first husband **Nako Spiru** was purged and committed
suicide, she was dismissed from all posts and sent to **Berat** to
teach school. After the fall of **Koçi Xoxe** in 1948, however, she
was rehabilitated and became a member of the Politburo from
1948 to 1960. She attended the Marxist-Leninist Institute in
Moscow with **Ramiz Alia** in 1952-1954 and was a member of the
party secretariat from 1954 to 1960. She was also married to
Maqo Çomo, minister of agriculture from 1954 to 1960.

On her return from **China** in 1960, Liri Belishova stopped
over in Moscow and allegedly spoke to Russian leaders about the
anti-Soviet intentions of the Chinese leadership. In September of
that year, when Albania was on the verge of breaking party relations with the Soviet Union, she was expelled from all party
functions as being pro-Soviet and a friend of Nikita Khrushchev,
and was placed under arrest. She spent the next thirty-one years
of her life, to 1991, in internment in Mallakastra.

BENEDICTINE ORDER. Order of **Catholic** monks adhering to the
rules of the Italian patriarch of monasticism, Benedict of Norcia
(ca. 480-547). Saint Benedict founded the order in 529 at the
Abbey of Monte Cassino where he died. It is not known when the
Benedictines sent their first missionaries to Albania but the order
was active in the country in the Middle Ages. The Benedictines
are credited with preserving Catholic influence in much of Albania against the pressure of rival Byzantine **Orthodoxy.** Though
in decline by the fourteenth century, the Benedictines are said to
have put up heroic resistance to the encroachment of **Islam** during the **Ottoman** conquest.

BERAT. Town in the District of Berat, of which it is the administrative center. **Population** in December 1999: 63,932. Berat is one
of the oldest settlements in Albania and a town of great historical
and cultural interest.

Founded in the fourth or third century B.C., Berat was known
in ancient Greek as *Antipatreia* and, in Latin, as *Antipatrea.* The
early Byzantine term for the town was *Pulcheriopolis* "beautiful
town," when it became the seat of a bishop under the Emperor
Theodosius II (408-450 A.D.). In the Middle Ages, it was succes-

sively under Byzantine, Bulgarian (ninth century), Norman (1082-1085), Angevin (1272-), Serb (1346-) and Turkish (1417-) control. The present name of the town derives from the Slavic *beli grad* "white town," ~ med. Lat. *Belogradum, Bellegradum,* Turkish *Belgrad* (1431), Ital. *Belgrado* (1515). To the Venetians, it was known as *Belgrado di Romania* and in Turkish as *Arnavud Belgrad* (1670), to distinguish it from Belgrade in Serbia.

The old town of Berat is situated on a hill with impressive Byzantine fortifications and contains some early **Orthodox** churches of note: the Vlachernes Church (ca. 1300), the church of St. Michael (ca. 1300), the Holy Trinity (ca. 1300), St. George (fourteenth century), St. Nicholas (1591), the Evangelism church (late sixteenth century), St. Demetrius (1607), St. Constantine and Helena (1644), the church of the Holy Virgin (1797), and foundations of the so-called Red Mosque (1417), said to be the earliest mosque in Albania.

The present town, which lies on the banks of the river **Osum**, ancient Apsus, is noted for the Sultan Mosque, Alb. *Xhamia e Mbretit* (1492); the Lead Mosque, Alb. *Xhamia e Plumbit* (1553-1555); and a *tekke* of the **Halveti order of dervishes** (1785). **Evliya Çelebi** who visited Berat in 1670, described it as having a "huge open town entirely outside the walls of the fortress... with 5,000 one- and two-story stonework houses with fine red tiled roofs. They are well-built and attractive houses with gardens and are spread over seven verdant hills and valleys. Among them are over 100 splendid mansions with cisterns and foundations and an invigorating climate."

In 1916, Berat had a population of 8,500 and in 1939 of 11,000. Known today as the "Town with the Thousand Windows," Berat was designated as an official museum city and is under monument protection.

BERAT, DISTRICT OF. Region of local government administration. The District of Berat (*Rrethi i Beratit*), with its administrative headquarters in the town of Berat, borders on the districts of **Fier** and **Mallakastra** to the west, **Lushnja, Kuçova** and **Elbasan** to the north, **Gramsh** and **Skrapar** to the east and **Tepelena** to the south. It has a surface area of 939 square kilometers and a present population of 140,914 (in 2000).

BERATI, DHIMITËR. *See* BERATTI, DHIMITËR.

BERATTI, DHIMITËR (1896-1970.09.06). Political figure. Dhimitër Beratti was from **Korça**. Having taken part in the declaration of Albanian independence in **Vlora**, he was made state secretary at the foreign ministry. From 24 August 1913 to 1914, he edited the biweekly Vlora newspaper *Përlindj' e Shqipënies* (Rebirth of Albania), which, as the voice of the provisional government, was devoted to "the defense of national rights." Beratti spent **World War I** in Bucharest and then served as secretary of the Albanian delegation at the Paris Peace Conference from 1919 to 1921. While in France, he published a sixty-nine-page book in English on *Albania and the Albanians,* Paris 1920, and a similar one in French entitled *La question albanaise* (The Albanian Question), Paris 1920, to make the Albanian cause better known. In 1923, Beratti was again at the foreign ministry and served as a member of the **International Boundary Commission**. After another period of stay in Romania, from 1925, he returned to the foreign ministry once more. In 1934, he was appointed as minister of economics. During the occupation, Dhimitër Beratti served as minister of education from December 1941 to January 1943. He fled to Italy after the war, where he died in a traffic accident in 1970.

BERISHA. Northern Albanian tribe and traditional tribal region. The Berisha region is situated south of the **Drin** River in the present District of **Puka**, to the west of the town of Fierza. It borders on the traditional tribal regions of **Dushmani** and **Toplana** to the west, Bugjoni to the north, Iballja to the east and Kabashi to the south. The Berishas are thought to be one of the oldest tribes in the northern mountains, with a genealogy reaching back to the year 1360. The name was recorded in 1691 as *Berisa.* Berisha is a common family name, in particular in **Kosova**. The Berisha tribe had a **population** of about 1,700 in 1917.

BERISHA, SALI (1944.10.15-). Political figure and high-ranking member of the **Democratic Party of Albania**. Berisha was born in Vuçidol in the **Tropoja** region of northern Albania and graduated from the Faculty of Medicine of the University of **Tirana** in 1967. He became a member of the communist **Party of Labor** in 1971 and, after specializing in cardiology, was appointed assistant professor of medicine and cardiologist at Tirana General Hospital. In 1978, he spent nine months of advanced training in Paris on a UNESCO fellowship.

In October 1989, Sali Berisha became one of a small group of Albanian intellectuals to voice open opposition to the collapsing **communist** system and, by early 1990, he was the leading spokesperson of the reform movement. In December 1990, following student protests, he founded the Democratic Party, the first opposition party in post-communist Albania. He was formally elected head of the party in February 1991 and became a member of **parliament** in the elections of 31 March 1991. On 9 April 1992, he was elected by parliament as president of Albania, the first noncommunist head of state since **World War II**.

Sali Berisha did much to transform Albania into a western democracy. He carried out badly needed institutional, economic and legal reforms, introducing basic democracy, the rule of law and a market economy. Radical changes in personnel took power out of the hands of the former communist ruling elite but polarized Albanian society. By mid-1994, however, his rule had become increasingly authoritarian and autocratic, and few decisions were made in the country without his approval. With the leader of the political opposition languishing in prison and the new **National Information Service** (SHIK) sniffing about in everybody's business, Albania had once again become a one-party state, though infringements on individual rights never reached the awesome proportions they had known under the communist dictatorship. While Berisha retained much sympathy in the north of the country, by 1995 he had lost all semblance of popular support in central and southern Albania. The end to his regime was finally brought about by the collapse of the **pyramid investment schemes**, which led to chaos and an angry popular uprising in the south of the country at the very moment he was having himself elected to a second term of office (3 March 1997). On 23 July 1997, after tense negotiations under international supervision, Sali Berisha resigned as president, turning power over to the Socialists under his arch-rival **Fatos Nano**. Since that time, he has continued to head the Democratic Party and is official leader of the opposition in parliament. Sali Berisha is a dynamic and determined political figure who has survived the vicissitudes of political life in his country.

BERLIN, CONGRESS OF. *See* CONGRESS OF BERLIN.

BESA. Popular custom. The *besa* (Alb. *besë*, def. *besa*) is one's word of honor, a sworn oath, a pledge or a cease-fire. In Albanian culture, the *besa* was regarded as something sacred and its violation was quite unthinkable. The *besa* was not only a moral virtue, but also a particularly important institution in Albanian customary law. Among the **feuding** tribes of the north it offered the only form of real protection and security to be had. A *besa* could be given between individuals or feuding families for a specific period of time in order for them to settle other urgent affairs. It could also be concluded between tribes as a cease-fire between periods of fighting.

The Croatian priest Lovro Mihačević O.F.M., who lived in the mountains of northern Albania in the late nineteenth century, described the institution of the *besa* in the following terms: "The *besa*, equivalent to our word of honor, is sacred to the Albanians. Anyone who does not keep his *besa* is no man at all, and certainly not a gentleman. The *besa* is made between individuals as a pledge that they will protect one another. It can happen that two or more individuals who are in the middle of a blood feud, will give one another their *besa* for a certain period of time, during which the feud and any other hostile actions must be put aside. The Albanian would rather die than break his word of honor, especially if he has taken someone under his protection."

The *besa*, taken to extremes, could have terrible repercussions. The **Rilindja** author **Sami bey Frashëri** also exemplified this in his Turkish-language play, *Besa yahud ahde vefa* (*Besa* or the Fulfilment of the Pledge), published in Istanbul in 1875 and translated into English as *Pledge of Honor, an Albanian Tragedy*, New York, 1945. In this rather melodramatic work, readers are confronted with the tragic dilemma of an Albanian father who prefers to kill his own son rather than break his *besa*.

Despite some excesses and exceptions, the Albanian *besa* is an institution which—until recently—was generally respected by the Albanians and of which they can still be proud.

BESA-BESË. *See* LEAGUE OF PEJA.

BIBERAJ, ELEZ (1952.11.15-). Albanian-American scholar and political commentator. Elez Hysen Biberaj was born in Krusheva near Plava in Montenegro a year after his family had escaped from **Tropoja**. He emigrated with his entire family to the United States in 1968. In December 1980, he began working for the Albanian Service of the Voice of America in Washington D.C. From 1982 to September 1986, he served as senior analyst for Soviet and East European affairs at the press division of the United States Information Agency, and since September 1986, he has been chief of the Albanian Service of the VOA. Biberaj received his Ph.D. in political science at Columbia University in New York in 1985, where he specialized in Soviet and Eastern European affairs, and first visited Albania in March 1991 as an election observer for the Helsinki Commission. Among his publications are: *Albania and China: A Study of an Unequal Alliance,* Boulder 1986; *Albania: A Socialist Maverick,* Boulder 1990; and *Albania in Transition: The Rocky Road to Democracy,* Boulder 1998. He has also published articles in journals such as *Conflict Studies, Problems of Communism, Survey* and *East European Quarterly.*

BIBLIOTEKA KOMBËTARE E SHQIPËRISË. *See* NATIONAL LIBRARY OF ALBANIA.

BIÇAKU, AQIF PASHA (1861-1926.02.10). Political figure. Aqif pasha Biçaku of Elbasan, also known as Aqif pasha Elbasani, was born in **Elbasan**. He is remembered for having raised the Albanian **flag** in Elbasan on 26 November 1912 at the request of **Ismail Qemal bey Vlora**. He supported Qemal in his attempt to form a stable administration and, having been minister of the interior for a brief period in 1914, took part in an unsuccessful congress in his native Elbasan in 1916 to restore Albanian independence. In 1920, he chaired the **Congress of Lushnja** and, as a representative of the **Bektashi**, was elected to the four-member High Regency Council (*Këshilli i Lartë i Regjencës*). Biçaku was a foe of Shefqet bey Vërlaçi and had often tenuous relations with **Ahmet Zogu**. Together with Dom **Luigj Bumçi,** he took part in a coup d'état in December 1921 and was later relieved of his duties on the High Council by Zogu. In 1923-1924, Biçaku represented **Korça** in **parliament** as a member of a pro-**Noli** faction. After the fall of the Noli government, he went into exile.

BJESHKËT E NAMUNA. *See* ACCURSED MOUNTAINS.

BLANCHUS, FRANCISCUS. *See* BARDHI, FRANG.

BLANCUS, FRANCISCUS. *See* BARDHI, FRANG.

BLAND, BILL (1916.04.28-2001). British Marxist-Leninist. Born in Ashton-under-Lyne, William B. Bland was head of the Stalinist-oriented **Albanian Society** in **Britain** for about thirty years. He was instrumental in the creation of the Society in 1957 and served as its secretary from 1960 almost without interruption until his resignation in July 1990.

Bland first visited Albania in 1962 at the invitation of the Central Committee of the **Party of Labor**. He was thereafter active for years in spreading information about Albania and in promoting the political objectives of the Albanian party leadership. He endeavored to foster ties between Albania and Britain and in 1980 launched a campaign to promote diplomatic relations between the two countries. He also edited the Society's small quarterly journal *Albanian Life* from his home in Ilford, Essex. Bland was, in addition, instrumental in the foundation of the Marxist-Leninist Organisation of Britain, which in 1975, was renamed the Communist League. From 1968 to 1978, Albania broke off relations with Bland and his Albanian Society because of the latter's opposition to the pro-Chinese stance of the Albanian party leadership, but close ties resumed after the disintegration of the Sino-Albanian alliance.

Bill Bland was the author of *Albania: World Bibliographical Series,* Oxford, 1988, and coauthor of *A Tangled Web: History of Anglo-American Relations with Albania, 1912-1955,* Ilford 1986.

BLLOK. Term from the **communist** period. The *Bllok,* a word related to the English "block," referred to the residential area of **Tirana,** which was reserved for the members and families of the country's political elite and their servants. It was blocked off by soldiers throughout the dictatorship and, though it is situated in the very heart of Tirana, most inhabitants of the capital had never seen it until 1990. Prominent in the *bllok* were the villas of **Enver Hoxha** and of **Mehmet Shehu**.

BLOOD FEUDING. Blood feuding or vendetta, Alb. *gjakmarrje,* def. *gjakmarrja,* lit. "blood taking," is a reflection of Albanian customary law as codified for instance in the *Kanun* **of Lekë Dukagjini.** It was and is practiced as a means of exercising tribal justice in wide regions of northern Albania and **Kosova**. Behind the blood feud is the principle of "male honor," i.e., that a man cannot cleanse his honor until he has given satisfaction in blood for a crime or infringement upon his honor or upon the honor of a member of his family. **Women** are exempt from such feuds. Vendettas usually occur between families, but they can also take place between entire tribes and may last for decades, even after the original cause of the feud has been forgotten. A murder committed in revenge is usually carried out according to specific customs and norms and is considered fully justified by the community in question. The murderer must inform the family of his victim and ensure that the body be transported home. He must also see that the victim's rifle be returned to the family and, after the arrangement of a *besa* for a twenty-four-hour cease-fire, he is even expected to attend his victim's funeral. The *Kanun* originally sanctioned the slaying of the murderer himself, but the practice was later extended so that male honor or blood could also be "cleansed" by the slaying of any male relative of the murderer. Many of the tribes in the north were once virtually decimated by feuding.

In 1909, **Edith Durham** described the custom of blood feuding as follows: "The unwritten law of blood is to the Albanian as is the Fury of Greek tragedy. It drives him inexorably to his doom. The curse of blood is upon him when he is born, and it sends him to an early grave. So much accustomed is he to the knowledge that he must shoot or be shot, that it affects his spirits no more than does the fact that 'Man is mortal' spoil the dinner of a plump tradesman in West Europe. The man whose honour has been soiled must cleanse it. Until he has done so he is degraded in the eyes of all—an outcast from his fellows, treated contemptuously at all gatherings. When finally folk pass him the glass of rakia behind their backs, he can show his face no more among them—and to clean his honour he kills."

Though substantially curtailed in Albania after **World War II**, blood feuding has remained a prominent feature of northern Albanian society. In Kosova, thousands of families remained discreetly entrapped in these bloody rites until the late 1980s. An anti-vendetta campaign in 1990, led by a committee of prominent Kosova-Albanian intellectuals, among whom was the venerable Anton Çetta (1920-1995), resulted in the "pacification" of over 900 blood feuds. In Albania itself, there has been a substantial revival of blood feuding in the north since the fall of the dictatorship. In 1991, it was estimated that some 60,000 people in northern Albania did not dare to leave the security of their homes because of blood feuds.

BOGA. Northern Albanian tribe and traditional tribal region. The Boga region is situated on the road from Koplik to Theth in the upper regions of the Përroi i Thatë river in the District of **Malësia e Madhe**. It borders on the traditional tribal regions of **Kastrati** to the west, **Kelmendi** to the north, **Shala** to the east, and Gimaj, Plani and **Shoshi** to the south. The small Boga tribe was closely related to the Kelmendi tribe, from which it stemmed, and had a **population** of about 700 at the end of the nineteenth century.

BOGDANI, PJETËR (ca. 1630-1689.12). Writer of early Albanian **literature**. Pjetër Bogdani, known in Italian as Pietro Bogdano, was the last and by far the most original writer of early literature in Albania. He is author of the *Cuneus prophetarum* (The Band of the Prophets), the first prose work of substance written originally in Albanian (i.e., not a translation). Born in Gur i Hasit near Prizren about 1630, Bogdani was educated in the traditions of the **Catholic Church** to which he devoted all his energy. His uncle Andrea or Ndre Bogdani (ca. 1600-1683) was archbishop of Skopje and author of a Latin-Albanian grammar, now lost. Bogdani is said to have received his initial schooling from the **Franciscans** at Čiprovac in northwestern Bulgaria and then studied at the Illyrian College of Loretto near Ancona, as had his predecessors **Pjetër Budi** and **Frang Bardhi**.

From 1651 to 1654, he served as a parish priest in Pult and from 1654 to 1656 studied at the College of the Propaganda Fide in Rome where he graduated as a doctor of philosophy and theology. In 1656, he was named bishop of **Shkodra**, a post he held for twenty-one years, and was also appointed administrator of the Archdiocese of Antivari (Bar) until 1671. During the most troubled years of the Turkish-Austrian war, 1664-1669, he hid out in the villages of Barbullush and Rjoll near Shkodra. A cave near Rjoll in which he took refuge still bears his name. In 1677, he succeeded his uncle as archbishop of Skopje and administrator of the Kingdom of Serbia. His religious zeal and patriotic fervor kept him at odds with Turkish forces, and in the atmosphere of war and confusion which reigned, he was obliged to flee to Ragusa (Dubrovnik), from where he continued on to Venice and Padua, taking his manuscripts with him. In Padua, he was cordially received by Cardinal Gregorio Barbarigo (1622-1697), whom he had served in Rome. Cardinal Barbarigo, bishop of Padua, was responsible for church affairs in the East and had a keen interest in the cultures of the orient, including Albania. He had also founded a printing press in Padua, the *Tipografia del Seminario*, which served the needs of oriental languages and had fonts for Hebrew, Arabic and Armenian. Barbarigo was thus well-disposed, willing and able to assist Bogdani in the latter's historic undertaking.

After arranging for the publication of the *Cuneus prophetarum*, Bogdani returned to the Balkans in March 1686 and spent the next years promoting resistance to the armies of the **Ottoman Empire**, in particular in **Kosova**. He contributed a force of 6,000 Albanian soldiers to the Austrian army, which had arrived in Prishtina, and accompanied it to capture Prizren. There, however, he and much of his army were met by another equally formidable adversary, the plague. Bogdani returned to Prishtina but succumbed to the disease there in December 1689. His nephew Gjergj reported in 1698 that his uncle's remains were later exhumed by Turkish and Tartar soldiers and fed to the dogs in the middle of the square in Prishtina. So ended one of the great figures of early Albanian culture, the writer often referred to as the father of Albanian prose.

It was in Padua in 1685 that the *Cuneus prophetarum*, his vast treatise on theology, was published in Albanian and Italian with the assistance of Cardinal Barbarigo. It is considered to be the masterpiece of early Albanian literature and is the first work in Albanian of full artistic and literary quality. In scope, it covers philosophy, theology and science (with digressions on geography, astronomy, physics and history). The work was reprinted twice under the title *L'infallibile verità della cattolica fede* (The Infallible Truth of the Catholic Faith), Venice 1691 and 1702.

BOGOMILISM. Religious movement. This dualistic sect is said to have been founded by a priest called Bogomil who was active in Bulgaria from 927 to 950. The Bogomils believed in a good God the Father and in an evil God or devil named Satanael, who was the son of the former and was the creator of mankind. Since the visible world was the creation of evil, the Bogomils condemned worldliness. Marriage, for example, was regarded as an abominable obstacle to holiness and a capitulation to the flesh. The Bogomils, who also condemned eating meat and drinking wine, were convinced that they alone could save the world through activities inspired by Jesus, the second son of God the Father.

The Bogomil movement spread from Philippopolis (Plovdiv) to Byzantium, where its adherents were brutally suppressed in the early twelfth century, not only for their religious beliefs but also apparently for their Slavic nationalism and resentment of Byzantine culture. Despite this, they managed to survive in the Balkans and Asia Minor up to the time of the Ottoman conquest. Bogomil beliefs, condemned by the Christian Church as heresy, also spread to Italy and the West. The Bogomils were widely considered to be the forerunners of the Cathar movement of southern France. Among the Cathar communities of western

Europe in 1250 was an *Ecclesia Albanensis*, a dualistic religious community based around Milan, Verona and Desenzano, whose founders, judging by the name, may have come from Albania.

The cradle of medieval Bogomilism in the Balkans corresponds approximately to the territory of the present Republic of Macedonia (FYROM) and part of southwestern Bulgaria. By the end of the twelfth century, the movement had spread to Serbia, Bosnia and Hercegovina. To what extent it exerted its influence in Albania is uncertain. Since Macedonian Bogomilism had declined and virtually disappeared by the fourteenth century, an age in which the nomadic Albanian tribes were still in a phase of early consolidation, it is unlikely that this predominantly Slavic belief had any profound effect on the native population of Albania.

BOJAXHIU, AGNES GONXHE. *See* TERESA, MOTHER.

BOLETINI, ISA BEY (1864.01.15-1916.01.23). Nationalist figure and guerrilla fighter. Isa bey Boletini, born in the village of Boletin near Mitrovica, was one of the great freedom fighters of **Kosova** at the turn of the last century. After the rise of the **League of Prizren**, he took part as a young man in the Battle of Slivova against **Turkish** forces on 22 April 1881. In 1902, Boletini was appointed head of the personal "Albanian guard" of Sultan Abdul Hamid II (r. 1876-1909) in Istanbul, where he spent most of the next four years and acquired the title "bey." He was loyal to the sultan, but, in 1908, he gave his initial support to the Young Turks. When Xhavid Pasha sent an army of 7,000 men to subdue Kosova in November 1908, however, he and a handful of friends put up fierce resistance. After their escape, Turkish troops burned his house down in revenge. In 1909 Boletini led fighting in Prishtina, Prizren and elsewhere, and played an important role in the general uprising in Kosova in the spring of 1910, where he held Turkish forces at bay in Caraleva, between Ferizaj and Prizren, for two days. During the first **Balkan War** in 1912, he led armed guerrillas in Kosova and later in Albania proper, in support of the provisional government which proclaimed Albanian independence in **Vlora** on 28 November 1912.

In March 1913, Boletini accompanied Ismail Qemal bey Vlora to London to seek British support for the new country. **Edwin Jacques** (1995, p. 339) reports the anecdote that "upon entering the British Foreign Office building to plead his nation's cause, the security police asked him to remove the pistol from his belt and check it in the vestibule. He complied with no objection. Following the interview, the foreign secretary, Sir Edward Grey, accompanied Boletini to the vestibule where he put the pistol back in his belt. The foreign secretary remarked with a smile, 'General, the newspapers might record tomorrow that Isa Boletini, whom even Mahmut Shefqet Pasha could not disarm, was just disarmed in London.' Boletini replied with a broad smile, 'No, no, not in London either,' and he withdrew from his pocket a second pistol." Boletini returned to Albania, where his troops defended **Prince Wilhelm zu Wied** until the latter's departure from Albania. He was later interned in Podgorica where he is said to have been killed in a shoot-out.

BOPP, FRANZ (1791.09.17-1867.10.23). German scholar and linguist. Bopp was born in Mainz and taught linguistics at the University of Berlin, where he died. He is remembered as one of the fathers of Indo-European studies with his *Vergleichende Grammatik* (Comparative Grammar), Berlin 1833-1852. Of particular significance to Albanian studies was his treatise *Über das Albanesische in seinen verwandtschaftlichen Beziehungen* (On Albanian in its Genetic Relations), Berlin 1854, in which he was the first to convince the scholarly world that Albanian was an Indo-European language.

BRITAIN, RELATIONS WITH. *See* UNITED KINGDOM, RELATIONS WITH.

BUCHHOLZ, ODA. German scholar and linguist. Originally from East Germany, Buchholz was able to study in Albania before political relations between Albania and the Warsaw Pact were frozen in 1961. She subsequently became a leading figure of Albanian studies in the German Democratic Republic, working for the Academy of Sciences in Berlin, where she still lives. Oda Buchholz, who is an expert in verb morphology, is the author of *Zur Verdoppelung der Objekte im Albanischen* (On the Doubling of the Object in Albanian), Berlin 1977, and is coauthor of *Wörterbuch Albanisch Deutsch* (Albanian-German Dictionary), Leipzig 1977; *Albanische Grammatik* (Albanian Grammar), Leipzig 1987; and of literary translations from the Albanian.

BUDA, ALEKS (1910.09.07-1993.07.07). Scholar and historian. Aleks Buda was born in **Elbasan**, apparently of a merchant family of **Jewish** origin, and went to school in Lecce in southern

Italy. He finished secondary school in Salzburg in Austria in 1930 and completed his university studies in Vienna in 1938. He returned to Albania in February 1939 and taught school in **Korça**, and, in 1943, in **Tirana**. After **World War II,** he was appointed director of the **National Library** (1945-1946). Although he had specialized in literature up to this point, he was to make a name for himself as a historian, in particular for the ancient, medieval and **Rilindja** periods. Much lauded during the **communist** period, he was also a member of the People's Assembly and from January 1973 was president of the **Academy of Sciences**. Buda edited many standard works of Albanian history and published numerous "representative" articles. His writings were collected in the volume *Shkrime historike* (Historical Writings), Tirana 1986.

BUDI, PJETËR (1566-1622.12). Writer of early Albanian **literature**. Pjetër Budi, known in Italian as Pietro Budi, was the author of four religious works in Albanian. He was born in the village of Gur i Bardhë in the **Mat** region of the north-central Albanian mountains. He could not have benefited from much formal education in his native region, and trained for the priesthood at the so-called Illyrian College of Loretto (*Collegium Illyricum* of Our Lady of Luria), south of Ancona in **Italy**, where many Albanians and Dalmatians of renown were to study. At the age of twenty-one he was ordained as a **Catholic** priest and sent immediately to Macedonia and **Kosova**, then part of the ecclesiastical province of Serbia under the jurisdiction of the archbishop of Antivari (Bar), where he served in various parishes for an initial twelve years. In 1610, he was referred to as "chaplain of **Christianity** in Skopje" and, in 1617, as chaplain of Prokuplje. In Kosova, Budi came into contact with **Franciscan** Catholics from Bosnia, connections, which in later years, proved fruitful for his political endeavors to mount support for Albanian resistance to the **Ottoman Empire**. In 1599, Budi was appointed vicar general (*vicario generale*) of Serbia, a post he held for seventeen years. As a representative of the Catholic church in the Turkish-occupied Balkans, he lived and worked in what was no doubt a tense political atmosphere. His ecclesiastical position was in many ways only a cover for his political aspirations.

In 1616, Pjetër Budi traveled to Rome, where he resided until 1618 to oversee the publication of his works. From March 1618 until ca. September 1619, he went on an eighteen-month pilgrimage to Santiago de Compostela in Spain. Back in Rome in the autumn of 1619, he endeavored to draw the attention of the Roman curia to the plight of Albanian Christians and to raise support for armed resistance. On 20 July 1621, he was made bishop of Sapa and **Sarda** (*Episcopus Sapatensis et Sardensis*), i.e., of the **Zadrima** region, and returned to Albania the following year. His activities there were often more political than religious in nature. One of his interests was to ensure that foreign clergymen were replaced by native Albanians, a step which could not have made him particularly popular with some of his superiors in Italy. In December 1622, some time before Christmas, he drowned while crossing the **Drin** River.

Pjeter Budi's first work is the *Dottrina Christiana* or *Doktrina e Kërshtenë* (Christian Doctrine), a translation of the catechism of Saint Robert Bellarmine (1542-1621). It was published in Rome in 1618 and is preserved in only one original copy. The Albanian Christian Doctrine was subsequently reprinted by the Congregation of the Propaganda Fide in Rome in what would seem to be relatively large editions in 1636, 1664 and in 1868. In 1759, it is known that there were still a total of 960 copies of the book in the depository of the Propaganda Fide. Of more literary interest than the catechism itself are Budi's fifty-three pages of religious poetry in Albanian, some 3,000 lines, appended to the Christian Doctrine. It constitutes the earliest poetry in **Gheg** dialect. Much of it was translated from Latin or Italian, though some is original.

Budi's second publication entitled *Ritvale Romanvm et Specvlvm Confessionis* (Roman Ritual and Mirror of Confession) contains his three other religious works: the *Rituale Romanum* or *Rituali Roman* (Roman Ritual), a 319-page collection of Latin prayers and sacraments with comments in Albanian; a short work entitled *Cusc zzote mesce keto cafsce i duhete me scerbyem* (Whoever Says Mass Must Serve This Thing), a sixteen-page explanation of mass, and; the *Speculum Confessionis* or *Pasëqyra e t'rrëfyemit* (The Mirror of Confession), a 401-page translation or, better, adaptation of the *Specchio di Confessione* of Emerio de Bonis, described by Budi as "some spiritual discourse most useful for those who understand no other language than their Albanian mother tongue." Both the Roman Ritual and the Mirror of Confession are supplemented by verse in Albanian.

Pjetër Budi is the first writer from Albania to have devoted himself to poetry. His works include some 3,300 lines of religious verse, almost all in quatrain form with an alternate rhyme. This verse, nineteen poems in all, comprises both poetic translations and original poetry by Budi himself. Though his religious verse is not without style, its content, being imitations of Italian and Latin moralist verse of the period, is not excessively original. He prefers Biblical themes, eulogies and universal motifs such as the inevitability of death.

BUFI, YLLI (1948.05.25-). Political figure and high-ranking member of the **Socialist Party of Albania**. Ylli Bufi was born in **Tirana** and studied chemistry at the University of Tirana, finishing his doctorate in 1971. He worked in the **oil** and food industries from 1972 to 1982. From 1983 to 1990, he was deputy head, and from 1990 to 1991, head of the ministry of light industry and food production. From 5 June to December 1991, he served as prime minister, heading the so-called stability government in the transitional period between the fall of the **communist** regime and the rise of pluralist structures. In the cabinet of July 1997, he was appointed minister of economics and privatization. Ylli Bufi has been a member of **parliament** for the Socialist Party since 1991.

BULGARIA, ALBANIANS IN. The first group of Albanians known to have emigrated to Bulgaria settled in the village of Arbanasi near the ancient Bulgarian capital of Veliko Tărnovo in the early fourteenth century. In 1480, after the death of **Scanderbeg**, thousands more Albanians fled eastwards through Bulgaria, and many of them settled on the western slopes of the Rhodope mountains. Later, more **Orthodox** Albanians settled in different regions of Bulgaria and Thrace, in particular in Dyevna, Veliko Tărnovo, Oryahovitsa, Lyaskovets, Stara Zagora, Nova Zagora and Gorno Dolno, many of them forced into exile by the **Ottoman** authorities. A group of **Catholic** Albanians moved to the region of Mihaylovgrad in northwestern Bulgaria and settled in the villages of Kopilovets, Chiprovtsi and Zhelezna. A good portion of the Albanians of Bulgaria was later forced to flee to Romania and Russia. In the late nineteenth century, however, Sofia served as a rallying point for the Albanian nationalist movement. Today, Albanian can still be heard in the Bulgarian-Greek-Turkish border region, notably in the village of Mandrica. In 1951, there were 1,000 Albanians there. According to the 1992 Bulgarian census, there were 3,197 Albanians in the country.

BULKU, RAIMONDA (1958.08.16-). Actress. Raimonda Bulku was born in **Tirana** and graduated with a degree in acting from the Academy of Fine Arts (*Instituti i Lartë i Arteve*) there in

September 1985. Her first successful role was in the film *Dimri i fundit* (The Last Winter), 1976. From then to 1994, she played in eighteen feature films, mostly in major roles.

BULO, JORGO (1939.04.27-). Scholar. Jorgo Bulo was born in Sheper in the southern **Gjirokastra** region. He attended secondary school in Gjirokastra and graduated from the University of **Tirana** with a degree in Albanian **language** and **literature**. He finished his doctorate in 1982 and worked for years as a research expert at the Institute of Linguistics and Literature, which he now heads. His research has focused, in particular, on literary typology and the works of **Naim Frashëri**. Among his monographs are: *Romani shqiptar i realizmit socialist për luftën nacionalçlirimtare* (The Socialist Realism Novel on the National Liberation War), Tirana 1982; *Magjia dhe magjistarët e fjalës* (Magic and the Verbal Magician), Tirana 1998; and *Tipologjia e lirikës së Naim Frashërit* (Typology of the Poetry of Naim Frashëri), Tirana 1999.

BULQIZA, DISTRICT OF. Region of local government administration. The District of Bulqiza (*Rrethi i Bulqizës*), with its administrative headquarters in the town of Bulqiza, borders on the districts of **Mat** and **Tirana** to the west, **Dibra** to the north, **Librazhd** to the south and the Republic of Macedonia to the east. It has a surface area of 469 square kilometers and a present **population** of 52,140 (in 2000). It possesses considerable chromite deposits.

BUMÇI, LUIGJ (1872.11.07-1945). Political and **Catholic** religious figure. Dom Luigj Bumçi of **Shkodra** was the nephew of writer **Pashko Vasa**. He trained for the priesthood in his native Shkodra and, in January 1912, was made bishop of **Lezha**. In 1919, he was sent by the government to preside over the Albanian delegation to the Paris Peace Conference. He also participated in the **Congress of Lushnja** in January 1920 and, as a representative of the Catholic community, was elected to the four-member High Regency Council (*Këshilli i Lartë i Regjencës*). Together with **Aqif pasha Biçaku** he took part in a coup d'état in December 1921 and was later relieved of his duties on the High Council by **Ahmet Zogu**. He thereafter withdrew from politics and returned to his ecclesiastical duties.

BUSHATI, MALIQ BEY (?-1945). Political figure from **Shkodra**. Maliq bey Bushati from Shkodra edited the newspaper *Populli* (The People) in 1919-1920, together with Salih Nivica. In 1921-1923 and from 1925 on, he was a member of **parliament**. After the Italian invasion, he gave his support to the occupation and was made minister of the interior in the cabinet of **Shefqet bey Vërlaci**. **Sir Andrew Ryan**, British minister in Albania from 1936 to 1939, describes him as a man of character, but of no great intelligence. On 13 February 1943, despite his alleged membership in the *Balli Kombëtar*, he was appointed prime minister by the Italian authorities. Under his administration, an Albanian army and an Albanian gendarmerie were set up, thus creating the illusion of a certain autonomy within the country. On 12 May 1943, after three months in power, he was replaced by his predecessor, **Eqrem bey Libohova**. In 1943, he also became head of the National Fascist Party of Albania. Bushati was executed in the spring of 1945 as a collaborator.

BUSHATI, ZEF (1953.10.11-). Actor and political figure. Born in **Tirana**, Zef Bushati finished his studies in acting at the Academy of Fine Arts (*Instituti i Lartë i Arteve*) in 1976. He worked initially as a stage actor for the **National Theater** in Tirana and then moved on to **film**, in which he starred in six major roles, in particular *Njeriu me top* (The Man with the Cannon), 1977; and *Këmishët me dyllët* (The Shirt with Wax), 1987. Since the fall of the dictatorship, he has abandoned his acting career for politics and is currently head of the Albanian Christian Democratic Party.

BUSHATLLIU, KARA MAHMUD PASHA (1749-1796.09.22). Historical figure. Kara Mahmud Bushatlliu was the son of Mehmed Pasha Bushatlliu (d. 1775), who, as bey of Bushat, founded the dynasty of Ottoman pashas, which rose to prominence in and around **Shkodra** in the late eighteenth century. Kara Mahmud Pasha ruled over much of northern and central Albania for over twenty years and gave the region autonomy within the **Ottoman Empire**, battling both Ottoman and Montenegrin forces. He promoted trade and commerce and brought new prosperity to the region. Kara Mahmud Pasha was succeeded by his brother, Ibrahim Pasha Bushatlliu (d. 1809), who reigned from 1796 to 1809, and his brother's son, Mustafa Pasha Bushatlliu (1796-1860), who reigned from 1815 to 1831, when the dynasty was overcome by Turkish troops.

BUTRINT. Archeological site south of **Saranda**. Butrint (Greek *Buthrotos,* Latin *Buthrotum*) is the most impressive archeological site in Albania. According to the legend recorded in Vergil's Aeneid (III 292 sq.), the site was founded by the seer Helenos after the fall of Troy for refugees from Asia Minor. Helenos is said to have married Hector's widow Andromache and reigned as king of Butrint. The site does not seem to have been founded by the Greeks at any rate. Archeological evidence points rather to the seventh and sixth centuries B.C. as the actual age of foundation. Butrint reached its zenith in the fourth and third centuries B.C. Under Julius and Augustus Caesar, Butrint, then known as Colonia Iulia and Colonia Augusta, served as a base for the Roman fleet and as a grain depot. The town grew substantially in the first and second centuries A.D. It is mentioned by Cicero in his letters to Atticus. The first Christian bishop was consecrated here in 451 A.D. Butrint remained inhabited throughout the Middle Ages. **Ali Pasha Tepelena** constructed a small fortress here in 1807 to protect his merchant vessels from the French fleet.

Butrint was excavated between 1928 and 1941 by Italian archeologists under Luigi M. Ugolini (1895-1936). Preserved at this splendid, though compact site between the lake and a channel leading to the Ionian Sea are Cyclopean-scale walls and gateways, a finely preserved theater for 2,000 spectators dating from the third century B.C., the remains of a third-century Ionian temple of Asclepios, a bath from the second century B.C., an acropolis, as well as a basilica from the early sixth century A.D., and a well-preserved early Christian baptistry with fine mosaics.

Butrint was visited in 1991 by British Lord Sainsbury of Preston Candover and Lord Rothchild, who set up the **Butrint Foundation** in London to help protect the site and promote archeological research there. The British School of Archaeology in Rome has since discovered numerous Roman villas in the surrounding area, as well as the ancient and medieval harbor. Butrint was declared a World Heritage Site in 1992.

BUTRINT FOUNDATION (1993-). International foundation set up in 1993 by Lord Rothchild and Lord Sainsbury of Preston Candover (1927-) for the conservation and preservation of the ancient site of **Butrint** and its hinterland. The prime objective of the foundation is the preservation and development of the Butrint site for the benefit of the public generally. Also connected to the Butrint Foundation as director of archeology is Professor Richard Hodges, director of the Institute of World Archaeology at the

University of East Anglia. He carried out excavations in Butrint and was active on behalf of the British School of Archaeology in Rome from 1988 to 1995. *See* www.butrintfound.dial.pipex.com.

BUZA, ABDURRAHIM (1905.12.22-1986.11.07). Painter. Abdurrahim Buza was born in Skopje of a family from Gjakova in **Kosova**. With the help of **Bajram Curri**, he was able to get a basic education in **Shkodra** and **Tirana** and then attend the Normal School (*Shkolla Normale*) in **Elbasan** (1923-1928). As a student there, he took an active part in the so-called **Democratic Revolution** of June 1924. He was subsequently able to study in Italy with an Albanian government scholarship. Together with sculptor **Odhise Paskali**, he attended the Academy of Fine Arts in Turin for a year, and then continued his training as a painter in Florence (1933). On his return to Albania, he taught art at a school in Tirana and from 1947 at the Jordan Misja Academy, where he remained until his retirement in 1966. Buza's works were first exhibited at the national level in April 1945. They are characterized by bright colors and a certain peasant naivety. He dealt with a wide range of themes in his painting, from portraits to landscapes in **Pogradec** and Tirana, as well as historical, legendary and nationalist subjects. The spirit of his native Kosova is reflected in many of the ca. 500 oil paintings and 10,000 drawings of his, which have been preserved.

BUZUKU, GJON (sixteenth century). Early Albanian writer. Gjon Buzuku was the author of the first book (1555) published in Albanian, at least the first one known. This 188-page Albanian translation of the **Catholic** missal, commonly known as *Meshari* (The Missal), is considered by many observers to be the most spectacular creation of all the history of Albanian writing. Since the frontispiece and the first sixteen sheets of the only extant copy of the book are missing, neither its exact title nor its place of publication are known.

Little is known about the author of this old Albanian missal. The scant information available about Gjon Buzuku comes from the colophon (postscript) of the missal, which Buzuku wrote in Albanian, not unaware of the historic dimensions of his undertaking: "I, Don John, son of Benedict Buzuku, having often considered that our language had in it nothing intelligible from the Holy Scriptures, wished for the sake of our people to attempt, as far as I was able, to enlighten the minds of those who understand, so that they may comprehend how great and powerful and forgiving our Lord is to those who love him with all their hearts... I began it in the year 1554 on the twentieth day of March and finished it in the year 1555 on the fifth day of January."

It has been put forth convincingly that Gjon Buzuku did not live in Albania itself but rather somewhere on the northern Adriatic in the Republic of San Marco, perhaps in the Venetian region itself, where families of Albanian refugees had settled after the Turkish conquest of **Shkodra** in 1479. In Venice, Buzuku would have had greater access to a literary education and to training as a priest than in Albania itself. Judging from the traits of the northwestern **Gheg** dialect used in the text, Gjon Buzuku's family must have stemmed from one of the villages on the western bank of Lake **Shkodra**, possibly around Shestan, which is now in Montenegro. Elements of other dialects also occur, which would seem to confirm the assumption that Buzuku was born and raised outside of Albania, unless of course he was consciously endeavoring to employ a language more widely intelligible than his native dialect.

The mystery of Buzuku's missal is compounded by the fact that only one copy of the book has survived the centuries. It was discovered by chance in 1740 in the library of the College of the Propaganda Fide. The first complete publication of the text was undertaken in 1958 by **Namik Ressuli**, including a photocopy and a transcription. Ten years later, historical linguist **Eqrem Çabej** published another, two-volume critical edition in **Tirana**.

BYLLIS. Archeological site near the present-day village of Hekal in the District of **Mallakastra**. Byllis was founded from Nikaia in the mid-fourth century B.C. The toponym derives from the Greek tribal name, *Bylliónes, Byllydeis.* The hill-site town reached its zenith in the fourth and third centuries B.C. In the second century B.C., it became a Roman colony and was known as Colonia Byllidensium. Mentioned by Pliny in the first century A.D., Byllis was still going strong in the sixth century A.D. The present site includes 2.5 kilometers of perimeter walls three meters thick and nine to ten meters high, eight towers, an agora, a theater dating from the third century B.C., two stoas and two early Christian basilicas from the early sixth century. Little of Byllis has been properly excavated.

BYRON, GEORGE GORDON, Lord (1788-1824). British poet. In the course of his extensive travels to the Mediterranean region, the flamboyant and scandalous romantic poet Lord Byron visited southern Albania in 1809, in particular to see the tyrant **Ali Pasha Tepelena**, the so-called Lion of Janina. The visit made a tremendous impression on him.

Byron is remembered in English literature primarily for his long verse tale *Childe Harold's Pilgrimage* (1812-1819),which was inspired by his travels there and in other parts of the Mediterranean. In Canto II, he writes of the Albanians: *"Land of Albania! where Iskander rose, / Theme of the young, and beacon of the wise, / And he his namesake, whose oft-baffled foes / Shrunk from his deeds of chivalrous emprize: / Land of Albania! let me bend mine eyes / On thee, thou rugged nurse of savage men! / The cross descends, thy minarets arise, / And the pale crescent sparkles in the glen, / Through many a cypress grove within each city's ken."* (xxxviii), and later: *"Fierce are Albania's children, yet they lack / Not virtues, were those virtues more mature. / Where is the foe that ever saw their back? / Who can so well the toil of war endure? / Their native fastnesses not more secure / Than they in doubtful time of troublous need: / Their wrath how deadly! but their friendship sure, / When Gratitude or Valour bids them bleed / Unshaken rushing on where'er their chief may lead"* (lxv).

In the summer of 1813, Byron put on an Albanian costume which he had purchased during his stay in Albania and sat for the portrait painter, Thomas Phillips. The resultant painting in three-quarter length, entitled "Portrait of a Nobleman in the Dress of an Albanian," was exhibited at the Royal Academy and is now at the British Embassy in Athens. A copy of this painting, made in 1836, is on permanent display at the National Portrait Gallery in London. The original Albanian costume, rediscovered in 1962 and now in the possession of the Landsdowne family, is preserved at their family home at Bowood House in Wiltshire.

- C -

ÇABEJ, EQREM (1908.08.06-1980.08.13). Scholar and historical linguist. Çabej was born in Eskişehir, Turkey, and finished his elementary schooling in **Gjirokastra** in 1921. He studied in Austria—in Klagenfurt (1923-1926), Graz (1927) and, in particular, in Vienna (1930-), where he received a solid training in historical linguistics. It was there that he attended the lectures of Paul Kretschmer (1866-1956), Carl Patsch (1865-1945), Nikolai Trubetzkoy (1890-1938) and especially **Norbert Jokl**, who instilled in him an interest in the historical development of his native language. He completed his doctorate in Vienna on 7 October 1933 with a dissertation on *Italoalbanische Studien* (Italo-Albanian Studies), Vienna 1933. On his return to Albania, he worked as a secondary school teacher in **Shkodra** (1934), and later in **Elbasan** (1935), **Tirana** and Gjirokastra, and thereafter was considered one of the country's leading scholars. From 1939 to 1940 he taught once again in Tirana but in September 1942 refused to join the newly created Institute of Albanian Studies there for political reasons. He was in Rome until July 1944 but then returned to Albania. In 1947, he was appointed as a member of the Institute of Sciences, forerunner of the University of Tirana, and served from 1952 to 1957 as professor for the history of Albanian and historical phonology. In 1972, he became a founding member of the Academy of Sciences. Despite the isolation in which he lived during the long years of the Stalinist dictatorship in Albania, he achieved renown as a linguist and scholar at home and abroad. He died in Rome. The University of Gjirokastra now bears his name.

Eqrem Çabej is the author of over 200 publications, many on the Albanian **language**, but also of writings on **literature** and folklore. His earliest scholarly publications of substance date from the mid-1930s. He is remembered in particular for his two-volume critical edition of *Meshari i Gjon Buzukut, 1555* (The Missal of **Gjon Buzuku**, 1555), Tirana 1968, and his seminal etymological research as in *Studime etimologjike në fushë të shqipes* (Etymological Studies in the Field of Albanian), Tirana 1976, 1996. Much of his work was republished in the nine-volume edition *Studime gjuhësore* (Linguistic Studies), Prishtina 1986-1989.

ÇAJUPI, ANDON ZAKO (1866.03.27-1930.07.11). Poet and playwright. Born in Sheper, a village in the Upper Zagoria region of southern Albania, Çajupi was the son of a rich tobacco merchant, Harito Çako, who did business in Kavala and Egypt. The young Andon Zako, who was later to adopt the pseudonym Çajupi, attended Greek-language schools in the region and in 1882 emigrated to Egypt where he studied for five years at the French lycée "Sainte Catherine des **Lazaristes**" in Alexandria. In 1887, he went on to study law at the University of Geneva.

Çajupi remained in Switzerland for two or three more years, during which time he married a girl named Eugénie, who gave birth to their son, Stefan. He completed his law degree on 24 October 1892, but Eugénie died that same year, a tragic loss for the poet. Çajupi returned to Kavala to leave his small son to the charge of his mother, Zoica.

About 1894-1895, he went back to Egypt and articled for three years with a German law firm in Cairo. His legal career came to a swift conclusion, however, when he made the strategic mistake of defending a French company in a dispute against the interests of the khedive. Financially independent, however, Çajupi bore this professional calamity with ease. He withdrew to his villa in Heliopolis near Cairo and devoted himself subsequently to literature and to the consolidation of the thriving Albanian nationalist movement in Egypt. In the years following Albanian independence, Çajupi continued to play an active role in the Albanian community on the Nile, organized as it was in various patriotic clubs and societies at odds with one another over political issues. The poet died at his home in Heliopolis. His remains were transferred to Albania in 1958.

The most significant phase of Çajupi's literary and nationalist activities was from 1898 to 1912. By 1902, he was an active member of the Albanian Fraternity of Egypt (*Vëllazëria e Egjiptit*) and that same year published the poetry volume for which he is best remembered, *Baba-Tomorri* (Father Tomorr), Cairo 1902. This collection, named after Mount **Tomorr** in central Albania, the Parnassus of Albanian mythology, contains light verse on mostly nationalist themes and is divided into three sections: Fatherland, Love, and True and False Tales. The work was an immediate success. Indeed, no volume of Albanian poetry had proven so popular among Albanians at home and abroad since the collections of **Naim bey Frashëri**. Çajupi did not confine himself to the romantic nostalgia of earlier poets in exile. Nationalist he was, but he was also aware of the dreary realities of life in his homeland. One of the most memorable ballads in this collection, *Fshati im* (My Village), focuses for instance on the inequalities of patriarchal society. Though by far the most significant volume of verse in the early years of the twentieth century, *Baba-Tomorri* was not Çajupi's only publication. In 1921, he translated 113 fables of La Fontaine (1621-1695) in *Perralla* (Fables), Heliopolis 1920-1921, and soon thereafter completed a selection of Sanskrit verse, *Lulé te Hindit* (The

Flowers of India), Cairo 1922, which he had adapted from a French anthology and dedicated to **Faik bey Konitza**.

Çajupi was also a playwright, author of a verse tragedy on **Scanderbeg** entitled *Burr' i dheut* (The Earthly Hero), written in 1907. This was followed by a one-act original comedy *Pas vdekjes* (After Death), written in 1910. Another drama in verse, which remained unpublished during his lifetime, was the four-act situation comedy, *Katërmbëdhjetë vjeç dhëndër* (A Bridegroom at Fourteen).

CAMAJ, MARTIN (1925.07.21-1992.03.12). Scholar, linguist and writer. Martin Camaj was an emigrant writer of significance both to Albanian scholarship and to modern Albanian prose and poetry. He was born in the village of Temal, in the **Dukagjini** region of the northern Albanian Alps, and benefitted from a classical **education** at the **Jesuit** Saverian college in **Shkodra**. Camaj managed to flee Stalinist Albania in 1949, and after an initial period in Kosova, he studied at the University of Belgrade. From there he went on to do postgraduate research in Italy, where he taught Albanian and finished his education in linguistics at the University of Rome in 1960. From 1970 to 1990, he was professor of Albanian studies at the University of Munich and lived in the mountain village of Lenggries in Upper Bavaria until his death on 12 March 1992.

Camaj's academic research focused on the Albanian **language** and its dialects, in particular those of southern Italy. He was also active in the field of folklore. Among his major publications in these fields are: *Il Messale di Gjon Buzuku: contributi linguistici allo studio della genesi* (The Missal of **Gjon Buzuku**: Linguistic Contributions to the Study of the Genesis), Rome 1960; *Albanische Wortbildung: die Bildung der älteren Nomina im Albanischen* (Albanian Morphology: The Construction of the Older Substantives in Albanian), Wiesbaden 1966; *Lehrbuch der albanischen Sprache* (Handbook of the Albanian Language), Wiesbaden 1969; *La parlata albanese di Greci in provincia di Avellino* (The Albanian Dialect of Greci in the Province of Avellino), Florence 1971; *Die albanische Mundart von Falconara Albanese in der Provinz Cosenza* (The Albanian Dialect of Falconara Albanese in the Province of Cosenza), Munich 1977; *Albanian Grammar with Exercises, Chrestomathy and Glossary*, Wiesbaden 1984; and *La parlata arbëreshe di San Costantino Albanese in provincia di Potenza* (The Arbëresh Dialect of San Costantino Albanese in the Province of Potenza),

Rende 1993. He was also the coauthor of a volume of Albanian folk tales in German, *Albanische Märchen* (Albanian Folk Tales), Düsseldorf 1974.

Martin Camaj began his literary career with poetry, a genre to which he remained faithful throughout his life, though in later years, he devoted himself increasingly to prose. His first volumes of classical verse, *Nji fyell ndër male* (A Flute in the Mountains), Prishtina 1953, and *Kânga e vërrinit* (Song of the Lowland Pastures), Prishtina 1954, were inspired by his native northern Albanian mountains to which he never lost his attachment, despite long years of exile and the impossibility of return. His collections *Legjenda* (Legends), Rome 1964, and *Lirika mes dy moteve* (Lyrics between Two Ages), Munich 1967, which contained revised versions of a number of poems from *Kânga e vërrinit*, were reprinted in *Poezi 1953-1967* (Poetry 1953-1967), Munich 1981. Camaj's mature verse shows the influence of the hermetic movement of Italian poet Giuseppe Ungaretti (1888-1970), who was his teacher in Rome. The metaphoric and symbolic character of his language increased with time as did the range of his poetic themes. Camaj's language is discreet, reserved and trying at times, although the author himself regarded the term hermetic as coincidental. He relies on the traditional and colorful linguistic fountainhead of his native **Gheg** dialect in order to convey a poetic vision of his pastoral mountain birthplace near the **Drin** River, with its sparkling streams and shining forests. His verse has appeared in English in the volumes *Selected Poetry*, New York 1990, and *Palimpsest*, Munich 1991.

Camaj's first major prose work was *Djella* (Djella), Rome 1958, a novel interspersed with verse about the love of a teacher for a young girl of the lowlands. This was followed, twenty years later, by the novel *Rrathë* (Circles), Munich 1978, which has been described as the first psychological novel in Albanian. After *Shkundullima* (Quaking), Munich 1981, a collection of five short stories and one play, came the novel *Karpa* (Karpa), Rome 1987, which is set on the banks of the River Drin in the year 2338, a long prose work which Camaj preferred to call a parable. General themes which occur in Martin Camaj's work are the loss of tradition, loneliness in a changing world and the search for one's roots. Needless to say, his works only became known to the Albanian public after the fall of the dictatorship. Up until then, only a handful of people in Albania had ever heard of him. His prose and poetry were first made widely available in the Balkans in the five-volume edition, *Vepra letrare* (Literary Works), Tirana 1996.

CAMARDA, DEMETRIO (1821.10.23-1882.04.13). Arbëresh philologist. Among the cultural leaders of the Arbëresh in the nineteenth century whose publications on Albanian **language** and **literature** gave impetus not only to the Albanians of Italy but also to the **Rilindja** movement in the motherland was philologist and folklorist Demetrio Camarda, known in Albanian as Dhimitër Kamarda. He was born in Piana degli Albanesi in Sicily and studied for the priesthood at the college of the Propaganda Fide in Rome. After being ordained in the Byzantine rite in 1844, he lived in Naples and in his native village until 1848 when he was expelled from the Kingdom of the Two Sicilies by the Bourbon authorities for allegedly having collaborated with the liberals. He fled first to Rome and then to the **Benedictine** monastery of Cesena. In 1852, he was appointed teacher at a secondary school in Leghorn (Livorno), where he spent the rest of his life as a parish priest of the Greek Catholic community.

Camarda is remembered for his *Saggio di grammatologia comparata sulla lingua albanese* (Essay on the Comparative Grammar of the Albanian Language), Leghorn 1864, one of the first works of Albanian diachronic philology, in which he attempted to prove the strong affiliation of the Albanian language with Greek, in contradiction to German comparative linguist **Franz Bopp**, who had demonstrated its direct Indo-European origin in 1854. This work was followed by *Appendice al saggio di grammatologia comparata* (Appendix to the Essay on Comparative Grammar), Prato 1866, a collection of Arbëresh folksongs. Camarda also wrote a grammar of Albanian and published a book of Albanian poetry dedicated to **Dora d'Istria**, entitled *A Dora d'Istria gli Albanesi* (To Dora d'Istria, the Albanians), Leghorn 1870. He died in Leghorn.

ÇAMËRIA. Geographical region extending from the southern tip of Albania into what is now northern Greece, the region of Janina. The city of Janina and much of the Çamëria region, formerly populated to a large extent by Albanian Muslims, was given to Greece on the basis of the report of the **International Boundary Commission** in 1913. In June 1944, the Albanian Muslim population of Çamëria, a total of 40,000 individuals, was expelled en masse from Greece to Albania, and their property and assets were confiscated by the Greek authorities. They have not yet been given official permission to return.

The so-called Çamërian question and the issue of **minority** rights in the two countries in general, have long constituted an element of discord in Greek-Albanian relations. The problem of return, and restitution of or compensation for lost property, long taboo in Greece, was brought up by the Council of Europe for the first time in late 2002.

ÇAMI, FOTO (1925.10.04-). Political figure of the **communist** period. Foto Çami was born in Labova in the **Gjirokastra** region and served as the political commissar of a partisan unit during **World War II**. He studied philosophy at the University of **Tirana** and was thus given the honorary title "professor." On 7 November 1971, he became a full member of the Central Committee and in 1986 a full member of the Politburo. Çami was chairman of the foreign relations committee of the Albanian **parliament** from 1983 to 1990 and secretary of the Central Committee from 1985 to 1990. He was tried together with nine other members of the Politburo and sentenced to prison on 30 December 1993. On 20 June 1996, he was then sentenced to life in prison for crimes against humanity.

ÇAMI, MUHAMET. *See* KYÇYKU, MUHAMET.

ÇARÇANI, ADIL (1922.05.05-1997.10.13). Political figure of the **communist** period. Adil Çarçani was born in the village of Fushë-Bardhë in the district of **Gjirokastra** and took part in the communist resistance movement during **World War II** as the assistant commander of an assault brigade. He studied economics, and in 1955-1965, he was minister of industry, mining and geology. In 1965-1982, he served as deputy prime minister, and from 4 January 1982 to 22 February 1991 as prime minister of Albania.

Çarçani was a full member of the Central Committee from 1956 to 1991 and a full member of the Politburo from 1961 to 1991. He was chairman of the commission for the total electrification of the country from 1966 to 1971, and headed economic delegations to **China** to sign credit agreements in September 1968 and July 1975. On 2 July 1994, after the fall of the dictatorship, he was sentenced to five years of prison for abuse of power, but the term was suspended due to his age and failing health. He died in **Tirana**.

ÇASHKU, KUJTIM (1950.08.05-). Film director. Born in **Tirana**, Çashku studied directing at the Academy of Fine Arts (*Instituti i Lartë i Arteve*) in Tirana and at the Institute for Theater and Cinematography in Bucharest, Romania. As a **film** director, he began his career with the documentary, *Pranverë në zemrat tona* (Spring in our Hearts), 1977, which was banned by the authorities for a long time for ideological reasons. He was then codirector with **Piro Milkani** of the successful *Ballë për ballë* (Face to Face), 1979. His film, *Dorë e ngrohtë* (Warm Hand), 1983, was well received by the public because it broke political taboos by focusing on negative aspects of contemporary Albanian society. Equally successful was his *Të paftuarit* (The Uninvited), 1987, based on **Ismail Kadare**'s novel "Broken April."

Kujtim Çashku was a major intellectual and moral leader of the democratic movement in 1991 and was one of the first intellectuals to speak out openly against the **communist** dictatorship. He was also one of the founders of the Albanian Helsinki Committee for the Defense of Human Rights. In 1993, he did a postgraduate course in international relations at Columbia University in New York but has returned to film making. His feature film, *Koloneli Bunker* (Colonel Bunker), 1996, received numerous international awards and was nominated for an Oscar. During the **Kosova War**, he made the moving documentaries *Sytë e Kosovës* (The Eyes of Kosova), 1998, and *Lotët e Kosovës* (The Tears of Kosova), 1999.

CASTRIOTTA, GEORGE. *See* SCANDERBEG.

CATHOLICISM. Religion. The final rupture between Roman Catholicism and Byzantine **Orthodoxy** took place in 1054 after Pope Leo IX (r. 1048-1054) directed his representative in Constantinople to leave a papal bull on the altar of the Church of Saint Sophia, anathematizing the "seven mortal heresies" of the Greeks and excommunicating the patriarch of Constantinople. The patriarch, in turn, anathematized the pope, thus making the Oriental or Eastern Schism inevitable. Most of central and southern Albania opted for the Byzantine rite, while northern Albania, under the influence of Italy, Venice and the Crusaders, remained in communion with the Latin Church. With the creation of the Slav principality of Dioclea (corresponding to modern Montenegro), the metropolitan See of Bar (Antivari), which was set up in 1089, became responsible for most of the dioceses in northern Albania, and, consequently, for most Albanian Catholic settlements at the time: Ulcinj, **Shas**, **Shkodra**, **Drisht** (Drivastum), Pult (Polatum), Sapa and Shurdhah (**Sarda**). During the ephemeral Venetian occupation of the early thirteenth century (1204-1212), an archdiocese was also established in **Durrës** (1204), with a number of suffragans.

The Catholic Church put up much resistance to the **Ottoman** occupation of Albania, which began in 1393 with the conquest of the fortress of Shkodra. Opposition was at its height in the age of **Scanderbeg**, who initially received much support from Venice, the pope and the Kingdom of Naples. Scanderbeg was widely admired in the Christian world for his resistance to the Turks and was given the title "Athleta Christi" by Pope Calixtus III (r. 1455-1458). After Scanderbeg's death in 1468 and the collapse of organized Albanian resistance to the Turks, however, the position of the Catholic Church in Albania became much more precarious. In 1577, it is known that northern and central Albania were still staunchly Catholic, but by the early decades of the seventeenth century, an estimated thirty to fifty percent of the **population** of northern Albania had "turned Turk," i.e., had converted to **Islam**. In 1599, there were no more than 130 Catholic priests left in the country, most of whom had little education. It can be assumed that the Albanians converted to Islam not for theological reasons, but primarily to escape oppression and the harsh taxes imposed by the Porte on the "infidels." Many Albanian Catholics initially retained their Christian faith in the privacy of their homes but adopted Muslim names and customs for use in public. This **Crypto-Christianity** proved to be a pragmatic and very Albanian solution to an existential problem faced by Catholics living in the Ottoman-occupied Balkans.

The survival of Catholicism in the northern mountains can subsequently be attributed to the untiring missionary activities of the **Franciscans**. The Albanian tribesmen themselves never seem to have taken the intricacies of Catholic dogma too seriously though, and apostolic visitors to the country were often scandalized by the moral and ecclesiastical conditions in the mountains. In 1703, during the reign of the albanophile Pope Clement XI (r. 1700-1721), himself said to have been of Albanian descent on his mother's side, the Croatian archbishop and visitor apostolicus, Vincentius Zmajevich (1670-1745), convoked an **Albanian Council** in 1703 and attempted to inculcate the provisions of the Council of Trent upon the rather lax tribesmen.

Despite the activities of the **Jesuits**, who opened a pontifical seminary in Shkodra in 1859, conversions to Islam continued unabated throughout the nineteenth century. The majority of the highland tribes, however, resisted conversion to Islam. In 1881, among the nineteen tribes north of the **Drin** River, there were 35,000 Catholics, 15,000 Muslims and 220 Orthodox. In 1886, Shkodra replaced Bar as the metropolitan see for most of Albania.

In 1940, the structure of the Catholic hierarchy was as follows: an archbishop in Shkodra with sees in Pult, Sapa, **Lezha**, an archbishop in Durrës with no suffragans, the Abbey Nullius of Saint Alexander of Orosh directly subordinate to the Holy See in Rome, and an apostolic administration for central and southern Albania under the jurisdiction of the archbishop of Durrës. At the end of **World War II**, there were 253 Catholic churches and chapels in Albania, two seminaries, ten monasteries, twenty convents, fifteen orphanages and asylums, sixteen Catholic schools and ten charitable institutions. Catholics today make up ten percent of the population of Albania and **Kosova**.

With the **communist** takeover in 1944 under a largely **Tosk** leadership, the Catholic Church, with its power base in Shkodra, began to be the object of substantial persecution. General **Mehmet Shehu**, in a public address there on 28 January 1945, called the Catholic Church a "nest of reaction" and warned that its leaders would receive their "just" rewards before the people's court. The apostolic nuncio to Albania, Monsignor Leone G. B. Nigris, was arrested in May 1945 and expelled from the country as a persona non grata. Most native priests and Italian missionaries were imprisoned and some were put to death after show trials in 1946. The Church was cut off from all ties with Rome and the outside world.

Virtually all Scutarine clergymen and intellectuals suffered under the new regime. The priest and playwright **Ndre Zadeja**, the priest and poet Lazër Shantoja (1892-1945), the priest and poet **Bernardin Palaj**, the novelist **Anton Harapi**, and the publicist Gjon Shllaku (1907-1946) were executed, and the priest, prose writer and publisher Dom **Ndoc Nikaj**, the father of twentieth-century **Gheg** prose, died in prison.

On 24 April 1949, a large show trial was held in the *Republika* cinema in Shkodra during which a number of Catholic dignitaries were accused of spying for Yugoslavia and were executed. According to a report by the National Committee for a Free Albania in 1953, of the ninety-three Catholic clergymen in Albania in 1945, ten were free, twenty-four had been murdered, thirty-five were in prison, ten had died or disappeared, eleven had been drafted and three had escaped abroad. The Albanian Catholic

Church, isolated from support abroad, was thus virtually decimated by the early 1950s, although it continued to function formally over the next decade and a half. The pressure decreased after 1951 but resumed again towards the end of the 1950s. In 1967, the Catholic Church in Albania was dissolved entirely when all forms of organized **religion** were banned.

Diplomatic relations with the Vatican were reestablished on 7 September 1991 after the definitive fall of the dictatorship. Among the orders to have returned to Albania are the **Jesuits**, the Franciscans and the Salesians. Pope John Paul II visited **Tirana** and Shkodra on 25 April 1993 and laid the cornerstone for a new St. Paul's Cathedral in Tirana, which was inaugurated on 26 January 2002.

CEKA, HASAN (1900.08.25-1998.11.01). Archeologist. Hasan Ceka was born in **Elbasan**. He attended a Turkish-language school in Macedonia before returning to his native town in 1910. In November 1919, his family sent him to Austria, initially to Wels and Linz. After secondary school graduation in 1925, he studied at the Faculty of History of the University of Vienna, from which he graduated in 1930, specializing in archeology. On his return to Albania, he was appointed to the tiny museum of archeology, and later, representing the Albanian authorities, took part in archeological expeditions and excavations under Léon Rey in **Apollonia** and Luigi M. Ugolini in **Butrint**. From 1942 to November 1944, he served as secretary-general at the ministry of **education**. After the war, he continued to work for the museum of archeology and became a member of the Institute of Sciences. He led excavations in Apollonia from 1947 to 1972, when he retired.

Hasan Ceka is the author of numerous scholarly articles on archeology published from 1948 onwards. He is remembered in particular for *La question de numismatique illyrienne: avec un catalogue des monnaies d'Apollonie et de Dyrrachium* (Question of Illyrian Numismatics: With a Catalog of Coins from Apollonia and Durrës), Tirana 1972. His final years saw the publication of his manuscript *Në kërkim të historisë ilire* (In Search of Illyrian History), Tirana 1998.

CEKA, NERITAN (1941.02.11-). Archeologist, political figure and high-ranking member of the **Democratic Alliance Party**. Neritan Ceka was inspired by his father, **Hasan Ceka**, to devote his energies to archeology. He is currently one of the most influential archeologists in Albania as well as a leading political figure. He was a founding member of the **Democratic Party** in 1990, and in 1992 became head of the Democratic Alliance Party, which broke away from **Sali Berisha**'s Democratic Party. Ceka served as minister of the interior from 25 July 1997 to 18 April 1998. In 2002, he was chairman of the **parliamentary** commission on public order and the intelligence service. As an archeologist, he has published: *Ilirët* (The Illyrians), Tirana 2000; and in coauthorship with **Muzafer Korkuti**, *Arkeologjia: Greqia, Roma, Iliria* (Archeology: Greece, Rome, Illyria), Tirana 1993.

ÇEKREZI, KOSTANDIN. *See* CHEKREZI, CONSTANTINE ANASTASI.

ÇELEBI, EVLIYA. *See* EVLIYA ÇELEBI.

CENTRAL COMMITTEE FOR THE DEFENSE OF THE RIGHTS OF THE ALBANIAN PEOPLE (*KOMITET QENDROR PËR MBROJTJEN E TË DREJTAVE TË KOMBËSISË SHQIPTARE*) (1877). Association founded by a group of leading Albanian intellectuals, among whom are: **Abdyl bey Frashëri, Naim bey Frashëri, Sami bey Frashëri, Jani Vreto, Pashko Vasa**, Zija Prishtina, Mehmet Ali Vrioni (1842-1895) and Koto Hoxhi (1824-1895), in Istanbul in December 1877 with a view to obtaining a certain autonomy for the Albanians within the **Ottoman Empire**. The national question became more urgent for Albanian intellectuals following the Russian and Serbian victory over the Ottoman Empire on 31 January 1878 and the Treaty of San Stefano of March 1878, which provided for the annexation of much Albanian-speaking territory by the newly autonomous Bulgarian state and by the now independent Kingdoms of Montenegro and Serbia. The subsequent **Congress of Berlin** on 13 June 1878 confirmed the independence of Romania, Serbia and Montenegro and an autonomous government in Bulgaria, but the interests of the Albanians had been entirely overlooked. The Central Committee for the Defense of the Rights of the Albanian People can be seen as a precursor to the **League of Prizren**.

CHAMERIA. *See* ÇAMËRIA.

CHEKREZI, CONSTANTINE (1892-1959.01.10). Albanian-American publisher and writer, known in Albanian as Kostandin or Kost Çekrezi. Constantine Anastas Chekrezi was born in the village of Ziçisht in the **Korça** area and graduated from a Greek secondary school in 1909. He studied in Salonika and Athens, and after losing his job as an interpreter for the **International Control Commission** as a result of the outbreak of **World War I**, he emigrated via Italy to the United States at the invitation of the **Vatra federation**. In Boston, he was put in charge of the Vatra newspaper *Dielli* (The Sun) for a time until the latter was taken over by **Fan Noli**. Like **Faik bey Konitza**, Chekrezi studied at and graduated from Harvard University, 1916-1918. It was in Boston, too, that he published an ephemeral semimonthly periodical called *Illyria* from March to November 1916, and in early 1919 took over editorship of Fan Noli's monthly *Adriatic Review*. He served as Albanian high commissioner to Washington, where he died.

Chekrezi was the author of a number of monographs in Albanian and English, in particular of several lengthy works of history in Albanian, which, in their scope, were quite impressive for the time. These monographs include: *Albania Past and Present*, New York 1919; *Kendime per rjeshten e funtme te shkollave filltare* (Readings for the Last Grade of Elementary Schools), Boston 1921; *Histori e Shqipërisë* (History of Albania), Boston 1921; *Histori e vjetër që në kohërat e Pellasgëve gjer në rrënien e Perandorisë romane* (Ancient History from the Times of the Pelasgians up to the Fall of the Roman Empire), Boston 1921; *Histori e re e Evropës* (Modern History of Europe), Boston 1921; *Historia mesjetare e Evropes që në rënien e Romës gjer në rënien e Kostantinopojës 478-1453* (Medieval History of Europe from the Fall of Rome to the Fall of Constantinople 478-1453), Boston 1921; and the first English-Albanian dictionary, *Chekrezi's English-Albanian Dictionary, Fjalor inglisht-shqip*, Boston 1923.

CHETTA, NICOLA (1740?-1803.11.19). Arbëresh poet and writer. Nicola Chetta, known in Albanian as Nikollë Keta, was born in Contessa Entellina (Alb. *Kundisa*), the oldest Albanian settlement in Sicily, founded between 1450 and 1467. He was taught at the Greek seminary in Palermo by Giorgio Guzzetta (1682-1756) and the scholar Paolo Maria Parrino (1710-1765). In 1777, Chetta became rector of the seminary himself. As a poet, he wrote both religious and secular verse in Albanian and Greek, and has the honor of having composed the first Albanian sonnet (1777).

Chetta was an imaginative poet, though his verse, as far as can be judged for the moment, is not distinguished by any sublime inspiration or unusually refined metric or linguistic skill. His significance, on the whole, lies more in the variety and universality of his scholarly endeavors as a lexicographer and linguist, as a "creative" historian much influenced by Paolo Maria Parrino and Giorgio Guzzetta, as a theologian of Neoplatonic proclivities, and as a public and religious figure in his capacity as rector of the Greek seminary.

CHINA, RELATIONS WITH. Sino-Albanian relations began in the mid-1950s in the framework of solidarity and friendship between the countries of the **communist** bloc. On 14 October 1954, agreements were signed on scientific and technical cooperation, and on 3 December of that year, China granted Albania a long-term loan. **Enver Hoxha** and **Mehmet Shehu** visited China in October 1956.

The years 1961 to 1978 marked the Sino-Albanian alliance. The Albanian leadership had broken off relations with Moscow, and the People's Republic of China was more than glad to replace the Soviet Union as Albania's protector in Europe. An Albanian delegation to China under **Spiro Koleka** had already signed important economic loan and trade agreements with China in early 1961. The loans, amounting to US$123 million, were designed to cover the running costs of Albanian investment projects. By 1962, China accounted for sixty-five percent of Albanian imports and twenty-nine percent of Albanian exports. Most of these goods were shipped to and from China by a special Albanian-Chinese shipping company founded on 26 December 1961.

On 10-17 January 1964, the Chinese prime minister Chou En-Lai visited Albania, and on 11-12 February that year, the **Party of Labor** concentrated its twelfth plenary session on relations with China. In the following years, about 6,000 Chinese experts flooded into Albania to assist in economic development and to finish the large-scale industrial projects which the Russians had left behind them. Many young Albanians were also sent to China to study.

The Cultural Revolution, which broke out in China in November 1965, was echoed in Albania in March 1966 with a campaign for the revolutionizing of Albanian culture, which was directed against bureaucracy and corruption. In actual fact, however, there were few elements of Chinese socialism which the Albanian leadership followed, except denouncing the two superpowers. There was never a real cultural revolution in Albania, no Red Guards and certainly no destabilizing of the political leadership.

Good relations continued in the early 1970s. On 27 November 1974, regular flights were inaugurated between **Tirana** and Beijing. Albania imported far more from China than it exported, and the enormous trade deficit which it incurred soon became a problem. China, a developing country itself, was not in a position to keep Albania afloat forever. In 1975, it demanded that Albania begin paying back some of the loans, which Albania was not able to do. These financial problems marked the beginning of the end of the Sino-Albanian alliance. China gradually reduced its exports to Albania and stopped them completely in 1978.

Enver Hoxha had criticized the Chinese leadership at the seventh party congress from 1 to 7 November 1976, and on 7 July 1977, an article appeared in the daily newspaper, *Zëri i popullit* (The Voice of the People), denouncing the Chinese "theory of the three worlds" as anti-revolutionary. On 7 July 1978, China withdrew its experts and blocked all further economic and military assistance to the country. The Sino-Albanian alliance came to an official end on 29 July 1978 with an exchange of letters between the two central committees.

Diplomatic relations were, however, not interrupted, and since the fall of the communist dictatorship, normal commercial and political relations with China have resumed. In the mid-1990s, there was a small Chinese emigrant community in Albania and no less than five Chinese restaurants in Tirana at one time. All have since closed.

On 15 February 1993, a trade and investment agreement was signed in Beijing by foreign minister Alfred Serreqi. His visit was reciprocated by Chinese foreign minister Qian Qichen in Tirana on 10-12 September 1993. On 16-19 January 1996, President **Sali Berisha** paid an official visit to China at the invitation of Jiang Zemin.

In China, there are still some 200 people who can speak Albanian from the time of the alliance, and in Albania one can also find a number of people who can speak very good Chinese.

CHRISTIANITY. Religion. Christianity arrived early on Albanian soil. First to have preached the gospel in Albania may have been Saint Paul himself, who stated: *So from Jerusalem all the way around to Illyricum, I have fully proclaimed the gospel of Christ* (Romans 15:19). The Apostle, Andrew, is also believed to have preached in Epirus. By 58 A.D. the coastal port of **Durrës** is said, at any rate, to have been inhabited by seventy Christian families. It was a prominent **religion** in Albania in the fourth and fifth centuries, long before there were any traces of the Albanian people as we know them today. Christianity seems to have approached the Roman provinces of Praevalis, New Epirus and Old Epirus from southern Dalmatia (Salona) in the fourth and fifth centuries, and by the fifth century, the new religion had already begun to penetrate the interior of the country. Among the Church dignitaries who attended the first ecumenical Council of Nicaea in 325 A.D., called by the Emperor Constantine I (r. 307-337) to deal with the problems raised by Arianism, were a number of bishops from Dardania and Macedonia Salutare, which correspond to modern-day eastern Albania and **Kosova**. In 343-344 A.D., five or six bishops from Dardania, New Epirus and Old Epirus also attended the Council of Sardica.

The initial division of the Roman Empire took place in the year 395 A.D., with Illyria finding itself on the political and ecclesiastical border between the two new empires. As such, northern Albania came under the sway of the pope in Rome, and southern Albania fell under the ecclesiastical authority of the eastern Church in Constantinople. The Slavic invasion of Albania in around 600 A.D. brought any ecclesiastical structures that there may have been in Albania to an abrupt end, however, and little is known of the country in the following centuries. Albanian territory was attached to the patriarchate of Constantinople in 732 A.D. under the reign of Emperor Leo III the Isaurian (r. 717-741) and new bishoprics were set up early in the ninth century in **Kruja**, Stephaniaca at the mouth of the **Ishëm** River, **Lezha** and Chounavia.

The division of Christianity into two main faiths, western **Catholicism** and eastern **Orthodoxy**, became definitive with the condemnation of the patriarch of Constantinople by Pope Leo IX (r. 1048-1054) in 1054. In the following centuries, Albanian territory was to continue to constitute the ecclesiastical, political and often military border land between the Roman Catholic West and the Byzantine East. Northern Albania drifted into the Catholic fold under the influence of Italy, Venice, and, in particular, of the Crusaders, whereas most of central and southern Albania remained derivatively Byzantine Orthodox.

CHRISTOFORIDÊS, KÔNSTANTINOS. *See* KRISTOFORIDHI, KOSTANDIN.

CHROME. *See* MINERAL RESOURCES.

ÇIFTELI. Musical instrument. The mandolin-like *çifteli* is a lively, long-necked, two-stringed instrument popular in northern Albania and **Kosova**, where it is the epitome of folk **music**. The word *çifteli* is related to Alb. *çift* "in twos, a pair."

CIKO, ZHANI (1945.12.08-). Conductor and violinist. Zhani Ciko was born and raised in **Tirana**. He graduated from the state conservatory, now Academy of Fine Arts, in 1967. After years as a violin soloist and concert master, he was appointed director of the Tirana symphony orchestra in 1973. In 1989 he was also conductor of the orchestra of Radio Tirana.

CIMOCHOWSKI, WACŁAW (1912.12.22-1982.07.04). Polish scholar and linguist. Wacław Cimochowski was born in Kursk in Russia and moved with his mother to Vilnius in Lithuania in 1922. He studied classics at the university there and finished an M.A. thesis in Indo-European linguistics under Jan Otrębski. In 1936, he won a scholarship to continue his research in Vienna, where he studied classics and Indo-European philology under Paul Kretschmer (1866-1956), Slavic philology under Nikolai Trubetzkoy (1890-1938), and Albanian under **Norbert Jokl**. His studies of Albanian inspired him to visit the country in 1937. It was there that he gathered the material for his doctoral thesis on the northern Albanian dialect of **Dushmani**, material which was published many years later in a French-language version as *Le dialecte de Dushmani: description de l'un des parlers de l'Albanie du nord* (The Dialect of Dushmani: Description of One of the Dialects of Northern Albania), Poznań 1951.

After his return to Vilnius, Cimochowski worked as an assistant at the Department of Indo-European Linguistics until the outbreak of **World War II**. In the USSR, he joined the Polish Army and returned with it to Poland in 1945. In May 1948, he completed his doctorate in Poznań under Professor Otrębski and, beginning in November of that year, at the Department of General Linguistics there. Cimochowski was subsequently professor at the universities of Poznań and Toruń and, until recently, was the only Polish specialist in Albanian studies. He visited Albania twice and gave lectures on the origins of the Albanian **language**. He retired in 1978 and died in Gdynia after a long illness.

Cimochowski's primary field of interest was the Albanian language, in particular within the framework of Balkan and Indo-

European linguistics. In addition to the "Dialect of Dushmani," he is the author of over thirty articles, most of which deal with the Albanian language and Albanian studies in general.

CIVIL AVIATION. *See* AIR TRANSPORTATION.

CLIMATE. Albania has a primarily Mediterranean climate in coastal zones, characterized by hot and dry summers and by mild, wet winters, though there is much sunshine throughout the year. Inland, the climate becomes sub-Mediterranean and then increasingly continental, with shorter dry summers interrupted by thundershowers and cold winters. The temperatures are more extreme in the interior, both in summer and in winter, and there can be much snow at higher altitudes. There are not only east-west, but also north-south variations in general climatic conditions. The dry period in summer is substantially shorter in **Shkodra** than in **Himara**. In southern Albania, there are 2,600 hours of sunshine a year, in central Albania 2,200 hours, and in the northeast of the country only 2,000 hours. On the coast, there is little precipitation in summer. Most regions of the country receive over 900 millimeters of precipitation, but the northern Albanian Alps can get up to 3,500 millimeters.

COAL PRODUCTION. Albania has deep lignite reserves in four basins, in particular in the Tirana-Durrës basin, which represents eighty-six percent of total reserves. It is situated in the Krraba mountains southeast of **Tirana**. The thickness of the coal layer here is relatively limited, however. There are also lignite reserves in Memeliaj (**Tepelena**), Mborja and Denova (**Korça**), Alarup (**Pogradec**) and Priska (Tirana). There are no substantial hard coal reserves in the country.

The first lignite mine, that of Memeliaj, was established in 1918. In 1939, there was an annual production of just 7,000 tons. Coal was long used for brick-making and lime-burning, but it now only plays a minor role as a source of energy in the Albanian economy, compared to oil, **electricity** and wood. In 1998, coal satisfied only 0.8 percent of total primary energy consumption and only 0.3 percent of final energy consumption. From 1985 to 1990, production in the coal mining sector varied from 2 to 2.2 million tons per year. In 1990, it was 2.1 million tons and in 1991 only 1.1 million tons. Since 1992, there has been a drastic fall and current production is minimal. The coal sector currently employs 1,095 persons, down from 5,200 in 1991.

The coal mining industry is thus facing serious trouble. In addition to problems related to outdated technology and the lack of investment funds, the coal industry has had difficulty finding markets due to competitive prices and the better quality of imported coal. Many unprofitable coal mines have, therefore, shut down.

CODE OF LEKË DUKAGJINI. *See* KANUN OF LEKË DUKAGJINI.

COMMUNISM. Albania was and is a predominantly agricultural country. It had no **industry** until well into the 1930s and thus no proletariat to speak of. As such, communist ideas were slow to develop. The first Albanians to come into contact with Marxism and the ideals of the October Revolution in Russia were those who had been abroad, in particular in Russia, for a period of time in the 1920s. Among them were Bishop **Fan Noli** and his secretary, **Sejfulla Maleshova**, Llazar Fundo and **Tajar Zavalani**. Political figure **Mehmet Shehu** took part in the Spanish civil war as a member of the twelfth International Brigade from 1938 to 1939 and joined the Spanish communist party there. He was later a member of the Italian communist party and returned to Albania in 1942 to join the partisan movement. **Ali Kelmendi**, who had been schooled by the Comintern in Russia from 1925 to 1930 returned to Albania to found clandestine communist groups, in particular the **Korça** group, which was formed in June 1929 under the influence of the Greek Archeio-Marxist group. In 1934, there was also a communist group at the **Franciscan** secondary school in **Shkodra**. Among its members were Qemal Stafa (1921-1942) and Fadil Hoxha, who was later to become a member of the presidium of the Yugoslav communist party. In 1940, a more Trotskyite-oriented Youth group was created by Anastas Luli and Sadik Premtaj from the ranks of the Korça group.

In early **World War II** there were thus several, highly fragmented communist groups in Albania, but total membership probably did not exceed 200. It is doubtful whether many early members of the movement knew much about communist philosophy and theory because there were no Albanian translations of any Marxist writings before 1941.

An attempt was made in the autumn of 1939 to unite the communist groups, but to no avail, and it was only in 1941, after the Comintern in the Soviet Union had called on communist parties around the world to take part in the antifascist liberation struggle against **Germany**, that the Albanian communists, with strong support from Tito's emissaries Miladin Popović (1910-1945) and Dušan Mugoša (1914-1973), finally united to form a party which would lead the "people's liberation struggle." The Communist Party of Albania (*Partia Komuniste e Shqipërisë*) was thus born in **Tirana** on 8 November 1941. It actually remained an appendage of the **Yugoslav** communist party until June 1948. *See also* KONARE; PARTY OF LABOR.

COMMUNIST PARTY. *See* PARTY OF LABOR.

CONFERENCE OF AMBASSADORS (1912-1913). The Conference of the Ambassadors, as it is known in Albanian history, was a conference held in London and representing the six Great Powers (**Britain**, France, **Germany**, Austria-Hungary, **Russia** and **Italy**). It began its work on 17 December 1912 under the direction of the British foreign secretary, Sir Edward Grey (1862-1933), following the first **Balkan War** and the declaration of Albanian independence in **Vlora** on 28 November 1912. With regard to Albania, the ambassadors had initially decided that the country would be recognized as an autonomous state under the sovereignty of the sultan. After much discussion, however, they reached a formal decision on 29 July 1913 that Albania would be a sovereign state independent of the **Ottoman Empire**. It was to be ruled by a European prince to be selected by the Great Powers themselves, and an **International Control Commission** for Albania, composed of representatives of the six powers and one Albanian, would be set up to supervise the establishment of a government administration. The new gendarmerie was to be organized by Dutch officers. For the Albanians, the most momentous decision taken at this conference was the fixing of the borders where, in order to appease the exaggerated territorial claims of Albania's neighbors, the Great Powers gave the whole of **Kosova**, **Dibra**, Ohrid and Monastir to **Serbia**, and, in the north, gave Hoti, **Gruda**, much of **Kelmendi** territory, as well as Plava and Gucia to Montenegro. In the south, the Conference constituted an **International Boundary Commission** in August 1913 to study the ethnicity of the local population and fix an exact border between Albania and **Greece**.

CONFERENCE OF PEZA (1942). In the summer of 1942, the **communists** called for a meeting to be held to unite all the resistance groups, communist and noncommunist, in order to present a united front against the Axis forces. The conference took place in the village of Peza near **Tirana** on 16 September 1942, in the home of resistance fighter **Myslim Peza**. A total of twenty people took part, among whom were Myslim Peza, **Haxhi Lleshi**, Baba Faja Martaneshi and royalist leader **Abaz Kupi**. **Mehdi bey Frashëri** was honorary chairman of the gathering, a fact which was later suppressed in communist historiography. The conference set in place a joint national liberation movement (*Lëvizje Nacionalçlirimtare*) with a provisional eight-member council, among whom were **Enver Hoxha** and Abaz Kupi, though the movement was increasingly dominated by the communists and eventually broke apart.

CONGREGATION OF THE MISSION. *See* LAZARIST CONGREGATION.

CONGRESS OF BERLIN (1878). The Congress of Berlin was held by the Great Powers (**Britain**, France, **Germany**, Austria-Hungary, **Italy** and **Russia**) in June and July 1878 to revise the Treaty of San Stefano, which Russia had forced upon the **Ottoman Empire** in that year, and to create stable political relations in the Balkans. It was chaired by Bismark, acting as an "honest broker." The Congress recognized the independence of **Serbia**, Montenegro and Romania, and made arrangements for a smaller, though autonomous Bulgaria, but Albanian concerns were completely ignored. All Albanian territories were returned to the control of the Ottoman Empire. The Albanians reacted to the Congress of Berlin by the creation of the **League of Prizren**.

CONGRESS OF LUSHNJA (1920). This conference of about fifty delegates from the various political factions and regions of Albania was held in late January 1920 in the central Albanian town of **Lushnja** to put an end to the seven years of anarchy which had followed the declaration of independence in November 1912. It designated a new government to be run by **Sulejman bey Delvina** and a four-man High Regency Council (*Këshilli i Lartë i Regjencës*), composed of representatives of the four main religious groups in the country: **Aqif pasha Biçaku (Bektashi)**, Abdi bey Toptani (Sunni **Islam**), Mihal Turtulli (**Orthodox**), and **Luigj Bumçi (Catholic)**, to act as head of state. In order to outdo the previous and now illegal government in **Durrës**, Delvina set up his administration in **Tirana**, then a little town of 12,000 inhabitants, which from that year on, was to serve as the capital of Albania. The Congress of Lushnja thus laid the foundations for a modicum of political stability in Albania.

CONGRESS OF MONASTIR (1908). The lack of a definitive and universally accepted alphabet for the Albanian **language** was long an impediment to national unity and indeed to the goal of Albanian independence. On 14-22 November 1908, a congress was held in the Macedonian city of Monastir (Bitola) to decide upon a definitive alphabet for the Albanian language. The congress was convoked at the initiative of the *Bashkimi* (Unity) literary society under **Gjergj Fishta** and presided over by **Mid'hat bey Frashëri**, son of **Abdyl bey Frashëri**. It was attended by **Catholic**, **Orthodox** and Muslim delegates from Albania and abroad, among them Shahin Kolonja (1865-1919), **Ndre Mjeda**, **Hilë Mosi** and **Sotir Peci**. The three main alphabets under discussion were the Istanbul alphabet devised by **Sami bey Frashëri**, the Bashkimi alphabet supported by Gjergj Fishta and his *Bashkimi* literary society of **Shkodra**, and the Agimi alphabet of the *Agimi* literary society represented by Ndre Mjeda. A committee of eleven delegates headed by Fishta was elected, and, after three days of deliberations, they resolved to support two alphabets: a modified form of Sami Frashëri's Istanbul alphabet, which was most widely used at the time, and a new Latin alphabet almost identical to the Bashkimi in order to facilitate printing abroad.

CONGRESS OF TRIESTE (1913). Gathering held in Trieste, then part of Austria-Hungary, on 1 March 1913. The Congress of Trieste, Alb. *Kongresi i Triestit*, was convened to show solidarity among Albanians from Albania and abroad for their country following the declaration of independence in **Vlora** on 28 November 1912. About 150 representatives from Albania, Romania, Bulgaria, **Italy**, **Egypt**, **Turkey** and the **United States** attended to discuss the affairs of the nation. The congress recognized the provisional government set up by **Ismail Qemal bey Vlora** and discussed the various candidates for the new vacant throne. Among the candidates being discussed at the time were Ferdinand François Bourbon Orléans-Montpensier of France, Albert Ghika of Romania, Count Urach of Württemberg, the Egyptian prince Ahmed Fuad, and the son of the Marchese Castriota from Naples. Austria-Hungary promoted the congress, in particular to ensure the selection of a prince of its choice.

Scholar **Franz Nopcsa**, who subsequently proposed himself as candidate for the throne, was present at the congress and noted ironically in his memoirs: "After welcoming ceremonies the first evening, Marchese Castriota was chosen as honorary president of the congress and **Faik bey Konitza** was elected chairman. **Hilë Mosi**, Fazil Toptani and **Dervish Hima** were also elected to the chair. The nomination of Konitza was not to the liking of Ghika since, when the latter was on the point of bringing up the issue of candidates to the Albanian throne, his old rival Faik prevented him from doing so. In order to have an ace in his hand, Ghika, who like many a Romanian had a long career as an impostor behind him, had cunningly succeeded in getting control of Ismail Qemali's retarded son. Before the congress started, he traveled to Nice, where the Qemali family resided in virtual poverty, and, as Qemali himself was unable to attend, invited the son Tahir to the Albanian Congress in Trieste at his own expense, or, to be more precise, at the expense of Montpensier... All in all, there was nothing but hot air at the congress, aside from a dispute between the **Vlachs** and Albanians, during which the little nation of Vlachs, not even officially born yet, gave substantial proof of its fanaticism and Balkan megalomania, and from a further clash between the chairman Faik bey Konitza and the rather crooked **Nikolla Ivanaj**, who endeavored unsuccessfully to challenge the authority of the chairman simply in order to draw attention to himself. The day before the congress was to end, I therefore felt compelled to call Faik bey Konitza aside and inform him that the congress had as yet done no work at all and that the least one could expect from a political congress was a resolution. Faik agreed and I dictated to him a resolution which the congress was to telegraph to all the Great Powers the next day. The matter was attended to within half an hour, and the next day, Faik presented the document to the congress as a resolution. After a debate on the position of the Vlachs at the congress and in a future Albania, which Faik overcame in favor of the Albanians by presenting the Vlachs more or less with an ultimatum, the resolution was accepted and, as such, my text was sent to the Great Powers as the congress resolution."

COPPER. *See* MINERAL RESOURCES.

CORDIGNANO, FULVIO (1887.10.19-1952.05.09). Italian scholar. Fulvio Cordignano was born in Moggia near Udine and entered the **Jesuit** order in Cremona on 19 October 1905. There he studied literature in 1908 and philosophy from 1909 to 1911. From 1912 to 1916, he taught seminarists at the Saverian college in **Shkodra,** and from 1917 to 1920, having been ordained as a priest on 23 December 1918, pursued his studies in theology at **Catholic** establishments abroad: in Moravia, Hastings in southern England, Dublin in Ireland, and Leuven (Louvain) in Belgium. In 1921, he was in Rome where, in the following year, he worked for the church periodical *Civiltà Cattolica* (Catholic Civilization). In 1924, he returned to Shkodra where he taught philosophy and literature. From 1926 to 1941, he served as a missionary for the Jesuit Visiting Mission (Missione Volante) and traveled widely in northern Albania. These years provided him with an in-depth knowledge of Albanian folklore and customs. The Highland people called him Pater Milan because of his northern Italian origins. He returned to Italy in 1942 and served in Padua until 1949, and then in Palermo in 1950, and finally Goricia in 1951. He died in Rome the following year.

Father Cordignano was an impassioned scholar and collector of Albanian folklore, and over the years built up an impressive library, archive and museum. Impressive, too, are his publications in the field of Albanian studies. Among his major monographs are: *Epopeja komtare e popullit shqyptar* (The National Epic of the Albanian People), Shkodra 1925; *Lingua albanese [dialetto ghego]: grammatica, saggi di letteratura, fraseologia e proverbi* (The Albanian Language (Gheg Dialect): Grammar, Samples of Literature, Phraseology and Proverbs), Milan 1931; his three-volume, 1,300-page *magnum opus* entitled *L'Albania attraverso l'opera e gli scritti di un grande missionario italiano, il P. Domenico Pasi S. J. 1847-1914* (Albania through the Works and Writings of a Great Italian Missionary Pater Domenico Pasi S. J. 1847-1914), Rome 1933, 1934; *Dizionario albanese-italiano e italiano-albanese* (Albanian-Italian and Italian-Albanian Dictionary), Milan 1934; *Geografia ecclesiastica dell'Albania: dagli ultimi decenni del secolo XVI alla metà del secolo XVII* (Ecclesiastical Geography of Albania: From the Last Decades of the Sixteenth Century to the Middle of the Seventeenth Century), Rome 1934; *Dizionario italiano-albanese* (Italian-Albanian Dictionary), Shkodra 1938; *Catasto Veneto di Scutari e registrum concessionum 1416-1417* (Venetian Land Register of Shkodra and the Registry of Concessions, 1416-1417), Rome 1942, Tolmezzo 1944-1945; and *La poesia epica di confine nell'Albania del Nord, 1-2* (The Epic Frontier Poetry of Northern Albania, 1-2), Venice 1943. He was also the author of numerous scholarly articles on northern Albanian culture published in Italian and Albanian periodicals.

CORFU CHANNEL INCIDENT (1946). On 14 October 1946, during the Cold War which had begun between East and West after the conclusion of **World War II**, Albanian guns fired at British minesweepers which were cleaning the Corfu Channel, a narrow waterway which separates the Greek island of Corfu from the southern Albanian mainland. The Albanian government, which was largely under the control of **Yugoslavia** at the time, claimed that the ships had been in Albanian territorial waters. In reaction, the British government sent four destroyers to the channel as a show of force, no doubt to put **communist** forces in the region on the defensive. On 22 October, two of these destroyers hit mines and sank, resulting in the deaths of forty-four men. Albania disclaimed any responsibility for the mines, which were probably laid by the Yugoslav armed forces. **Britain**, however, took the issue to the International Court and was awarded £843,947 in damages.

The result of this incident was not only the freezing of relations between Britain and Albania, but also problems with Albania's gold reserves. During the Italian occupation, the Albanian treasury (an estimated 2.5 tons of gold) had been taken to Rome. In 1943, German troops transferred the treasury to a salt mine in Germany for safekeeping. When the territory in question was captured by the Allies, the gold was sent for storage to the Bank of England. A joint commission was set up with representatives from the **United States**, Britain and France to deal with the issue, and all three sides agreed in principle that the reserves were to be returned to Albania. However, in view of Albania's sudden debt to Britain as a result of the Corfu Channel Incident, the issue was not solved until the 1990s when diplomatic relations between the two countries were restored.

COSMAS AITOLOS (1714-1779.08.24). Greek Orthodox saint. Born in Epirus in 1714, Cosmas Aitolos, Gk. *Κοσμᾶς ὁ Αἰτωλός*, came to be a respected figure of eighteenth-century Greek culture. He traveled widely, preached and strove to defend Greek civilization and **Orthodoxy** in an age of mass conversion to **Islam**. Towards the end of his life he returned to Epirus and, during the rule of Kurd Ahmed Pasha, traveled and preached throughout southern Albania. Journeying from **Himara** and **Vlora** to **Berat**, Myzeqeja, **Durrës** (1777), **Kruja** and as far as **Pogradec** and

Voskopoja, he did his best to keep up the spirit of Greek Orthodoxy until his death. He was revered in Berat in particular and is still remembered in Epirus in general. In Himara, there once stood a little building called the Hut of Father Cosmas, where the saint is said to have taken his rest and preached to the masses. Saint Cosmas was buried at the small church, built in 1813, which bears his name in Kolkondas near the mouth of the **Seman River**. The site is presently being restored. The remains of Cosmas Aitolos were transferred from there to the archeological museum of **Fier** in 1984 and, rumor has it, were recently being sold by the custodian to the highest bidder. Other relics of Saint Cosmas are kept in a special shrine at the main Metropolitan Cathedral in Athens. Though a purveyor of Hellenic culture, Cosmas Aitolos is still highly regarded among Orthodox Albanians in Albania and in the United States for his spiritual message.

CROATIA, ALBANIANS IN. The first group of Albanians to migrate to Croatia was an **Orthodox** community which settled near Pula in Istria in 1655. More substantial groups of Albanians settled in Croatia during the years 1723-1726. One notable Albanian foundation was that of Arbanas (Ital. *Borgo Erizzo*), a southern suburb of Zadar on the Dalmatian coast. This settlement was founded in 1726 by Albanians from Brisk and Shestan on the west bank of Lake **Shkodra**. In the 1950s, there were about 4,000 of them living there and speaking a very archaic **Gheg** dialect. It is still spoken today.

CRYPTO-CHRISTIANITY. Form of popular belief. Crypto-Christians were those Albanians and other inhabitants of the Balkans under the **Ottoman Empire** who, though adhering to their Christian beliefs in the privacy of their homes, professed **Islam** in public. In northern Albania and **Kosova** they were also known as *laramanë*, lit. "motley, multicolored, insincere." Many of them had two names: a Christian name for private use and a Muslim name for public use. Crypto-Christianity, which arose out of historical necessity, was particularly common in the region around Peja, on the plain of Kosova and in the Shpat region of central Albania. It often resulted in a syncretism of folk beliefs and rituals.

ÇUKO, LENKA (1938.07.08-). Political figure of the **communist** period. Lenka Çuko was born in Fieri i Ri in the **Lushnja** region. She worked her way up the party hierarchy in 1957-1968. She was considered an expert in **agriculture** and was appointed in 1968 to head the J. V. Stalin Collective Farm in Krutja (Lushnja), the country's first collective farm, created in 1946. She graduated from the V. I. Lenin Higher Party School in **Tirana** in 1971. Lenka Çuko was a full member of the Central Committee from 1976 to 1991 and a full member of the Politburo from 1981 to December 1990. She was tried together with nine other members of the Politburo and sentenced to prison on 30 December 1993. On 30 September 1996, she was then sentenced to fifteen years in prison for crimes against humanity.

CURRI, BAJRAM (1862-1925.03.29). Political figure and guerrilla fighter from Gjakova in **Kosova**. Bajram Curri is one of the best-known guerrilla commanders and was early to make a name for himself in the fight against Serb rule in Kosova. He was among the founders of the Albanian **League of Peja** in 1899-1900. He also organized and took part in numerous open uprisings, in particular the Kosova uprising of 1913. In 1918, he was forced with Hasan Prishtina to flee to Vienna. In 1920, he was appointed minister without portfolio by the **Congress of Lushnja** and assisted in suppressing the forces of **Essad Pasha Toptani**. He also led the National Defense of Kosova committee. After the coup d'état of December 1921 and the uprising which he himself initiated in March 1922, he supported the **Democratic Revolution** of **Fan Noli** and the latter's short-lived government. A price was put on Bajram Curri's head when **Ahmet Zogu** took over power, and he was surrounded by government troops on 29 March 1925 while he was hiding in a cave in Dragobi, near the town now named after him. After a shootout, he killed himself in order to avoid capture.

CUSTOMARY LAW. *See* KANUN OF LABËRIA; KANUN OF LEKË DUKAGJINI; KANUN OF THE MOUNTAINS; KANUN OF SCANDERBEG.

- D -

DADE, ARTA (1953.03.15-). Political figure and high-ranking member of the **Socialist Party of Albania**. Arta Dade was born in **Tirana** and studied English at the University of Tirana. She taught English at a secondary school from 1975 to 1985 and at the University of Tirana from 1985 to 1997. She joined the Socialist Party in 1991, was a member of its executive in 1992, and played an important role for that party in the tumultuous events of 1997. In 1998, she was appointed minister of culture, youth and sports, and from 15 February to 24 July 2002 she served as foreign minister, thereafter resuming her position at the Ministry of Culture, Youth and Sports.

DAIJA, TISH (1926.01.30-). Composer. Tish Daija was born in **Shkodra** and began composing at an early age. From 1951 to 1956, he studied composition at the Tchaikovsky Conservatory in Moscow. He led the Albanian folk **music** and dance ensemble from 1962 to 1980, and was long a professor of composition at the Academy of Fine Arts. In 1999, he was finally made a member of the Academy of Sciences. Daija is the author of songs, symphonies, operettas, operas such as *Pranvera* (Spring), 1960, and *Vjosa* (Vjosa), 1980, and the first Albanian ballet, *Halili dhe Hajrija* (Halili and Hajrija), 1963.

DAJA, FERIAL (1946.11.05-). Scholar and ethnomusicologist. Daja was born and raised in **Tirana**, where he studied **music** at the Jordan Misja Academy from 1960 to 1964. He continued his studies at the state conservatory in Tirana from which he graduated in 1969. From 1969 to 1994, when he emigrated, Ferial Daja served as a research expert at the Institute of Folk Culture in Tirana. Among his major publications in the field of traditional Albanian music are: *Këngë popullore djepi* (Cradle Folk Songs), Tirana 1982; *Rapsodi kreshnike: tekste e melodi* (Epic Rhapsodies: Texts and Melodies), Tirana 1983; and *Muzika e eposit heroik legjendar shqiptar* (The Music of the Albanian Legendary Heroic Epic), Tirana 1991.

DAKO, CHRISTO ANASTAS (1878.12.21-1941.12.26). Albanian-American journalist and activist. Christo Anastas Dako first became involved in the nationalist movement while a student in

Bucharest and was imprisoned for a time for his activities. He married Sevasti **Qiriazi** (1871-1949), a noted figure in **women's education**, and emigrated to the **United States** in 1907. There, he vied with **Fan Noli** for leadership of the Albanian community in Massachusetts, and in 1913 became president of the **Vatra federation** and editor of its principal medium, the Boston weekly *Dielli* (The Sun). He also edited the short-lived periodical *Biblioteka zëri i Shqipërisë* (The Voice of Albania Library) published in 1916 in Southbridge, Massachusetts. Dako was, in addition, the author of school texts and works of political history such as the essay *Cilët janë Shqipëtarët* (Who Are the Albanians?), Monastir 1911; *Albanian, the Master Key to the Near East*, Boston 1919; the short historical study *Liga e Prizrenit* (The League of Prizren), Bucharest 1922; and in later years *Shënime historike nga jeta dhe veprat e Nalt Madhërisë së tij Zogu i parë Mbreti i Shqiptarvet* (Historical Notes from the Life and Works of His Majesty, Zog the First, King of the Albanians), Tirana 1937, translated by the author into English as *Zogu, the First King of the Albanians: a Sketch of his Life and Times*, Tirana 1937. Needless to say, the latter work did not make his memory particularly cherished in postwar Stalinist Albania.

DALLIU, HAFIZ IBRAHIM (1878-1952.05.25). Muslim writer and publisher. Dalliu was born in **Tirana** and studied theology in Turkey. In 1901, he returned to Tirana as an Albanian teacher at Tirana's first school. He was a member of the *Bashkimi* (The Union) organization, which strove for Albanian autonomy at the time of the Young Turks. In 1909, he took part in the Congress of Elbasan and taught at the newly opened Normal School (*Shkolla Normale*) there. The **Ottoman** authorities imprisoned him several times for his nationalist activities in 1909-1911. He supported **Prince Wilhelm zu Wied** and remained politically active in later years. During the witch hunts which followed the **communist** takeover in 1944, he was arrested and sentenced to prison. Dalliu is remembered in particular for his nationalist tract *Patriotizma në Tiranë* (Patriotism in Tirana), 1930, and for his writings on **Islam**.

DARA, GABRIELE (1826.01.08-1885.11.19). Arbëresh writer. Gabriele Dara, known in Albanian as Gavril Dara i Ri, was born in Palazzo Adriano in Sicily to an old Arbëresh family, reputed to have been one of the first to leave Albania after the death of **Scanderbeg** in 1468. He studied at the Greek seminary in

Palermo and later received a degree in law, practicing for a time in Agrigento. Dara became increasingly active in the turbulent political events of Garibaldi's overthrow of the Kingdom of the Two Sicilies and held a variety of offices. After an initial appointment as first councillor of the prefecture of Palermo, he served from 1867 to 1869 as prefect, or governor, of the city of Trapani. From 1871 to 1874, he was also director of the periodical *La Riforma* in Rome. Dara's literary and scholarly interests were wide-ranging, spanning poetry, folklore, philosophy, archeology and jurisprudence. He wrote some Italian verse and one religious poem in Albanian dedicated to Saint Lazarus but is remembered primarily for his romantic ballad *Kënka e sprasme e Balës*, Catanzaro 1906 (Engl. *The Last Lay of Bala,* Tirana 1967).

It was no doubt under the late effects of Ossianism generated by Scottish poet James Macpherson (1736-1796) that Gabriele Dara claimed to have recognized in his grandfather's collection of folk song fragments an old Albanian epic by a mountain bard called Bala. The four-part poem, recounting the adventures of Nik Peta and Pal Golemi, Albanian heroes during the *moti i madh*, the "great age" of Scanderbeg, was first published in installments in 1887 in the periodical *Arbri i ri* (Young Albania) by **Giuseppe Schirò** and appeared in full in Italian and Albanian in the journal *La Nazione albanese* (The Albanian Nation) from July 1900 on.

The Last Lay of Bala, with its nine cantos, was soon recognized to be from Gabriele Dara's own pen. One may regard his allusion to the discovery of fragments of a nonexistent old Albanian epic more as a romantic enhancement typical of the period than as a conscious forgery. Whatever the author's intentions may have been, the poem is not without literary merits in its own right and is in any case more unified and harmoniously balanced than the works of Dara's predecessor and guide, **Girolamo De Rada**. The Last Lay of Bala makes quite pleasant reading within the context of the nineteenth-century romantic literature of the Arbëresh and is still enjoyed by Albanians today.

DARA I RI, GAVRIL. *See* DARA, GABRIELE.

DAUGHTERS OF CHARITY. *See* LAZARIST CONGREGATION.

DAVIES, EDMUND FRANK. British military officer and writer. Brigadier "Trotsky" Davies was a senior British officer of the Royal Ulster Rifles, who had trained at Sandhurst and was parachuted into Albania by the **Special Operations Executive** in 1943 to promote contacts with Albanian resistance fighters and encourage them to fight the Germans instead of one another. His sympathies were more with the **communist** partisans than with the nationalist and royalist movements, and he brought his influence to bear upon the Foreign Office for the support of the former. Having set up base in Çermenika, he was in Albania from 1943 until he was wounded and captured by the Germans in 1944. Davies was later held in a German prisoner-of-war camp in Colditz in Saxony until it was liberated by American troops in April 1945. His experience in Albania is recounted in his memoirs: *Illyrian Venture: The Story of the British Military Mission to Enemy-Occupied Albania, 1943-1944,* London 1952.

DELVINA, DISTRICT OF. Region of local government administration. The District of Delvina (*Rrethi i Delvinës*), with its administrative headquarters in the town of Delvina, borders on the districts of **Saranda** to the west, and **Gjirokastra** to the east. It has a surface area of 348 square kilometers and a present **population** of 29,862 (in 2000).

DELVINA, SULEJMAN BEY (1884.10.05-1932.08.01). Political figure. Sulejman bey Delvina was born in the southern **Delvina** region and went to secondary school in Janina. He then got a job with the Ottoman administration, working for the ministry of the interior. Delvina supported initiatives for Albanian cultural autonomy and, later, for the right to self-determination. The Albanians of the **Ottoman Empire** sent him as their representative to the Paris Peace Conference in 1919. He had considerable experience in administration and talent in reconciling various political factions. As a result he was elected prime minister by the **Congress of Lushnja** in January 1920. Although his government made some progress in restoring stability and national sovereignty and in ridding the country of the many foreign troops occupying it, he was soon thereafter, on 14 November 1920, forced to resign under pressure from **Ahmet Zogu**. From July to October 1921, he served as minister of the interior and was a member of **parliament** until 1924, when he was more closely affiliated with **Fan Noli** than Zogu. During Noli's **Democratic Revolution**, he served as foreign minister and, as Noli's deputy, introduced some modest reforms. He opposed diplomatic recognition of the USSR but was outvoted on the subject. Delvina went into exile after the fall of the Noli government and joined the *Bashkimi Kombëtar*

(The National Union). Ailing, he returned to Albania in 1928 and died in a hospital in **Vlora**.

DE MARTINO, LEONARDO (1830-1923.07.12). Arbëresh poet. Leonardo De Martino was from the Campanian village of Greci (Alb. *Greçi*) in the province of Avellino. He was sent as a **Franciscan** priest to **Shkodra** on missionary work in 1865. There, having secured the support of the Italian minister of education, Francesco Crispi (himself of Albanian descent), De Martino took an active part in the opening of the first Italian school in Albania. For most of his years of service in the rugged mountains of northern Albania, he was assigned to the diocese of **Zadrima** and **Lezha**. For a time, he served as secretary to Prenk Pasha, prince of **Mirdita**, and tutored his son, **Prenk Bibë Doda**. He was also mentor to the young **Gjergj Fishta**, who was to take the traditions of northern Albanian verse to far greater heights. De Martino left Albania at the end of the century, whether for retirement or having been actively encouraged to do so by the Austro-Hungarian government, which was enforcing its jurisdiction under the *Kultusprotektorat*. He died at the convent of Sarno in Italy at the ripe old age of ninety-three.

Leonardo De Martino was a born poet whose talent for verse surprised many of his contemporaries, in particular since he wrote not in his mother tongue but in the **Gheg** dialect of northern Albania, which he learned during his forty years as a missionary there. He is the author of Albanian translations of Italian religious **literature** and of poetry of primarily religious inspiration both in Albanian and Italian. His poetry, following the tradition of nineteenth-century **Catholic** literature in Albania established by **Zadrima** abbot Pjetër Zarishi (1806-1866), circulated for years on leaflets until his friend, parish priest Ndue Bytyçi (1847-1917) of **Kosova**, persuaded De Martino to publish it in a collection. The resulting volume, entitled *L'Arpa di un italo-albanese* (The Harp of an Italo-Albanian), Venice 1881, is an impressive 442-page compilation of De Martino's mature and polished verse in Italian and Albanian. His importance as a poet lies not so much in any unusual poetic fantasy or inspiration but in his prosodic finesse. It was Leonardo De Martino who introduced new meters such as the iambic into Albanian and popularized Sapphic verse. He was also the author of several other religious works, among which are a short nativity play entitled *Nata Këshnellavet* (Christmas Night), Shkodra 1880, the first of its kind in Albanian, and

Arbenorve t'kersctén t'Grisciun Festuér (Festive Appeal to Albanian Christians), Shkodra 1896.

DEMIRAJ, BARDHYL (1958.03.29-). Scholar and linguist. Bardhyl Demiraj was born in **Tirana,** where he finished his schooling in 1976. His father, linguist Shaban Demiraj, instilled in him a passion for the historical development of his native language. From 1976 to 1981, he studied Albanian **language** and **literature** at the University of Tirana, finishing his masters in 1982, and in 1984-1986, he specialized in Indo-European, Romanian, and Balkan linguistics at the University of Vienna. On his return to Tirana, Demiraj was appointed to the Institute of Linguistics and Literature of the Academy of Sciences as a research expert for the history of the Albanian language and onomastics. From December 1991 to August 1993, he did postgraduate research at the Linguistics Institute of the University of Bonn, and finished his doctorate in Tirana in 1994 with a dissertation on the historical development of the number system in Albanian. In 1994-1995, he collaborated on a research project for an Indo-European Dictionary under the direction of Robert Beekes in Leiden, Holland, and carried on with etymological research in Bonn until 2000. In March 2001, he was appointed professor of Albanian at the Institute for Comparative and Indo-European Linguistics of the University of Munich. Bardhyl Demiraj is considered one of the leading experts in the field of Albanian etymology. Foremost among his publications is *Albanische Etymologien: Untersuchungen zum albanischen Erbwortschatz* (Albanian Etymologies: Research into the Hereditary Vocabulary), Atlanta 1997.

DEMIRAJ, SHABAN (1920.01.01-). Scholar and linguist. Shaban Demiraj has been Albania's most noted specialist in the field of historical linguistics since the death of **Eqrem Çabej**. He was born in **Vlora** and finished secondary school in **Tirana** in 1939. A man with a rare passion for language history, Demiraj managed to study Latin, ancient Greek and the major languages of Europe and the Balkans despite the difficult social and political environment in his country. From 1948 to 1954, he worked as a teacher of Albanian **literature** in **Gjirokastra** and Tirana, and from 1954 to 1990 taught at the Institute of Education (*Instituti i Lartë Pedagogjik*), and then at the newly created University of Tirana, at which he became a professor in 1972. In 1989, he was appointed a member of the Albanian Academy of Sciences and, after his retirement in 1990, served as its president from 1993 to 17 August 1997.

Among his many monographs on the history and in particular morphology of the Albanian **language**, mention may be made of *Gramatika e gjuhës shqipe: fonetika e morfologjia* (Grammar of the Albanian Language: Phonetics and Morphology), Prishtina 1969; *Historia e gjuhës së shkruar shqipe* (History of Written Albanian), Prishtina 1970; *Morfologjia e gjuhës së sotme shqipe* (Morphology of Modern Albanian), Prishtina 1971; *Çeshtje të sistemit emëror të gjuhës shqipe* (Questions of the Noun System of Albanian), Tirana 1972; *Gramatikë historike e gjuhës shqipe* (Historical Grammar of Albanian), Tirana 1986; *Gjuha shqipe dhe historia e saj* (The Albanian Language and its History), Tirana 1988; *Eqrem Çabej: një jetë kushtuar shkencës* (**Eqrem Çabej**: A Life Devoted to Scholarship), Tirana 1990; *Historische Grammatik der albanischen Sprache* (Historical Grammar of Albanian), Vienna 1993; *Gjuhësi ballkanike* (Balkan Linguistics), Skopje 1994; *Gramatika e gjuhës shqipe: vëllimi 1, morfologjia* (Grammar of Albanian, Volume 1, Morphology), Tirana 1995; *La lingua albanese: origine, storia, struttura* (The Albanian Language: Origins, History, Structure), Cosenza 1997; *Fonologjia historike e gjuhës shqipe* (Historical Phonology of Albanian), Tirana 1997; *Prejardhja e shqiptarëve nën dritën e dëshmive të gjuhës shqipe* (The Origin of the Albanians in the Light of the Records of the Albanian Language), Tirana 1999; and *Gramatikë historike e gjuhës shqipe* (Historical Grammar of Albanian), Tirana 2002.

DEMOCRAT PARTY. *See* NEW DEMOCRATIC PARTY.

DEMOCRATIC ALLIANCE PARTY (*PARTIA ALEANCA DEMOKRATIKE, PAD*) (1992-). The Democratic Alliance Party evolved out of the **Democratic Party** of **Sali Berisha** on 19 September 1992. Its leaders, among whom are Gramoz Pashko, **Neritan Ceka**, **Arben Imami**, Shahin Kadare, and most of the intellectuals in the Democratic Party, strove for a more moderate course to promote national reconciliation, at a time when the mainstream elements of the Democratic Party were increasingly characterized by nationalist fundamentalism and political revanchism. The Democratic Alliance remained a small party, however. In 1996, it won a mere 1.6 percent of the popular vote, in 1997 2.7 percent and in 2001 2.6 percent.

DEMOCRATIC PARTY OF ALBANIA (*PARTIA DEMOKRATIKE E SHQIPËRISË, PDSH*) **(1990-).** The Democratic Party was formed on 12 December 1990 as the first non-communist political party in the country after half a century of totalitarian rule. Among its founding members were **Sali Berisha**, Gramoz Pashko, **Azem Hajdari** and **Neritan Ceka**. In the elections of 1991 it won 38.7 percent of the popular vote. In 1992 it won 62.1 percent, in 1996 55.5 percent, in 1997 25.8 percent, and in 2001 (as part of the **Union for Victory** alliance) 36.8 percent. The leading political figure of the **Socialist Party**, Sali Berisha, took over power as president of Albania on 8 April 1992. The Democratic Party ruled Albania, under Berisha's authoritarian style, until the disastrous events of 1997. Though it has suffered some splits (the **Democratic Alliance Party** broke off in September 1992, and the **New Democratic Party** was formed in 2001 under **Genc Pollo**), it has remained the leading opposition party.

DEMOCRATIC REVOLUTION (*REVOLUCIONI DEMOKRATIK*) **(1924).** The capital of Albania was moved to **Tirana** after the **Congress of Lushnja** in 1920 when the first serious attempts were made to form a stable Albanian government. No stability was achieved, however, and political infighting continued for the next four years. A pro-Zogist faction won the parliamentary elections held in November-December 1923, but political leaders hesitated to appoint the power-hungry landowner **Ahmet Zogu** as head of government. On 23 February 1924, just before **parliament** was to discuss the issue, Zogu was shot and seriously wounded but managed to have his conservative ally, **Shefqet bey Vërlaci**, appointed prime minister on 3 March, supported by other feudal landowners. The political situation in the country had become extremely tense when, on 6 April 1924, two American tourists, G. B. de Long and R. L. Coleman, were murdered at Mamurras, north of **Tirana**. The nation was outraged and accused Zogu of being behind the murders to show that he was the only person who could bring law and order to the country. On 20 April, the revolutionary **Avni Rustemi** was then shot in Tirana and died of his injuries two days later. It was assumed once again that Zogu was behind the murder, Rustemi having been indirectly involved in the assassination attempt against him on 23 February. Over 10,000 people took part in Rustemi's funeral in **Vlora** on 30 April, including twenty-six members of parliament. Bishop **Fan Noli** gave a fiery oration on the occasion which provoked the liberal opposition into such a fury that the

Vërlaci government fell on 27 May, and Ahmet Zogu and 500 of his followers were obliged to flee to **Yugoslavia**. Army commander Kasëm Qafëzezi and his forces then took Tirana on 10 June 1924, inducing the so-called Democratic or June Revolution.

A new democratic government was formed by Fan Noli, and on 19 June 1924 it proclaimed an ambitious, twenty-point program, including plans for a number of radical reforms. Among these plans were: disarming the population, including leaders who supported Noli, ending feudalism, improving the lot of the peasants, downsizing the administration, reducing taxes, reforming the administration, the justice system, **health care** and **education**, as well as promoting friendly relations with all, especially with neighboring countries.

In the summer of 1924, Ahmet Zogu and his allies in Yugoslav exile gathered their forces. Mercenaries from General Piotr Nikolayevich Wrangel's White Russian army, and volunteers from **Kosova**, were assembled to form a force of some 3,000 men, which the Yugoslav army equipped with weapons. In mid-December, this army, accompanied by Yugoslav troops, marched on Albania. Other volunteer units under **Kostaq Kota** and **Myfit bey Libohova** attacked from **Greece**. Noli and his government protested bitterly about Yugoslav aggression to the League of Nations and withdrew to Vlora on 23 December, from where, two days later, they were forced to flee to Italy after Zogu and his forces took Tirana on 24 December 1924.

Noli's twenty-point program for the modernization and democratization of Albania, including agrarian reform, had proven to be too rash and too idealistic for a backward country with no parliamentary traditions. In a letter to an English friend, he was later to note the reasons for his failure: "By insisting on the agrarian reforms I aroused the wrath of the landed aristocracy; by failing to carry them out I lost the support of the peasant masses."

DE RADA, GIROLAMO (1814.11.29-1903.02.28). Arbëresh poet and figure of the Albanian nationalist movement in nineteenth-century Italy. Girolamo De Rada, known in Albanian as Jeronim De Rada, was born the son of a parish priest of Greek rite in Macchia Albanese (Alb. *Maqi*) in the mountains of Cosenza. He attended the College of Saint Adrian in San Demetrio Corone. In October 1834, in accordance with his father's wishes, he registered at the Faculty of Law of the University of Naples, but the main focus of his interests remained folklore and **literature**. It was in Naples in 1836 that De Rada published the first edition of his best-known Albanian-**language** poem, the Songs of Milosao, under the Italian title *Poesie albanesi del secolo XV. Canti di Milosao, figlio del despota di Scutari* (Albanian Poetry from the Fifteenth Century: Songs of Milosao, Son of the Despot of Shkodra).

His second work, *Canti storici albanesi di Serafina Thopia, moglie del principe Nicola Ducagino* (Albanian Historical Songs of Serafina Thopia, Wife of Prince Nicholas Dukagjini), Naples 1839, was seized by the Bourbon authorities because of De Rada's alleged affiliations with conspiratorial groups during the Italian Risorgimento. The work was republished under the title *Canti di Serafina Thopia, principessa di Zadrina nel secolo XV* (Songs of Serafina Thopia, Princess of Zadrina in the Fifteenth Century), Naples 1843, and in later years in a third version as *Specchio di umano transito, vita di Serafina Thopia, Principessa di Ducagino* (Mirror of Human Transience, Life of Serafina Thopia, Princess of Dukagjini), Naples 1897. De Rada founded the newspaper *L'Albanese d'Italia* (The Albanian of Italy), which included articles in Albanian. This bilingual "political, moral and literary journal" with a final circulation of 3,200 copies was the first Albanian-language periodical anywhere.

Girolamo De Rada's fame as a catalyst of Albanian national awareness spread in the mid-nineteenth century. He corresponded with leading figures of the **Rilindja** movement such as **Thimi Mitko**, **Zef Jubani**, **Sami bey Frashëri** and **Dora d'Istria**, and with foreign scholars and writers interested in Albania such as French Albanologist **Auguste Dozon**, Baroness Josephine von Knorr and Austrian linguist **Gustav Meyer**.

Discouraged by the events of 1848, he abandoned publication of *L'Albanese d'Italia*, left Naples and returned to San Demetrio Corone to teach school. In 1868, he managed to get a position as director of the Garopoli secondary school in Corigliano Calabro, a job he was to hold for ten years. It was during these years that a number of further works appeared in print, mostly in Italian.

In 1883, he founded the bilingual monthly journal *Fiàmuri Arbërit—La bandiera dell'Albania* (The Albanian **Flag**). This periodical, published initially in Macchia Albanese and later in Cosenza "by a committee of gentlemen from Albania and its colonies," lasted until November 1887 and was widely read by Albanians in the Balkans despite Turkish and Greek censorship.

In 1892, De Rada was reappointed to teach Albanian language and literature at the College of Saint Adrian in San Demetrio

Corone and in 1895 organized the first Albanological congress in Corigliano Calabro. He also took an active part in the second Albanological congress in Lungro (Alb. *Ungra*) two years later in which he appealed for the setting up of a much-needed chair of Albanian studies at the Oriental Institute in Naples.

Before Albania had become a political entity, it was already a poetic reality in the works of Girolamo De Rada. His vision of an independent Albania grew in the second half of the nineteenth century from a simple desire to a realistic political objective to which he was passionately committed. De Rada was the harbinger and first audible voice of the Romantic movement in Albanian literature, a movement which, inspired by his unfailing energy on behalf of national awakening among Albanians in Italy and in the Balkans, was to evolve into the romantic nationalism characteristic of the Rilindja period in Albania. His journalistic, literary and political activities were instrumental not only in fostering an awareness for the Arbëresh minority in Italy but also in laying the foundations for an Albanian national literature.

DERVISH ORDERS. Religious communities or brotherhoods. The medieval movement of **Islamic** mysticism known as Sufism gave rise to a number of dervish sects, Arabic *tariqat* "paths," in the Shi'ite tradition. Many of these sects and sub-sects penetrated into Albania and **Kosova** during the five centuries of **Ottoman** rule. Their centers or monasteries were known as *tekkes,* Alb. *teqe.* The two most important dervish sects to have found a home in Albania were the **Bektashi** and the **Halveti**. These are followed in importance by the **Rifa'i**, the **Sa'di**, the **Kadiri** and to a much lesser degree by the Tidjani. There is also some information as to the presence on Albanian soil, most often in Kosova, of the Djelveti, the Sinani, the Bayrami, the Mevlevi, the Melami, the Naqshbandi, the Badavi, the Jezevi, the Shahzeli and the Desuki. Each of the *tariqat* had its own particular origin, but the spiritual differences between them in Albania were often minimal, mostly concerning matters of detail and specific rites. As such, there was no open rivalry between the sects, in Albania at least, and members of one sect were traditionally wont to participate in the ceremonies of the others.

The dervish orders lost much of their significance when independent Albania began looking increasingly towards the West, though most of the major sects referred to above survived up to **World War II**. Their history in Albania and in the Balkans in general has been superbly documented in recent years by the

French scholars Alexandre Popovic, Nathalie Clayer and Gilles Veinstein, although much remains obscure.

With the **communist** rise to power in 1944, the sects were initially given the status of an independent religious community and were then gradually liquidated. The smaller orders had virtually disappeared by 1950, whereas the Bektashi survived, at least nominally, until 1967, when **religion** in Albania was banned entirely. Since the removal of the ban on religious activity in December 1990, the Bektashi have managed to return to life, and some of the other *tariqat* have also begun to show signs of revival.

DESNICKAJA, AGNIJA (1912.08.23-1992.04.18). Russian scholar and linguist. Until her death, Agnija Vasiljevna Desnickaja was the leading Russian specialist in Albanian studies. She was born in the Černigov region and specialized in German studies at the A. J. Herzen Institute in Leningrad in 1928 under V. M. Žirmunski. Thereafter, she was active for many years at the Leningrad Institute of Linguistics, finishing her masters in 1935 and her doctorate in 1946. From 1963 to 1976, Desnickaja headed the Leningrad branch of the Institute of Linguistics of the Soviet Academy of Sciences. She was also an active teacher and lecturer. In 1957, she founded the Department of Albanian **Language** and **Literature** at the University of Leningrad. From the early 1950s onwards, Desnickaja's research activities concentrated increasingly on Albanian and Balkan studies, with particular attention to comparative linguistics. She is the author of 187 articles and monographs, 73 of which are devoted to Albanian language, literature and folklore.

Among her major publications in this field are: *Slavjanskie zaimstvovanija v albanskom jazyke* (Slavic Loanwords in the Albanian Language), Moscow 1963; *Rekonstrukcija elementov drevnealbanskogo jazyka i obščebalkanskie lingvističeskie problemy* (Reconstruction of the Elements of the Paleo-Albanian Language and General Balkan Linguistic Problems), Moscow 1966; *Albanskij jazyk i ego dialekty* (The Albanian Language and its Dialects), Leningrad 1968; and *Albanskaja literatura i albanskij jazyk* (Albanian Literature and the Albanian Language), Leningrad 1987. She was also the author of countless articles on the historical development and dialects of Albanian. Madame Desnickaja can be considered the founder of Albanian studies in **Russia**. Her contacts with Albania were unfortunately cut off due to the break in political and party relations between the two countries in 1961, and her work was ignored in Albania for political reasons throughout the 1970s and 1980s.

DESTANI, BEJTULLAH (1960.08.13-). British-Albanian scholar. Bejtullah D. Destani was born in Blaç near Prizren in **Kosova** and went to school in Prizren and Dragash. He studied political science in Belgrade in the 1980s, where he published a *Selektivna bibliografija knjiga o Albaniji, 1850-1984* (Selective Bibliography of Books about Albania, 1850-1984), Belgrade 1986. In the 1990s, in view of the increasingly perilous situation in his native Kosova, he emigrated to London, where he has lived since 1991. He has devoted himself to Albanian studies, in particular to research on British-Albanian cultural relations. Destani has made many significant discoveries in British archives and libraries. He is the author of the 1,100-page *Albania & Kosovo, Political and Ethnic Boundaries, 1867-1946: Documents and Maps,* Slough 1999.

In 1997, Bejtullah Destani founded the Centre for Albanian Studies in London, initially very much a one-man show, and has managed, as head of this center, to publish or republish a number of important works in Albanian studies: *The Truth on Albania and the Albanians: Historical and Critical Issues by Wassa Effendi,* London 1999; *Harry Hodgkinson: Scanderbeg,* London 1999; *Faik Bey Konitza: Selected Correspondence 1896-1942,* London 2000; *Wadham Peacock: The Wild Albanian,* London 2000; *M. Edith Durham: Albania and the Albanians, Selected Articles and Letters, 1903-1944,* London 2001; and *Dayrell R. Oakley-Hill: An Englishman in Albania, Memoirs of a British Officer, 1929-1955,* London 2002.

DEVOLL, DISTRICT OF. Region of local government administration. The District of Devoll (*Rrethi i Devollit*), with its administrative headquarters in the town of Bilisht, borders on the districts of **Kolonja** and **Korça** to the west, and the Republic of Greece to the east and south. It has a surface area of 429 square kilometers and a present **population** of 36,669 (in 2000). The word Devoll was recorded in Byzantine sources in 1028 A.D. as Deabolis.

DIBRA, DISTRICT OF. Region of local government administration. The District of Dibra (*Rrethi i Dibrës*), with its administrative headquarters in the town of Peshkopia, borders on the districts of **Mat** and **Mirdita** to the west, **Kukës** to the north, **Bulqiza** to the south and the Republic of Macedonia to the east.

It has a surface area of 1,088 square kilometers and a present **population** of 104,782 (in 2000). The word "Dibra," also Alb. indef. Dibër, is known is Macedonian Slavic as Debar, and as a geographic region, it extends into Macedonia. The term was first recorded in Latin as Deborus.

DILO, KSENOFON (1932.01.15-). Painter. Ksenofon Dilo was born in **Gjirokastra** and studied in the 1950s at the Academy of Fine Arts in Prague. He is remembered not only as a painter, but also for his activities in cinematography, including film scripts. In 1975, he left the **film** industry and became artistic secretary of the **Union of Writers and Artists**. Dilo also served as director of the national art gallery in **Tirana**.

DINE, SPIRO (1846?-1922.04.12). Albanian folklorist. Spiro Risto Dine was from Vithkuq in the **Korça** region and emigrated to Egypt in 1866, at the age of twenty, approximately one year after **Thimi Mitko**, whom he met there and with whom he soon collaborated on Mitko's collection of Albanian folk songs and tales. He was also a founding member of the Egyptian section of the **Society for the Publication of Albanian Writing** in 1881. While in Shibîn el Kôm, Spiro Dine corresponded with **Girolamo De Rada** and was inspired by the activities of the **Frashëri** brothers. Later in life he was particularly enthused by the publication of Naim Frashëri's epic *Istori e Skenderbeut* (History of Scanderbeg), Bucharest 1898, which became his favorite work of poetry.

The book for which Spiro Dine is remembered, and indeed his only significant publication, is a monumental 856-page collection of Albanian folklore and **literature** entitled *Valët e detit* (The Waves of the Sea), Sofia 1908. At the time of publication, it was the longest book ever printed in Albanian.

DISRAELI, BENJAMIN, Earl of Beaconsfield (1804.12.21-1881.04.19). British political figure and writer. Disraeli was one of the most colorful and influential figures of British politics in the nineteenth century. He was also a well-known and much-read author of Victorian prose. Born in London of a noted **Jewish** family, he was elected to parliament in July 1837 and became prime minister of **Great Britain** in 1868.

As a young man, Disraeli made a grand tour of the Mediterranean and the Middle East, ostensibly for health reasons. This seventeen-month tour (from June 1830 to October 1831), which took him to Spain, Malta, Albania, Greece and the Middle East, proved to be one of the most formative experiences of his early years. Towards the end of September 1830, he sailed with two traveling companions to Corfu, from where they intended to proceed to Janina, then the capital of southern Albania under **Ottoman** rule, which **Lord Byron** had visited in the days of **Ali Pasha Tepelena**. Disraeli's official pretext for the journey into the wilds of Albania was to deliver a letter to the grand vizier from Sir Frederick Adam, the British governor of the Ionian Isles. Sir Frederick also gave him a "very warm letter" of recommendation for the British consul general in Preveza on the Greek mainland. Disraeli paid a visit to the Albanian governor in Arta in order to ask for an additional escort on to Janina and departed with a sense of awe at having entered the divan of the Great Turk. The Albanian officers in the bey's household were described as "finely shaped men, with expressive countenances and spare forms." Disraeli delighted in particular in the Albanian costumes: "Their picturesque dress is celebrated, though, to view it with full effect, it should be seen upon an Albanian... The long hair and the small cap, the crimson velvet vest and jacket, embroidered and embossed with golden patterns of the most elegant and flowing forms, the white and ample kilt, the ornamented buskins, and the belt full of silver-sheathed arms; it is difficult to find humanity in better plight." The bey granted them "a guard of Albanians" who like the rest were "armed to the teeth with daggers, pistols and guns, invariably richly ornament-ed, and sometimes entirely inlaid with silver, even the barrel." With them, he finally reached the fabled city of Janina, which was nestled in the mountains at the edge of a sparkling lake. Much of what Disraeli saw and experienced in southern Albania was used in his prose writings, in particular in *The Rise of Iskander,* London 1833, a short novel based on the life of the Albanian prince and national hero **Scanderbeg**.

D'ISTRIA, DORA. *See* GJIKA, ELENA.

DOCCI, PRIMUS. *See* DOÇI, PRENG.

DOÇI, PRENG (1846.02.25-1917.02.22). Political and religious figure and poet. Doçi, known in Italian as Primus Docci, was born near **Lezha** and studied at the *Kolegjia Papnore Shqyptare* (Albanian Pontifical Seminary) in **Shkodra** and at the College of the Propaganda Fide in Rome. In 1871, he returned to the **Catholic**

Mirdita region to serve as a parish priest in Korthpula, Orosh, and, subsequently, in Kalivarja near Spaç. He was among the leaders of the **Mirdita** uprising against **Ottoman** rule in 1876-1877. In preparation for this rebellion, Doçi traveled to Cetinje, mountain capital of Montenegro, to seek financial and military assistance. Although the northern Albanian tribes were equally suspicious of Montenegrin designs on their homeland, they had agreed this time to "shake hands with their southern Slavic brothers in order to resist the burden they jointly bore." Though Doçi managed to return from Cetinje with a pledge of Montenegrin assistance and, what is equally important, a promise of noninterference, the rebellion proved a failure and was put down by Turkish troops in March 1877. Preng Doçi was captured, exiled to Istanbul, but was later released and expelled to Rome.

From the Vatican, Cardinal Simeoni of the Propaganda Fide sent him to the west coast of Newfoundland where he worked as a missionary until 1881. To Doçi goes the honor, as far as can be ascertained, of being the first known Albanian resident of North America. Western Newfoundland's rugged coastline and inhospitable climate, however, proved too much for Doçi, whose desire it was to return to his Mediterranean homeland. As an initial compromise, the Vatican transferred him to St. John in New Brunswick, where he worked from October 1881 to March 1883. After his return to Rome, he was sent on another missionary assignment, this time to India as secretary of the apostolic delegate to India, Cardinal Agliardi. In 1888, after years of petitioning and with the intercession of the patriarch of Constantinople, Preng Doçi finally received permission from the Ottoman authorities to return to Albania. In January of the following year, he was consecrated head of the Abbey Nullius of St. Alexander of Orosh in Mirdita, a position which enabled him to exercise considerable political and religious influence in the region for many years to come. In 1897, he traveled to Vienna to propose the creation of an autonomous Catholic principality in northern Albania under Mirdita leadership.

Two years later, in 1899, he founded the *Shoqnia e bashkimit të gjuhës shqipe* (Society for the Unity of the Albanian **Language**), usually known as the *Bashkimi* (Unity) literary society, together with **Ndoc Nikaj** and **Gjergj Fishta**, and devised the so-called Bashkimi alphabet.

DODA, PRENK BIBË (1858-1920). Tribal leader and political figure. Prenk Bibë Doda was born in Orosh in **Mirdita** and spent his youth in Istanbul. In 1876, he returned to his native Mirdita region, where he inherited the hereditary title of Kapidan (captain) of Mirdita. Immediately after accession, he made contact with Montenegro and instigated a revolt in Mirdita, which was put down by the Turks in 1877. Doda continued to play an important role in Mirdita during the time of the **League of Prizren**. In 1881, he was arrested and banned to Anatolia where he remained for seventeen years. He returned to Albania in 1908 after the Young Turk Revolution. Doda had hoped to accede to the throne of Albania after independence in 1912, but nonetheless remained loyal to **Prince Wilhelm zu Wied**, under whom he served for a short time as foreign minister. After **World War I**, he served as deputy prime minister in the government of Turhan Pasha Përmeti.

DOKLE, NAMIK (1946.03.11-). Political figure and high-ranking member of the **Socialist Party**. Namik Dokle was born in **Durrës** and studied agrarian economy in 1965-1970 and journalism from 1968 to 1970. From 1983 to 1989 he was editor-in-chief of the newspaper *Puna* (Work) and in 1991 was briefly editor-in-chief of the daily *Zëri i popullit* (The People's Voice). He has been a member of **parliament** and a leading figure of the Socialist Party since 1991. From 1992 to 1996, he served as deputy head of the party in the absence of **Fatos Nano**, who was in prison. In July 1997, he was appointed deputy speaker of parliament and was later speaker of parliament. In 1999-2000, he was also general secretary of the Socialist Party. He resigned as speaker of parliament on 29 April 2002.

DOMI, MAHIR (1915.03.12-2000.09.19). Scholar and linguist. Mahir Domi was born in **Elbasan** and graduated from the French lycée in **Korça**. He studied language and literature at the University of Grenoble from which he graduated in 1941. After a period of internment by the Italians in Porto Romano, he returned to Albania and served as director of the Normal School (*Shkolla Normale*) in Elbasan. In 1947, he began teaching and lecturing at the Institute of Sciences. When the University of **Tirana** was founded in 1957, he was appointed to the chair of Albanian **language**. As a member of the Albanian Academy of Sciences, he was also active in the Section for Grammar and Dialectology at the Institute of Linguistics and Literature.

Mahir Domi was the author of a number of works devoted to Albanian syntax and to diachronic and comparative linguistics.

Mention may be made in this connection of: *Gramatika e gjuhës shqipe, II: sintaksa* (Grammar of the Albanian Language, II: Syntax), Tirana 1954; and *Morfologjia historike e gjuhës shqipe* (Historical Morphology of the Albanian Language), Tirana 1961. He also edited the series *Dialektologjia shqiptare* (Albanian Dialectology), Tirana 1974-1990.

DOMINICAN ORDER. Order of the **Catholic Church.** The Dominican order of Friar Preachers was established in 1215 by Saint Dominic (1170-1221). Born in Spain, Saint Dominic established his headquarters in Toulouse to convert the Albigenses. Approved by Rome in 1216, the order superseded his activities there and spread to Italy and later throughout Europe, playing a major role in the religious and intellectual life of the later medieval period. In Albania the Dominicans followed on the heels of the **Benedictines.** It is known that they settled in **Durrës** in 1278 and were active there from 1304, when the town fell to the West after twenty years of Byzantine rule. In a letter dated 31 March 1304, Pope Benedict XI (r. 1303-1304) asked the head of the Dominican order in Hungary to send to Albania some of his subordinates of "good moral character, active and eloquent" for missionary activities. With the support of the Holy See, the Dominicans acquired full power to set up a Latin hierarchy to their own liking on the Albanian coast to replace the **Orthodox** Church, which had been forced to abandon its position. Of the Dominican order were the anonymous authors of two important fourteenth-century historical texts on Albania: the *Anonymi Descriptio Europae Orientalis* of 1308 and the *Directorium ad passagium faciendum* of 1332.

DONES, ELVIRA (1960.07.24-). Writer. Elvira Dones was born in **Durrës**. She studied at the University of **Tirana** and worked for a time for the television and **film** industry there. In 1988, she managed to flee the country, then still under Stalinist rule, and now lives in Switzerland. Her first novel *Dashuri e huaj* (A Foreign Love), Tirana 1997, was followed by *Kardigan* (Cardigan), Tirana 1998, the short story collection *Lule të gabuara* (Mistaken Flowers), Tirana 1999, and in particular *Yjet nuk vishen kështu* (Stars Don't Dress Up Like That), Elbasan 2000. The candid description of the Albanian mafia and the realities of Albanian prostitution in Italy in the latter novel, translated into Italian as *Sole bruciato* (Burning Sun), Milan 2001, caused a furor in her home country. Much of her writing, not without autobiographical elements, deals with the theme of **women** in emigration.

DOZON, AUGUSTE (1822.08.02-1890.12.31). French scholar and diplomat. Auguste Dozon was born in Châlons-sur-Marne. He studied ancient and modern literature at the Sainte-Barbe college in Paris and, after further studies in law, worked for the ministry of the interior. He was later transferred to the Directorate for Fine Arts and was responsible there for the protection of historical monuments. Dozon was passionately interested in foreign languages and peoples, and embarked upon a career as a professional diplomat. The French foreign ministry seconded him to the Balkans, where he served as French consul in Belgrade (1854-1863), Mostar (1863-1865, 1875-1878), Plovdiv (1865-1869), Janina (1869-1875), Cyprus (1875-1881), and Salonika (1881-1885). He was particularly interested in the Albanian **language,** which he had begun to learn in Janina after meeting **Johann Georg von Hahn** and young Albanians studying in the one-time "capital of Albania." The fruits of his research into the Albanian language and folklore, in particular Albanian oral **literature**, are to be seen in his *Manuel de la langue chkipe ou albanaise* (Handbook of the *Shqip* or Albanian Language), Paris 1879; and *Contes albanais, recueillis et traduits* (Albanian Folk Tales, Collected and Translated), Paris 1881. Dozon died in Versailles on New Year's Eve 1890.

DRAGUA. Figure of northern Albanian mythology. This semi-human being, Alb. *dragúa*, def. *dragói*, **Gheg** *drangue,* stems etymologically from Lat. *draco(nem)* "dragon" or Ital. *dracone* "dragon." *Draguas* are born wearing shirts, symbolic of the caul, and have two to four invisible wings under their armpits. The prime aim in life of a *dragua* is to combat and slay dragon-like *kulshedras*. Their struggle with the *kulshedras* is reminiscent of the combat between the giants and gods of ancient Greece.

DRENOVA, ALEKS STAVRE. *See* ASDRENI.

DRIN. River in northern Albania. The Drin is the largest river in Albania and the southwestern Balkans. It is formed by the confluence of two rivers, the Black Drin, Alb. *Drini i Zi*, which takes its source at Struga in Lake **Ohrid** and flows 150 kilometers northwards through **Dibra**, and the White Drin, Alb. *Drini i Bardhë*, which takes its source in the mountains of Kosova north of Peja and is 128 kilometers in length. The two rivers join at **Kukës** and flow through the mountains of northern Albania to the Adriatic Sea. Arriving at the coastal plain, part of the Drin flows into the Buna River near **Shkodra** and another part uses its traditional bed southwards through the **Zadrima** plain and flows into the Adriatic Sea near **Lezha**. It has a total length of 285 kilometers. The hydroelectric dams built on the Drin at Fierza in 1971-1978, Koman in 1979-1985, and Vau i Dejës in 1967-1971 provide most of the country's **electricity** and have transformed much of the Drin into a lake. There is a car ferry connection up the Drin from Koman, east of Shkodra, to Fierza and the **Tropoja** region. The name of the river, which was referred to by Pliny as *Drinius* and by Strabo as *Drilôn*, is considered a pre-Slavic toponym.

DRINO. River in southern Albania. The Drino takes its source in northern Greece and flows in a northwesterly direction through the District of **Gjirokastra** into the **Vjosa** River near **Tepelena**. It has a total length of eighty-five kilometers in Albania.

DRISHT. Archeological site, medieval fortress, and village in the mountains above the Kir valley east of **Shkodra**. In the ninth century, Drisht, medieval Drivastum, Drivasto, was a hillside settlement in the realm of Zeta and, in the course of the next four centuries, was to become one of the major settlements of northern Albania. In the eleventh century, it owed its allegiance to the metropolitan See of Bar (Antivari), which was founded in 1089. Though Byzantine up to the mid-twelfth century, it pledged allegiance to **Serbia** in 1185. It was ravaged by the Mongols in 1242 and acquired by the Venetians in 1396 when it issued its own coins marked Civitas Drivasti. Drisht was finally destroyed when it was taken by the Ottomans in 1478. Remaining at the site are the hillside fortifications and walls.

DUCELLIER, ALAIN. French scholar and historian. Ducellier, an expert in Byzantine and Balkan history, is professor at the University of Toulouse. He is the author of several works on Albanian history, in particular, his masterful 700-page *La Façade maritime de l'Albanie au moyen age: Durazzo et Valona du XIe au XVe siècle* (The Coastline of Albania in the Middle Ages: Durrës and Vlora from the Eleventh to the Fifteenth Century), Thessalonika 1981; and *L'Albanie entre Byzance et Venise, Xe-XVe siècles* (Albania between Byzantium and Venice, Tenth to

Fifteenth Centuries), London 1987. Ducellier is also noted for a number of standard works of Byzantine history.

DUKAGJINI. Geographical and ethnographical region of northern Albania. Dukagjini in Albania refers to the isolated mountain region east of **Shkodra** and north of the **Drin** River. It is the traditional land of the **Shala** and **Shoshi** tribes, through which the Shala and Kir Rivers flow. In **Kosova**, Dukagjini refers, however, to a different region, that of western Kosova (Peja, Gjakova, Prizren). As a toponym, Dukagjini is said to derive from *duka* "duke" and *Gjin* "John," i.e., Duke John.

DUMA, DERVISH (1908.07.04-1998.05.06). Historical figure. Dervish Duma was born in Borsh on the southern coast of Albania and attended an Italian school in **Vlora**. In 1921, he began studies at the **American Vocational School** and worked briefly for an Italian **oil** company. He was later employed by **Sir Jocelyn Percy** as an English interpreter for the British staff of the Royal Albanian Gendarmerie. With Percy's assistance, Duma was able to study in England. In 1933, he embarked upon a two-year course of public administration at the London School of Economics and returned to Albania in 1935 to join the diplomatic service.

Dervish Duma served as second secretary at the Albanian legation in London and, concurrently, as first secretary of the Albanian delegation to the League of Nations in Geneva. He was chargé d'affaires of the Albanian Embassy in London in 1939. In 1940, after the Italian occupation, he began a series of nightly broadcasts on the BBC's new Albanian service, and assisted **King Zog** and his family in London in 1941. In later years, he worked for the Bowater paper mills and steamship company, in particular in the United States and Canada. Dervish Duma was a prominent figure of the Albanian exile community in London until his death in Surrey in May 1998.

DURAZZO. *See* DURRËS.

DURHAM, EDITH (1863.12.08-1944.11.15). British writer and traveler. Mary Edith Durham stemmed from a large and prosperous middle-class family of North London. All of her eight brothers and sisters were successful in their careers: medicine, engineering, and the civil service. She attended Bedford College in London (1878-1882) and then trained to be an artist at the Royal Academy, illustrating a volume of the *Cambridge Natural His-*

tory. As the last child living at home in the family, she was entrusted with the duty of caring for her ailing mother, a monotonous life which took her to the edge of a nervous breakdown. Her doctor recommended travel, and Edith, at the age of thirty-seven, set off in 1900 with a female companion on a cruise down the Adriatic coast, where, after some time in Montenegro, she became fascinated with the Balkans. On her return to London, she immersed herself in the study of the Serbian language and Balkan history. In 1902-1903, Durham traveled through **Serbia** collecting material for her first book *Through the Lands of the Serbs,* London 1904. She also visited **Shkodra** and **Kosova** in Ottoman territory, a rare journey which at the time entailed a good deal of courage and stamina. At the end of 1903, she returned to Montenegro for a five-month stay in the Balkans on behalf of the Macedonian Relief Committee. The journey and appalling humanitarian situation in the region are described in her *The Burden of the Balkans,* London 1905. It included her first lengthy expedition to Albania. For three summers, she then traveled widely in Montenegro, Bosnia and Hercegovina, collecting ethnographical material, which was later, much later, to be published in her *Some Tribal Origins, Laws and Customs of the Balkans,* London 1928, which included illustrations by the author.

An in-depth knowledge of the Machiavellian politics of the Balkans caused her to turn away from the Slavic nationalism that she encountered on her travels through Serbia, and to focus her attention and her sympathies increasingly on Albania and the Albanians. In the summer of 1908, she traveled once more to Montenegro and from there to Shkodra and through the Albanian Highlands, a journey she described in her most delightful and widely read book, *High Albania,* London 1909. *High Albania* is regarded by many people as the best English-language book ever written on Albania.

Edith Durham acquired quite a reputation among the northern Albanians for her interest in and support for their cause. She was soon known throughout the mountains as *Kraljica e Malesorëvet* "The Queen of the Highland Peoples," and rumor spread that she was the sister of the King of England.

Her next book, *The Struggle for Scutari: Turk, Slav and Albanian*, London 1914, focused on the Montenegrin siege of Shkodra in the wake of the declaration of Albanian independence. It is a harrowing description of war, starvation and humanitarian catastrophe. She also visited **Vlora** in southern Albania only to find that conditions were no better there. Durham was forced to leave

Albania at the outbreak of **World War I**. She traveled by steamer to Biscay, worked initially in a hospital in the Pyrenees, and later for the YMCA in Port Said in Egypt. After the war, she published *Twenty Years of Balkan Tangle*, London 1920, which was subsequently translated into German, Italian and Albanian. She is also the author of countless articles on Albanian folklore.

Edith Durham's last visit to Albania was in 1921. After that, she was not able to travel for health reasons. She did, however, continue to campaign on Albania's behalf over the next two decades. She was a founding member of the **Anglo-Albanian Association** and wrote many press articles and countless "letters to the editor" to counter ignorant views and to focus public attention on Albania and its plight. It was also in this period that her controversial book *The Sarajevo Crime,* London 1925, appeared, which dealt with the background of the Sarajevo assassination and the causes for the outbreak of World War I.

In later years, her home in London became a rallying point for friends of Albania and for Albanians in exile. She died in November 1944, two weeks before the **communist** takeover of the country. Edith Durham is well remembered in Albania and Kosova, where many towns have a Miss Durham Street.

DURRËS. Town in the **District of Durrës**, of which it is the administrative center. **Population** in Dec. 1999: 142,511. It is known as Durazzo in Italian, Dyrrhachion in Greek, and Drač in Serbian. Durrës is the major port of Albania, the second largest town in the country, and one of the oldest settlements.

Originally known as Epidamnos, Durrës was settled in about 627 B.C. by Greek colonists from Corinth and Corfu. In 229 B.C., it came under Roman protection and was called Dyrrachium. It served from the Roman period onwards as the point of departure of the **Via Egnatia** and of most sea communication with Italy. The poet Catullus called the town "the tavern of the Adriatic" (*Adriae taberna*), and Cicero, who stayed there in 58 B.C., referred to it as an *admirabilis urbs*, but very crowded. It was south of the town in 48 B.C. that a naval battle between Julius Caesar and Pompey took place. Under Augustus Caesar, Durrës was settled by Roman veterans and received the status of a colony, which was called *Colonia Iulia Augusta Dyrrachinorum*. In the fourth century, A.D. Durrës was the seat of a Christian bishop. In the late Middle Ages, the city, a virtual island with the Adriatic on one side and marshland on the other, was conquered by the Normans (1082-1085), the Venetians (1205-1214), the

Despot of Epirus, the Angevins (1272-1368, 1392-1501) and the Turks (1501-), though it gradually lost its significance due to several major earthquakes. In 1912, it served as the capital of the newly independent Kingdom of Albania under **Prince Wilhelm zu Wied**. In 1916, it had a population of 600 and in 1939, 9,000.

Durrës is noted for its cultural monuments from the Roman and Venetian periods, in particular fortifications and an amphitheater, the largest of its kind in the Balkans, which dates from the reign of the Emperor Hadrian (117-138 AD). The town has a new archeological museum and an eleven-kilometers-long sandy beach to the south, traditionally the most popular one in the country.

DURRËS, DISTRICT OF. Region of local government administration. The District of Durrës (*Rrethi i Durrësit*), with its administrative headquarters in the town of **Durrës**, borders on the Adriatic Sea to the west, on the districts of **Kruja** and **Tirana** to the east, and **Kavaja** to the south. It has a surface area of 433 square kilometers and a present **population** of 195,766 (in 2000). It has the second highest population density in the country.

DUSHMANI. Northern Albanian tribe and traditional tribal region. The Dushmani region is situated north of the **Drin** River in the present District of **Shkodra**. It borders on the traditional tribal regions of **Shoshi** to the west, **Toplana** to the north, **Berisha** to the east, and Kabashi and **Shllaku** to the south. The name was recorded in the sixth century by Procopius as *Dousmanes*. The Dushmani tribe, said to be originally from the area of Tuz, south of Podgorica in Montenegro, was related to the Thaçi tribe and was reputed to be one of the wildest of the north. It had a population of about 1,400 in the late nineteenth century.

- E -

ECONOMY. *See* AGRICULTURE; COAL PRODUCTION; ELEC-
TRICITY PRODUCTION; FOREIGN TRADE; INDUSTRY;
OIL PRODUCTION; MINERAL RESOURCES; NATURAL
GAS PRODUCTION; TOURISM.

EDUCATION. Eight years of public schooling are mandatory and
financed by the government in Albania. In 2000, there were about
777,000 people attending institutions of education, equaling
twenty-three percent of the **population**. As a result of domestic
migration and other factors, there was a drastic drop in school
attendance in the 1991-2001 period. In 2000, only thirty-
eight percent of children were attending preschool institutions;
eighty-nine percent attended the compulsory, so-called eight-year
schools, i.e., elementary school; only forty-three percent went to
secondary school; and fifteen percent attended university or
college. Expenditures for education amount to ten percent of total
budget spending, with an annual increase of seventeen to
twenty percent. In general, the education system is in desperate
need of reform. The extremely low salaries made by teachers and
professors, especially in the early 1990s, meant that it was often
easier for students to buy a diploma than to pass a test.

About forty-one percent of elementary school pupils and
eighty-two percent of secondary school students study a foreign
language, the main languages being English (seventy percent) and
French (twenty-nine percent), with a very few studying Russian
and German. Most children in coastal towns know Italian well by
the time they enter school due to the pervasive influence of Italian
television, so it is not usually taught as a subject in schools.

As to the structure of Albanian education, in 2000 there were
2,151 kindergartens, 1,855 so-called eight-year schools, 410
secondary schools, and eleven institutions of higher education.
Since 1991, there have also been private schools in Albania and
steps have been taken recently to create private institutions of
higher education. In 2000, there were eighty-three private schools
and nineteen other private institutions of education, and by June
2001, a total of 159 private institutions. The proportion of Albanian students studying at such schools and institutions is, however, low due to the high cost of tuition.

In 2002, there were 40,125 students (24,030 female and 16,095 male) attending the eleven institutions of higher education. The institutions in question are: the University of **Tirana** (14,683 students), the Polytechnic University of Tirana (2,558 students), the Agricultural University of Tirana centered in Kamza (1,929 students), the University of **Elbasan** (6,059 students), the University of **Shkodra** (6,312 students), the University of **Gjirokastra** (3,562 students), the University of **Korça** (2,449 students), the University of **Vlora** (1,210 students), the Academy of Fine Arts (544 students), the Institute of Physical Education (355 students) and the Academy of Nursing (464 students). Female students make up a noticeable majority in most of these institutions, with the number of male students dominating only at the Polytechnic University, the Agricultural University, the Academy of Fine Arts and the Institute of Physical Education. For the academic year 1999-2000, there were 1,679 university teachers (1,045 male and 634 female), of which 200 were full professors (192 male and eight female).

EGNATIA, VIA. *See* VIA EGNATIA.

EGYPT, ALBANIANS IN. The first Albanians arrived in Egypt as soldiers and mercenaries in the second half of the eighteenth century and made a name for themselves in the **Ottoman** struggle to expel French troops in 1798-1801. Thousands of Albanians left their impoverished homeland and poured into the country with the advent of Mehmed Ali Pasha (1769-1849), who took power as governor of Egypt and as founder of an Albanian dynasty, which lasted there until 1952. Mehmed Ali made good use of their services as mercenaries and troops to ensure his reign. Albanian immigration to Egypt continued throughout the nineteenth century and indeed into the first three decades of the twentieth century.

The Albanian community in Egypt, with their patriotic societies and publishing activities, played an important role in the Albanian national awakening at the end of the nineteenth century. The first Albanian society of Egypt was founded there in 1875, and many others were to follow. Nationalist figures and writers such as **Thimi Mitko**, **Spiro Dine**, Filip Shiroka (1859-1935), Jani Vruho (1863-1931), Stefan Zurani (1865-1941), **Andon Zako Çajupi**, Milo Duçi (1870-1933), Loni Logori (1871-1929) and **Fan Noli** were all active in Egypt at some point in their careers. In 1922, Milo Duçi founded the Albanian Publishing

Society (*Shoqeria botonjesé shqipetaré*) in Cairo. Later in the twentieth century, the Albanian **Bektashi** community had its own *tekke* in Egypt, the famed Magauri *tekke* on the outskirts of Cairo, which was headed by Baba Ahmet Serri Glina of **Përmet**. The Albanian community survived in Egypt until after **World War II**. When **King Zog** and the Albanian royal family were forced out of Albania during the war, it was in Egypt that they finally took up residence from 1946 to 1955 and were received by King Farouk (r. 1936-1952), who, as a descendant of Mehmed Ali Pasha, was himself of Albanian origin. With the advent of Gamal Abdel Nasser and the Arab nationalization of Egypt, not only the royal family but also the whole Albanian community —some 4,000 families—were forced to leave the country, thus bringing the chapter of the Albanians on the Nile to a swift close.

ELBASAN. Town in the **District of Elbasan**, of which it is the administrative center. **Population** in Dec. 1999: 116,466. Elbasan is a major town in the middle of Albania, situated on the northern bank of the **Shkumbin** River, on the site of the ancient Roman fortification of Scampa. It was the seat of a bishop in the fifth century. Elbasan flourished in particular after the **Ottoman** conquest in 1466, when the thick fortress walls of the town were constructed. It was known originally as "new town," Greek *Neokastron,* Slavic *Novigrad,* Italian *Terra Nuova,* but later retrieved its older name Elbasan, based on the root **alb,* as in Albania, though the term is commonly associated with the Ottoman Turkish *il-basan* "the fortress."

Elbasan developed into a center of trade and of strong Muslim tradition and culture. **Evliya Çelebi,** who visited it in 1670, called it the "bride of the world" and the "home of scholars and virtuous men, poets and mystics." The town is still considered a center of learning and **education**. According to **Lef Nosi,** there were still thirty-one mosques in Elbasan in 1931, but only five of them survived the ravages of the Cultural Revolution in 1967. Four of these were destroyed in the following decade. The Long Market, Elbasan's famed oriental bazaar, which had 900 shops in the late seventeenth century and which was restored in 1935-1936, was razed to the ground in 1970-1972. Elbasan had a population of 12,000 in 1916 and of 14,000 in 1939.

The principal cultural monuments of the town which survived the **communist** period are the Sultan Mosque, Alb. *Xhamia e Mbretit,* built in 1492, the Naziresha Mosque outside the center of town, and the Turkish bathhouse near the hotel, which Evliya

Çelebi reported as being a "spacious, agreeable and clean building with lovely serving-boys."

During the communist period, Elbasan was the site of the colossal metallurgical complex called the "Steel of the Party" (*Çeliku i Partisë*), constructed with Chinese assistance in 1971-1974. It was the largest industrial complex in the country, producing not only steel but also ferro-nickel, and was the greatest pollutant. It was abandoned to a large extent after the fall of the dictatorship and has left Elbasan with a high level of unemployment and serious environmental problems.

ELBASAN, DISTRICT OF. Region of local government administration. The District of Elbasan (*Rrethi i Elbasanit*), with its administrative headquarters in the town of **Elbasan**, borders on the districts of **Peqin** and **Lushnja** to the west, **Tirana** to the north, **Librazhd** to the east, and **Gramsh**, **Berat** and **Kuçova** to the south. It has a surface area of 1,372 square kilometers and a present **population** of 225,174 (in 2000). It is the second most populated district in Albania.

ELBASANI, AQIF pasha. *See* BIÇAKU, AQIF.

ELECTRICITY PRODUCTION. Electricity production is one of the oldest major industries in Albania. Production began in 1923 with the installation of the first diesel engines in **Tirana**. The first hydroelectric plant was built in Vithkuq in the **Korça** region in 1936.

The electrical energy sector was created in 1957 and major hydroelectric dams were built over the following years: the Friedrich Engels dam on the **Mat** River, built in 1959-1963; the J. V. Stalin plant in Bistrica, now in the District of **Delvina**, built in 1960-1965; the Vau i Dejës dam and power plant on the lower **Drin** River near **Shkodra**, built in 1967-1971; the *Drita e Partisë* (The Light of the Party) dam and power plant on the upper Drin River at Fierza, constructed in 1971-1978; and the **Enver Hoxha** dam and power plant on the lower Drin River at Koman, built in 1979-1986. Electricity was first supplied to all consumers on 25 October 1970, and the electrical energy system reached a maximum production of 5,027 billion kWh in 1986, of which 2,138 billion kWh were exported. Transmission lines were built to Titograd (Podgorica) in Montenegro and Igoumenitsa in Greece in 1974, another to Greece in 1985 and one to Prizren in Kosova in 1988. The Albanian system thus functioned with those of the neighboring countries by 1985 and is now connected to the European grid via a new 400 kV line from **Elbasan** to Greece.

At present, there are twenty main power plants in the country with a total capacity of 1670 MW: eleven hydro-power (1,446 MW) and eight thermo-power plants (224 MW). The main sources of electricity are the three above-mentioned plants on the Drin River at Vau i Dejës (250,000 kWh), Koman (600,000 kWh) and Fierza (500,000 kWh), which represent eighty percent of the total electricity production in Albania.

In recent years, due to a lack of investment and maintenance and because of rapidly increasing consumer demand, the energy system has fallen into great disrepair, and power cuts have become increasingly frequent, especially in the winter months. The new state-owned Albanian Electrical Energy Corporation, KESH (*Korporata Elektroenergjetike Shqiptare*), created in 1992, has not succeeded in solving the country's many urgent problems in this sector. At the same time, private energy consumption has risen dramatically, from eleven percent in 1990 to forty percent in 1999. In the winter of 2001-2002, many regions of the country had no electricity supply for ten to eighteen hours a day. Tirana itself was without power for eight hours a day.

ELSIE, ROBERT (1950.06.29-). Canadian scholar. Robert Elsie was born in Vancouver, Canada. He studied at the University of British Columbia, graduating in 1972 with a diploma in Classical Studies and Linguistics. In the following years, he did his postgraduate research at the Free University of Berlin, at the Ecole Pratique des Hautes Etudes and at the University of Paris IV in Paris, at the Dublin Institute for Advanced Studies in Ireland, and at the University of Bonn, where he finished his doctorate (Dr. Phil.) in 1978 at the Linguistics Institute. From 1978 on, he was able to visit Albania several times with a group of students and professors from the University of Bonn, visits which first awakened in him an interest in the culture of the tiny and, at the time, exotic Balkan country. For several years in a row, he also attended the International Seminar on Albanian Language, Literature and Culture, held in Prishtina (Kosova). From 1982 to 1987, he worked for the German Ministry of Foreign Affairs in Bonn. Since that time he has worked as a freelance conference interpreter, primarily for Albanian and German. In 2002, he interpreted the Slobodan Milošević trial at the International Criminal Tribunal for the former Yugoslavia (ICTY) in The Hague. He lives in the Eifel mountains of Germany, not far from the Belgian border.

Elsie is the author of numerous books and articles, in particular on various aspects of Albanian culture and affairs, and of literary translations from the Albanian. Among his major works are: *Dictionary of Albanian Literature*, New York 1986; *Migjeni, Freie Verse: Gedichte aus Albanien* (Migjeni, Free Verse: Poetry from Albania), Idstein 1987; *Einem Adler gleich: Anthologie albanischer Lyrik vom 16. Jahrhundert bis zur Gegenwart* (Like an Eagle: Anthology of Albanian Poetry from the Sixteenth Century to the Present), Hildesheim 1988; *An Elusive Eagle Soars: Anthology of Modern Albanian Poetry*, London 1993; *History of Albanian Literature*, New York 1995; *Një fund dhe një fillim: vëzhgime mbi letërsinë dhe kulturën shqiptare bashkëkohore* (An End and a Beginning: Observations on Contemporary Albanian Literature and Culture), Tirana / Prishtina 1995; *Studies in Modern Albanian Literature and Culture*, New York 1996; *Histori e letërsisë shqiptare* (History of Albanian Literature), Tirana 1997; *Kosovo: In the Heart of the Powder Keg*, New York 1997; *Evliya Çelebi in Albania and Adjacent Regions: Kosovo, Montenegro, Ohrid*, Leiden 2000 (with Robert Dankoff); *Who Will Slay the Wolf: Selected Poetry by Ali Podrimja*, New York 2000; *Dictionary of Albanian Religion, Mythology and Folk Culture*, London 2001; *Flora Brovina —Call Me by My Name: Poetry from Kosova in a Bilingual Albanian-English Edition*, New York 2001; *Albanian Folktales and Legends*, Peja 2001; *Migjeni —Free Verse: A Bilingual Edition*, Peja 2001; *Handbuch zur albanischen Volkskultur: Mythologie, Religion, Volksglaube, Sitten, Gebräuche und kulturelle Besonderheiten* (Handbook of Albanian Folk Culture: Mythology, Religion, Popular Beliefs, Habits, Customs and Cultural Particularities), Wiesbaden 2002; *Gathering Clouds —the Roots of Ethnic Cleansing in Kosovo and Macedonia: Early Twentieth-Century Documents*, Peja 2002; *Gjergj Fishta: The Highland Lute, the Albanian National Epic, Cantos I-V*, Peja 2003; and *Eqrem Basha —Neither a Wound nor a Song: Poetry from Kosova*, Peja 2003. He has also edited: *Reisen in den Balkan: die Lebenserinnerungen des Franz Baron Nopcsa* (Travels in the Balkans: The Memoirs of Baron Franz Nopcsa). Peja 2001; *Jean-Claude Faveyrial: Histoire de l'Albanie* (Jean-Claude Faveyrial: History of Albania), Peja 2001; *Der Kanun: Das albanische Gewohnheitsrecht nach dem sogenannten Kanun des Lekë Dukagjini* (The Kanun: Albanian Customary Law according to the so-called Kanun of Lekë Dukagjini), Peja 2001; and *Berit Backer: Behind Stone Walls,* Peja 2003.

EPIC VERSE. *See* SONGS OF THE FRONTIER WARRIORS.

ERZEN. River in central Albania. The Erzen takes its source in the Mali me Gropa region east of **Tirana** and flows south of Tirana and past Shijak into the Adriatic Sea north of **Durrës.** It has a total length of 109 kilometers. The Erzen was known in ancient times as the *Ardanaxus.* It was referred to by Anna Comnena in 1148 as *Charzanes* and in 1308 as *Ersenta* (Anonymi Descriptio Europae Orientalis).

EVANGJELI, PANDELI (1858-1949.09). Political figure. Born in **Korça** of an **Orthodox** family, Pandeli Evangjeli, also known as Pandeli Vangjeli, spent his early years in Bucharest where a large Albanian community had settled. In 1895, he became chairman of the *Dituria* (Knowledge) Society and, in 1907 helped found a Committee for the Freedom of Albania. Evangjeli returned to Albania after independence. In 1914, he was prefect of Korça and in 1920 took part in the Albanian delegation to the Paris Peace Conference on behalf of the government of **Sulejman bey Delvina.** In 1921, he became a member of **parliament,** then foreign minister and, finally, prime minister briefly from 16 October to 6 December 1921, heading a short-lived liberal administration. In September 1922, he was foreign minister once more, a post he retained under **Ahmet Zogu.** In the autumn of 1925, he was made president of the senate and thus Zogu's deputy. In 1928, he headed the constitutional asssembly and the commission to prepare for the proclamation of the monarchy. He served as prime minister again from 6 March 1930 to 15 October 1935. During the final years of the Zog regime, Evangjeli served as parliamentary president.

EVIL EYE. Popular belief. Alb. *syri i keq,* **Gheg** *syni i keq,* also *mësysh.* As in the Middle East, it is thought in Albania that a malicious glance can do damage in itself. Accordingly, people who are believed to have such a glance, the evil eye, are to be avoided. It is also thought that people with blue eyes are more likely to have the evil eye.

One must avoid praising little children, farm animals, or things of value in public so that the evil eye is not attracted to them. Anyone who does look at a child attentively may spit or wipe his eyes with his hands to save the child from harm. The attention of the evil eye can be deflected by small objects placed on or nearby the person or thing in question. A wooden spoon was often hung around the neck of a farm animal, and a coin was stuck onto the forehead of a baby in its cradle, or a dot of rust was painted on its nose. Coins and blue glass beads could also be attached to the front locks of a child's hair. **Edith Durham** reports that the head of a snake, cut off with the sharpened edge of a silver coin, also served ás a good amulet against the evil eye. It had to be dried and fastened between two medals or images of Saint George, and then blessed by a priest. Garlic and wolves' teeth were also effective against the evil eye. Until recently, families who had lost a son would dress a second male infant up as a girl and let his hair grow long so as to protect him from a second attack by the evil eye. Fields and farms could be protected by placing the skull of a horse or steer on a high pole. In **Kosova,** it is still customary to dress children with their undershirts on backwards so that the evil eye cannot penetrate their bodies.

Even today, many homeowners in Albania, and certainly anyone constructing a new house or building, will hang some sort of amulet from its girding or eaves in order to deflect the evil eye. The most common objects used to this end nowadays are buffalo horns, garlic, dolls or even a **flag.** People who buy new clothes will often carry an amulet in their pocket to defend themselves from envious glances.

Belief in the evil eye is not restricted to the southern Balkans, though it is interesting to note that the Roman author Pliny the Elder (23-79 A.D.) recorded its presence among the **Illyrians** who inhabited the region in antiquity. He states that there were Illyrians "who could gaze with the evil eye, cast a spell and even kill someone" (*Historia Naturalis* 7.16). Aulus Gellius (123-165 A.D.) recounts the same thing a century later (*Noctes Atticae* 9.4, 8) .

EVLIYA ÇELEBI (1611-1684). Turkish writer and traveler. Evliya Çelebi or Chelebi, pseudonym of Dervish Mehmed Zillī, was the son of a goldsmith at the court of the sultan in Istanbul. From 1640 to 1676, he traveled extensively through the **Ottoman Empire** and neighboring countries, both in a private capacity and at the service of the Sublime Porte. The account of his travels is recorded in his ten-volume Turkish-language *Seyahatname* (Travel Book), which he completed in Cairo. The *Seyahatname* contains a wealth of information on the cultural history, folklore, and **geography** of the countries to which he traveled. For seventeenth-century Albania it is of inestimable significance. Çelebi visited regions of Albanian settlement three times: **Kosova** in December 1660, northern Albania and **Montenegro** in February 1662, and finally southern Albania in November 1670. His descriptions of the central Albanian towns of **Berat** and **Elbasan** during the latter journey can be regarded as no less than sensational, in particular for those who know the towns today. One can only marvel at the refined oriental culture that he encountered in Albania, of which very few traces remain. Evliya Çelebi's travels in Albania have been edited by **Robert Elsie** and Robert Dankoff in the volume *Evliya Çelebi in Albania and Adjacent Regions: Kosovo, Montenegro, Ohrid*, Leiden 2000.

- F -

FALASCHI, NERMIN VLORA (1921.04.18-). Writer. Nermin Vlora Falaschi, Alb. Nermin Vlora Falaski, the great granddaughter of **Ismail Qemal bey Vlora**, was born in **Tirana** where she spent her youth. In 1934, she attended the Queen Mother Pedagogical Institute (*Instituti Nanë Mbretneshë*) there. As the wife of an Italian officer who had been stationed in Albania, she emigrated to Italy and studied law in Siena, where she was later to be recipient of a doctorate *honoris causa*. She has lectured widely, in particular on her rather controversial views of the ties between the Albanian **language** and early Mediterranean languages. In June 2000, she and her husband Renzo Falaschi founded an **Illyrian** Cultural Academy (*Accademia Culturale Iliria*) in Rome for the promotion of such studies.

Nermin Vlora Falaschi is the author of numerous books – poetry, fiction and nonfiction. Among them are: *Il signore del tempo* (The Lord of the Age), Rome 1976; *Antiche civiltà mediterranee: pelasgi, iliri, etruschi, albanesi* (Ancient Mediterranean Civilization: Pelasgians, Illyrians, Etruscans, Albanians), Rome 1984; *L'Etrusco lingua viva* (Etruscan, a Living Language), Rome 1989; *Lashtësia e gjuhës shqipe: sipas dokumenteve epigrafike nga Egjeu deri në Atlantik* (The Antiquity of the Albanian Language: According to Epigraphic Documents from the Aegean to the Atlantic), Rome 1991; and *Linguis-*

tic and Genetic Heredities: Probability of Monogenesis of Words,
Tirana 1997. She has also published the memoirs of her great
grandfather.

FAN. River of northern central Albania. The Fan River flows
through the **Mirdita** region past the towns of Rrëshen and Rubik
into the **Mat** River. It has a length of ninety-four kilometers and
is fed primarily by the Great Fan River, Alb. *Fani i Madh,* and the
Lesser Fan River, Alb. *Fani i Vogël.* The Fan was referred to in
1515 as *Fanti* and in 1610 as *Fandi.*

FANKO, SERAFIN (1937.05.24-). Actor and **film** director. Fanko
was born in **Shkodra** and studied at the Academy of Fine Arts in
Prague, Czechoslovakia, and at the Academy of Fine Arts
(*Instituti i Lartë i Arteve*) in **Tirana.** He began his film career as
an actor in *Fijet që priten* (Broken Threads) in 1976. He interpreted nine roles in Albanian films and has also been successful
as a stage director.

FAVEYRIAL, JEAN-CLAUDE (1817.03.25-1893.11.26). French
priest and historian. Faveyrial was born in Usson en Forez, a
mountain village in Auvergne in central France. He attended a
seminary in Lyon and was admitted to the **Lazarist** Congregation
in Paris in 1843. The congregation seconded him as a missionary
to Greece (March 1845) and Constantinople (July 1847). It was
at the Maison Saint-Benoît in Constantinople that he became
passionately interested in the various ethnic groups of the southern Balkans and began collecting rare books about the Albanians,
Bulgarians and **Vlachs.** In 1867, he was sent to Monastir (Bitola),
now in the Republic of Macedonia, where he spent most of the
rest of his life teaching French and philosophy at a Vlach secondary school. He visited Albania in 1884 as an inspector for
Romanian-language education, and founded schools in **Berat,**
Korça and Prizren.

Faveyrial is the author of the the first work to trace the entire
history of Albania from antiquity to the nineteenth century, written in Monastir between the years 1884 and 1889. It has been
published by **Robert Elsie** as *Histoire de l'Albanie* (History of
Albania), Peja 2001.

FEUDING. *See* BLOOD FEUDING.

FIEDLER, WILFRIED (1933.05.07-). German scholar and linguist. Born in the town of Oberfrohna near Chemnitz in Saxony, Fiedler studied Slavic and East European philology at the Humboldt University in (East) Berlin from 1951 to 1955. From 1955 to 1963, he worked as a research assistant at the Institute for German Folklore of the Academy of Sciences there and finished his doctorate at the Humboldt University in 1961 with a dissertation on plural formations in Albanian. He had visited Albania for the first time in 1957 as part of an East German expedition to gather folk songs, and returned to the country for several months in 1959. In the following years, Fiedler was active as a research expert for the East German Academy of Sciences in Berlin, in particular from 1968 to 1990 as a member of the Central Institute for Linguistics, where he specialized in Albanian and Balkan philology. In January 1991, he was appointed professor of Albanian at the Institute for Comparative and Indo-European Linguistics of the University of Munich, as a successor to **Martin Camaj**. He also lectured regularly on Albanian in Vienna, Berlin and Jena. After retirement in September 1998, he returned to Berlin and currently lives in Jena. Wilfried Fiedler is the author of numerous articles on the Albanian **language**, in particular on verb morphology. He is coauthor of *Wörterbuch Albanisch Deutsch* (Albanian-German Dictionary), Leipzig 1977; *Albanische Grammatik* (Albanian Grammar), Leipzig 1987; *Wörterbuch Deutsch-Albanisch* (German-Albanian Dictionary), Leipzig 1997; and of literary translations from Albanian into German.

FIER. Town in the **District of Fier**, of which it is the administrative center. **Population** in Dec. 1999: 80,183. Site of the ancient *Ad Novas*, Fier lies in the center of the fertile coastal plain of Myzeqeja. It was founded as a market town by the **Vrioni** family, the beys of **Berat**, in the eighteenth century and is situated near **oil**, gas and bitumen deposits. It thus evolved as an industrial and agricultural center, in particular during the **communist** period.

FIER, DISTRICT OF. Region of local government administration. The District of Fier (*Rrethi i Fierit*), with its administrative headquarters in the town of **Fier**, borders on the Adriatic Sea to the west, the districts of **Lushnja** to the north, **Berat** to the east, and **Mallakastra** and **Vlora** to the south. It has a surface area of 785 square kilometers and a present **population** of 215,471 (in 2000).

FILM. The first public movie theater in Albania was set up in **Shkodra** in August 1912 by the Josef Stauber company of Austria, with local assistance from painter and photographer **Kolë Idromeno**, and showed films until 1914 when **World War I** broke out. In the autumn of 1920, the *Përparimi* (Progress) movie theater was opened in **Vlora**, followed by cinemas in **Tirana**, Shkodra and **Berat**, and by 1939 there were eighteen cinemas in the country.

The Albanian film industry itself stems from the **communist** period. The first Albanian documentary film, *Komandanti viziton Shqipërinë e Mesme dhe të Jugut* (The Commander visits Central and Southern Albania), on **Enver Hoxha**, was produced in 1947. In 1952, the New Albanian Film Studios were opened on the outskirts of Tirana. The first major film undertaking of the period was a grandiose Soviet-Albanian co-production called *Skënderbeu* (Scanderbeg), directed in 1953 in Russian by Sergey Yutkevich, though with Albanian actors. The first real Albanian film, *Tana* (Tana), followed five years later in 1958, directed by Kristaq Dhamo, with roles by **Tinka Kurti**, Naim Frashëri, **Kadri Roshi** and Pjeter Gjoka.

For a small country such as Albania, the film industry made astounding progress, in particular from 1975 to 1990, when an average of thirteen feature films a year were being produced. As there were few other forms of entertainment to be had in Stalinist Albania, the movie theaters were widely attended throughout the country. In 1972, no less that 20,000,000 seats were sold at 450 venues, meaning an average of ten visits for every inhabitant of the country. In 1982, there were 102 movie theaters in the country, and by 1995, the Albanian film industry had produced some 270 feature films.

The aesthetic qualities of many of these feature films would seem questionable from a contemporary point of view, in particular due to the heavy-handed propaganda they contained. Rarely missing in Albanian films were partisan heroism from the communist resistance movement of **World War II** or the moral-izing convictions of the "new man" striving for a better socialist society. Nonetheless, seen within the context of what could be expected of an underdeveloped country with a Stalinist leadership, the Albanian film industry made impressive advances until 1990-1991.

With the opening of the country, the structures of the state-owned film industry collapsed in the early 1990s, and only in recent years have Albanian films begun to reappear. It has only been since 1999, on the initiative of the former minister of culture, **Edi Rama**, that there have once again been decent movie theaters in Albania. The Millennium Cinema was opened in Tirana in July 1999 on the site of the former Republika Cinema. This was followed by a movie theater in **Elbasan** and a Millennium II in Tirana in 2002.

Of the dozen or so Albanian films produced since 1995, mention may be made in particular of *Koloneli Bunker* (Colonel Bunker), 1996, by **Kujtim Çashku**; *Nata* (The Night), 1998, by Roland Gjoza; *Dasma e Sakos* (Sako's Wedding), 1998, by Vladimir Prifti; *Funeral Business,* 1999, by **Gjergj Xhuvani**; and *Tirana viti zero* (Tirana Year Zero), 2002, by **Fatmir Koçi**.

FINO, BASHKIM (1962.10.12-). Political figure and high-ranking member of the **Socialist Party of Albania**. Bashkim Fino was born in **Gjirokastra** and studied economics and finance at the University of **Tirana**, graduating in 1986. From 1992 to 1996, he was mayor of Gjirokastra and, in the wake of the **uprising of 1997** and chaos, served as prime minister (13 March - 25 July 1997), heading a short-lived government of national reconciliation. He later served as deputy prime minister and is a leading figure of the Socialist Party.

FISCHER, BERND JÜRGEN (1952.01.27-). American scholar and historian. Bernd Fischer was born in Bünde, Germany. He completed his Ph.D. on Balkan history at the University of California in Santa Barbara and taught at the universities of Hartford, in Connecticut, and McGill in Montreal. He currently holds the chair of history at Indiana University in Fort Wayne. In addition to numerous scholarly articles on twentieth-century Albanian history, he is author of *King Zog and the Struggle for Stability in Albania,* New York 1984; and *Albania at War, 1939-1945*, London 1999, and is coeditor with **Stephanie Schwandner-Sievers** of *Albanian Identities: Myth and History,* London 2002.

FISHTA, GJERGJ (1871.10.23-1940.12.30). Poet, writer, religious and political figure. **Franciscan** pater Gjergj Fishta was by far the greatest and most influential figure of Albanian **literature** in the first half of the twentieth century. He was born in the **Zadrima** village of Fishta near Troshan in northern Albania where he was baptized by Franciscan missionary and poet **Leonardo De Martino**. In 1886, when he was fifteen, Fishta was sent by the Order of the Friars Minor to Bosnia, as were many young Albanians destined for the priesthood at the time. In 1894, he was ordained as a priest and admitted to the Franciscan order. On his return to Albania in February of that year, he was given a teaching position at the Franciscan college in Troshan and subsequently a posting as parish priest in the village of Gomsiqja. On 14-22 November 1908, he participated in and presided over the **Congress of Monastir** as a representative of the *Bashkimi* literary society.

In October 1913, almost a year after the declaration of Albanian independence in **Vlora**, Fishta founded and began editing the Franciscan monthly periodical *Hylli i Dritës* (The Day-Star), which was devoted to literature, politics, folklore and history. In 1916, together with **Luigj Gurakuqi**, **Ndre Mjeda** and **Mati Logoreci**, Fishta played a leading role in the **Albanian Literary Commission**. Throughout these years, he continued teaching and running the Franciscan school in **Shkodra**, known from 1921 on as the *Collegium Illyricum* (Illyrian College), which had become the leading educational institution of northern Albania. He was now also an imposing figure of Albanian literature.

In August 1919, Gjergj Fishta served as secretary-general of the Albanian delegation, attending the Paris Peace Conference and, in this capacity, was asked by the president of the delegation, Msgr. **Luigj Bumçi**, to take part in a special commission to be sent to the **United States** to attend to the interests of the young Albanian state. There he visited Boston, New York and Washington. In 1921, Fishta represented Shkodra in the Albanian **parliament** and was chosen in August of that year as vice-president of this assembly. His talent as an orator served him well in his functions both as a political figure and as a man of the cloth. In later years, he attended Balkan conferences in Athens (1930), Sofia (1931) and Bucharest (1932) before withdrawing from public life to devote his remaining years to the Franciscan order and to his writing. From 1935 to 1938, he held the office of provincial of the Albanian Franciscans. These most fruitful years of his life were now spent in the quiet seclusion of the Franciscan monastery of Gjuhadol in Shkodra. As the poet laureate of his generation, Gjergj Fishta was honored with various diplomas, awards and distinctions both at home and abroad. He was awarded the Austro-Hungarian *Ritterkreuz* in 1911, was decorated by Pope Pius XI with the *Al Merito* award in 1925, was given the prestigious *Phoenix* medal of the Greek government, was honored with the title *Lector jubilatus honoris causae* by the Franciscan order and was made a regular member of the Italian Academy of Arts and Sciences in 1939.

Although Gjergj Fishta is the author of a total of thirty-seven literary publications, his name is indelibly linked to one great work, indeed to one of the most astounding creations in all the history of Albanian literature, *Lahuta e malcis* (The Highland Lute), Shkodra 1937. The Highland Lute is a 15,613-line historical verse epic focusing on the Albanian struggle for autonomy and independence. It constitutes a panorama of northern Albanian history from 1862 to 1913. This literary masterpiece was composed for the most part between 1902 and 1909, though it was refined and amended by its author over the following quarter of a century. It constitutes the first Albanian-language contribution to world literature and has been translated into English in part as *The Highland Lute: The Albanian National Epic,* Peja 2003. The definitive edition of the original work in thirty cantos was published in Shkodra in 1937 to mark the twenty-fifth anniversary of Albanian independence. Despite the success of *The Highland Lute* and the preeminence of its author, this and all other works by Gjergj Fishta were banned after **World War II** when the **communists** came to power.

Fishta's achievements are actually no less impressive in other genres, in particular as a lyric and satirical poet. Indeed, his lyric verse is regarded by many scholars as his best. Among his poetic works are the lyric collections: *Vierrsha i pershpirteshem t'kthyem shcyp* (Spiritual Verse Translated into Albanian), Shkodra 1906; *Mrizi i zâneve* (Noonday Rest of the Zanas), Shkodra 1913; *Vallja e Parrîzit* (The Dance of Paradise), Shkodra 1925; and the satirical volumes *Anxat e Parnasit* (The Wasps of Parnassus), Sarajevo 1907; and *Gomari i Babatasit* (Babatasi's Ass), Shkodra 1923.

The Scutarine **Catholic** school of letters, which Gjergj Fishta dominated, entered a golden age in the first decades of the twentieth century, and much credit for this blossoming of **Gheg** culture goes to him. At the outbreak of World War II, Gjergj Fishta was universally recognized as the "national poet." Austrian Albanologist **Maximilian Lambertz** described him as "the most ingenious poet Albania has ever produced" and Gabriele D'Annunzio called him "the great poet of the glorious people of Albania." For others he was the "Albanian Homer."

After the war, Fishta was nonetheless attacked and denigrated perhaps more than any other prewar writer and fell into prompt oblivion. The national poet became an anathema. The official

Tirana History of Albanian Literature of 1983, which carried the blessing of the Albanian **Party of Labor**, restricted its treatment of the country's "national poet" to an absolute minimum.

The real reason for Fishta's fall from grace after the "liberation" in 1944 is to be sought, however, not in his alleged pro-Italian or clerical proclivities, but in the origins of the Albanian Communist Party (ACP) itself. The ACP, later to be called the Albanian Party of Labor, had been founded during World War II under the auspices of the Yugoslav envoys Dušan Mugoša (1914-1973) and Miladin Popović (1910-1945). On 9 July 1946, Albania and **Yugoslavia** signed a treaty of friend-ship, cooperation and mutual assistance and, later, a number of other agreements, which gave Yugoslavia effective control over all Albanian affairs, including the field of culture. It is no doubt the alleged anti-Slavic sentiments expressed in *The Highland Lute* which caused the work and its author to be proscribed by the Yugoslav authorities, even though Fishta was educated in Bosnia and largely inspired by Serbian and Croatian literature. Gjergj Fishta, who but a few years earlier had been lauded as the national poet of Albania, disappeared from the literary scene, seemingly without a trace. Such was the fear of him in later years that his bones were even dug up and secretly thrown into the river.

Yet, despite four decades of unrelenting Party harping and propaganda endeavoring to reduce Fishta to the rank of a minor "clerical poet," the people of northern Albania, and in particular the inhabitants of his native Shkodra, did not forget him. After almost half a century of silence, Gjergj Fishta was commemorated openly on 5 January 1991 in Shkodra. During this first public recital of Fishta's works in Albania in forty-five years, the actor at one point hesitated in his lines, and was immediately and spontaneously assisted by members of the audience—who still knew many parts of *The Highland Lute* by heart.

FLAG, ALBANIAN. The Albanian flag portrays a double-headed black eagle centrally positioned on a red background. The eagle was a common heraldic symbol for many Albanian dynasties in the late Middle Ages, and came to be the symbol of the Albanians in general. It is also said to have been the flag of **Scanderbeg**. The double-headed eagle was also the symbol of Byzantium and was later used in other countries, in particular Austria-Hungary. As a symbol of modern Albania, the flag began to be seen during the years of the national awakening and was in common use during the uprisings of 1909-1912. It was this flag that **Ismail**

Qemal bey Vlora raised in **Vlora** on 28 November 1912 for the proclamation of Albanian independence. During the reign of **King Zog**, a crown was added, during the Italian occupation two axes, and during the **communist** period a five-pointed golden star (the latter was removed on 8 April 1992). The red flag with the double-headed black eagle is both the official symbol of the Republic of Albania and the national symbol of all Albanians.

FLLOKO, TIMO (1948.04.26-). Film actor. Born in Peja, Timo Flloko graduated from the Academy of Fine Arts (*Instituti i Lartë i Arteve*) in **Tirana** before embarking on a career as a film actor. He has appeared in major roles in numerous Albanian **films**, among which are *Ngadhjnim mbi vdekjen* (Victory over Death), 1967; *Lulëkuqet mbi mure* (Red Poppies on Walls), 1976; *Njeriu me top* (The Man with the Cannon), 1977; *Vdekja e kalit* (The Horse's Death), 1991; and *Përdhunuesit* (The Rapists), 1994. Flloko emigrated to the United States in 1997.

FLOQI, KRISTO (1873-1951). Playwright. Kristo Floqi of **Korça** was the most popular of all Albanian dramatists in the first half of the twentieth century. He studied law in Athens until graduation in 1899 and returned to his native Korça to practice for six years. He spent some time in Istanbul, ostensibly to learn Turkish, but his intimate involvement with the nationalist movement forced him to keep on the move—back to Korça, to Greece where his father worked as a merchant, to **Vlora**, where he took part in an attempt to declare Albanian independence, and on to the **United States**. In Boston, Floqi became editor of the Albanian-language weekly *Dielli* (The Sun) in September 1911 and was cofounder with **Fan Noli** and **Faik bey Konitza** of the **Vatra** society. In New York, he also published the short-lived weekly *Zër' i popullit* (The People's Voice) in the winter of 1912-1913.

At the time of independence, Kristo Floqi returned to Albania to join **Ismail Qemal bey Vlora** in Vlora and endeavored to set up a new legal system for the sovereign little nation. He is said to have been the first person to record legal proceedings in Albanian. When Vlora fell under occupation, Floqi moved to **Shkodra** where he started a legal practice during **World War I**. In May 1919, he began publishing the monthly *Agimi* (The Dawn), medium of the *Vellazenija* (Brotherhood) society. In 1920, he became president of the Shkodra Court of Appeal. In December of that year, he took over as minister of **education** and was later appointed counsellor of state. After **World War II**, Floqi was arrested by the **communists**, as were most prewar intellectuals who had not fled the country, and died in or around 1951 after several years in prison.

Kristo Floqi was a prolific writer, whose popularity is due on the whole not so much to the literary quality of his works, but to the whole-hearted pleasure his plays gave to audiences and to the reading public. He is the author of four tragedies on nationalist and historical themes, seventeen comedies and sketches, as well as several volumes of poetry, legal, political and educational texts, and translations of Sophocles, Euripides and Molière.

FOREIGN TRADE. In 1939, on the eve of **World War II**, **Italy** outranked all other countries in Albania's foreign trade. It accepted about sixty-five percent of Albanian exports and was responsible for about forty percent of Albanian imports. Total per capita commerce was, however, low, as it remains today.

In the **communist** period, there was, as could be expected, a substantial increase in trade with the East bloc countries. This process has been reversed, and Italy has once again become Albania's major trading partner, accounting in 1999 for thirty-four percent of all imports and almost seventy percent of all Albanian exports. Substantial imports also come from **Greece** (twenty-four percent) and, to a lesser extent, from the other countries of the European Union. Aside from Italy, substantial Albanian exports also go to Greece and Germany. Albanian foreign trade is expected to improve dramatically once preferential trading agreements are reached with the European Union.

FORTINO, ITALO COSTANTE (1947-). Arbëresh scholar. Italo Costante Fortino was born in San Benedetto Ullano (Alb. *Shën Benedhiti*) in the southern Italian province of Cosenza. He worked initially for the government and then for the department of Albanian at the University of Calabria. He is now professor of Albanian at the Oriental Institute of the University (Istituto Universitario Orientale) in Naples. Fortino is the author of numerous articles on Albanian and Italo-Albanian **literature**. He has also edited the works of early Arbëresh authors such as **Giulio Variboba** and Francesco Santori, and the volumes *Albanistica: novantasette* (Albanistica: Ninety-seven), Naples 1997; and *Albanistica - duemiladue* (Albanistica: Two Thousand Two), Naples 2002. He lives in Rome.

FRAKULLA, NEZIM (ca. 1680-1760). Muslim poet. Nezim Frakulla, the first major poet among the *Bejtexhinj*, was born in the village of Frakull near **Fier** and lived a good deal of his life in **Berat**, a flourishing center of Muslim culture at the time. Frakulla studied in Istanbul where he wrote his first poetry in Turkish, Persian, and perhaps Arabic, including two *divans*. About 1731, he returned to Berat where he is known to have been involved in literary rivalry with other poets of the period, notably with Mulla Ali, mufti of Berat. Between 1731 and 1735 he composed a *divan* and various other poetry in Albanian, as well as an Albanian-Turkish dictionary in verse form. Although the whole of the original divan did not survive, there are copies of approximately 110 poems from it. Some of his verse was put to **music** and survived the centuries orally. Nezim Frakulla tells us himself that he was the first person to compose a *divan* in Albanian.

Frakulla's *divan* includes verse ranging from panegyrics on local pashas and military campaigns, to odes on friends and patrons, poems on separation from and longing for his friends and (male) lovers, descriptions of nature in the springtime, religious verse and, in particular, love lyrics. The imagery of the latter *ghazal*, some of which are devoted to his nephew, is that of Arabic, Persian and Turkish poetry with many of the classical themes, metaphors and allusions: love as an illness causing the poet to waste away, the cruel lover whose glance could inflict mortal wounds or the cupbearer whose beauty could reduce his master to submission.

Nezim Frakulla enjoyed the patronage and protection of Sulejman Pasha of Elbasan and of Ismail Pasha Velabishti, the latter a poet himself. At some point after 1747, having returned to Istanbul in search of work, he was sent to Khotin in Bessarabia (now in the Ukraine), probably into exile. There he composed several *qasîde*, one of them celebrating the *firman* authorizing his return home and another about his journey back. Whether due to political intrigue or to the often caustic literary polemics in which he engaged, Frakulla fell into disfavor and left Berat once again to settle in **Elbasan** for a number of years. On his subsequent return to Berat, he seems to have been imprisoned. At any rate, he died in old age as a prisoner in Istanbul in 1760 [1173 A.H.].

Frakulla not only considered himself the first poet to write in Albanian, but also lauded himself as the Sa'dî and Hâfiz of his times. His *qasîde* in Albanian, he tells us, are comparable to those of 'Urfî in Persian and Nef'î in Turkish. Most experts would consider this comparison somewhat exaggerated. While Nezim

Frakulla doubtlessly had initiative and talent, his Albanian verse did not by any means reach the level of literary perfection of the Persian classics, nor was the clumsy mixture of Albanian, Turkish and Persian that he employed refined enough to enable him to do so. What he did accomplish was to lay the foundations for a new literary tradition in Albania, one which was to last for two centuries.

FRANCISCAN ORDER. Order of the **Catholic Church**. The history of the Franciscan order, founded by Saint Francis of Assisi (1181-1226) in 1209, dates in Albania from 1248 when a group of monks was brought to the country by the noted missionary Giovanni da Piano Carpine (1182-1252). A document dating from 1283 lists a number of Franciscan monasteries in Albania and by 1402 the Franciscans, also known as the Order of Friars Minor (*Ordo Fratrum Minorum* [O.F.M.]), had founded their own protectorate in **Durrës**, the *Custodia Durracensis*. They subsequently declined. A new Franciscan mission to Albania was authorized by a papal decree of 22 June 1634 and in August of that year, a group of nine Franciscans and two lay brothers set out for Dubrovnik in order to make their way to Ottoman-occupied Albania. On 15 December 1634, they landed in Shëngjin and managed with great difficulty to establish themselves in **Mirdita** for a short time again.

In the mid-nineteenth century, the order became increasingly active in the field of **education** and culture. In 1855, it established a Franciscan school in **Shkodra**, later to be known as the *Collegium Illyricum*, which became the first institute of education in which the Albanian **language** was taught. In 1861, it opened a Franciscan seminary, which also provided instruction in Albanian. In later years, the Franciscans operated a printing press and produced a number of religious and secular books in Albanian as well as periodicals of great literary and cultural interest such as *Hylli i Dritës* (The Day-Star), 1913-1944, and *Zâni i Shna Ndout* (The Voice of Saint Anthony), 1913-1944. The order continued its religious and educational activities up to the end of **World War II**, which saw the **communist** takeover. Soon after the war, many leading Franciscans were arrested. Among those who were tortured and executed were the writer **Anton Harapi**, who died on 4 February 1946, and father Gjon Shllaku (1907-1946), who died on 4 March 1946. In April 1946, all Fran-ciscan schools and monasteries were then closed down and their property confiscated. In January 1947, the communist secret police, **Sigurimi**, planted a cache of arms and ammunition in the main Franciscan church of Gjuhadol in Shkodra and was thereby given a pretext to arrest many of the remaining Franciscan brothers. The order was thereafter disbanded entirely.

After almost half a century of interruption, the Franciscan order resumed its activities in Albania in the early 1990s after the rescinding of the law on the public practice of **religion** in December 1990.

FRASHËRI, ABDYL BEY (1839.08.17-1892.10.11). Political leader. Abdyl Frashëri, like his brothers **Naim Frashëri** and **Sami Frashëri**, was born in the southern Albanian village of Frashër. In 1877, he entered the public service, being appointed to head the customs office in Janina. In the same year, he was elected as a member of the Turkish parliament to represent Janina, where his family had moved in 1865. In December 1877, together with other Albanian intellectuals, among them his younger brother Sami, he founded the **Central Committee for the Defense of the Rights of the Albanian People** in Istanbul with a view to obtaining a certain autonomy for the Albanians within the **Ottoman Empire**. Following the Russian and Serbian victory over the Ottoman Empire on 31 January 1878 and the Treaty of San Stefano of 3 March 1878, which provided for the annexation of much Albanian-speaking territory by the newly autonomous **Bulgarian** state and by the now independent kingdoms of Montenegro and Serbia, Abdyl turned his energy and talent increasingly and more urgently to the Albanian question. It was his articles in Turkish and Greek newspapers which first voiced the concerns and dismay of the Albanian population in the Balkans about the repercussions of the treaty and the **Congress of Berlin**.

On 10 June 1878, delegates from all over Albania assembled in Prizren to work out a common political platform in the **League of Prizren**, no doubt initially with the tacit support of the Ottoman government. Abdyl Frashëri, representing the central committee from Istanbul, held the opening speech. After this historic meeting, Abdyl Frashëri returned to southern Albania where he organized a League committee and began gathering troops to oppose the annexation of the south of the country by **Greece**. In 1879, he traveled to Berlin, Paris, Vienna and Rome with Mehmet Ali Vrioni (1842-1895) to seek support for the Albanian cause and to submit a memorandum of Albanian demands to the Great Powers. In October 1879, he cofounded the Istanbul **Society for the Publication of Albanian Writing**. In mid-1880, a program for Albanian autonomy was passed with his assistance by delegates of the national movement in **Gjirokastra**.

Although by this time his movements were under strict surveillance by the Istanbul authorities, he managed to get to Prizren in December 1880 and in the following month set up a Provisional Government (*Kuvernë e përdorme*), which extended its authority throughout Kosova down to Skopje. In **Dibra**, Abdyl Frashëri deposed the Turkish mutasarrif and placed the town under the administration of the League, but at the end of April 1881, the Sublime Porte had had enough and sent in troops to quell the uprising. Following resistance in Gjakova and the suppression of the League, Abdyl Frashëri was obliged to flee westward towards the Adriatic where he hoped to escape to Italy. While crossing the **Shkumbin** River near **Elbasan**, he was captured by Turkish forces and sentenced to life in prison. After four years in a Turkish jail, Abdyl bey Frashëri was pardoned at the intercession of Gazi Osman Pasha at the end of 1885. He died in Istanbul after a long illness.

FRASHËRI, KRISTO (1920.12.04-). Scholar and representative historian of the **communist** period. Kristo Frashëri was born in Istanbul and went to school in **Tirana**. He studied in Italy for two years but was forced to interrupt his education there because of **World War II**. He graduated from the Faculty of History in Tirana in 1955. Frashëri has focused his research on the **Rilindja** period of Albanian history. Among his publications are: *History of Albania, a Brief Survey,* Tirana 1964; *Lidhja shqiptare e Prizrenit, 1878-1881* (The Albanian League of Prizren, 1878-1881), Tirana 1979; *Abdyl Frashëri, 1839-1892* (Abdyl Frashëri, 1839-1892), Tirana 1984; and *Skënderbeu, jeta dhe vepra* (Scanderbeg, Life and Deeds), Tirana 2003.

FRASHËRI, MEHDI BEY (1874.02.28-1963.05.25). Political figure, publisher and writer. After studies in Monastir (Bitola) and Istanbul, where he graduated in economics, Mehdi bey Frashëri held various positions in the **Ottoman** administration, as bey of Jerusalem and governor-general of Palestine (1911) and as deputy high commissioner of Egypt (1912). After Albanian independence, he became prefect of **Berat** and in August of 1913 was appointed as a member of the **International Control Commission**. Following the departure from Albania of **Prince Wilhelm zu Wied** on 3 September 1914, Frashëri went into exile, joining his cousin Mid'hat bey Frashëri in Lausanne, and after an unsuccessful attempt to return to Albania in March 1915, he spent the war years in San Demetrio Corone (Alb. *Shën Mitri*), an **Arbëresh** settlement in southern Italy.

After World War I, Mehdi bey returned to Albania as a public figure, supporting a policy of close ties with **Italy**. He held various political positions, including minister of the interior (1918), member of the Albanian delegation to the Paris Peace Conference (June 1919), foreign minister (1919), minister of the interior once again and minister of public works (1921) and representative at the League of Nations in Geneva (1923) and on the **International Boundary Commission**. In 1927, he taught economics at the School of Law in **Tirana** and was subsequently made minister of economics (1930-1931) and prime minister (21 October 1935 to 7 November 1936). His short-lived, so-called liberal administration, not receiving sufficient support from **King Zog**, fell to conservative pressure. Despite his italophile proclivities, Mehdi bey spoke out against Mussolini's occupation of Albania in 1939 and was interned for a period in Rome. On 22 October 1943, he was elected for the last time to the uncom-fortable position of chairman of the so-called High Regency Council (*Këshilli i Lartë i Regjencës*) under the German occupation, a post he accepted in spite of the fact that his sympathies were more with the Allies than with the Axis. With the **communist** victory in 1944, Mehdi bey fled to Italy and died in Rome.

As a writer, Mehdi bey is remembered for the 144-page romantic novel *Nevruzi* (Nevruzi), Tirana 1923, a five-act historical drama entitled *Trathëtia* (Treason), Tirana 1926, set in the age of **Scanderbeg**, both devoid of literary merit, and of works on economics, philology, history and politics, including a three-part history of Albania, the first part of which survived and has been recently published as: *Historia e lashtë e Shqipërisë dhe e Shqiptarëve* (Ancient History of Albania and the Albanians), Tirana 2000.

FRASHËRI, MID'HAT BEY (1880.03.25-1949.10.03). Publicist, political figure and prose writer. Mid'hat bey Frashëri, also known by his pen name Lumo Skendo, was the son of **Rilindja** politician and ideologist **Abdyl bey Frashëri** and nephew of the equally illustrious **Naim bey Frashëri** and **Sami bey Frashëri**. He is thought to have been born in Janina (Iôannina) in northern Greece and, from 1883, was raised in Istanbul where his family was the focus of the nationalist movement. At the age of seventeen, he assisted **Kristo Luarasi** and Kosta Jani Trebicka

(d. 1944) in the publication of the Albanian cultural almanac known as the *Kalëndari kombiar* (The National Calendar) printed at Luarasi's press in Sofia. A year after the death of his uncle, Naim bey Frashëri, he published a short biography of the latter entitled *Naim Be Frashëri* (Naim Bey Frashëri), Sofia 1901, using the pseudonym Mali Kokojka. From 1905 to 1910, having given up his studies of pharmacy, he worked for the Ottoman administration in the vilayet of Salonika as director of political affairs. In July 1908, this time under the pen name of Lumo Skendo, he began publishing the weekly newspaper *Lirija* (Freedom) in Thessalonika, which lasted until 1910. He presided over the **Congress of Monastir** in 1908, and in January of the following year began editing a monthly magazine entitled *Diturija* (Knowledge), an illustrated periodical of cultural, literary and scholarly interest which appeared in 1909 in Thessalonika, in 1916 in Bucharest, and from 1926 to 1929 in **Tirana**. Frashëri played a major role in the patriotic club of Thessalonika, which was noted for its relatively conciliatory attitude towards the Young Turks and which was consequently opposed by more extreme nationalists.

Frashëri's political activities took on a more nationalist character during the **Balkan Wars** and the final collapse of the **Ottoman Empire** when Albania was at the point of being gobbled up by its Balkan neighbors. After Albanian independence in November 1912, he became his country's first minister of public works, and later Albanian consul general in Belgrade and postmaster general. At the start of **World War I**, he was interned in Romania for a time, but after his release, he returned to publishing. From 5 May 1916, he headed the fortnightly Bucharest periodical *L'indépendance albanaise* (Albanian independence), one of the many ephemeral media of the Albanian nationalist movement that sprang up during World War I. Mid'hat bey was later to be found in Lausanne, where he lived with his cousin **Mehdi bey Frashëri** and where he was author of a number of newspaper articles and essays. On 25 November 1920, he was nominated chairman of the Albanian delegation to the Paris Peace Conference, where he remained until 1922. In Paris he continued his journalistic activities in the French press to publicize Albania's position in the postwar restructuring of Europe. His lucid articles appeared in journals such as *France-Orient, L'Europe nouvelle, Mercure de France, Revue de Genève,* and *Les Peuples libres*. He subsequently held other ministerial posts and was Albanian ambassador to Greece and to the United States from 1922 to 1926.

Under the **Zog** dictatorship, Mid'hat bey left politics for a time and opened a bookstore in Tirana in 1925. He himself possessed an exceptionally large private library of some 20,000 volumes, the largest collection in the country at the time, which in February 1938 he offered to donate for the creation of an institute of Albanian studies. Unfortunately, nothing came of the project over the following few years. At the end of 1942, he reentered the political arena, at the age of eighty-two, to fight the Axis occupation, and was named leader of the conservative republican organization, *Balli Kombëtar*. In the autumn of 1944 with the **communist** victory apparent in Albania, he fled to southern Italy. His library in Tirana was confiscated and later came to form the core of the **National Library** of Tirana.

The early years of the cold war found Mid'hat bey Frashëri in the West trying to patch together a coalition of anticommunist opposition forces in **Britain** and the **United States**. In August 1949, he was elected as head of a **Free Albania Committee**. He died of a heart attack at the Lexington Hotel on Lexington Avenue in New York.

Mid'hat bey Frashëri was also the author of a wide variety of educative works: school texts, translations, newspaper articles, political tracts, and a collection of prose poems, short stories and reflections entitled *Hî dhe shpuzë* (Ashes and Embers), Sofia 1915.

FRASHËRI, NAIM BEY (1846.05.25-1900.10.20). Poet. Naim Frashëri is nowadays widely considered to be the national poet of Albania. He spent his childhood in the village of Frashër, where he no doubt began learning Turkish, Persian and Arabic and where, at the **Bektashi** monastery, he was imbued with the spiritual traditions of the Orient. In Janina (Iôannina), Naim Frashëri attended the Zosimaia secondary school, which provided him with the basics of a classical education along Western lines. As he grew in knowledge, so did his affinity for his pantheistic Bektashi **religion**, for the poets of classical Persia and for the Age of Enlightenment. After finishing secondary school in 1870, he spent some time in Istanbul, but for health reasons he soon returned to Albania, hoping to find relief in the mountain air from the tuberculosis he had contracted as a child. Naim bey worked as a civil servant initially in **Berat** and from 1874 to 1877 as a customs official in **Saranda** across from Corfu. In 1881 or 1882, he returned to Istanbul and, following the arrest of his brother **Abdyl Frashëri** in Janina at the end of April 1881, began to play a serious role in the activities of Albanian nationalists there. He participated in the work of the **Central Committee for the Defense of the Rights of the Albanian People** and in the **Society for the Publication of Albanian Writing**. He and his younger brother **Sami Frashëri** were soon to become the focal point of the Albanian nationalist movement on the Bosporus.

Naim Frashëri is the author of a total of twenty-two works: four in Turkish, one in Persian, two in Greek and fifteen in Albanian. The poetry collections for which he is primarily remembered are: *Bagëti e bujqësija* (Bucolics and Georgics), Bucharest 1886, which is a 450-line pastoral poem reminiscent of Vergil; *Luletë e verësë* (The Flowers of Spring), Bucharest 1890; *Parajsa dhe fjala fluturake* (Paradise and Winged Words), Bucharest 1894, published together with the spiritual essays *Mësime* (Teachings), Bucharest 1894; *Istori' e Skenderbeut* (History of Scanderbeg), Bucharest 1898, an historical epic of 11,500 verses, which Frashëri regarded as his masterpiece; and *Qerbelaja* (Kerbela), Bucharest 1898, a Shi'ite religious epic in twenty-five cantos.

The significance of Naim Frashëri as a **Rilindja** poet and indeed as a "national poet" rests not so much upon his talents of literary expression nor upon the artistic quality of his verse but rather upon the sociopolitical, philosophical and religious messages it transmitted, which were aimed above all at national awareness and, in the Bektashi tradition, at overcoming religious barriers within the country. His influence upon Albanian writers at the beginning of the twentieth century was enormous.

FRASHËRI, SAMI BEY (1850.06.01-1904.06.05). Writer, publisher and ideologist of the nationalist movement. Sami Frashëri, known in Turkish as Şemseddin Sami, was the Frashëri brother with the most diverse and universal talent. After schooling in Janina, he moved to Istanbul to join his brother **Abdyl bey Frashëri**. There he promoted the **Central Committee for the Defense of the Rights of the Albanian People**, which supported Albanian demands for autonomy at the time of the **League of Prizren**. At the beginning of 1879, the Central Committee set up an alphabet commission under Sami Frashëri's direction to tackle the orthography problem. The alphabet that Sami Frashëri devised, which was subsequently approved by the commission, was a phonetic system relying primarily on Latin letters, though with the addition of a number of Greek/Cyrillic characters. On 12 October 1879, leading members of the Alban-ian community in

Istanbul also set up the **Society for the Publication of Albanian Writing**. It, too, was headed by Sami Frashëri.

Sami Frashëri is the author of about fifty works as well as numerous newspaper articles. His interests were on the whole more scholarly than literary. Between 1882 and 1902, he published six teaching manuals in Turkish and Arabic. His publications in Turkish are indeed of greater universal significance than his Albanian-language works. In 1872, Sami Frashëri published what is widely regarded as the first Turkish novel and, at the same time, the first novel written and published by an Albanian, the 180-page *Taaşşuk-u Tal'at ve Fitnat* (The Love of Tal'at and Fitnat). It is a period piece, a sentimental love story which was in full accord with the tastes of the time. While by no means realistic, the combination of oriental and occidental elements it contained did provide a good deal of social criticism, in particular of the status of **women** in **Ottoman** society. More than anything, Sami Frashëri was an educator.

Sami Frashëri's play, the 180-page *Besa yahud ahde vefa* ("Besa" or the Fulfilment of the Pledge), published in Istanbul in 1875, and translated into Albanian by Abdyl Ypi Kolonja in 1901 and into English by Nelo Drizari (1902-1978) as *Pledge of Honor, an Albanian Tragedy*, New York 1945, was premiered on 6 April 1874 at the "Osmanli Tiyatrosu" (Ottoman Theater). In this, for modern tastes somewhat melodramatic work on a very Albanian theme, the spectator observes the tragic dilemma of an Albanian father who prefers to kill his own son rather than break his *besa*, his word of honor.

As a Turkish lexicographer, Sami Frashëri published a 1,630-page *Kamûs-u fransevî, fransizcadan türkçeye lugat* (French-Turkish Dictionary), Istanbul 1882 [1299 A.H.]; a *Kamûs-u fransevî, türkçeden fransizcaya lugat* (Turkish-French Dictionary), Istanbul 1885 [1301 A.H.]; and a two-volume *Kamûs-u türkî* (Turkish Dictionary), Istanbul 1900-1901 [1317 A.H.], reprint Istanbul 1979, which is still regarded as useful and which was consulted by the Turkish Philological Society (Türk Dil Kurumu) in 1932 as a guideline for the creation of the modern Turkish literary **language**. Lack of money caused him to abandon his vast project of a *Kamûs-u Arabî* (Arabic dictionary). After twelve years of preparation, he was, however, able to publish his monumental six-volume Turkish-language encyclopedia of history and **geography**, *Kamûs al-a'lâm* (Dictionary of the World), Istanbul 1889-1896 [1306-1313 A.H.]. With a total of 4,830 pages, the *Kamûs al-a'lâm* was an exceptional work of reference for the period and also contained extensive information on the history and geography of Albania.

Of major significance to the Albanian national movement was Sami Frashëri's much-read political manifesto *Shqipëria—Ç'ka qënë, ç'është e ç'do të bëhetë? Mendime për shpëtimt të mëmëdheut nga reziket që e kanë rethuarë* (Albania—What It Was, What It Is and What Will Become of It? Reflections on Saving the Motherland from Perils which Beset It), Bucharest 1899. The immediate goal of his manifesto was full autonomy for Albania within the empire, though it served to promote the ideal of full independence.

FREE ALBANIA COMMITTEE, FAC (1949-). Anticommunist organization. The Free Albania Committee was originally founded in Italy after **World War II** as a forum and movement of anticommunist resistance to the regime of **Enver Hoxha** in Albania. It reformed in New York in 1949, where it was headed briefly by **Mid'hat bey Frashëri**. From 1956 to 1992, it was headed by **Rexhep Krasniqi**, who published a periodical called *Shqiptari i lirë* (The Free Albanian), which appeared monthly from November 1957 to 1970, and later sporadically. The FAC acted as a rare voice from the free world to the silenced and oppressed people of Albania. Its activities diminished over the years, but it continued to organize political gatherings, conferences and seminars. Over 15,000 Albanian refugees were resettled in the **United States** through its efforts. With the demise of **communism**, the board of directors of the FAC decided that its functions would no longer be needed, and it was disbanded in 1992.

- G -

GALERIA KOMBËTARE E ARTEVE. *See* NATIONAL GALLERY.

GASHI. Northern Albanian tribe and traditional tribal region. The Gashi region is situated in the District of **Tropoja**, from east of the town of Bajram Curri into **Kosova**. It borders on the traditional tribal regions of **Krasniqi** to the west, and Bytyçi to the south. The Gashis, whose name was recorded in 1634 as *Gaasi*, were a Muslim tribe and were the traditional enemies of the Catholic **Shalas**. Gashi is a common family name, in particular in Kosova.

GEG. *See* GHEG.

GEGAJ, ATHANAS (1904-1988.02). Scholar. Athanas Gegaj was born in Triepsh, now in Montenegro, and studied at the Illyrian college of **Shkodra**. He was then able to continue his education in Italy and at the Catholic University of Leuven (Louvain) in Belgium, and became a **Franciscan** priest. In 1938, he returned to Albania and taught at the Franciscan college until the Italian invasion. Because of his opposition to Italian rule, he was interned in **Italy** and never returned to Albania. After **World War II**, Gegaj served as secretary to **King Zog** while the latter was in exile in France. In 1962, he emigrated to the **United States** and became editor of the Boston weekly *Dielli* (The Sun) until 1971. He died in Santa Monica, California, in February 1988. Athanas Gegaj is remembered primarily for his monograph *L'Albanie et l'invasion turque au XVe siècle* (Albania and the Turkish Invasion in the Fifteenth Century), Louvain 1937, and for numerous scholarly articles in the **Catholic** and exile press.

GENTHIUS. Last Illyrian king of **Shkodra**. He was vanquished by the Romans in 168 B.C., a date which marked the conclusion of the three **Illyrian** wars with Rome. Many of today's Albanian men bear the name Gent in his honor.

GEOGRAPHICAL POSITION. The Republic of Albania is a European country in the southwestern part of the Balkan peninsula. It is situated on the eastern bank of the Adriatic Sea between 42°39' and 39°38' degrees of latitude north, and 19°16' and 21°40' degrees of longitude east. The geographical extremes of the country are the village of Vermosh in the District of **Malësia e Madhe** in the north, the town of Konispol in the District of **Saranda** in the south, the island of **Sazan** off the coast of **Vlora** in the west, and the village of Vërnik in the District of **Devoll** in the east. Albania has a surface area of 28,748 square kilometers, being roughly the size of Belgium or the U.S. state of Maryland. It borders to the north on **Montenegro**, to the northeast on **Kosova**, to the east on the Republic of **Macedonia**, to the south on Greece, and to the west on the Adriatic and Ionian Seas. At the closest point, it is a mere seventy kilometers from the coast of southern **Italy**. It has a maximum north-south distance of 340 kilometers and a maximum east-west distance of 180 kilometers Albania has a total border length of 1,094 kilometers, of which 657 kilometers are land borders, 316 kilometers sea border, and the rest, rivers and lakes.

The major rivers of Albania are the **Drin, Seman, Vjosa, Shkumbin, Mat,** and **Erzen**. It has three major lakes: **Shkodra, Ohrid** and **Prespa**, all of which form part of the borders.

Albania is a primarily mountainous country, with flat land only along the coastal plain. The highest mountain is Mt. Korab, 2,751 meters, in the District of **Dibra**, which forms the border to Macedonia, and the highest peaks in the northern Albanian Alps are Mt. Jezerca, 2,694 meters and Mt. Radohima, 2,570 meters in the District of **Shkodra**. Other important peaks are Mt. Gramoz, 2,523 meters in the District of **Kolonja**, which forms the border with Greece, and Mt. **Tomorr**, 2,417 meters in the central District of **Berat**.

GERALDINE, Queen. *See* APPONYI, GERALDINE.

GERMANY, RELATIONS WITH. Although there were certain contacts between German rulers and **Scanderbeg** during the mid-fifteenth century, the first German recorded as having visited Albania was **Arnold von Harff**, a knight from the Cologne region, who stopped off in **Durrës** on his way to the Holy Land in the spring of 1497. There he recorded not only his impressions, but also several words and phrases of the Albanian **language**.

Germans first became aware of Albania in the age of Scanderbeg, and, in particular, with the publication in Augsburg in 1533 of a German-language translation of the "History of Scanderbeg" by **Marinus Barletius**. Philosopher Wilhelm von Leibniz (1646-1716) dealt with the Albanian language in his research, and Johann Erich Thunmann (1746-1778) of the University of Halle first disseminated the theory of the autochthony of the Albanians in his monograph *Über die Geschichte und Sprache der Albaner und der Wlachen* (On the History and Language of the Albanians and Vlachs), Leipzig 1744. In the nineteenth and early twentieth centuries, German and Austrian scholars made further notable contributions to Albanian studies, including history, folk culture, and most importantly, language. **Johann Georg von Hahn**, born in Frankfurt am Main, was to be called the father of Albanian studies.

After Albanian independence in 1912, the Great Powers decided that the newly created Albanian throne would be given to a German prince. Their choice, **Prince Wilhelm zu Wied**, was of a noble Protestant family from Neuwied on the Rhine and was the nephew of Queen Elizabeth of Romania. He agreed to accept the Albanian throne on 1 November 1913, and arrived in Durrës on 7 March 1914 aboard an Austro-Hungarian naval vessel. After less than seven months, however, he abandoned Albania forever, though without formally abdicating. Such were Germany's first official contacts with the Albanian state. Other contacts were sporadic until **World War II**.

When **Italy** capitulated on 8 September 1943, German troops occupied Albania to fill the void. The occupation lasted until late 1944. Troops began evacuating the country on 2 October of that year as part of the German pullback from Greece and the southern Balkans, and the last German soldier left Albanian soil on 29 November 1944.

Diplomatic relations were established with the German Democratic Republic on 2 December 1949. Albania's high demands for reparations (US$2 billion) impeded relations with West Germany for many years. The last German and Austrian prisoners of war in Albania were repatriated on 31 May 1950, and, on 15 March 1955, the Albanian authorities declared the state of war with Germany officially over.

Relations with the GDR flourished in the 1950s. A trade agreement was signed on 4 April 1951, and an agreement for technical and scientific cooperation was concluded on 16 February 1952. Numerous Albanians studied at East German universities in the late 1950s and several East Germans studied and worked in **Tirana**. The rupture of relations with the **Soviet Union** in 1961 meant a break in relations with East Germany, too, and ambassadors were recalled to their respective countries on 18 December of that year.

In the late 1970s, an increasingly isolated Albania began to show an interest in normalizing relations with West Germany. On 15 March 1979, a note was issued on the prerequisites for normalization. An Albanian delegation under Sofoli Lazri visited Bonn on 27-28 April 1984 to discuss the issue, and the two sides later held secret talks in Vienna on 8-9 November of that year. In the meanwhile, the Bavarian prime minister Franz Joseph Strauss, who had ambitions of becoming German foreign minister himself, visited Albania on 18-20 August 1984, much to the displeasure of foreign minister Hans-Dietrich Genscher. Strauss visited

Albania once more on 19-29 May 1986 and was received by Albanian prime minister **Adil Çarçani**. Diplomatic relations with the Federal Republic of Germany were officially established on 2 October 1987, and an economic delegation under Fahrudin Hoxha visited Bonn and Salzgitter on 31 May-2 June 1988, when an economic agreement was signed. A first session of the German-Albanian economic commission was held in Tirana on 5-8 December 1988. **Foto Çami**, a high-ranking member of the Politburo then visited Bonn on 10 May 1989 and held talks with Genscher on further relations and on the situation in **Kosova**, but the German reaction was cool.

In July 1990, Germany agreed to accept the 3,200 Albanians who had taken refuge in the German embassy in Tirana. They were transported to Germany by three Red Cross trains from Brindisi. Foreign Minister Genscher visited Tirana on 15 June 1991, and on 22 April 1992. According to statistics of the United Nations Development Program, there were some 12,000 emigrants from Albania living in Germany in 1999.

Since the fall of the dictatorship, Germany has played a major role in providing economic and development assistance to Albania. In the early 1990s, per capita aid to Albania was higher than to any other country of eastern Europe. German President Roman Herzog visited Albania on 28 February - 1 March 1995, and President **Sali Berisha** reciprocated with a state visit to Bonn on 18-19 December of that year. President **Rexhep Meidani** visited Germany on 13-16 June 1999, after the **Kosova War**, at the invitation of the Friedrich Ebert Foundation. On 17-18 January 2001, Prime Minister **Ilir Meta** visited Berlin, Wolfsburg and Hamburg to promote trade ties and Albania's integration into the European Union.

GËRMENJI, THEMISTOKLI (1871-1917.11.07). Nationalist figure and guerrilla fighter. Themistokli Gërmenji was born in **Korça** and emigrated to Romania in 1892 in search of work, where he was influenced by the rise of patriotic societies in the Albanian community. He returned to Korça and Monastir where he and his brother opened the *Liria* (Freedom) Hotel, a center of the nationalist movement. He helped plan the **Congress of Monastir** in 1908 and the uprisings of the following years. In 1911, he traveled to Italy and Greece to find support and was imprisoned in Janina until early 1912. He then returned to Korça and led a guerrilla band in the fight against Ottoman troops. He subsequently led the guerrilla forces in the **Balkan Wars** and

World War I, which drove the Greeks out of his native Korça in 1914. He fled to Sofia when Greek troops re-occupied Korça in 1915. In October 1916, he traveled to **Pogradec,** which was occupied by Austrian and Bulgarian troops, to seek Austrian assistance. When he realized he would receive no help, he turned to the French, who had taken Korça in October 1916.

The French initially left the administration of Korça to their Greek allies, which caused much anger and increasingly strong resistance among the Albanians. Guerrilla bands under the leadership of Themistokli Gërmenji and Salih Butka were formed again and were on the point of fighting not only against the Greeks, but also against the French. The French command in Salonika soon realized that the Greeks had no support whatsoever in Korça and, understanding the increasingly difficult situation they were being faced with, sent Colonel Descoins to Korça. On 24 November of that year, Gërmenji met the French commander, who entrusted him with the post of prefect of the new autonomous republic, which was established there on 10 December 1916. This ephemeral creation under French auspices had its own government, gendarmerie and police force, and even stamps and paper money. Gërmenji set up Albanian schools throughout the villages of the region and discontinued the use of Turkish and Greek. The French Republic of Korça was not to survive long. When **Greece** joined the Entente in June 1917, Korça lost its autonomous status (officially on 16 February 1918) and Greek schools were re-opened.

Themistokli Gërmenji, accused of being an "Austrian agent working against the best interests of the allied cause," was arrested, imprisoned in Salonika and tried before a French military court. He was executed there by a firing squad. He is well-remembered in Korça, where his statue as a freedom fighter dominates the city.

GHEG. The term Gheg, Alb. *geg*, refers to the northern Albanians, i.e., all Albanians living north of the **Shkumbin** River and speaking Gheg dialects. The territory of the Ghegs is poetically referred to as Gegëria or Gegnia (pronounced with a hard *g*). The southern Albanians are called **Tosks.**

GHICA, HELENA. *See* GJIKA, ELENA.

GJEBREA, ARDIT (1963.06.07-). Singer and composer. Born in **Tirana**, Gjebrea graduated with a degree in **music** from the

Academy of Fine Arts (*Instituti i Lartë i Arteve*) in 1986. He is one of the most popular, talented and innovative singers in Albania today. His success derives in good part from his ability to combine modern pop music with traditional Albanian folk music, in particular southern Albanian polyphony, to create a style which has been widely admired. Gjebrea is also a well-known figure on Albanian television.

GJEÇOVI, SHTJEFËN (1874.07.12-1929.10.14). Folklorist and writer. Gjeçovi was the first Albanian folklorist to collect oral **literature** in a scholarly and systematic manner. He was born in the village of Janjeva south of Prishtina in **Kosova** on 12 July 1874 (according to some sources 3 October 1873). Gjeçovi was considered the best pupil in his local school and one of exceptional talent. For this reason, the church authorities in Skopje sent him as a young boy to the **Franciscan** seminary in Troshan north of **Lezha**. In 1888, at the age of fourteen, he was sent on for further schooling to Franciscan educational establishments in Bosnia. On 15 August 1892, he entered the seminary of Fojnica near Sarajevo, continued on to Derventa (1893) and Banja Luka (1893) in northern Bosnia, and subsequently entered the Franciscan seminary in Kreševo, again near Sarajevo, where he studied theology together with his classmate Pashko Bardhi (1870-1948), who was later to become a noted journalist and contributor to the **Shkodra** cultural periodical *Hylli i dritës* (The Day-Star).

The young Gjeçovi was ordained as a priest of the Franciscan order in 1896 and returned to Albania the same year. He served as a parish priest in Peja and in 1905-1906 replaced his friend Pashko Bardhi as an Albanian teacher in the Albanian-speaking village of Borgo Erizzo, now called Arbanasi, a southern suburb of Zadar on the upper Dalmatian coast. In the following years, his most productive, Gjeçovi lived in a number of rugged mountain settlements in northern Albania, including Laç at the foot of the **Kurbin** mountains (ca. 1899-1905), Gomsiqja east of Shkodra (1907-1915), Theth in the far north (1916-1917) and Rubik in the **Mirdita** district (ca. 1919-1921). It was here among the mountain tribes that he began compiling material on oral literature, tribal law, archeology and folklore, and collecting objects of folk culture.

Among the more interesting of Gjeçovi's literary publications is the 144-page *Agimi i gjytetniis* (The Dawn of Civilization), Shkodra 1910, dedicated to **Gjergj Fishta**, a collection of didactic articles and aphorisms on Albania and its **language**. He is also the author of numerous essays and studies, published and unpublished, on Albanian history, ethnography and archeology. A reflection of his enthusiasm for archeology can be found in his *Trashigime thrako-ilirjane* (Thracian-Illyrian Heritage), a series of essays published under the pseudonym Komen Kanina in *Hylli i dritës* (The Day-Star) in 1924.

It is, however, not primarily through his work in the field of archeology that Shtjefën Gjeçovi made his mark on Albanian culture, but through his monumental codification and publication of Albanian tribal law, the *Kanuni i Lekë Dukagjinit* (The *Kanun* of Lekë Dukagjini), Shkodra 1933, which he originally published in part in **Faik bey Konitza**'s periodical *Albania* in 1898 and 1899, and then more extensively in the Shkodra periodical *Hylli i dritës* (The Day-Star) from 1913 to 1924.

In 1926, Father Shtjefën Gjeçovi was transferred to the parish of Zym, one of the **Catholic** villages in Has territory between Prizren and Gjakova in Kosova. There, with his reputation as a strong Albanian nationalist and as a scholar interested in digging up his people's ancient past, he incurred the wrath of the local Serbian population and/or authorities, and was murdered near Zym on his way home from Prizren. Gjeçovi's death was a loss to Albanian ethnography and archeology and came as a great shock to people throughout the nation. In **Tirana**, the **parliament** commemorated his passing in a series of moving speeches on 11 November of that year. Gjergj Fishta proclaimed the following day, "We do not wish to mourn the death of Father Gjeçovi; on the contrary, we are proud, because it is in the blood of martyrs that ideas are reinforced and states are consolidated." Shtjefën Gjeçovi's grave at Karashëngjergj near Prizren remains a site of pilgrimage for Albanians of all faiths to this very day.

GJERGJI, ANDROMAQI (1928-). Scholar and ethnographer. Andromaqi Gjergji studied history and philology in **Tirana** and finished her habilitation in ethnology in 1980. She has done field work throughout Albania and taken part in many international conferences. In 1993, she was appointed professor and worked until retirement for the Institute of Folk Culture. Gjergji is the author of over 130 scholarly articles and specializes in Albanian costumes and dress. Among her publications are: *Bibliografi e etnografisë shqiptare, 1944-1979* (Bibliography of Albanian Ethnography, 1944-1979), Tirana 1980; *Veshet shqiptare në shekuj: origjina, tipologjia, zhvillimi* (Albanian Costumes over the Centuries: Origins, Typology, Development), Tirana 1988;

and *Ligjerata për etnologjinë shqiptare* (Lectures on Albanian Ethnology), Tirana 2001.

GJIKA, ELENA (1828.02.28-1882.11.20). Writer of Albanian origin. Elena Gjika, known in Romanian as Helena Ghica, and more commonly as Dora d'Istria, was an interesting figure in mid-nineteenth century Albanian and European culture. This Romanian writer of Albanian origin was born in Bucharest of the aristocratic Ghica family originally from **Macedonia**. Her uncle, Grigore IV, was voivode of Wallachia. As a young woman, Dora d'Istria traveled with her parents to the courts of Vienna, Dresden and Berlin, and was widely admired for her talents and beauty. In 1849, her marriage to Prince Alexander Masalsky took her to Russia where she spent almost six years. After her separation from him in 1855, she moved to **Switzerland**, where she was the first woman to climb the Jungfrau, and in 1860 she traveled to **Greece**. Most of the rest of her life was spent in **Italy**. She died in Florence.

Dora d'Istria's untiring devotion to the aspirations of national minorities in the Austro-Hungarian Empire, to equality for **women**, and to popular **education**, made her quite well-known all over Europe. Although some have regarded her as a dilettante in her various writings, there can be no doubt that her essay *La nationalité albanaise d'après les chants populaires*, published in 1866 in the Parisian literary *Revue des deux mondes*, made an impact on the Albanian nationalist movement in the **Rilindja** period. On the history of her own family, Dora d'Istria also published a 455-page work entitled *Gli Albanesi in Rumenia: storia dei principi Ghica nei secoli XVII, XVIII e XIX* (The Albanians in Romania: History of the Ghica Princes in the Seventeenth, Eighteenth and Nineteenth Centuries), Florence 1873.

GJIKA, VIKTOR (1937.06.23-). Film director. Viktor Gjika was born in the village of Trebicka near **Korça** and studied at the Institute of Cinematography in Moscow. His first independent production was the documentary *Bistricë '63* (Bistrica '63). He was head of the **New Albania Film Studios** from 1984 to 1991. In the course of his career, he has produced ten documentary and fourteen feature films, among which were *I teti në bronx* (The Bronze Bust), 1970; *Rrugë të bardha* (White Roads), 1974; *Përballimi* (The Face-Up), 1976; *Gjeneral gramafoni* (General Gramophone), 1978; and *Nëntori i dytë* (The Second November),

1982. His most recent film, *Kur ikin korbat* (When the Crows Depart), 2000, is devoted to **Kosova**.

GJINUSHI, SKËNDER (1949.12.24-). Political figure and high-ranking member of the **Social Democratic Party of Albania**. Skënder Gjinushi was born in **Vlora** and studied mathematics at the University of **Tirana**, graduating in 1972. From 1973 to 1977, he studied in France where he finished his doctorate in science. In 1977, he taught at the Faculty of Science in Tirana and, in 1986, was a full professor there. His political career began in the **communist** period. From 1987 to February 1991, he served as minister of **education** in the last communist government. He played an important role in the democracy movement in 1990-1991, and in 1991 founded the Social Democratic Party of Albania, serving as party leader from 1992 to 1996. From 23 July 1997 to 2001, he was speaker of the Albanian **parliament**.

GJIROKASTRA. Town in the **District of Gjirokastra**, of which it is the administrative center. **Population** in Dec. 1999: 32,724. The town was referred to in Byzantine records in 1336 as *Argyrokastron*, meaning "silver fortress" in Greek. It was also known as *Argirocastro* in Italian and *Ergiri* in Turkish.

   Gjirokastra on the mountainside (*"Gjirokastra në shpatë mali"*) is the most attractive town of southern Albania. Situated in the Dropulli valley to the west of the **Drino River**, it was taken by the Turks in 1419, and most of the monuments date from the **Ottoman** period. **Ali Pasha Tepelena** conquered the town in 1812, fortified its impressive citadel and used it as an administrative center.

   Gjirokastra is known for its Ottoman architecture, in particular for its large nineteenth-century stone mansions. In 1961, it was designated a museum city under monument protection and is now a UNESCO World Heritage Site. It was the birthplace of **communist** dictator **Enver Hoxha** and writer **Ismail Kadare**. There is a substantial **Greek minority** in the villages to the south of the town.

GJIROKASTRA, DISTRICT OF. Region of local government administration. The District of Gjirokastra (*Rrethi i Gjirokastrës*), with its administrative headquarters in the town of **Gjirokastra**, borders on the districts of **Saranda** and **Delvina** to the west, **Tepelena** to the north, **Përmet** to the east and the Republic of

Greece to the south. It has a surface area of 1,137 square kilometers and a present **population** of 65,841 (in 2000).

GODIN, MARIE AMELIE, Freiin von (1882.03.07-1956.02.22). German writer and publicist. Baroness Godin was born and raised in Munich in the traditions of the **Catholic Church** as the daughter of a family of Bavarian aristocrats. In 1905-1906, she traveled with her younger brother to Athens, Istanbul and Palestine. It was on board a vessel bound for Istanbul that she first met an Albanian, Avdi bey Delvina, who invited her to visit his country. In 1908, she finally got to Albania where she met **Eqrem bey Vlora** with whom she was to be a lifelong intimate friend. It was no doubt he who inspired her to devote her life to Albania. Baroness Godin traveled to visit him in 1910 and once again from September 1912 to April 1913 when she was caught up in the chaos of the **Balkan War**. In the spring of 1914, she served as a lady of the court and interpreter to **Prince Wilhelm zu Wied** in **Durrës**.

In the 1920s, as the author of novels and tales of adventure, Godin was one of the most popular female writers in Germany. Many of her stories have Albanian themes. She spent most of the years between **World War I** and **World War II** in her native Munich, though she traveled to Albania whenever she could.

Among her many publications, mostly popular prose, mention may be made of: *Aus dem Lande der Knechtschaft: albanische Novellen* (From the Land of Servitude: Albanian Short Stories), Vienna 1913; *Aus dem neuen Albanien: politische und kulturhistorische Skizzen* (From the New Albania: Political, Cultural and Historical Sketches), Vienna 1914; *Befreiung: Roman aus dem modernen Albanien* (Liberation: Novel from Modern Albania), Regensburg 1920; *Wörterbuch der albanischen und deutschen Sprache* (Dictionary of the Albanian and German Language), Leipzig 1930; *Auf Apostelpfaden durch das schöne Albanien* (On Apostolic Paths through Fair Albania), Münster 1936; *Der tolle Nureddin: Roman aus Albanien* (Mad Nureddin: Novel from Albania), Cologne 1936; and *Gjoka und die Rebellen: geschichtlicher Roman aus dem Albanien unserer Tage* (Gjoka and the Rebels: Historical Novel from the Albania of our Times), Trier 1939. In collaboration with Eqrem bey Vlora, she also translated the *"Kanun* of Lekë Dukagjini" into German.

GODO, SABRI (1929.08.08-). Writer, political figure and high-ranking member of the **Republican Party**. Sabri Godo was born in Delvina and went to school in **Gjirokastra** and **Tirana**. After a military career, he became a professional writer and is remembered in particular for his historical novels. His first work, *Plaku i Butkës* (The Old Man from Butka), Tirana 1964, was a biography of Sali Butka (1852-1938), a minor nationalist figure and poet who led Albanian forces against both the Greeks and the Young Turks. His *Ali Pashë Tepelena* (Ali Pasha of Tepelena), Tirana 1970, dramatized the life of the "Lion of Janina" whose shrewd and ruthless rule held the sultan and Napoleon at bay and so captivated the young **Lord Byron**. The best-known of his works is *Skënderbeu* (**Scanderbeg**), Tirana 1975, an epic portrayal of the Albanian national hero from birth to death. Godo's other prose works include the short story collection *Zëra nga burime të nxehta* (Voices from the Hot Springs), Tirana 1971; and a collection of literary wanderings and sketches entitled *Kohët që shkojnë, kohët që vijnë* (Times Come, Times Go), Tirana 1985. Other novels include *Ujërat e qeta* (Tranquil Waters), Tirana 1988 and *Koha e njeriut* (The Age of Man), Tirana 1990, which revived the culture of the Albanian **Bektashi** community.

One month after the fall of the **communist** dictatorship in December 1990, Sabri Godo was elected head of the Republican Party of Albania, which was founded on 17 January 1991. He held the position until 5 November 1997, but has remained active in politics since that time. He was a member of **parliament** from 1997 to 2001 and chaired the parliamentary commission for foreign affairs. Sabri Godo is remembered for his contribution to Albanian parliamentary and political life in reconciling the various political factions and in attaining requisite agreements in times of extreme political confrontation. He also played a major role in the drafting of the Albanian constitution.

GORAN MINORITY IN ALBANIA. *See* SLAVIC MINORITY IN ALBANIA.

GRADILONE, GIUSEPPE. Arbëresh scholar. Gradilone was born in San Demetrio Corone (Alb. *Shën Mitri*) in the southern Italian province of Cosenza. He studied classical philology and literature at the University of Rome and was influenced in his interests in Albanian studies by **Ernest Koliqi**. In 1952 he was appointed professor of Albanian **language** and **literature** at the University of Rome, a position he held until retirement. Gradilone is the author of many works on Albanian and Italo-Albanian literature, among which are: *Studi di letteratura albanese* (Studies in Albanian Literature), Rome 1960; *Racconti popolari di S. Sofia* *d'Epiro, S. Demetrio Conrone, Macchia Albanese, S. Cosmo Alb., Vaccarizzo Alb. e S. Giorgio Alb.* (Folk Tales from Santa Sofia d'Epiro, San Demetrio Corone, Macchia Albanese, San Cosmo Albanese, Vaccarizzo Albanese and San Giorgio Albanese), Florence 1970; *Altri studi di letteratura albanese* (Further Studies in Albanian Literature), Rome 1974; *La letteratura albanese e il mondo classico: quattro studi* (Albanian Literature and the Classical World: Four Studies), Rome 1983; *Contributo alla critica del testo dei canti di Giuseppe Serembe* (Contribution to the Textual Criticism of the Songs of Zef Serembe), Rome 1989; *Miscellanea di albanistica* (Albanological Miscellany), Rome 1997; and *Studi di letteratura albanese contemporanea* (Studies in Contemporary Albanian Literature), Rome 1997.

GRAMENO, MIHAL (1871.01.13-1931.02.05). Writer, publisher and nationalist figure. The literary and patriotic activities of Mihal Grameno span the **Rilindja** and independence periods. Grameno was born in **Korça** of a merchant family and studied at the Greek school there before emigrating as a lad to Romania in 1885. It was in Bucharest that he became involved with the nationalist movement and in 1889 became secretary of the burgeoning *Drita* (The Light) society. Mihal Grameno was not only an ideologist of the Rilindja movement, but he was also a man of action. In 1907, he joined the **Çerçiz Topulli** band, an early guerrilla unit fighting against Turkish troops in southern Albania. With his fiery eyes and flowing beard, he was the very epitome of the Balkan freedom fighter and bandit.

In July 1909, he published the first issue of *Lidhja orthodhokse* (The **Orthodox** League) in his native Korça, a fortnightly newspaper of nationalist aspiration which lasted until June 1910 when it was closed down by the censors. On 1 February 1911, he began editing another newspaper in Korça entitled *Koha* (The Time), a weekly political and literary journal published to defend the rights of the Albanian people.

In 1915, Mihal Grameno emigrated to the **United States** and continued publishing the weekly in Jamestown, New York, until 1919 under the subtitle "the organ of the nationalist Albanian." Deeply concerned about Albania's very survival following the convulsions of **World War I** and the continued lack of a stable government there, the Albanian-American community sent Mihal Grameno and five other Albanian delegates to attend the 1919 Paris Peace Conference and represent Albania's interests.

As a literary figure, Mihal Grameno first became known in 1903 for his patriotic poem *Vdekja* (Death), though the political fervor of this and later verse was never matched by any particular linguistic finesse. More readable are his plays and short stories. On the eve of Albanian independence, he printed a volume of fiery nationalist verse entitled *Plagët* (The Wounds), Monastir 1912, and in later years published the memoirs of his experience as a guerrilla fighter in *Kryengritja shqiptare* (The Albanian Uprising), Vlora 1925.

Mihal Grameno was a typical figure of late Rilindja culture, full of romantic nationalism and creative energy to improve the sorry lot of his people and defend their rights. He personifies the nationalist hero-writer of this age and is thus much admired in Albania.

GRAMSH, DISTRICT OF. Region of local government administration. The District of Gramsh (*Rrethi i Gramshit*), with its administrative headquarters in the town of Gramsh, borders on the districts of **Berat** to the west, **Elbasan** to the north, **Librazhd** and **Pogradec** to the east, and **Korça** and **Skrapar** to the south. It has a surface area of 695 square kilometers and a present **population** of 45,026 (in 2000). The word "Gramsh" was recorded in 1610 as Gramsi.

GREAT BRITAIN, RELATIONS WITH. *See* UNITED KINGDOM, RELATIONS WITH.

GREATER ALBANIA. The Albanians are currently at home on their own ethnic territory in no less than six countries: Albania, **Montenegro, Kosova, Serbia, Macedonia,** and **Greece**. The concept of a Greater Albania, i.e., the unification of all Albanian-settled territories into one state, was launched by Benito Mussolini when, on 12 August 1941, Italian forces, having occupied Kosova and the Albanian-speaking regions of Plava, Gucia and Ulqin (Ulcinj) in Montenegro, reunited these territories with Albania itself.

The Albanians do not use the term "Greater Albania" and never have. The term has only been kept alive in recent years by Belgrade in order to justify its push for a Greater Serbia. The Albanians speak, at the most, of an Ethnic Albania, in line with the writings of Kosova scholar Rexhep Qosja (1936-), i.e., one corresponding simply to the areas of majority Albanian settlement.

There is no predominant view or opinion among the Albanians on the necessity or even the desirability of an Ethnic Albania. The opening of borders and the freer flow of goods and people in the region since the **Kosova War** have, at any rate, made any desire for political unification or reunification much less urgent.

GREECE, ALBANIANS IN. There are three distinct groups of Albanians in Greece: the old Arvanitika settlements dating from the late Middle Ages; Albanian speakers in the Greek-Albanian border region, in particular in **Çamëria**; and Albanian immigrants who have arrived in Greece in large numbers since 1990.

The traditional Albanian settlements in Greece are among the oldest diaspora settlements anywhere. In the mid-fourteenth century, Albanian tribes in large numbers migrated southwards into Greece, first into Epirus, Thessaly (1320), Acarnania and Aetolia. From there they continued eastwards into Boeotia (1350) and Attica, where, in 1382, the Catalonian rulers of the region gave them permission to settle and work the land. They also moved southwards across the gulf of Corinth into the Morea (Peloponnese). Manuel Cantacuzene (r. 1348-1380) of Mystra invited Albanian colonists to settle in the sparsely populated regions of Arcadia and Laconia and to serve as mercenaries against the Frankish principalities to the south. In 1402 and 1425, the Venetian rulers of Negropont (Euboea) also encouraged Albanian colonists to settle in southern Euboea. By the mid-fifteenth century, which marks the end of this process of colonization, the Albanians had settled in over half of Greece and indeed in such great numbers that in many regions they constituted the majority of the population. Only in the mid-nineteenth century did the Albanian **language** begin to give way to Greek. Austrian consul **Johann Georg von Hahn** reported in 1854 that "on the islands of Hydra, Spetsai, Poros and Salamis, the Albanians have such ethnically compact settlements that during the Greek war of liberation there were apparently no women at all who could understand Greek."

Although it has now disappeared from these islands, the Albanian language, known here as *Arbërisht* and in Greek as *Arvanitika*, can still be heard in many parts of central Greece. In all, there are said to be about 320 villages where *Arvanitika* is or until recently was spoken. Notable among them are settlements in Boeotia (especially around Levadhia), southern Euboea, Attica, Corinth and northern Andros. No official statistics exist as to the number of speakers, since the language does not enjoy any official status. *Arvanitika,* which is dying out rapidly, is thought to be the most archaic form of Albanian spoken anywhere today.

Aside from the Arvanitika settlements themselves, there are speakers of southern Albanian dialects, in particular Çamërian, in many settlements along the border region, from Florina (Alb. *Follorina*) and Kastoria (Alb. *Kosturi*) in the east, to Parga (Alb. *Parga*), Igoumenitsa (Alb. *Gumenica*) and Filiates (Alb. *Filati*) in the west on the Ionian Sea.

The third and most recent group, that of immigrants from Albania, far surpasses the first two in number and range of settlement. Since the opening of Albania in 1990-1991, virtually hundreds of thousands of Albanians have moved to Greece, legally or illegally, in search of work and a better life. Albanian is now the second most widely spoken language in Greece. According to statistics of the United Nations development Program, there were 350,000 to 400,000 Albanian emigrants in Greece in 1999. On 13 January 1998, an agreement was reached between the Greek and Albanian governments enabling Albanian children in Greece to be taught in their mother tongue.

GREECE, RELATIONS WITH. Greek colonists from Corfu and Corinth settled on the coast of Albania in the seventh century B.C. The colony of Epidamnos (**Durrës**) was founded in 627, and **Apollonia** a little later. Trade relations existed between Albania and Greece throughout antiquity. For centuries, Albania formed the political, military and cultural border between East and West, i.e., between the Roman Empire of the western Mediterranean, including much of the northern Balkans, and the Greek Empire of the eastern Mediterranean, including the southern Balkans. In the Middle Ages, most of Albania was once again under the sway of the Byzantine Greek Empire. In the mid-fourteenth century, Albanian tribes in large numbers migrated southwards into Greece, and by the mid-fifteenth century, they had settled in over half of Greece and indeed in such great numbers that in many regions they constituted the majority of the population. There were also Greek settlements in southern Albania, though they are difficult to date. At any rate, Albanian and Greek settlements were mixed throughout much of Epirus during the Ottoman period. In the first half of the nineteenth century, in particular in the age of **Ali Pasha Tepelena**, Janina was known as the capital of Albania.

Because of the mixed settlement patterns, the Greek-Albanian border region proved to be a stumbling block in Greek-Albanian relations throughout the twentieth century. Relations were particularly tense during the **Balkan Wars** and **World War I**, the period in which Albania attained independence. Indeed, on 27 November 1912, one day before the declaration of Albanian independence, Greek troops landed in **Saranda** and occupied the island of **Sazan**. Agreeing on a borderline between Greece and the new Albanian state proved to be a major problem, and the **Conference of Ambassadors** in London set up an **International Boundary Commission** (August to December 1913) to decide the matter.

In World War I, Greece was among the seven countries which invaded Albania in order to fill the power vacuum created by the collapse of **Turkey** in Europe, though Greek positions were soon occupied by **Italian** troops in the **Gjirokastra** region and French troops in **Korça**. Greece formally renounced possession of the Korça region in the Kapshtica agreement of 15 May 1920.

Despite some tension caused by the treatment of the **minorities**—the Albanian Çam minority in northwestern Greece and the **Greek minority** in southern Albania—relations between the two world wars were generally quiet.

On 28 October 1940, Italian troops, including 50,00 Albanian conscripts, invaded Greece from Albanian territory. By the end of 1940, they were driven back by Greek forces, which occupied Gjirokastra, Leskovik, Korça, and **Pogradec**. Greek positions in Albania were abandoned when **Germany** invaded Greece a year later, on 6 April 1941. In June 1944, the Albanian Muslim population of **Çamëria**, a total of 40,000 individuals, was expelled from Greece to Albania en masse and their property and assets were confiscated by the Greek authorities.

Greek-Albanian relations were complex after the **communist** takeover in Albania, due in particular to the long civil war in Greece and to resentment caused in Albania by the mass expulsion of the Albanian Çams, and in Greece by the miserable living conditions of the Greek minority in southern Albania. Border tensions were heightened by attempts made during the Cold War to infiltrate Albania from Greece. An agreement to clear mines in the **Corfu Channel** was finally reached between the two countries on 8 February 1958, but it was only in the 1970s that relations were normalized to some extent.

A trade agreement was signed on 24 June 1970, and diplomatic relations were resumed on 6 May 1971. On 18 July 1977, an aviation agreement was also signed, enabling regular flights between the two countries. Political relations stabilized in the

1980s, signaled in Albania by **Enver Hoxha**'s monograph *Two Friendly Peoples: Excerpts from the Political Diary and other Documents on Albanian-Greek Relations, 1941-1944* (Tirana 1985). Some practical border problems were settled and trade ties improved substantially. An Albanian trade delegation under Nedin Hoxha visited Greece on 18 to 22 November 1980, and this was reciprocated by a Greek delegation in Tirana on 11 to 15 December 1981.

Tension on the minorities' issue flamed up from time to time, stoked in particular by irredentist groups in Greece calling for *enosis*, the unification of so-called **Northern Epirus** with Albania. A bomb exploded at the Albanian embassy in Athens on 24 June 1983, and in a speech in Janina on 21 February 1984, Prime Minister Andreas Papandreou proclaimed that Greece would never tolerate infringements on the rights of the Greeks in Albania, but relations calmed down once again after a visit to **Tirana** by Greek foreign minister Karolos Papoulias. On 12 January 1985, the Kakavia border crossing was opened, and, on 28 August 1985, the state of war which still officially existed between the two countries, was finally declared over.

Since the fall of the dictatorship, relations with Greece have intensified in every sense. President Konstantinos Mitsotakis visited Albania on 13 to 14 January 1991, a year which saw the beginning of a mass and unprecedented exodus of Albanians to Greece. It is said that one-tenth of the population of Albania now lives in Greece, legally or illegally. The Albanian economy has been kept afloat to a good extent by remittances from Albanian workers in Greece, so good relations with Greece are essential. There are, however, still many problems to be solved—integrating Albanian immigrants in Greece, deciding on a legal status for them and reducing the high levels of crime they have brought with them.

GREEK MINORITY IN ALBANIA. The Greeks are the only substantial ethnic minority in Albania. They constitute over ninety percent of all non-Albanians in the country. The size of the Greek minority is traditionally estimated at about 50,000-80,000, although there are no reliable statistics, and some irredentist organizations in Greece indeed claim there are up to 200,000 Greeks in what they regard as Albanian-occupied **Northern Epirus**. According to the census of April 1989, there were 58,758 members of the Greek minority in Albania. Most Greek-speakers in Albania live in the southern districts of **Gjirokastra**, **Saranda**, and **Delvina**. In particular, there are compact, Greek-speaking villages in the **Drino** valley south of Gjirokastra and along the coast of **Himara**.

The Greek minority was officially recognized and well-integrated during the **communist** dictatorship. Many leading political figures in the country, then as now, were of Greek origin. The Greek government rightly complained about infringements on the human rights of the Greek minority in Albania, problems related primarily to schooling and **religion**, but most infringements under the dictatorship seem to have applied equally to Greeks and Albanians.

In February 1991, the **Omonia** association was officially recognized as the Democratic Union of the Greek Minority and won five seats in the **parliamentary** elections that year. At the same time, with the opening of the border, many Greeks, indeed probably the majority of them, emigrated to Greece in search of jobs and a better life.

In April 1994, political relations between the Albanian and Greek governments deteriorated substantially, primarily due to the effects of the mass immigration of Albanians to Greece and to the question of minority rights in the two countries, and this exacerbated in the situation of the remaining Greeks for a time during the regime of **Sali Berisha**. Things have since settled down, although latent tension remains, fostered primarily by irredentist groups in Greece which still call for the annexation of southern Albania by Greece.

GREZDA, QAMIL (1917-1992). Painter. Qamil Grezda was born in Gjakova. He moved to **Shkodra** at an early age with his family, and later to **Tirana**. He went to Italy to study economics but was accepted instead at the Academy of Fine Arts in Rome (1939), where he specialized as a painter. Grezda finished his studies in 1943 and returned to Albania, working first as a painter for the **National Theater**, then as a **museum** director and finally as an arts teacher at the Jordan Misja Academy. He is remembered primarily as a landscape painter, though he also did portraits of national heroes and revolutionary themes for the Party in the 1970s and 1980s.

GRUDA. Northern Albanian tribe and traditional tribal region. The Gruda region is now situated in Montenegro in the mountains along the Albanian border, east of Podgorica. It borders on the traditional tribal regions of **Hoti** and **Kelmendi** to the south and east, and on Slavic tribal regions to the north. The name was recorded in 1648 as *Grudi* and is related to Alb. *grudë* "soil, sod," from Slav. *gruda*. Gruda was a primarily **Catholic** tribe and, according to Baron **Franz Nopcsa**, had a **population** of some 7,000 in 1907.

GURAKUQI, KARL (1895.03.24-1971.12.06). Scholar. Karl Gurakuqi was born and raised in **Shkodra** where he attended the **Franciscan** college. In about 1908, he was sent to Austria where he attended a Franciscan seminary in Salzburg and the University of Graz. In 1917, he returned to Albania to teach and work as a school inspector in **Vlora** (1920). In December 1922, he was appointed as the first director of the **National Library**. In the following years, he edited a number of influential newspapers and periodicals. He also worked for the ministry of **education** and taught Albanian and Latin at the Queen Mother Pedagogical Institute (*Instituti Nanë Mbretneshë*) in **Tirana**. After **World War II**, he emigrated to **Italy** and served as professor of Albanian at the University of Palermo. Karl Gurakuqi is remembered not only for his many articles, school texts and translation, but also for his *Grammatica albanese dell'uso moderno* (Albanian Grammar for Modern Usage), Palermo 1958; and for his masterful anthology *Shkrimtarët shqiptarë* (Albanian Writers), Tirana 1941.

GURAKUQI, LUIGJ (1879.02.19-1925.03.02). Writer and major political figure of the **Rilindja** movement. Gurakuqi studied at the Saverian College run by the **Jesuits** in his native **Shkodra**. Encouraged by his teachers **Anton Xanoni** and Gaspër Jakova Merturi (1870-1941), he began writing poetry in Italian, Latin and Albanian, the latter being published in the Jesuit periodical of religious culture, *Elçija i Zemers t'Jezu Krisctit* (The Messenger of the Sacred Heart). In 1897, he left for **Italy** to study at the Italo-Albanian college of San Demetrio Corone under **Girolamo De Rada**, who was to exercise a strong influence on him. He also studied medicine in Naples for three years, but his interests were focused more on science and the humanities. In Naples, he came into contact with Arbëresh literary and political figures and published Albanian school texts and a book on prosody.

In 1908, after the revolution of the Young Turks, Gurakuqi returned definitively to Albania and soon became a leading figure in the nationalist movement, which led to the country's independence in 1912. Together with **Gjergj Fishta**, he represented the *Bashkimi* (Unity) literary society of Shkodra at the **Congress of Monastir** in 1908, and, in September 1909, he attended the Congress of Elbasan, which was held to organize Albanian-language teaching and education. When Albania's first teacher-training college, the Normal School (*Shkolla Normale*), was set up in **Elbasan** on 1 December 1909, it was Luigj Gurakuqi who was appointed its director. Gurakuqi was also one of the leaders of the northern Albanian uprising around Shkodra in 1911. He also took part in the uprising in southern Albania in 1912, and in March of that year traveled to Skopje and Gjakova to stir up support for open resistance to Turkish rule and for the inclusion of **Kosova** in a new Albanian state. Gurakuqi took part in the declaration of Albanian independence in **Vlora** on 28 November 1912 and served as minister of **education** in the first Albanian government, headed by **Ismail Qemal bey Vlora**.

In 1915, when his native Shkodra was occupied by Montenegrin troops, Gurakuqi was taken prisoner and jailed in Montenegro until after the invasion of Austro-Hungarian forces. In 1916, he played a role in the **Albanian Literary Commission** on Albanian orthography which also served to encourage the publication of Albanian-**language** school texts. During the Austro-Hungarian occupation of Shkodra, he served as director-general of education and assisted in establishing about 200 elementary schools. In 1918, Gurakuqi was again appointed minister of education in the newly formed **Durrës** government. The following year he attended the Paris Peace Conference. In 1921, he was appointed minister of the interior in the government of **Hasan bey Prishtina**, and, in 1924, minister of finance in the short-lived government of **Fan Noli**. In August 1924, Gurakuqi traveled to Geneva to defend Albanian interests at the League of Nations, but with the overthrow of Fan Noli's democratic administration by the more authoritarian Zogu forces, he was forced to flee to Italy and was murdered in Bari by one Baltjon Stambolla, no doubt an agent of **Ahmet Zogu**.

Luigj Gurakuqi served the national cause not only by playing an active role in public life but also by contributing informative articles to a good number of Albanian periodicals. He was, in addition, the author of both didactic and educational works and of poetry, much of which he published under the pseudonyms Lek Gruda and Jakin Shkodra. A collection of his verse, imbued with the strong patriotic emotion and sentimentality of romantic nationalism, was published posthumously in the ninety-four-page *Vjersha* (Verse), Bari 1940, by Gjikam, under the pseudonym of

Gjon Kamsi. The town of Shkodra has always been proud of Luigj Gurakuqi, and, on 29 May 1991, it named the newly founded university there after this great figure.

GUSHO, LLAZAR. *See* PORADECI, LASGUSH.

GUZZETTA, ANTONINO (1922-). Arbëresh scholar from Sicily who for many years held the chair of Albanian studies at the University of Palermo. Guzzetta is the author of *Tracce della lingua albanese del secolo XV nella documentazione veneta dell'epoca* (Traces of the Albanian Language in the Fifteenth Century in Venetian Documents of the Period), Palermo 1973, and *La parlata di Piana degli Albanesi* (The Dialect of Piana degli Albanesi), Palermo 1978, as well as many articles, in particular on the Albanian **language**. For years he organized international congresses of Albanian studies in Palermo and edited the publications thereof.

GYPSY MINORITY IN ALBANIA. *See* ROMA MINORITY IN ALBANIA.

- H -

HAHN, JOHANN GEORG VON (1811.07.11-1869.09.23). German scholar and father of Albanian studies. Hahn was born in Frankfurt am Main and studied law in Giessen and Heidelberg. From 1834 to 1843, he worked for the legal authorities of the newly founded Kingdom of Greece. From 1843 to 1847, he represented the Prussian consulate in Athens, and then transferred to the Austrian vice-consulate in Janina where he came into contact with the Albanians and began learning Albanian. Finally, in 1851, he was appointed Austrian consul on the island of Syros.

It was during his years in Janina that Hahn toured Albania three times and gathered information on Albanian history, philology and folklore. This vast amount of material was published in the seminal three-part *Albanesische Studien* (Albanian Studies), Jena 1854, which laid the foundations for multidisciplinary Albanian studies. He is also remembered for his *Griechische und albanesische Märchen* (Greek and Albanian Folk Tales), Leipzig

1864, and for accounts of his travels in the Balkans *Reise von Belgrad nach Salonik* (Journey from Belgrade to Salonica), Vienna 1861, and *Reise durch die Gebiete des Drin und Vardar* (Journey through the Region of the Drin and Vardar), Vienna 1867, 1869.

HAJDARI, AZEM (1963.03.11-1998.09.12). Political figure. Azem Hajdari was born in Bajram Curri in the District of **Tropoja**, which he later represented in **parliament**. He studied philosophy and law and was a leading figure of the democracy movement among the students in **Tirana** in 1990. He was a cofounder of the **Democratic Party** and was elected to parliament in 1991. From February 1991 to September 1992, he was vice-chairman of the Democratic Party, second only to **Sali Berisha**. From 1993 to 21 November 1996, he was head of the parliamentary committee for defense, public order and the secret service. On 5 November 1996, he was elected head of the independent trade union BSPSH. Though he remained a member of the Democratic Party, he was increasingly at odds with President **Berisha**.

　　Azem Hajdari was a controversial figure in politics and public life, with many friends and many foes. He was shot and injured on 18 September 1997 by fellow member of parliament, Gafur Mazreku, who was taking revenge for an earlier public insult by Hajdari. He was also shot at in Tropoja on 3 June 1998. A few months later, on 12 September 1998, Hajdari was then murdered, together with one of his bodyguards, by a police officer from Tropoja as he was leaving the headquarters of the Democratic Party in Tirana. This murder, which took place at a time of extreme political confrontation between the parties, was interpreted by the Democratic Party as a political assassination and Hajdari was made a martyr to the cause.

HALVETI ORDER OF DERVISHES. Islamic Sufi sect, or *tariqa*. The Halveti movement arose among Turkish, Kurdish and Iranian Sufis some time after the fourteenth century, founded according to legend by Ömer Halveti of Tabriz (d. 1397). The sect spread rapidly from the Caucasus to Egypt and Anatolia and from there into the Balkans. In Albania, the Halveti order was second only to the **Bektashi**. It is estimated to have had several thousand adepts at the beginning of the twentieth century, at about twenty-two sites throughout the country. The Halveti themselves, who were prone to asceticism and retreats, gave rise to a number of sub-groupings, many of which were present in Albania: the

Symbyli, the Gylçeni, the Karabashi, the Hayati and the Akbashi, the latter two being found exclusively in the Balkans.

The oldest Albanian Halveti *tekke* is that of Sheh Hashim in Janina, now in northern Greece, which was founded in 1390 by Ghazi Evrenos under the authority of Sultan Bayezid I (r. 1389-1403). This *tekke* continued to function up to 1943. There was also a Halveti *tekke* founded in **Vlora** in 1490 by Imrahor Ilyas bey, horse-master of Sultan Bayezid II (r. 1481-1512). The Halveti order spread through southern Albania in the first half of the sixteenth century. Of significance in its history were the *tekke* of Ohrid (1600), and the *tekke* of **Tirana**, said to have been founded in 1605 by Sheh Ali Pazari (1581-1615).

The Turkish traveler **Evliya Çelebi**, who visited Albania in the summer of 1670, noted the presence of the Halveti in **Gjirokastra**: "Around the courtyard (of the *Tekke* Mosque) are the cells of a Halveti *tekke* and on one side are the graves of many saints and notables" (*Seyahatname*, VIII, 354b). In **Berat**, Evliya Çelebi visited the two-storey Halveti *tekke* of Sheikh Hasan in the courtyard of the Sultan Mosque, Alb. *Xhamia e Mbretit*, and, in Vlora, he mentions the Halveti *tekke* of Yakub Efendi "with hundreds of devout dervishes, barefooted and bareheaded, with patched woollen cloaks." In **Elbasan**, Evliya Çelebi also visited the Halveti *tekke* of Sinan Pasha inside the mighty fortress, noting that it had numerous dervishes and endowments and was unmatched anywhere else.

With time, Vlora, Berat and Delvina became Halveti centers in themselves, and in the eighteenth century the sect spread from Albania to **Kosova** and Macedonia. Halveti *tekkes* were founded in Ohrid in 1667 and in Prizren in 1699-1700, the latter by Osman Baba of Serres. From there, the movement extended westwards back into Albania proper. Frederick William Hasluck (1878-1920) refers to Halveti pilgrimage sites at Nanga in the **Luma** region near **Kukës**, where Sheikh Hasan was the object of veneration, and at Vrepska. Of the many other Halveti *tekkes* known to have existed in Albania, mention may be made of those in Fshat, Surroj, Mat, Peshkopia, **Shkodra**, Tirana (the *tekke* of Sheikh Suleyman dating from ca. 1705), Elbasan (three *tekkes* from the late seventeenth century, of which two still existed before **World War I**), Berat (the above-mentioned *tekke* of Sheikh Hasan at the Sultan Mosque, the present building of which was constructed by Kurd Ahmed Pasha in 1785, and the *tekke* of Sheikh Musa Efendi at Kara Kasim), Bilisht (two or three *tekkes* dependent on Ohrid), Progër, Shëngjergj between Bilisht and **Pogradec**, **Korça** (a *tekke* founded at the end of the fifteenth century), Leskovik (a *tekke* founded in 1796-1797, but which burnt down in the early years of the twentieth century), **Përmet, Tepelena**, Luzat, Mezhgoran, Ramica, Vinokash, Tosk-Martalloz, Maricaj, Gjirokastra, Delvina and **Saranda**. The two latter *tekkes* were destroyed in the 1950s.

The Halveti order was reestablished in Albania in 1990 and is presently led by Sheh Muamer Pazari (1929-) of Tirana, where a *tekke* was opened in 1992. In 1998, there were a total of forty-two Halveti *tekkes* in Albania, most of which are in the south, though there are also sites in **Tropoja**, Burrel and Peshkopia.

HARALLAMBI, KRISTO. *See* NEGOVANI, KRISTO (PAPA).

HARAPI, ANTON (1888.01.05-1946.02.15). Writer and political figure. Anton or Ndue Harapi was born in Shiroka and educated in **Shkodra** and in Tyrol by the **Franciscans**. From 1923 to 1931, he taught at the Franciscan college in Shkodra and was its director. In October 1943, he was appointed as a member of the High Regency Council (*Këshilli i Lartë i Regjencës*) under German occupation. He was executed in **Tirana** by the **communist** regime. As a writer, Harapi is remembered for the short novel *Valë mbi valë* (Wave upon Wave) serialized in the periodical *Hylli i dritës* (The Day-Star) from 1939 to 1942, and for the 222-page *Andrra e Prêtashit* (Prêtashi's Dream), Rome 1959, a prose work published posthumously in twenty-two chapters.

HARAPI, TONIN (1928.07.08-1992.07.30). Composer. Tonin Harapi was born in **Shkodra** and attended the **Jesuit** Saverian college there, initially wanting to become a priest. He later attended the Jordan Misja Academy in **Tirana** from 1946 to 1951, and studied composition at the Tchaikovsky Conservatory in Moscow from 1959 until political relations between Albania and the **Soviet Union** were broken off in 1961. He finally graduated from the Tirana conservatory in 1964. From then on, until retirement, he taught composition at the Academy of Fine Arts, making a significant contribution to modern Albanian **music**. Harapi is the author of vocal and instrumental works, including operas, rhapsodies, suites, cantatas and light music.

HARFF, ARNOLD VON (ca. 1471-1505). German traveler and chronicler. Arnold von Harff was a German knight, traveler, and writer born of a noble family in the lower Rhineland (at Harff on the Erft, northwest of Cologne) who was one of the first people to put the Albanian **language** in writing. In the autumn of 1496, von Harff had set out on a journey, ostensibly a pilgrimage to the Holy Land, which took him to Italy, down the Adriatic coast to Greece, Egypt, Arabia, Palestine, Asia Minor and then back through central Europe to France and Spain. He returned to Cologne in the autumn of 1498 or 1499 and died in 1505. During his travels, von Harff collected material on the languages he encountered. On a stopover in the port of **Durrës** in the spring of 1497, he jotted down twenty-six words, eight phrases, and twelve numbers in Albanian, which he recorded in his travel journal with a German translation. The account of his journey is considered one of the best examples of the period of this genre of travel narrative, which was very popular at the end of the Middle Ages. Von Harff showed a consistent interest in foreign customs and languages during his travels, giving, in addition to the Albanian material, short lexicons of words and phrases in Croatian, Greek, Arabic, Hebrew, Turkish, Hungarian, Basque and Breton.

HAS, DISTRICT OF. Region of local government administration. The District of Has (*Rrethi i Hasit*), with its administrative headquarters in the town of Kruma, borders on the districts of **Puka** to the west, **Tropoja** to the north, and **Kukës** to the south, and on **Kosova** to the east. It has a surface area of 393 square kilometers and a present **population** of 21,043 (in 2000). It is the least populated district in Albania. The term, in the definitive form "Hasi," was recorded in 1570 as Hassi. The Hasi tribe are noted in Kosova for the colorful costumes of their women, in particular on market day in Prizren.

HASLUCK, MARGARET (1885-1948.10.18). Scottish scholar and anthropologist. Margaret Masson Hardie Hasluck was born in Drumblade of a strict Christian family and grew up in the Moray countryside near Elgin in northern Scotland. She studied at Aberdeen University and then at Newnham Collage, Cambridge, where she completed a degree in Classics. In 1910, she won a scholarship to study at the British School of Archaeology in Athens and took part in archeological excavations in Anatolia under William Ramsay. It was at the British School that she met archeologist and orientalist Frederick William Hasluck (1878-1920), whom she married in 1912. In 1915, her husband quit the British School and joined the Intelligence Department of the British Legation in Athens. He died in a Swiss sanatorium of tuberculosis in 1920, and it was Margaret who edited and published his *magnum opus* entitled *Christianity and Islam under the Sultans,* Oxford 1929. In 1921, Margaret Hasluck received two fellowships from Aberdeen University, which enabled her to travel and work in the Balkans, initially to collect folk tales in Macedonia.

From 1923 onwards, she spent most of her years in Albania. In 1935, she settled in **Elbasan,** where she bought land and built a house. She was a close friend and, as rumor has it in Elbasan today, the lover of scholar **Lef Nosi. Enver Hoxha,** at any rate, called her "Nosi's mistress." Hasluck spent thirteen years in Elbasan, returning once or twice a year to Britain to give lectures at the Folklore Society and to visit her family.

In April 1939, she was forced to flee Albania in the wake of the **Italian** invasion, leaving her home and her 3,000-book library to the care of Nosi. In Athens, she worked for the Press Office of the British Embassy and, in view of her unique knowledge of Albania, was able to establish contacts with Albanian resistance leaders. In February 1943, she was recruited in Cairo to help set up an Albanian section of the **Special Operations Executive** (SOE). There, until February 1944, she was active writing reports and assessments on Albania and in briefing SOE operatives. In May of that year, she returned to London, ill with leukemia, and died in Dublin.

Of Margaret Hasluck's scholarly publications, mention may be made of the now rather outdated *Këndime Englisht-Shqip or Albanian-English Reader: Sixteen Albanian Folk-stories, Collected and Translated, with two Grammars and Vocabularies.* Cambridge 1931; and the rare *Albanian Phrase Book,* London 1944. She published numerous articles on Albanian folk culture in *Man—the Journal of the Royal Anthropological Society* and elsewhere. Hasluck is now remembered primarily for her *The Unwritten Law in Albania: A Record of the Customary Law of the Albanian Tribes,* Cambridge 1954, the first English-language monograph devoted to Albanian **customary law** and the *Kanun.*

HAXHIADEMI, ET'HEM (1902.03.08-1965.03.17). Playwright and poet. Et'hem Haxhiademi from **Elbasan** is remembered as the best playwright of the independence period. He was sent to Italy in 1919, where he attended school in Lecce before moving on to Austria. He finished secondary school in Innsbruck in 1924 and studied political science in Berlin. In 1927, he returned to Albania and was appointed deputy prefect of **Lushnja.** Haxhiademi worked for the **prefectures** of **Gjirokastra** and

Berat in 1933-1936. In 1940, he was appointed director of municipal government at the ministry of the interior and was a member of the new Institute of Albanian Studies in **Tirana**. In 1945, immediately after the war, he was made an executive member of the newly formed **Writers' Union** and became head of its Elbasan chapter. He also taught Albanian at the Normal School (*Shkolla Normale*) in Elbasan in 1946.

In the witch hunts of 1946-1947, Haxhiademi was arrested and sentenced to death. His library and manuscripts were confiscated. At the intercession of the influential **Aleksandër Xhuvani** and **Omer Nishani**, his sentence was converted to life in prison. He died in 1965, having worked in Burrel concentration camp for many years as a translator.

Haxhiademi was the author of a remarkable hexameter translation of Vergil's Bucolics (1932) and of a seventy-three-page volume of wistful poetry entitled *Lyra* (The Lyre), Tirana 1939. His solid western European education nonetheless found its optimal expression in his classical tragedies based on Greek and Latin models. Haxhiademi's first three five-act tragedies were published as a trilogy: *Ulisi* (Ulysses), Tirana 1931, written in Berlin in 1924; *Akili* (Achilles), Tirana 1931, written in Vienna in 1926; and *Aleksandri* (Alexander), Tirana 1931, written in Lushnja in 1928. Next came *Pirrua* (Pyrrhus), written in Gjirokastra in 1934, a tragedy on a theme already treated by **Mihal Grameno** in 1906 and **Kristo Floqi** in 1923. The five-act *Skënderbeu* (Scanderbeg), Tirana 1935, completed in Gjirokastra on 1 May 1935, was followed by two elegant masterpieces, *Diomedi* (Diomedes), Tirana 1936; and *Abeli* (Abel), 1939, in hendecasyllabic verse. Though treating figures of ancient history and mythology, Haxhiademi regarded them as somehow part of Albania's own heritage.

With the tragedies of Haxhiademi, Albanian actors for the first time had material which transcended the trite nationalist dramas and sentimental outpourings of the late **Rilindja** period. Though the general public may have preferred the light-hearted farces of middle-class mores offered to them by Kristo Floqi, the hollow nationalism of Mihal Grameno, and the pathetic sentimentality of **Foqion Postoli**, Etëhem Haxhiademi's tragedies were not unappreciated. They were much performed throughout the 1930s and early 1940s, initially by amateur groups stemming from the Normal School (*Shkolla Normale*) in Elbasan, but later also in Tirana and elsewhere.

HAXHIHASANI, QEMAL (1916.08.16-1991.02.02). Scholar and folklore expert. Qemal Haxhihasani was born in **Elbasan**, where he attended the Normal School (*Shkolla Normale*). He studied at the University of Florence and, in 1949, was appointed to the Institute of Science, forerunner of the University of **Tirana**. From 1960 on, he served as head of the section for oral **literature** and thereafter at the Institute of Folk Culture. Haxhihasani was the leading specialist in oral literature in Tirana for almost half a century and collaborated in virtually all publications in the field there. Among the many volumes of oral literature he edited alone or with colleagues are: *Këngë popullore legjendare* (Legendary Folk Songs), Tirana 1955, *Këngë popullore historike* (Historical Folk Songs), Tirana 1956; *Epika legjendare: cikli i kreshnikëve, 1-3* (The Legendary Epic: the Cycle of the Frontier Warriors, 1-3), Tirana 1966, 1983; *Tregime dhe këngë popullore për Skënderbeun* (Tales and Folk Songs on **Scanderbeg**), Tirana 1967; *Epika historike, 1-3* (Historical Epic, 1-3), Tirana 1981, 1983, 1990; *Balada popullore shqiptare* (Albanian Folk Ballads), Tirana 1982; *Chansonnier épique albanais* (Albanian Epic Songs), Tirana 1983; *Folklor kosovar 1: epikë historike kosovare* (Kosova Folklore, 1: Kosova Historical Epic), Tirana 1985; and *Lirika popullore, 1* (Folk Lyrics, 1), Tirana 1988.

HAZBIU, KADRI (1922.07.15-1983.09). Political figure of the **communist** period. Hazbiu was born in Mavrova near **Vlora**, where he graduated from the commercial school in 1942. He joined the communist partisan movement during **World War II** and trained at a Soviet military academy from 1946 to 1948. On his return to Albania, he served as deputy minister of the interior from 1949, and minister of the interior from 1954 to April 1980. He was also head of the notorious secret service, **Sigurimi**. Hazbiu was a full member of the Central Committee from 1952 to 1982 and a full member of the Politburo from 1971 to 1982. He served as minister of defense from April 1980 to 14 October 1982 when, having been accused of involvement in a purge against the "anti-**Shehu** group," he was tried for high treason and executed the following year at Linza near **Tirana**.

HEALTH CARE. Albania now spends 2.4 percent of its gross domestic product on health care (1999), though, as in most countries, needs are much greater than the funds available. There are fifty-one hospitals in the country and 2,191 other health care centers. As of 1999, the country had a total of 4,325 physicians,

1,425 dentists, 1,042 pharmacists and 12,774 nurses and midwives. As to other institutions, there were 779 pharmacies, 99 medical clinics, 621 dental clinics and fifteen medical laboratories. Under the **communist** dictatorship, there was a local, though very basic public health care center in almost every village in the country, with at least one nurse and midwife on duty. Since that time, in view of urbanization and funding problems in the health care sector, there has been a tendency to centralize services, i.e., less local and more regional hospitals and health care centers.

HERBERT, AUBREY (1880.04.03-1923.09.23). British public figure, diplomat and writer. Aubrey Nigel Henry Molyneux Herbert was the half-brother of Lord Carnarvon of Tutenkhamen fame. Born of an aristocratic family, he attended Eton from April 1893 to 1898 when he went on to study history at Balliol College in Oxford. He worked as an honorary attaché at the British embassies in Tokyo (1902) and Constantinople (1904), and traveled extensively throughout the **Ottoman Empire**. In Thessalonika, he first met the Albanian Kiazim Kokeli, who became his servant and intimate longtime companion. It was Kokeli, described as a wild Albanian highlander, who instilled in him an interest in Albania.

As a conservative candidate, Herbert was elected to the British Parliament in November 1911 and helped make the Albanian cause known there over the next decade. In 1912 and 1913, he traveled to the Balkans. At the time of the **Conference of Ambassadors** in London in 1913, he founded an Albanian Committee to guide the Albanian delegation in its negotiations with the Great Powers and to act as a pressure group to raise funds and draw attention to the appalling situation in Albania. This Albanian Committee evolved into the Anglo-Albanian Society (1918), of which Herbert was president, and finally into the **Anglo-Albanian Association**. It was in 1913 that Herbert first met **Edith Durham** with whom he collaborated in relief efforts. He was also a friend of Isa Boletini. By this time, he had become something of a national hero in Albania, and his name was being mentioned increasingly in connection with the vacant Albanian throne. During his final stay in Albania, as an army colonel, he spent three months in **Vlora** (June to August 1918). From the end of **World War I** to his death, he served as a champion of the Albanian cause, acting, among other things, as an advisor to the Albanian delegation at the Paris Peace Conference.

After Herbert's untimely death, his mother, Elizabeth, Countess of Carnarvon, founded a British-Albanian Relief Committee and carried on relief work in Albania herself, in particular in the fight against malaria. She also financed the first public library in the country, the Herbert Library in **Tirana**, which later became known as the Herbert Institute. In **Kavaja**, Lady Carnarvon founded a village for refugees from **Kosova**. This village, now called Helmas, was known at the time by the name of Herbert in honor of her son.

Aubrey Herbert is the author of the volume *Ben Kendim, a Record of Eastern Travels,* London 1924. His biography, written by his granddaughter Margaret Fitzherbert, was published under the title *The Man Who Was Greenmantle,* London 1983.

HETZER, ARMIN (1941.12.27-). German scholar, linguist and literary historian. Armin Hetzer was born in Bad Godesberg near Bonn. He graduated from secondary school at St. Wendel in the Saarland in 1961 and studied at the universities of Bonn, Cologne and Göttingen, specializing in Slavic, Chinese and philosophy. He completed his masters in Sinology in 1969, his doctorate in 1972 and his habilitation in 1994. He has been actively involved in Albanian studies since 1975. Armin Hetzer worked from 1972 to 2000 as a librarian at the university library in Bremen. Since November 2002, he has been professor of general linguistics at the University of Bremen, specializing in the languages of southeastern Europe. His Albanological monographs have been concentrated in the fields of **language**: *Lehrbuch der vereinheitlichten albanischen Schriftsprache* (Manual of the Unified Albanian Literary Language), Hamburg 1989; *Albanisch-deutsches und deutsch-albanisches Taschenwörterbuch* (Albanian-German and German-Albanian Pocket Dictionary), Hamburg 1990; and *Nominalisierung und verbale Einbettung in Varietäten des Albanischen* (Nominalization and Verbal Embedding in Varieties of Albanian), Wiesbaden 1995; and cultural studies: *Aspekte der Subjektivität in der albanischen Kulturpolitik, 1965-1975* (Aspects of Subjectivity in Albanian Cultural Policies, 1965-1975), Bremen 1979; and *Geschichte des Buchhandels in Albanien: Prologomena zu einer Literatursoziologie* (History of the Book Trade in Albania: Prolegomena to a Sociology of Literature), Berlin 1985. Hetzer is also the coauthor of the bibliography *Albania: A Bibliographic Research Survey with Location Codes,* Munich 1983. His many articles on Albanian literary history have been refreshingly critical.

HIBBERT, REGINALD Sir (1922.02.21-2002.10.05). British military officer and historian. Born in Hertfordshire, Sir Reginald Alfred Hibbert was educated at Queen Elizabeth College in Barnet and at Worcester College, Oxford, where he completed a degree in history in 1946. During **World War II**, he served as a British liaison officer at the Stables Mission of the **Special Operations Executive** in northern Albania and was parachuted into the country in December 1943 to help maintain contacts with Albanian resistance fighters. After the war, he joined the foreign service and held appointments in Bucharest, Vienna, Guatemala, Ankara, Brussels, Ulan Bator (1964-1969), Singapore (1969) and Bonn. He ended his diplomatic career as British ambassador to France (1979-1982) and retired in Wales. Hibbert's insider view of the Albanian civil war during German occupation in 1943-1944 is described in his book *Albania's National Liberation Struggle: The Bitter Victory,* London 1991, the first objective history of the period.

HIMA, DERVISH (1873-1928). Publisher and nationalist figure. Dervish Hima, pseudonym of Ibrahim Mehmet Naxhi, was from Struga on Lake **Ohrid**. He attended school in Monastir (Bitola) and Thessalonika, and studied medicine for two years in Istanbul, where he initially supported the Young Turk movement and began to reflect on the Albanian question. From 1895 until **World War I**, he wandered indefatigably from country to country, propagating the Albanian cause with articles and pamphlets. Dervish Hima was an extreme opponent of Ottoman rule in Albania and author of a number of radical manifestos calling for an all-out struggle against the Porte. As such, his movements were carefully observed by the Ottoman authorities and he was imprisoned on several occasions. In Bucharest, he edited the short-lived periodical *Pavarësia e Shqipërisë* (The Independence of Albania), which appeared in 1898 in Albanian, French and Romanian. In October of the following year, he was obliged to leave Romania for Rome where he collaborated with Mehmed bey Frashëri in the fortnightly *Zën'i Shqipënisë* (Voice of Albania), which was issued in French and Albanian. In 1903, Dervish Hima published the fortnightly periodical *L'Albanie* in Geneva, which he continued as a monthly from 1905 to 1906 in Brussels. In 1909, he was in Istanbul, where he ran the weekly *Shqipëtari-Arnavud* (The Albanian) with **Hilë Mosi**, a periodical in Turkish and Albanian subsidized by Austria-Hungary. This journal lasted until it was banned at the end of 1910. Dervish Hima took an active interest in public life even after Albanian independence in November 1912. In the autumn of 1917, he was appointed school inspector for the **Tirana** district by the Austro-Hungarian authorities and, in 1920, became the first director of the Albanian press office.

HIMARA. Geographical region. Himara refers to the mountainous coastal region of southern Albania from the Llogara Pass south of **Vlora** down to **Saranda**. The rugged coast of Himara, with several beautiful Albanian and Greek-speaking villages, including the little town of Himara itself, is considered to be one of the most attractive parts of Albania and has great potential for **tourism**. The word "Himara" derives from ancient Greek χειμάρροος, meaning "ravine."

HOBHOUSE, JOHN CAMERON (1786.06.17-1869.06.03). British traveler and writer. John Cameron Hobhouse, also known as Lord Broughton, was born near Bristol. He was educated at Westminster School and attended Trinity College, Cambridge, where he founded the Whig Club and an Amicable Society. It was at Cambridge that he met and befriended the poet **Lord Byron**. In 1809-1810, he accompanied Byron on a tour to Albania, Greece and Turkey, in particular to the court of **Ali Pasha Tepelena** in Janina and as far north as **Tepelena**. Hobhouse later became a member of parliament, served as secretary for war in the cabinet of Earl Grey in 1832 and held positions in later governments. The memoirs of his travels to Albania with Byron were published in the volume *A Journey through Albania and Other Provinces of Turkey in Europe and Asia to Constantinople during the Years 1809 and 1810,* London 1813, which was re-edited as *Travels in Albania and the Other Provinces of Turkey in 1809 and 1810,* London 1858, and as *A Journey through Albania,* New York 1971.

HODGKINSON, HARRY (1913.03.15-1994.10.02). British journalist and writer. Harry Hodgkinson was born in Kirkham, Lancashire, and began writing for newspapers at an early age. In 1936, he walked on foot from Charing Cross in London to Damascus Gate in Jerusalem and published short stories of his travels in the *Christian Science Monitor, The Times* and the *Guardian*. He visited Albania in 1937, fell in love with the country, and joined the **Anglo-Albanian Association** on his return to England, corresponding for many years with **Edith Durham**. Hodgkinson joined the Navy in 1942 and with the collapse of

Benito Mussolini's regime in Italy was transferred to the **Special Operations Executive** in Bari. He operated in Yugoslavia and Albania during and after the German occupation. After the war, he continued working for Naval Intelligence under Ian Fleming and took charge of the Yugoslav and Albanian desk, being closely involved in the **Corfu Channel incident** in 1946. In 1955, he left the Navy and worked in the petroleum industry until retirement in 1972. Thereafter, he devoted most of his time to the Anglo-Albanian Association, of which he became president in 1985. Hodgkinson is the author of *The Adriatic Sea,* London 1955; and a biography of *Scanderbeg,* London 1999. Other manuscripts of Albanological interest have remained unpublished.

HOTI. Northern Albanian tribe and traditional tribal region. The Hoti region is situated in the District of **Malësia e Madhe** along the road from the Albanian-Montenegrin border-crossing Han i Hotit ("The Inn of Hoti") and Bajza up the valley to the northeast to Rapsh-Starja, leading towards Vermosh. It borders on the traditional tribal regions of **Gruda** to the north, **Kelmendi** to the northeast and **Kastrati** to the south. The name Hoti was recorded in 1330. In 1474, the region was mentioned as *montanee octorum, montanea ottanorum* (Mountain of the Hotis). The Hoti tribe, traditionally **Catholic,** had a **population** of about 4,000 in 1842.

HOXHA, ENVER (1908.10.16-1985.04.11). Political figure and leader of **communist** Albania. Enver Hoxha was the son of a merchant. He was born and raised in **Gjirokastra** and went to secondary school at the French lycée in **Korça** from 1927 to 1930. In 1930-1931, he won a government scholarship to study biochemistry in Montpellier in southern France. According to communist hagiography, he was expelled from the university for his revolutionary activity. Recent information has shown, however, that he simply failed his first-year exams, and the Albanian minister of **education, Mirash Ivanaj,** cut off his scholarship as of the end of March 1934. Hoxha later worked for a time as a watchman at the Albanian consulate in Brussels. In 1936, he returned to Albania and made his living as a teaching assistant in **Tirana** and Korça.

It was in Korça that Enver Hoxha came into direct contact with the communist movement, which sent him to Tirana to set up a group there. In Tirana, he worked at the Flora tobacco shop as a front for the new communist cell (1940-1941). He was a founding member of the Albanian communist party on 8 November 1941 and was elected to its initial central committee. He also edited the first edition of the communist newspaper *Zëri i popullit* (The People's Voice) on 25 August 1942. In 1943, he became general secretary of the party, and in May 1944, was chairman of the Antifascist National Liberation Army, leading communist forces to victory both against German troops and against the rival **Balli Kombetar**.

After the liberation of Tirana and communist takeover on 28 November 1944, Enver Hoxha assumed the position of prime minister in several successive administrations and was initially also minister of defense (1944-1953) and minister of foreign affairs (1946-1953). He was commander-in-chief of the Albanian armed forces from 1945 to 1985.

In the immediate postwar years, Hoxha vied with other communist figures for party leadership, notably with **Koçi Xoxe**, who had the support of Tito during the brief Albanian-Yugoslav alliance from 1946 to 1948. Hoxha allied himself tactically with Joseph Stalin, whom he met five times between 1947 and 1951 and whom he came to emulate. It was only after the rupture of relations with Yugoslavia and the beginning of the Soviet-Albanian alliance that Enver Hoxha was certain of complete control. His personal identification with Stalin was so strong that the Albanian party leadership refused to de-Stalinize with the rest of eastern Europe in 1956 when the extent of Stalin's crimes in Russia became more than apparent. In October 1956, Hoxha and his closest party ally **Mehmet Shehu** traveled to **China** to lay the foundations for a new alliance in order to offset Albania's increasing dependence on the Soviet Union. This new Sino-Albanian alliance came into force in 1961 and lasted for seventeen years, during which Hoxha reigned unchallenged over his little Balkan country, now hermetically isolated from the rest of Europe.

Enver Hoxha's uncompromisingly radical policies of Marxist revolution and perpetual class struggle, involving purge after purge until no one, even within the party, dared to oppose him, were not a reflection of conviction or ideology, but rather simply a means of maintaining personal power. By the time of his death on 11 April 1985, the nation was exhausted, the few surviving intellectuals were intimidated, passive and silent, and the economy was on the verge of collapse.

A reliable biography of Enver Hoxha and his times has yet to be written, but history will certainly not treat him kindly. He had an inestimable influence on the country's development for four decades and is regarded by most Albanians today as personally responsible for the nation's woeful state.

Enver Hoxha was a prolific writer, author of seventy-one volumes of "Works" published in Tirana from 1968 to 1990. He was survived by his wife **Nexhmije Hoxha**, two sons, and one daughter.

HOXHA, NEXHMIJE (1921.02.08-). Political figure of the **communist** period. Nexhmije Hoxha, birth name Nexhmije Xhuglini, was born in Monastir (Bitola), now in the Republic of Macedonia. She graduated from the Queen Mother Pedagogical Institute (*Instituti Nanë Mbretneshë*) in 1941 and taught elementary school in **Tirana** from 1941 to 1942. She joined the communist party in 1941 and took part in the resistance movement as a youth and **women**'s organizer. From 1946 to 1955 Nexhmije Hoxha headed the Albanian Women's Union and, from 1952 to 1966, occupied a variety of party functions in propaganda, press, **education** and culture. From 1966 to 1992, she headed the Institute of Marxist-Leninist Studies in Tirana and, from 1986 to 1990, was president of the Democratic Front (*Fronti Demokratik*).

Nexhmije Hoxha was a member of the Central Committee from 1948 to 1991. As the wife of party leader **Enver Hoxha**, she played a major role in the political life of the country both during her husband's lifetime and in the years following his death. After the fall of the dictatorship, she was arrested on 5 December 1991 and, after a trial in Tirana lasting from 8 to 27 January 1993, she was sentenced to nine years in prison, officially for corruption in the misfeasance of about US$75,000 in state funds. After release from prison on 10 January 1997, she lived as a recluse in the Tirana suburb of Lapraka and now has an apartment in the former *Bllok* neighborhood.

HULD, MARTIN. American scholar and linguist. Martin E. Huld finished his B.A. in English at California State University in Los Angeles in 1972. In 1979, he completed his doctorate there in Indo-European linguistics with, as his dissertation, *An Etymological Glossary of Selected Albanian Terms.* This work served as the basis for his best-known publication in Albanian studies: *Basic Albanian Etymologies,* Columbus 1984. Huld is currently assistant professor at the Department of English of California State University in Los Angeles.

HYDROELECTRIC POWER. *See* ELECTRICITY PRODU-
CTION.

- I -

IBRAHIMI, FEIM (1935.10.20-1997.08.02). Composer. Feim
Ibrahimi was born in **Gjirokastra** and studied at the state conservatory in **Tirana** from 1962 to 1966, where he worked until 1977.
From 1977 to 1991, he was **music** secretary of the Albanian
Union of Writers and Artists, and from 1991 to 1992 was artistic director of the national **Opera and Ballet Theater.** From
1989 to 1992, he headed the Albanian music committee as part of
the International Council of Music. Ibrahimi is remembered for
his vocal and symphonic compositions, in particular contemporary chamber and **film** music.

IDROMENO, KOLË (1860.08.15-1939.12.12). Painter, photographer and architect. Kolë Idromeno is perhaps the best-known of
the early figures of Albanian painting. He was born in **Shkodra**
and began drawing and doing water colors at an early age (1871-
1874). With the help of **Pjetër Marubi,** from whom he also
learned the art of photography, he was able to travel to Venice in
1875 to attend the Academy of Fine Arts, but he did not survive
the rigors of formal training and gave up after six months. He
remained in Venice, though, and worked for a couple of years as
the assistant to an established Venetian painter, returning to
Albania in 1878. In 1883, he opened a photo studio with cameras
imported from the Pathé company in France. In 1912, he became
the first person in Albania to import moving picture equipment
and to show **films.** In August of that year, he signed a contract
with the Josef Stauber company in Austria to set up the country's
first, rudimentary public cinema. As a painter, Idromeno preferred urban subjects, such as in his *Dasma shkodrane* (Shkodra
Wedding), 1924, but also did portraits of intellectuals and nationalist figures. Particularly well-known is the portrait of his half-
veiled *Motra Tone* (Sister Tone), 1883. Landscapes and religious
subjects also occur. His paintings were shown at international art
exhibitions in Budapest (1898), Rome (1925), Bari (1931), Rome

(1936) and New York (1939). Kolë Idromeno is also remembered as a sculptor and as an architect of public buildings in Shkodra.

ILLIA, FRANO (1918.02.21-1997.10.22). Catholic religious figure and writer. Dom Frano Illia was appointed by the pope on 25 April 1993 as Archbishop of **Shkodra** and Primate of the Catholic Church in Albania. He had been sentenced to death by the regime of **Enver Hoxha** for spying for the Vatican, i.e., refusing to renounce his faith during the **communist** party's campaign against **religion**, and spent decades in prison. Illia was also a writer and scholar. Aside from religious works, he is remembered for his publication of the *Kanuni i Skanderbegut* (The Kanun of **Scanderbeg**), Brescia 1993, as well as for the novel *Dava* (The Dispute), Shkodra 1996, written in **Gheg** dialect.

ILLYRIANS. Ancient inhabitants of the western Balkans. The Illyrians of the fifth and fourth centuries B.C. were a collection of tribes who have not been entirely identified by archeologists. They spoke an Indo-European language, of which few remains have survived, mostly personal and place names. Their territory stretched from the northern Adriatic down to Albania, the three main districts being Dalmatia, Iapydia and Liburnia. An Illyrian kingdom was created ca. 383 B.C. and survived, despite internal dissension and a growing conflict with Macedon and Rome, until it was conquered and subjected by the Romans in about 168 B.C. Among the rulers of Illyria who have entered the annals of Albanian history are Agron, Teuta and **Genthius**. The Albanians derive their ethnic origins from the ancient Illyrians, although there is no convincing proof of this, one way or the other.

IMAMI, ARBEN (1958.01.21-). Actor, political figure and high-ranking member of the **Democratic Alliance Party**. Arben Imami was born in **Tirana** and, after studies at the Academy of Fine Arts (*Instituti i Lartë i Arteve*), worked for the **National Theater**, 1980-1987. In the **film** industry, he appeared in major roles in *Ballë per ballë* (Face to Face), 1979; *Në çdo stinë* (In Every Season), 1980; and *Të shoh në sy* (I'm Looking into Your Eye), 1985.

Imami played an important part in the democracy movement in 1990, and became a leading figure of the **Democratic Party** and a member of **parliament** for that party from 1991 to 1992. In 1992, he joined the Democratic Alliance Party, which evolved out of the Democratic Party, and from 1992 to 1997 was its general secretary. In the government cabinet of 25 July 1997, he was appointed state secretary for legislation reform and relations with the national assembly.

INDUSTRY. Albania had little industry to speak of until the **communist** period. Before **World War II**, there were only cottage industries catering to **agriculture** and animal husbandry, as well as to the direct needs of private consumers. Among these existing small industries were dairies, soap factories, flour mills, fish canneries, wagon works, cigarette factories, brick works, breweries and distilleries.

Things changed dramatically in the communist period. Adhering to Soviet economic theory, the Albanian leadership gave priority to the exploitation of natural resources (mining and hydroelectric power) and to setting up heavy industry rather than light industry and manufacturing. The processing of natural resources began in the 1960s. Among the notable industrial projects of the communist period were the first **oil** refineries in Ballsh and **Fier**; a copper wire plant in **Shkodra**, 1965; and finally, the largest of all, the huge iron and steel works at **Elbasan**, 1978, called *Çeliku i Partisë* (The Steel of the Party), with 12,000 employees. The Elbasan project was begun by the **Russians** and after 1961 was carried on by the **Chinese**. Though operational by 1978, it was never really finished and closed down in 1991.

Since 1991, there has been no new production, though many attempts have been made to maintain existing industries (energy, mining and oil). *See also* MINERAL RESOURCES.

INTERNATIONAL BOUNDARY COMMISSION (1913). The International Boundary Commission was set up in August 1913 by the **Conference of Ambassadors** in London to study the ethnicity of the **population** of southern Albania and northern **Greece (Northern Epirus)**, and fix an exact border between Albania and Greece. **Edwin Jacques** (1995, p. 337-338), quoting Sevasti **Qiriazi**-Dako, noted, "Their work was greatly complicated in the south by the obsession of the Greeks that persons identified with the Greek **Orthodox** religion were therefore Greeks. Sevasti Kyrias Dako reported that when the commissioners reached Monastir that October en route to Korcha, she contacted an acquaintance of Mr. Bilinski, the Austrian representative, to inform him of the Greek strategy to represent Korcha population as Greek. After the colorful Greek-inspired demonstrations, Mr. Bilinski suggested to his colleagues a stroll in the city. When they entered the Greek school yard where the children were playing, he threw in their midst a handful of small coins. The children rushed to pick them up, and in their excitement forgot to speak Greek, but spoke Albanian, their mother tongue. This was enough to convince the commission." The Commission finished its work in December 1913 and submitted its report in Florence, Italy. The resulting border line satisfied no one, with much traditional Albanian territory and many Albanian settlements (Albanian **Çamëria**) given to Greece, and many Greek settlements (Northern Epirus) left in Albania.

INTERNATIONAL CONTROL COMMISSION (1913). The International Control Commission for Albania was set up by the **Conference of Ambassadors** in London on 29 July 1913 to supervise the establishment of a government administration in Albania after the Great Powers recognized the declaration of independence. It was to be composed of one representative from each of the six Powers and one Albanian, **Mehdi bey Frashëri**, and was to supervise the country for a period of ten years. It also set forth that the new gendarmerie was to be organized by Dutch officers. In March 1914, it turned over authority to **Prince Wilhelm zu Wied**, but resumed it on 3 September 1914 when the prince departed.

IPPEN, THEODOR (1861.11.29-1935.01.31). Austrian scholar and diplomat. Theodor Ippen was born in Vienna and studied at the Consular Academy there. In 1884, he served at the Austro-Hungarian consulate in **Shkodra**, where, in 1887, he was appointed vice-consul. In 1893, he headed the consulate general in Jerusalem and was subsequently in Istanbul. In 1895, he was appointed consul in Shkodra once again. From 1905, he served in Athens and, from 1909, in London, where he took part in the **Conference of Ambassadors** as representative of Austria-Hungary. From 1921 to 1927, he was an important member of the International Danube Commission. He died in Vienna.

Theodor Ippen is the author of a number of monographs on early northern Albanian history and ethnography, with particular attention to the Middle Ages. Among them are: *Novibazar und Kossovo: das alte Rascien* (Novi Pazar and Kosova: Ancient Rascia), Vienna 1892; *Stare crkvene ruševine u Albaniji* (Old Church Ruins in Albania), Sarajevo 1898; *Skutari und die nordalbanische Küstenebene* (Shkodra and the Northern Albanian

Coastal Plain), Sarajevo 1907; *Die Gebirge des nordwestlichen Albaniens* (The Mountains of Northwestern Albania), Vienna 1908; and numerous scholarly articles on early northern Albania, published primarily in German and Serbo-Croatian.

ISAI, HEKURAN (1933.05.07-). Political figure of the **communist** period. Hekuran Isai was born in **Peqin** and worked as a specialist at the **oil** refinery in Cërrik in 1962. He graduated from the V. I. Lenin Higher Party School in 1967 and worked as party secretary in **Elbasan** from 1967 to 1970. He thereafter held a variety of party offices. In 1975, he headed a delegation of the Sino-Albanian friendship association to **China**. After the elimination of **Mehmet Shehu**, he served from January 1982 to 2 February 1989 as minister of the interior, and from 8 July 1990 to 22 February 1991, both as minister of the interior and deputy prime minister. Hekuran Isai was a powerful figure in the communist party hierarchy throughout the 1980s. He was a full member of the Central Committee from 1971 to 11 June 1991 and a full member of the Politburo from 1976 to 11 June 1991. He was arrested on 3 October 1991. On 2 July 1994, he was sentenced to five years of prison for abuse of power.

ISHËM. River in central Albania. The Ishëm takes its source from the **Tirana**, Gjole and Zeza Rivers west of the towns of Tirana and **Kruja** and flows into the Adriatic Sea in the District of **Kurbin**, north of Cape Rodon. It has a length of seventy-four kilometers. The Ishëm is the ancient *Isamnus* (Vibius Sequester 149). It was recorded in 1302 as *Yssamo*.

ISLAM. Religion. Before the arrival of the Turks in the Balkan peninsula, all the Albanians were encompassed within the sphere of **Christianity**: **Catholicism** in the north and **Orthodoxy** in the south. By the end of the fourteenth century, the third great **religion** of the Balkan peninsula, Islam, had entered the ring, unfolding its banners on the eastern horizon. By 1431, the Turks had incorporated all of southern Albania into the **Ottoman Empire** and set up a sandjak administration with its capital in **Gjirokastra**, captured in 1419. Mountainous northern Albania remained under the control of its autonomous tribal leaders, though now under the suzerain power of the sultan. The new religion, Islam, had wedged itself between the Catholic north and the Orthodox south of Albania and, with time, was to become the dominant faith. The coming four centuries of Ottoman colonization changed the face of the country radically.

During the first decades of Ottoman rule, there were few Muslims among the Albanians themselves. In 1577, it is known that northern and central Albania were still staunchly Catholic, but by the early decades of the seventeenth century, an estimated thirty to fifty percent of the **population** of northern Albania had converted to Islam. By 1634, most of **Kosova** had also converted. Of the inhabitants of the town of Prizren at the time, for instance, there were 12,000 Muslims, 200 Catholics and 600 Orthodox. By the close of the seventeenth century, Muslims began to outnumber Christians throughout most of the country. Roman Catholicism and Greek and Serbian Orthodoxy had, after all, been the vehicles of foreign cultures in Albania, propelled by foreign languages. They were religions to which the Albanians, as opposed to their Serbian, Bulgarian and Greek neighbors, had only been superficially converted and with which they could not so easily identify. The mass conversion of the Albanian population to Islam is all the more understandable in view of the heavy *haraç* or poll taxes imposed on the *rayah*—Christian inhabitants of the Empire. With these taxes in mind, many Albanians preferred the best of both worlds and became so-called **Crypto-Christians**, i.e., Christian in the privacy of their homes, but Muslim in public. Characteristic of the Albanian attitude to matters of religion was the motto: "Where the sword is, there lies religion," Alb. *Ku është shpata, është feja*. Pressure to convert to Islam increased during the Russo-Turkish wars of the eighteenth century, although the situation improved for the Orthodox community somewhat in 1774 with the Treaty of Küçük Kaynarci, according to which **Russia** became protectress of all Orthodox Christians in the Ottoman Empire. At the dawn of Albanian independence in 1912, about two-thirds of the Albanian population were Muslim.

Up to 1929, the Muslim community was headed by the grand mufti of **Tirana** with a five-member supreme council of the Sheriat. Later, a general council was established with the chief of the community and four grand muftis, representing **Shkodra**, Tirana, **Korça** and Gjirokastra. Organized Sunni Islam was somewhat weakened in the 1930s when **King Zog** severed all official ties with Muslims outside the country. Nonetheless, according to Italian statistics from the year 1942, of the total population of Albania of 1,128,143, there were 779,417 (sixty-nine percent) Muslims, including the **Bektashi**, 232,320 (twenty-one percent) Orthodox and 116,259 (ten percent) Catholics. As such, one can estimate today that approximately seventy percent of Albanians in the Republic of Albania and about eighty percent of all Albanians in the Balkans are of Muslim background. The most devout of these Muslims are no doubt the Albanians of western Macedonia (the region of Tetova and Gostivar), where more elements of traditional culture have been preserved and maintained than in Albania itself.

There were 1,127 mosques, 1,306 imams and muftis and seventeen Islamic primary schools in Albania at the end of **World War II**. From 1945 onwards, the Muslim community, divided as it was into four districts with a grand mufti for each, came increasingly under the control of the state, particularly by virtue of the law of 26 November 1949. This decree required all the religious communities to instil in their members a feeling of loyalty towards the **communist** regime. The head of the Muslim community now also had to be approved by the government council of ministers. Some Muslim leaders, such as the mufti of **Durrës**, Mustafa Efendi Varoshi, and the mufti of Shkodra, refused to cooperate with the communist leaders and were liquidated. Others were imprisoned. An estimated 1,050 mosques survived in Albania unscathed up to 1967, but then, in an unprecedented act of extremism and cultural suicide, Islam and all other religions were banned by the communist authorities.

The destruction of Islamic culture in Albania during the late 1960s and early 1970s was ruthless and thorough. Almost all the mosques in the country, including some which had just been restored and which were of inestimable cultural value, were demolished or transformed for other uses. A few buildings were simply locked up, and thus survived the cultural massacre in a more or less recognizable form. Among the latter are the Mirahor Mosque of Korça (1495), the Sultan Mosque (1492) and the Lead Mosque (1553-1554) of **Berat**, the Murad Mosque of **Vlora** (1537-1542), the Naziresha Mosque of **Elbasan** (pre-1599), the Lead Mosque of Shkodra (1773-1774) and the Et'hem Bey Mosque in Tirana (1793-1794). Islam had ceased to exist, at least in Albanian public life.

The public practice of religion was first authorized again in December 1990 and the few remaining mosques, after twenty-four years of closure, began to reopen from January to mid-March 1991. It was also in this period that the first public celebration of *Ramadan* was held. In December 1992, Albania joined the Organization of the Islamic Conference, a move which was widely criticized in the country at the time, even among Muslims. The

Albanians were reluctant to jeopardize their country's western orientation and new ties with the rest of Europe for the sake of religious tradition.

The reestablished Sunni Muslim community is now headed by **Hafiz Sabri Koçi,** who spent over twenty years of his life in prison and at hard labor. Islamic groups from abroad—Saudi Arabia, Kuwait, Abu Dhabi and Egypt and others, have done much to provide humanitarian assistance and to revive Islamic traditions in Albania. Virtually all towns and villages with a Muslim population now have a mosque or a modest Islamic community center.

Despite the new freedoms, there still seems to be more interest in the revival of Islam among foreign missionaries and groups than there is among the Albanians themselves. As opposed to their Greek and Serbian neighbors, the Albanians have never had a "national" religion with which they could identify as a people. For the last century and a half, national, i.e., ethnic identity, has predominated conspicuously over religious identity, and this situation is unlikely to change in the coming years, given that Albania is a small and struggling nation surrounded by hostile neighbors. Organized religion still only plays a very marginal role in public life in Albania. The Albanians have indeed on occasion been described as tenacious pagans who can only be superficially converted and, after a fifty-year break in religious traditions, there is some justification for this view. Many a missionary and preacher has been driven to despair by them, especially over the last few years. Religious fervor is rare and religious extremism is still virtually unknown.

Despite the often-expressed concerns among western publicists, fundamentalism is not a problem among the Albanians nor is it likely to arise in Albania in any form. Isolated acts of religious extremism, such as the throwing of pig heads into the courtyards of mosques, the knocking down of Catholic tombstones, the bombing of an Orthodox church in Shkodra or the damaging of Orthodox frescoes, have been just that—isolated acts. The sad incident in **Voskopoja** near Korça on 11 August 1996 was typical. Three Albanian adolescents, aged sixteen to eighteen, all of them educated by Islamic extremists from abroad, broke into the beautiful Orthodox Church of Saint Michael (1722-1725) while on holiday at a summer camp there. The boys took knives to the eighteenth-century frescoes and, in true centuries-old Balkan tradition, scarred the faces and scratched out the eyes of twenty-three serene Orthodox saints. This act of cultural barbarism shocked and dismayed the Albanian public, Christians and Muslims alike, and caused a minor wave of irritation between the religious communities. However, such acts have remained sporadic instances and do not represent any particular trend. Confrontation in Albania is more at the political and regional level than at the confessional.

Despite the current lack of open religious fervor among the Albanians, Islam has contributed substantially to making the Albanians what they are today. It is now an inherent feature of Albania's national culture and ought to be treated and respected as such. At the dawn of the twenty-first century, the Albanian nation found itself in a state of profound turmoil, indeed of anarchy: economically, politically and culturally. Only time will tell whether mainstream Islam and the Sufi *tarikat* can contribute once again to giving the Albanian people a sense of identity.

ISLAMI, KASTRIOT (1952.08.18-). Political figure and high-ranking member of the **Socialist Party of Albania**. Kastriot Islami was born in **Tirana** and studied physics, in particular atomic and molecular physics, in Tirana and in Paris. He later worked at the Geological and Geodesical Institute and taught theoretical physics at the Faculty of Science. In 1991 he was minister of **education**.

Islami was speaker of **parliament** from March 1991 to March 1992, has been a leading member of parliament for the Socialist Party since 1992 and was appointed minister of finance on 24 July 2002. He is author of *Për një konfiguracion të ri politik* (Towards a New Political Configuration), Tirana 2000.

ISMAILI, VEHBI, Imam (1919.11.25-). Muslim religious figure. Vehbi Ismaili was born in **Shkodra**. He completed his religious training at the Medresa of **Tirana** and moved to Cairo in 1937 to continue his training in **Islamic** theology at Al-Azhar University. By the time he finished his studies, Albania had been taken over by the **communists**, and his father, a mufti, advised him not to return. During his stay in Egypt, he wrote on Islamic topics and translated literary works from Albanian into Arabic.

In 1949, Ismaili emigrated to the **United States** and became imam of the Albanian Muslim community in Detroit. There he establish the first Albanian mosque and Islamic center and edited two quarterly journals. He has written and translated many Islamic religious publications, and in 1993 was chosen as president of the Albanian Muslim Communities of the United States and Canada.

ISUFI, ELEZ (1861-1924.12.29). Nationalist figure and guerrilla fighter. Elez Isufi was born in the village of Sllova in the **Dibra** region. He and his guerrilla band resisted Serb forces in 1912. A close ally of **Bajram Curri**, Isufi led an armed uprising in Dibra on 15 August 1921 to free the region from Serb forces. The fighting continued up to December 1921. He was involved in a further uprising on 1 March 1922 against the regime of **Ahmet Zogu**, and his Dibran fighters were able to cross the mountains and take **Tirana**. He took the side of **Fan Noli** during the **Democratic Revolution** and was killed by Yugoslav troops at the end of 1924.

ITALY, ALBANIANS IN. There are two distinct groups of Albanians in Italy: the traditional ethnic minority of the Italo-Albanians or Arbëresh in southern Italy, and the substantial wave of new immigrants from Albania since 1990.

The Italo-Albanians, or Arbëresh, are the descendants of sporadic groups from Albania who had found their way to Italy as early as 1272, 1388 and 1393. It was, however, not until the mid-fifteenth century that notable settlements were established, when Albanian troops under the command of Demetrius Reres were summoned to Italy by Alfonso I of Aragon (r. 1435-1458), the King of Naples, to put down a revolt in Calabria. For his assistance, Reres was offered land in Calabria in 1448, and there his soldiers and their families immigrated. His sons, George and Basil, are said later to have made their way to Sicily to establish the first Albanian colonies there. Mass settlement began, however, with the **Ottoman** invasion of the Balkans which resulted in a great exodus of Albanians to Italy. This exodus became all the more acute after the collapse of Albanian resistance and the death in 1468 of **Scanderbeg**, who had found a generous patron in the House of Aragon. Between 1468 and 1478, waves of refugees abandoned southern Albania to establish themselves in Basilicata, Molise, Apulia and particularly in Calabria. More Albanians fled **Greece** in 1532-1533 after Turkish encroachments in the Morea and settled mostly in Sicily. These waves of refugees formed the core of Albanian colonization in southern Italy, although other emigrants followed in later years.

All in all, the Albanians founded or repopulated about 100 towns and villages in southern Italy, over half of which are to be located in the mountains of Calabria. Today, there are about fifty towns scattered throughout the *mezzogiorno* where Albanian is still to be heard. These communities, comprising an estimated Albanian-speaking population of about 90,000, are located in seven regions: Abruzzi, Molise, Campania, Apulia, Basilicata, Calabria and Sicily. They are:

Province of Pescara (Abruzzi):
   Villa Badessa (Alb. *Badhesa*)
Province of Campobasso (Molise):
   Campomarino (Alb. *Këmarini*), Montecilfone (Alb. *Munxhifuni*), Portocannone (Alb. *Portkanuni*) and Ururi (Alb. *Ruri*)
Province of Avellino (Campania):
   Greci (Alb. *Greçi*)
Province of Foggia (Apulia):
   Casalvecchio di Puglia (Alb. *Kazallveqi*) and Chieuti (Alb. *Qeuti*)
Province of Taranto (Apulia):
   San Marzano di San Giuseppe (Alb. *Shën Marxani*)
Province of Potenza (Basilicata):
   Barile (Alb. *Barilli*), Ginestra (Alb. *Xhinestra*), Maschito (Alb. *Mashqiti*), San Costantino Albanese (Alb. *Shën Kostandini*) and San Paolo Albanese (Alb. *Shën Pali*)
Province of Cosenza (Calabria):
   Acquaformosa (Alb. *(Firmoza)*, Castroregio (Alb. *Kastërnexhi*), Cavallerizzo (Alb. *Kajverici*), Cerzeto (Alb. *Qana*), Civita (Alb. *Çifti*), Eianina or Poicile (Alb. *Ejanina* or *Purçilli*), Falconara Albanese (Alb. *Fallkunara*), Farneta (Alb. *Farneta*), Firmo (Alb. *Ferma*), Frascineto (Alb. *Frasnita*), Lungro (Alb. *Ungra*), Macchia Albanese (Alb. *Maqi*), Marri (Alb. *Marri*), Plataci (Alb. *Pllatani*), San Basile (Alb. *Shën Vasili*), San Benedetto Ullano (Alb. *Shën Benedhiti*), San Cosmo Albanese (Alb. *Strigari*), San Demetrio Corone (Alb. *Shën Mitri*), San Giacomo di Cerzeto (Alb. *Shën Japku*), San Giorgio Albanese (Alb. *Mbuzati*), San Martino di Finita (Alb. *Shën Murtiri*), Santa Caterina Albanese (Alb. *Picilia*), Santa Sofia d'Epiro (Alb. *Shën Sofia*), Spezzano Albanese (Alb. *Spixana*) and Vaccarizzo Albanese (Alb. *Vakarici*)
Province of Catanzaro (Calabria):
   Caraffa di Catanzaro (Alb. *Garafa*), Carfizzi (Alb. *Karfici*), Pallagorio (Alb. *Puhëriu*), San Nicola dell'Alto (Alb. *Shën Kolli*) and Vena di Maida (Alb. *Vina*)
Province of Palermo (Sicily):

Contessa Entellina (Alb. *Kundisa*), Piana degli Albanesi (Alb *Hora e Arbëreshëvet*) and Santa Cristina Gela (Alb. *Shëndhastini*). Though the Albanian **language** is by no means moribund in Italy after 500 years of existence, Italian is gaining the upper hand even in these often isolated mountain villages. In a number of the above-mentioned communities, Albanian is still spoken by virtually all the inhabitants. In other settlements, the adult population is bilingual and the children speak only Italian. In still other communities, it is only the old people who understand Albanian. Several factors have contributed to the gradual transition from Albanian to Italian in village communication: the compulsory use of Italian in all schools, the lack of support by the Italian government, the discontinuity of Albanian-speaking territory, the Italian-language mass media and, in particular, seasonal emigration due to chronic unemployment in southern Italy. For written communication, Albanian has only been used by an intellectual minority, as school education and external cultural stimulation have always been in Italian. The substantial difference between the Albanian dialects spoken in southern Italy and the standard literary language of Albania (*gjuha letrare*) has also made it difficult for the Arbëresh to adapt to standard Albanian for written communication.

The second wave of Albanian emigration to Italy occurred in the 1990s. In March 1991, 20,000 Albanians fled by sea to Brindisi and, on 6 to 8 August of that year, another 12,500 arrived by boat in Bari. Emigration slowed down somewhat after the forced repatriation of the August group, but continued over the following years. Speedboats crossing the Adriatic at night from **Kavaja** and **Vlora** were the main source of clandestine immigration, and the practice was only stifled in late 2002. According to statistics of the United Nations Development Program, there were some 100,000 to 150,000 Albanian emigrants in Italy in 1999.

ITALY, RELATIONS WITH. Albania's relations with Italy are traditionally extremely close, and indeed nowadays are closer than with any other country. Relations between the two banks of the Adriatic date from the Roman period, initially from Roman endeavors to suppress **Illyrian** piracy. **Durrës** came under Roman protection in 229 B.C. and most of Illyria was conquered and subjected by the Romans by 168 B.C. Durrës itself served from the Roman period onwards as the point of departure for the **Via Egnatia** and for most sea communication with Italy. It was settled by Roman veterans under Augustus Caesar and received the status of a colony. That the period of Roman colonization in Albania was intense can be inferred from the Albanian **language**, which underwent extreme Latin influence, almost to the point of romanization, like modern Romanian.

For centuries, Albania formed the political, military and cultural border between East and West, i.e., between the Roman Empire of the western Mediterranean including much of the northern Balkans, and the Greek Empire of the eastern Mediterranean, including the southern Balkans. In the Middle Ages, Albania was once again a buffer zone, this time between Catholic Italy, especially Venice, and the Byzantine Greek Empire. Venetian influence in Albania was primordial up to and well after the **Ottoman** conquest in the early fifteenth century. One direct result of the Ottoman conquest was the Albanian colonization of southern Italy. Today the mountains of Calabria and Sicily are inhabited by about 200,000 Italo-Albanians, including about 90,000 speakers of an archaic dialect of Albanian.

In **World War I**, Italy was among the seven countries which invaded Albania in order to fill the power vacuum created by the collapse of Turkey in Europe. Italian troops occupied the island of **Sazan** and the town of **Vlora** in the autumn of 1914 where they stayed until August 1920.

Italy's influence in Albania grew steadily between the two world wars. Italian predominance in Albanian affairs was ensured by the first Pact of **Tirana**, signed by dictator **Ahmet Zogu** on 27 November 1926. The second Pact of Tirana, signed on 22 November 1927, ensured Italian military influence in the country, which Italy needed in order to counter **Yugoslav** expansion. It was with Italian support on 1 September 1928 that Zogu was able to declare himself Zog I, King of the Albanians. Subsequent attempts by the new king to elude Italian influence were met by economic, political, or indeed military pressure, such as the arrival of the Italian fleet off Durrës on 23 June 1934. On 19 March 1936, the two countries signed economic and financial agreements, as well as a secret military protocol which gave fascist Italy even more control over Albania. It was then only a matter of time before Albania became part of Benito Mussolini's new Roman empire.

On 7 April 1939, Italian troops invaded the country and took swift control. Five days later, the Albanian **parliament** offered the crown of **Scanderbeg** to King Victor Emmanuel III of Italy, thus making the latter King of Albania in "personal union." Italy ruled Albania until its capitulation on 8 September 1943.

Relations between the two countries cooled substantially during the **communist** period. In early 1946, all Italian companies in Albania were nationalized and heavy demands were made for reparations. The new regime also closed down all institutions of the **Catholic Church** and, on 19 February 1946, expelled all Italian priests from the country. A peace treaty was nonetheless signed on 10 February 1947, including the return of the island of Sazan, and diplomatic relations were resumed on 3 May 1949.

Despite the low level of official relations and a modicum of trade, in particular in the 1980s, Italian cultural influence in Albania was stronger than ever at the end of the dictatorship, due to the influence of Italian television, the only window on the outside world for the isolated and impoverished population of Albania.

When the dictatorship collapsed, the greatest desire of most Albanians was to see and enjoy the marvels of the West with their own eyes. In March 1991, in an unprecedented exodus, 20,000 Albanians fled by sea to Brindisi, and, in April, more and more boats started arriving. On 6-8 August 1991, another 12,500 Albanians turned up in Bari. The very foundations of the Italian republic were being shaken by these tidal waves of poor and unwanted Albanian emigrants, washed up on the coast of southern Italy. Italian Foreign Minister Gianni de Michelis hastened to Tirana on 12 August 1991, and President Francesco Cossiga a day later, to offer emergency assistance to the country in order to stem the tide of emigrants. From 25 September 1991 to 31 March 1992, Italy provided Albania with 130,000 tons of emergency humanitarian aid in the so-called Pelican Operation.

On 15 April 1997, 6,000 United Nations troops of **Operation Alba** under Italian command landed in Durrës to restore order in the country after the general **uprising**. Since that time, Italian influence in Albania has been substantially greater than that of any other country. Italy is now by far Albania's number one trading partner, accounting in 1999 for thirty-four percent of all imports and almost seventy percent of all Albanian exports. It also provides more economic assistance than any other country.

IVANAJ, MIRASH (1891.03.12-1953.09.22). Political figure. Mirash Ivanaj was born in Podgorica. He graduated from secondary school in Belgrade in 1912 and set off for Italy the following year to study in Rome where he completed two doctorates, one in law and one in literature. On his return to Albania in 1923, he assisted in the publication of his cousin Nikolla bey Ivanaj's weekly newspaper *Republika* (The Republic). He fled to Yugoslavia in May 1924 and, upon his return in late December of that year, worked as the principal of a secondary school in **Shkodra** and later taught in **Tirana**. From 1932, onwards he was a member of **parliament** and, in 1933, was appointed as minister of **education**, a post he held for two and a half years. It was during his time as minister, on 6 February 1934, that he cut off **Enver Hoxha**'s scholarship in France when the latter failed his exams. Mirash Ivanaj is remembered primarily for having attempted to nationalize the school system in Albania, but his efforts were opposed by **Italy** and especially by **Greece** because of the particular interests of the **Greek minority** in southern Albania. Greece won a court case against Albania on the matter at the International Court of Justice in The Hague on 6 April 1935, and Ivanaj, as a result, resigned from his post on 30 August of that year.

On 7 April 1939, during the Italian invasion, Ivanaj fled to Greece and spent the early war years in Istanbul. He later traveled to Lebanon, Egypt and Jerusalem in search of work. In September 1945, having received a guarantee from the new government, he returned to Albania, one of the few intellectuals to do so, and began teaching at a school of education in Tirana in November of that year. His return, alas, coincided with the zenith of the witch hunts against intellectuals carried out by **Koçi Xoxe**. Ivanaj was arrest on 15 May 1947 and, after much mistreatment and torture, was sentenced to seven years in prison. He worked in prison as a translator (most genuine intellectuals with a knowledge of foreign languages were in prison at the time, so the new **communist** government, in a rare sign of pragmatism, set up its first translation unit in Tirana prison). He died twelve days before he would have been released. Mirash Ivanaj was the author of a volume of poetry and a play, both unpublished.

IVANAJ, NIKOLLA BEY (1879-1951.11.23). Publisher and nationalist figure. Nikolla bey Ivanaj, cousin of Mirash Ivanaj, was born in **Gruda** territory in the present Albanian-Montenegrin border region and grew up in Podgorica in Montenegro. He is said to have studied in Belgrade, Vienna, Zagreb and Dalmatia and held various positions as a civil servant in Serbia, including that of secretary and interpreter (dragoman) at the Serbian foreign ministry. Ivanaj is remembered as editor-in-chief of the weekly newspaper *Shpnesa e Shcypeniis* (The Hope of Albania), published from 1905 to 1908 in Albanian, Italian and Serbo-Croatian. This periodical which was important in diffusing the ideals of independence and Albanian-**language** schooling throughout the Balkans appeared initially in Dubrovnik, later in Trieste and, finally, in Rome. After Albanian independence, Ivanaj published the **Shkodra** weekly newspaper *Lidhja kombëtare* (National League) in 1915 in defense of Albanian self-government and national rights. In 1919, he attended the Paris Peace Conference and returned to Albania to found and publish the biweekly newspaper *Koha e re* (New Age) in 1919 and 1925, and the weekly *Republika* (The Republic) from 1923 to 1925, both in Shkodra. During **World War II**, he published an autobiographical *Historija e Shqipëniës së ré: vuejtjet e veprimet e mija—Pjesa e parë* (History of Modern Albania: My Sufferings and Activities —Part I), Tirana 1943; and *Historija e Shqipëniës së ré—Pjesa e II-të* (History of Modern Albania—Part II), Tirana 1945, which dealt in particular with the role of the **Catholic** clergy; as well as a volume of verse in **Tirana**, where he died.

- J -

JACQUES, EDWIN (1908-1996). American scholar and historian. Edwin E. Jacques was a **Protestant** missionary who worked as a teacher in **Korça** from 1932 to 1940, where he began collecting material on Albanian history. He was in Rome in 1940 and then returned to the **United States** to obtain a master's degree at Boston University in 1941 with a thesis on *The Islamization of Albania under the Turks*. He visited Albania in 1986. Jacques' major contribution to Albanian studies is his 700-page history of Albania, entitled *The Albanians: An Ethnic History from Prehistoric Times to the Present,* Jefferson, North Carolina 1995. This work is the longest and most complete history of Albania written in English. It has recently appeared in an Albanian translation.

JAKOVA, PRENKË (1917.07.27-1969.09.16). Composer. Prenkë Jakova was the author of a wide range of creative **music** in Albania. He was born and raised in **Shkodra**, where he attended the **Franciscan** secondary school. From 1936 to 1942, he taught school in Bërdica and Orosh and, in 1943, spent several months at the Accademia di Santa Cecilia in Rome, where he studied clarinet. From 1945 to his death, he headed the music department at the House of Culture in his native Shkodra. He is remembered as the composer of the first Albanian opera, *Mrika* (Mrika) in 1956-1958, and of the opera *Gjergj Kastrioti Skënderbeu* (George Castriotta Scanderbeg) in 1966-1967.

JAKOVA, TUK (1914.04.26-1959.08.27). Political figure of the early **communist** period. Tuk Jakova was raised in **Shkodra** and worked there as a carpenter. He was a founding member of the communist party and took part in the resistance movement during **World War II**. He was a member of the Central Committee from 1943 to 1955. Jakova served as minister of economics from 23 March 1946 to 2 February 1947; ambassador to **Yugoslavia** from March to October 1947; minister of finance from 2 February 1947 to 7 February 1948 and from August 1953 to July 1954; and deputy prime minister from 29 November 1948 to 24 June 1953. In 1955 he was purged with **Bedri Spahiu** on charges of revisionism and pro-Yugoslav activities, and interned in **Berat**. He died in the prison hospital in **Tirana** in the summer of 1959.

JANULATOS, ANASTAS (1929.11.04-). Greek Orthodox religious figure. Anastas Janulatos was born in Piraeus in Greece and finished his studies in theology in 1952 at the University of Athens. He then did postgraduate research in Hamburg and Marburg in Germany and worked from 1965 to 1969 in Uganda. In 1966-1969, he taught modern Greek and philosophy at the University of Marburg. In 1972, he was appointed an archbishop and, thereafter, held various offices in the hierarchy of the Greek Orthodox Church. From January 1991 to June 1992, he worked in **Tirana** to set up a new **Orthodox** Church administration in Albania, and since June 1992, he has been Archbishop of Tirana and all Albania, thus the highest office of the Orthodox Church in Albania. His election caused a furor at the time because he was Greek and not Albanian. The Orthodox population of Albania was fearful that the Greek Orthodox hierarchy would attempt to assimilate the Albanian Church, as it had done in the past. With time, however, Archbishop Janulatos came to be accepted by the Orthodox faithful in his new country.

JARNIK, JAN (1848-1923). Czech linguist. Jan Urban Jarnik, known in German as Johann Jarnik, studied Romance philology in Vienna, where he first began learning Albanian. He was later appointed professor of Romance philology at the University of Prague and specialized in Romanian. In the field of Albanian studies, Jarnik collected oral **literature** (folk tales, anecdotes and sayings) in the **Shkodra** region and published much of the material with a precise interlinear translation. He is thus considered to be the founder of Albanian studies in Czechoslovakia. Among his Albanological publications are: *Zur albanischen Sprachenkunde* (On Albanian Philology), Leipzig 1881; *Přspěvky ku poznání nářečí albánských* (Contributions to an Understanding of Albanian Dialects), Prague 1883; and *Albanesische Märchen und Schwänke* (Albanian Folk Tales and Jokes), 1890-1892.

JESUIT ORDER. Order of the **Catholic** Church. Founded by Saint Ignatius Loyola (1491-1556) in 1540, the Jesuit order first came to Albania in the mid-nineteenth century. It was in 1841 that the first three Italian Jesuit missionaries, Giuseppe Guagliata (ca. 1814-?), Vincenzo Basile (1818-1882) and Salvator Bartoli, arrived in the country from Sicily to set up a mission. Despite its late arrival, the Society of Jesus (*Societas Jesu* - S.J.), as the order is known, played an inestimable role in **education** and culture in northern Albania for about a century. Though the prime objectives of the Jesuits were the training of seminarians for the priesthood and the propagation of the faith, for which they set up schools, churches and publishing facilities, their activities and their formidable intellectual talents also contributed substantially to raising the educational and cultural level of their new homeland.

In 1859, the Jesuits opened the *Kolegjia Papnore Shqyptare* (Albanian Pontifical Seminary) in **Shkodra** and, in 1870, set up a printing press called the *Shtypshkroja e Zojës s'Paperlyeme* (Press of the Immaculate Virgin), which six years later was to produce its first book in Albanian, the *Dotrina e kerscten* (Christian Doctrine) of Ëngjell Radoja (1820-1880). By 1928, the Jesuit press had published a total of 471 works in Albanian, Italian and Latin. Like the **Franciscans**, the Jesuits also edited periodicals of note such as *Elçija i Zemers t'Jezu Krisctit* (The Messenger of the Sacred Heart), 1891-1944, known from 1914 on as *Lajmtari i Zemers t'Jezu Krishtit*, a magazine of religious culture; *Përparimi* (Progress), 1914-1916, a short-lived historical and scholarly journal; and *Leka*, 1929-1944, a monthly cultural review.

In 1877, they founded the College of Saint Francis Xavier, also known as the Saverian College, Alb. *Kolegja Saveriane*, in Shkodra, which evolved into a major center of higher education for all of Albania and which, by stressing instruction in Albanian in addition to Italian, produced many great Albanian writers and national figures in the early twentieth century. Among the figures to have studied at the Saverian College were the poet **Ndre Mjeda**; the writer and publisher **Faik bey Konitza**; the political leader and writer **Luigj Gurakuqi**; the poet and folklorist **Vinçenc Prennushi**; the poet, prose writer and scholar **Ernest Koliqi**; the playwright Kolë Jakova (1916-2002); the **communist** revolutionary and poet Qemal Stafa (1920-1942); and the poet and critic Mark Gurakuqi (1922-1977).

In 1932, with the founding of the Jesuit Apostolic Preparatory School in Shkodra, there were forty-five Jesuits in the country. One year later, a Jesuit alumni association called Don Bosco was founded in Shkodra, and, in June 1941, the Jesuits opened the Sacred Heart cathedral in **Tirana**.

Soon after the communists entered Shkodra on 29 November 1944, a virulent propaganda campaign was unleashed against the Jesuits, who were accused of being "Vatican and Anglo-American spies." General **Mehmet Shehu**, speaking from the balcony of the main square post office in Shkodra on 28 January 1945, called the Jesuits "perfidious conspirators against the people's power." The expulsion of foreign Jesuits and the arrest of Albanian Jesuits soon followed. On 4 March 1946, fathers Gjon Fausti (1889-1946) and Dajan Dajani (1906-1946) were executed after a mock trial, and in April of that year, the Jesuit order was banned entirely by the new communist authorities, with all its remaining schools and property being confiscated.

In August 1990, the Jesuit order returned to Albania and reopened the Albanian Pontifical Seminary of Shkodra in September 1991. A new diocesan seminary called Our Lady of Good Counsel was opened in Shkodra on 17 October 1998.

JEWISH MINORITY IN ALBANIA. *See* JUDAISM.

JIREČEK, KONSTANTIN (1854.07.24-1918.01.10). Czech scholar and historian. Balkan specialist Konstantin Jireček was born in Vienna where he learned Slavic, Greek and Italian as a child. From 1872 to 1875, he studied history and classical philology at the University of Prague and finished his doctorate with a thesis on the *Geschichte der Bulgaren* (History of the Bulgarians). In 1877, he was appointed lecturer for Balkan history and geography at the University of Prague. He later carried out research at the archives of Dubrovnik and, in 1879, moved to Bulgaria, where he served as minister of education and in 1883-1884 as director of the national library. From 1884 to 1893, he was professor of history at the Czech University of Prague and, from 1893, was professor of Slavic studies and history at the University of Vienna, where he died. Although primarily a Slavist, Jireček was also interested in Albanian history. Among his Albanian publications are articles on early Albanian history in the collection *Illyrisch-Albanische Forschungen* (Illyrian-Albanian Research), Munich 1916, and *Studien zur Geschichte und Geographie Albaniens im Mittelalter* (Studies on the History and Geography of Albania in the Middle Ages), Budapest 1916.

JOCHALAS, TITOS (1942-). Greek scholar. Titos P. Jochalas studied classical philology and philosophy at the University of Athens and went on to do linguistics and Albanian at the University of Palermo in Sicily. He finished his doctorate in Balkan history and comparative linguistics at the University of Munich in 1968. Since 1975, Jochalas has been director of the Greek Center for Southeast European Studies in Athens. Among his Albanological publications are: *Ho Geôrgios Kastriôtês Skentermpeês eis tên neoellênikên historiografian kai logotechnian* (George Castriotta Scanderbeg in Modern Greek Historiography and Literature), Thessalonika 1975; *To hellênoalbanikon lexikon tu Marku Mpotsarê* (The Greek-Albanian Lexicon of Mark Boçari), Athens 1980; *Stoicheia hellênoalbanikês grammatikês kai hellêno-albanikoi dialogoi* (Elements of Greek-Albanian Grammar and Greek-Albanian Dialogues), Thessalonika 1985; *Symbolê stê balkanikê bibliografia* (Contribution to Balkan Bibliography), Athens 1987; *Albanologia kai erasitechnismos* (Albanology and Amateurism), Athens 1988; *Hellênoalbanika keimena gia glôssikê proseggisê* (Greek-Albanian Texts for Linguistic Comparison), Athens 1992; *Hellênika epônyma, onomata kai topônymia tôn albanikôn koinotêtôn tês Katô Italias kai tês Sikelias* (Greek Surnames, Names and Place Names of the Albanian Community in Lower Italy and Sicily), Athens 1993; *Albano-Italika: thematikê bibliografia* (Albano-Italica: Subject Bibliography), Athens 1996; and *Arbanitika paramythia kai doxasies* (Arvanitika Folk Tales and Beliefs), Athens 1997.

JOKL, NORBERT (1877.02.25-1942.05.06). Austrian scholar and linguist. Norbert Jokl was born of **Jewish** parents in Bzenec in southern Moravia. He graduated from a German-language secondary school in July 1895 and moved to Vienna to study law and political science, finishing his doctorate there in 1901. He then embarked upon a legal career but soon abandoned it to return to university studies. Jokl took up Indo-European philology under Paul Kretschmer (1866-1956), Romance philology under Wilhelm Meyer-Lübke (1861-1936) and Slavic philology under Vratoslav Jagić and W. Vondrák, finally choosing Slavic as his main field. In 1903, he got a position as a trainee at the Vienna University Library and, after finishing a second doctorate in March 1908, worked there as a librarian until the end of his career. In 1913, he was authorized by the university to hold lectures in Albanian, Slavic and Baltic philology and, in 1923, was made a full professor, a position he retained until 1938, when he was fired on racial grounds.

Jokl had begun learning Albanian with the help of **Gjergj Pekmezi** and other Albanians in Vienna. From a preliminary report on the study of **Gheg** dialects, which he prepared in 1914 for the Austrian Academy of Sciences, it is evident that he was particularly fascinated by the regional variants of northern Albanian. In the spring of that year, he had heard about a group of Albanians working as confectioners in Hungary. Without losing any time, he set off to meet them to make notes on their dialects. With the support of the Balkan Commission of the Austrian Academy of Sciences, Jokl invited one of the workers, a certain Mustafa Abdyli from Vrapçishta near Gostivar in Macedonia, to Vienna for a month to make a sound recording of the **language** at the Phonogram Archives there. This five-minute recording, made on 4 April 1914, constitutes the earliest audio recording ever made of the Albanian language. It is still preserved at the Phonogram Archives of the Austrian Academy of Sciences in Vienna. _

Norbert Jokl taught at the University of Vienna from 1913 to 1938 and was the leading figure of Albanian scholarship in the German-speaking world. On the occasion of the twenty-fifth anniversary of Albanian independence, he was awarded the **Scanderbeg** Order by the Albanian government and visited Albania for the first and last time. In 1941, when life for the Jews in the Third Reich had become intolerable, he tried to get a job in Albania as supervisor of Albanian libraries. Aware of his great contribution to Albanian studies, the Albanian government under Italian occupation approved his request, and the Italian foreign minister, at the insistence of **Carlo Tagliavini**, sought an exit visa for him. The German authorities, however, refused to let Jokl leave the country. On 4 March 1942, he was arrested by the Nazis in their campaign against the Jews and was deported towards an unknown destination. He died on or about 6 May of that year, having been murdered either in a barracks near Vienna or in a camp in Minsk or Riga, or possibly by putting an end to his own life.

Norbert Jokl is the author of about sixty scholarly articles on the Albanian language, published primarily in German. Of particular note is his monograph *Linguistisch-kulturhistorische Untersuchungen aus dem Bereiche des Albanischen* (Research in Linguistic and Cultural History from the Field of Albanian), Berlin 1923. His *Einführung in die vergleichende historische Grammatik des Albanischen* (Introduction to the Comparative Historical Grammar of Albanian), which he worked on painstakingly from 1913 to 1937, remained unpublished. It is preserved at the Manuscript Division of the Austrian National Library, together with several other manuscripts by the author.

JUBANI, ZEF (1818-1880.02.01). Poet and writer. Zef Jubani, known in Italian as *Giuseppe Jubany*, is thought to have been born in **Shkodra** of an Albanian father and Maltese mother. In about 1830, he was sent for schooling to his uncle in Malta, where he remained until 1838. Having finished his studies at a school of commerce there, he returned to Shkodra and, from 1848, served for several years as "dragoman" (interpreter) to Louis Hyacinthe Hécquard (1814-1866), French consul in Shkodra, who was preparing a book on northern Albania. Hécquard was very interested in folklore and took the young Zef Jubani and Halil Kopliku with him on his exhausting journeys through the northern Albanian mountains. A number of the folk songs they collected appeared in French translation in Hécquard's pioneer work, *Histoire et description de la Haute Albanie ou Guégarie* (History and Description of High Albania or Gegaria), Paris 1858. Jubani's own first collection of folklore, no doubt the original Albanian texts of the songs published by Hécquard, was unfortunately lost in the flood which devastated the city of Shkodra on 13 January 1866. Jubani later fled to Italy for a time, for reasons unknown, and was assisted there by **Girolamo De Rada**, also passionately interested in Albanian oral literature, with whom he had corresponded.

The work for which Zef Jubani is best remembered is his *Raccolta di canti popolari e rapsodie di poemi albanesi* (Collection of Albanian Folk Songs and Rhapsodies), Trieste 1871. This book constitutes the first collection of **Gheg** folk songs, indeed the first work of folklore to be published by an Albanian from

Albania itself. The introduction to Jubani's collection contains political reflections on the state of the country, an explanation of his "new system of Albanian writing in the Latin alphabet," which, it must be noted, was none too practical, and several paradigms. Among the songs included are those published previously in French by Hécquard, material which had appeared in **Pjetër Bogdani**'s *Cuneus prophetarum* (The Band of the Prophets) in 1685, and some specimens of *Bejtexhinj* lyrics. Jubani was also the author of an unfinished history of **Scanderbeg**, which remained unpublished. Of his own verse, only two poems have survived: one dedicated to **Dora d'Istria** and the other about Scanderbeg.

JUBANY, GIUSEPPE. *See* JUBANI, ZEF.

JUDAISM. Religion. The first reports of Jews living in Albania date from the twelfth century. Benjamin Ben Jonah of Tudela (d. 1173) noted at the time that, "they are not strong in the faith of the Nazarenes and call each other by Jewish names, and some say that they are Jews." By the early sixteenth century, there were definite Jewish settlements in most of the major towns of Albania, including **Berat**, **Elbasan**, **Vlora,** and **Durrës**, as well as in **Kosova**. Many of these Jewish merchant families, who were of Sephardic origin and descendants of the Spanish and Portuguese Jews expelled from Iberia in the 1490s, had close ties with Jewish communities in Split, Dubrovnik, Corfu and Thessalonika. In 1519-1520, there were 609 Jewish households in Vlora alone, mostly refugees from Spain. Vlora was also the site of Albania's only synagogue, which was destroyed in **World War I**. In 1673, the charismatic Jewish prophet **Sabbetai Sevi**, the so-called mystical messiah, was exiled by the sultan to the Albanian port of Ulcinj, now in Montenegro, and died there two years later.

According to the census of 1930, there were 204 Jews registered in Albania. On 2 April 1937, the Jewish community, now consisting of some 300 members, was granted official recognition in the country. With the rise of Adolf Hitler, a number of families of German and Austrian Jews took refuge in Albania. Indeed the Albanian Embassy in Berlin continued to issue visas to Jews up to the end of 1938, at a time when no other European country was willing to take them in. Jewish refugees were mostly well looked after by the local population and survived the German occupation of Albania (1943-1944) unscathed. Indeed, it is said that during the Nazi occupation not one single Jew in hiding in Albania was betrayed or handed over to the Germans, an admirable reflection of how well the Albanians adhered to their traditional customs of hospitality and *besa*.

For the Jews of Kosova, however, the situation turned out much worse. During **World War II**, many Jews from Croatia and Serbia who had sought refuge in Kosova during its short-lived reunification with Albania (ironically under the auspices of fascist **Italy** and Nazi **Germany**) and who were initially well treated there, were returned by the Italians to Belgrade and executed. In the spring of 1944, 281 Jews of Kosova were arrested by the SS "Skanderbeg" Division and imprisoned at a camp in Prishtina before being transported to the Reich. Others joined them later. Of the 400 Jews sent to Bergen Belsen concentration camp, only about 100 survived.

During the **communist** dictatorship, there were about 200 Jews in Albania (seventy-three according to the official census of April 1989), most of them were well integrated into Albanian society. In 1991, after the fall of the dictatorship, the vast majority of Jews and their family members (ca. 400 persons), emigrated en bloc to Israel, where they now form a tiny ethnic community of their own.

JUNE REVOLUTION. *See* DEMOCRATIC REVOLUTION.

- K -

KABALLIÔTÊS, THEODÔROS ANASTASIOS. *See* KAVALIOTI, THEODHOR.

KACELI, SADIK (1914-2000). Painter. Sadik Kaceli was born in **Tirana** of a large family from the nearby Dajti region. From 1929, he attended the **American Vocational School**, where he specialized in drawing. He acquired an initial knowledge of world art from the art books and magazines that he discovered at the new **Herbert** Library, the first public library in Albania, founded by Lady Carnarvon. Wishing to study art in France, he wrote a letter to French painter Henri Matisse (1869-1954), who replied to him on 12 April 1936, recommending that he contact art critic André Lhote (1885-1962) and study at the Ecole Nationale

Supérieure des Beaux Arts in Paris. In September 1936, assisted financially by his brothers, Kaceli thus left for Paris and continued his training there until 1941. On his return to Tirana, he taught art at a secondary school and then, from 1946 until his retirement in 1973, at the Jordan Misja Academy. Sadik Kaceli was a realist painter though he was never willing or able to adapt his style completely to the prerequisites of socialist realism and was thus marginalized for many years during the dictatorship. He is remembered for both portraits and landscape paintings.

KADARE, ISMAIL (1936.01.28-). Prose writer and poet. Born in the museum-city of **Gjirokastra**, Kadare studied at the Faculty of History and Philology of the University of **Tirana** and subsequently at the Gorky Institute of World Literature in Moscow until 1960 when relations between Albania and the **Soviet Union** became tense. On his return to Albania he worked as a journalist, became editor-in-chief of the French-language literary periodical *Les Lettres Albanaises* (Albanian Letters) and carried out several formal political functions.

Kadare began his literary career in Albania with poetry but turned increasingly to prose, of which he soon became the undisputed master and by far the most popular writer of the whole of Albanian **literature**. His works were extremely influential throughout the 1970s and 1980s and, for many readers, he was the only ray of hope in the chilly, dismal prison that was **communist** Albania. Ismail Kadare, who is also the only Albanian writer to enjoy a broad international reputation, lived the next thirty years of his life in Tirana, constantly under the Damocles Sword of the Party. He was privileged by the authorities, in particular once his works became known internationally. Indeed, he was able to pursue literary and personal objectives for which other writers would certainly have been sent into internal exile or to prison. But Kadare knew well that liberties in Albania could be withdrawn easily, by an impulsive stroke of the tyrant's quill. At the end of October 1990, a mere two months before the final collapse of the dictatorship, Ismail Kadare left Tirana and applied for political asylum in France. This departure enabled him for the first time to exercise his profession with complete freedom. His years of Parisian exile have been productive and have accorded him further success and recognition, as a writer both in Albanian and in French. After twelve years in Paris, he returned in Tirana in 2002.

Though Kadare is admired as a poet in Albania, his reputation and, in particular, his international reputation now rests entirely upon his prose. Of his works which have been translated into English, mention may be made of the following: *Gjenerali i ushtrisë së vdekur,* Tirana 1963 (*The General of the Dead Army,* London 1971); *Prilli i thyer,* 1978 (*Broken April,* New York 1990); *Nëpunësi i pallatit të ëndrrave,* 1981 (*The Palace of Dreams,* New York & London 1993); *Krushqit janë të ngrirë,* 1986 (*The Wedding Procession Turned to Ice,* Boulder 1997); *Koncert në fund të dimrit,* Tirana 1988 (*The Concert,* New York & London 1994); *Dosja H,* Tirana 1990 (*The File on H,* London 1997); *Piramida,* 1993 (*The Pyramid,* London & New York 1996); *Tri këngë zie për Kosovën,* Tirana 1998 (*Three Elegies for Kosovo,* London 2000); and *Lulet e ftohta të marsit,* Tirana 2000 (*Spring Flowers, Spring Frost,* New York 2002). Kadare has recently published his collected works in eleven thick volumes, each in an Albanian-**language** and a French-language edition, and has been given membership in the prestigious Académie Française (28 October 1996) and in the French Legion of Honor. He has also been nominated on several occasions for the Nobel Prize for Literature.

There can be no doubt that Ismail Kadare was a profoundly dissident writer who, at the same time, led an extremely conformist, if you will, collaborationist life. Dissent in Kadare's prose up to the fall of the dictatorship is very discreet but ubiquitous. Notwithstanding its subtle nature, it was sufficiently evident at all times to the educated Albanian reader, and this is one of the major factors which contributed to his popularity at home. He left no opportunity untouched to attack the follies, weaknesses and excesses of the Albanian communist system, yet many of his subtle barbs are difficult to grasp for those who did not grow up in or live through that system. The very treatment in a conformist manner of a taboo subject, i.e., of virtually anything beyond the very narrow scope of socialist realism and communist partisan heroism, constituted in itself an act of extreme dissent, amounting to treason in Albania. Though some observers in Albania silently viewed him as a political opportunist, and many Albanians in exile later criticized him vociferously for the compromises he made, it is Ismail Kadare more than anyone else who, from within the system, dealt the death blow to the literature of socialist realism. There can certainly be no doubt that he made use of his relative freedom and his talent under the dictatorship to launch many a subtle but effective fusillade against the regime in the form of political allegories which occur throughout his works. Ismail Kadare was thus the most prominent representative of Albanian literature under the dictatorship of **Enver Hoxha** and, at the same time, the regime's most talented adversary.

KADIRI ORDER OF DERVISHES. Islamic Sufi sect or *tariqa.* The Kadiri order, Alb. *Kadri,* is named after a twelfth-century Hanbalite theologian called Abd al-Qâdir al-Jîlâni (1077-1166) of Baghdad. After he died, his legend and his doctrines spread throughout the Islamic world as far as the Indian subcontinent, in particular in the fifteenth century. The Kadiri order appeared in Istanbul in the seventeenth century when Sheikh Ismail Tumi, known as Pîr Thânî, founded a *tekke* at Tophane. The Balkan branch of the sect, also called the Zindjiri, was founded by Ali Baba of Crete, whose death helped to propagate the order in Albania, initially from within the **Bektashi** movement. According to **Eqrem bey Vlora**, the Kadiri were the fifth most important dervish sect in Albania, after the Bektashi, the **Halveti**, the **Rifa'i** and the **Sa'di**.

　　We know of their presence in at least five towns of central Albania: in **Berat**, where a Kadiri *tekke* was situated in the Baba Kadi quarter and was headed up to 1708 by one Sheh Ahmet; in **Elbasan**, where their *tekke* seems to have been associated with the Tanners' Mosque, Alb. *Xhamia e Tabakëve,* in the former Market quarter; in Peqin; in Tirana, where the Kadiri poet Haxhi Ymer Mustafa Kashari was active in the early eighteenth century and where the mausoleum of Dervish Hatixhe was built around 1798; and in Peshkopia. Peshkopia may perhaps have been the most important center of the Kadiri sect, where, in about 1900, a sheikh from **Dibra** is said to have been the head sheikh of the *tariqa.*

　　The Kadiri formed part of the *Drita Hyjnore* (Divine Light) organization in 1936, and after 1945 became a recognized religious community, led by a Sheikh Besim Selimi of Peshkopia. In the 1990s, they reestablished themselves in Albania and now have a center in Peshkopia, led by Sheikh Mesur Shehu.

KADRIU, HOXHA. *See* PRISHTINA, KADRI.

KAMARDA, DHIMITËR. *See* CAMARDA, DEMETRIO.

KANUN OF ARBËRIA. *See* KANUN OF SCANDERBEG.

KANUN OF LABËRIA. System of customary law. The *Kanun* of **Labëria**, Alb. *Kanuni i Labërisë*, was adhered to in the southern Albanian districts of **Vlora**, Kurvelesh, **Himara** and **Tepelena**, in particular, within the area of the so-called three bridges (Drashovica, Tepelena and Kalasa), and regulated social norms and property relations in this region. It is traditionally associated with a priest called Papa Zhuli, founder of the village of Zhulat near **Gjirokastra**, and is thus also known as the *Kanun* of Papa Zhuli, Alb. *Kanuni i Papa Zhulit*.

KANUN OF LEKË DUKAGJINI. System of customary law. The *Kanun* or Code of Lekë Dukagjini, Alb. *Kanuni i Lekë Dukagjinit*, is the most famous compilation of Albanian customary or consuetudinary law. This initially unwritten code of law governed social behavior and almost every facet of life in the isolated and otherwise lawless terrain of the northern highlands, and was adhered to throughout much of northern Albania for centuries. Indeed, it is widely respected even today. The heartland of the *Kanun* was **Dukagjini**, the highlands of **Lezha**, **Mirdita**, **Shala**, Shosh, Nikaj-Merturi and the plain of Dukagjini in present-day western **Kosova**. Lekë Dukagjini (1410-1481), after whom the code was named, is a little-known and somewhat mysterious figure thought to have been a fifteenth-century prince and comrade in arms of **Scanderbeg**. Whether he compiled the code or simply gave his name to it is not known.

The *Kanun* was strictly observed by the tribes of northern Albania and had priority over any other laws, ecclesiastical or secular, which tried to impose themselves in the mountains. With the help of this ancient code, the highland tribes were able to preserve their identity, their autonomy and their way of life though they were ostensibly part of the **Ottoman Empire** for five centuries.

In its definitive form, the *Kanun* had twelve chapters: church; the family; marriage; house, livestock, and property; work; transfer of property; the spoken word; honor; damages; the law regarding crimes; judicial law; exemptions and exceptions. Some aspects of the code may appear harsh, indeed barbaric, to the modern observer. Vengeance, for instance, was accepted as the prime instrument for exacting and maintaining justice. This led to a perpetuation of **blood feuding**, which decimated the northern tribes in the early years of the twentieth century and which has once again become a major problem of social life in the north. **Women** had a vastly inferior status, being deprived of virtually all male rights and privileges but also of all male duties. The code states explicitly, "a woman is a sack for carrying things," Alb. *grueja âsht shakull për me bajtë.* These aspects, however, simply mirrored social realities among the patriarchal tribes. One concept of this tribal law, which still arouses a certain admiration or at least astonishment today is that of the *besa*, an absolute fidelity to one's word, come what may.

The *Kanun* of Lekë Dukagjini was first codified by Father **Shtjefën Gjeçovi,** who published parts of it in **Faik bey Konitza**'s periodical *Albania* in 1898 and 1899, and then more extensive sections of it in the Shkodra periodical *Hylli i dritës* (The Day-Star) from 1913 to 1924. The definitive version was published under the title *Kanuni i Lekë Dukagjinit* (The Code of Lekë Dukagjini), Shkodra 1933.

The code has been the object of much interest among historians, legal experts and ethnographers, not only in Albania and Kosova but also abroad. The Scottish scholar **Margaret Hasluck,** for instance, dealt with it in her monograph *The Unwritten Law in Albania* (Cambridge 1954). It has been translated into English by Leonard Fox (New York 1989).

The *Kanun* of Lekë Dukagjini is not the only compilation of customary law among the Albanians, but it is by far the best-known. There is also a similar *Kanun* **of the Mountains**, a southern Albanian *Kanun* **of Labëria** and the so-called *Kanun* **of Scanderbeg**.

KANUN OF THE MOUNTAINS. System of customary law. The *Kanun* of the Mountains, Alb. *Kanuni i Maleve* or *Kanuni i Malësisë së Madhe,* was adhered to by the Albanians of the mountains north of the area of the *Kanun* **of Lekë Dukagjini,** i.e., primarily by the tribes of **Kastrati, Hoti, Gruda, Kelmendi,** Kuç, **Krasniqi, Gashi** and Bytyçi, thus extending in influence from Lake **Shkodra** through the northern Alps to the Gjakova highlands. It is quite similiar in content to the *Kanun* of Lekë Dukagjini.

KANUN OF PAPA ZHULI. *See* KANUN OF LABËRIA.

KANUN OF SCANDERBEG. System of customary law. The *Kanun* of **Scanderbeg,** Alb. *Kanuni i Skënderbeut,* also known as the Kanun of Arbëria, Alb. *Kanuni i Arbërisë,* was adhered to by the Albanians of northern central Albania, south of the area of the *Kanun* **of Lekë Dukagjini,** primarily in the regions of **Dibra,**

Kruja, **Kurbin**, Benda, and Martanesh, i.e., the territory once part of the principality created by Scanderbeg.

KANUNI I ARBËRISË. *See* KANUN OF SCANDERBEG.

KANUNI I LABËRISË. *See* KANUN OF LABËRIA.

KANUNI I LEKË DUKAGJINIT. *See* KANUN OF LEKË DUKAGJINI.

KANUNI I MALËSISË SË MADHE. *See* KANUN OF THE MOUNTAINS.

KANUNI I MALEVE. *See* KANUN OF THE MOUNTAINS.

KANUNI I PAPA ZHULIT. *See* KANUN OF LABËRIA.

KANUNI I SKËNDERBEUT. *See* KANUN OF SCANDERBEG.

KAPO, HYSNI (1915.03.04-1979.09.23). Political figure of the **communist** period. Hysni Kapo was born in Tërbaç near **Vlora**, where he attended the commercial school. He was a founding member of the communist party in 1941 and took part in the resistance movement during **World War II.** In 1945, he married Vito Kondi (1922-), who was a full member of the Central Committee from 1961 to 1991. Kapo served as ambassador to Yugoslavia from 1945 to 1947; deputy minister of foreign affairs from 1947 to 1949; deputy prime minister from 1950 to 1956; and minister of agriculture from 1951 to 1954.

Hysni Kapo was a member of the Central Committee from 1943 to 1979 and a member of the Politburo from 1946 to 1979. He played a major role in **Enver Hoxha**'s clash with Nikita Khrushchev and the Soviet party leadership in 1960-1961 and, as one of Hoxha's most trusted aides and allies, he remained an influential figure until his retirement in 1979. He died in Paris.

KASTRATI. Northern Albanian tribe and traditional tribal region. The Kastrati region is situated in the District of **Malësia e Madhe** east and northeast of Bajza. It borders on the traditional tribal regions of **Hoti** to the north, **Kelmendi** to the northeast, and the Koplik region to the south. The name was recorded as *Kastrati* in 1416 and *Castrati* in 1635, and is thought to be related to Lat.

castrum "Roman camp." The Kastrati tribe had a **population** of about 2,000 in the late nineteenth century.

KASTRATI, JUP (1924.04.15-). Scholar. Kastrati was born and raised in **Shkodra**, where he taught at the university. He is a well-known bibliographer and has written much on the history of Albanian studies. Among his major works are: *Bibliografi shqipe, 29.XI.1944-31.XII.1958* (Albanian Bibliography 29.XI.1944-31.XII.1958), Tirana 1959; *Histori e gramatologjisë shqiptare, 1635-1944* (History of Albanian Grammatology, 1635-1944), Prishtina 1980; *Zef Jubani: jeta dhe vepra* (Zef Jubani: Life and Works), Tirana 1987; *Faik Konica, monografi* (Faik Konitza: Monograph), New York 1995; and *Historia e Albanologjisë, 1497-1997: vëllimi i parë, 1497-1853* (History of Albanian Studies, 1497-1997, volume one, 1497-1853), Tirana 2000.

KASTRIOTI, GJERGJ. *See* SCANDERBEG.

KAVAJA. Town in the **District of Kavaja**, of which it is the administrative center. **Population** in Dec. 1999: 33,864. Kavaja is situated on the coastal plain south of **Durrës**. It was recorded as *Kavalye* in 1431 and as *Borgo Cavaglia* in the sixteenth century. The present settlement dates from the **Ottoman** period, when **Durrës** had fallen into decay. **Evliya Çelebi**, who visited Kavaja in 1670 called it a "charming town...with 400 one- and two-storey stonework houses, with tiled roofs and embellished with delightful gardens, ponds and fountains. There are also exquisite mansions with towers and pleasure-domes. Many noble families live here." Kavaja, like **Elbasan**, is a town with a traditionally strong Muslim culture, though there are **Catholics** here, too. It was in Kavaja that the first anticommunist demonstrations took place on 26 March 1990. It has grown substantially since that time as a result of migration from the mountains and the development of **tourism** along the nearby sandy beach, but it still suffers from high unemployment.

KAVAJA, DISTRICT OF. Region of local government administration. The District of Kavaja (*Rrethi i Kavajës*), with its administrative headquarters in the town of **Kavaja**, borders on the Adriatic Sea to the west, the districts of **Durrës** and **Tirana** to the north, **Peqin** to the east, and **Lushnja** to the south. It has a surface area of 414 square kilometers and a present **population** of 91,274 (in 2000).

KAVALIOTI, THEODHOR (ca. 1718-1789). Vlach scholar and publisher. Kavalioti, known in Greek as Theodôros Anastasios Kaballiôtês, was a Vlach scholar from **Voskopoja** who made an important contribution to Albanian writing in the field of lexicography. Kavalioti studied mathematics, theology and philosophy in Janina (Iôannina) between 1732 and 1734, famil-iarizing himself with the works of Descartes, Malebranche and Leibniz. He returned to his native Voskopoja, which was itself beginning to flourish in the mid-eighteenth century, and became director of the New Academy in 1746. He is the author of several works of philosophy written in Greek, of an elementary grammar of Greek, and of a scholarly work entitled *Prôtopeiria* (Primer), Venice 1770, which contains a three-language lexicon in Greek, Aromanian and Albanian of about 1,170 words. A copy of the work is in the possession of the Library of the Romanian Academy in Bucharest. This lexicon was republished by the German scholar Johann Thunmann from Halle with a Latin translation in 1774 and is of linguistic interest for students of both Albanian and Aromanian.

KËLCYRA, ALI BEY (1891.05.28-1963.09.24). Political figure. Ali bey Këlcyra, also known as Ali bey Klissura, was born in Këlcyra, formerly Klissura, in the **Përmet** district of southern Albania. He studied in Istanbul and finished his doctorate in law in Rome. Këlcyra took part in the **Congress of Lushnja** and in the fight in the summer of 1920 to rid **Vlora** of Italian troops. From 1921 to 1924, he was a member of **parliament** where he supported **Fan Noli** but was less reform oriented. He is remembered in particular as a great speaker who used his rhetorical skills to attack **Ahmet Zogu** and his cohorts. He fled the country after the fall of the Noli government and headed the *Bashkimi Kombëtar* (The National Union) organization abroad. The Zogu regime sentenced him to death in absentia on several occasions. Ali bey Këlcyra was also among the leading figures of the *Balli Kombëtar* resistance movement during **World War II**, and was forced to flee the country in 1944 when the **communists** took power. Together with **Mid'hat bey Frashëri**, he endeavored to keep the anticommunist *Balli Kombëtar* alive from abroad until it inevitably split into various factions and lost its significance. Këlcyra later broadcast Albanian-language news programs from the West and died in Rome.

KËLLEZI, ABDYL (1919-1975). Political figure of the **communist** period. Abdyl Këllezi was born in **Tirana** and studied business administration at the University of Florence in Italy. He also attended a military school in Rome. He was interned on the Italian island of Ventotene in 1939-1941 for his antifascist activities and was rearrested in 1942 but later took part in the resistance movement during **World War II**. After the war, he served as director of the state bank, 1945-1946; minister of finance, 1948-1953 and 1954-1958; chairman of the state planning commission, Dec. 1968-1975; deputy prime minister, June 1958–3 March 1966; and chairman of the Sino-Albanian friendship association, 1959-1975. He was a member of the Central Committee from June 1956 to 1975 and a full member of the Politburo from 1971 to 1975.

Abdyl Këllezi, together with Koço Theodhosi, minister of industry and mines, and **Kiço Ngjela**, trade minister, fell victim to the purge at the seventh Congress of the Central Committee on 26-29 May 1975, allegedly for grave "revisionist" mistakes and sabotage of the economy. He was swiftly relieved of his posts, expelled from the party, arrested and executed.

KELMENDI. Northern Albanian tribe and traditional tribal region. The Kelmendi region is situated in the District of **Malësia e Madhe** in the most northerly and isolated portion of Albania. It borders on the traditional tribal regions of **Gruda** to the west, **Hoti** to the southwest, **Boga** to the south and **Shala** to the east. The administrative center of this isolated mountain region is now Vermosh. The name "Kelmendi," recorded in 1485 as *Kelmente* and in 1689 as *Clementi*, is related to the Latin personal name *Clementus,* borrowed into Albanian through the influence of the **Catholic Church**.

In the mid-1580s, the Catholic Kelmendi tribe ceased paying taxes to the **Ottoman** state and, as fierce and independent-minded warriors, gradually came to dominate all of northern Albania. They were exceptionally mobile and went raiding and marauding not only in the mountains, but deep into the territories of **Kosova**, Bosnia and **Serbia**, indeed as far as Plovdiv in Bulgaria. The Kelmendi played a prominent role in various anti-Ottoman rebellions, especially in the first half of the seventeenth century. They allied themselves with the Hapsburg forces invading Kosova in 1689, and after the withdrawal of the Imperial Army in 1690, were surrounded by Ottoman forces and compelled to leave their mountain homeland and settle in the Pešter region of the Sandjak in 1702. During the Austrian campaign of 1730, they were then obliged to retreat with the Hapsburg army to Austrian-controlled territory near Belgrade, where many of them settled. Though they remained a powerful tribe in northern Albania over the following 150 years, they never regained the power they had enjoyed in the seventeenth century. In the late nineteenth century, the Kelmendi tribe had a modest **population** of some 4,000.

KELMENDI, ALI (1900-1939.02.11). Early figure of the Albanian **communist** movement. Ali Kelmendi was born in Peja in **Kosova** as the son of a peasant farmer. He was early to join the communist movement and fled to Albania in 1920 when the Yugoslav communist party was banned. In 1925-1930, he lived in the Soviet Union, where he was schooled by the Comintern. After his return to Albania in 1930, he founded some clandestine communist groups, in particular the **Korça** group, and took part in communist agitation and anti-royalist demonstrations. He fled the country in 1936, returning to Moscow, and later died in Paris.

KEMAL, ISMAIL. *See* VLORA, ISMAIL QEMAL BEY.

KEMP, PETER (1915.08.19-1993). British military officer and writer. Peter Mant Macintyre Kemp was born in Bombay and was educated at Trinity College, Cambridge. He fought with the Nationalists in the Spanish Civil War in 1938 and was called to the War Office in the spring of 1940. In 1943, he was recruited by the **Special Operations Executive** (SOE) and was parachuted into Albania to join the British military mission there. He traveled on foot to **Kosova** and, after ten months in Albania, escaped to Montenegro. He later worked for the SOE in Southeast Asia. After retirement from the army, he took a job with a life insurance company but left its employ in 1980. Kemp was also active as a journalist over the years, and reported Albania and Kosova after a visit there in 1990. His wartime experiences, including much on Albania, were recorded in the volumes *No Colours or Crest* (London 1958) and *The Thorns of Memory* (London 1990).

KËNGË KRESHNIKESH. *See* SONGS OF THE FRONTIER WARRIORS.

KETA, NIKOLLË. *See* CHETTA, NICOLA.

KINOSTUDIO "SHQIPËRIA E RE." *See* NEW ALBANIA FILM STUDIOS.

KLISSURA, ALI BEY. *See* KËLCYRA, ALI BEY.

KLOSI, ARDIAN (1957-). Scholar and author. Ardian Klosi was born in **Tirana** of a ruling **communist** family. He studied language and literature in Tirana and, from 1986 to 1990, attended the University of Innsbruck in Austria, where he finished his doctorate in comparative literature with a dissertation entitled *Mythologie am Werk: Kazantzakis, Andrić, Kadare* (Mythology in the Making: Kazantzakis, Andrić, Kadare), Munich 1991. He spent several years in Munich, where he taught Albanian, translated German literature into Albanian and coauthored a *Wörterbuch Deutsch-Albanisch* (German-Albanian Dictionary), Leipzig 1997.

Klosi was a leading intellectual figure of the democracy movement in 1990-1991, and, after his return to Albania, he headed Albanian Radio and Television from 23 July 1998 to 24 March 1999. He currently writes for the newspaper *Shekulli* (The Century). Among his other publications are the critical anthologies *Shqipëria zgjim i dhimbshëm* (Albania Painful Awakening), Tirana 1991; and *Quo vadis, Shqipëri?* (Whither Goest Thou, Albania?), Tirana 1993; and, with German photographer Jutta Benzenberg, the album *Albanisches Überleben* (Surviving the Albanian Way), Salzburg 1993.

KOÇA, VANGJEL (1900-1943). Writer and political figure. Vangjel Koça of **Korça** was the cofounder of **Neo-Albanianism**. He translated Epictetus, Lucian and Descartes and was known as a journalist under the playful oriental pseudonyms of Vangjo Nirvana and Vangjo Knishna. Koça became a leader of the fascist party after Benito Mussolini's invasion of Albania in 1939. He drowned while trying to escape to **Italy** in 1943.

KOÇI, FATMIR (1959.11.30-). **Film** director. Fatmir Koçi was born in **Tirana** and graduated in drama from the Academy of Fine Arts (*Instituti i Lartë i Arteve*) in 1982. His first full-length film was the well-received *Nekrologji* (Obituary), 1994, which got special mention at the Montreal film festival. His documentary *Koka alternative* (Alternative Head), 1997, also received two awards at the Mediterranean film festival in Aubagne. After the film *Superballkan* (Super Balkan), 1997, based primarily on archive footage, he directed the delightful social comedy *Tirana Viti Zero* (Tirana Year Zero), 2001, which received the Silver Wave award at the Mediterranean film festival in Cologne, Germany, in December 2002.

KOÇI, SABRI (1921.05.13-). Muslim religious figure. Haxhi Hafiz Sabri Koçi was born in the village of Orenja near **Librazhd**. His parents died at an early age. He finished his schooling and religious training in **Shkodra**. Still at a young age, he worked as an imam in **Drisht** from 1938 to 1939 and was then transferred to Shkodra. He was later active as a mufti in **Kruja** (1955), and **Kavaja** (1956). On 14 June 1966, Koçi was arrested and sentenced to twenty-two years in prison. He was released on 26 October 1986. When the **Islamic** community was officially recognized in early 1991, Sabri Koçi was chosen as its new leader.

KODRA, IBRAHIM (1918.04.18-). Painter. Ibrahim Kodra was born in **Ishëm** near **Durrës** and studied at the **American Vocational School** in **Tirana**, specializing in drawing and design. With the assistance of the Italian consulate, he received a scholarship to study abroad and spent four years at the Academy of Fine Arts in Brescia in northern Italy. In 1944, he opened an art studio in Milan and gradually made a name for himself with a style all his own. In 1948, he met Picasso at an international peace conference in Rome and studied architecture over the following years. Ibrahim Kodra is the author of over 2,000 works of art created over a period of fifty years. He is the only Albanian painter of international renown. French surrealist poet Paul Eluard (1895-1952) wrote of him "Kodra is the primitive of a new civilization."

KODRA, LAME. *See* MALËSHOVA, SEJFULLA.

KOKALARI, MUSINE (1917.02.10-1983.08.14). Prose writer. Musine Kokalari of **Gjirokastra** is the first female writer of Albania and was the only one up until the 1960s. Born in Adana in southern Turkey to a family of Gjirokastrite origin, Kokalari returned to Albania with her family in 1920. She acquired a taste for books and learning early in life because her brother Vejsim operated a bookstore in **Tirana** in the mid-1930s. In January 1938, she left for Rome to study **literature** at the university there and graduated in 1941 with a study on **Naim bey Frashëri**. Her stay in the eternal city gave her an ephemeral glimpse into a fascinating world of intellectual creativity, and her sole aim in life upon her return to Albania was to become a writer. In 1943, she declared to a friend, "I want to write, to write, only to write literature, and to have nothing to do with politics." At the age of twenty-four, she published an initial eighty-page collection of ten youthful prose tales in her native Gjirokastrite dialect: *Siç më thotë nënua plakë* (As My Old Mother Tells Me), Tirana 1941. This historic collection, strongly inspired by **Tosk** folklore and by the day-to-day struggles of **women** in Gjirokastra, is thought to be the first work of literature ever written and published by a woman in Albania. Three years later, despite the vicissitudes of the civil war, Kokalari published a longer collection of short stories and sketches entitled *...sa u-tunt jeta* (...How Life Swayed), Tirana 1944, which established her—ever so briefly—as a writer of substance. A third volume of her folksy tales was entitled *Rreth vatrës* (Around the Hearth), Tirana 1944.

As **World War II** came to an end, Kokalari opened a bookstore herself and was invited to become a member of the **Writers' Union**, created on 7 October 1945 under the chair-manship of **Sejfulla Malëshova**. All this time, she was haunted by the execution without trial of her two brothers, Mumtaz and Vejsim, on 12 November 1944 by the **communists** and candidly demanded justice and retribution. Having herself been closely associated in 1943 with the founding of the fledgling Albanian **Social Democratic Party** and its press medium *Zëri i lirisë* (The Voice of Freedom), she was arrested on 17 January 1946 in an age of terror concomitant with the fall of Malëshova, and on 2 July 1946 was sentenced by the military court of Tirana to twenty years in prison as a "saboteur and enemy of the people." The next eighteen years of her life were spent in the infamous concentration camp of Burrel in the **Mat** region, isolated and under constant surveillance, persecuted and provoked by boorish and uneducated prison officers. A broken woman, she was released around 1964 and given a job as a street sweeper in the provincial town of Rrëshen. Musine Kokalari, once a gifted young teller of tales, was persecuted to the end of her days. Terminally ill with cancer, she was even refused a hospital bed before her death in 1983.

KOLEKA, SPIRO (1908.07.07-2001.08). Political figure of the **communist** period. Koleka was born in Vuno on the coast of **Himara** in the 1920s, son of a government minister. He went to college in Cosenza in 1928-1929 and studied at the University of Pisa in 1930-1934, graduating with a degree in civil engineering.

In 1936-1937, he worked for an Italian engineering company and was arrested during the **Fier** strike against the **Zog** administration. He took part in the communist partisan movement during **World War II**. After the communist takeover, he served as minister of public works, 1944-1948; minister of communications, Nov. 1948 - July 1950; chairman of the state planning commission, Nov. 1949 - July 1950, 1954-1958, 1966-1968; deputy prime minister, 1950-1953, 1956-1966, 1968-1978; and chairman of the Sino-Albanian friendship association, 1975. A leading figure of the communist hierarchy to the end, Spiro Koleka was a member of the Central Committee from 1948 to June 1991 and of the Politburo from 1948 to 1981.

KOLIQI, ERNEST (1903.05.20-1975.01.15). Prose writer, scholar and public figure. Ernest Koliqi was the most imposing and influential prose writer of the period before **World War II**. He was born in **Shkodra** and was educated at the **Jesuit** college of Arice in the Lombardian town of Brescia. With the formation of a new regency government in Albania under **Sulejman bey Delvina** and the return of a semblance of stability in the country with the **Congress of Lushnja**, the young Ernest arrived back in Shkodra to rediscover and indeed to relearn his mother tongue and the culture of his childhood in a newly independent country.

When conservative landowner **Ahmet Zogu** took power in a coup d'état in December 1924, Koliqi escaped to **Yugoslavia**, where he lived for a total of five years, three of them in Tuzla. These years were to have a profound influence on his later academic and literary career. From 1930 to 1933, Koliqi taught at a commercial school in **Vlora** and at the state secondary school in Shkodra until he was obliged, once again by political circumstances, to depart for **Italy**.

Ernest Koliqi's solid Jesuit **education** enabled him from the start to serve as a cultural intermediary between Italy and Albania. In later years, he was to play a key role in transmitting Albanian culture to the Italian public by publishing, in addition to numerous scholarly articles on literary and historical subjects, the following monographs: *Poesia popolare albanese* (Albanian Folk Verse), Florence 1957; *Antologia della lirica albanese* (Anthology of Albanian Poetry), Milan 1963; and *Saggi di letteratura albanese* (Essays on Albanian Literature), Florence 1972. He also published a large two-volume Albanian-**language** anthology of Italian verse entitled *Poetët e mëdhej t'Italis* (The Great Poets of Italy), Tirana 1932, 1936, to introduce Italian literature to the new generation of Albanian intellectuals eager to discover the world around them.

Koliqi registered at the University of Padua in 1933. After five years of studying under linguist **Carlo Tagliavini** and of teaching Albanian there, he graduated in 1937 with a thesis on the *Epica popolare albanese* (Albanian Folk Epic). He was then a recognized Albanologist, perhaps the leading specialist in Albanian studies in Italy. In 1939, as the clouds of war gathered over Europe, he was appointed to the chair of Albanian language and **literature** at the University of Rome, at the heart of Mussolini's new Mediterranean empire.

Koliqi's strong affinity for Italy and Italian culture, in particular for poets such as Giosuè Carducci, Giovanni Pascoli and Gabriele D'Annunzio, may have contributed to his acceptance of fascist Italy's expansionist designs. As much of an Albanian nationalist as any other, Koliqi, now the country's *éminence grise*, chose to make the best of the reality with which he was faced and did what he could to further Albanian culture under Italian rule. Accepting the post of Albanian minister of education from 1939 to 1941, much to the consternation of large sections of the population, he founded and subsequently ran the literary and artistic monthly *Shkëndija* (The Spark) in **Tirana**. Under Koliqi's ministerial direction, Albanian-language schools, which had been outlawed under **Serbian** rule, were first opened in **Kosova**, which was reunited with Albania during the war years. Koliqi also assisted in the opening of a secondary school in Prishtina and arranged for scholarships for Kosova students to be sent abroad to Italy and Austria for training. He also made an attempt to save **Norbert Jokl**, renowned Austrian Albanologist of **Jewish** origin, from the hands of the Nazis by offering him a teaching position in Albania.

From 1942 to 1943, Koliqi was president of the newly formed Institute of Albanian Studies (*Istituti i Studimevet Shqiptare*) in Tirana, a forerunner of the Academy of Sciences. In 1943, on the eve of the collapse of Mussolini's empire, he succeeded Terenc Toçi as president of the Fascist Grand Council in Tirana, a post which of course did not endear him to the victorious **communist** forces which "liberated" Tirana in November 1944. With the defeat of fascism, Koliqi managed to flee to Italy again, where he lived, no less active in the field of literature and culture, until his death in 1975.

It was in Rome that Ernest Koliqi published the noted literary periodical *Shêjzat / Le Plèiadi* (The Pleiades) from 1957 to 1973.

Shêjzat was the leading Albanian-language cultural periodical of its time. Ernest Koliqi served as a distant voice of opposition to the cultural destruction of Albania under Stalinist rule. Because of his activities and at least passive support of fascist rule and Italian occupation, Koliqi was virulently attacked by the postwar Albanian authorities—more so even than **Gjergj Fishta** who had the good fortune of being dead—as the main proponent of bourgeois, reactionary and fascist literature. The 1983 party history of Albanian literature refers to him only in passing as "Koliqi the traitor."

Ernest Koliqi first made a name for himself as a prose writer with the short story collection *Hija e maleve* (The Spirit of the Mountains), Zadar 1929, twelve tales of contemporary life in Shkodra and in the northern Albanian mountains. *Tregtar flamujsh* (Flag Merchant), Tirana 1935, his second collection of tales, is considered by many to rank among the best Albanian prose of the prewar period. A quarter of a century later, Koliqi also published a short novel, *Shija e bukës së mbrûme* (The Taste of Sourdough Bread), Rome 1960. This 173-page work revives the theme of nostalgia for the homeland felt by Albanian immigrants in the **United States**. Not devoid of political overtones, the novel was little known in Albania during the dictatorship.

The literary production of Ernest Koliqi was by no means restricted to prose. *Gjurmat e stinve* (The Traces of the Seasons), Tirana 1933, is a verse collection composed for the most part during Koliqi's years of exile in Yugoslavia. *Symfonija e shqipevet* (The Symphony of Eagles), Tirana 1941, is prose poetry on historical and nationalist themes reminiscent of his earlier *Kushtrimi i Skanderbeut* (**Scanderbeg**'s War Cry). Koliqi's final volume of verse entitled *Kangjelet e Rilindjes* (Songs of Rebirth), Rome 1959, was composed again in his refined **Gheg** dialect and published with an Italian translation.

As a literary and cultural figure, Ernest Koliqi was and remains a giant, in particular for his role in the development of northern Albanian prose. Literary production in Gheg dialect reached a high point in the early 1940s from every point of view —style, range, content, volume—and much credit for this development goes to publisher, prose writer and scholar Ernest Koliqi.

KOLOMBI, ZEF (1907.03.03-1949.01.23). Painter. Zef Kolombi was born in Sarajevo of a father from **Shkodra** and a mother from Slovenia. His parents died when he was very young and he was raised in Shkodra by his grandmother. After a difficult youth, he got a state scholarship from minister **Hilë Mosi** to study at the Academy of Fine Arts in Rome in 1929. He returned to Albania in 1933 and worked as an arts teacher at the Normal School (*Shkolla Normale*) in **Elbasan**. In 1941, he moved back to Shkodra, where he died at the age of forty-two. About fifty of his paintings and drawings, the earliest dating from 1926, are preserved today. Among them are portraits and tranquil landscape paintings, often infused with a touch of melancholy.

KOLONJA, DISTRICT OF. Region of local government administration. The District of Kolonja (*Rrethi i Kolonjes*), also known as the district of Erseka, with its administrative headquarters in the town of Erseka, borders on the districts of **Përmet** to the west, **Korça** to the north, **Devoll** to the east and the Republic of Greece to the south. It has a surface area of 805 square kilometers and a present **population** of 25,022 (in 2000). It is the second least populated district in Albania, after Has, and has the lowest population density. The word "Kolonja" was recorded in Byzantine Greek in 1382 as Kolôneía.

KOLSTI, JOHN (1935.09.30-). Albanian-American scholar. John Sotter Kolsti was born in Boston, Massachusetts, of a family of southern Albanian descent. He studied at Harvard University, where he finished his doctorate in 1968 under the supervision of folklorist Albert Bates Lord. Since 1966, he has been professor of Slavic languages and literatures at the University of Austin in Texas. Kolsti is the author of *The Bilingual Singer: A Study in Albanian and Serbo-Croatian Oral Epic Traditions,* New York 1990, and of articles on Albanian epic poetry and politics.

KOMISIJA LETRARE SHQYPE. *See* ALBANIAN LITERARY COMMISSION.

KOMITET QENDROR PËR MBROJTJEN E TË DREJTAVE TË KOMBËSISË SHQIPTARE. *See* CENTRAL COMMITTEE FOR THE DEFENSE OF THE RIGHTS OF THE ALBANIAN PEOPLE.

KONARE (1925-). Organization. The KONARE or National Revolutionary Committee (*Komiteti Nacional Revolucionar*) heralds the beginning of the Albanian **communist** movement. It was set up in Vienna in 1925 by exile groups, including writer and politician **Fan Noli** and **Omer Nishani** as a sign of opposition to dictator **Ahmet Zogu,** who seized power in December 1924. From 29 July 1925, the committee published an anti-Zog weekly newpaper in Geneva called *Liria Kombëtare* (National Freedom). This committee established links with the Communist International (Comintern) in Moscow which provided financial backing. Among the early figures of this Albanian communist movement was **Ali Kelmendi.**

KONGOLI, FATOS (1944-). Prose writer. Fatos Kongoli has become one of the most convincing representatives of contemporary Albanian **literature** in recent years. He was born and raised in **Elbasan** and studied mathematics in **China** during the tense years of the Sino-Albanian alliance. Kongoli chose not to publish any major works during the dictatorship. Instead of this, he devoted his creative energies at the time to an obscure and apolitical career as a mathematician and waited for the storm to pass. His narrative talent and individual style only really emerged in the 1990s, after the fall of the **communist** dictatorship.

Kongoli's first major novel, *I humburi* (The Loser), Tirana 1992, was set in March 1991, when some 20,000 refugees scrambled onto decrepit and heavily rusting freighters to escape the past and to reach the marvelous West. This was followed by *Kufoma* (The Corpse), Tirana 1994, which has clear affinities with its predecessor, both with respect to Kongoli's now crystallized and more elaborate narrative style, and to his innate preoccupations. Protagonist Festim Gurabardhi is another loser, caught up in the inhumane machinery of the last decade of the Stalinist dictatorship in Albania. The third novel, *Dragoi i fildishtë* (The Ivory Dragon), Tirana 1999, focuses primarily on the life of an Albanian student in **China** in the 1960s. Kongoli's works have been translated into French, German and Greek.

KONICA, FAIK. *See* KONITZA, FAIK BEY.

KONICA, MEHMET BEY. *See* KONITZA, MEHMET BEY.

KONITZA, FAIK BEY (1875.03.15-1942.12.15). Writer and publisher. Faik bey Konitza, also spelled Konica, was the most influential of all Albanian writers and publishers of the turn of the century. He was born in 1875 in the now Greek village of Konitsa in the Pindus mountains, not far from the present Albanian border. After elementary schooling in Turkish in his native village, he studied at the **Jesuit** Saverian College in **Shkodra.** From there, he continued his schooling at the French-language Imperial Galata secondary school in Istanbul. In 1890, at the age of fifteen, he was sent to study in France, where he spent the next seven years. After initial education at secondary schools in Lisieux (1890) and Carcassonne (1892), he registered at the University of Dijon, from which he graduated in 1895 in Romance philology. After graduation, he moved to Paris for two years where he studied medieval French, Latin and Greek at the Collège de France. He finished his studies at Harvard University in the **United States**, although little is known about this period of his life. As a result of his highly varied educational background, he was able to speak and write Albanian, Italian, French, German, English and Turkish. Konitza's stay in France, a country of long-standing liberal democratic traditions, was to have a profound effect on him and he was able to acquire and adopt the patterns of Western thinking as no Albanian intellectual had ever done before.

In 1897, he moved to Brussels, where at the age of twenty-two he founded the periodical *Albania*, which was soon to become the most important organ of the Albanian press at the turn of the century. He moved to London in 1902 and continued to publish the journal in that city until 1909. It was there that he made friends with French poet and critic Guillaume Apollinaire (1880-1918) who stayed with him in 1903 and 1904.

In the autumn of 1909, Faik Konitza emigrated to the United States. In Boston he became editor of the newspaper *Dielli* (The Sun), founded that year. *Dielli* was the medium of the important Pan-Albanian **Vatra** (The Hearth) federation of Boston, of which Konitza became general secretary in 1912. He also edited another short-lived periodical, the fortnightly *Trumbeta e Krujës* (The Trumpet of Croya) in St. Louis, Missouri, which he ran for a short time (three editions) in 1911. In 1912, he traveled to London on behalf of the Vatra federation to defend Albania's interests at the **Conference of Ambassadors**. At the beginning of March 1913, Konitza, who had quarreled with **Ismail Qemal bey Vlora** and had initially given his support to the government of **Essad Pasha Toptani**, spoke before 300 delegates at the Albanian **Congress of Trieste** who had gathered to discuss their country's fate during the political anarchy precipitated by the **Balkan Wars**.

In 1921, back in the United States, he was elected president of the *Vatra* federation in Boston and resumed editing the newspaper *Dielli* (The Sun) there, in which he now had his own column, *Shtylla e Konitzës* (Konitza's Column). In the summer of 1926,

Faik Konitza was appointed Albanian ambassador to the United States by the dictator **Ahmet Zogu**, a post he held until the Italian invasion of his country over Easter 1939. He died in Washington and was buried in Forest Hills cemetery in Boston. His remains were repatriated to **Tirana** after the fall of the **communist** dictatorship.

Faik Konitza unfortunately wrote little in the way of **literature** per se, but as a stylist, critic, publicist and political figure he had a tremendous impact on Albanian writing and culture at the turn of the century. His periodical *Albania*, published in French and Albanian, not only helped make Albanian culture and the Albanian cause known in Europe, but also set the pace for literary prose in **Tosk** dialect. It is widely considered to be the most significant Albanian periodical to have existed up to **World War II**. The biting sarcasm with which he expressed his intransigent views on the naivety of his compatriots and on the many sacred cows of Albanian culture and history ushered a breeze of fresh air into Albanian letters. A selection of his work was posthumously edited in English by Qerim M. Panarity in the 175-page volume *Albania, the Rock Garden of Southeastern Europe and other Essays*, Boston 1957. Little of his impulsive and sophisticated prose was available in Albania until recently.

KONITZA, MEHMET BEY (1881-). Political figure. Mehmet bey Konitza, brother of **Faik bey Konitza**, was born in the village of Konitsa, now in northern Greece. He was appointed foreign minister on 22 June 1914 for a short period. In 1918, he headed the Congress of Durrës and served again as foreign minister. In 1920, after the **Congress of Lushnja**, he was made foreign minister once more and accompanied **Fan Noli** on his journey to the League of Nations. In March 1922, he was seconded to London as Albania's diplomatic representative there. Although originally an opponent of Ahmet Zogu, Mehmet bey conducted negotiations in Rome on his behalf in 1926. He served thereafter as an informal political advisor and intermediary and represented Albania at the Balkan conferences of 1931. During **World War II**, Mehmet bey Konitza was initially interned in Rome by the Italians and, later, under the German occupation, was appointed Albanian foreign minister but refused to take up the position.

KORÇA. Town in the **District of Korça**, of which it is the administrative center. **Population** in Dec. 1999: 79,528. Korça is situated on the Plain of Korça, elev. 890 meters, in southeastern Albania, not far from the Greek and Macedonian borders. It was traditionally considered the most prosperous and civilized part of the country due to early emigration.

Korça was first referred to in 1280. The present town was founded by Iljaz bey, the son of an **Orthodox** priest, who was taken as a hostage to the court of the sultan and took part in the conquest of Constantinople in 1453. The town grew in the seventeenth and eighteenth centuries as a center of trade. It was in Korça that the first Albanian-**language** school was opened in 1887. During the **Balkan wars**, the town was occupied by the Greeks and during **World War I** by French forces, which set up a semi-autonomous but short-lived Republic of Korça in 1916. In 1916, the town of Korça had a population of 10,000 and, in 1939, of 22,500.

Among the points of interest in the town are the Mirahor Mosque, dating from the year 1496, the **National Museum of Medieval Art** and the **National Museum of Education**. The town in known in Greek as *Koritzá,* in Italian as *Còrizza,* in Turkish as *Körice* and in Aromanian as *Curceaua.*

KORÇA, DISTRICT OF. Region of local government administration. The District of Korça (*Rrethi i Korçës*), with its administrative headquarters in the town of **Korça**, borders on the districts of **Skrapar** to the west, **Gramsh, Pogradec** and the Republic of Macedonia to the north, **Devoll** and **Kolonja** to the south, and Lake **Prespa** to the east. It has a surface area of 1,752 square kilometers and a present **population** of 172,011 (in 2000). It is the second largest district in Albania, after **Shkodra**.

KORKUTI, MUZAFER (1936.05.17-). Scholar and archeologist. Muzafer Korkuti was born in Fterra in the **Saranda** region and went to school in **Shkodra**. He studied history at the University of **Tirana** from 1957 to 1962 and spent nine months in **China**, specializing in archeology. Korkuti took part in various archeological expeditions and excavations in Albania from the 1960s onwards. He is an internationally recognized expert on the prehistoric period in Albania, and some of his works have appeared abroad in translation. Korkuti is currently head of the Institute of Archeology at the Academy of Sciences in Tirana. Among his publications are: *Shqipëria arkeologjike* (Archeological Albania), Tirana 1971; and in German: *Neolithikum und Chalkolithikum in Albanien* (The New Stone Age and Bronze Age in Albania), Mainz 1995.

KOSOVA, ALBANIANS IN. It is impossible to determine when the Albanians first settled in Kosova, whether there was an unbroken continuity of settlement from ancient times—before the Slav invasions—or whether Albanian tribes first descended onto the fertile plains of Kosova from the mountains of northern Albania after the Serb Empire fell into decline and the **Ottoman** Turks took control of the region following the Battle of Kosovo Polje in 1389. The Albanians were, at any rate, a significant element of the population of Kosova from the late Middle Ages onwards, although they never governed the land themselves. They were always under Serb or Turkish rule.

After the **Conference of Ambassadors** in London in 1912-1913, at which the Great Powers de facto recognized the existence of the fledgling Albanian state, about forty percent of the Albanian population, i.e., the Albanians of Kosova, found themselves excluded from this new country. Kosova, which had been "liberated" by the Serbian army, was given to the Kingdom of **Serbia**, an error which haunted the Balkans until the very end of the twentieth century.

The history of the Kosova Albanians from the beginning of Serb rule in 1913 to its very end in 1999 is one of tragedy and injustice. Since the campaign of the North Atlantic Treaty Organization (NATO) of the spring of 1999, Kosova has been a United Nations protectorate on the road to independence. The Albanians now form the absolute majority (ninety to ninety-five percent) of the population. Albanian speakers are to be found throughout Kosova, though they are a clear minority in the Serb-speaking area of Leposavić, north of Mitrovica.

KOSOVA WAR, EFFECTS ON ALBANIA (1998-1999). The Kosova conflict between the majority Albanian population in Kosova and the Serb authorities in Belgrade dates from the uprising in Prishtina in March and April 1981, which was violently suppressed by the Serb government. At the end of the 1980s, the Serbian side succeeded in revoking the autonomy status of Kosova and in incorporating the province into **Serbia**, against the will of the population. In view of the refusal of the Serb government to address any of the wishes and complaints of the Albanian population, a general uprising was only a matter of time.

The government and people of the Republic of Albania had always shown strong emotional solidarity with the people of Kosova, but there was never much willingness to intervene in the conflict directly. At the practical level, Albania had so many overwhelming problems of its own. Yugoslavia was, by comparison, an uncontested military superpower, capable of crushing not only Kosova, but also Albania if it wished.

The Albanian government, therefore, concentrated its efforts on drawing international attention to the crisis and on seeking mediation to put increasing pressure on the regime of Slobodan Milošević and to avoid the coming catastrophe. It called for international intervention on 1 March 1998 when open conflict broke out in the Drenica region. On 4 March, the Kosova Liberation Army appealed to all Albanians to join the struggle against Serb forces, and thousands of Kosova Albanians in exile began returning home to join up, most of them entering Kosova through Albania. The **Democratic Party** in Albania gave its immediate support to the armed struggle, while Foreign Minister **Paskal Milo** demanded an urgent negotiated settlement. On 6 March, 10,000 people demonstrated in **Tirana** against Serb oppression in Kosova.

On 16-17 April 1998, there was initial fighting along the Albania-Kosova border between the Serb army and Kosova-Albanian resistance fighters. Serbia accused Albania of providing weapons to the "rebels," an accusation which Tirana denied. On 23 April, fifteen to thirty Kosova-Albanians were killed trying to enter Kosova from Albania. In view of the mass concentration of Serb troops in the area, Albania seconded its elite units to the border region. By 31 May 1998, the first 1,000 refugees had crossed the border into the **Tropoja** region, and thousands of others followed in June. In the following months, the government began moving refugees down into safer areas, but more and more Kosova Albanians entered Albania every week to take their place.

On 6 August 1998, the Albanian **parliament** demanded immediate NATO intervention, and on 17-21 August, 1,700 troops from the **United States**, France, **Germany, Russia, Britian, Greece, Italy,** Lithuania, Spain and **Turkey** held initial NATO maneuvers near Tirana. On 21 September, Ahmet Krasniqi, minister of defense of the self-proclaimed Republic of Kosova, was murdered in Tirana, allegedly by Serb agents.

The exodus of Kosovar civilians to Albania increased dramatically with the failure of the Rambouillet negotiations in February 1999 and especially with the beginning of the NATO bombing campaign on 24 March. On 25 March, soldiers in Albania were shot at by Yugoslav troops from across the border, and on 13 April, Yugoslav soldiers crossed the border and burned down houses in the locality of Kamenica. Diplomatic relations between

Albania and Yugoslavia were broken off on 18 April and the conflict took its course.

According to Albanian government statistics, by the end of the NATO campaign and the defeat of Serbia, there were 446,371 Kosova refugees in Albania. Of these, 294,771 were sheltered by local Albanian families, destitute themselves in most cases. The other 151,600 refugees ended up in tents and public buildings and were provided for by international relief agencies. The total population of Albania had increased by almost one-sixth within the space of two months. The achievement of the people of Albania in coming to terms with this unprecedented humanitarian catastrophe was all the more impressive given the extremely limited resources and primitive infrastructure in the country. Traditional solidarity and the unwritten law of Albanian hospitality prevailed, despite desperate circumstances for all.

KOTA, KOSTAQ (1899-1949). Political figure. Kostaq Kota, also known as Koço Kotta, was born in **Korça,** where he worked as an elementary teacher and was active in cultural affairs. In 1913, he was appointed secretary-general at the ministry of **education** under **Luigj Gurakuqi** and, in 1920, took part in the **Congress of Lushnja**, later representing his hometown in the senate. In October 1920, he became one of the founders of the pro-Zog People's Party. From 1921 to 1923, he headed the **prefecture** of **Berat** and returned to **parliament** in 1924, becoming minister of public works. Kota fled to Greece during the **Democratic Revolution** and organized troops from Florina and Janina to invade southeastern Albania in December 1924. When the government of Fan Noli fell, he returned to his ministerial post. He later served as minister of education (January 1925), minister of the interior (February and March 1925), president of the parliament (from 3 October 1925), minister of the interior again (May-September 1928) and, finally, prime minister under **King Zog** (1928-March 1930 and November 1936-April 1939). The pro-Italian Kota was loyal to Zog, but repressive and brutal towards the population. During **World War II**, he joined the royalist **Legality** movement and fled to Greece at the end of 1944. Kota is later said to have been kidnaped by agents of the **communist** regime, taken back to Albania and sentenced to a long term in prison, where he died ca. 1949.

KOTTA, KOÇO. *See* KOTA, KOSTAQ.

KOVAÇI, LORO (1909-1979.09.19). Actor. Kovaçi was born in Podgorica, Montenegro and began his acting career with amateur roles in 1924. He joined the People's Theater in **Tirana** when it was created in 1945. He played a minor role in the Soviet-Albanian **film** *Skënderbeu* (**Scanderbeg**) in 1953 but is best remembered for his role as Tuç Maku in the film *Toka e jonë* (Our Land), 1964.

KRAJA, MARIE (1911.09.24-1999.11.21). Singer. Marie Kraja was born in Zadar on the Dalmatian coast of a family from Kosova. She studied at the **music** conservatory in Graz, Austria, from 1929 to 1934. As a soprano, Kraja gave concerts and recitals throughout central Europe: Vienna (1934), Bari (1937), Munich (1938) and Florence (1939), before returning to Albania, where she taught at the Jordan Misja Academy after **World War II**. She also sang for many years at the **Opera and Ballet Theater** in **Tirana**, in particular in the first Albanian opera *Mrika* (Mrika), performed in 1959. Marie Kraja is remembered not only as an operatic soloist and teacher, but also for her renditions of northern Albanian folk **music**, some of which have survived as recordings.

KRANTJA, ERMIR (1947.03.06-). Conductor. Son of conductor Mustafa Krantja, Emir Krantja was early to devote himself to the world of **music**. He studied at the Jordan Misja Academy from 1962 to 1966 and majored in conducting in 1966-1970 at the Academy of Fine Arts (*Instituti i Lartë i Arteve*) under his father's direction. He thereafter worked as a conductor of the orchestra of Radio **Tirana** until 1975 and as conductor of the **Shkodra** philharmonic orchestra from 1975 to 1979. Krantja then returned to Tirana to head the symphony orchestra of the **Opera and Ballet Theater** until 1990, when he emigrated to Italy. He is among Albania's leading conductors.

KRANTJA, MUSTAFA (1921.04.10-2002.01.04). Conductor. Mustafa Krantja was born in **Kavaja**. After schooling in **Elbasan**, he taught in Laç, Prishtina and **Gjirokastra**. From 1947 to 1950, he studied **music** in Prague and was subsequently appointed as conductor of the Albanian symphony orchestra. In later years, he played a significant role in the development of the Albanian **Opera and Ballet Theater**. In 1962, he founded the symphony orchestra of Radio **Tirana** and, subsequently, the orchestra of the Tirana state conservatory. He is remembered as a major conductor of foreign and Albanian operatic music and as the author of a number of well-known songs.

KRASNIQI. Northern Albanian tribe and traditional tribal region. The Krasniqi region is situated in the District of **Tropoja** north of the **Drin** River, from Fierza eastwards to the District of Has, and northwards to the Montenegrin border, including most of the upper Valbona valley. It borders on the traditional tribal regions of **Nikaj** and **Merturi** to the west, Bugjoni to the south, Bytyçi to the east and **Gashi** to the northeast. The name, of Slavic origin, was recorded in 1634 as *Crastenigeia*. The Krasniqi tribe was primarily Muslim.

KRASNIQI, REXHEP (1906.04.24-1999.02.12). Political figure. Rexhep Krasniqi was born in Gjakova in Kosova. In 1921, he was sent under an Albanian government scholarship to Austria to study. After schooling in Graz and Vienna until 1929, he studied history at the University of Vienna in 1929-1934, finishing his doctorate with a dissertation on *Der Berliner Kongreß und Nordostalbanien* (The **Congress of Berlin** and Northeastern Albania), Vienna 1934, under the supervision of Carl Patsch. On his return to Albania, he taught school in **Shkodra, Gjirokastra** (1936) and **Tirana** (1937). From 1938 to the outbreak of **World War II,** he worked for the ministry of **education.** In 1941, during the early Italian occupation, he was interned in Porto Palermo but then returned to teaching, this time as the principal of the first Albanian secondary school in Prishtina. In October 1943, he was elected as a member of **parliament** and was later appointed minister of education in the government of Fiqiri Dine. After the war, he fled to Austria, **Italy, Turkey** (1947) and Syria. In 1954, he emigrated to the **United States** and was elected in 1956 as head of the **Free Albania Committee,** a post he held until retirement in 1992. He died in New York.

KRISTOFORIDHI, KOSTANDIN (1826-1895). Writer and Bible translator. Kostantin Kristoforidhi, known in Greek as Kônstantinos Christoforidês, was a leading figure of Albanian scholarship in the nineteenth century. He was the son of a silversmith from **Elbasan,** where he went to school. From 1847 to 1850, he attended the Zosimaia secondary school in Janina and collaborated there with the Austrian vice-consul **Johann Georg von Hahn** on the latter's monumental *Albanesische Studien* (Albanian Studies), Jena 1854. The following years took him to

Athens, **Durrës**, perhaps to London, Izmir, Istanbul, Malta and Tunis, where he married and taught at a Greek school.

It was during the 1860s that he began working for the British and Foreign Bible Society, for whom he translated the New Testament into a **Gheg** version (1872 in the Latin alphabet) and a **Tosk** version (1879 in the Greek alphabet) and several books of the Old Testament. These translations helped serve as a basis for the creation of a modern literary **language**, in two dialect variants, and conferred upon him the title of "father of the Albanian language." Kristoforidhi also wrote a grammar of the Albanian language in Greek *Grammatikê tês albanikês glôssês* (Grammar of the Albanian Language), Istanbul 1882, and compiled an Albanian-Greek dictionary *Lexikon tês albanikês glôssês* (Dictionary of the Albanian Language), Athens 1904. The latter, regarded as one of the best Albanian dictionaries until recent times, was transliterated and republished by **Aleksandër Xhuvani** in 1961. Kristoforidhi was also the author of children's works, such as *Historia e shenjtësë shkroyë për dielmt* (History of Holy Script for Children), Istanbul 1870, and of the children's tale *Gjahu i malësorëvet* (The Hunt of the Mountaineers), Istanbul 1884.

Kostandin Kristoforidhi was a significant figure in the **Rilindja** culture of the national awakening and is still honored in Albania today, especially in his native Elbasan.

KRUJA. Town in the **District of Kruja**, of which it is the administrative center. **Population** in Dec. 1999: 14,240. Kruja, with its mountainside fortress north of **Tirana**, was first referred to as *Kroai* in a Byzantine document in the early seventh century. In medieval Latin it was called *Croya* or *oppidum Croarum*.

Kruja formed the heart of the kingdom of Arbanon in the twelfth and thirteenth centuries and of the Angevin realm, which was set up thereafter. In 1343, it was conquered by the Serbs and later ruled by the Balsha and **Thopia** families. Historically, Kruja is associated primarily with **Scanderbeg**, who seized the fortress in 1443 and withstood three **Ottoman** sieges there. After Scanderbeg's death in 1468, Kruja fell to the Venetians and then to the Turks in 1478. It is a center of the **Bektashi** order. Most of the sites of interest are in the fortress: the Dollma mosque and baths dating from 1533 to 1534, the **museum** of folk art in the mansion of the **Toptani** family and, in particular, the Scanderbeg Museum designed in 1982 by architect Pranvera Hoxha, daughter of the dictator **Enver Hoxha**. Also of interest is a well-restored market street abounding in traditional handicrafts. The people of Kruja are considered to be excellent merchants.

The word "Kruja" is related to Alb. *kroi* "fountain, spring." In Italian it was known as *Croia* and in Turkish as *Akçahisar, Akhisar* "the white fortress," from Turk. *akça, ak* "white" and *hisar* "castle, fortress."

KRUJA, DISTRICT OF. Region of local government administration. The District of Kruja (*Rrethi i Krujës*), with its administrative headquarters in the town of **Kruja**, borders on the districts of **Durrës** to the west, **Kurbin** to the north, **Mat** to the east and **Tirana** to the south. It has a surface area of 333 square kilometers and a present **population** of 61,500 (in 2000).

KRUJA, MUSTAFA (1887.03.15-1958.12.27). Political and nationalist figure. Kruja, whose real name is Mustafa Merlika, attended a school of administration in Istanbul from which he graduated in 1910 with a diploma in political and social sciences. After his return to Albania, he was appointed head of **education** for the district of **Elbasan**. He took part in the uprising of 1912 and was among the signatories of the declaration of independence on 28 November 1912. During the short reign of **Prince Wilhelm zu Wied**, he was one of the few political leaders of the country to support the new monarch. Kruja spent **World War I** in **Italy** and thereafter maintained a strong pro-Italian stance in politics. In 1921, he was elected as a member of **parliament** for the Progress Party and, in 1924, supported the **Democratic Revolution**, fleeing to Italy when **Ahmet Zogu** seized power. There, with Italian support, he was groomed as a possible successor to Zogu. He returned to Albania in 1939 and was made a member of the Italian senate. In 1940, during the Italian occupation, he became president of the newly founded *Istituti i Studimevet Shqiptare* (Institute of Albanian studies) in **Tirana**. On 3 December 1941, the Italian viceroy Francesco Jacomoni di San Savino appointed him as prime minister of Albania, a position he held until 10 January 1943, when he was forced out of office because he was unable to maintain order in difficult times. In May 1942, an attempt was made to assassinate him, which resulted in the imposition by the Italian authorities of a state of siege and in new and harsher restrictions for the population. He fled to Italy after the **communist** takeover and later died in Niagara Falls, leaving behind numerous manuscripts and translations.

KUÇOVA, DISTRICT OF. Region of local government administration. The District of Kuçova (*Rrethi i Kuçovës*), with its administrative headquarters in the town of Kuçova, formerly called *Qyteti Stalin* (Stalin City), borders on the districts of **Lushnja** to the west, **Elbasan** to the north and **Berat** to the east and south. It has a surface area of eighty-four square kilometers and a present **population** of 40,236 (in 2000). It is the smallest district in Albania but the one with the highest population density.

KUKËS, DISTRICT OF. Region of local government administration. The District of Kukës (*Rrethi i Kukësit*), with its administrative headquarters in the town of Kukës, borders on the districts of **Mirdita** and **Puka** to the west, **Has** to the north, **Dibra** to the south and on **Kosova** to the east. It has a surface area of 938 square kilometers and a present **population** of 75,421 (in 2000).

KUKUZELI, JOHN (thirteenth-fourteenth centuries). Orthodox saint and figure of Byzantine **music**. John Kukuzeli, Alb. *Jan Kukuzeli,* was probably born around the year 1280 in **Durrës** and was of Macedonian Slav descent. He is said to have had an "angel-voice" as a boy and attended an imperial school in Constantinople, subsequently serving as choir director in the chapel of the imperial palace. According to his *vita,* Kukuzeli or Koukouzeles, deriving from Gk. *koukia* "beans" and Slav. *zeliya* "cabbage," was a nickname given to him by his school companions in view of his difficulties with the Greek language. A great musician of his time, Kukuzeli was known as the "master" or the "second source" of Greek music after the hymnographer Saint Romanus. He introduced a major reform in the transcription of Byzantine music, elaborating a system of his own. This so-called Kukuzelian transcription, utilized up to the first half of the nineteenth century, constituted an important step in the preservation and solidification of the traditions of Byzantine musical paleography. At the height of his fame as a singer, Kukuzeli left Constantinople to retire to monastic life on Mount Athos, where he died ca. 1360-1375. He was buried at the Grand Lavra monastery. John Kukuzeli is depicted in the frescoes of the monastery of **Ardenica**.

KULLURIOTI, ANASTAS (1822-1887). Nationalist figure, publisher and writer. Kullurioti was born in the Plaka district of Athens. He inaugurated the weekly newspaper *Hê fônê tês Albanias* (The Voice of Albania), a fervently nationalist periodical in Greek with the occasional article in Albanian. It was published from September 1879 to August 1880 in a total of forty issues. The three main goals of this newspaper and of Kullurioti's nationalist activities in general were the founding of an Albanian political party in **Greece**, the opening of Albanian-**language** schools and the liberation of Albania from the Turkish yoke.

In the early 1880s, Kullurioti journeyed to southern Albania to win support for the nationalist cause, an activity which inevitably brought him into conflict with both the Turkish and Greek authorities. In **Gjirokastra**, at the request of the Greek consul, he was arrested by the **Ottoman** authorities and extradited to Corfu. He was imprisoned in Greece for some time and is rumored to have died of poisoning at the beginning of 1887.

Kullurioti is remembered not only as a publisher but also for his *Albanikon alfabêtarion* or *Avabatar arbëror* (Albanian Primer), Athens 1882, a bilingual primer or speller of his native dialect. It included an introduction to Albanian grammar and a selection of folk tales, poetry and proverbs of the Albanians of Greece. Both as a publisher and as a nationalist figure, Anastas Kullurioti contributed substantially to an awakening of national identity among the Albanians of Greece and southern Albania.

KULSHEDRA. Figure of Albanian mythology. This female dragon, Alb. *kulshedër,* def. *kulshedra,* derives from Latin *chersydrus* "amphibious snake." The *kulshedra,* usually described as a huge serpent with seven to twelve heads, is one of the most popular figures of Albanian mythology, being well known throughout the Albanian-speaking Balkans and among the Arbëresh in southern **Italy**. She is extremely ugly. Her face and body are covered in red woolly hair and her long, hanging breasts drag along the ground. She lives in a mountain cave, in an underground lake or in a swamp, and spits fire out of all her mouths. When a *kulshedra* approaches, storm clouds will fill the sky. She thus fulfils the role of an ancient storm demon. The term *kulshedra* is also used in Albanian to refer to a quarrelsome woman.

KULTUSPROTEKTORAT. German term for Austrian patronage of **Catholics** in the **Ottoman Empire**. The Albanian Catholic Church, with its power base in the north of the country, i.e., **Shkodra** and the highlands, was traditionally Italian-oriented. In the mid-nineteenth century, the Catholics in this region also came under the influence of Austria in the *Kultusprotektorat* (religious protectorate), a right which Vienna had wrested from the Porte in a series of peace treaties with the sultans beginning in 1616. The *Kultusprotektorat*, which was reconfirmed after the Austrian-Turkish war of 1683-1699, authorized Austria to serve as protectress to the Catholic population in the Balkans, among whom were the Catholics of northern Albania. Always more with political pragmatism than with altruistic evangelization in mind, Austria promoted her activities under the protectorate as a means of wielding political influence in northern Albania, to check the Ottoman Empire from within and to counter any political ambitions which the **Orthodox** southern Slavs might have. With Austrian assistance, schools and churches were built and repaired in northern Albania and the Catholic Church began to play a more active role in the fields of **education** and culture. The northern Albanian town of Shkodra was soon to develop into the literary and cultural capital not only for Albanian Catholics, who represented only about one-tenth of the **population** of Albania but for all of the country.

KUMBARO, SAIMIR (1945.05.05-). Film director and actor. Saimir Kumbaro graduated from the Academy of Fine Arts (*Instituti i Lartë i Arteve*) and began work for **New Albania Film Studios**. Among the best feature films he has directed are: *Koncert në vitin '36* (Concert in the Year 1936),1978; *Rrethimi i vogël* (The Small Siege), 1986; and *Vdekja e kalit* (The Horse's Death), 1992, the latter dealing with the absurdities of life under the **communist** dictatorship. Saimir Kumbaro has also produced numerous documentary films.

KUPI, ABAZ (1892.02.06-1976.01.09). Political figure and resistance fighter. Abaz Kupi, also called Bazi i Canës, was born in **Kruja**. He supported **Essad Pasha Toptani** from 1912 on and, in the 1920s, took the side of **Mustafa Kruja** against **Ahmet Zogu**. Zogu, however, later made Kupi commander of Kruja, which he actually already was, and thereby brought about an improvement in their relations. As a gendarmerie officer in **Durrës**, Abaz Kupi put up fierce resistance to the Italian invasion of 1939 and was then forced to flee to Istanbul. On 7 April 1941, he returned to Albania and founded the monarchist resistance movement, **Legality**. He was a leading figure at the **Conference of Peza** on 16 September 1942, which was intended to unite the various antifascist resistance movements into one national liberation front. He later withdrew from joint resistance in November 1943 when the movement became increasingly dominated by the

communists, and eventually joined sides with the puppet government under **German** occupation. In November 1944, government forces were overpowered by the communist partisans, and Kupi and his officers were forced to flee by boat from the coast of **Mat** to **Italy.** They were adrift for six days without food or water until they were picked up by a Canadian minesweeper and towed to Brindisi. In Italy and elsewhere in western Europe, he continued to organize anticommunist resistance during the initial years of the Cold War. He was involved in particular in the work of the **Free Albania Committee.** In 1968, he moved to the **United States** and later died in New York. Abaz Kupi lies buried in Kew Gardens Cemetery in Queens, New York.

KURBIN, DISTRICT OF. Region of local government administration. The District of Kurbin (*Rrethi i Kurbinit*), also known as the district of Laç, with its administrative headquarters in the town of Laç, borders on the Adriatic Sea to the west, the districts of **Lezha** and **Mirdita** to the north, **Mat** to the east and **Kruja** to the south. It has a surface area of 273 square kilometers and a present **population** of 58,542 (in 2000). The word "Kurbin" was recorded in Latin as *Corvinus* and, in 1570, as *Curbin.*

KURTI, DONAT (1903-1983). Scholar and folklorist. Donat Kurti was from **Shkodra.** He studied theology and philosophy at the Collegium Antonianum in Rome and was ordained as a **Franciscan** priest in 1927. After his return to Shkodra, he taught at the Illyrian college. Kurti was particularly interested in Albanian folklore and epic verse. Together with **Bernardin Palaj**, he published the best-known cycles of epic poetry in *Kângë kreshnikësh dhe legenda* (The Songs of the Frontier Warriors and Legends),Tirana 1937.

    Like many other **Catholic** priests, Kurti was arrested by the **communists** in 1946 and spent the next seventeen years in prison (Shkodra, Burrel, Beden and other internment camps). It was during this period that he translated the New Testament into Albanian. He is also remembered for his two-volume *Prralla kombtare mbledhë prej gojës së popullit* (National Folk Tales Collected from the Mouth of the People), Shkodra 1940, 1942.

KURTI, TINKA (1932.12.17-). Film and stage actress. Tinka Kurti was born in Sarajevo. She graduated from the Jordan Misja Academy in 1947 and worked as a professional actress at the **Migjeni** Theater in **Shkodra** from 1949. She played the leading role in the first full-length Albanian film, *Tana* (Tana), 1958. From then to 1993, she appeared in thirty roles in Albanian feature films, mostly emotional or stoic portrayals of mothers, grandmothers and aunts. She is best remembered for her roles in *Yjet e netëve të gjata* (Stars of Long Nights), 1972; *Operacioni Zjarri* (Operation Fire), 1973; *Gjeneral gramafoni* (General Gramophone), 1978; and *Zemra e Nënës* (A Mother's Heart), 1992.

KUSHI, ANDREA (1884.04.04-1959.04.17). Painter. Andrea Kushi was born in **Shkodra** and studied art in Belgrade from 1912 to 1914. In the 1920s, he taught school in Shkodra before moving to **Tirana** to set up the first drawing school there (1931-1937). Kushi lived in **Korça** from 1937 to 1943, where he was in close contact with the painters **Vangjush Mio** and Foto Stamo (1916-1989), and in **Elbasan** from 1944 to 1947, when he moved back to Tirana. He is remembered for his portraits and landscape paintings. Well known among his works are the portraits *Bariu me shkop* (The Shephard with the Staff) and *Vajza me kordele* (The Girl with the Ribbon).

KUTELI, MITRUSH (1907.09.13-1967.05.04). Prose writer. Mitrush Kuteli, pseudonym of Dhimitër Pasko, known in Romanian as Dimitrie Pascu, was born in **Pogradec** and attended a Romanian commercial college in Thessalonika. He later moved to Bucharest, where he studied economics and graduated in 1934 with a dissertation on the banking systems of the Balkans.

It was there that he began publishing the collections of short stories for which he is best known. His first book, *Nete shqipëtare* (Albanian Nights), Bucharest 1938, was a compilation of eight tales on village life in and around his native Pogradec. He also arranged for the publication of **Lasgush Poradeci**'s verse collection *Ylli i zemrës* (The Star of the Heart) in 1937. In the autumn of 1942, Kuteli returned to Albania, which was itself on the verge of disintegrating into open civil war. It was during these war years that Kuteli, at his own expense, was able to publish most of his major works such as: *Ago Jakupi e të tjera rrëfime* (Ago Jakupi and Other Tales), Tirana 1943, a collection of seven tales of peasant life; *Kapllan Aga i Shaban Shpatës: rrëfime—rrëfenja* (Kapllan Aga of Shaban Shpata: Tales—Stories), Tirana 1944, five short stories written between 1938 and 1944; *Këngë e brithma nga qyteti i djegur* (Songs and Cries from a Charred City), Tirana 1944, a collection of folk songs; *Shënime letrare*

(Literary Notes), Tirana 1944; and *Sulm e lotë* (Assault and Tears), Tirana 1944, a collection of modest nationalist verse.

Mitrush Kuteli set the pace for the short story in southern Albania and managed to attain a higher level of literary sophistication than most other sentimental prose writers of the period. The peasant themes and the mixture of folksy humor and old-fashioned adventure made his tales popular with broad sections of the reading public during the war and thereafter. In some of his short stories, one senses the atmosphere of nineteenth-century Russian prose, of Nikolay Gogol and Ivan Turgenev, whom the author had read and particularly enjoyed in his earlier years, and of Romanian prose writer Mihail Sadoveanu (1880-1961).

At the end of **World War II**, Mitrush Kuteli, now an executive at the Albanian State Bank, was a leading figure of Albanian letters. On 15 February 1944, together with Vedat Kokona (1913-1998), Nexhat Hakiu (1917-1978) and **Sterjo Spasse**, he founded the fortnightly literary periodical *Revista letrare* (Literary Review), which had a significant impact on Albanian culture during its short life. He was also a founding member of the Albanian **Writers' Union** and a member of the editorial board of Albania's first postwar literary journal *Bota e re* (New World).

Kuteli managed to survive the transition of political power in Albania until the real terror began in 1947. During a purge which ensued after the Albanian **communist** party had come under Yugoslav domination, he unwisely disapproved of the proposed customs and monetary union between Albania and **Yugoslavia**. As a member of an official delegation to Yugoslavia, received among others by writer Ivo Andrić (1892-1975), he is also said to have expressed a critical attitude to the Serb reoccupation of **Kosova**, a stance reflected earlier in his *Poem kosovar* (Kosovar Poem), published in 1944.

Upon his return to Albania, he was arrested and sentenced to fifteen years in prison. For Kuteli, as for most writers of the late 1940s, life had become a nightmare. He survived the first two years of his prison sentence (April 1947 to April 1949) in a labor camp near **Korça**, where inmates were put to work draining the infamous mosquito-infested swamp of Maliq. Working and living conditions for the prisoners were unimaginably harsh, and Kuteli, amidst such horror, attempted suicide. But with the elimination of Yugoslav influence in Albanian party politics, the open persecution of Kuteli subsided and he was released. He returned to **Tirana** and was allowed, like Lasgush Poradeci and a number of other suspicious intellectuals, to work as a literary translator for the state-owned Naim Frashëri publishing company.

Mitrush Kuteli died of a heart attack in Tirana, bereft of the honor and recognition due to the man who had made the short story a popular genre in Albania and who, had politics not interfered, might otherwise have been the leading prose writer of the 1950s.

KUVENDI I ARBËNIT. *See* ALBANIAN COUNCIL.

KYÇYKU, MUHAMET (1784-1844). Muslim poet. Muhamet Kyçyku marks the transition between the classical verse of the early *Bejtexhinj* and the **Rilindja** poets of the second half of the nineteenth century. Kyçyku, who is also known as Muhamet Çami, i.e., the **Çamërian**, was from Konispol in what is now the southern tip of Albania. He studied theology for eleven years in Cairo, where a sizeable Albanian colony had settled. On his return to his native village, he served as a hodja (Muslim priest) and died in 1844 [1260 A.H.]. Kyçyku was a relatively prolific author who wrote in his native dialect of Çamëria and, as it seems, was the first Albanian author to have written longer poetry. The work for which he is best remembered is a romantic tale in verse form known as *Erveheja* (Ervehe), originally entitled *Ravda* (Garden), written in about 1820. This poetic tale follows the adventures of the fair Ervehe, who manages to defend her chastity and virtue through many a trial and tribulation. It is also one of the rare works of the *Bejtexhinj* to have been published in the nineteenth century, though in an altered version. Rilindja publicist **Jani Vreto** not only transliterated and published *Erveheja* in Bucharest in 1888, but adapted it to late nineteenth-century tastes, seeing fit to purge it of all its Turkish, Persian and Arabic vocabulary.

Erveheja is not Kyçyku's only surviving work, though it was the only one known for many years. Most of the over 4,000 lines of his verse (ca. 200 pages), which have survived, were discovered within the last fifty years. Kyçyku's other major work is *Jusufi i Zelihaja* (Joseph and Zeliha), a moralistic verse tale in 2,430 lines based on the biblical story recounted in Genesis 39 and the twelfth Sura of the Koran, of the attempted seduction of the handsome Joseph by the wife of his Egyptian master Potiphar. This "most beautiful tale," as the Koran calls it, served as a common motif in Arabic, Persian and Turkish literature. Kyçyku's *Jusufi i Zelihaja* evinces a higher level of literary sophistication than *Erveheja*. Its language is more ornate and many of the descriptive passages transcend the constraints of a simple narrative. It also relies more on character analysis as a means of conveying dramatic suspense, in particular with respect to the passions of the enamored Zeliha.

KYRIAS FAMILY. *See* QIRIAZI FAMILY.

- L -

LABËRIA. Geographical and ethnographical region of southwestern Albania, south of the **Vjosa** River. It is traditionally defined as the area within the three bridges of Drashovica, **Tepelena,** and Kalasa. Its cultural center is **Vlora.** The term "Labëria" and the adjective Lab are related through metathesis to the root **alb-,* as in Albania.

LAÇO, TEODOR (1936.09.27-). Prose writer, political figure and high-ranking member of the Social Democratic Union. Teodor Laço, from the village of Dardha near **Korça**, studied agronomy, which he taught for several years in Korça. From 1986 to 1992, he worked for **New Albania Film Studios** and, in 1990, was appointed director of *Albafilm.*

Laço established his reputation as a major prose writer of the socialist period with his novel *Tokë e ashpër* (Rough Land), Tirana 1971, which dealt with the collectivization of **agriculture** in mountain regions. He has since published at least a dozen collections of short stories, five other novels, numerous plays and has written nine **film** scripts. His short stories have appeared in English as *A Lyrical Tale in Winter*, Tirana 1988.

Teodor Laço has been active in politics since the fall of the dictatorship, as head of the **parliamentary** group of the Social Democratic Union (*Bashkimi Socialdemokrat*) from 1992 to 1994, and as minister of culture, youth and sports from December 1994. On 27 June 1998, his party was renamed the Liberal Union (*Bashkimi Liberal*).

LAHUTA. Musical instrument. The lahuta is a one-stringed musical instrument with a long neck and an egg-shaped body. It is played with a bow and used in northern Albania and **Kosova** to accompany epic songs, such as the **Songs of the Frontier Warriors** (*këngë kreshnikesh*). The *lahuta* is similar to the south Slavic *gusle*, also used for epic **music**. The top of the instrument is usually decorated with a ram's head. The word *lahuta* is related etymologically to the Engl. "lute."

LAKO, NATASHA (1948.05.13-). Writer and poet. Natasha Lako was born in **Korça** and studied journalism at the University of **Tirana**. She worked for many years in the **film** script division of **New Albania Film Studios**. In 1992, she was elected to **parliament**, representing the **Democratic Party**, and is now director of the national film archives in Tirana.

Lako is also a prominent representative of the first generation of **women** writers in Albania. She has published the following volumes of poetry: *Marsi brenda nesh* (March within Us), Tirana 1972; *E para fjalë e botës* (The World's First Word), Tirana 1979; *Këmisha e pranverës* (The Spring Shirt), Prishtina 1984; *Yllësia e fjalëve* (Constellation of Words), Tirana 1986; and *Natyrë e qetë* (Quiet Nature), Tirana 1990; as well as the novel *Stinët e jetës* (The Seasons of Life), Tirana 1977.

LAMBERTZ, MAXIMILIAN (1882.07.27-1963.08.27). Austrian scholar and philologist. Max Lambertz was born and raised in Vienna. He studied comparative linguistics and classics at the university there from 1900 to 1905, finishing his doctorate on *Die griechischen Sklavennamen* (Greek Slave Names), Vienna 1907. A government scholarship enabled the young classical scholar to visit **Italy** and **Greece**, where, listening in on the conversations of the shepherds and fishermen of Attica, he first came into contact with the Albanian **language**. On his return to Vienna, he began teaching school but soon moved to Munich to collaborate on the great *Thesaurus Linguae Latinae* (Thesaurus of the Latin Language). In 1911, he returned to Vienna to continue working as a high school teacher. In 1913 and 1914, he traveled to southern Italy for several weeks to study the Albanian dialects there. His earliest Albanological publication, together with **Gjergj Pekmezi**, was a *Lehr- und Lesebuch des Albanischen* (Manual and Reader of Albanian), Vienna 1913.

In 1916, Max Lambertz visited northern and central Albania for the first time as a member of the Balkan Commission of the Austrian Academy of Sciences. Soon after his first visit, he returned to Albania with Austro-Hungarian troops during **World**

War I to do his military service and was charged with supervising schools in the part of the country under Austro-Hungarian occupation. He was also a member of the **Albanian Literary Commission,** which was set up by the Austro-Hungarian authorities to create a literary norm and a standard orthography for Albanian. While in **Shkodra,** he served with **Gjergj Fishta** on the editorial board of the biweekly newspaper *Posta e Shcypniës* (The Albanian Post), 1916-1918. He also collected Albanian folklore material, some of which appeared in his *Volkspoesie der Albaner: eine einführende Studie* (The Folk Poetry of the Albanians: An Introductory Study), Sarajevo 1917.

Lambertz returned to Austria after the war and taught school until 1934, continuing all the while to write books and articles on various aspects of Albanian culture, in particular folklore. At the age of fifty-three, he returned to university to study **Protestant** theology, but his dissertation was rejected by the Faculty for racial reasons—his mother stemmed from a **Jewish** family. In 1939, Lambertz went back to Munich to continue his work on the Thesaurus and remained there until 1942. In 1943, he moved to Leizpig, where he taught French and Italian and collaborated on the Pauly-Wissowa *Realenzyklopädie der Altertumswissenschaften* (Encyclopedia of Classical Antiquity). In June 1945, having become a member of the communist party, he was made director of the Leipzig School of Foreign Languages, and, in October 1946, he became professor for comparative studies and dean of the new Faculty of Education at the Karl Marx University of Leipzig. He was also director of the Institute of Indo-European Studies until retirement in 1957.

Although Max Lambertz was a classical scholar, and later a theologian by training, his greatest scholarly passion was and remained Albanian philology. He is considered the most prominent German-language exponent of Albanian studies in the twentieth century and has left behind him an impressive list of publications: *Albanische Märchen und andere Texte zur albanischen Volkskunde* (Albanian Folk Tales and other Texts on Albanian Folklore), Vienna 1922; *Zwischen Drin und Vojusa: Märchen aus Albanien* (Between the Drin and the Vjosa: Folk Tales from Albania), Leipzig 1922; a two-volume *Albanisches Lesebuch mit Einführung in die albanische Sprache* (Albanian Reader with an Introduction to the Albanian Language), Leipzig 1948; *Gjergj Fishta und das albanische Heldenepos "Lahuta e Malcis," Laute des Hochlandes: eine Einführung in die albanische Sagenwelt* (Gjergj Fishta and the Heroic Epic "Lahuta e Malcís," the Highland Lute: An Introduction to the World of Albanian Legendry), Leipzig 1949; *Die geflügelte Schwester und die Dunklen der Erde: albanische Volksmärchen* (The Winged Sister and the Dark Spirits of the Earth: Albanian Folk Tales), Eisenach 1952; a three-volume *Lehrgang des Albanischen* (Manual of Albanian), Berlin 1954-1955, Halle/Saale 1959; *Albanien erzählt: ein Einblick in die albanische Literatur* (Albania Narrates: A View of Albanian **Literature**), Berlin 1956; and *Die Volksepik der Albaner* (The Folk Epic of the Albanians), Halle 1958. Unpublished remained his 187-page manuscript *Das Drama im albanischen Theater von heute* (Drama in Modern Albanian Theater), written in 1963.

LANE, ROSE WILDER (1886-1968). American writer. Rose Wilder Lane was born in South Dakota, the daughter of Laura Ingalls Wilder, author of the *Little House on the Prairie* books, and was raised in Missouri. At the age of seventeen, she went to work at the Western Union in Kansas City and, in 1908, moved to San Francisco, where she began writing for the women's page of the *San Francisco Bulletin.* With her short stories for women's magazines, she was soon to become the highest-paid woman writer in the **United States**. After the publication of her first book, she accepted a job at the American Red Cross and Near East Relief, investigating and reporting to the press on conditions in Europe and the Near East in order to raise money for relief work. She began work at the Red Cross office in Paris and, from there, traveled to Italy, Greece, Yugoslavia and Albania, which was her lasting interest. She was shortly to move on from the refugee camp that she was visiting in **Shkodra** when a fellow American Red Cross worker, Frances Hardy, persuaded her to join a small party which was about to embark on an expedition to the northern Albanian mountains to set up schools.

It was this journey in 1921 which inspired her book *The Peaks of Shala, Being a Record of Certain Wanderings among the Hill-tribes of Albania,* London 1922, one of the most delightful contributions to America's discovery of Albania in the early decades of the twentieth century. Rose Wilder Lane was not an anthropologist with a profound knowledge of the Balkans, nor was she an experienced political commentator like her scholarly though witty British predecessor, **Edith Durham**; she was not even a specialist in travel literature as such. But what she was able to do was to bring the very foreign world of the highland tribes of northern Albania home to the American reading public, and this she accomplished with eminent skill and simplicity. Despite its exotic subject matter, the *Peaks of Shala* was an immediate success when it was published. Indeed, it went through three printings soon after its first appearance on the book market.

In 1926, five years after her trip to the **Shala** district, she returned to Albania with her friend, the author Helen Dore Boylston, and their reluctant French maid, Yvonne, with the intention of building a house and settling there for good. The narrative of her journey from Paris to **Tirana** in a Model T Ford called Zenobia was published by William Holtz in the volume *Travels with Zenobia, Paris to Albania in a Model T Ford: A Journal by Rose Wilder Lane and Helen Dore Boylston*, Columbia 1983. For family reasons, Rose's dream of living in Albania permanently was not be to fulfilled and she was forced to sail back to America a year and a half later. The Great Depression soon set in and all hopes of return to her beloved Albania had to be abandoned. She died in 1968 at the age of eighty-one on the eve of a planned trip around the world.

LANGUAGE, ALBANIAN. The Albanian language (*shqip*) is spoken by over six million people in the southwestern Balkans, primarily in the Republic of Albania and in the neighboring countries which once formed part of the Yugoslav federation (**Kosova**, Macedonia, Montenegro and **Serbia**). In Albania itself, the language is spoken by the entire **population** of 3,087,159 inhabitants (census of April 2001), including some bilingual ethnic **minorities**.

In Kosova, where there are as yet no reliable population statistics, Albanian is spoken by almost the entire population of about two million individuals, including some bilingual minorities: Bosnians, Turks, Croats and **Roma**. Ethnic Serbs in Kosova (now about five percent of the population) have traditionally refused to learn or speak Albanian, but attitudes may change once traditional hostilities and ethnic tensions subside.

The Republic of **Macedonia** is estimated to have at least half a million Albanian speakers, equaling about thirty percent of the total population of the republic, although there are, again, no reliable statistics. The Albanian population is to be found in and around Skopje (Alb. *Shkup*), where it constitutes a substantial minority, Kumanova (Maced. *Kumanovo*) and, in particular, from Tetova (Maced. *Tetovo*), Gostivar and **Dibra** (Maced. *Debar*) down to Struga, where it forms the majority.

A minority of about 50,000 Albanian speakers is also to be found in Montenegro, mostly along the Albanian border. There are also at least 70,000 to 100,000 Albanian speakers scattered throughout southern Serbia, primarily in the Presheva Valley near the borders of Macedonia and Kosova.

To the south of Albania, in **Greece**, there are traditional settlements of **Çamërian** dialect speakers, in particular around Parga and Igoumenitsa in Epirus. Despite border changes and deportations to Albania, the Albanian population here may be as high as 100,000, although they are highly assimilated. In central Greece, the Albanian language, known in Albanian as *Arbërisht* and in Greek as *Arvanitika*, languishes in about 320 villages, primarily those of Boeotia (especially around Levadhia), southern Euboea, Attica, Corinth and northern Andros. These speakers are the descendants of large-scale Albanian emigration to Greece during the late Middle Ages. No official statistics exist as to their numbers. This exceptionally archaic form of Albanian is dying out rapidly.

In southern **Italy**, there is a small but well-established Albanian-speaking minority, the so-called *Arbëresh,* or Italo-Albanians. These are the descendants of refugees who fled Albania after the death of **Scanderbeg** in 1468. As a linguistic group, the Arbëresh now consist of about 90,000 speakers, most of whom live in the mountain villages of Cosenza in Calabria and in the vicinity of Palermo in Sicily. The Arbëresh speak an archaic dialect of Albanian, which differs substantially from the Albanian now spoken in the Balkans, to the extent that communication is difficult if Arbëresh speakers are not familiar with standard literary Albanian.

Traditional Albanian settlements can be encountered sporadically elsewhere in the Balkans: in a suburb of Zadar on the Dalmatian coast of Croatia, in some villages in the Sandjak in Serbia and in the Bulgarian-Greek-Turkish border region, notably in the Bulgarian village of Mandrica. A few Albanian speakers are also to be found in the Ukraine, notably in villages in the regions of Melitopol' and Odessa.

Little remains of the once extensive colonies of Albanians scattered throughout the **Ottoman Empire**. The Albanian minority in Egypt has now dissipated, though Albanian communities still exist in large numbers in Turkey (Istanbul, Bursa and elsewhere) and to an extent in Syria, notably in Damascus.

Since the late 1980s in Kosova and since the opening of Albania in 1990-1991, there has been a substantial emigration of

Albanian speakers from their traditional areas of settlement to other countries, in particular to Greece and Italy. There are also large numbers of Albanian emigrants to be found in western Europe, Germany and Switzerland, in particular, as well as in North America.

Albanian is a language of the extensive Indo-European family and is thus distantly related to almost all other languages of Europe. The Indo-European character of the language was first recognized in 1854 by the German linguist **Franz Bopp**. At the same time, Albanian shows no particularly close historical affinity to any other language or language group within the Indo-European family. Despite Albania's **geographical** proximity to Greece, linguistic contacts with ancient Greek seem to have been sporadic. Roman trading settlements on the **Illyrian** coast and Albania's absorption into the Roman Empire, however, left noticeable traces in the language. Borrowings from Latin, which took place over a period of several centuries, were so massive as to threaten the very structure of the language. Cultural contacts with the Slavs (Bulgarians and Serbs), Turks and Italians have also left substantial strata of vocabulary in Albanian.

Not only in its vocabulary, but also in its morphology and syntax, Albanian shows many traits in common with other Balkan languages, due both to extinct substrata languages (Illyrian, Thracian, Dacian) and to centuries of parallel development. Among these traits are: a postpositive definite article; the fusion of the genitive and dative case endings; the formation of the numbers 11-19 by "one on ten"; the absence of a grammatical infinitive; and the formation of the future tense with the verb "to want."

Whether or not Albanian is a direct successor of the language of the ancient Illyrians, as is broadly assumed nowadays, is difficult to determine since very few records of the Illyrian language have been preserved.

The Albanian language is divided into two basic dialect groups: **Gheg** in the north of the country and **Tosk** in the south. The **Shkumbin** River in central Albania, flowing past **Elbasan** into the Adriatic, forms the approximate boundary between the two dialect regions. Here, in a zone ten to twenty kilometers wide, intermediate dialects are also found. The Gheg dialect group, characterized by the presence of nasal vowels, by the retention of the older *n* for Tosk *r* (e.g., *venë* "wine" for Tosk *verë*; *Shqypnia* "Albania" for Tosk *Shqipëria*) and by several distinct morphological features, can be further classified into a northwestern (**Shkodra** and surrounding region), a northeastern (northeastern Albania and Kosova), a central (between the **Ishëm** and **Mat** Rivers and eastwards into Macedonia, including Dibra and Tetova) and a southern (**Durrës, Tirana**) Gheg dialect. The Tosk dialect group is in general more homogenous, though it can be subdivided into a northern (from **Fier** to **Vlora** on the coast and all of inland southern Albania north of the **Vjosa** River), a **Labërian** or Lab (south of the Vjosa to **Saranda**), and a **Çamërian** or Çam (the southern tip of Albania and into Greece) dialect.

The modern literary language (*gjuha letrare*), agreed upon at the Orthography Congress of 20 to 25 November 1972, is a combination of the two dialect groups, though based about eighty percent on Tosk. It is now a widely accepted standard both in Albania and elsewhere, though there have been increasing tendencies in recent years to revive literary Gheg.

In its structure, Albanian is a synthetic language similar to most other Indo-European languages. Nouns are marked for gender, number, case and also have definite and indefinite forms. The vast majority of nouns are masculine or feminine, though there are rare examples of neuter nouns, which now function increasingly as masculine in the singular and feminine in the plural. As to number, nouns appear in the singular and plural, as in most other European languages. There are approximately 100 plural formations, including suffixes, umlauts, final consonant changes, and combinations thereof.

The nominal system distinguishes five cases: nominative, genitive, dative, accusative and ablative. The genitive and dative endings are always the same. Attributive genitives are in addition linked to the nouns that they qualify by a complicated system of connective particles: *i, e, të* and *së*, of ten reflecting the ending of the preceding word, e.g., *bulevardi i qytetit* "the city boulevard," *bukuria e bulevardit të qytetit* "the beauty of the city boulevard." The definite and indefinite forms of the noun are shown by the presence or absence of a postpositive definite article. The noun declension thus shows two sets of endings: definite and indefinite. Most adjectives follow the noun either directly or are preceded by a connective particle, e.g., *djali nervoz* "the irritable boy," *djali i vogël* "the little boy."

The Albanian verb system has the following categories: three persons, two numbers, ten tenses, two voices and six moods. Unusual among the moods is the admirative, which is used to express astonishment on the part of the speaker, e.g., *ra shi* "it rained," *rënka shi* "why, it's been raining!"

LA PIANA, MARCO (1883-1958). Arbëresh scholar from Piana degli Albanesi (Alb. *Hora e Arbëreshëvet*) near Palermo in Sicily. He is the author of a number of studies in Albanian philology, including: *Il catechismo albanese di Luca Matranga, 1592, da un manoscritto Vaticano* (The Albanian Catechism of Lekë Matrënga, 1592, from a Vatican Manuscript), Grottaferrata 1912; *Prolegomeni allo studio della linguistica albanese* (Introduction to the Study of Albanian Linguistics), Palermo 1939; and *Studi linguistici albanesi: i dialetti siculo-albanesi* (Albanian Linguistic Studies: The Albanian Dialects of Sicily), Palermo 1949.

LAZARIST CONGREGATION. Congregation of the **Catholic** Church. The Lazarist congregation, also known as the Congregation of the Mission, was founded by the French saint Vincent de Paul (1581-1660) in 1625 to preach missions among the poor and to work for the formation of the clergy in France and elsewhere. The French Lazarists extended their activities into the southern Balkans in the second half of the nineteenth century from their headquarters in Thessalonika. Under Fulgence Czarev, who was appointed Catholic archbishop of Skopje on 8 November 1879, following the death of Dario Bucciarelli (1827-1878), they promoted missionary activities among the Bulgarians and **Vlachs** in Monastir (Bitola) and among the Albanians in Prizren. Lazarist missions were also founded in **Korça** and **Pogradec** by Thomas Brunetti. The Sisters of St. Vincent de Paul, also known as the Daughters of Charity, were founded in 1633 and began their missionary activities among the Albanians in 1888 when the first native Albanian sisters, Agatha Shënkolli, known as Sister Philomena, Suzana Sopi and Xhuliana Sopi, arrived in Prizren after training abroad. The Daughters of Charity were granted freedom of action by the **Ottoman** authorities in 1890 but were apparently opposed to some extent by the **Franciscans** and **Jesuits**. The group survived in Prizren until 1891. Among the leading figures of the Lazarist community in Monastir was father **Jean-Claude Faveyrial**, author of a recently published *Histoire de l'Albanie* (History of Albania), and of works concerning the Vlachs.

LEAGUE OF PEJA (*LIDHJA E PEJËS*) (1899). The League of Peja was established at a meeting of Albanian leaders, which was organized in Peja on 23-29 January 1899 by the Muslim cleric and nationalist figure, Haxhi Zeka, to recreate and reform the defunct **League of Prizren**. Most of the ca. 500 delegates to the meeting came from **Kosova**, though invitations were sent out to leaders from all Albanian lands. The purpose of the Albanian League of Peja, also known as *Besa-Besë* (Pledge for a Pledge), which was to function throughout the four Albanian-inhabited vilayets, was to create a *besa*, a general truce on **blood feuding** so that the Albanians could concentrate their energies on defending their territory rather than on fighting among themselves. One delegate proclaimed its aim as being "to unite everyone in a general *besa* in order to be able to stand up to the Bulgarians, Serbs and Montenegrins, and reject all other sorts of reforms." Other objectives of the league were, in fact, to preserve the Albanians from the western-oriented reforms, which were being carried out in Istanbul and to protect the Muslim **religion**. The meeting came up with a twelve-point program for territorial defense, beginning with loyalty to the sultan, and not expressly mentioning autonomy at all. Local Muslim committees were to guard public order and enforce sharia law. Many delegates wanted the courts to pronounce judgment only in accordance with the **Kanun of Lekë Dukagjini**.

LEAGUE OF PRIZREN (*LIDHJA E PRIZRENIT*) (1878-1881). On 10 June 1878, delegates from all over Albania assembled in Prizren to work out a common political platform to counter the Treaty of San Stefano and the resolutions of the **Congress of Berlin**, which had ignored the Albanian wish for self-determination. It no doubt initially had the tacit support of the **Ottoman** government. Among the most prominent participants of the League of Prizren were **Abdyl bey Frashëri**, Sulejman Vokshi and Ymer Prizreni. On 13 June 1878, the League submitted an eighteen-page memorandum to **Benjamin Disraeli**, the British representative at the Congress of Berlin, announcing: "Just as we are not and do not want to be Turks, so we shall oppose with all our might anyone who would like to turn us into Slavs or Austrians or Greeks. We want to be Albanians." The *Kararname*, resolutions of the League of Prizren, were passed and signed by forty-seven Albanian beys on 18 June 1878. They included: a refusal to give up any territory to **Serbia**, Montenegro, or **Greece**; a demand for the return of all Albanian-speaking land annexed by Serbia and Montenegro; Albanian autonomy within the Empire;

and no more conscription for, and taxation by, the central government in Constantinople.

After this historic meeting, which served to promote the national awakening, Abdyl bey returned to southern Albania where he organized a League committee and began gathering troops to oppose the annexation of the south of the country by Greece. A key assembly of Muslim and Christian landowners at the **Bektashi** monastery of his native village of Frashër adopted a program for autonomy, which was accepted by the League in Prizren on 27 November 1878. Its program was later published by **Sami bey Frashëri** in the Constantinople daily newspaper *Tercümân-i-Şark*. In 1879, Abdyl bey traveled to Berlin, Paris, Vienna and Rome with Mehmed Ali Vrioni to seek support for the Albanian cause and to submit a memorandum of Albanian demands to the Great Powers. In mid-1880, a program for Albanian autonomy was passed by delegates of the national movement in **Gjirokastra**. At the end of April 1881, the Ottoman authorities had had enough and sent in troops to quell the uprising, and the League of Prizren was suppressed.

The League of Prizren is considered the beginning of the long struggle against the Ottoman Empire and against Albania's neighbors for the country's self-determination and independence. The original venue of the League of Prizren is commemorated by a small **museum,** which has now been rebuilt, after being razed to the ground by Serb forces during the **Kosova War** in 1999.

LEAGUE OF WRITERS AND ARTISTS. *See* UNION OF WRITERS AND ARTISTS.

LEAKE, WILLIAM MARTIN (1777.01.14-1860.01.10). British writer and diplomat. Leake was born near Colchester and, after training as an English artillery officer, worked as a military instructor for the **Ottoman** army in Istanbul in 1799. After serving in Egypt (1800), Malta and the Morea, he worked as British consul to the court of **Ali Pasha Tepelena** in Janina in the early years of the nineteenth century. He is the author of two works, which include much fascinating material on southern Albania: *Researches in Greece,* London 1814; and the four-volume *Travels in Northern Greece,* London 1835, reprint Amsterdam 1967. The former is of particular interest to Albanian studies because it includes a grammar of the Albanian **language** and a rare, 2,000-word Greek-English-Albanian dictionary compiled by Jani Evstrat Vithkuqari (d. 1822). In a preface to his section on Albanian grammar, Leake writes: "The greater part of the information upon which the following remarks are founded, was derived from Evstratio of Viskuki, who holds the rank of Hieroceryx in the Greek church, and had been many years school-master in Moskhopoli" (Voskopoja).

LEAR, EDWARD (1812.05.12-1888.01.29). British poet and painter. Lear was born in Highgate (London), the twentieth of twenty-one children. He was a passionate painter from an early age and received a commission from the Earl of Derby to paint landscapes in the Mediterranean. He traveled to Albania in the autumn of 1848 on an originally unplanned journey. It was the British ambassador in Constantinople who managed to get the requisite papers for him to travel through what was then considered the wilds of the **Ottoman Empire**. Starting from Thessalonika, he arrived in Monastir on 20 September, accompanied by his temperamental dragoman Giorgio. From there, they continued on to Ohrid, Struga, **Elbasan, Tirana**, **Kruja**, **Lezha** and **Shkodra,** which they reached on 2 October. After several days there, they returned to Tirana and continued southwards to **Kavaja, Berat** (14-18 October), **Ardenica, Apollonia, Vlora**, the coast of **Himara** (21-30 October), **Tepelena, Gjirokastra** and on to Janina (5 November). The delightful account of the journey was published in his *Journals of a Landscape Painter in Greece and Albania,* London 1851, reprint 1988. Many of the landscape paintings and sketches he made during the journey provide an accurate topographical record of mid-nineteenth century Albania.

LEGALITY (*LEGALITETI*) (1943-). Resistance movement and political organization. The Legality movement, Alb. *Legaliteti,* is associated with **Abaz Kupi**. It arose on 21 November 1943 as a third force of resistance, after the **communist**-dominated National Liberation Front and the republican *Balli Kombëtar*. Among the other leading founders of the movement were **Muharrem Bajraktari**, Fiqri Dine and Cen Elezi. The Legality movement maintained that only the prewar **Zog** regime was legitimate, and supported the return of the king. Its supporters were mostly former Zogist army officers and officials. When the communists took power in 1944, most Legality members fled the country or were killed. As a political force, it revived after the fall of the dictatorship as the **Movement for Legality Party** (*Partia Lëvizja e Legalitetit*).

LEGRAND, EMILE (1841-1904.11.14). French scholar and bibliographer. Legrand was born in Paris and taught Greek at the Ecole des Langues Orientales (School of Oriental Languages). He was the first to compile a major Albanian bibliography, *Bibliographie albanaise: description raisonnée des ouvrages publiés en albanais ou relatifs à l'Albanie du quinzième siècle à l'année 1900* (Albanian Bibliography: Reasoned Description of Works Published in Albanian or Concerning Albania from the Fifteenth Century to the Year 1900), Athens 1912, which he completed just before his death. His bibliographical work on Albanian was later carried on by Henri Gûys.

LEK. Albanian currency. The *lek* was introduced as the national currency of Albania on 16 February 1922, replacing the gold francs and other currencies which had been used previously. It was revalued in 1964, one new *lek* being then equal to ten old *leks*. All prices are since written in new *leks*, but, although forty years have passed, old *leks* are still more common in Albania for verbal communication. The *lek* is divided into 100 *qindarkas*. In 2003, a U.S. dollar was worth ca. 136 *leks*.

LEKA. *See* ZOGU, LEKA.

LEKA, DHORA (1923.02.23-). Music composer. Dhora Leka was born in **Korça** and finished her schooling in 1942 at the Queen Mother Pedagogical Institute (*Instituti Nanë Mbretneshë*). She took part in the resistance movement during **World War II** and composed numerous partisan songs which are still played today. From October 1948 to November 1953, she studied composition at the Tchaikovsky Conservatory in Moscow and taught at the Jordan Misja Academy upon her return to Albania. In February 1954, she was appointed secretary of the **Union of Writers and Artists** but was fired and expelled from the **communist** party in May 1956, and interned in **Gjirokastra** in June of that year. In May 1957, she was arrested and sentenced to twenty-five years in prison for treason. All her compositions to date, including opera and ballet, were removed from libraries and destroyed. After her release in 1963, she was interned in various villages until the end of the **communist** dictatorship. In 1992, she founded and headed the Dhora Leka Cultural Foundation for young musicians. Aside from her partisan songs, little of her **music** is widely known due to her long years of imprisonment and internment, but some pieces have been revived recently.

LEKA, GAZMEND (1953.10.11-). Painter. Gazmend Leka studied painting at the Academy of Fine Arts (*Instituti i Lartë i Arteve*) in **Tirana**, where he later taught art. He has also worked for the animated **films** division of **New Albania Film Studios** and produced films of note. His painting has been inspired in part by Albanian legendry.

LEZHA. Town in the **District of Lezha**, of which it is the administrative center. **Population** in Dec. 1999: 20,859. As a settlement, Lezha with its fortified acropolis dates back at least to the eighth century B.C. In 385 B.C., Dionysios I, the tyrant of Syracuse, is said to have founded a Greek colony here, called Lissos. In 168 B.C. it was settled by the Romans under Julius Caesar and received the status of a *municipium*. Between the third and fifth centuries A.D., it was the seat of a bishop. In 1343, Lezha was conquered by the Serbs and in 1393, by the Venetians. Like **Kruja**, Lezha is primarily associated with the figure of **Scanderbeg** who convened an assembly of Albanian nobles here on 2 March 1444 to counter an impending **Ottoman** invasion. Scanderbeg died in Lezha in 1468 and was buried in the church of St. Nicholas, where his grave can be seen. In 1979, the town was destroyed by an earthquake and is still subject to flooding every year from the **Drin** River. The town is known in Italian as *Alessio*.

LEZHA, DISTRICT OF. Region of local government administration. The District of Lezha (*Rrethi i Lezhës*), with its administrative headquarters in the town of **Lezha**, borders on the Adriatic Sea to the west, the districts of **Shkodra** and **Puka** to the north, **Mirdita** to the east and **Kurbin** to the south. It has a surface area of 479 square kilometers and a present **population** of 68,318 (in 2000).

LIBOHOVA, EQREM BEY (1882.01.24-1948). Political figure. Eqrem bey Libohova, brother of Myfit bey Libohova, stemmed from one of the richest landowning families in Albania. He was born in **Gjirokastra**, attended school in Istanbul and trained at a military academy in Brussels. He was active in the **Ottoman** administration and army until 1912, and after independence, he served in Albania. Eqrem bey was one of the leading political figures of Albania who traveled to Germany in 1914 to pay their respects to the new monarch, **Prince Wilhelm zu Wied**. He later served as Wied's aide-de-camp and was Albanian envoy in Rome and Vienna. In 1929, after the declaration of the monarchy, he was appointed minister of court and accompanied **King Zog** to Vienna, where he was wounded during the assassination attempt on the steps of the opera house on 20 February 1931. In the late 1930s, the italophile Libohova served as foreign minister in the government of **Kostaq Kota**. In April 1939, he fled to **Italy**, where he was detained for some time but was soon able to return to Albania. He served as prime minister and minister of the interior for three weeks in February 1943 and once again in May of that year. Libohova fled to Italy with Lieutenant General Alberto Pariani during the **German** invasion of September 1943, and died in exile in Rome.

LIBOHOVA, MYFIT BEY (1876-1927.02.10). Political figure. Myfit bey Libohova, brother of Eqrem bey Libohova, was born in the southern Albanian village of Libohova, scion of a wealthy landowning family. He served in the **Ottoman** administration and represented Albania in the parliament of the Young Turks in 1908. It was in Istanbul that he published a 219-page book on **Ali Pasha Tepelena** in Turkish. Back in Albania, he took part in the Congress of **Vlora** and was appointed minister of the interior and **education**, and later foreign minister. Under the short reign of **Prince Wilhelm zu Wied** he was minister of justice, then war minister and in 1918, deputy prime minister. In March of 1924, he was appointed minister of justice and de facto finance minister. Libohova fled to **Italy** in June 1924 during the **Democratic Revolution** and returned to Albania via Greece in December of that year when **Ahmet Zogu** overthrew **Fan Noli**. Thereafter, he held several other ministerial posts until his death in **Saranda** in February 1927.

LIBRARIES. *See* NATIONAL LIBRARY OF ALBANIA.

LIBRAZHD, DISTRICT OF. Region of local government administration. The District of Librazhd (*Rrethi i Librazhdit*), with its administrative headquarters in the town of Librazhd, borders on the districts of **Elbasan** and **Tirana** to the west, **Bulqiza** to the north, **Pogradec** and **Gramsh** to the south and the Republic of **Macedonia** to the east. It has a surface area of 1,023 square kilometers and a present **population** of 72,286 (in 2000). The word Librazhd was recorded as *Liborasi* in 1515.

LIDHJA E SHKRIMTARËVE DHE E ARTISTËVE TË SHQIPËRISË. *See* UNION OF WRITERS AND ARTISTS.

LIOLIN, ARTHUR (1943.06.19-). Orthodox religious figure. Arthur Evans Liolin was born in New York of a family originally from Boboshtica near **Korça.** He graduated from secondary school in New York in 1961 and attended the Albert Schweitzer Institute in Chur, Switzerland, in 1964-1965. In 1967, he graduated from Princeton University with a degree in in religion, art and archeology and on 16 September 1970, was ordained as a priest at St. George Cathedral in Boston. In 1975, after various posts in the church hierarchy, Arthur Liolin was appointed chancellor of the Albanian **Orthodox** Archdiocese in America, with its headquarters in Boston. He is also founder of the **Fan Noli** Library of Albanian Culture and the Albanian Humanitarian Aid Committee.

LITERATURE, ALBANIAN. The rise of early Albanian literature, that of the sixteenth and seventeenth centuries, is closely linked to the fortunes of the **Catholic Church** in the southwestern Balkans and to the spread of Italian civilization. The first books in Albanian were Latin and Italian texts translated into an as yet unsophist-icated **language**, but later, more polished ecclesiastical texts were written in Albanian itself. The authors of the major works of early Albanian literature were all clerics trained in **Italy**. The earliest book written and published in Albanian, at least the first one we know of, is a 188-page Albanian translation of the Catholic missal, commonly known as the *Meshari* (The Missal). It was written in 1555 by one **Gjon Buzuku**, a northern Albanian Catholic cleric.

Other works of early Albanian literature include translations of Christian Doctrines by **Lekë Matrënga** of Sicily in 1592 and by **Pjetër Budi** in 1618; a Latin-Albanian dictionary, 1635, by **Frang Bardhi**; and the so-called *Cuneus prophetarum,* a theological treatise by **Pjetër Bogdani**, the latter being con-sidered the masterpiece of early Albanian literature and the first work in Albanian of artistic and literary quality.

With the **Ottoman** conquest of the Balkans, early Albanian literature suddenly died, and the first notable chapter of Albanian literary history came to a rapid and definitive close. Not until the so-called **Rilindja** movement of national rebirth in the second half of the nineteenth century was literature in Albania to regain the vitality it experienced in the sixteenth and seventeenth centuries.

The literature of the Ottoman period consisted almost exclusively of verse. This poetry, composed in Arabic script, was strongly influenced by Turkish, Persian and Arabic literary models, which were in fashion at the time both in Istanbul and the Middle East. The subject matter was often religious, either meditatively intimate or openly didactic, serving to spread the faith. The first major poet among the so-called *Bejtexhinj* was **Nezim Frakulla**.

One strong branch of Albanian literature to evolve on its own outside the Balkans was that of the **Arbëresh** of southern Italy. **Giulio Variboba** from the mountains of Calabria is regarded by many as the first genuine poet in the whole of Albanian literature with his long lyric poem on the life of the Virgin Mary, 1762. **Girolamo De Rada** is not only the best-known writer of Italo-Albanian literature but also the foremost figure of the Albanian nationalist movement in nineteenth-century Italy. He was the harbinger and first audible voice of the Romantic movement in Albanian literature. His journalistic, literary and political activities were instrumental not only in fostering an awareness for the Arbëresh minority in Italy but also in laying the foundations for an Albanian national literature.

The struggle for political autonomy within the languishing Ottoman Empire, and the will for cultural identity and survival among a backward and religiously divided people, crystallized in the second half of the nineteenth century into the so-called Rilindja movement of national awakening. There was an intrinsic link between the goals of the nationalist movement in this period and the creative force of Albanian literature. Romantic nationalism accordingly became a dominant trait of expression. The main reason for the sluggish evolution of Albanian literature throughout the Ottoman period was the ban imposed by the Turkish authorities on Albanian writing and publishing and on Albanian-language schools. Even into the twentieth century, the authorities often went so far as to open people's handbags and correspondence and to search homes for anything written in Albanian. Therefore, very little literature was able to develop.

Naim bey Frashëri is nowadays widely considered to be the national poet of Albania. He is the author of twenty-two literary works, fifteen of which are in Albanian. The most influential of all Albanian writers and publishers of the early years of the twentieth century was most certainly **Faik bey Konitza**, who founded the periodical *Albania*, which was soon to become the most important medium of the Albanian press. **Fan Noli** was not only a politician and an outstanding leader of the Albanian-American community, but also a preeminent and multitalented figure of Albanian literature. He has not been forgotten as a poet, though his powerful declamatory verse is far from prolific. His main contribution to Albanian literature was that of a stylist, as seen especially in his translations.

By far the greatest and most influential figure of Albanian literature in the first half of the twentieth century was the **Franciscan** pater **Gjergj Fishta**, who more than any other writer gave artistic expression to the searching soul of the now sovereign Albanian nation. Lauded and celebrated up until **World War II** as the "national poet of Albania" and the "Albanian Homer," Fishta was to fall into sudden oblivion when the **communists** took power in November 1944. The very mention of his name became taboo for forty-six years. Fishta is the author of a total of thirty-seven literary publications, though his name is indelibly linked to one great work, indeed to one of the most astounding creations in all the history of Albanian literature, the long verse epic *Lahuta e malcís* (The Highland Lute), Shkodra 1937.

The road to modernity was to be taken by two poets of a new generation, two outsiders who broke with the traditions of mainstream literature and gave Albanian culture its place in a contemporary Europe: the messianic **Migjeni** and the pantheistic **Lasgush Poradeci**.

For almost a quarter of a century after the declaration of political independence in 1912, Albanian writers and intellectuals continued to draw their inspiration from the ideas and ideals of the nineteenth-century Rilindja movement. By the 1930s and early 1940s, intellectual life had reached unprecedented heights, a zenith in Albanian written culture. A modern literature had been created in Albania and the nation had finally come of age. But it was a brief blossoming in the shadow of the apocalypse to come, an apocalypse which would snuff out all genuine literary production for about twenty years.

Enver Hoxha and the new partisan leaders who took power in 1944 were suspicious of Albanian writers and intellectuals of all political hues, regarding the vast majority of them as representatives of the "ancien régime." Many figures of note in Albanian intellectual life fled the country before or during the **communist** takeover, among them: **Ernest Koliqi**, **Mehdi bey Frashëri**, **Mid'hat bey Frashëri**, **Karl Gurakuqi**, **Branko Merxhani** and **Tajar Zavalani**.

Others cherished the illusion that, having survived the war, they could come to some sort of arrangement with the new communist leaders and work actively with them on the building of a new Albania, a new socialist society. The immediate postwar period soon, however, became a nightmare for Albanian writers and intellectuals. Writers of the Catholic school of **Shkodra** suffered particularly. Playwright **Ndre Zadeja**, poet Lazër Shantoja (1892-1945), poet **Bernardin Palaj**, novelist **Anton Harapi** and publicist Gjon Shllaku (1907-1946) were executed. Poet and archbishop **Vinçenc Prennushi** died in prison after gruesome torture, as did prose writer and publisher Dom **Ndoc Nikaj**. Other intellectuals of note to be executed included Arbëresh publisher **Terenzio Tocci**, editor Nebil Çika (1893-1944), **Bektashi** writer Baba Ali Tomori (1900-1947) and poet Manush Peshkëpia (1910-1951). Among the many other writers and intellectuals who were arrested and imprisoned during the witch hunts after World War II were noted playwrights **Kristo Floqi** and **Etëhem Haxhiademi**, Muslim writer and publisher **Hafiz Ibrahim Dalliu**, **Mirash Ivanaj,** and poet Gjergj Bubani (1899-1954), all of whom died in prison; short story writer **Mitrush Kuteli**, novelist **Petro Marko**, poet **Sejfulla Malëshova**, short story writer **Musine Kokalari**, poet and scholar **Arshi Pipa**, Bektashi poet Ibrahim Hasnaj (1912-1995), poet Nexhat Hakiu (1917-1978), poet Andrea Varfi (1914-1992), translators **Jusuf Vrioni** and Pashko Gjeci (1918-), novelist Mustafa Greblleshi (1922-1986), publicist Dionis Miçaço, poet Kudret Kokoshi (1907-1991), novelist and editor Andon S. Frashëri (1892-1965), humorist and indefatigable translator Mid'hat Araniti (1912-1992), linguist **Selman Riza**, critic Filip Fishta (1904-1973), folklorists **Donat Kurti** and Stavro Frashëri of **Kavaja** and writer Lazër Radi (1916-1998), who was released in 1991 after an incredible forty-five years of prison and internment.

The persecution of intellectuals, in particular of all those who had been abroad before 1944, and the break with virtually all cultural traditions, created a literary and cultural vacuum in Albania which lasted until the 1960s, the results of which can still be felt today. The first turning point in the evolution of Albanian prose and verse, after a quarter century of stagnation, came in the stormy year of 1961 which, on the one hand, marked the definitive political break with the **Soviet Union** and thus with Soviet literary models and, on the other hand, witnessed the publication of a number of trend-setting volumes by **Ismail Kadare, Dritëro**

Agolli and **Fatos Arapi**. The long years of Stalinist dictatorship which were to follow, however, impeded Albanian writing from evolving into a literature comparable to that of the more developed countries of Europe. A high degree of conformity continued due to the extreme level of pressure exerted upon writers and intellectuals throughout the rule of Enver Hoxha. Successful writers learned how to lie low and present what they wished to express in thick layers of political wrapping, so that only the trained eye of an experienced reader could comprehend the analogies being drawn. Despite the constraints of socialist realism, Albanian literature did make some progress in the 1970s and 1980s.

The best example of creativity and originality in contemporary Albanian letters is that of Ismail Kadare, still the only Albanian writer to enjoy a broad international reputation. Among other figures of contemporary Albanian prose, mention may be made of Dritëro Agolli, **Fatos Kongoli**, **Kasëm Trebeshina**, Mira Meksi (1960-), **Elvira Dones** and Ardian-Christian Kyçyku (1969-). In the field of modern verse, mention may be made, among many others, of Fatos Arapi, **Xhevahir Spahiu**, Visar Zhiti, Flutura Açka, **Mimoza Ahmeti** and **Luljeta Lleshanaku**.

Written literature in **Kosova** and **Macedonia** was late to develop because of widespread illiteracy and Slav cultural hegemony. It flourished, however, in the mid-1970s when access to Albanian-language **education** and cultural facilities was finally granted, a brief blossoming in which tremendous progress was made within a short period of time, in education, culture and literature.

Literature in Kosova and Macedonia evolved without the. severe ideological constraints imposed upon writers in Albania itself. Emigration also brought about contacts with the outside world, which enabled the written word to develop in a more cosmopolitan manner from the start. Literature here is, as such, more experimental and offers the reader a much wider range of styles, subject matter and ideas. Though the level of formal training for prose writers in Kosova was never to reach **Tirana** standards, young Kosova writers were eager to assimilate foreign influences and the currents of contemporary European thought that were rejected out of hand in Tirana. At the same time, this much more eclectic literature has lost surprisingly little of its traditional Albanian flavor. Its strength and dynamism are a direct result of the need perceived by Kosova Albanians to defend their cultural values in a region plagued by political turmoil and ethnic conflict.

While some monographs were published in the 1950s, it was not until the mid-1960s that Albanian and Kosova Albanian literature began to appear in print in **Yugoslavia** on a significant scale. Among prose writers, mention may be made of Hivzi Sulejmani (1912-1975) of Mitrovica; Ramiz Kelmendi (1930-) of Peja; writer and longtime political prisoner Adem Demaçi (1936-), whose controversial novel *Gjarpijt e gjakut* (The Snakes of Blood), Prishtina 1958, established his literary reputation; Rexhep Qosja (1936-), one of the most eminent and prolific literary critics in the Balkans; Anton Pashku (1938-1995) a writer who relished the hermetic observations of the psychological novel; Nazmi Rrahmani (1941-) from the Podujeva region, a prolific and popular novelist of Kosova village life; Luan Starova (1941-) of Skopje, whose novels have been translated into French and German; Teki Dërvishi (1943-) of Gjakova; Beqir Musliu (1945-1996) from Gjilan; Jusuf Buxhovi (1946-) of Peja; Eqrem Basha (1948-) from Dibra; and Kim Mehmeti (1955-) of Skopje.

Poetry has always been the vanguard of literature in Kosova and has enjoyed more popularity among writers and the reading public there than prose. This poetic imagination has solid roots in the soil, in the land and in its people with their aspirations, sufferings and dreams. The writer widely considered to be the father of modern Albanian poetry in Yugoslavia, Esad Mekuli (1916-1993), founded the literary periodical *Jeta e re* (New Life) in 1949 and was a committed poet of social awareness. Of the many other contemporary poets of Kosova, mention may be made of Enver Gjerqeku (1928-) of Gjakova; Besim Bokshi (1932-) of Gjakova; Din Mehmeti (1932-); Azem Shkreli (1938-1997) from the Rugova mountains near Peja; Ali Podrimja (1942-) from Gjakova, whose masterful collection *Lum Lumi* (Lum Lumi), Prishtina 1982, marked a turning point not only in his own work but also in contemporary Kosova verse as a whole; Sabri Hamiti (1950-) of Podujeva, a leading and innovative literary critic, prose writer, playwright and now political figure; Eqrem Basha; and Lindita Ahmeti (1973-) of Skopje.

LLESHANAKU, LULJETA (1968-). Poet. Luljeta Lleshanaku was born in **Elbasan** and is the author of four poetry collections. She studied **literature** at the University of **Tirana** and was editor-in-chief of the weekly magazine *Zëri i rinisë* (The Voice of Youth). She then worked for the literary newspaper *Drita* (The Light). In 1996, she received the best book of the year award from the Eurorilindja Publishing House, and, in 1999, she took part in the International Writers Program at the University of Iowa. Her verse has been published in English in the volume *Fresko: Selected Poetry of Luljeta Lleshanaku*, New York 2002.

LLESHI, HAXHI (1913.05.01-1998.01.01). Political figure of the **communist** period. Haxhi Lleshi was born in the village of Reshan in the **Dibra** region of a wealthy Muslim family. He studied at the University of Belgrade from 1936 to 1939 and served as a partisan commander in Dibra in 1941-1943. He attended the **Conference of Peza** in 1942 and became a leading member of the communist resistance. After the communist takeover, he served as minister of the interior, 1944-1946; minister without portfolio, 1946-1948; chairman of the party control commission, 1948-1949; and member of **parliament** from 1950. He also held high positions in the army and was a member of the Central Committee from 1956. In August 1953, he was elected to the post of chairman of the presidium of the People's Assembly and was thus formally head of state in Albania until November 1982. He was placed under house arrest on 16 December 1995, and was accused of manslaughter for the deaths of Albanians trying to escape across the border illegally.

LOGORECI, ANTON (1910.07.19-1990.09.23). Writer. Anton Pjetër Logoreci was born in **Shkodra**, where he was educated by the **Franciscans**. He attended the **American Vocational School** in **Tirana**, from which he graduated in 1927. He worked as an English teacher in the mountains and then served as an interpreter to General **Sir Jocelyn Percy** who was charged with organizing a new Albanian police force under **King Zog**. Thereafter, Logoreci moved to England to study at the London School of Economics. With the outbreak of **World War II**, he got a post as head of the tiny Albanian section of the BBC's new overseas service, broadcasting news reports to his country under fascist occupation. He retired from the job in 1974 and died in London. Logoreci is remembered for numerous articles and, in particular, for his book *The Albanians: Europe's Forgotten Survivors,* London 1977.

LOGORECI, MARIE (1920.09.23-1988.06.19). Stage and **film** actress. Marie Logoreci was born in **Shkodra** and began her artistic career as a singer in 1940. From 1947, she worked as a professional actress at the **National Theater** in **Tirana**, of which she became one of the best-known female interpreters. She also played in twelve full-length feature **films**, in particular in: *Tana* (Tana) 1958; *Toka jonë* (Our Land), 1964; and *Operacioni Zjarri* (Operation Fire), 1973.

LOGORECI, MATI (1867.02.10-1941.02.07). Educator and publisher. Mati Logoreci was born on 10 February 1867 of a **Catholic** family in **Shkodra**. As a young man, he worked as an apprentice for the Italian trading company Parruca, which sent him as an accountant to Monfalcone near Trieste. It was there that he also trained as a teacher. After his return to Albania, he opened a school in Prizren on 1 May 1889, said to be the first Albanian school in **Kosova**. In 1899, he founded another Albanian private school, which is reported to have received wide public support. The two schools were merged in 1900. He taught in Prizren until 1903, when he transferred to the **Franciscan** school in Shkodra. On 14 November 1907, he began publication of the short-lived fortnightly newspaper *Dašamiri* (The Patron), which he had printed in Trieste in the so-called *Agimi* alphabet. In November 1908, Logoreci represented the *Agimi* (The Dawn) society of Shkodra at the **Congress of Monastir**, together with poet **Ndre Mjeda**.

After independence, Logoreci taught in **Tirana**, and from 1916 to 1918 worked for the **education** authorities in Shkodra. In 1916, he was also a member of the Albanian Literary Commission and attended the **Congress of Lushnja** as a delegate for Shkodra. From 1922 to 1923, he was secretary-general at the ministry of education and devoted himself to teaching until retirement in 1930. Late in life, Mati Logoreci returned to publishing with a new newspaper, *Drita* (The Light), which printed its first edition on 28 November 1936 and lasted until 1939. *It was* the largest Albanian newspaper until the end of **World War II**. Mati Logoreci died in Tirana at the age of seventy-four, a noted figure of northern Albanian **education**.

LOHJA. Northern Albanian tribe and traditional tribal region. The small Lohja region is situated in the District of **Malësia e Madhe** near Dedaj on the road from Koplik to Theth. It borders on the traditional tribal regions of **Kastrati** to the west and north, and Reç and Rrjoll to the south. The Lohja tribe had a **population** of some 2,500 in the last years of the nineteenth century.

LONDO, BARDHYL (1948.12.25-). Poet. Bardhyl Londo, from Lipa near **Përmet**, built up a reputation as a leading Albanian poet in the 1980s. He studied **language** and **literature** at the University of **Tirana**, taught school for some years in his native district of Përmet, and later worked for the literary journal *Drita* (The Light). He also served as president of the Albanian **Union of Writers and Artists** until 21 February 1998, when he was replaced by **Xhevahir Spahiu**. He is the author of eight poetry collections from 1975 to 1996. Londo's lyrics depart from the concrete: details and moments of existence which he has experienced, lived through intensely, and transformed into verse in a controlled, erudite manner. His poetry, which is written in standard meters and is mostly rhymed, echoes the rich traditions of **Tosk** verse. In recent years he has been active in politics.

LORECCHIO, ANSELMO (1843.11.03-1924.03.22). **Arbëresh** publisher, writer and public figure. Lorecchio was born in Pallagorio (Alb. *Puhëriu*) in the Calabrian province of Catanzaro and studied law at the University of Naples. Very soon, he devoted himself to the study of Albanian culture and took an active part in the political and cultural movements of the period. He presided over the second Albanological congress in Lungro (Alb. *Ungra*) in 1897, was elected president of the Società Nazionale Albanese (Albanian National Society), and published the works of many Arbëresh writers at his own expense. Lorecchio was also a writer and poet himself. He was the author of *La questione albanese* (The Albanian Question), Catanzaro 1898; *Il pensiero politico albanese in rapporto agli interessi italiani* (Albanian Political Thought in Relation to Italian Interests), Rome 1904; and countless articles. His fame rests nonetheless on his activities as publisher of the influential Arbëresh periodical *La Nazione albanese* (The Albanian Nation), a fortnightly review of political and cultural affairs which lasted from 1897 to his death.

LUARASI, KRISTO (1879.12.15-1934). Publisher. Kristo Luarasi, from the village of Luaras southwest of **Korça**, went to school in the village of Hotova where he was taught by educator and publisher **Petro Nini Luarasi**. In 1892, after the **Ottoman** authorities closed down Albanian schools, he emigrated to Romania and found work as a printer. In 1896, he moved to Sofia and set up the *Mbrothësia* (Progress) Press, which was to have an enormous impact on the diffusion of Albanian **literature**. Together with Kosta Jani Trebicka (d. 1944) and **Mid'hat bey Frashëri**, he published the cultural almanac *Ditërëfenjës* or *Kalëndari kombiar* (The National Calendar) which appeared annually, with some lengthy interruptions, from 1897 to 1928. The national calendars were relatively significant works in the history of Albanian literature since, like nineteenth-century family almanacs in farming communities on the North American prairies, they were read in many homes. These almanacs created an awareness of the existence of Albanian literature amongst the general public which otherwise had little contact with contemporary works of Albanian prose and verse. But for Kristo Luarasi, this was only a start. At the *Mbrothësia* Press, he also published a total of thirty-seven monographs of Albanian literature, including works of **Spiro Dine**, **Mihal Grameno**, Papa **Kristo Negovani**, Mid'hat bey Frashëri and **Hilë Mosi**. He also republished the works of **Naim bey Frashëri** and **Sami bey Frashëri,** making them available to a larger public.

After the Young Turk revolution, Luarasi transferred his printing press to Thessalonika where about sixty works were produced in the course of one year: books, newspapers, magazines, and over 10,000 spellers, which were distributed free of charge among the Albanian-speaking population. In March 1910, when the Turkish authorities had begun to grow wary of his activities, he transferred the press back to Sofia. Here he published a weekly newspaper called *Liria e Shqipërisë* (The Freedom of Albania) from 1911 until 1915. In 1921, he returned to Albania and founded the Luarasi Press, which was to be the largest printing press in the country.

LUARASI, PETRO NINI (1865.04.22-1911.08.17). Publisher and educator. Luarasi, one of the first Albanian teachers of the national awakening, was in the vanguard of the movement for the creation of Albanian schools. He was born in Luaras in the **Kolonja** region of southern Albania, and attended Greek schools in Nokova and Hotova near **Gjirokastra**. After completing his teacher training in Qestorat, he was given an initial posting as a Greek teacher in the village of Bezhdan in 1882, where he also began teaching the children Albanian, using the so-called Istanbul alphabet. Despite the fierce opposition of the Greek **Orthodox** church and of the **Ottoman** authorities in Istanbul, he managed, with the financial assistance of Nikolla Naço (1843-1913) in Bucharest, to found several schools in southern Albania over the next years.

Petro Nini Luarasi was one of the teachers at the first Albanian school officially recognized by the Porte which was opened in **Korça** on 7 March 1887. He took over the management of this national school from Pandeli Sotiri (1852-1890) in the spring of 1891 and assisted in the financing of other schools in southern Albania. On 20 September 1892, he was excommunicated once again, this time by Philaretos, the metropolitan of Kastoria, for allegedly promoting freemasonry and **Protestantism**. In a circular letter to the Orthodox community, Philaretos condemned Luarasi's endeavors to recruit teachers for Albanian, a **language** which "does not exist," and threatened anyone accepting such a post or receiving "masonic" and "Protestant" books with an anathema from the Almighty himself. In 1903-1904, when the Ottoman government began closing down all Albanian schools, Luarasi was imprisoned, but managed to escape with a false passport and emigrated to America under the pseudonym Petro Kostandini. His admission to the **United States** proved complicated because he steadfastly refused to be registered as a Greek national.

In the year of the revolution of the Young Turks, 1908, Luarasi returned to Albania under an amnesty and continued his activities. In Korça, he resumed management of the national school in 1908-1909, and in the following school year moved to Monastir (Bitola), where he taught Albanian at a Turkish school. Petro Nini Luarasi is remembered not only for his work on behalf of Albanian **education**, but also for one monograph in Greek and Albanian entitled *Mallkim i shkronjavet shqip dhe çpërfolja e shqipëtarit* (Curse of Albanian Writing and Scorn of the Albanians), Monastir 1911, in which he defended Albanian-language education against the Orthodox church, which had threatened to excommunicate any Christian recognizing the Albanian alphabet.

LUARASI, SKËNDER (1900.01.06-1982.04.27). Public figure and translator. Skënder Luarasi was born in the village of Luaras as the son of **Petro Nini Luarasi** and studied at Robert College in Istanbul. In 1915, he returned to **Vlora**, from where he emigrated to the United States, studying at Springfield College near Boston. In 1922, he was in Vienna, where he continued his studies in modern literature. He went back to Albania in 1924, during the **Fan Noli** administration, but returned, after the Noli's fall, to finish his studies in Vienna. He subsequently taught in **Vlora**, **Shkodra** and at the **American Vocational School** in **Tirana**. Luarasi took part in the Spanish Civil War with a group of some forty Albanians, and was interned from 1939 to 1944. He then returned to Albania. After the war, in October 1945, he participated in the formation of the **Writers' Union**, but was expelled during the purge of Malëshova. Thereafter, he kept a low profile and worked as a literary translator until the end of his days. He is remembered as a leading intellectual in a difficult era.

LUBONJA, FATOS (1951.04.27-). Writer, journalist and intellectual figure. Fatos Lubonja was born in **Tirana**, the son of Todi Lubonja, general director of Albanian radio and television who was purged in 1974. That same year, Fatos Lubonja, who had just graduated in theoretical physics from the University of Tirana, was arrested himself and sentenced to seven years' imprisonment for "agitation and propaganda," after police found writings which contained criticism of the regime of Enver Hoxha, in his uncle's attic. He began serving his sentence in the copper mine of Spaç. In 1979, while still incarcerated, he was sentenced to a further sixteen years in prison for having, with nine other prisoners, created a counterrevolutionary organization. After his release on 17 March 1991, he became involved in the human rights movement and served as secretary of the Albanian Helsinki Committee.

Fatos Lubonja was a major intellectual figure in the democracy movement. In 1994, he founded the critical cultural periodical *Përpjekja* (The Endeavour), which caused a fury in many circles. His experience in the **communist** prison camps has been described in his memoirs: *Në vitin e shtatëmbëdhjetë* (In the Seventeenth Year), Tirana 1994, and *Ridënimi* (The Second Sentence), Tirana 1996. The latter has been translated into English as *The Second Sentence: A Prison Memoir*, but remains unpublished. Fatos Lubonja is also the author of the drama *Ploja e mbramë* (The Final Slaughter), Tirana 1994, written in Burrel prison in 1988-1989, and of *Liri e kërcënuar: publicistika a viteve 1991-1997* (Threatened Freedom: Current Affairs Writings from the Years 1991-1997), Tirana 1999. On 3 December 2002, Lubonja was awarded the prestigious Italian Alberto Moravia Prize for International Literature.

LUBONJA, TODI (1923.02.13-). Public figure of the **communist** period. Todi Lubonja was raised in **Tirana**. He joined a communist **Korça** cell in Tirana in 1940 and took part in the resistance movement during **World War II**. He worked as a party secretary in **Elbasan** from 1951 to 1953 and in **Kukës** from 1954 to 1955. From 1955 to February 1964, he was first secretary of the party youth organization and became a close colleague and friend of **Ramiz Alia**. From 1964 to 1968, he then served as editor-in-chief of the daily newspaper *Zëri i popullit* (The People's Voice).

After three and a half years in Korça, Todi Lubonja was appointed by Ramiz Alia as general director of Albanian radio and television in early 1972. On 25 December of that year, the eleventh national song festival was held in a relatively liberal atmosphere. Western pop music was to be heard increasingly in Albania and was even being broadcast on Radio Tirana. This "liberalization" served as a pretext for Todi Lubonja's downfall. At the fourth plenary session of the Central Committee on 26-28 June 1973, he and **Fadil Paçrami** were singled out by **Enver Hoxha** in a campaign against liberal and foreign influence in Albanian culture. The two of them were the main victims of the so-called purge of the liberals. Lubonja was arrested on 24 July 1974 and sentenced to fifteen years of prison, of which he served thirteen years from 1974 to 1987, mostly in Burrel. He was released on 7 June 1987 and sent into internment until 1990. He has since written his memoirs in the volumes *Nën peshën e dhunës* (Under the Weight of Violence), Tirana 1993; *Ankthi pa fund i lirisë* (The Unending Fear of Freedom), Tirana 1994; and *Pse hesht shtëpia e muzikës* (Why Is the Music House Silent), Tirana 2002.

LUCA, NDREK (1927.09.03-1993). Stage and film actor. Luca was born in the **Dukagjini** region and worked from 1950 to the end of his life as a stage actor for the **National Theater** in **Tirana**. He also played in thirty Albanian films, among which are: *Duel i heshtur* (The Silent Duel), 1967; *Plagë të vjetra* (Old Wounds), 1969; *Pylli i lirisë* (The Forest of Freedom), 1976; and *Udha e shkronjave* (The Road of Writing), 1978.

LULI, DEDË GJO' (1840-1915.09.24). Nationalist figure and guerrilla fighter. Dedë Gjo' Luli was a Highland warrior of the **Hoti** tribe, born in Traboin. He resisted Montenegrin incursions in Hoti and **Gruda** after the **League of Prizren**. Many years later, he participated in the northern Albanian uprising of 1911. Dedë Gjo' Luli, who was immortalized in **Gjergj Fishta**'s epic poem *Lahuta e Malcís* (The Highland Lute), was murdered by Montenegrin forces near Orosh in **Mirdita**.

LUMA. Northern Albanian tribe and traditional tribal region. The Luma region is situated in the **District of Kukës** south of the White **Drin** River and east of the Black Drin River. It borders on **Kosova** to the east. The name is no doubt related to Alb. *lumë* "river."

LUSHNJA, CONGRESS OF. *See* CONGRESS OF LUSHNJA.

LUSHNJA, DISTRICT OF. Region of local government administration. The District of Lushnja (*Rrethi i Lushnjes*), with its administrative headquarters in the town of Lushnja, borders on the Adriatic Sea to the west, the districts of **Kavaja** and **Peqin** to the north, **Elbasan** and **Kuçova** to the east and **Berat** and **Fier** to the south. It has a surface area of 712 square kilometers and a present **population** of 144,933 (in 2000).

- M -

MACEDONIA, ALBANIANS IN. The Republic of Macedonia is estimated to have at least half a million Albanian speakers, equaling about thirty percent of the total population of the republic, although there are no reliable statistics. The Albanian population is to be found in and around Skopje (Alb. *Shkup*), where it constitutes a substantial minority, Kumanova (Maced. *Kumanovo*), and in particular in the west from Tetova (Maced. *Tetovo*), Gostivar and Dibra (Maced. *Debar*), down to Struga, where it forms the majority. With the declaration of Macedonian independence, the status of the Albanian community was demoted from that of official equality to that of a national minority, and widespread discrimination occurred in all walks of life there. The equally widespread frustration and dissatisfaction of the Albanians of Macedonia at being treated as second-class citizens brought the country to the brink of civil war in 2000. With the mediation of the international community, an agreement was signed in Ohrid on 13 August 2001 to give the Albanian people in Macedonia basic linguistic and cultural rights and a modicum of equality, an agreement which may now prove decisive in preserving the territorial integrity of the country.

MACEDONIAN MINORITY IN ALBANIA. *See* SLAVIC MINORITY IN ALBANIA.

MADHI, GURI (1921.05.15-1988.06.10). Painter. Guri Madhi was born in **Korça** and finished his studies in art in the Soviet Union in 1956. He taught for many years at the Academy of Fine Arts (*Instituti i Lartë i Arteve*) in **Tirana** and is among the best-known painters of his generation.

MAJKO, PANDELI (1967.11.15-). Political figure and high-ranking member of the **Socialist Party**. Pandeli Majko was born in **Tirana** and studied mechanical engineering and law at the University of Tirana. In 1992-1996, he was a member of **parliament** for the Socialist Party and head of the socialist youth organization FRESSH. In 1996-1997, he was public relations secretary for the party and, in 1997, served as head of the parliamentary group and general secretary of the Socialist Party (from 10 August). From 28 September 1998 to 29 October 1999, during the **Kosova War**, he was prime minister of Albania, and at the age of thirty-one, the youngest prime minister in Europe. In 2002, he served briefly as prime minister from 7 February to 24 July, when, under **Fatos Nano**, he was appointed minister of defense.

MALCOLM, NOEL (1956.12.26-). British scholar and historian. Noel Malcolm was born in Berkshire, England, and studied at Peterhouse and Trinity College, Cambridge, where he completed his Ph.D. in history. He taught at Gonville and Caius College, Cambridge, from 1981 to 1988, and became foreign editor of the *Spectator*, 1987-1992, and political columnist for the *Daily Telegraph*, 1992-1995. In 2001, he was elected to the British Academy, and, in 2002, he became a Fellow of All Souls College in Oxford where he currently lives. After the success of his *Bosnia: A Short History,* London 1994, he authored the first comprehensive and objective history of Kosova: *Kosovo: A Short History,* London 1998, which was widely acclaimed during the **Kosova War**. He is currently president of the **Anglo-Albanian Association** in London.

MALËSHOVA, SEJFULLA (1901-1971.06.09). Poet and political figure of the **communist** period. Originally from the **Përmet** region of southern Albania, Sejfulla Malëshova spent a good deal of his early life abroad. He had studied medicine in Italy and in 1924, at the age of twenty-three, became **Fan Noli**'s personal secretary in the latter's democratic government. With the over-throw of Noli, Malëshova fled to Paris and from there, inspired by the October Revolution, he continued on to Moscow, where he studied and later taught Marxism. In the Soviet Union he joined the communist party (1930-1932) but was subsequently expelled as a Bukharinist. Most of the verse of this self-styled rebel poet was written in exile under the pseudonym Lame Kodra and was published in the now rare volume *Vjersha* (Verse), Tirana 1945.

As minister of culture in the first communist-controlled provisional government after **World War II**, Malëshova fol-lowed a relatively liberal and conciliatory course for the times in order to encourage the reintegration of noncommunist forces into the new structures of power. He was not one to condemn all prewar writers such as **Gjergj Fishta** as reactionaries, nor was he in favor of a total break with the West. Malëshova soon became the spokesperson of one of the two factions vying for power within the party. With the backing of the Yugoslav communists, however, the faction of his adversary **Koçi Xoxe** gained the upper hand by early 1946 and Malëshova fell into disgrace. At a meeting of the Central Committee on 21 February 1946, Malëshova was accused of opportunism and right-wing deviationism and was expelled both from the Politburo and from the Central Committee.

Strangely enough, Malëshova survived his fall. This left-wing idealist, who had once been a member of the Comintern, was interned in Ballsh for two or three years and spent all his later life in internal exile as a humble stock clerk in **Fier**, where, for years, no inhabitant of the town dared speak to him. His only social contact was to play soccer with the children. Whenever anyone approached he would pinch his lips with his fingers, signifying the vow of eternal silence which ensured his survival. Malëshova died of appendicitis in unimaginable isolation. Although everyone in town knew his poems by heart, no one dared to attend his funeral. He was buried in the presence of his sister, the gravedigger, and two **Sigurimi** agents.

MALËSIA E MADHE, DISTRICT OF. Region of local government administration. The District of Malësia e Madhe (*Rrethi i Malësisë së Madhe*), with its administrative headquarters in the town of Koplik, borders on Lake **Shkodra** to the west, the Republic of Montenegro to the north and east and the **District of Shkodra** to the south. It has a surface area of 555 square kilometers and a present **population** of 45,718 (in 2000). The term "Malësia e Madhe" means great mountain range.

MALILE, REIS (1922.08.12-). Political figure of the **communist** period. Malile headed the political department of the Albanian foreign ministry in 1952-1953. He served as ambassador to the United Nations in 1956-1961 and ambassador to the People's Republic of **China** in 1962-1963. His wife and his two children died in a plane crash in China in 1963. On 30 June 1982, he was appointed minister of foreign affairs, a post he held until 21 February 1991, and was a member of the Central Committee from 1986.

MALLAKASTRA, DISTRICT OF. Region of local government administration. The District of Mallakastra (*Rrethi i Mallakastrës*), with its administrative headquarters in the town of Ballsh, borders on the district of **Fier** to the west and north, **Berat** to the east and **Tepelena** and **Vlora** to the south. It has a surface area of 393 square kilometers and a present **population** of 44,107 (in 2000).

MANDALÀ, MATTEO. Arbëresh scholar. Mandalà is from the Arbëresh settlement of Piana degli Albanesi (Alb. *Hora e Arbëreshëvet*) in Sicily and currently holds the chair of Albanian studies at the University of Palermo. He has edited the works of **Giuseppe Schirò** in nine volumes, *Opere I-IX* (Works I-IX), Soveria Mannelli 1997, and is author of *La diaspora e il ritorno: mito, storia, cultura tradizionale nell'opera di Giuseppe Schirò* (Diaspora and Return: Myth, History, Traditional Culture in the Work of Giuseppe Schirò), Palermo 1990.

MANI, PIRO (1932-). Stage and **film** actor and director. Piro Mani was born in **Korça** and graduated in drama from the Lunicharsky Institute in Moscow in 1954. From then on, he worked as an actor and, later, as director at the **National Theater** in **Tirana**. He also played in two film roles.

MANN, STUART (1905-1986). British scholar. Stuart E. Mann was born in Nottingham and studied at English schools and universities. He graduated with a degree in Germanic philology from the University of Bristol in 1927. In 1929, he traveled to Albania on a ferry from Brindisi in order to learn Albanian and familiarize himself with the culture. He got a job in **Tirana** as an English teacher at the **American Vocational School** run by Harry Fultz and stayed in the country until 1931. In the 1930s, he later taught English at the Mazaryk University of Brno in Czechoslovakia.

Mann returned to England during **World War II** and worked for the Information Ministry and subsequently for the Foreign Office. In 1947, he also became reader in Czech and Albanian at the School of Slavonic and East European Studies of the University of London, where he worked until his retirement in 1972.

Stuart Mann's primary interest in Albanian studies was in phonology and **language** history. Among the main Albanological publications are: *A Short Albanian Grammar,* London 1932; *An Historical Albanian-English Dictionary,* London 1948; *Albanian Literature, an Outline of Prose, Poetry and Drama,* London 1955; *English-Albanian Dictionary,* London 1957; and *An Albanian Historical Grammar,* Hamburg 1977. He was also the author of numerous articles devoted primarily to Albanian language and literature.

MARITIME TRANSPORTATION. *See* PORTS.

MARKO, PETRO (191311.25-1991). Prose writer. Petro Marko from Dhërmi on the coast of **Himara,** is an author who paved the road to modernity in Albanian **literature** before the time of **Ismail Kadare** and influenced the latter's early development. Marko began writing when he was twenty. His first short stories appeared in journals of the period with the assistance of his mentor **Ernest Koliqi.** From 1 March 1936, Marko edited the short-lived periodical *ABC* in **Tirana,** a fortnightly literary journal which was soon to be shut down by the Zogist authorities. Always something of a revolutionary and an anarchist in spirit, Marko set off in 1936 for the Spanish Civil War with a group of forty Albanians to join the Garibaldi Unit of the International Brigades. In Madrid, the twenty-three-year-old Marko and **Skënder Luarasi** started up a twenty-page Albanian-language periodical called *Vullnetari i lirisë* (The Volunteer of Freedom), of which only two issues appeared. Marko met Ernest Hemingway at a congress of writers held in Valencia in 1937, which was also attended by Aleksey Tolstoy, Ludwig Renn, Anna Seghers, André Malraux and Pablo Neruda. It was Petro Marko's experience in the Spanish Civil War that formed the basis of his best-known novel *Hasta la vista* (Hasta la vista), Tirana 1958.

In 1940, Marko was forced to return home from exile in France. Arrested by the Italian occupants the following year, he was interned with 600 other Balkan prisoners on the isolated island of Ustica in the Tyrrhenian Sea north of Sicily. The 380-page novel *Nata e Ustikës* (Ustica night), Tirana 1989, is the literary digestion of this period of internment. In October 1944, Marko returned to Albania as a partisan. After a couple of years as editor-in-chief of the periodical *Bashkimi* (Unity), he was arrested in 1947, by the **communists** this time, and imprisoned in Tirana. After the fall of **Koçi Xoxe**, he was released and allowed to teach in Tirana. It was in the late 1950s and early 1960s that several volumes of prose and a collection of Marko's verse first appeared.

As the author of eight novels, Petro Marko is considered by many critics to be one of the founding fathers of modern Albanian prose. Though some writers have criticized his telegraphic style, the passion of his search for new descriptive techniques and his treatment of original subjects met with wide approval, and many of this works are still read today.

MARKO, RITA (1920.02.17-). Political figure of the **communist** period. Rita Marko was born in Dishnica in the **Korça** region as the son of a shepherd of Macedonian Slav origin. He joined the communist party in 1942 and took part in the resistance movement during **World War II**. In 1949-1950, he was first secretary of the party for Korça and served as minister of industry from July 1950 to March 1951. He became a full member of the Central Committee in April 1952 and a full member of the Politburo in June 1956. Marko subsequently served as chairman of the People's Assembly in 1956-1958; vice-chairman of the People's Assembly from September 1966 to December 1976; first secretary of the party for **Durrës**, 1966-1970; and chairman of the trade union council, April 1970-1982. He was related by marriage to **Pilo Peristeri**. Marko was arrested on 5 December 1991 after the fall of the dictatorship. On 2 July 1994, he was sentenced to eight years of prison for abuse of power.

MARTINI, NDOC (1880.01.17-1916.12.06). Painter. Ndoc Martini was born in **Shkodra** and, with the help of **Kolë Idromeno**, studied art in Rome in 1902. From 1904 to 1906, he attended the College of Saint Adrian in San Demetrio Corone in Calabria, where he seems to have been very active as a painter. The ceilings in one of the halls of the college are covered in frescoes done by him. He is thought to have moved to France in 1913, but soon fell ill of tuberculosis and died there during **World War I**. Well known is his portrait of Dr. Prelë Martini, the only one of his works to be preserved in the **National Gallery** in **Tirana**.

MARUBI PHOTO COLLECTION. The Marubi Photo Collection (*Fototeka Marubi*) in **Shkodra** comprises over 100,000 negatives of great historical, artistic and cultural significance. It was compiled by three generations of photographers. Pietro Marubi (1834-1903) was an Italian painter and photographer, who, as a supporter of Garibaldi, had emigrated from Piacenza in Italy to Shkodra for political reasons around the year 1850. There, he founded a photo business, *Foto Marubi*, in Shkodra with cameras he had brought with him. The oldest photos in the collection date from 1858 to 1859. Some of them were published in *The London Illustrated News*, the *La Guerra d'Oriente* and *L'Illustration*.

Marubi was assisted by the young Rrok Kodheli (1862-1881) and his brother Kel Kodheli (1870-1940), the latter of whom took over the family business after Pietro's death and changed his name to Kel Marubi. He furthered techniques with special effects and by retouching the negatives. He also began photographing outside the studio with more advanced cameras. The third generation of photographers in the family was Kel's son, Gegë Marubi (1907-1984). He studied in Lyon in 1923-1927 at the first school of photography and cinema, founded by the Lumière brothers, and worked in Shkodra as a professional photographer from 1928 to 1940. He was the first to work with **film** instead of glass plates. Unfortunately, he took no more pictures during the **communist** dictatorship.

The Marubi Photo Collection documents northern Albanian history from the **League of Prizren** onwards. It contains fascinating photographs of tribal leaders, highland uprisings, town life in Shkodra and public events. Only a few of the photos have been published, most recently in *Albanie—Visage des Balkans, Ecrits de lumière: Photographies de Pjetër, Kel et Gegë Marubi* (Albania—Face of the Balkans, Writings in Light: Photographs of Pjeter, Kel and Gegë Marubi), Paris 1995. Attempts are currently underway to preserve the collection.

MAT. River in northern central Albania. The Mat takes its source in the Martanesh region in the southern part of the **District of Mat** and flows northwest past the town of Burrel and into the Adriatic Sea south of **Lezha**. It is 115 kilometers in length and is dammed at Ulza and Shkopet. The Mat is the ancient *Mathis* (Vibius Sequester). It was recorded in 1380 as *Mathia* (Anonymi Descriptio Europae Orientalis) and seems to be a pre-Slavic toponym, possibly related to Alb. *mat* "beach, riverbank."

MAT, DISTRICT OF. Region of local government administration. The District of Mat (*Rrethi i Matit*), with its administrative headquarters in the town of Burrel, borders on the districts of **Kruja** and **Kurbin** to the west, **Mirdita** to the north, **Dibra** and **Bulqiza** to the east and **Tirana** to the south. It has a surface area of 1,029 square kilometers and a present **population** of 68,623 (in 2000).

MATRËNGA, LEKË (1567-1619.05.06). Arbëresh writer. Lekë Matrënga, known in Italian as Luca Matranga, is the author of the second major work of early Albanian **literature**, entitled *E mbsuame e krështerë* (Christian Doctrine), Rome 1592. He was born either in Piana dei Greci (now Piana degli Albanesi) or in Monreale near Palermo in Sicily, as the scion of an Arbëresh family who had emigrated to the island, probably from the Peloponnese, in about 1532-1533. The exact date of his birth is not known. He studied for five years, probably from 1582 to 1587, at the Greek College of Saint Athanasius in Rome, and then returned to his native Sicily. He is mentioned in the "Chronicle of all the students of the Greek College from its foundation to the year 1640," which states tersely: "Luca Matragna (sic) of Monreale in Sicily of Albanian nationality was of a mediocre temperament, studied Greek and Latin humanities, then departed due to an indisposition, having been at the college for five years." Not much is known of Matrënga's life except that he was engaged in pastoral duties among the Arbëresh in Piana dei Greci in December 1601 and that he died as an archpriest on 6 May 1619.

The manuscript form of his translation of the Latin catechism of the Spanish **Jesuit** priest Jacob Ledesma (1516-1575) survives in three differing versions, the first of which is apparently in Matrënga's own handwriting. The published version, of which, like **Buzuku**'s missal, only one copy survived, was discovered by **Mario Roques**. It is based on one of the badly revised versions of the manuscript and contains many mistakes.

Matrënga's work contains an introduction in Italian, an eight-line poem, which constitutes the earliest specimen of written verse in Albanian, and the catechism itself, being religious instruction on church doctrines in the form of questions and answers. In his introduction, Matrënga explains that the translation was for the use of the Arbëresh who could not understand the Italian version of the catechism in circulation, noting that it would be useful for the "hundreds of families in Calabria and Apulia" of Albanian origin. Though short in comparison with other works of early Albanian literature, a mere twenty-eight pages, Lekë Matrënga's Christian Doctrine is of historical and literary significance not only as the second oldest publication of Albanian literature, but also as the first work by an Italo-Albanian and the first one written in the southern **Tosk** dialect.

MCLEAN, BILLY (1918-1986.11.17). British military officer. Lieutenant-Colonel Neil L. D. McLean, known as Billy Mclean, was from the western Highlands of Scotland. He was educated at Eton and Sandhurst and was commissioned into the Royal Scots Greys in 1938. After duty in Palestine and Ethiopia, he was recruited by the **Special Operations Executive** in 1943 to go to Axis-occupied Albania and support resistance movements there. Together with **David Smiley**, he was one of the first British officers to enter the country, which he did on foot from Greece in April 1943. He was recalled in a period of calm, but returned to Albania with Smiley and **Julian Amery** in early 1944 after the German occupation. McLean, an enthusiastic anticommunist, had close contacts both with **Abaz Kupi**, whom he admired and wished to support, and with **Enver Hoxha** and the **communist** partisans. He established and maintained a radio link with British military headquarters to coordinate activities and arms supplies. In September 1944, he withdrew from Albania, forced by higher authority to abandon Abaz Kupi and his forces to the mercy of the communists.

After **World War II**, McLean was involved with Smiley and Amery in Western efforts to overthrow the communist regime by training anticommunist agents to infiltrate Albania. He was also active as a military adviser in Chinese Turkistan, Vietnam, Algeria and Yemen and, in 1954, was elected as a Conservative member of parliament for Inverness.

MEIDANI, REXHEP (1944.08.17-). Political figure and scholar. Rexhep Meidani was born in **Tirana** and graduated from the University of Tirana with a degree in physics in 1966. He subsequently did postgraduate research at the Universities of Caen and Paris in France. He finished his doctorate in 1984 and was appointed professor in 1987. From 1966 to 1996 he taught various branches of physics at the University of Tirana and, from 1988 to 1992 served as dean of the Faculty of Science. On 30 August 1996, Meidani was elected head of the **Socialist Party** and on 25 July 1997 became president of Albania, replacing **Sali Berisha**. Meidani consciously and radically transformed the presidency from the political office it had been under Berisha to a more representative office, transferring political power back to the prime minister and to the elected government. Meidani held the presidency until 24 July 2002, when he was replaced by **Alfred Moisiu**.

MEKSI, ALEKSANDËR (1939.03.08-). Political figure and scholar. Aleksandër Meksi was born in **Tirana** and studied construction engineering at the University of Tirana. As a specialist in medieval architecture and Byzantine church restoration, he worked from 1962 to 1987 for the Institute of Monuments of Culture (*Instituti i Monumenteve te Kulturës*) and from 1987 to 1991 for the Institute of Archeology (*Instituti Arkeologjik*). He is the author of numerous articles, primarily on Albanian **Orthodox** church architecture, in the scholarly periodical *Monumentet* (The Monuments) from 1971 to 1987.

Meksi was an early activist and founding member of the **Democratic Party** in December 1991. He served as deputy speaker of **parliament** from April 1991 to April 1992 and then as prime minister from 13 April 1992 to 25 March 1997. He withdrew from politics after the collapse of the regime of **Sali Berisha**.

MEKSI, ERMELINDA (1956-). Political figure and high-ranking member of the **Socialist Party**. Ermelinda Meksi was born in **Tirana** and studied economics at the University of Tirana, specializing in demography. From 1978 to 1980, she worked for the Geological Institute in Tirana and from 1980 to 1982, taught statistics and demography at the Faculty of Economics. She became a member of the leadership of the Socialist Party in 1991 and has been a member of **parliament** since 1992. For several years now, Ermelinda Meksi has held the post of minister of economic cooperation.

MELO, VASIL (1932.09.30-2002.05.12). Political figure and high-ranking member of the **Union for Human Rights Party**. Vasil Melo was born in Delvina. He went to school in **Tirana** and studied Albanian **language** and **literature** at the university there. He taught at the Academy of Fine Arts (*Instituti i Lartë i Arteve*) from 1970 to 1976 and worked for the literary periodical *Drita* (The Light). In 1991, he was a founding member of the small Union for Human Rights (*Bashkimi për të Drejtat e Njeriut*) Party, which he led until 10 February 2002. Melo was a member of **parliament** from 1996 and headed the parliamentary committee for human and **minority** rights.

MERLIKA, MUSTAFA. *See* KRUJA, MUSTAFA.

MERTURI. Northern Albanian tribe and traditional tribal region. The Merturi region is situated north and south of the **Drin** River in the Districts of **Puka** and **Tropoja**, basically the area to the west of the town of Fierza. It borders on the traditional tribal regions of **Shoshi** to the west, **Nikaj** to the north and northwest, **Krasniqi** to the east and **Berisha**, with whom it is closely related, and **Toplana** to the south. The name was recorded in 1629 as *Marturi*. The Merturi tribe had a **population** of some 2,000 in the early years of the twentieth century.

MERXHANI, BRANKO (1894-1981.09.25). Publisher. Branko Merxhani was one of the most interesting figures of Albanian culture during the 1930s. He collaborated in the weekly *Illyria* under the editorship of **Karl Gurakuqi** from March 1934 to 1936 before beginning publication of his own influential *Përpjekja shqiptare* (The Albanian Endeavor) in October of 1936. This monthly, which continued publication into 1939, offered Albanian readers not only excerpts of contemporary Albanian poetry and prose and translations of world literature, but also book reviews and well-formulated articles on philosophy, sociology, history, linguistics, archeology and teaching, intro-ducing the Albanian public to the works of philosopher René Descartes and of sociologists Auguste Comte and Emile Durkheim. It strove for serious literary criticism and a new intellectual effort to reflect contemporary realities. Merxhani was painfully aware of the intellectual underdevelopment of his country and appealed for a spiritual revival, which he called **Neo-Albanianism** (*Neo-Shqiptarizmi*). Merxhani had first championed the nationalist ideology of Neo-Albanianism with **Vangjel Koça** in 1929 in the pages of the much-read **Gjirokastra** weekly newspaper *Demokratia* (Democracy) and in his short-lived monthly periodical entitled *Neo-Shqiptarizmi* (Neo-Albanianism), which had begun publication in July 1930. He fled to Turkey at the end of **World War II** and lived in exile from then on.

META, ILIR (1969.03.24-). Political figure and high-ranking member of the **Socialist Party**. Ilir Meta was born in **Skrapar** and studied economics at the University of **Tirana**, where he subsequently taught. Meta has been a member of **parliament** for the Socialist Party since 1992 and was head of the party's youth organization FRESSH in 1995-2001. He served as chairman of the parliamentary committee for foreign relations, 1996-1997; secretary of state for European integration, May 1998 - October 1998; deputy prime minister from October 1998 to October 1999; and prime minister of Albania from 29 October 1999 to 29 January 2002. Later in 2002, after a power struggle with **Fatos Nano**, he became deputy prime minister and minister of foreign affairs. He resigned from the government in July 2003.

MEYER, GUSTAV (1850.11.25-1900.08.28). Austrian scholar and linguist. Gustav Meyer was born in Gross-Strehlitz in Upper Silesia (now in Poland) and studied classical philology, German, modern Greek and Sanskrit from 1867 to 1871 in Breslau (now Wrocław) and Leipzig. From 1875 on, he traveled extensively in the Balkans. In 1876, Meyer was appointed professor of Sanskrit and comparative linguistics at the University of Prague and, in 1881, professor of comparative linguistics at the University of Graz in southern Austria. He was dean of the faculty there from 1890 to 1897, when he fell ill with a severe brain disease. He died in a mental asylum near Graz in 1900. Meyer's main fields of research were ancient and modern Greek and Albanian, though he was also interested in Balkan literature, folklore and folk tales. In addition to numerous articles on the Albanian **language**, he is the author of a *Kurzgefaßte albanesische Grammatik, mit Lesestücken und Glossar* (Short Albanian Grammar with Texts and Glossary), Leipzig 1888, and, in particular, of an *Etymologisches Wörterbuch der albanesischen Sprache* (Etymological Dictionary of the Albanian Language), Strasbourg 1891, for which he is remembered primarily. In this dictionary, the first of its kind for Albanian, he analyzed the origins of 5,140 Albanian words and asserted that only 400 of them were of direct Indo-European origin, the rest being loanwords or of unknown origin. By stressing the Latin influence in Albanian, he came to the conclusion that Albanian was a semi-Romance **language**, a hypothesis which is generally rejected nowadays. His contribution to Albanian linguistic studies and Albanian etymology is, nonetheless, still highly valued.

MIGJENI (1911.10.13-1938.08.26). Poet and prose writer. Migjeni, an acronym of **Millosh Gjergj Nikolla**, was born in **Shkodra**. As a young lad, he attended a Serbian **Orthodox** elementary school in Shkodra and from 1923 to 1925 a secondary school in Bar (Tivar) on the Montenegrin coast, where his eldest sister, Lenka, had moved. In the autumn of 1925, when he was fourteen, he obtained a scholarship to attend a secondary school in Monastir (Bitola) in southern Macedonia and entered the Orthodox Seminary of St. John the Theologian, also in Monastir, where, despite incipient health problems, he continued his training and studies until June 1932. On his return to Shkodra in 1932, after failing to win a scholarship to study in the West, he decided to take up a teaching career rather than join the priesthood for which he had been trained. On 23 April 1933, he was appointed to teach Albanian at a school in the Serb village of Vraka, seven kilometers from Shkodra. It was during this period that he also began writing prose sketches and verse which reflected the life and anguish of an intellectual in what certainly was and has remained the most backward region of Europe.

Soon though, in the summer of 1935, the twenty-three-year-old Migjeni fell seriously ill with tuberculosis, which he had contracted earlier. In January 1936, he was transferred to the mountain town of Puka and, in April 1936, began his activities as the headmaster of the rundown school there. After eighteen hard months in the mountains, the consumptive poet was obliged to put an end to his career as a teacher and as a writer and to seek medical treatment in Turin in northern Italy, where his sister Ollga was studying mathematics. He set out from Shkodra and arrived in Turin before Christmas Day 1937. There he had hoped, after recovery, to register and study at the Faculty of Arts. The breakthrough in the treatment of tuberculosis, however, was to come a decade too late for Migjeni. After five months at San Luigi sanatorium near Turin, Migjeni was transferred to the Waldensian hospital in Torre Pellice, where he died. His demise at the age of twenty-six was a tragic loss for modern Albanian letters.

Migjeni made a promising start as a prose writer. He is the author of about twenty-four short prose sketches, which he published in periodicals, for the most part between the spring of 1933 and the spring of 1938. Ranging from one to five pages in length, these pieces are too short to constitute tales or short stories. Although he approached new themes with unprecedented cynicism and force, his sketches cannot all be considered great works of art from a literary point of view. It is far more as a poet that Migjeni made his mark on Albanian **literature** and culture, though he did so posthumously. His verse production was no more voluminous than his prose, but his success in the field of poetry was no less than spectacular in Albania at the time.

Migjeni's only volume of verse, *Vargjet e lira* (Free Verse), Tirana 1944, was composed over a three-year period from 1933 to 1935. The main theme of Free Verse, as with Migjeni's prose, is misery and suffering. It is poetry of acute social awareness and despair. Previous generations of poets had sung the beauties of the Albanian mountains and the sacred traditions of the nation, whereas Migjeni now opened his eyes to the harsh realities of life, to the appalling level of misery, disease and poverty which he discovered all around him. Though he did not publish a single book during his lifetime, Migjeni's works, which circulated privately and in the press of the period, were an immediate success. Migjeni paved the way for a modern literature in Albania. His works have appeared in English in the volume *Free Verse*, Peja 2001.

MILKANI, PIRO (1939.01.05-). Film director. Piro Milkani was born in **Korça** and studied at the Academy of Fine Arts in Prague, Czechoslovakia. Among his best films are: *Ngadhjnim mbi vdekjen* (Victory over Death), 1967; *Kur zbardhi një ditë* (Once at Dawn), 1971; *Zonja nga qyteti* (The Lady from the City), 1976; *Ballë për ballë* (Face to Face), 1979, with **Kujtim Çashku**; and *Besa e kuqe* (The Red Pledge), 1982. From 1991 to 1993, he was director of *Albafilm* Distribution and, in 1999, was appointed Albanian ambassador to the Czech Republic.

MILO, PASKAL (1949.02.22-). Political figure, scholar and high-ranking member of the **Social Democratic Party**. Paskal Milo was born in **Himara** and studied history and **geography** at the University of **Tirana**. He worked for the newspaper *Zëri i popullit* (The People's Voice) from 1971 to 1975, taught school in **Fier** from 1975 to 1979, and was professor of history at the University of Tirana from 1980 to 1992. He is the author of the book *Shqipëria dhe Jugosllavia, 1918-1927* (Albania and Yugoslavia, 1918-1927), Tirana 1992.

In his political career, Paskal Milo joined the Social Democratic Party of Albania in 1991 and has been a member of **parliament** since 1992. He served as secretary of state for **education** in the coalition government of June 1991; deputy head of the Social Democratic Party from 1992 to 1997; and minister of foreign affairs in the government of 25 July 1997 to 2001. In 2002, he was minister of state for European integration.

MINERAL RESOURCES. Albania is comparatively rich in minerals. It is estimated to have the fourth largest chrome reserves on earth, after South Africa, Russia and Zimbabwe. The chromite ore deposits, usually in serpentine and other basic igneous rock structures, are situated primarily in the western part of the District of **Bulqiza**, near the town of Bulqiza, though there are smaller reserves in Kam (**Tropoja**), Kalimash (**Kukës**), in the Shebenik region (**Librazhd**), and near **Pogradec**. First exports of chromite ore were shipped to Italy in 1940 by the Azienda Minerali Metallici Italiani (AMMI).

Albania was once the third largest producer of chrome in the world, but output began declining in 1985. After years of stagnation in the 1990s, chrome production has now revived somewhat. The Italian Darfo company received the concession for this sector in 2000 and reopened the mines at Përrenjas and Pojska. There is a current production of about 5,000 tons of chrome and 1,500 tons of ferro-chrome per month, but a monthly production of 40,000 tons of ferro-chrome is envisaged for the future.

Albania also has substantial copper reserves in the **Mat** and **Drin** valleys, in particular in Rubik (**Mirdita**), Kurbnesh (Mirdita) and Gjegjan (Kukës). The **Italians** had an initial copper concession in Mirdita in 1926 and opened a mine near Puka in 1929, but it was only under the Italian occupation after 1939 that real production began. Copper ore production has been in decline since 1985.

There are also reserves of iron-nickel and nickel silicate in Guri i Kuq (Pogradec), Pishkash (Librazhd), Përrenjas (Librazhd) and Bitincka (Devoll), as well as in the region of Kukës. These metals were processed at the metallurgical complex in **Elbasan**.

Also of economic significance are deposits of petroleum, **natural gas**, bitumen and **coal.**

MINGA, ALBERT (1946.03.04-). Film director. Albert Minga was born in **Vlora** and finished acting school in 1968. He worked for many years thereafter as a television director, producing dramas and television series. Among his recent feature films are: *Unë e dua Erën* (I love Era), 1990; and *Porta Eva* (Porta Eva), 2000. In 1997, he was appointed director general of Albanian Radio and Television.

MINORITIES IN ALBANIA. According to the census of April 1989, there were 64,816 Albanian citizens of non-Albanian ethnicity, equal to about two percent of the **population**. The vast majority of these non-Albanians (about ninety percent) were members of the **Greek** community in southern Albania. Other ethnic minorities include **Slavs** (Serb-speaking Montenegrins, Macedonians and Gorans), **Vlachs** or Aromanians and **Roma**. Not to be forgotten are very small groups of **Jews** and **Armenians**.

MIO, VANGJUSH (1891.03.05-1957.12.30). Painter. Vangjush Mio is regarded as the finest Albanian landscape painter of the twentieth century. He was born in **Korça** and moved with his brother to Bucharest, Romania, in 1908, where, in 1915, he studied at the national school of fine arts. He finished his training there in 1919. In the same year, he opened his first personal exhibition, initially in Bucharest and then in Korça—probably the first exhibition of figurative art ever held in Albania. From 1920 to 1924, he studied at the Academy of Fine Arts in Rome and traveled widely in **Italy** in the 1920s. Mio was a great admirer of nineteenth and early twentieth century Italian realist art and of impressionism. Back in Korça, the most refined and cultured town in Albania at the time, he founded a fine arts society and exhibited his works on numerous occasions, becoming one of the best-known Albanian painters of the period. From 1934, he also taught art at the French-language secondary school there. Over 400 of his paintings are preserved, both in **museums** and galleries in **Tirana** and Korça and at his home in Korça, which now serves as a museum. He is remembered in particular for his landscape paintings: poplars glowing in the autumn sunlight beside the waters of Lake **Ohrid** and floodlit plains of Korça covered in snow.

MIRDITA. Northern central Albanian tribe and traditional tribal region. The Mirdita region corresponds broadly to the present **District of Mirdita**, though, as tribal land, it originally referred most specifically to the mountains north of Blinisht. The name was recorded in 1571 as *Mirdita* and in 1610 as *Miriditti* and is often said to be related to Alb. *mirë dita* "good day," though this is probably a folk etymology. Mirdita is traditionally a staunchly **Catholic** region, with its religious center at the church of Saint Alexander in Orosh.

MIRDITA, DISTRICT OF. Region of local government administration. The District of Mirdita (*Rrethi i Mirditës*), with its administrative headquarters in the town of Rrëshen, borders on the districts of **Lezha** to the west, **Puka** to the north, **Kukës** and **Dibra** to the east and **Mat** to the south. It has a surface area of 867 square kilometers and a present **population** of 45,228 (in 2000).

MIRDITA, RROK (1939.09.28-). Catholic religious figure. Rrok Mirdita was born in Klezna, Yugoslavia. He was ordained as a Catholic priest in New York on 2 July 1965 and was appointed as Archbishop of **Durrës** and **Tirana** on 25 December 1992, thus becoming the highest-ranking Catholic dignitary in Albania.

MISHA, PIRO. Public figure. Piro Misha worked from 1983 to 1991 as a translator for the **Tirana**-based Naim Frashëri Publishing Company. In 1991-1993, he was director of international relations at the Albanian ministry of culture and, from 1993 to 2001, was program director of the Open Society Foundation for Albania (Soros Foundation). He is currently executive director of the Libri e Komunikacioni (Book and Communication) publishing house, which evolved out of the Soros Foundation. Piro Misha has published prose, essays and studies and is the author, in particular, of *Duke kërkuar rrënjët ose kthimi i shqiptarëve në histori* (Searching for Roots or the Return of the Albanians to History),Tirana 1997.

MISKA, PALI (1931.05.19-). Political figure of the **communist** period. Pali Miska was born in Bradvica in the **Korça** region and studied economics. He became a communist party member in 1951 and served as director of a sawmill in Fushë-Arrëz, 1964; first secretary of the party in **Puka,** 1969-1975; first secretary in **Elbasan,** 1982; first secretary in **Fier** 1983; minister of industry and mining, 1975-1978; and minister of agriculture, from 2 February 1989 to 22 February 1991. He was also deputy prime minister from 1978 to 23 November 1982 and from 2 February 1989 to 31 January 1991, as well as chairman of the People's Assembly from 22 November 1982 to 19 February 1987.

Pali Miska was considered a party expert in economic affairs. He was a full member of the Central Committee from November 1976 to 1991 and a full member of the Politburo from June 1975 to 1991. He was tried together with nine other members of the Politburo and sentenced on 30 December 1993 to seven years in prison for the misappropriation of state funds.

MISSIONARIES OF CHARITY. Order of the **Catholic Church**. The Missionaries of Charity were founded in 1950 by **Mother Teresa**, originally Agnes Gonxhe Bojaxhiu, an ethnic Albanian from Skopje. It is devoted in particular to orphans, leprosy patients and the terminally ill, and has over 3,370 sisters in 443 branches worldwide. In 1990, Mother Theresa visited Albania and established a branch of her order there the following year.

MITKO, THIMI (1820-1890.03.22). Folklorist and nationalist figure. Thimi Mitko of **Korça** was the author of an important collection of Albanian oral **literature**. After receiving his education at a Greek school in his native Korça, he left Albania in 1850, moving first to Athens, then to Plovdiv and finally to Vienna, where he worked for several years as a tailor. In 1865, in the prime of his life, Mitko emigrated to Egypt, where he set up a successful trading business in Beni Suef and subsequently died of throat cancer.

Mitko began to take an interest in folklore about 1859 while he was in Vienna. From **Spiro Dine** it is known that Mitko had begun recording folklore material by 1866. He provided **Demetrio Camarda** with folk songs, riddles and tales for the latter's collection. Mitko's own collection of Albanian folklore, consisting of 505 folk songs, and 39 tales and popular sayings primarily from southern Albania, was finished in 1874 and was published in Greek script four years later, the year of the **League of Prizren**, under the Greek title *Albanikê melissa* (The Albanian Bee), Alexandria 1878. This work, bearing the Albanian subtitle *Bëlietta shqipëtare* (Albanian Bee), was not only the first compilation of oral literature designed for the Albanian public but also the first such collection of genuine scholarly interest. A copy of the book is said to have been burnt in public in Athens. Mitko compiled a supplementary collection of Albanian oral literature known as the Little Bee, but he never succeeded in publishing it. Also unpublished was his Albanian-Greek dictionary, some 3,000 pages in manuscript form, which was later discovered in Alexandria.

MITROVICA, REXHEP BEY (1887-1967.05.21). Political figure. Rexhep Mitrovica was born in Mitrovica (**Kosova**) of a wealthy, landowning family. He took part in the declaration of independence in 1912 as a representative of Peja. From 1921 to 1923, he served as minister of **education**. After the fall of the government of Fan Noli in December 1924, he took part in a plot to overthrow

Ahmet Zogu but was amnestied in 1927. He returned to Albania after the Italian invasion and joined the *Balli Kombëtar* in 1942. After the capitulation of **Italy**, Mitrovica was head of the so-called Second League of Prizren, which supported ethnic Albania, i.e., the reunification of all Albanian territory. From November 1943 to mid-June 1944, he was prime minister of Albania and endeavored to maintain a stable government amidst the chaos of war and civil war. During the **communist** takeover, he managed to flee to Turkey, where he headed the Albanian community in exile. He died in Istanbul.

MJEDA, NDRE (1866.11.20-1937.08.01). Poet. Ndre Mjeda was born in **Shkodra** and, like so many other **Gheg** writers of the period, was educated by the **Jesuits**. The Society of Jesus sent him abroad for studies and training. He studied in France, Italy, Slovenia, Poland and Croatia. It was in 1898 that a conflict is said to have broken out among the Jesuits of Kraljevica on the Dalmatian coast, apparently concerning their loyalties to Austria-Hungary and the Vatican. The exact details of the incident are not known, but Ndre Mjeda is said to have resigned or been expelled from the Jesuit Order.

He returned to Albania and in 1899 was given a teaching position in Vig in the mountainous **Mirdita** region. He also participated initially in the activities of the *Bashkimi* (Unity) literary society, which had been founded that year in Shkodra. In 1901, due to differing opinions on the alphabet question, Ndre and his brother Lazër Mjeda founded an alternative organization, the *Agimi* (Dawn) literary society, which encouraged the use of Albanian in school texts and **literature**, and which supported a spelling system using Croatian as a model. It was in this alphabet that Ndre Mjeda and **Anton Xanoni** published a number of readers for Albanian schools. Mjeda's passionate interest in the Albanian alphabet question led, in addition to problems with the **Ottoman** authorities, to his participation at the **Congress of Monastir** in 1908 at which his *Agimi* alphabet lost out to **Gjergj Fishta**'s *Bashkimi* alphabet. Mjeda was a member of the Albanian Literary Commission set up in Shkodra on 1 September 1916, and, from 1920 to 1924, he served as a member of **parliament**. After the defeat of **Fan Noli**'s **Democratic Revo-lution** at the end of 1924 and the definitive rise of the dictatorship of **Ahmet Zogu**, he withdrew from politics and served as a parish priest in Kukël, a village between Shkodra and Shëngjin. From

1930, he taught Albanian **language** and literature at the Jesuit college in Shkodra, where he died.

Mjeda's poetry, in particular his collection *Juvenilia* (Juvenilia), Vienna 1917, is noted for its classical style and for its purity of language. A second cycle of poetry begun by Mjeda was to be devoted to the ancient cities of Illyria: *Lissus* (**Lezha**), *Scodra* (Shkodra), *Dyrrachium* (**Durrës**) and *Apollonia* (Pojan). However, only the first two parts of this cycle ever saw the light of day. Though not covering an especially wide range of themes, Mjeda's poetry evinces a particularly refined language under the influence of the nineteenth-century Italian classics and, in general, a high level of metric finesse.

MOISIU, ALFRED (1929.12-). Political figure. Alfred Moisiu was born in **Shkodra**, the son of **communist** military figure Spiro Moisiu (1900-1980), and embarked upon a military career. He studied at the military academy (*Shkolla e Bashkuar e Oficerëve*) in **Tirana** in 1949-1952, and went through military studies in Leningrad, 1952-1958, graduating as a military engineer in Moscow. On his return to Albania, he taught at the military academy and held a variety of military posts until retirement in 1984. Later, in the so-called technical government of 1991, he was appointed minister of defense (January to March 1992) and was subsequently advisor to the minister until 1998. On 24 June 2002, **parliament** elected him president of Albania as a successor to **Rexhep Meidani**. He assumed his position on 24 July 2002.

MOISSI, ALEXANDER (1879.04.02-1935.03.22). Actor. Alexander Moissi, known in Albanian as Aleksandër Moisiu, was born in Trieste, then part of Austria-Hungary, of an Albanian father from **Kavaja** and an **Arbëresh** mother. After a childhood in Trieste, **Durrës** and Graz, the twenty-year-old Alexander finally settled with his mother and two sisters in Vienna. It was there, with the encouragement and support of Austrian actor Josef Kainz (1858-1910), that Moissi's career as one of the great European stage actors of the early decades of the twentieth century began. The following years took him to Prague and then to Berlin, where he became a protégé of Max Reinhardt (1873-1943). Moissi accompanied the Reinhardt Ensemble to Russia in 1911 and was acclaimed in St. Petersburg by critic and dramatist Anatoly Lunacharsky (1875-1933) for his interpretation of Oedipus. Among other roles for which Alexander Moissi is remembered in particular are Hamlet, Faust, Fedya in Tolstoy's *The*

Living Body, and Dubedat in George Bernard Shaw's *The Doctor's Dilemma*. Though primarily a stage actor, Moissi also appeared in ten **film** productions from 1910 to 1935, of which seven were silent and three talking films. His own play "The Prisoner," about Napoleon's later years on St. Helena, proved to be a failure. Alexander Moissi lies buried at the Morcote cemetery overlooking Lake Lugano in Switzerland.

MONASTIR, CONGRESS OF. *See* CONGRESS OF MONASTIR.

MONTENEGRIN MINORITY IN ALBANIA. *See* SLAVIC MINORITY IN ALBANIA.

MONTENEGRO. *See* SERBIA AND MONTENEGRO, RELATIONS WITH.

MONTENEGRO, ALBANIANS IN. There is a minority of about 50,000 Albanian speakers in the Republic of Montenegro, mostly along the Albanian border. Albanian communities stretch from the region of Guci (Serb. Gusinje) and Plava (Serb. Plav) in the east, to Tuz (Serb. Tuzi) south of Podgorica, and the Ulqin (Serb. Ulcinj) region on the southern Montenegrin coast. In the Ulqin area, where they constitute a majority of the population, the Albanians now have good political representation at the local level. Ulqin has benefitted from mass tourism from **Kosova** in recent years.

MOSCHOPOLIS. *See* VOSKOPOJA.

MOSI, HILË (1885.04.22-1933.02.22). Poet and political figure. Hilë Mosi was born in **Shkodra** and attended an Italian elementary school and the Saverian College, founded by the **Jesuits** in 1877. For four years, ca. 1904-1908, he studied in Klagenfurt in southern Austria, training as a teacher. There, under the direction of linguist **Gjergj Pekmezi**, he was involved in organizing Albanian students studying in Austria in the patriotic club *Lirija* (Freedom), known later as *Dija* (Knowledge). After his return to Albania in April 1908, he served as secretary to the **Congress of Monastir** and lived in **Korça** for a time. At the end of December 1909, together with nationalist figure **Dervish Hima**, he began publishing a weekly newspaper *Shqipëtari-Arnavud* (The Albanian) in Istanbul, with articles in Albanian, Turkish and French. In 1911, he took an active part in the uprising in northern Albania and taught for a year at the Normal School (*Shkolla Normale*) in **Elbasan**. In late 1912, he was back in Austria, where he participated in the Albanian **Congress of Trieste** in early March 1913. He thereupon returned to Albania to found another nationalist weekly, this time in Shkodra, *Shqypnia e re* (New Albania).

Mosi was a member of the **Albanian Literary Commission** in 1916, represented his native Shkodra in **parliament** from 1920 to 1924, and served as a member of the Albanian delegation to the League of Nations from November 1920. In 1921, he was appointed minister of **education** but never seems to have assumed his activities as such. Under the **Fan Noli** government of 1924, Hilë Mosi served as prefect of Korça and of **Gjirokastra** until he was obliged to flee to Brindisi when **Ahmet Zogu** seized power during Christmas of that year. In 1927, Mosi returned to Albania under the amnesty proclaimed by Zogu and was made minister of public works. The following year, he worked as director general of public security and, in 1930, as minister of education, a post he held until his death.

Hilë Mosi is the author of patriotic verse and love lyrics written primarily between the years 1900 and 1925 and which were published in periodicals and in a small number of monographs. *Këngat shqipe* (Albanian Songs), Thessalonika 1909, his first poetry collection, was followed by *Zân' i atdheut* (The Voice of the Homeland), Trieste 1913, on nationalist themes. More interesting was the poetry volume *Lotët e dashtnies* (Tears of Love), Shkodra 1916, which helped introduce the genre of love poetry. Together with **Andon Zako Çajupi** and **Asdreni**, Hilë Mosi was one of the earliest twentieth-century poets to publish love verse, which was a relatively new and shocking phenomenon in Albanian letters. In the second edition of this collection, published now under the more respectable title *Lule prendvere* (Flowers of Spring), Tirana 1927, Mosi included his translations of love verse by a number of foreign poets, no doubt with a view to demonstrating to the Albanian public that love poetry was an acceptable literary genre.

MOVEMENT FOR LEGALITY PARTY (*PARTIA LËVIZJA E LEGALITETIT, PLL*) (1992-). The Movement for Legality is a small monarchist party which was formed in the summer of 1992 to promote the return of the monarchy under pretender **Leka Zogu**. It derives its inspiration from the **Legality** resistance movement of **World War II**. In the **parliamentary** elections of 1996, it won 2.1 percent of the popular vote and, in 1997,

3.3 percent. It now forms part of the opposition coalition **Union for Victory** but has recently suffered a dramatic loss of support.

MULA, AVNI (1928.01.04-). Singer and composer. Avni Mula was born in Gjakova in **Kosova** and taught in **Shkodra** from 1945 to 1947, where he came into contact with composer **Prenkë Jakova.** From 1952 to 1957, he studied at the Tchaikovsky Conservatory in Moscow and worked from then on for the **Tirana** opera and ballet company. He provided great stimulus in various fields of Albanian **music.** *See also* OPERA AND BALLET THEATER.

MULA, INVA (1963.07.27-). Soprano. Daughter of singers Avni Mula and Nina Mula, Inva Mula studied **music** at the Jordan Misja Academy from 1978 to 1982 and continued in the field of music at the Albanian Academy of Fine Arts from 1982 to 1986. In 1987, she was appointed as a soloist to the Albanian opera company in **Tirana** and is now considered to be the best-known Albanian opera singer. In 1996, she won first prize at the Placido Domingo "Concours International de Voix d'Opéra" and gave several concerts with him, which enabled her to embark upon an international career in opera. She now lives in France.

MURRA, PROKOP (1921.11.24-). Political figure of the **communist** period. Prokop Murra was born in **Tirana.** He joined the communist party in 1943 and took part in the partisan movement during **World War II.** After the communist takeover, he studied economics, worked in the petroleum industry, and later served as vice-chairman of the state planning commission, 1966-1969; first secretary of the party for **Shkodra,** 1968-1970; minister of industry and mining, 1980-1982; and minister of defense from November 1982 to February 1991, following the purge and arrest of **Kadri Hazbiu.**

  Prokop Murra, elevated in particular by **Ramiz Alia,** was a member of the Central Committee from 1956 to 1991 and a full member of the Politburo from 1986 to 1990. He was arrested on 31 August 1991, tried together with nine other members of the Politburo, and sentenced on 30 December 1993 to five years in prison for the misappropriation of state funds. On 20 June 1996, he was then sentenced to life in prison for crimes against humanity.

MUSACHI, JOHN (early sixteenth century). Historical figure. John Musachi, known in Italian as Giovanni Musachi and now in

Albanian as Gjon Muzaka, is the author of a chronicle or memoir which constitutes the oldest substantial text ever written by an Albanian. Musachi, despot of Epirus, was of a noble, landowning family from the **Myzeqeja** region of central Albania. He was forced to abandon his land and take flight to **Italy** when Albanian resistance to the **Ottoman** conquest collapsed and the country was occupied by the Turks. The prime objective in his chronicle, entitled *Breve memoria de li discendenti de nostra casa Musachi, per Giovanni Musachi, despoto d'Epiro* (Brief Chronicle on the Descendants of our Musachi Dynasty, by John Musachi, Despot of Epirus) 1515, was not to provide a history of his times, but simply to prove to his descendants that they were of an important, landowning family so that they should not forget their origins and property rights. The chronicle is an important source not only for late fifteenth-century Albania, but also for Albanian toponyms and the names of local Albanian rulers. Indeed it is significant as proof of the rise of the Albanians as a distinct ethnic group. It was first published by Charles Hopf in *Chroniques gréco-romanes inédites ou peu connues* (Unpublished or Little Known Greco-Roman Chronicles), Paris 1873.

MUSEUMS. There are nine national museums in Albania: the **National Museum of History** in **Tirana**; the **Scanderbeg Museum** in **Kruja**, the so-called **Residence of Scanderbeg Museum** in **Lezha**, the **Museum of Independence** in **Vlora**, the **Museum of Medieval Art** in **Korça**, the **Museum of Education** in Korça, the **Museum of Ethnography** in Kruja, the **Onufri Museum** in **Berat,** and another **Museum of Ethnography** in **Berat**. There are also municipal and other museums around the country, many of which were, however, plundered and devastated during the **uprising of 1997**. The new Museum of Archeology in **Durrës** was finally opened on 14 April 2002, after sixteen years of construction.

MUSIC, ALBANIAN. Traditional folk music in Albania is still very popular and offers a wealth of regional styles and variations. The rousing heroic songs of the northern mountains and **Kosova** sung to the accompaniment of a *çifteli* have little in common with the flowing rhythms of **Kolonja**, the droning **polyphonic** choirs of **Vlora** or the mandolin serenades of **Korça**. In general, it can be said that the vocal music of northern Albania is homophonic, i.e., one-voiced, whereas in southern Albania polyphonic (several voices together) music is preferred, although there are, of course, exceptions.

Among the traditional forms of vocal music, mention can be made of the centuries-old epic **Songs of the Frontier Warriors** (*këngë kreshnikesh*), sung by one male voice to the accompaniment of a one-stringed *lahuta*, which to foreign ears may sound monotonous. More popular throughout the north and especially in Kosova is vocal music, often with heroic or nationalist texts, accompanied by a two-stringed mandolin-like *çifteli*. The favorite form of vocal music in southern Albania is Albanian polyphony, known especially in the regions of Vlora, **Tepelena**, **Gjirokastra** and **Përmet**. This is perhaps the best known and, for foreign ears, certainly the most unusual type of music in Albania. Here, too, the texts are often heroic, concerned with patriotic figures of the past.

There are other regional variations in folk music. The town of Korça is known for its elegant serenades, often to the accompaniment of guitars and mandolins, which are more western in style, almost Neapolitan. **Elbasan**, on the other hand, specializes in vocal music of a more **Ottoman**, oriental nature. Almost every region of Albania has its own specifically recognizable style of music.

Instrumental music, which was traditionally independent of vocal music, is more a speciality of the north. Aside from the above-mentioned *lahuta* and *çifteli*, use is also made of the long-necked, ten-string *saze* and of the three-stringed, guitar-like *bakllama*. Flutes and clarinets are also very prevalent.

Traditional Albanian folk music is still very popular, though now perhaps more so in Kosova than in Albania itself. The authenticity and originality of Albanian music was promoted under the dictatorship in particular at a National Folklore Festival (*Festivali folklorik kombëtar*), which was held every five years in the fortress of Gjirokastra. The tradition of the folklore festival, in which groups from all over the country gather to compete, has been carried on to the present day. *See also* OPERA AND BALLET THEATER.

MUSLIU, ESAT (1945.04.22-). Film director. Musliu was born in the District of **Dibra**, attended the Jordan Misja Academy in **Tirana**, and studied at the Academy of Fine Arts (*Instituti i Lartë i Arteve*). He gained a reputation as a leading Albanian film director in the late 1980s. Best known among his feature films are: *Hije që mbeten pas* (The Lingering Shadows), 1985; *Vitet e* *pritjes* (The Years of Waiting), 1990; and *Nata* (The Night), 1998. Musliu is also noted as a director of documentary films.

MUZAKA, GJON. *See* MUSACHI, JOHN.

MYFTIU, MANUSH (1919.01.16-). Political figure of the **communist** period. Myftiu was born in **Vlora**. He graduated from secondary school in Rome in 1939 and studied medicine at the University of Turin for one year in 1940. He joined in the foundation of the communist party in 1941, though he was still a member of the Albanian fascist youth at the time, and took part in the communist partisan movement during **World War II**. After the war, as a protege of **Mehmet Shehu** and thus immune from **Enver Hoxha**'s many purges, he served as chairman of the People's Assembly, 1947-1949; deputy minister of foreign affairs from May 1950 to April 1951; deputy prime minister, 1950-1966; acting minister of justice, 1951; minister of health, 1956-1958; minister of **education**, 1958-1965; first secretary of the party for **Tirana**, 1966-1976; deputy prime minister from 1976 to 8 July 1990; and chairman of the state control commission from 2 February 1989.

Manush Myftiu was considered a party expert in the fields of education, culture and science. He was a member of the Central Committee from November 1948 to June 1991 and a full member of the Politburo from June 1956 to July 1990. He was related by marriage to **Besnik Bekteshi**, **Pilo Peristeri** and **Adil Çarçani**. On 2 July 1994, after the fall of the dictatorship, he was sentenced to five years of prison for abuse of power.

MYZEQEJA. Coastal region of southern central Albania. Myzeqeja, definite form *Myzeqe,* the coastal plain extending from the southern bank of the **Shkumbin** River in the north down to **Vlora** in the south, is the breadbasket of Albania. It is about sixty-five kilometers long (north-south) and about fifty kilometers wide (east-west), covering a total area of about 1,350 square kilometers. Its population centers are **Lushnja** and **Fier**. The toponym Myzeqeja was recorded in 1417 as *Musachia* and derives from the name of the aristocratic family **Musachi** of the period from 1280 to 1600.

- N -

NANO, FATOS (1952.09.16-). Political figure and high-ranking member of the **Socialist Party of Albania**. Fatos Nano was born in **Tirana** and studied economics at the University of Tirana. He worked as an economist at the metallurgical plant in **Elbasan** from 1975 to 1978; as a member of the Institute of Marxist-Leninist Studies in Tirana from 1978 to 1981; as an economist for an agricultural cooperative in Priska near Tirana from 1981 to 1983; and for the Institute of Marxist-Leninist Studies once again from 1984 to 1990.

In his political career, Fatos Nano was a leading member of the Socialist Party from its foundation, heading it from June 1991 to 1998. He served as prime minister from 22 February until 4 June 1991. When the **Democratic Party** took power, Nano was arrested on 30 July 1993 by his arch-rival **Sali Berisha**, tried in March 1994, and sentenced on 3 April to twelve years in prison on charges of corruption and appropriating state property. Although nominally head of the Socialist Party and the official opposition in **parliament**, he spent the years of the **Berisha** regime in prison in Bënça near **Tepelena**. He was released and granted amnesty on 14 March 1997 in the wake of the **uprising** that year. From 25 July 1997 to 28 September 1998, and since 24 July 2002, he has been prime minister and is currently considered the most powerful politician in the country.

NATIONAL ALBANIAN AMERICAN COUNCIL, NAAC (*KËSHILLI KOMBËTAR SHQIPTARO-AMERIKAN*) (1996-). The National Albanian American Council is an independent, non-profit association which lobbies for and promotes Albanian interests in the **United States**. It opened its office in Washington D.C. on 1 October 1996 and was particularly active in the following years on behalf of Kosova. Its current executive director is Martin Vulaj. *See* www.naac.org.

NATIONAL CENTER OF CINEMATOGRAPHY. *See* NEW ALBANIA FILM STUDIOS.

NATIONAL GALLERY, TIRANA (*GALERIA KOMBËTARE E ARTEVE*). The national gallery, situated on the main boulevard of **Tirana** beside the old Hotel Dajti is the most important art gallery in the country. Originally called the Gallery of Figurative Art (*Galeria e Arteve Figurative në Tiranë*), it was opened in 1954 to replace the Tirana *Pinakoteka* of 1952. The national gallery hosts 4,132 paintings by over 500 artists and has possibly the best collection of Albanian art in the world. It also organizes most major art exhibitions in the capital and is responsible for the restoration and conservation of works of art in public ownership. The present building was inaugurated in 1976.

NATIONAL INFORMATION SERVICE (*SHËRBIMI INFORMATIV KOMBËTAR* - SHIK). The National Information Service was the intelligence service of the regime of Sali Berisha. It was created in July 1991 after the banning of its predecessor, the notorious **Sigurimi** of the **communist** regime. Its original head, Irakli Koçollari, was replaced by mathematician Bashkim Gazidede on 6 July 1992. Koçollari himself was sentenced to six years in prison on 4 December 1996 for dereliction of duty. In the later years of the **Berisha** regime, the SHIK disintegrated into an organization almost as notorious as the original Sigurimi. Its last director was Arben Karkini, appointed by President Berisha on 29 May 1997. It was disbanded after the fall of the Berisha regime later that year and replaced by a new State Information Service (Shërbimi Informativ Shtetëror), headed by Fatos Klosi until August 2002.

NATIONAL LIBRARY OF ALBANIA (*BIBLIOTEKA KOMBËTARE E SHQIPËRISË*). The National Library in **Tirana** possesses the world's largest collection of Albanian-language books. The origins of the library go back to 16 April 1917 when the **Albanian Literary Commission** in **Shkodra**, under the auspices of the Austro-Hungarian administration there, set up the Library of the Literary Commission, which later became known as the Library of Albania. This first state library was transferred to Tirana in 1920 when the latter town became the capital and seat of the Albanian government. It was originally attached to the fledgling ministry of **education** and was then reinaugurated on 10 December 1922 as the National Library of Albania, with a collection of approximately 6,000 books. In 1947, the National Library was in possession of about 100,000 volumes, derived in good part from the confiscation of stocks from private bookshops and, in particular, of the private collections of some anticommunist figures who had fled the country or who had been executed by the new **communist** authorities. Of particular significance was the collection of **Mid'hat bey Frashëri,** which found its way into the National Library after he fled to Italy.

On 31 December 2002, the National Library possessed 286,674 Albanian-language books, 432,208 foreign-language books, 29,914 Albanian-language periodicals, 95,829 foreign-language periodicals, 1,502 manuscripts, 6,297 microfilms, 1,007 maps of Balkanological interest and 4,755 scholarly dissertations. The current director of the National Library is **Aurel Plasari,** appointed on 3 May 1998.

Of particular interest is the so-called Albano-Balkanological Collection of material dealing with Albania, the Albanians and the other peoples of the Balkans. This collection currently comprises 40,987 volumes, in addition to substantial archive material.

NATIONAL MUSEUM OF EDUCATION, KORÇA (*MUZEU KOMBËTAR I ARSIMIT*). The museum of **education,** inaugurated in 1967, is located where the first Albanian-language school was opened in March 1887 in **Korça.** It displays the history of writing and publishing in the Albanian **language** and is much visited by school classes.

NATIONAL MUSEUM OF ETHNOGRAPHY, BERAT (*MUZEU KOMBËTAR ETNOGRAFIK*). The museum of ethnography in **Berat** is situated in the so-called Bachelor's Mosque (*Xhamia e Beqarëve*), built in 1827, and displays the cultural and traditional heritage of everyday life in the city of Berat and in southern Albania in general. Of particular interest are the objects for making olive oil.

NATIONAL MUSEUM OF ETHNOGRAPHY, KRUJA (*MUZEU KOMBËTAR ETNOGRAFIK*). The museum of ethnography in **Kruja** is situated in the fortress of Kruja in the manor of the once ruling **Toptani** family. The building was constructed in traditional style in 1764. Displayed are handicrafts and objects of the period, including rich interiors such as the *oda e burrave* (men's counsel room), designed in oriental motif.

NATIONAL MUSEUM OF GEORGE CASTRIOTTA SCANDERBEG, KRUJA (*MUZEU KOMBËTAR GJERGJ KASTRIOTI SKËNDERBEU*). The Scanderbeg Museum was designed by architect Pranvera Hoxha, daughter of dictator **Enver Hoxha,** and was opened on 1 November 1982 in the fortress of **Kruja.** It is devoted to the fifteenth-century Albanian national hero, **Scanderbeg**. The museum displays many objects associated with the life and times of Scanderbeg. The helmet of Scanderbeg, which is the centerpiece of the museum, is a copy of the original in the Hofburg in Vienna. It is often lamented that there are many reconstructions and very few original objects in the museum. As such, visitors learn more about the cult of Scanderbeg as a national hero than they do about Scanderbeg himself.

NATIONAL MUSEUM OF HISTORY, TIRANA (*MUZEU HISTORIK KOMBËTAR*). The museum of history, situated imposingly on the main square in **Tirana**, is the largest and most important museum in the country. It was inaugurated on 28 October 1981 and hosts about 3,600 objects of Albanian cultural heritage, as well as over 4,000 archeological items from the paleolithic age to antiquity, and over 300 objects from the medieval period, including the fourteenth-century Epitaph of Glavenica, and Byzantine icons. It also has a section devoted to the **communist** dictatorship. Its current director is Moikom Zeqo.

NATIONAL MUSEUM OF INDEPENDENCE, VLORA (*MUZEU KOMBËTAR I PAVARËSISË*). The independence museum in **Vlora**, which was opened in 1962, is situated in the original building, which served as the headquarters of the first independent Albanian government in 1912. It commemorates the declaration of Albanian independence by **Ismail Qemal bey Vlora** on 28 November 1912 and contains some original furnishings and objects of the period.

NATIONAL MUSEUM OF MEDIEVAL ART, KORÇA (*MUZEU KOMBËTAR I ARTIT MESJETAR*). The museum of medieval art in **Korça**, with over 7,000 objects at its disposal, is devoted to the development of Byzantine icon painting and art in Albania over a period of five centuries. Displayed are the works of **Onufri**, **David Selenica** and other noted icon painters. The museum was opened on 26 April 1980, despite the extreme anti-religious orientation of the ruling **Party of Labor**.

NATIONAL MUSEUM ONUFRI, BERAT (*MUZEU KOMBËTAR ONUFRI*). The Onufri Museum was opened in 1986 in the **Orthodox** Church of Saint Mary's, built in 1797, which is situated within the walls of the old fortress of **Berat**. It hosts a rich collection of Byzantine icon paintings and other religious objects, including of course the works of the painter **Onufri**.

NATIONAL MUSEUM OF THE RESIDENCE OF SCANDERBEG, LEZHA (*MUZEU KOMBËTAR I VENDBANIMIT TË SKËNDERBEUT*). The so-called museum of the residence of **Scanderbeg** is actually a memorial site in the ruins of the Church of Saint Nicholas in **Lezha** and serves to commemorate the foundation of the League of Lezha in 1444 and Scanderbeg's death there in 1468.

NATIONAL REVOLUTIONARY COMMITTEE. *See* KONARE.

NATIONAL THEATER, TIRANA (*TEATRI KOMBËTAR SHQIPTAR*). The Albanian National Theater, formerly known as the People's Theater (*Teatri Popullor*), is situated in a modest building near the **National Gallery** in **Tirana** and is the principal venue for Albanian drama. It is currently under reconstruction. It was founded in Tirana on 25 May 1944, originally under the name of State Theater, and began functioning in 1946 under the direction of Sokrat Mio and Pandi Stillu.

NATURAL GAS PRODUCTION. The natural gas industry began operations in 1955. Maximum gas production was attained in 1982 with 938.8 million m^3N. Up to 1999, Albania had produced and consumed almost 7.7 billion m^3N, forty-one percent of this being natural gas and fifty-nine percent accompanying gas. Until 1990, gas represented eight percent of the country's total energy production and was used by the fertilizer industry, in particular by the nitrogen fertilizer plant in **Fier**. After 1993, the production of natural gas declined substantially, as did the **oil** industry. In 1999, it reached an all-time low of 14 million m^3N, a mere two percent of domestic energy resources and 0.2 percent of final energy consumption.

NAXHI, IBRAHIM MEHMET. *See* HIMA, DERVISH.

NDRENIKA, ROBERT (1942.01.10-). Stage and **film** actor. Robert Ndrenika was born in **Tirana** where he finished his studies in acting in 1964. He worked for seven years at the Skampa theater in **Elbasan** before returning to the **National Theater** in Tirana. Aside from his activities as a leading stage actor, he appeared in thirty-two film roles up to 1989. Best remembered among them are his roles in: *Koncert në vitin '36* (Concert in the Year 1936), 1978; *Mesonjëtorja* (The Schoolhouse), 1979; and *Përrallë nga e kaluara* (Tale from the Past), 1987. He played a role in the democracy movement in 1990 and was elected a member of **parliament** in 1992.

NEGOVANI, KRISTO (1875-1905.02.12). Writer and educator. Papa Kristo Negovani, also known as *Kristo Harallambi*, was born in Negovan near Florina in northern Greece. In 1894, he migrated to Brăila in Romania, where he worked for three years as a carpenter. It was there that he first came into contact with the nationalist movement and learned to write Albanian (in the Istanbul alphabet). In 1897, he returned to his native village, and was ordained as a parish priest. Negovani transformed his house into a school and taught over 100 children and adults to read and write Albanian. He also preached and said mass in Albanian, much to the displeasure of the Greek **Orthodox** hierarchy.

On 10 February 1905, Negovani held a church service in Albanian in the presence of Kara-Vangjelis, bishop of Kastoria, who, on leaving the church, is said to have pronounced the fatal words, "May the coming year no longer find you among the living." Two days later, the village was surrounded by bandits who forced the thirty-year-old Negovani out of his house in the middle of the night and hacked him and five other persons to death with axes. To avenge this bloody deed attributed by the Albanians to the Greek Orthodox hierarchy, the Albanian guerrilla **Bajo Topulli** waylaid and murdered Photios, bishop of **Korça,** on 22 September 1906.

Papa Kristo Negovani is the author of early prose and poetry in Albanian, including school texts, translations and fables. Some of his work appeared in journals of the period, in particular in the *Kalëndari kombiar* (The National Calendar).

NEO-ALBANIANISM (*NEO-SHQIPTARIZMI*). Neo-Albanianism was a current of intellectual thought which arose in Albanian society around 1928, though its roots, as its proponents pointed out, were to be found in the **Rilindja** movement. It was propagated in particular by **Branko Merxhani** as a spiritual revival for an intellectually underdeveloped country. The Albanian nationalists of the nineteenth century had concentrated all their energies on the attainment of independence from the **Ottoman Empire**, but independence itself was only half the job. What was now needed was a revival to create and cement a national identity, an Albanian conscience, in order to lead the people out of darkness and ignorance, i.e., a second nationalist movement. He called Albania "an entity bound externally but boundless internally" (*një qënie e kufizuar së jashtëmi dhe e pakufishme së brëndshmi*). Merxhani had first championed the nationalist ideology of Neo-Albanianism with **Vangjel Koça** in 1929 in the pages of the much-read **Gjirokastra** weekly newspaper *Demokratia* (Democracy) and in his short-lived monthly periodical entitled *Neo-Shqiptarizmi* (Neo-Albanianism), which had begun publication in July 1930.

Neo-Albanianism was based on ideological nationalism. It called for social progress as a foundation for intellectual process, but did not advocate a direct political commitment to social change or the elimination of traditional political and social structures. In its original form it was a cultural, nonpolitical movement, as evident in Merxhani's slogan "There are no politics! Only culture!" (*Politikë s'ka! Vetëm kulturë!*). Inevitably, however, Neo-Albanianism evolved into a counter-weight to the much more political ideology of socialism and left-wing internationalism. Though an Albanian creation, Neo-Albanianism must nonetheless be seen within the context of the other nationalist ideologies which arose throughout Europe in the 1920s and 1930s and which slowly but surely merged to form and promote European fascism. Among these were the Greek *hellênikótêta*, especially under the 1936-1940 dictatorship of General Joannis Metaxás (1871-1941), *italianità* under Italian dictator Benito Mussolini (1883-1945) and *hispanidad* in fascist Spain under General Francisco Franco (1892-1975).

NEW ALBANIA FILM STUDIOS (*KINOSTUDIO "SHQIPËRIA E RE"*) (1952-). The history of the Albanian **film** industry began on 10 July 1952 with the founding, with Soviet support, of the "New Albania" Film Studios in **Tirana**. The film studios were given property and a delightfully Stalinist building on the eastern outskirts of Tirana, and students were sent abroad, principally to Czechoslovakia and the **Soviet Union**, to study directing and filmmaking. The first Albanian feature film *Tana* (Tana) followed five years later in 1958, directed by Kristaq Dhamo. From that time until 1995, 270 feature films, 700 documentary, and 150 animated films were produced in Albania, the vast majority of which were by New Albania Film Studios. The first animated film, *Zana dhe Miri* (Zana and Miri), was shown in 1975. The studios had exclusive responsibility for the export and import of films during the dictatorship. They also organized various film festivals. The New Albania Film Studios have recently been renamed the National Center for Cinematography (*Qendra Kombëtare e Kinematografisë*).

NEW DEMOCRATIC PARTY (*PARTIA DEMOKRATIKE E RE, PDR*) (2001-). This political formation arose as a reform movement from within the **Democratic Party** of Albania. Its leaders, among whom were **Genc Pollo** and Dashamir Shehi, were frustrated by the continued authoritarian style of **Sali Berisha** and by the refusal of the latter to take part in **parliament** and play a positive, active role in politics. It broke away from the Democratic Party in early 2001, originally calling itself the New Democratic Party (*Partia Demokratike e Re*). On 4 April 2001, however, it registered under the name *Partia Demokrate* (as opposed to *Demokratike*), i.e., Democrat Party or Party of Democrats, but is now generally known as the New Democratic Party. In the elections of 2001, the New Democratic Party, with an extremely liberal platform, won 5.1 percent of the popular vote and is represented in **parliament** by six seats. It is thus currently the third largest formation in the assembly.

NEWMARK, LEONARD (1919-). American scholar and linguist. Leonard Newmark, born in Indiana, is professor emeritus of linguistics at the University of California in San Diego and was a research linguist at the Center for Research in Language there. He has been involved in the study of Albanian since 1951 when he began to teach the **language** as a graduate student at Indiana University. Since then, he has participated in seminars in Albanian language and culture in both Albania and **Kosova**. He is the author of *Structural Grammar of Albanian,* Bloomington 1957; and *Albanian-English Dictionary*, Oxford 1998, no doubt the best Albanian dictionary ever to have appeared; and is coauthor of *Spoken Albanian,* Ithaca, N.Y. 1980; and *Standard Albanian: A Reference Grammar for Students,* Stanford 1982.

NGJELA, KIÇO (1917.12.25-2002.06.16). Political figure of the **communist** period. Kiço Ngjela was minister of trade in the 1970s. Together with **Abdyl Këllezi**, head of the state planning commission, and Koço Theodhosi, minister of industry and mines, he fell victim to the purge at the seventh Congress of the Central Committee on 26-29 May 1975, allegedly for grave "revisionist" mistakes and sabotage of the economy. He was relieved of his posts, expelled from the party, arrested and imprisoned on 10 October 1975. His sons were also imprisoned, and the whole family was interned during the communist period. He was released in February 1991. Kiço Ngjela is the father of politician Spartak Ngjela, who was minister of justice in 1997 and who is currently public relations secretary of the **Democratic Party**.

NIKAJ. Northern Albanian tribe and traditional tribal region. The Nikaj region is situated north of the **Drin** River in the western part of the District of **Tropoja**. It borders on the traditional tribal regions of **Shala** to the west, **Krasniqi** to the east and **Merturi** to the south. The Nikaj were the hereditary enemies of the Shala and **Shoshi**, and were considered, together with the **Dushmani**, to be among the wildest inhabitants of the northern mountains. The name was recorded in 1703 as *Nicagni, Nichagni* and seems to derive from the personal name Nicholas. The Nikaj tribe had a **population** of some 2,200 in the early years of the twentieth century.

NIKAJ, NDOC (1864.03.08-1951.10.14). Prose writer and publisher. Dom Ndoc Nikaj has been called the father of the Albanian novel. He studied at the **Jesuit** *Kolegjia Papnore Shqyptare* (Albanian Pontifical Seminary) in **Shkodra**, was ordained in 1888, and subsequently worked as a parish priest in the **Shkreli** mountains. As a publisher, he began his career by founding the weekly newspaper *Koha* (The Time) in January 1910. In the spring of 1913, he founded another newspaper, the *Besa Shqyptare* (The Albanian Pledge), which was published two to four times a week until 1921.

In addition to running newspapers, Ndoc Nikaj also had his own small publishing company, the *Shtypshkroja Nikaj* (Nikaj Press), founded in 1909, at which many of his own works and those of others were published. Although the publishing company was not a financial success, businessman Nikaj was able to compensate for the loss with profits earned in other more lucrative fields such as lumber and gunrunning. After **World War I**, Nikaj turned increasingly to writing and published both educative works for schools, religious works for the church and some literary prose. Little is known of his personal life in later years.

In the realm of creative **literature**, Nikaj is the author of numerous now rare volumes of prose in the main, though also of some dramatic works. Best known are the novelettes *Marzia e* *ksctenimi n'filles t'vet* (Marzia and the Origins of Christianity), Shkodra 1892; *Fejesa n'djep a se Ulqini i mârrun* (Marriage in the Cradle or Ulcinj Captured), Shkodra 1913; and *Shkodra e rrethueme* (Shkodra under Siege), Shkodra 1913.

During the persecution of the **Catholic** clergy in northern Albania in 1946, Dom Ndoc Nikaj was arrested by the **communists**, at the age of eighty-two, on the absurd charge of "planning the violent overthrow of the government," and died in Shkodra prison in 1951.

NIKOLLA, MILLOSH GJERGJ. *See* MIGJENI.

NISHANI, OMER (1887.02.05-1954.05.26). Political figure. Omer Nishani was born in **Gjirokastra** and studied medicine in Istanbul. He began his political career in the early 1920s. In 1924, during **Fan Noli**'s democratic government, he participated in a trial in absentia against **Ahmet Zogu** and his cohorts and, in 1925, he cofounded the **KONARE** and ran its Geneva weekly newspaper *Liria Kombëtare* (National Freedom) from June 1926 to April 1932. The Zog regime sentenced him to death in absentia. Nishani returned to Albania after the **Italian** invasion in 1939 and was elected to the Council of State. He later joined the resistance movement and cofounded the National Liberation Front. In May 1944, he was chosen by the Congress of Përmet as president of the antifascist national liberation council and on 12 January 1946, after the **communist** takeover, became chairman of the people's constituent assembly. Omer Nishani thus served as Albanian head of state until he retired in July 1953. His articles and speeches from the communist period were published in the volume *Për Shqipërinë e popullit* (For Albania of the People), Tirana 1988.

NOLI, FAN (1882.01.06-1965.03.13). Political figure, church leader, writer, poet and translator. Fan Noli, also known as Theophan Stylian Noli, was not only an outstanding leader of the Albanian-American community, but also a preeminent and multi-talented figure of Albanian **literature**, culture, religious life and politics. Noli was born in the village of Ibrik Tepe (Alb. *Qyteza*), south of Edirne (Adrianopole) in European Turkey. He lived from 1903 to 1906 in Egypt, from where he emigrated to the **United States**.

On 9 February 1908 at the age of twenty-six, Fan Noli was made a deacon in Brooklyn and was ordained as an **Orthodox** priest on 8 March of that year. A mere two weeks later, on 22 March 1908, the young Noli proudly celebrated the liturgy in Albanian for the first time at the Knights of Honor Hall in Boston. This act constituted the first step towards the official organization and recognition of an Albanian Autocephalic **Ortho-dox** Church.

From February 1909 to July 1911, Noli edited the newspaper *Dielli* (The Sun), mouthpiece of the Albanian community in Boston. Together with **Faik bey Konitza,** he founded the Pan-Albanian **Vatra Federation** of America on 28 April 1912, which was soon destined to become the most powerful and significant Albanian organization in America. Fan Noli had now become the recognized leader of the Albanian Orthodox community and was an established writer and journalist of the nationalist movement. In November 1912, Albania was declared independent, and the thirty-year-old Noli, having graduated with a B.A. from Harvard University, hurriedly returned to Europe. In March 1913, among other activities, he attended the Albanian **Congress of Trieste**, which was organized by his friend and rival Faik bey Konitza.

In July 1913, Fan Noli visited Albania for the first time, and there, on 10 March 1914, he held the country's first Orthodox church service in Albanian in the presence of **Prince Wilhelm zu Wied**. From 21 December 1915 to 6 July 1916, he was again editor-in-chief of the Boston *Dielli* (The Sun), now a daily news-paper. In July 1917, he once more became president of the *Vatra* federation which, in view of the chaotic situation and political vacuum in Albania, now regarded itself as a sort of Albanian government in exile. On 27 July 1919, Noli was appointed bishop of the Albanian Orthodox Church in America, now finally an independent diocese. In the following year, in view of his grow-ing stature as a political and religious leader of the Albanian community and as a talented writer, orator and political commen-tator, it was only fitting that he be selected to head an Albanian delegation to the League of Nations in Geneva where he was successful in having Albania admitted on 17 December 1920. Noli rightly regarded Albania's admission to the League of Na-tions as his greatest political achievement. Membership in that body gave Albania worldwide recognition for the first time and was in retrospect no doubt more important than **Ismail Qemal bey Vlora**'s declaration of independence in 1912.

Noli's success at the League of Nations established him as the leading figure in Albanian political life. From Geneva, he re-turned to Albania and, from 1921 to 1922, represented the *Vatra*

Federation in the Albanian **parliament** there. In 1922, he was appointed foreign minister in the government of **Xhafer bey Ypi** but resigned several months later. On 21 November 1923, Noli was consecrated bishop of **Korça** and metropolitan of **Durrës**. He was now both head of the Orthodox Church in Albania and leader of a liberal political party, the main opposition to the conservative forces of **Ahmet Zogu**, who were supported primarily by the feudal landowners and the middle class. On 23 February 1924, an attempt was made in parliament on the life of Ahmet Zogu and two months later, on 22 April 1924, nationalist figure and deputy **Avni Rustemi** was assassinated, allegedly by Zogist forces. At Rustemi's funeral, Fan Noli gave a fiery oration, which provoked the liberal opposition into such a fury that Zogu was obliged to flee to **Yugoslavia**.

On 17 July 1924, Fan Noli was officially proclaimed prime minister and shortly afterwards regent of Albania. For six months after this so-called June or **Democratic Revolution**, he led a democratic government which tried desperately to cope with the catastrophic economic and political problems facing the young Albanian state. With the overthrow of his government by Zogist forces on Christmas Eve 1924, Noli left Albania for good. In November 1927, he visited Russia as a Balkan delegate to a congress of "Friends of the Soviet Union" marking the tenth anniversary of the October Revolution, and in 1930, having obtained a six-month visa, he returned to the United States.

Back in Boston, he withdrew from political life and henceforth resumed his duties as head of the Albanian Autocephalic Orthodox Church. In 1935, he returned to one of his earlier passions—**music**—and, at the age of fifty-three, registered at the New England Conservatory of Music in Boston, from which he graduated in 1938 with a Bachelor of Music. On 12 April 1937, Noli's great dream of an Albanian national church was fulfilled when the patriarch of Constantinople officially recognized the Albanian Autocephalic Orthodox Church. Not satisfied with ecclesiastical duties alone, Noli turned to postgraduate studies at Boston University, finishing a doctorate there in 1945 with a dissertation on **Scanderbeg**. In the early years following **World War II**, Noli maintained reasonably good relations with the new **communist** regime in **Tirana** and used his influence to try to persuade the American government to recognize the latter. His reputation as the "red bishop" indeed caused a good deal of enmity and polarization in emigré circles in America. In 1953, at the age of seventy-one, Fan Noli was presented with the sum of US$20,000 from the *Vatra* Federation, with which he bought a house in Fort Lauderdale, Florida, where he died at the age of eighty-three.

Politics and **religion** were not the only fields in which Fan Noli made a name for himself. He was also a dramatist, poet, historian, musicologist and, in particular, an excellent translator who made a significant contribution to the development of the Albanian literary language.

NOPCSA, FRANZ Baron (1877.05.03-1933.04.25). Hungarian scholar. Franz Nopcsa was born the son of Hungarian aristocrats at the family estate in Szacsal (Săcel) near Hatzeg in Tran-sylvan-ia. He was able to finish his schooling at the Maria-Theresianum in Vienna with the support of his uncle and godfather, Franz von Nopcsa, who was headmaster of the court of the Empress Elisabeth.

Nopcsa developed quickly into a talented scholar. On 21 July 1899, at the age of twenty-two, he held his first lecture at the Academy of Sciences in Vienna on *Dinossaurierreste in Siebenbürgen* (Dinosaur Remnants in Transylvania) and attracted much attention with it. He is considered one of the founders of paleophysiology, in particular because of his internationally renowned studies on reptile fossils. Well known were his hypotheses on the "running proavis," on the warm-bloodedness of the pterosaurus, and on the significance of a number of endocrine processes, which he considered to have had an important influence on the evolution and extinction of dinosaurs. Not all of his theories were accepted at the time, but they did succeed in advancing and stimulating a wide range of fields of paleontology. Equally important were Nopcsa's achievements in the field of geology, an example of which was his research into the tectonic structures of the western Balkan mountain ranges, where he defended some rather unusual theories.

Nopcsa traveled extensively in the Balkans and lived in **Shkodra** for some time in the early years of the twentieth century. Later, he became one of the leading Albania specialists of his times and was even a candidate for the Albanian throne in 1913. His publications in the field of Albanian studies from 1907 to 1932 were concentrated primarily in the fields of prehistory, early Balkan history, ethnology, **geography**, modern history and Albanian customary law, i.e., the *Kanun*. His early works such as *Das Katholische Nordalbanien* (Catholic Northern Albania), Budapest 1907; *Aus Šala und Klementi* (From Shala and Kelmendi), Sarajevo 1910; *Haus und Hausrat im katholischen*

Nordalbanien (House and Household Equipment in Catholic Northern Albania), Sarajevo 1912; and *Beiträge zur Vorgeschichte und Ethnologie Nordalbaniens* (Contributions to the Prehistory and Ethnology of Northern Albania), Sarajevo 1912, contain a myriad of fascinating observations, although from a modern perspective the material may not always seem well organized. In his later years, when he had settled down and was no longer traveling in the Balkans, he produced ambitious works of more sound scholarly quality. Among the best known of these are *Bauten, Trachten und Geräte Nordalbaniens* (Buildings, Costumes and Tools of Northern Albania), Berlin 1925, and, in particular, the 620-page *Geologie und Geographie Nordalbaniens* (Geology and Geography of Northern Albania), Öhrlingen 1932, which may be considered the *magnum opus* of the Albanological studies that he published during his lifetime. The list of Nopcsa's publications includes over 186 works, primarily in the fields of paleontology, geology, and Albanian studies. At least fifty-four of these works are related specifically to Albania.

Suffering from depression, Baron Nopcsa committed suicide at his home in Vienna on 25 April 1933 and killed his longtime Albanian secretary and lover Bajazid Elmaz Doda (ca. 1888-1933). His manuscripts *Die Bergstämme Nordalbaniens und ihr Gewohnheitsrecht* (The Mountain Tribes of Northern Albania and Their Customary Law), Vienna 1993, and *Reisen in den Balkan: die Lebenserinnerungen des Franz Baron Nopcsa* (Travels in the Balkans: The Memoirs of Baron Franz Nopcsa), Peja 2001, were published posthumously.

NORTHERN EPIRUS. Region. Northern Epirus, Greek *Vorio-Epiros*, is a term used primarily by the Greeks to refer to the region of southern Albania extending from the Greek border northwards to about **Vlora**. The designation is often used to reflect the territorial claims to this ethnically mixed region which were made by Greek nationalists in the first decades of the twentieth century. The Albanians usually refer to the region simply as southern Albania. *See* GREECE, RELATIONS WITH.

NOSI, LEF (1873-1946.02.15). Political figure and scholar. Lef Nosi was born of a wealthy **Orthodox** family in **Elbasan**. He supported the Congress of Elbasan of August 1909 and was director of the respected Normal School (*Shkolla Normale*) in his native town. On 25 March 1910, he began editing the weekly newspaper *Tomorri* (Tomorr) and was present at the declaration of independence in **Vlora** in 1912, after which he was made postmaster general. In 1918, Nosi took part in the Congress of Durrës, was briefly minister of national economy and attended the Paris Peace Conference in 1919 as part of the Albanian delegation led by Msgr. **Luigj Bumçi.** He retired from politics and lived in Elbasan between 1929 and 1938, where he divided his time between business and historical research.

Lef Nosi was a scholar and collector of manuscripts and early twentieth-century documents. He had a passionate interest in archeology and ethnography. **Edith Durham** called him the only Albanian who understood the value of folklore. He is remembered in particular as editor, from 1924 on, of a collection of historical documents under the title *Dokumenta historike për t'i shërbye historiës tone kombëtare* (Historical Documents to Serve Our National History), Elbasan. Nosi was a good friend, and reportedly the lover of Scottish anthropologist **Margaret Hasluck,** who lived in Albania for thirteen years, principally in Elbasan.

In June 1943, Lef Nosi joined the *Balli Kombëtar* and became a leading figure of the anticommunist resistance. In October 1943, during the **German** occupation, he was chosen as president of the national assembly and was elected to the High Regency Council (*Këshilli i Lartë i Regjencës*). He resigned from the position in October 1944 when German troops were evacuating Albania and when it became evident that the **communist** partisans would soon take control. Nosi was arrested in August 1945 while trying to escape from **Tirana** and was brought to trial in February 1946, together with **Anton Harapi** and former prime minister **Maliq bey Bushati.** According to the British Military Mission, which covered the trial: "The trial took place, in eight sessions, in a squalid cinema in Tirana before a house packed by Party members who constantly interrupted and jeered, while three military judges on the stage kept hurling accusations and abuse at the defendants, jointly and severally. All three were held responsible for, among other things, Albania's entire war losses.... Defendant's counsel was howled down as a 'fascist' and never succeeded in making himself heard.... The three accused were shot two days afterwards, on 15 February."

NUSHI, GOGO (1913.02.15-1970.12.04). Political figure of the **communist** period. Gogo Nushi was born in Vuno on the coast of **Himara.** He lived in Lyon, France, from 1928 to 1940 and was a member of the French communist party from 1935. Back in

Albania in 1940, he was a founding member of the Albanian communist party in 1941 and took part in the partisan movement during **World War II**. After the war he served as minister of industry 1948-1949; head of the trade union, 1949-1951 and 1958-1970; minister of trade, 1947-1948 and 1953-1954; minister of industry and mines, 1948; chairman of the People's Assembly, 1954-1956; deputy prime minister, 1956-1958; first secretary of the party for **Berat**, 1966; and vice chairman of the People's Assembly, 1962-1970. Gogo Nushi was a member of the Central Committee from 1948 and was one of the rare communist leaders of the period to have survived all the purges unscathed. He died a natural death.

- O -

OAKLEY-HILL, DAYRELL (1898-1985.11.05). British colonel. Dayrell R. Oakley-Hill was among the British officers who were assigned the task of organizing the Albanian police force in the 1930s under the direction of General **Sir Jocelyn Percy**. He was born in South Africa, completed his military training at Sandhurst, and served with the Indian Army in Mesopotamia from November 1917 until after the end of **World War I**. Oakley-Hill was recruited for the Albanian mission in 1929 and served principally in **Elbasan,** where he learned Albanian and traveled extensively. He was forced to leave Albania with the withdrawal of all British officers in November 1938. During the early years of **World War II**, he worked for the **Special Operations Executive** in Belgrade and **Kosova** as a specialist for Albanian affairs to help organize the resistance. He was obliged to surrender to the Germans in Belgrade in 1941 and was held as a prisoner of war until October 1943. At the end of World War II, he headed the mission of the United Nations Relief and Rehabilitation Administration (UNRRA) to Albania to provide humanitarian assistance there until work became impossible and he resigned in 1946. From January 1951 to 1955, he was posted to the British Embassy in Athens and worked for M16. In later years, he served as chairman of the **Anglo-Albanian Association** in London. His memoirs have been published in the volume *An Englishman in Albania: Memoirs of a British Officer, 1929-1955*, London 2002.

OHRID, LAKE. Lake Ohrid, the ancient *Lacus Lychnidus,* is situated on the southeastern border of Albania and is considered to be exceptionally old. It has a surface area of 363 square kilometers, of which 111.4 square kilometers are in Albanian territory, the rest being in the Republic of **Macedonia**. The lake is 695 meters above sea level and is fed by springs deriving in good part from Lake **Prespa**. Water from the lake flows into the Black **Drin** River at Struga. Lake Ohrid is known for its rich and varied marine wildlife and, in particular, for its delicious *koran* "Ohrid trout" (*Salmo letnica*), which is very popular with connoisseurs of fish.

OIL PRODUCTION. The Albanian oil industry dates back to the 1930s and is thus one of the oldest industries in the country. Italian marine officers had reported on seepages of heavy oil east of **Vlora** during **World War I** and, although some borings were made in 1918, is was only in 1925 that a concession was granted, initially to the Anglo-Persian Oil Company. A second concession was given to the Azienda Italiana de Petroli Albania (AIPA), an Italian company subsidized by Rome. It began drilling and eventually found oil in two fields, one near **Kuçova** and one near Vlora. By 1938, 445 wells had been sunk. The Italians then constructed a seventy-four-kilometers-long pipeline from the Kuçova field to Vlora and shipped the crude oil to refineries in Trieste, Bari and Leghorn. Annual production in 1940 reached 1.6 million barrels.

The oil industry reached its peak of production in 1974 with 2.2 million tons. High levels were also attained in the period 1976-1990, with an average annual production of 1.3 million tons. It used to cover a complete cycle: extraction, transportation, processing of final products and by-products, and distribution, and to an extent still does. It also used to satisfy demands in almost all sectors: industrial, domestic and other services.

With the transition to a market economy, price liberalization and privatization in the 1990s, the industry declined due to inadequate exploration and drilling technology and extremely outdated equipment. There was a drastic fall in production, from 1,067,000 tons in 1990 to 323,000 tons in 1999, and the oil processing industry slumped accordingly. Increasing demands for oil and petroleum by-products were met by imports. Thus, from an oil-exporting country, with ca. 200,000 tons exported in 1982, Albania became an oil importing country, with 184,800 tons imported in 1999.

Petroleum and its by-products accounted for 41.1 percent of final energy consumption in 1990 but only twenty-nine percent by 1999.

The state-owned petroleum enterprise Albpetrol was transformed into a joint stock-owning venture on 26 November 1998, with controlling shares in the new Albpetrol, Armo (processing) and Servcom (drilling) companies, which together cover the full cycle.

Albania had an oil-processing capacity of 2.5 million tons per year. Of the four oil-processing plants in the country, only two are currently in operation: the Ballsh and **Fier** refineries with a total capacity of 1.5 million tons per year. The most important processing plant is that of Ballsh.

Most oil reserves in Albania are found in the region in and around Ballsh, seventy-seven percent of total explored reserves being in sandy structures and the other twenty-three percent in calcareous structures. One negative characteristic of domestic oil is its viscosity and high bitumen content.

In about mid-1993, five foreign companies (Agip, Deminex, ÖMN, Occidental and Chevron) began conducting offshore explorations, but the deposits discovered to date have been too deep for serious commercial exploitation.

OMONIA (1990-). Political association of the **Greek minority**. The Omonia association was officially recognized as the Democratic Union of the Greek Minority on 22 February 1991. It presented five candidates in **Gjirokastra** and **Saranda** in the 1991 **parliamentary** elections and won all five seats, though it only gained 0.73 percent of the popular vote. It thereafter lost much public support because it was increasingly associated with efforts by political extremists in neighboring **Greece** to annex southern Albania (**Northern Epirus**) to Greece. Since the 1991 law on **political parties** banned parties formed on an ethnic basis, Omonia's supporters formed the **Union for Human Rights Party**, which was open to all Albanian citizens. On 20 April 1994, when political relations between the Albanian and Greek governments had deteriorated substantially, primarily due to the question of **minority** rights in the two countries, five Omonia leaders were arrested and tried for complicity in an armed attack carried out by Greek paramilitaries on a small military post in Gjirokastra on 10 April of that year, in which two Albanian soldier were killed. The trial in September 1994 caused outrage in Greece, which exerted pressure on Albania by blocking a desperately needed European Union loan of 34 million euros, and by expelling tens of thousands of Albanian workers from Greece.

ONUFRI (mid-sixteenth century). Painter. Onufri, Greek Onouphrios, Archpriest of **Elbasan** (medieval Neokastron), was the most important painter of icons and murals of the early post-Byzantine era in Albania. His works, influenced by the northern Greek painting of the Paleologus age, the Cretan School and western Gothic art, are to be seen in many churches in central Albania (Shelcan, Valsh and Shpat), in Greek Macedonia (Kastoria) and, in particular, at the Onufri **Museum** in **Berat**, which was opened in 1986. Characteristic for Onufri are strong colors, especially reds. Onufri's two sons, Joan and Nikolla, were also icon painters of note.

OPERA AND BALLET THEATER, TIRANA (*TEATRI I OP-ERAS DHE BALETIT*). The Opera and Ballet Theater, as a national institution for **music** and dance, was founded in 1953. Since that time, it has produced over 117 operas and ballets as well as thousands of concerts. The theater has a staff of approximately 260, including chorus, orchestra, musicians and performing artists. *See also* THEATER, ALBANIAN.

OPERATION ALBA (1997). Operation Alba (Ital. "dawn") was an international military undertaking to restore public order and security in Albania after the general **uprising** and political chaos of the early spring of 1997. The mission was led by Italian Admiral Guido Venturoni and General Luciano Forlani. On 15 April 1997, 6,000 troops began military and humanitarian operations in the country. In the contingent were 2,500 Italian, 1,000 French, 700-800 Greek, 500 Turkish, 400 Romanian, 325 Spanish, 120 Austrian and seventy Danish soldiers. The Operation Alba had the full support of the European Union, the United Nations and the Organization for Security and Cooperation in Europe. It was concluded on 11 August 1997 when the last Italian units left the country.

ORA. Figure of northern Albanian mythology, known primarily north of the **Drin** River. This popular female fairy is much like a fairy godmother. Every person has an *ora* to protect him or her. On the birth of a child, the *oras* gather at night beside a bonfire and decide what qualities to give him or her. *Oras,* whose actual names are often taboo, live in the forests, in the mountains, near streams and lakes or in caves.

OREL, VLADIMIR (1952.02.09-). Russian-born Israeli linguist. Vladimir Orel was born in Moscow and studied theoretical and computational linguistics at Moscow State University. He finished his doctorate in Slavic and Balkan linguistics with the Russian Academy of Sciences under the supervision of Balkanologist Leonid A. Gindin. From 1981 to 1990, he was a senior researcher at the Russian Academy of Sciences. Orel emigrated to Israel in 1990, where he worked as a senior lecturer in historical linguistics at Hebrew University and Tel Aviv University from 1991 to 1997, and at Bar-Ilan University from 1997 to 1999. He then emigrated to Canada and is currently living in Calgary, Alberta.

Vladimir Orel is a major figure in Albanian historical linguistics. He has taught courses and held seminars in Albanian historical grammar and the Albanian **language** at the Russian Academy of Sciences, Hebrew University and UCLA. Among his major publications, in addition to numerous scholarly articles on Albanian and the ancient languages of the Balkan region are a 700-page *Albanian Etymological Dictionary,* Leiden 1998; and *A Concise Historical Grammar of the Albanian Language: Reconstruction of Proto-Albanian,* Leiden 2000.

ORTHODOXY. Religion. The final rupture between Byzantine Orthodoxy and Roman **Catholicism** took place in the year 1054. Thirty-five years beforehand, in 1019, most of the dioceses of Byzantine rite in central and southern Albania had been placed under the autocephalic Archdiocese of Achrida (Ohrid). **Durrës** was subsequently reestablished as a metropolitan see of its own and took with it much Albanian territory along the coast. With the Turkish conquest of Albania in the early fifteenth century, **Islam** wedged itself between the Catholic north and the Orthodox south of Albania and, with time, became the dominant faith of the country. Nonetheless, twenty percent of the people of Albania remain faithful—nominally at least—to the Orthodox Church. As opposed to the Roman Catholics, Orthodox Christians were, to a certain extent, integrated into the structures of the **Ottoman Empire.** They were officially recognized as a religious community and their religious leaders, foremost of whom was the patriarch of Constantinople, acted under the direct authority of the Sublime Porte. The Orthodox community was allowed its own property, churches, schools, hospitals and monasteries, and had the right to use its Greek language.

During the Greek national awakening in the early nineteenth century, the Orthodox Church remained an expression of Greek civilization and was exclusively devoted to the Greek language as a cultural bulwark against the invading hordes of Islam. To be of Orthodox faith was to be Greek, just as to be of Islamic faith was to be Turkish. There was little room in either culture for the rising aspirations of Albanian nationalism half a century later during the Albanian national awakening. The use of the Albanian **language** was regarded by the Orthodox Church as eminently superfluous and in later years quite often as a heretical menace.

At the turn of the century, Orthodox Albanians in the United States, too, were growing increasingly impatient with Greek control of the Church. Tension reached its climax in 1907 when a Greek Orthodox priest refused to officiate at the burial of an Albanian called Kristo Dishnica in Hudson, Massachusetts. The young **Fan Noli**, who had arrived in America a year before, saw his calling and convoked a meeting of Orthodox Albanians from throughout New England at which delegates resolved to set up an autocephalic, i.e., autonomous Albanian Orthodox Church, with Noli as its first clergyman. On 9 February 1908, at the age of twenty-six, Fan Noli was made a deacon in Brooklyn and on 8 March 1908, Platon, the Russian Orthodox archbishop of New York, ordained him as an Orthodox priest. On 27 July 1919, Noli was appointed bishop of the Albanian Orthodox Church in America, now finally an independent diocese.

In Albania itself, the following years saw a struggle within the Orthodox Church between Albanian nationalists supporting an autocephalic church and the Greek hierarchy bitterly opposed to any change. In December 1921, Jakobos, Archbishop of Durrës and prime representative of Greek claims, was expelled from the country, as were the bishops of **Gjirokastra**, Korça and **Berat** the following year. The Albanian Autocephalic Orthodox Church was finally proclaimed in Berat on 12 September 1922 with four metropolitans, two seminaries and twenty-nine monasteries. The new church was placed under the provisional care of Fan Noli and, subsequently, of Archimandrite Visarion Xhuvani. It was, however, not immediately recognized by the patriarchate in Constantinople which, while conceding a certain autonomy, continued to insist on Greek as the language of the liturgy. Fan Noli, who was consecrated bishop of Korça and metropolitan of Durrës on 21 November 1923, and who was elected prime minister of Albania in 1924, endeavored to persuade the patriarch of the Orthodox Church to consecrate Albanian bishops, but failed. As such, he turned to the Serbian metropolitan of Peja (Peć), who agreed to his wishes. The patriarch, however, declared the action of the Serbian metropolitan to be null and void. New negotiations on the problem were first held again in 1935. On 12 April 1937, Fan Noli's great dream of an Albanian national church was fulfilled when the patriarch of Constantinople finally issued a *tomos*, officially recognizing the Albanian Autocephalic Orthodox Church. A synod then elected an Albanian, Kristofor Kissi (1908-1958) of Berat, as the first primate of this new autocephalic church. Noli himself, who had retired to America, continued to devote his energies to the Albanian Autocephalic Orthodox Church until his death in 1965 and made elegant Albanian translations of numerous Orthodox texts (liturgies, catechisms, psalms, etc.).

The Orthodox Church initially received somewhat better treatment than the Catholics when the **communists** came to power in Albania in 1944. It recognized the new regime and, like the Russian Orthodox Church in the **Soviet Union**, attempted to adapt to the new situation. There were still sixty-five monasteries on Albanian soil in the immediate postwar years. On 28 August 1949, however, Archbishop Kissi was forcibly relieved of his duties and sent into retirement to a monastery. His successor, Bishop Paisi or Pashko Vodica (d. 1966), chosen by the communist government, endeavored to strengthen relations with the patriarch of Moscow and received a visit from Bishop Nikon of Odessa in May 1951. Soon, however, the communists began to whittle away at the structures of the Orthodox Church, too. More and more churches were closed down and christenings and church marriages were made increasingly difficult. Paisios' successor, Damian Kokonesi (1886-1973), was arrested one year after taking up office and died in November 1973 at the age of eighty. The bishops of Elbasan, Pojan, Berat, Korça and Gjirokastra were also imprisoned, and some of them were shot. In 1967, Orthodoxy and all other forms of **religion** were banned entirely.

In January 1991, after the end of the dictatorship, the patriarch of Constantinople appointed the Greek bishop of Athens, **Anastas Janulatos**, as Patriarchal Exarch for the reestablishment of the Albanian Orthodox Church, and he was inaugurated as archbishop of the National Council in 1992. Many Orthodox Albanians were shocked and dismayed at the time by the appointment, once again, of a Greek to lead the Orthodox Church in Albania.

The patriarchate countered this with the argument that there were no suitable Albanian candidates available. Although Janulatos is well accepted as an individual and has followed a wise course of action in a delicate situation, the controversy continues. The Orthodox Church presently has four dioceses which form the synod in Albania (**Tirana**, Berat, Gjirokastra and Korça) and which runs a training seminary in Durrës, the *Shkolla Teologjike-Hieratike*, which opened on 7 February 1992. In July 1998, the Church appointed its first native Albanian bishop, Ioan Pelushi (1956-) of Tirana, as metropolitan of Korça. The Albanian Orthodox Archdiocese in America for its part, headed by Father **Arthur Liolin** of Boston, remains administratively part of the Orthodox Church of America. In 1999, there were about 100 Orthodox priests in Albania, 25 of whom were in the diocese of Korça alone.

OSUM. River in central Albania . The Osum takes its source in the District of **Kolonja** and flows in a northwesterly direction through **Skrapar** and past the town of **Berat** to join the Devoll River and form the **Seman**, which flows into the Adriatic Sea. The Osum is 161 kilometers long. It was known in antiquity as Greek *Apsos* (Strabo VII.5.8) and Latin *Apsus* (Livy 31.27). The subsequent form *Assamus* became Osum through Slavic transmission.

OTTOMAN EMPIRE. *See* TURKEY, RELATIONS WITH.

- P -

PAÇRAMI, FADIL (1922.05.25-). Political figure of the **communist** period and dramatist. Fadil Paçrami was born in **Shkodra** and, although of Muslim origin, was educated by the **Franciscans** who sent him to Bologna where he studied medicine. In 1942, he interrupted his studies to join the partisan movement back in Albania. After the war, he worked in the communist youth movement, became deputy minister of **education** and culture under **Sejfulla Malëshova**, and editor-in-chief of the daily newspaper *Zëri i popullit* (The People's Voice) from 1948 to 1957. In 1965-1966, he served as minister of culture and the arts and, from 1971 to 1973, as chairman of the People's Assembly. At the fourth plenary session of the Central Committee on 26-28 June 1973, Fadil Paçrami and **Todi Lubonja**, head of Albanian radio and television, were singled out by **Enver Hoxha** in a drive against liberal and foreign influence in Albanian culture. Relieved of all his positions, Fadil Paçrami was arrested on 21 October 1975 and spent an initial eighteen months in **Tirana** prison awaiting trial, only to suffer the very same fate which other intellectuals had suffered under his rule. In March 1977, he was convicted of sabotage in the field of culture for having introduced foreign influences and for having corrupted the youth, not to mention the standard charges of agitation and propaganda. He was sentenced to twenty-five years in prison. After fifteen years and five months, he was released on 17 March 1991.

As a playwright, Fadil Paçrami wrote thirteen dramas up to 1973, of which nine were published at the time. He continued to write while in prison in both Burrel and Kosova e Madhe and has recently published more plays.

PALAJ, BERNARDIN (1894.12.02-1947.12.08). Catholic poet and folklorist. The **Franciscan** cleric Bernardin Palaj is the author of classical lyric and elegiac verse, much of which was published in the 1930s in the periodical *Hylli i Dritës* (The Day-Star). In deference to his master **Gjergj Fishta**, Palaj did not compose much epic verse, although his affinity for the magical rhapsodic world of frontier heroes Mujo and Halili gave him both a talent and an inclination for it. Fishta died on 30 December 1940, and Palaj was moved by the occasion to compose the 1,180-line elegy *Kah nata e vetme* (Towards the Solitary Night) in his honor. Palaj was arrested in **Shkodra**, severely mishandled, and then sentenced to death for treason. He died in a Shkodra prison.

PANO, NICHOLAS (1934-). American scholar and historian. Nicholas Christopher Pano studied at Tufts University and pursued his M.A. at John Hopkins in Baltimore. He was subsequently professor of history at Western Illinois University in Macomb. His research has focused on twentieth-century Albanian history and politics. He is the author of the volume *People's Republic of Albania,* Baltimore 1968.

PAPAVRAMI, TEDI (1971-). Violinist. Born in **Tirana**, Tedi Papavrami was given a rare opportunity to leave Stalinist Albania at the age of eleven and to study **music** in Paris under Pierre Amayal. He has become an internationally known violinist and, in recent years, has also translated some of the works of **Ismail Kadare** into French. He has been living in Paris since 1986.

PARLIAMENT. Albania is not a country of longstanding or solid parliamentary traditions. It was the government of **Iljaz bey Vrioni** in 1920-1921 which first prepared a rudimentary law for national elections. The first constituent assembly, called the National Council (*Këshilli Kombëtar*), was convened on 21 April 1921 with seventy-eight deputies. The vast majority of the **population** (including the peasantry and the **women**) was not represented. Political factions arose among the delegates to this first parliament, but no real political parties were created. The rise of the dictatorship of **Ahmet Zogu,** later King Zog, in 1924 stifled the evolution of parliamentary life and no genuine multiparty elections were held in Albania until 1991. There was, however, a one-chamber parliament of fifty-seven deputies from 1928 to 1939.

After the **communist** takeover, elections were held on 2 December 1945 and a constitutional assembly was convened. This assembly promulgated a communist-style constitution on 14 March 1946 and transformed itself two days later into the People's Assembly (*Kuvendi Popullor*). The competencies of this chamber of 140 members in a one-party state were extremely limited. The deputies were elected every four years upon the proposal of the Democratic Front and were simply approved of by the electorate in pseudo-elections. The approval ratings in these national "elections" ranged from 99.28 percent in 1950 to 100 percent in 1987. There was no opposition, only the occasional, and extremely rare invalid ballot.

After the fall of the communist dictatorship, free elections were held on 31 March 1991, and a first pluralist parliament (*Kuvendi*) was convened on 15 April 1991 with 250 deputies. A new electoral law was passed on 4 February 1992, after which the **Democratic Party** took power away from the communists and set Albania on the road to parliamentary democracy. On the current Albanian Parliament, *see also* www.parlament.al.

PARTIES, POLITICAL. *See* POLITICAL PARTIES.

PARTY OF LABOR (*PARTIA E PUNËS, PPSH*) (1941-1990). The Party of Labor of Albania (*Partia e Punës e Shqipërisë*), originally known as the **Communist** Party of Albania (*Partia Komuniste e Shqipërisë*), was founded in **Tirana** on 8 November 1941 with strong support from Tito's emissaries Miladin Popović (1910-1945) and Dušan Mugoša (1914-1973). It actually remained an appendage of the Yugoslav communist party until June 1948. In the schism between Tito and Stalin, the Albanian communists took the Soviet side and split with their Yugoslav comrades. This was more a result of factional infighting within the party and, to an extent, of reticence about **Yugoslavia**'s growing influence in the country than of any ideological concerns.

The Party of Labor ruled Albania with an iron fist and without any organized opposition until 1991, for the most part under its unequivocal leader, **Enver Hoxha**. After Hoxha's death in 1985, the leadership was taken over by **Ramiz Alia**, who ruled the country until the end of the dictatorship. The original program, statutes and organizational structure of the Party of Labor were set forth at the first party congress in 1948. As opposed to all other ruling communist parties of the Eastern bloc, the Albanian Party of Labor did not de-Stalinize in the mid-1950s. It remained inspired to the very end by the "revolutionary" teachings of Marx, Engels, Lenin and Stalin, the so-called national liberation movement of **World War II**, class struggle and the voluminous works of Enver Hoxha. In 1961, the Party of Labor broke relations with Nikita Khrushchev, and thus with the rest of eastern Europe, and allied itself in its international relations with the Chinese communists under Mao Tse-Tung until 1978. Thereafter, there followed a period of isolation and gradual decay until the introduction of pluralist democracy in 1991.

In its formal structure, the highest organ of the Party of Labor was the party congress (*Kongresi i Partisë*). These highly ritualized mass meetings were held every four to five years in the first week of November. They involved about 800 delegates and were devoid of any open discussion. Between the party congresses, the highest organ of the party was the Central Committee (*Komiteti Qendror*) composed of ca. 110-130 members, of which two-thirds were full members and one-third candidate members. Although theoretically an executive organ, the Central Committee was completely dependent on the Politburo (*Byroja Politike*) for any decision-making. The Politburo and the first secretary of the party were elected by the Central Committee to lead the party. Actual power lay, however, in the hands of the Secretariat of the Central Committee (*Sekretariati i Komitetit Qendror*) composed of four to six loyal members responsible for various fields. The government ministries were directly subordinate to the members of the secretariat, thus guaranteeing the rule of the party in all affairs of government and state.

At the end of the dictatorship, the Party of Labor evolved into the **Socialist Party** of Albania. A small minority of communists under Razi Brahimi (1931-) and Hysni Milloshi (1948-) founded an Albanian Communist Party on 8 November 1991, which was subsequently banned from 16 July 1992 to 10 July 1998. *See also* KONARE.

PASKALI, ODHISE (1903.12.30-1985.12.29). Sculptor. Odhise Paskali was born in the **Përmet** region. In February 1919, after taking part in the funeral of nationalist leader **Ismail Qemal bey Vlora**, he set off for Italy to study in Turin. He finished secondary school there in 1923 and studied philology and art at the University of Turin from November 1923 to 1927, graduating with a degree in art history. On his return to Albania, he cofounded the "friends of art" society on 15 April 1931 and organized a major national art exhibition in **Tirana**. In the 1930s, he taught art and completed a number of national monuments in different Albanian cities, principally of figures of Albanian history: Ismail Qemal bey Vlora (Vlora 1932), **Themistokli Gërmenji (Korça** 1932), **Çerçiz Topulli (Gjirokastra** 1934), and **Scanderbeg (Kukës** 1939), etc. After **World War II**, as director of the **National Gallery**, he continued his work, with sculptures not only of historical figures, but also of **communist** partisans and leaders, including a well-known bust of **Enver Hoxha** (1966). He completed the Scanderbeg monument which now stands in the heart of Tirana in 1968, with two other sculptors. Odhise Paskali is by far the best-known Albanian sculptor of the twentieth century.

PASKO, DHIMITËR. *See* KUTELI, MITRUSH.

PATSCH, CARL (1865.09.12-1945.02.21). German-language historian and archeologist. Carl Patsch was born in Kowac in Bohemia and studied history, **geography** and classical philology at the University of Prague, where he finished his doctorate in 1889. He taught in Vienna and Sarajevo, and worked in the latter city for the Bosnian-Hercegovinian Museum. In 1908, Patsch founded the Institute for Balkan Research (Institut für Balkanforschung) in Sarajevo, where he remained until the end of **World War I**. In 1921, he became professor of Slavic history at the University of Vienna and was subsequently a member of the

Austrian Academy of Sciences. Patsch is remembered for his articles on **Illyrian** and Thracian antiquity and, in a closer connection with Albania, for the monograph *Der Sandschak Berat in Albanien* (The Sandjak of **Berat** in Albania), Vienna 1904.

PEÇI, ALEKSANDËR (1951.07.11-). Composer. Peçi was born in **Tirana**. He attended the Jordan Misja Academy from 1965 to 1969 and majored in composition in 1969-1974 at the Academy of Fine Arts (*Instituti i Lartë i Arteve*). From 1979 to 1986, he directed the Albanian folk **music** and dance ensemble, and subsequently taught music. Since the fall of the dictatorship, he has taken part in conductors' workshops in Amsterdam (1992) and Paris (1997), and is cofounder of the Albanian society for modern music. Aleksandër Peçi is noted in particular for his piano concerts, light music, rhapsodies and **film** soundtracks.

PEÇI, SHEFQET (1906.06.30-1995.10.22). Political figure of the **communist** period. Shefqet Peçi was born in the village of Picar near **Gjirokastra** and served as a military officer in **King Zog**'s army. He played an active role in the communist resistance movement in **World War II** and was commander of the third army corps in 1944. After the war he was promoted to the rank of major general, 1949, and served as minister of communications, 1949-1951; minister of industry and mining, 1951; chairman of the state planning commission, 1955; minister without portfolio, 1966-1968; vice-chairman of the People's Assembly, 1970-1982; and chairman of the war veterans' committee from December 1982 to 1991. Shefqet Peçi was a member of the Central Committee from June 1950. He was sent to prison in 1995 and died there.

PECI, SOTIR (1873-1932). Publisher. Sotir Peci, also spelled Sotir Pettsy, came from Dardha, a village near **Korça**. Like many people in the Korça region at the beginning of the twentieth century, he emigrated to America, where he published *Kombi* (The Nation), the first Albanian-language newspaper in North America. *Kombi* lasted for three years until 1909 when it was succeeded in February of that year by *Dielli* (The Sun), founded by **Fan Noli** and **Faik bey Konitza**. Peci also attended the **Congress of Monastir** from 14 to 22 November 1908. From 1909, he taught mathematics and science in **Elbasan**. Peci was elected as vice chairman of the **Congress of Lushnja** and was subsequently appointed minister of **education**, when he laid the foundations for a national system of public schooling. He remained in government office during the **Democratic Revolution** of Fan Noli in 1924, but blocked important reform legislation. When **Ahmet Zogu** took power at the end of that year, Peci fled abroad and joined the *Bashkimi Kombëtar* (The National Union). In 1927, he was pardoned by Zog as part of a general amnesty.

PEJA, LEAGUE OF. *See* LEAGUE OF PEJA.

PEKMEZI, GJERGJ (1872.04.23-1938.02.24). Linguist and publisher. Pekmezi was born in Tushemisht near **Pogradec** and studied in Monastir (1884) and Belgrade from 1890 to 1894. From 1894 to 1898, he studied at the University of Vienna and then began to teach Albanian. In 1916, he was a leading member of the **Albanian Literary Commission** in **Shkodra** under the auspices of Austro-Hungary. From 1920 to 1924 and 1926 to 1928, he served as Albanian consul in Austria. From 1928 until his death, he taught Albanian at the University of Vienna. Gjergj Pekmezi was the author of *Vorläufiger Bericht über das Studium des albanesischen Dialekts von Elbasan* (Preliminary Report on the Study of the Albanian Dialect of Elbasan), Vienna 1901; *Grammatik der albanesischen Sprache* (Grammar of the Albanian Language), Vienna 1908; *Bleta shqypëtare e Thimi Mitkos* (The Albanian Bee of Thimi Mitko), Vienna 1924; coauthor of *Bibliographija shqype / Albanesische Bibliographie* (Albanian Bibliography), Vienna 1909; *Sprachführer zur schnellen Erlernung der albanischen Sprache* (Manual for Learning the Albanian Language Quickly), Vienna 1913; and *Lehr- und Lesebuch des Albanischen* (Manual and Reader of Albanian), Vienna 1913.

PELASGIANS. The Pelasgians were reputed in antiquity to have been a people inhabiting Thessaly, Greece and the islands of the eastern Mediterranean before the arrival of the Greeks. Although often mentioned by ancient Greek authors, they are now thought to have been a legendary or mythical people rather than a concrete ethnic group. In the nineteenth and early twentieth centuries, there was a widely held theory of the Pelasgian origins of the Albanian people. This was subsequently replaced by the theory of the **Illyrian** origins of the Albanian people, although the former still surfaces sporadically.

PELLEGRINI, GIOVAN BATTISTA (1921.02.23-). Italian scholar and linguist. Pellegrini was born in Belluno and graduated in linguistics in 1945 from the University of Padua. A noted figure of Italian and Balkan linguistics, he was head of the chair of linguistics at the University of Padua for many years and taught Albanian linguistics there. Among his publications of Albanian interest are: *Introduzione allo studio della lingua albanese* (Introduction to the Study of the Albanian Language), Padua 1977; *Ricerche linguistiche balcanico-danubiane* (Balkan Danubian Linguistic Research), Rome 1992; and *Avviamento alla linguistica albanese* (Beginning Albanian Linguistics), Palermo 1995.

PËLLUMBI, SERVET (1936.12.14-). Political figure and high-ranking member of the **Socialist Party**. Pëllumbi was born in **Korça** and graduated in philosophy in 1960 from the University of Leningrad. He thereafter taught philosophy for thirty years at the **communist** party academy in **Tirana**. He is author of *Dritëhije të tranzicionit* (The Penumbras of the Transition), Tirana 2000, and *Të mendosh ndryshe* (Thinking Differently), Tirana 2001.

Servet Pëllumbi has been a member of the Albanian **parliament** since 1992 and is active in international affairs. He was deputy chairman of the Socialist Party from 1991 to 1996 (chairman **Fatos Nano** was in prison from 1993 to 1997), and headed the Albanian delegations to the parliamentary assemblies of the Black Sea Economic Cooperation Council from 1997 to 2001. He is currently speaker of the Albanian parliament.

PEQIN, DISTRICT OF. Region of local government administration. The District of Peqin (*Rrethi i Peqinit*), with its administrative headquarters in the town of Peqin, borders on the districts of **Kavaja** to the west, **Tirana** to the north, **Elbasan** to the east and **Lushnja** to the south. It has a surface area of 109 square kilometers and a present **population** of 32,518 (in 2000). It is the second smallest district in Albania, after **Kuçova**. The word Peqin was recorded in an **Ottoman** census in 1431 as Biklenet and in 1528 as Peklin.

PERCY, JOCELYN, Sir (1871.03.09-1952.08.25). British officer. Sir Jocelyn Percy embarked upon a military career at Sandhurst. He served in the Boer War in South Africa (1899-1901) and in Pakistan (1907-1912). During **World War I**, he rose to the rank of major-general and chief of staff of the Second Army. In 1919-1920, he then headed the British military mission with General Piotr Nikolayevich Wrangel in southern Russia. He retired from the army in 1920 and took up farming in Canada.

In the autumn of 1927, Sir Jocelyn Percy was appointed by **King Zog** as inspector general of the Albanian Gendarmerie. Assisted by a small group of British officers, he effected the complete pacification of the country, gradually establishing law and order and eradicating banditry. He was in Albania until October 1938, when the Inspectorate General was closed down. He died in Bishopsteignton in Devon.

PERISTERI, PILO (1909.12.10-). Political figure of the **communist** period. Pilo Peristeri was born in **Korça**, where he worked as a tinsmith and professional soccer player. He was a founding member of the Albanian Communist Party in 1941 and became a political commissar during the resistance movement of **World War II**. After the communist takeover, he served as chairman of the trade union, 1951-1958; vice chairman of the People's Assembly, 1956-1966; director of the **Enver Hoxha** Mechanical Plant in **Tirana**, 1966-1978; and vice-chairman of the Democratic Front (*Fronti Demokratik*), 1979-1991. Peristeri was a member of the Central Committee from 1948 to 1991 and a candidate member of the Politburo from 1952 to 1981. He was related by marriage to **Rita Marko** and **Manush Myftiu** and, despite his advanced age, was still in the top party hierarchy at the end of the dictatorship.

PËRMET, DISTRICT OF. Region of local government administration. The District of Përmet (*Rrethi i Përmetit*), with its administrative headquarters in the town of Përmet, borders on the districts of **Tepelena** to the west, **Skrapar** to the north, **Kolonja** to the east and **Gjirokastra** and the Republic of **Greece** to the south. It has a surface area of 930 square kilometers and a present **population** of 36,746 (in 2000). It has the second lowest population density in the country, after Kolonja. The word Përmet was recorded in 1431 as Premeti.

PËRNASKA, REMZI. Linguist. Remzi Përnaska worked for the Institute of Linguistics and Literature in **Tirana**. After the fall of the dictatorship, he emigrated to France and taught Albanian at the Ecole Pratique des Hautes Etudes in Paris until his retirement in 1998. He pursued his doctorate at the University of Paris VII in 1996 with a dissertation on *La syntaxe de l'énoncé en albanais contemporain: la syntaxe des formes atones des pronoms personnels* (The Syntax of the Utterance in Contemporary Albanian: The Syntax of the Unstressed Forms of the Personal Pronouns), Lille 1997. Përnaska is the author of *Kundranori me parafjalë në gjuhën e sotme shqipe* (The Object with Preposition iri Modern Albanian), Peja 1996; and coauthor of *Parlons albanais* (Let's Speak Albanian), Paris 1999.

PETROTTA, GAETANO (1882-1952.10.29). Italian scholar and literary historian from Palermo in Sicily. He began publishing in the field of Albanian studies before **World War II**. He is remembered in particular for his *Popolo, lingua e letteratura albanese* (Albanian People, Language and Literature), Palermo 1931; *Saggio di bibliografia albanese, 1500-1930* (Essay on Albanian Bibliography, 1500-1930), Palermo 1931; and *Svoglimento storico della cultura e della letteratura albanese* (The Historical Development of Albanian Culture and Literature), Palermo 1950.

PETTIFER, JAMES (1949.04.06-). British writer and journalist specializing in the southern Balkans. Pettifer was born in Hereford, did his masters at Oxford University, and was later visiting professor at the Institute of Balkan Studies of the University of Thessalonika in Greece. He was an honorary research fellow of the Byzantine and Greek Studies department of Birmingham University and a professor at the Conflict Studies Research Centre of the Royal Military Academy of Sandhurst. Pettifer is the author of *The New Macedonian Question,* London 1999; *Blue Guide: Albania and Kosovo,* London 2001; *Concept for a New Reality: Dialogue with Hashim Thaçi,* Prishtina 2001; and coauthor with **Miranda Vickers** of *Albania: From Anarchy to a Balkan Identity,* London 1996.

PEZA, CONFERENCE OF. *See* CONFERENCE OF PEZA.

PEZA, MYSLIM (1897.05.01-1984). Resistance fighter. Born in Peza near **Tirana**, Myslim Peza fought against **Ahmet Zogu** in the 1920s and shot the commander of Zogu's personal guards, Osman Bali, on 8 September 1926 in Tirana. He lived abroad from 1930 to 1939. In 1940, he organized one of the first guerrilla bands to fight openly against **Italian** rule. He was active during **World War II** in the Tirana region. It was due to his fame during the war that **Enver Hoxha** chose the village of Peza as a venue for the resistance conference of 16 September 1942. Myslim Peza is said to have been the only early guerrilla fighter to have later developed a close relationship with the **communists**. After the war, he was nominated deputy chairman of the presidium of the People's Assembly (1946-1982).

PHILBY, KIM (1912-1988.05.11). British intelligence agent and spy. Harold Adrian Russell Philby, known as Kim Philby, was born in Ambala, India. He finished Westminster School in 1928 and attended Trinity College, Cambridge, where he was recruited by Soviet agents in 1933-1934. He later worked for British intelligence while spying on behalf of the Soviet Union, and indeed became one of the most famous spies of the twentieth century. Philby defected to Moscow in 1963 and was rewarded the Order of Lenin and the title of general by the KGB. It was his reports to Moscow, that were sent on to **Tirana**, which foiled the efforts of anticommunist forces to penetrate Albania during the early 1950s. It is thought that hundreds of anticommunist fighters fell into the hands of the **communist** authorities as a result of his secret activities. His memoirs appeared in the volume *My Silent War*, London 1968.

PHOINIKE. Archeological site near the present-day town of Finiq in the southern District of **Delvina**. The ancient fortified settlement of Phoinike, known in Albanian as Finiq, is situated on the top of a 270-meter-high hill eight kilometers inland from **Saranda**, which was its port. In the third century B.C. its large acropolis, with walls seven times the length of those in Athens, was the most important settlement in **Northern Epirus** and was capital of the region of Chaonia, i.e., of the **Illyrian** Chaones tribe. Phoinike was probably founded in the sixth century B.C. but the earliest archeological evidence dates from the fourth century B.C. A peace treaty between Rome and Macedon was concluded here in 205 B.C. Phoinike is mentioned by Polybius who called it the richest, strongest and best fortified city in Epirus. The fortification walls and a small temple were excavated by Italian archeologist Luigi M. Ugolini (1895-1936) in 1924-1926. Subsequent excavations in the 1960s revealed the presence of a theater and an early Christian basilica dating from the sixth century A.D.

PIPA, ARSHI (1920.07.28-1997.07.20). Scholar and writer. Arshi Pipa was born in **Shkodra** where he attended school until 1938.

His first poetry, composed in the late 1930s in Shkodra, was collected in the volume *Lundërtarë* (Sailors), Tirana 1944. Pipa studied philosophy at the University of Florence, where he received the degree of "dottore in filosofia" in 1942 with a dissertation on Henri Bergson (1859-1941). He thereafter worked as a teacher in Shkodra and **Tirana**. In 1944, he was editor of the short-lived Tirana literary monthly *Kritika* (Criticism). Unwilling to conform after the radical transition of power at the end of the war, he was arrested in April 1946 and imprisoned for ten years. After his release in 1956, he escaped to Yugoslavia and emigrated to the **United States** two years later. He held teaching posts at various American universities and until his retirement was professor of Italian at the University of Minnesota in Minneapolis. Pipa digested his ten years of horror in the prisons and labor camps of **Durrës**, Vloçisht, **Gjirokastra** and Burrel in *Libri i burgut* (The Prison Book), Rome 1959, a 246-page collection of verse. He has published two other volumes of poetry in **Gheg** dialect: *Rusha* (Rusha), Munich 1968, and *Meridiana* (Meridiana), Munich 1969, the latter being a collection in the romantic and nostalgic vein of Giacomo Leopardi.

Of greater impact were Pipa's scholarly publications, in particular his literary criticism. Among such works are the three-volume literary study *Trilogia albanica*, Munich 1978, and a monograph on *Montale and Dante*, Minneapolis 1968. He also published a controversial sociolinguistic study on the formation of standard Albanian (*gjuha letrare*) as the official **language** of Albania, entitled *The Politics of Language in Socialist Albania*, New York 1989; a collection of fifteen political essays entitled *Albanian Stalinism: Ideo-political Aspects*, New York 1990; and a study on the Albanian **literature** of the socialist realist period, *Contemporary Albanian literature*, New York 1991. In later years, he edited the short-lived periodical *Albanica* in Washington, D.C., where he lived with his sister in retirement.

PLASARI, AUREL (1956-). Writer and intellectual figure. Aurel Plasari was born in **Tirana**, son of historian Ndreçi Plasari (1920-1996). He studied **language** and **literature** at the University of Tirana and worked from 1983 to 1992 for the literary and cultural periodical *Nëntori* (November). He has taught Albanian literature at the university and is currently director of the **National Library** in Tirana.

Aurel Plasari is a critical intellectual with many determined views, which have forced the Albanian public into much self-reflection. Apart from his translations of Latin American, Romanian and Russian literature and many refreshingly polemic articles, he is the author of *Don Kishoti zbret në Shqipëri dhe ese të tjera* (Don Quixote Lands in Albania, and Other Essays), Tirana 1990; *Letërsia dhe muret: dy përgjigje një ankëtë* (Literature and Walls: Two Answers One Inquiry), Tirana 1993; *Vija e Teodosit rishfaqet; nga do t'ia mbajnë shqiptarët?* (The Theodosius Line Reappears: Which Side Will the Albanians Take?), Tirana 1995; *Përballë një kulture të vdekjes* (In the Face of a Culture of Death); Tirana 1997; and *Biopolitika a ekziston në Shqipëri* (Do Biopolitics Exist in Albania?), Tirana 1999; as well as literary studies on **Anton Harapi**, Mitrush Kuteli and **Gjergj Fishta**.

PLURALISM, POLITICAL. After half a century of one-party dictatorship, political pluralism was introduced in Albania at the thirteenth congress of the Central Committee of the **Party of Labor** on 11 December 1990. A day later, the **Democratic Party** was formed, as the first noncommunist **political party** since **World War II**. In the first pluralist elections held on 31 March 1991, the Party of Labor and the Democratic Party won 94.88 percent of the votes. By 1992, about twenty-five political parties had been founded. Many of these soon amalgamated or vanished, but just as many others were formed over the following years. A total of twenty-eight political parties and formations took part in the elections of 24 June 2001.

POGONI, BARDHYL (1926.01.31-1985.10.24). Scholar. Bardhyl Pogoni was born in **Tirana** and went to school in **Korça** and, from 1935 to 1936, in Tirana. Having received a scholarship to study in Austria, he attended a secondary school in Vienna from 1942 to 1944. In 1945, he emigrated to the **United States**. In 1945-1949, he studied at the University of Western Kentucky and finished his doctorate in comparative literature at the University of Indiana with a dissertation on *Albanian Writing Systems* (1967). From 1961 to 1968, he chaired the School of English Language and Literature of the University of Tripoli in Libya and, in 1968, replaced **Namik Ressuli** as head of the chair of Albanian studies at the Oriental Institute of the University (Istituto Universitario Orientale) in Naples, Italy, where he worked until his death. He is the author of *Drithma dëshire* (The Quivering of Desire), Tirana 1944; and *Contemporary Albanian Poems*, Naples 1985. As a devout Muslim **Bektashi**, he also translated the writings of **Baba Rexhebi** in the volume *The Mysticism of Islam and Bektashism* (Naples 1984).

POGRADEC. Town in the **District of Pogradec**, of which it is the administrative center. **Population** in Dec. 1999: 33,559. Pogradec is situated on the south bank of Lake **Ohrid** and is the terminus of the **railway** line from **Durrës**, which was built to export ore from the large nearby lead, iron and nickel mine. The banks of the lake have been settled since prehistoric days. In **Illyrian** times, the region was inhabited by a tribe called the *Encheliae* "eel people." Pogradec was referred to briefly as *Pogradas* by **Evliya Çelebi** who passed through it in 1670. The word is Slavic and means "by the town."

Pogradec is remembered as the home of poet **Lasgush Poradeci**. It was a center of domestic **tourism** in Albania before and during the **communist** dictatorship and has a considerable potential for development if the environment is not further damaged, i.e., if the beach and water in this part of the lake are preserved from increasing pollution.

POGRADEC, DISTRICT OF. Region of local government administration. The District of Pogradec (*Rrethi i Pogradecit*), with its administrative headquarters in the town of **Pogradec**, borders on the districts of **Gramsh** to the west, **Librazhd** to the north, **Korça** to the south and Lake **Ohrid** and the Republic of **Macedonia** to the east. It has a surface area of 725 square kilometers and a present **population** of 73,930 (in 2000).

POLITICAL PARTIES. After half a century of one-party dictatorship in the **communist** period, Albania now has a myriad of political parties, most of which are run by elderly men and have only marginal support. The first opposition party to arise in postcommunist Albania was the **Democratic Party**, which has remained a major political force. The **Socialist Party**, also with major political support, arose from the ashes of the communist **Party of Labor**. Early to arise on the new political landscape in the first half of the 1990s were also the **Republican Party**, **Omonia** representing the **Greek minority**, and two social democratic currents: the **Social Democratic Party,** which has been in coalition with the Socialists, and the Social Democratic Union, which has been more allied with the Democratic Party. Other parties have evolved from splits in existing parties. The **Democratic Alliance Party** and the **New Democratic Party** both arose, for instance, from dissent within the ranks of the Democratic Party. Some pre-communist movements have also been revived as political parties: the National Front (**Balli Kombëtar**) derives its inspiration from the anticommunist resistance movement of **World War II**, and the **Movement for Legality** (*Lëvizja e Legalitetit*) is a faction seeking the restoration of the monarchy instituted in the late 1920s under **King Zog**. Most small parties represent special interest groups or, more often, the dynamics of particular public leaders.

The great number of tiny parties which has arisen in recent years reflects to a substantial extent the inherent inability of Albanians, and Albanian politicians in particular, to work together for a common good. Traditional concepts of "left" and "right" are difficult to apply in Albanian politics. The leading "leftist" Socialist Party and the leading "rightist" Democratic Party have, for instance, differed very little over the past decade in their concrete policies.

POLLO, GENC (1963-). Political figure. Genc Pollo, son of historian **Stefanaq Pollo**, was born in **Tirana** and graduated with a degree in history from the university there. He worked initially as a research expert at the Academy of Sciences, 1986-1988, and studied in Vienna from 1988 to 1990 on an Austrian government scholarship.

In his political career, Genc Pollo was cofounder of the **Democratic Party** and soon became its spokesman. In the period 1992-1996, he was a close advisor to President **Sali Berisha** and remained faithful to him to the end of the latter's regime in 1997 and thereafter. In 1999, he finally challenged Berisha for the party leadership and came to be the main proponent of the reform wing of the party. On 2 February 2001, this reform wing split away from Berisha and the Democratic Party to form the **New Democratic Party** (*Partia Demokratike e Re*), of which Genc Pollo is currently the head.

POLLO, STEFANAQ (1923.02.07-1997.05.15). Scholar and representative historian of the **communist** period. Stefanaq Pollo was born in **Përmet** and attended secondary school in **Korça**. After **World War II**, he became editor-in-chief of the newspapers *Zëri i rinisë* (The Voice of Youth) and *Bashkimi* (The Union). In 1945, he studied history in the Soviet Union and began teaching college in **Tirana** in 1951. For thirty-five years, he was director of the Institute of History at the Academy of Sciences. With **Aleks**

Buda, he was coauthor of the standard *Historia e popullit shqiptar* (History of the Albanian People), Tirana 1965-1967; and *Historia e Shqipërisë* (History of Albania), Tirana 1983-1984. In coauthorship with **Arben Puto**, he was also responsible for the French-language *Histoire de l'Albanie des origines à nos jours,* Roanne 1974, translated into English as *History of Albania from Its Origins to Present Day,* London 1981.

POLYPHONIC MUSIC. Albanian polyphony (*polifonia*) is a type of traditional vocal **music** specific to southern Albania and northern Greece, and is by far the most popular form of folk music in the south of the country. It is normally sung without the accompaniment of instruments and is often improvised by two or three lead singers who set forth the melody and text. The other singers accompany the lead singers as a chorus with a so-called *iso,* a drone at a constant pitch, which, to foreign ears, sounds something like a dissonant bleating of sheep. The drone must be continuous, not interrupted. Traditionally it is said that "the drone must be kept up all the time so that not even a bullet can get through, otherwise the voices get lost." As with other forms of folk music in Albania, men traditionally sing with men and **women** with women, though there are mixed polyphonic groups nowadays. The first lead singer is called the *marrës* "the taker" who alternates with the second, called a *mbajtës* "the holder" or *kthyes* "the returner." Though there are strict rules for the singing of Albanian polyphonic music, there are also many regional variations. Polyphony is unknown in the north of the country.

POPULATION. According to the survey of April 2001, there were 3,087,159 people in the Republic of Albania, down from 3,259,800 in 1991 due to emigration. If the population working abroad temporarily (primarily in **Greece** and **Italy**) is included, the total population comes to 3,401,200 (as of 1 January 2000).

Albania has a very young population. After **Kosova**, it is the youngest in Europe, with an average age of twenty-nine. The crude birth rate in 1999 was 17.2, down from 25.2 in 1990, and the abortion rate in 1999 was 344 per 1,000 live births. Average life expectancy rose for 1999 to 74.0 (71.7 for men and 76.4 for **women**).

Albania has a high, though decreasing, proportion of its population in rural areas. In 1989, only 35.7 percent of the Albanian population was urban; in 1999, this figure rose to 45.9 percent. This increase derives from the high level of internal migration, which has resulted in a clear and massive depopulation of the poorest areas of the country, i.e., the north and northeast regions, and in a higher concentration of people in the main urban centers, in particular **Tirana** and **Durrës**. The primary reasons for migration have been poverty, the limited opportunities for finding jobs and difficult living conditions.

PORADECI, LASGUSH (1899.12.27-1987.11.12). Poet. Lasgush Poradeci, pseudonym of Llazar Gusho, is now regarded by many as the greatest Albanian poet of the twentieth century. He was born in **Pogradec** and attended a Romanian-language school in Monastir (Bitola), Macedonia, from 1909 to 1916 and a French-language secondary school in Athens until 1920. He later moved to Bucharest, a stay which was to have a decisive influence on his literary development. It was here that he met and befriended the romantic poet **Asdreni**, whom he replaced as secretary of the Albanian colony in 1922, short-story writer **Mitrush Kuteli** and numerous Romanian writers and poets. He also began publishing verse in various Albanian-language periodicals: *Shqipëri' e re* (New Albania), an illustrated national weekly published in Constanza, and *Dielli* (The Sun) of Boston, among others. His verse of this period was already revealing a certain theosophical affinity to the Romanian lyric poet Mihai Eminescu (1850-1889).

A scholarship provided by the **Fan Noli** government in 1924 enabled him to continue his studies at the University of Graz in southeastern Austria where he spent a total of ten years. In May 1933, he finished his doctorate there with a dissertation on *Der verkannte Eminescu und seine volkstümlich-heimatliche Ideologie* (The Unappreciated Eminescu and His Native Folk Ideology). The following year, Poradeci returned to Albania and taught art at a secondary school in **Tirana**, where he remained during the war. From 1944 until 1947, the first turbulent years of **communist** rule, he was unemployed and lived with his wife in Tirana on the latter's meager salary as a teacher. After brief employment at the Institute of Sciences, forerunner of the University of Tirana, he got a job translating **literature** for the state-owned Naim Frashëri publishing company, where he worked, keeping a low profile, until his retirement in 1974.

Lasgush Poradeci is the author of two much-enjoyed collections of poetry. *Vallja e yjve* (The Dance of the Stars) and *Ylli i zemrës* (The Star of the Heart), published in Romania in 1933 and 1937, respectively, are indeed just as much a revolution in Albanian verse as was **Migjeni**'s *Vargjet e lira* (Free Verse). Apart from the two main poetry collections of the 1930s, Poradeci published some verse in literary journals of the late 1930s and 1940s, in particular in **Branko Merxhani**'s cultural monthly *Përpjekja shqiptare* (The Albanian Endeavor). With the rise of **Stalinism**, however, the venerable quill of Lasgushi, as he was to be affectionately known to posterity, began to run dry. A few works did appear from time to time in the Tirana literary periodicals *Drita* (The Light) and *Nëntori* (November), carefully perused beforehand by party censors, but Poradeci's main field of activity in the socialist period was, nolens volens, translation, a safer haven for literary heretics.

Primordial to the poetic work of Lasgush Poradeci are the waters of Lake **Ohrid** on the Albanian-Macedonian border. It was in his native town of Pogradec that he spent his last summers in a run-down little house, tending his garden, and strolling along the lake with his dog. Lake Ohrid never ceased to fascinate and enchant him. He died in absolute poverty in Tirana.

PORTS. Albania has four ports for maritime transportation: **Durrës**, **Vlora**, **Saranda** and Shëngjin, which were used increasingly in the 1990s. The loading and unloading volume of ports in 1999 was seventy-one percent greater than it was in 1991. The largest and by far most important port is Durrës, which in 1999 accounted for 72.5 percent of all loading and unloading.

International maritime passenger transportation has also grown. There was a seventy-eight percent increase in 1999 as compared to 1994. In 1999, 365,983 passengers entered Albania by sea. There are daily ferry services from Durrës to Bari in southern **Italy**, as well as frequent services to Ancona and Trieste. From Vlora, there are ferry connections to nearby Otranto and Brindisi, and from Saranda, there is a regular daily connection to Corfu.

POSTOLI, FOQION (1889-1927.10.02). Sentimental novelist and playwright. Postoli was born in **Korça** of a merchant family. He studied commerce for two years in Istanbul where he had relatives and, subsequently, like many people from Korça at the time, emigrated with his family to the **United States**, settling in Massachusetts. There he worked as a secretary for the Brockton chapter of the **Vatra federation** and collaborated in the latter's main medium, the Boston newspaper *Dielli* (The Sun), where much of his writing was first published. In 1921, after a fourteen-year absence, he returned to Albania to help found the Albanian

Autocephalic **Orthodox** Church. The two novels and one play for which Postoli are remembered were all written in America within the years 1910-1919 and were first published in the pages of *Dielli*. His first novel, *Për mprojtjen e atdheut* (In Defense of the Homeland), 1921, is a typical product of the romantic nationalism of the late **Rilindja** period, a sentimental love story full of patriotic ideals and virtue. The novel *Lulja e kujtimit* (The Flower of Remembrance), Korça 1924, though suffering from the same artificiality and triteness of plot, is, artistically speaking, a slight improvement. This two-part tale of romance and patriotism proved more popular and became one of the best-known Albanian novels of the 1920s and 1930s.

POUQUEVILLE, FRANÇOIS (1770.11.04-1838.12.20). French scholar, diplomat and historian. François Charles Hugues Laurent Pouqueville, born in Merlerault (Orne) in Normandy, was educated in Caen and Lisieux and studied medicine at the Sorbonne in Paris under Antoine Dubois. As a physician, he took part in the French expedition to Egypt. On 25 November 1798, on his way back to France, he was captured by pirates and sent to Navarino in the Peloponnese, where he was imprisoned and held for ransom by the Turks. He spent two years in prison in Istanbul and returned to France in 1801. It was in prison that he began writing his travel memoirs, which were dedicated to Napoleon and published in the three-volume edition: *Voyage en Morée, à Constantinople, en Albanie et dans plusieurs autres parties de l'Empire othoman pendant les années 1798, 1799, 1800 et 1801*, Paris 1805 (Engl. transl. *Travels through the Morea, Albania and Several Other Parts of the Ottoman Empire to Constantinople during the Years 1798, 1799, 1800 and 1801*, London 1806).

The book was exceptionally successful and attracted the attention of the French government, which appointed him consul general in Janina, to the court of **Ali Pasha Tepelena**. He remained there until 1815, had a close personal relationship with the "Lion of Janina" and was able to travel widely in southern Albania. Pouqueville's works, including detailed descriptions of southern Albania, have also been published in English in the editions: *Travels in Greece and Turkey, Comprehending a Particular Account of the Morea, Albania, etc.*, London 1820; and *Travels in Epirus, Albania, Macedonia and Thessaly*, London 1998.

PREFECTURES. The Republic of Albania is once again divided into larger units of local administration called prefectures. The prefecture, Alb. *prefektura*, also known as a *qark*, groups an average of two to four of the districts, Alb. *rreth*, which continue to exist and were previously the only units of local administration during the **communist** period. There are now twelve prefectures in Albania. They are: **Berat**, population 193,020, composed of the Districts of Berat, **Kuçova** and **Skrapar**; **Dibra**, population 189,854, composed of the Districts of Dibra, **Bulqiza** and Mat; **Durrës**, population 245,112, composed of the Districts of Durrës and **Kruja**; **Elbasan**, population 381,213, composed of the Districts of Elbasan, **Gramsh**, **Librazhd** and **Peqin**; **Fier**, population 382,483, composed of the Districts of Fier, **Lushnja** and **Mallakastra**; **Gjirokastra**, population 93,934, composed of the Districts of Gjirokastra, **Përmet** and **Tepelena**; **Korça**, population 265,125, composed of the Districts of Korça, **Pogradec**, **Devoll** and **Kolonja**; **Kukës**, population 111,393, composed of the Districts of Kukës, Has and **Tropoja**; **Lezha**, population 159,169, composed of the Districts of Lezha, **Kurbin** and **Mirdita**; **Tirana**, population 597,676, composed of the Districts of Tirana and **Kavaja**; **Shkodra**, population 256,022, composed of the Districts of Shkodra, **Malësia e Madhe** and **Puka**; and **Vlora**, population 192,739, composed of the Districts of **Vlora**, **Delvina** and **Saranda** (population statistics from the 2001 census).

PRENNUSHI, VINÇENC (1885.09.04-1949.03.19). Catholic religious figure, poet, folklorist and translator. Prennushi was born in **Shkodra** and studied at a **Catholic** college in Austria. He was ordained as a **Franciscan** priest on 25 March 1908. Fascinated by the oral culture of northern Albania, Prennushi began collecting folk songs from the mountain tribes. His compilation of folklore material was published by the Austrian archeologist and historian **Carl Patsch** in the volume *Kângë popullore gegnishte* (Gheg folk songs), Sarajevo 1911, and made a major contribution to the study of Albanian oral **literature**. In 1924, he published a volume of elegant lyric verse in **Gheg** dialect entitled *Gjeth e lule* (Leaves and Flowers), Shkodra 1924, which was reprinted in 1931. This collection of sixty-five poems contains verse of both nationalist and religious inspiration. In his ecclesiastical career, Vinçenc Prennushi served as a provincial from 1929 to 1936. On 19 March 1936, he was made bishop of Sapa, and, in 1940, he was appointed archbishop of **Durrës**, thus becoming one of the two highest dignitaries of the Catholic Church in Albania. According to his contemporaries, he was a man of virtue and humility and enjoyed great respect among the Catholic population. Apparently not politically active despite his lofty position in the Church hierarchy, Prennushi was arrested by the **communist** authorities after the war, tortured and sentenced by a military court in Durrës to twenty years of imprisonment and hard labor as an enemy of the people. Weakened by prison conditions and suffering from asthma and heart disease, the sixty-three-year-old archbishop died in the prison hospital.

PRESPA, LAKE. Lake Prespa is situated in southeastern Albania and forms the border of three countries (Albania, Macedonia and Greece). There are actually two lakes: Greater Prespa (285 square kilometers) and Lesser Prespa (44 square kilometers). They are at an altitude of 853 meters and are comparatively deep, up to 54 meters. The water from Lake Prespa flows underground into Lake **Ohrid**. It is in the villages on the western banks of Greater Prespa that the Macedonian **Slavic minority** in Albania lives.

PRIFTI, NAUM (1932.03.07-). Writer. Naum Prifti was born in the village of Rehova in the southeastern District of **Kolonja** of a family of stonemasons. He originally studied medicine at the Polytechnic University in **Tirana** and worked for some time there and in **Korça** as a medical assistant. His love of writing, however, caused him to leave the medical profession and return to college to study **language** and **literature** at the University of Tirana. He later worked for the satirical journal *Hosteni* (The Goad) and became a full-time professional writer. Among his many volumes of short stories are: *Tregime të fshatit* (Village Tales), Tirana 1956; *Lëkura e ujkut*, Tirana 1958 (Engl. transl. *The Wolf's Hide*, Tirana 1988); *Çezma e floririt* (The Golden Fountain), Tirana 1960; *Njerëz të kësaj toke* (People of This Land), Tirana 1975; *Njëqind vjet* (A Hundred Years), Tirana 1983; and *Yjet ndritin lart* (Stars Shine High), Peja 2002. Naum Prifti has also written plays and was particularly noted for his numerous volumes of literature for children. Not all of his prose is inspiring, but he produced a number of quite readable short stories. In 1991, he emigrated to the **United States** and has been active on behalf of the **Vatra federation**.

PRIFTI, PETER (1924.11.24-). Albanian-American scholar. Peter Rafael Prifti was born of an **Orthodox** family in Rehova in the southeastern district of **Kolonja**. On 28 March 1940, at the age of fifteen, he emigrated to the **United States** to join his father and older brother, settling initially in Philadelphia. He graduated from Penn State College in 1949 with a bachelor of arts degree and got his masters in philosophy from the University of Pennsylvania in 1955. In 1958, at the invitation of the **Vatra federation**, he moved to Boston to work for the Albanian newspaper *Dielli* (The Sun) for two years. From 1961 to 1976, with the exception of a year of studies in Paris, Prifti worked at the Center for International Studies of the Massachusetts Institute of Technology, where his interests were focused on his Albanian homeland. In 1976, he moved to San Diego to teach Albanian at the Department of Linguistics of the University of California there. Prifti is the author of the following studies: *Albania's Cultural Revolution,* Cambridge 1968; *Albania and Sino-Soviet Relations,* Cambridge 1971; *Socialist Albania since 1944,* Cambridge 1978; *Confrontation in Kosovo: The Albanian-Serb Struggle, 1969-1998,* Boulder 1999; and *Remote Albania: The Politics of Isolationism,* Tirana 1999, as well as of literary translations and numerous articles on Albanian politics and history. He is also coauthor of *Readings in Albanian,* San Diego 1979; *Spoken Albanian,* Ithaca 1980; and *Standard Albanian: A Reference Grammar for Students,* Stanford 1982.

PRISHTINA, HASAN BEY (1873-1933.08.14). Political figure. Born in Vushtrria (Vuçitern) in **Kosova**, Hasan bey Prishtina attended a French secondary school in Salonica and a college of administration in Istanbul. He initially supported the Young Turks and was elected to the Turkish **parliament** in 1908, but lost his position in 1912 as did all the other Albanian deputies. Prishtina took an active part in the 1912 uprising in Kosova and formulated the autonomy demands which were submitted to the Turkish government in August 1912, the so-called fourteen points of Hasan Prishtina. In December 1913, after independence, he served as minister of **agriculture**, and later as minister of postal services. He spent **World War I** organizing divisions of volunteers to fight for Austria-Hungary. In 1918, after the Serb occupation of his native Kosova, he fled abroad with **Bajram Curri** to Vienna and then to Rome, where he was in contact with Macedonian, Croatian and Montenegrin opponents of the new kingdom of **Yugoslavia** and became head of a committee for the National Defense of Kosova.

In 1919, having participated in the Paris Peace Conference on behalf of the committee, Hasan bey Prishtina returned to Albania and in 1921 became a member of parliament for **Dibra**. He took part in a coup d'état that year and served as prime minister for a brief five days from 7 to 12 December. Thereafter, he headed uprisings in Kosova and led several anti-government insurrections in Albania, the latter being suppressed easily by the administrations of **Xhafer bey Ypi** and **Ahmet Zogu**. He returned to **Tirana** during the **Democratic Revolution** under **Fan Noli**, whom he accompanied to the League of Nations. Like most Kosova politicians, Hasan bey Prishtina was a sworn enemy of Ahmet Zogu, the two having attempted to assassinate one another. King Zog eventually won out when Hasan bey was murdered by Zog's agents in Salonica.

PRISHTINA, KADRI (1878-1925). Political figure. Kadri Prishtina, often known as Hoxha Kadriu, was born in Prishtina. He studied education and law in Istanbul, returning home in 1914. At the **Congress of Lushnja**, he was appointed minister of justice and, in 1921, was deputy secretary of the Albanian **parliament**. In December of that year, he was made minister of justice once again in the government of **Hasan bey Prishtina**. In **Shkodra** in 1921, he published the periodical *Udha e së vertetës* (Road of the Truth) and worked as a lawyer.

PRIZREN, LEAGUE OF. *See* LEAGUE OF PRIZREN.

PROGON (late twelfth century). Medieval ruler. Progon reigned over the early Albanian principality of Arbanon, centered around **Kruja**, which lasted from 1190 to 1216. Arbanon itself seems to have attained full political independence in 1204 when the Crusaders defeated the Byzantine Empire in the wake of the Fourth Crusade. Progon's son, Demetrios (r. 1208-1216), married the daughter of the King of Serbia and maintained relations with Dubrovnik and the pope.

PROSI, SANDËR (1920.01.06-1985.03.25). Stage and **film** actor. Sander Prosi was born in **Tirana** and studied dentistry in Austria. In 1948, he made his debut as a stage actor at the **National Theater** in Tirana and, in the course of his career which comprised eighty stage and thirty film roles, was to become one of the best-known actors of his time. He is remembered in particular for the following films: *Në fillim të verës* (At the Beginning of Summer),

1975; *Gjenerali i ushtrisë së vdekur* (The General of the Dead Army), 1975; *Udha e shkronjave* (The Road of Writing), 1978; and *Nëntori i dytë* (The Second November), 1982.

PROTESTANTISM. Religion. The British and Foreign Bible Society began its activities in the **Ottoman Empire** and the Balkans in the nineteenth century when the Sublime Porte grudgingly permitted it to translate and sell bibles and Christian literature. During the 1860s, it hired **Kostandin Kristoforidhi**, a noted figure of Albanian scholarship from **Elbasan**. Kristoforidhi translated the New Testament into a **Gheg** version (1872 in the Latin alphabet) and a **Tosk** version (1879 in the Greek alphabet) as well as several books of the Old Testament. These translations enabled the gospel to be read widely and to be understood in Albania for the first time, and indeed served as a basis for the creation of a modern literary **language**. Also active in the 1860s was the Protestant missionary Padget, whose home in the center of **Shkodra**, complete with tower, was built in 1868.

The early history of Albanian Protestantism is closely linked to the **Qiriazi** or Kyrias family of Monastir (Bitola), now in the Republic of Macedonia. Gjerasim Qiriazi and his brother Gjergj Qiriazi studied at an American bible college in Samokov, Bulgaria, and worked for the British and Foreign Bible Society.

From 1890 to 1912, the American board of missions carried out missionary activities in several towns in the southern Balkans that were still under Ottoman control, and trained further preachers for missionary work at the Samokov bible seminary. Beginning with the Bulgarians, their activities spread to the Albanians with the help of the above-mentioned Qiriazis and of the Luarasi and Treska families. There was also preaching in **Kosova**, though mainly among the Serbs at the time. A Protestant church existed in Prishtina until the Italian occupation during **World War II**.

In the 1980s, young foreign missionaries of various denominations gathered in Prishtina to learn Albanian at the university there. Many of them moved to Albania in 1991 when the dictatorship collapsed to begin missionary activities in **Tirana** and elsewhere. Numerous denominations are now active in Albania.

PUKA, DISTRICT OF. Region of local government administration. The District of Puka (*Rrethi i Pukës*), with its administrative headquarters in the town of Puka, borders on the districts of **Shkodra** to the west, **Tropoja** to the north, Has and **Kukës** to the east and **Mirdita** to the south. It has a surface area of 1,034 square kilometers and a present **population** of 42,766 (in 2000). Puka is the poorest district of Albania.

PUTO, ARBEN (1924-). Scholar and historian. Puto was born in **Gjirokastra** and, after attending the French lycée in **Korça** in the 1930s, studied in Italy from 1940 to 1942. In 1952, he finished his doctorate in international law at the University of Moscow and was appointed professor of international law at the newly created University of **Tirana** in 1957. With the fall of the dictatorship, in December 1990, he helped to induce democratic values as chairman of the Albanian Helsinki Committee for the Defense of Human Rights.

Arben Puto is the author of numerous publications on the history of diplomacy and Albanian politics, including: *Pavarësia shqiptare dhe diplomacia e fuqive të mëdha, 1912-1914* (Albanian Independence and Great Power Diplomacy, 1912-1914) Tirana 1978, French-language version, Tirana 1982; *From the Annals of British Diplomacy,* Tirana 1981; *Çështja shqiptare në aktet ndërkombëtare të periudhës së imperializmit* (The Albanian Question in International Documents of the Imperialist Period), Tirana 1984, 1987, French-language version, Tirana 1985, 1988; and *Demokracia e rrethuar: qeveria e Fan Nolit në marrëdhëniet e jashtme, qershor-dhjetor 1924* (Democracy under Siege: The Government of **Fan Noli** in Foreign Relations, June-December 1924), Tirana 1990. He was also coauthor, with **Stefanaq Pollo**, of the **communist** government's standard *History of Albania from Its Origins to the Present Day,* London 1981.

PYRAMID INVESTMENT SCANDAL AND THE 1997 UPRISING. Despite the years of economic freedom after the fall of the isolationist **communist** dictatorship in 1990-1991, the Albanians were still inexperienced in the ways of a free market economy and were thus easy prey for pyramid investment schemes, which had caused chaos in Bulgaria, Romania and Russia. In the 1990s, such "get rich quick" ventures spread like wildfire through the Albanian economy. The principal investment company was VEFA Holding, established in 1991. It was followed by Kamberi, Cenaj and Gjallica in **Vlora** in 1992, Sudja in 1994, and Xhaferri, Populli, Leka and Silva in 1996. The companies promised from eight to twenty-five percent interest on three-month investments. Some of them, such as Populli and Xhaferri claimed to be charitable organizations to assist the poor, thus making themselves look more reliable to the public. In October 1996, Vehbi Alimuçaj, head of VEFA Holding, stated that 800,000 Albanians had invested their savings in his company.

By the autumn and winter of 1996, such investments had created a mass psychosis in the population. Everyone wanted to get rich quick and no one was willing to listen to the warnings of the international financial community that the bubble would soon burst, least of all the Albanian government.

The investment companies grew rapidly. Populli, for instance, founded on 20 April 1996, had seventeen offices in **Tirana** within the first few months, and Silva, which was founded in the autumn of that year had 200 employees within the first eighteen days of its existence. Huge line-ups of small investors formed outside the offices day after day, and more and more money was poured in. In view of the lucrative interest, tens of thousands of families invested all their savings, many having sold their homes and property to invest even more. Bank loans for other investment projects were swiftly diverted to the investment companies until there was no more real investment capital in the country.

The Albanian government under the **Democratic Party** and President **Sali Berisha** did nothing to stop the scandal, stating that it was a free market. It is evident that the Democratic Party itself was receiving massive financial support from the investment companies.

On 20 November 1996, the small Grunjasi investment company of **Shkodra** collapsed when its owner disappeared with an estimated US$13 million, and a week later, on 26 November, there was panic in front of the offices of Sudja in Tirana. She was, however, able to pay investors out for a couple of weeks, and the market calmed. On 17 December 1996, Sudja then ceased payments and there were initial violent demonstrations in Tirana on the following days. An estimated 100,000 small investors had lost a total of US$60 million.

In January 1997, the situation got worse and panic spread. Sudja declared bankruptcy on 15 January, and there were further demonstrations on **Scanderbeg** Square. At the general assembly of the Democratic Party, President Berisha assured the population that all investments would be returned, down to the last *qindarka*. The government, now realizing the seriousness of the situation, closed the offices of Xhaferri and Populli to freeze their assets, and Xhaferri announced bankruptcy on 21 January. The huge VEFA Holding also showed its first signs of weakness.

The general panic, coupled by widespread anger and opposition to the now intolerably corrupt and authoritarian Berisha regime, quickly transformed itself into a political protest movement and soon into a general uprising in the country.

The police in the south of the country lost control of the situation on 25 January after mass demonstrations. There was plundering in **Berat, Lushnja** and **Gramsh**. On 26 January, 50,000 people gathered at the Dynamo Stadium in Tirana to protest.

Gjallica declared bankruptcy on 5 February, resulting in a demonstration of 30,000 people in Vlora. By 11 February, the police had lost control of Vlora and withdrew. Soon thereafter, government representatives and forces evacuated from most of southern Albania. The fury of the masses transformed itself into a rebellion, and, soon thereafter, into a military movement to advance on Tirana and throw Berisha and the Democratic Party out of office. The north of the country, which had been less affected by the financial scams, continued to support Berisha. Albania was on the brink of civil war.

On 1 March 1997, protesters in Vlora burned down the headquarters of the **National Information Service**, Berisha's much feared secret service, and the government of **Aleksandër Meksi** spoke of "armed communist insurgency in the south." Arms depots were plundered. A state of siege was declared on the next day throughout Albania.

On 3 March 1997, **parliament** dutifully reelected Sali Berisha for a second term of office as president, and on 4 March, press censorship was introduced, except for the Democratic Party newspaper *Rilindja Demokratike*. **Berat** and **Fier** fell to rebel forces on 10 March and by the next day the rebels had reached the **Shkumbin** River dividing the north from the south.

Bashkim Fino of the **Socialist Party** was suddenly appointed prime minister on 11 March, but it was too late to restore order. On 12 March, representatives of the rebel forces met in **Gjirokastra** and formed a National Committee of Public Salvation, and in Tirana the Military Academy was plundered by supporters of the Democratic Party, looking for weapons to defend themselves against an inevitable invasion from the south. Police stations and army barracks in and around the capital were vacated and looted the next day, and the minister of defense, Safet Zhulali, fled the country, as did Sali Berisha's children. Foreign countries also started evacuating their citizens from the country. Public order had collapsed and Albania had descended into an unprecedented chaos, which lasted for several weeks.

Order in Albania was gradually restored with the arrival of 6,000 foreign troops under Italian command on 15 April 1997, as part of **Operation Alba**. After much negotiation and political confrontation between the parties, Sali Berisha was forced into resignation on 23 July, and power was turned over to his archrival, **Fatos Nano**.

In all, the 1997 uprising caused 1,200 deaths and 6,000 injuries and set the Albanian **economy** back five years.

PYRRHUS (319-272 B.C.). King of the Molossi in Epirus. Pyrrhus was driven from his kingdom at the instigation of Cassander but returned to power in 297 B.C. with the help of Ptolemy I. He aspired to win the throne of Macedon and to emulate Alexander the Great. Though he gained much territory in Macedonia, he lost out to his brother-in-law Demetrius Poliorcetes and was forced to flee. He is remembered in particular for having aided the Tarentines in their battle against Rome in 280. At Heraclea he defeated the Roman consul Laevinus, but with such heavy losses, that the battle entered history as a "Pyrrhic victory." He was finally defeated by the Romans at Beneventum in 275, and withdrew to his native Epirus, where he made himself master of Macedonia once again in 273. The following year he was killed in a riot in Argos, reportedly by a tile flung by a woman from a rooftop.

- Q -

QEMALI, ISMAIL. *See* VLORA, ISMAIL QEMAL BEY.

QENDRA KOMBËTARE E KINEMATOGRAFISË. *See* NEW ALBANIA FILM STUDIOS.

QIRIAQI, AGIM (1951.01.27-). Stage and **film** actor and director. Qiriaqi graduated from the Academy of Fine Arts (*Instituti i Lartë i Arteve*) in 1973 and began acting for the **National Theater** in **Tirana**. He also directed numerous plays. He played in nineteen Albanian films and by the late 1980s was one of the country's best-known actors. He is remembered for his role in *Lulëkuqet mbi mure* (Red Poppies on Walls), 1976; *Tela për violinë* (Strings for a Violin), 1987; and most recently in *Koloneli Bunker* (Colonel Bunker), 1996. In 1992, he was elected head of the national actors' association.

QIRIAZI FAMILY. Educators, publishers and public figures of the nationalist movement. The four members of the **Protestant** Qiriazi or Kyrias family of Monastir (Bitola) in Macedonia are remembered for their activities towards the consolidation of Albanian national awareness. Gjerasim Qiriazi (1858-1894) attended a Greek school in his native Monastir and, with the assistance of his English teacher, the American missionary Jenney, studied at an American bible college in Samokov, Bulgaria. After four years of training there, he was offered a job by the British and Foreign Bible Society for whom he began working in **Korça** in 1883. He also began writing an Albanian grammar and is known to have preached in Albanian. On 12 November 1884, while traveling in the mountains southwest of Lake **Ohrid**, he was attacked by bandits and held for ransom for half a year. The narrative of his six-month ordeal was translated into English by one J. W. Baird of Monastir as *Captured by Brigands* (London 1902).

The opening of the first officially recognized Albanian school in Korça in 1887 inspired him and his sisters Sevasti Qiriazi-Dako (1871-1949) and Parashqevi Qiriazi (1880-1970) to open a girls' school. With the assistance of **Naim bey Frashëri** and, in particular, of American and English missionaries, they received the appropriate authorizations in Istanbul and on 15 October 1891 opened the first Albanian girls' school in Korça. The following summer, they moved the premises to a larger building to make room for more pupils. The Greek **Orthodox** hierarchy was fanatically opposed to the school from the start and went so far as to refuse to bury the son of one of its patrons. On 4 January 1894, Gjerasim Qiriazi died, aged thirty-six, of the pleurisy he had contracted during his period of captivity. He was the author of poetry, songs, sketches, dialogues and school textbooks. A selection of his writings was published by his younger brother Gjergj in the collection *Hristomathi më katër pjesë* (Chrestomathy in Four Parts), Sofia 1902.

Gjergj Qiriazi (1868-1912), known in English as George Kyrias, like his brother Gjerasim, attended a Greek school in his native Monastir and the American bible college at Samokov, and was hired by the British and Foreign Bible Society. He took over the direction of the Albanian girls' school in Korça upon the death of his brother in 1894 and, in 1908, was a delegate at the

Congress of Monastir. The politically active Gjergj Qiriazi was one of the founders of the Albanian-language newspaper *Bashkim' i Kombit* (Unity of the Nation) in 1909. In addition to his brother's chrestomathy, he published a collection of religious verse entitled *Kënkë të shenjtëruara* (Sacred Songs), Sofia 1906.

It was Naim bey Frashëri who enabled Sevasti Qiriazi-Dako (1871-1949) to study at the prestigious Robert College in Istanbul and to play an active role in **women**'s **education**. She was the first Albanian woman to study at this American institution, from which she graduated in June 1891. Immediately upon her return to Albania, she was instrumental in the founding of the Korça girls' school. After **World War I** this school was still known by the family name as the Kyrias School. Sevasti Qiriazi-Dako is said to have published a beginners' grammar for elementary schools (Monastir 1912) and edited a series of history texts. With her husband, journalist and writer **Christo Anastas Dako**, and her sister Parashqevi, she left for Romania and from there emigrated with them to the **United States**, where she collaborated in the fortnightly periodical *Yll' i mëngjezit* (The Morning Star).

Parashqevi Qiriazi (1880-1970), also known as Paraskevi D. Kirias, studied at Robert College in Istanbul, too, and returned to Albania to teach. In 1909, she published a speller for elementary schools. She later organized both children's **education** and night schools in southern Albania and helped set up the rudiments of a library system. In the United States, she helped found the *Yll' i mëngjezit* (The Morning Star) society and published the illustrated periodical of the same name, issued in Boston from 1917 to 1920. Parashqevi Qiriazi also took part in the Paris Peace Conference of 1919 as a representative of the Albanian-American community.

- R -

RAIL TRANSPORTATION. In 1947, Albania was the only country in Europe without a railway. Initial efforts had been made in 1927 to build a standard-gauge line from **Durrës** to **Tirana**, but the track was not completed until 1949. It was primarily in support of Albanian **industry**, in particular the mining and metallurgical industry, that the **communist** authorities embarked after

World War II on the building of a railway network departing southwards from Durrës. The first section of track, from Durrës to **Peqin**, was inaugurated with **Yugoslav** support on 7 November 1947. On 23 February 1949, the line from Durrës to Tirana was opened, thus connecting the country's main port to the capital city, and the Peqin-**Elbasan** section was inaugurated on 21 December 1950 (Stalin's birthday). This line was further extended to the mines of Përrenjas in March 1974 and now runs through a tunnel to Gur i Kuq near **Pogradec** on Lake **Ohrid**. Southwards down the coastal plain, a line was extended to **Fier** in October 1968 and from there to Ballsh, center of the **oil** industry, in March 1975. There is also a line from Fier to **Vlora**. Another rail connection extends northwards from Durrës to **Lezha**, with a sideline inland to Rrëshen and Klos in the **Mat** district, built for the transportation of chrome ore. From Lezha, the railway line was extended to **Shkodra** in November 1981 and, on 26 November 1985, the track between Shkodra and Titograd (Podgorica) was opened for international freight traffic, thus linking the Albanian railway system to the rest of Europe. With the exception of Korça, all major Albanian cities are now linked by rail. In 1996, there were 697 kilometers of tracks, of which 477 kilometers were main lines and 220 kilometers were for industrial freight only.

In the late 1980s, trains were responsible for one-third of freight and passenger transportation in the country, but the network was primitive and decrepit from the start, and train speeds rarely surpassed thirty to forty kilometers an hour. In the early 1990s, the system, with its vastly outdated locomotives and carriages, suffered much destruction, and broke down several times. Engines and carriages were demolished and looted for anything that could be sold and, in many parts of the country, impoverished peasants even stole the rails to sell them as scrap iron. New rails were laid and new carriages were imported from Italy, but in 1997, the entire railway network was devastated once again by the general **uprising** and anarchy. It has now recovered once more and freight is regularly transported from Durrës to Shkodra, Tirana, Pogradec and Vlora. There are also passenger services, but most travelers prefer buses, which are much faster and more frequent. The line to Montenegro has never been used for passenger traffic.

RAMA, EDI (1964-). Artist, political figure, and high-ranking member of the **Socialist Party**. Edi Rama was born in **Tirana**

and studied art at the Academy of Fine Arts (*Instituti i Lartë i Arteve*), where he graduated in 1986 and taught from 1987 to 1996. His paintings, sculptures and installations have been acclaimed at home and abroad. He was a major intellectual figure of the transition to democracy and a conspicuous leader of the student movement in early 1990. He is known in his country as a nonconformist and has done much to liberalize thinking. On 21 January 1997, he was seriously injured in a politically motivated attack and fled abroad until the end of the **Sali Berisha** regime. Rama returned under the socialists to serve as a nonparty minister of culture. On 1 October 2000, he was elected mayor of Tirana, where he has managed to push through many reforms.

RAMA, LUAN (1952.01.05-). Publicist, writer and diplomat. Luan Rama was born in **Tirana**, where he studied journalism. He worked for many years as a **film** scriptwriter for the **New Albania Film Studios**, of which he later became director. In 1989, he joined the ministry of foreign affairs, and in 1997, was appointed Albanian ambassador in Paris. Rama is the author of the following studies: *Metamorfoza e fjalës* (Metamorphosis of the Word), Tirana 1997; *Shkëlqimi i meteoreve* (The Glare of Meteors), Tirana 1997; and *Le long chemin sous le tunnel de Platon: le destin de l'artiste sous la censure en Albanie, 1945-1990* (The Long Path under Plato's Tunnel: The Fate of Artists under Censorship in Albania, 1945-1990), Nantes 1999

REINHOLD, KARL HEINRICH THEODOR (1834-1880). German scholar, physician and collector of Albanian folklore. Reinhold was born in Göttingen and worked as a doctor for the Greek navy at a time when the newly independent Kingdom of Greece was under Bavarian tutelage. It was in Greece, in particular, on the traditionally Albanian-speaking islands of Poros, Hydra and Spetsai, that he came into contact with Albanian sailors, who made up a substantial part of the Greek navy. He collected their folk tales, songs and sayings, which he published in a collection entitled *Noctes pelasgicae vel symbolae ad cognoscendas dialectos Graeciae Pelasgicas* (Pelasgian Nights or Contributions to a Knowledge of the Pelasgian Dialects of Greece), Athens 1855, which now constitutes a major source for the now extinct Albanian dialect of Poros and Hydra. Further, as yet unpublished material of his is to be found in the manuscript collection of the Biblioteca Marciana in Venice.

RELIGION. There are four traditional religious communities of significance in Albania: Sunni **Islam, Orthodoxy, Catholicism** and **Bektashism**. According to Italian statistics from the year 1942, of the total **population** of Albania of 1,128,143 at the time, there were 779,417 (sixty-nine percent) Muslims including the Bektashi, 232,320 (twenty-one percent) Orthodox and 116,259 (ten percent) Catholics. Today, although reliable statistics are still lacking, it is generally assumed that approximately seventy percent of Albanians in the Republic of Albania are of Muslim background, twenty percent (predominantly in the south) are of Orthodox background and the remaining ten percent (predominantly in and around **Shkodra** in the north) are of Catholic background.

The Albanians are not a particularly religious people, in particular after having gone through three decades of **Stalinist** dictatorship in which organized religion was banned and virtually every sign of religious activity was suppressed. Religious fervor and religious extremism are rare.

Since the fall of the dictatorship in 1991, there has been a modest revival of interest in religion and religions. It seems, however, to have been promoted more by the zeal of foreign missionaries (Muslim, Catholic, Orthodox and **Protestant**) than by a need in the population for traditional religious values. In addition to the traditional religious communities which have been reestablished, various Protestant denominations and the **Baha'i** have also entered the country and formed communities. Freedom of religion is guaranteed by the state and there do not seem to be any political problems in this field.

REPISHTI, SAMI (1925.07.05-). Albanian-American scholar and human rights activist. Sami Repishti was born in **Shkodra** where he attended school until 1944. He studied modern history at the University of Florence in Italy from 1942 to 1943, and returned to his native Shkodra. Together with most other Albanian intellectuals who had studied abroad before or during **World War II**, he was arrested in the witch hunts of late 1946 and, accused of having "western ideas," was sentenced on 28 November 1946 to fifteen years in prison. From 1946 to July 1956, he worked in various labor camps (in **Kavaja, Berat, Fier** and at Rinas airport) until he was released. After three years as an assistant carpenter, he managed to escape to **Yugoslavia** on 22 August 1959, where he was imprisoned for eleven months by the Yugoslav authorities. On 1 September 1961, he escaped to Italy from where he emigrated to the **United States** on 9 April 1962. From 1962 to 1964, he studied French language and literature at the City University of New York and, after a year of studies in Paris in 1970-1971, he finished his doctorate at CUNY in 1977. From 1966, he taught French and Italian at Malverne High School in New York and from 1978 to his retirement in 1991, taught French at Adelphi University in Garden City, New York. He currently lives in Baldwin, New York.

Sami Repishti has been active in the field of human rights, in particular for **Kosova**. He was a founding member of the **Albanian-American Civic League**, serving as its executive director until 1992 and, from 1996 to 1998, was the first president of the **National Albanian American Council**. He is coauthor with **Arshi Pipa** of *Studies on Kosova*, New York 1984, and has written numerous articles on Albanian history and the human rights situation. His memoirs were published in the volume *Pika loti: tregim burgu* (Teardrops: Prison Memoirs), Shkodra 1997.

REPUBLICAN PARTY (*PARTIA REPUBLIKANE SHQIPTARE, PRSH*) (1991-). The Albanian Republican Party, the second opposition formation to arise in the country after the **Democratic Party**, was established on 10 January 1991 by a group of intellectuals, the most prominent of whom was **Sabri Godo**. It was inspired in good part by the **Democratic Revolution** of **Fan Noli** in 1924 and has been noted for its support for the radical return of property and land to former owners. The Republican Party has taken part in government coalitions, mostly allied with the Democratic Party, but has remained a small political force. In the elections of 1991, it won a mere 1.5 percent of the popular vote. In 1992 it won 3.1 percent, in 1996 5.7 percent, in 1997 2.4 percent, and in 2002 2.7 percent. The Republican Party was headed by Sabri Godo from its foundation in 1991 to 5 November 1997, when he was succeeded by Fatmir Mediu.

RESSULI, NAMIK (1908-1985.09.12). Scholar, linguist and literary historian. Ressuli was born in **Berat** of a prominent Muslim family (his date of birth is given variously as 1908, 1910 or 1912) and went to secondary school in Bari in southern Italy. In 1935, he graduated in linguistics from the University of Turin. After his return to Albania, he taught Albanian **language** and **literature** in **Elbasan**, **Shkodra** and **Tirana**. From 1939 to 1950, he taught at the University of Rome, and, from 1955 to 1975, he served as professor of Albanian at the Oriental Institute of the University

(Istituto Universitario Orientale) in Naples. In 1975, upon the death of **Ernest Koliqi**, he returned to Rome to head the Institute of Albanian Studies until 1981, when he retired. He died in Turin. Among Ressuli's major publications are: *Il "Messale" di Giovanni Buzuku: riproduzione e trascrizione* (The Missal of **Gjon Buzuku**: Reproduction and Transcription), Vatican City 1958; *I più antichi testi albanesi* (The Oldest Albanian Texts), Turin 1978; *Le strutture del nome nell'odierna lingua letteraria albanese* (The Structure of Nouns in the Modern Albanian Literary Language), Turin 1978; *Grammatica albanese* (Albanian Grammar), Bologna 1985; and *Albanian Literature,* Boston 1987. He also edited volume one of the masterful anthology *Shkrimtarët shqiptarë* (Albanian Writers), Tirana 1941.

REXHEBI, BABA (1901-1995.08.14). Bektashi holy man. Baba Rexhebi, born in **Gjirokastra**, was the nephew of Baba Selim Ruhi (1907-1945). At the age of sixteen, he entered the nearby Bektashi *Teqe e Zallit,* where he completed his studies in **Islamic** theology, law and literature with private tutors, notably Ragip Effendi of Delvina. Taking a vow of celibacy, he became a **dervish** at the age of twenty-one and served the Bektashi community in southern Albania until **World War II**. Forced to flee Albania in 1944 because of his public stance against **communism**, he found refuge initially in a camp for displaced persons in Italy, continued from there to the Magauri *tekke* near Cairo in Egypt, and finally emigrated to the **United States**. Baba Rexhebi arrived in New York as a dervish in 1952 and soon moved on to Detroit where, in 1953, he assembled a group of fifteen Albanians, who agreed to collect funds to buy land for an Albanian *tekke*. The following year, the First Albanian *Teqe Bektashiane* in America was duly founded in Taylor, Michigan, and was presided over by Baba Rexhebi until his death in August 1995. Respected by Albanians of all faiths as a spiritual master and community leader, Baba Rexhebi was also the author of two books on Bektashism: *Misticizma Islame dhe Bektashizma* (New York 1970) translated into English by **Bardhyl Pogoni** as *The Mysticism of Islam and Bektashism* (Naples 1984), and *Kopshti i të përsosërvet* (Gjakova 1997), a translation of the *Hadîqatû's-su'adâ* (The Garden of the Blessed) by the great Azeri poet Fuzûlî (1494-1556).

RIFA'I ORDER OF DERVISHES. Islamic Sufi sect or *tariqa*. The Rifa'i, or Rufa'i, Alb. *Rufai,* sect first evolved in Iraq towards the end of the twelfth century following the teachings of the jurist Sheikh Ahmad ibn 'Ali al-Rifâ'i (1106-1182). The movement then spread to Syria, Egypt and Turkey and gave rise to a number of suborders, including the Badavi, the Desuki and the Shahzeli. The Rifa'i, often referred to as the "howling dervishes," are known in the Balkans for their rather violent practices of ritual mortification, including the piercing of lips and cheeks with needles, the eating of glass and the burning of skin. Such ceremonies are still carried out in Prizren.

Little is known of how and when the Rifa'i spread to the Balkans and of their early history in Albania. Many of their centers, among which were Peqin with a *tekke* founded by a certain Baba Hasan in 1701 [1113 A.H.], **Tirana**, **Shkodra** and **Gjirokastra**, were abandoned or taken over by the **Bektashi** by the early years of the twentieth century. Despite stagnation of the sect elsewhere, a Rifa'i center was founded and it flourished in Gjakova in **Kosova** at the end of the nineteenth century, giving rise to a second wave of Rifa'i *tekkes* throughout Kosova, Macedonia and Albania. The presence of second-wave Rifa'i centers is recorded in Shkodra, where the holy Mehmet Efendi was venerated in a *tekke* at the foot of the citadel and where a Rifa'i community was formed in the 1930s; **Tropoja**, Tirana and Petrela with a *tekke* dating from before 1907; Gjirokastra, and **Berat,** where the *tekke* of Sheikh Riza, also known simply as the Rifa'i *Tekke*, Alb. *Teqeja e Rufaive,* founded after 1785, was situated to the west of the Murad Çelepia quarter. In the early 1980s, there were still Rifa'i *tekkes* in Skopje, Gjakova, Prizren, Rahovec, Peja and Mitrovica. The Rifa'i community was re-established in Albania in the late 1990s under Sheh Xhemal Reka of Tirana, where a *tekke* was opened in 1998. The Rifa'i in Tirana hold a *zikr* every Thursday evening and have a modest publication entitled *Dashuria e Ehli-Bejtit* (The Love of the Prophet's Family).

RILINDJA. National movement. The struggle for political autonomy within the languishing **Ottoman Empire**, and the will for cultural identity and survival among a backward and religiously divided people, crystallized in the second half of the nineteenth century into the so-called *Rilindja* "rebirth" movement of national awakening. This *Rilindja* period, which in its classical phase spans the years from the formation of the **League of Prizren** in 1878 to the declaration of Albanian independence in 1912, woke the Albanian people and united them into one linguistic identity, one culture and one nation. *Rilindja* also refers to the corresponding period of Albanian **literature**, characterized primarily by works of romantic nationalism.

RIZA, SELMAN (1909.12.21-1988.12.16). Scholar and linguist. Selman Riza was born in Gjakova and went to school in **Tirana**, 1922-1924. He attended secondary school in **Korça**, 1925-1931. He continued his studies in Toulouse in southern France, 1932-1935, where he graduated with a degree in German and law, and briefly in Vienna, 1936. From 1936 to 1939 he taught French, Latin and German at the secondary school in Korça. Because of his antifascist activities, he was interned from February to October 1941 by the Italians on the island of Ventotene in the Tyrrhenian Sea but was able to return to Albania the following year. He settled in Prizren, where he worked as a lawyer but returned to Tirana in December 1944. Soon thereafter, in early January 1945 he was arrested by the Albanian authorities for being "anti-Yugoslav." In January 1948, he was then handed over to the Yugoslav authorities and was kept in prison in Prishtina until August 1951. In 1952-1953, he was interned in Sarajevo but was able to teach French at the university there. In 1954-1955, he worked in research at the Albanological Institute in Prishtina, which had been founded on 29 July 1953, but the institute was soon closed by the Yugoslav authorities, and, in December 1955, he was deported back to Albania.

In 1956, Selman Riza got a job at the Institute of Linguistics and Literature in Tirana and taught Albanian morphology and early Albanian **literature** at the newly founded university. In 1960, he was finally appointed professor and, in 1964, was honored with the Prize of the Republic for his monograph *Emrat në shqipen: sistemi i rasave dhe tipet e lakimit* (Nouns in Albanian: Case System and Declension Types), Tirana 1965. In 1967, however, in a period of political turbulence influenced by the Cultural Revolution in **China**, with which Albania was allied, he was denounced by revolutionary extremists and was ostracized to **Berat**, where he was put to work as a local museum guide. He was also forbidden to publish anything further. He retired in 1970 and returned to Tirana where he died.

Selman Riza was one of the leading intellectuals of his period, but because of the vicissitudes of political life, he was not able to publish as much as he might have. Among his major monographs are: *Tri monografina albanologjike* (Three Albanological Monographs), Tirana 1944; *Fillimet e gjuhësisë shqiptare* (The Beginnings of Albanian Linguistics), Prishtina 1952; *Gramatikë e sërbo-kroatishtes* (Grammar of Serbo-Croatian), Prishtina 1952; *Pesë autorët më të vjeter të gjuhës shqipe* (The Five Earliest Authors of the Albanian **Language**), Tirana 1960; and posthumously, *Sistemi foljor i letrarishtes shqiptare bashkëkohore* (The Verb System of Contemporary Literary Albanian), Tirana 1995.

ROMA MINORITY IN ALBANIA. There are no reliable statistics as to the size of the Roma (Gypsy) community in Albania. Their numbers have been estimated at between 60,000 and 100,000. The Roma (*rromët*) are divided into two distinct groups: the *jevgj* who are more assimilated and speak only Albanian, and the *gabel* who also speak Romani and who lead a more traditional Roma existence. The Roma in Albania specialize in metal handicrafts and urban hauling services, and are famed throughout the country as musicians. In the latter connection, they are especially sought after for wedding celebrations. A school for Roma children was opened in Baltëz near **Fier** on 9 April 1995.

ROMANIA, ALBANIANS IN. The first reference to Albanians in Romania dates from 1595, when Michael the Brave (Mihai Viteazul), prince of Walachia, invited a large group of Albanians to settle on the northern banks of the Danube. Of significance to Romanian history was the noble dynasty of Ghika, Alb. Gjika, of Albanian origin from **Përmet**, which ruled over Moldavia and Walachia for three centuries. A scion of this family was the Romanian publicist Elena Ghika (1828-1882), also known as **Dora d'Istria**, who did much to make the Albanian nation known in nineteenth-century Europe.

It was in the mid-nineteenth century that Albanians, in particular **Orthodox** Albanians from the **Korça** region, began to emigrate in large numbers to Romania, which had a much higher standard of living and development than impoverished Albania. In 1888, there were said to be 40,000 Albanians in the country. Substantial Albanian colonies arose in particular in Bucharest, Constanza and Brăila, and many figures of the Albanian community there played an important part in the nationalist awakening in the final decades of the nineteenth century. Among them in particular was Nikolla Naço (1843-1913), who founded an Albanian-Romanian cultural institute to train Albanian teachers. In 1884, the *Drita* (The Light) cultural society was formed in Bucharest, which, with Naço's support, gave much impetus to the national movement. In the twentieth century, many Albanian writers and intellectuals, especially from the Korça region, lived in Romania, among whom were **Asdreni, Lasgush Poradeci** and **Mitrush Kuteli**. Even today, there is a small Albanian community in Bucharest.

ROQUES, MARIO (1875-1961). French scholar and philologist. Mario Roques was a member of the French Academy of Sciences and Arts. He is remembered for his edition of the dictionary of **Frang Bardhi**, *Le dictionnaire albanais de 1635* (The Albanian Dictionary of 1635), Paris 1932, and *Recherches sur les anciens textes albanais* (Research on Ancient Albanian Texts), Paris 1932, as well as for a number of articles on early Albanian texts.

ROSHI, KADRI (1924.01.04-). Stage and **film** actor. Kadri Roshi was born in Ballsh. From 1947 to 1950, he studied acting at the Academy of Fine Arts in Prague, Czechoslovakia, and, with eighty stage and thirty film roles, he was to become a major actor of the 1970s and 1980s. Among his best-known films are: *Fijet që priten* (Broken Threads), 1976; *Lulëkuqet mbi mure* (Red Poppies on Walls), 1976; *Njeriu me top* (The Man with the Cannon), 1977; *Gjeneral gramafoni* (General Gramophone), 1978; *Koloneli Bunker* (Colonel Bunker), 1996, and *Mirupafshim* (Farewell), 1997, the latter a Greek-Albanian coproduction.

RROTA, JUSTIN (1889.02.17-1964.12.21). Scholar and linguist. Justin Rrota was born and raised in **Shkodra**, where he attended a **Franciscan** school. From 1907 to 1911, he studied **Catholic** theology in Villach and elsewhere in Austria. In 1911, he was ordained as a Franciscan priest and returned to Albania. After a period as a parish priest, he taught Albanian and Latin at the Illyrian college in Shkodra for twenty-five years. Rrota is the author of philological studies, in particular on early Albanian **literature**. Indeed, it was he who first made early authors known to the Albanian public at large. He survived the transition to the **communist** period, as opposed to many Catholic priests trained abroad who were shot, but was only allowed to publish the occasional article after 1945. Among his major publications are: *Letratyra shqype per shkolla të mjesme* (Albanian Literature for Secondary Schools), Shkodra 1925; *Monumenti mâ i vjetri i gjûhës shqype: D. Gjon Buzuku, 1555* (The Oldest Monument of the Albanian Language: Dom **Gjon Buzuku**, 1555), Shkodra 1930; *Shkrimtari mâ i vjetri i Italo-Shqyptarvet: Lukë Matranga, 1592* (The Oldest Italo-Albanian Writer, Lukë Matranga, 1592), Shkodra 1931; *Vjollca parrizit: liber uratësh per fëmi e të* *rritshem* (The Violets of Paradise: Prayer Book for Children and Grown-ups), Winterberg 1932; *Letratyra shqype* (Albanian Literature), Shkodra 1934; *Per historín e alfabetit shqyp* (On the History of the Albanian Alphabet) Shkodra 1936; and *Rreth votrës* (Around the Hearth), Tirana 1945.

RROTA, SIMON (1887.10.23-1961.01.27). Painter. Simon Rrota was born in **Shkodra** and was educated by the **Franciscans**. He learned to draw and paint under **Kolë Idromeno**. He studied at the Brera Academy of Fine Arts in Milan until 1915 and later traveled in France. On his return to Albania, he worked as a photographer in **Lushnja** and then taught school in his native Shkodra until retirement. He is remembered for his paintings of town life in Shkodra, of which the best known are *Te pusi i fshatit* (At the Village Fountain), 1934, and *Portë në Shkodër* (Gate in Shkodra),1936.

RUSSIA, RELATIONS WITH. As a Slavic nation, Russia has traditionally supported its Slavic brethren in the Balkans—nations such as **Serbia**, Montenegro, Bulgaria and **Macedonia**—which at many times were in conflict with Albania, a non-Slavic nation. As such, relations with Russia in the nineteenth century were characterized primarily by mutual distrust.

Diplomatic relations with the Soviet Union were established in December 1924 during the short-lived **Democratic Revolution** of **Fan Noli**, the so-called red bishop. Though contacts continued under dictator **Ahmet Zogu**, it was Noli who was later accused of having "introduced Bolshevism" to Albania. Russia's role in Albania up to **World War II** was limited to training **communist** cadres in Moscow and fostering the creation of communist groups in the country.

With the communist takeover, party relations and thus political relations between the two countries intensified dramatically. Diplomatic relations with the Soviet Union were reestablished on 10 November 1945 and, after a period of strong Titoist, i.e., Yugoslav influence in Albania until late June 1948, Albania and the Soviet Union became close political allies until 1961.

Enver Hoxha met Joseph Stalin on five occasions between July 1947 and April 1951. Several agreements were signed, and Soviet influence became all-pervasive in Albania for a decade. Over 3,000 Soviet military and economic advisors were sent to Albania to assist the country and bind it to the Soviet bloc. On 4 August 1953, the two countries raised their respective legations to the status of embassies, and on 14 May 1955, Albania became a founding member of the Warsaw Pact. Enver Hoxha and Nikita Khrushchev met unofficially on 18 July 1955, though relations were not always smooth after the death of Stalin. Hoxha and the Albanian leadership were first criticized openly at the twentieth congress of the Soviet communist party on 14-16 April 1956 for their unwillingness to reject the heritage of Stalin.

Despite friction between the parties, relations continued, in particular because Albania was in desperate need of Soviet economic assistance and Russia needed Albania in view of its strategic geopolitical position on the Mediterranean. Nikita Khrushchev visited Albania on 25 May-4 June 1959, when an economic agreement for 300 million rubles was signed.

In a speech on 16 November 1960 at a conference of eighty-one communist and workers' parties in Moscow, Enver Hoxha, however, denounced the Soviet leadership under Khrushchev, and relations with the Soviet Union began to deteriorate rapidly. Ideology was only one of several factors. On 3 December 1961, diplomatic relations between the two countries were ruptured and all Soviet advisors left the country. Albania broke its formal ties with the Warsaw Pact on 13 September 1968 after the Soviet invasion of Czechoslovakia, fearing that the Warsaw Pact countries might invade Albania, too.

From 1961 to the end of the communist dictatorship in 1990, relations with the Soviet Union were virtually nonexistent. Russia and the **United States**, the two superpowers, were the only countries on earth whose citizens were not allowed to visit Albania as a matter of principle. Russia made overtures to Albania from time to time for the restoration of ties, notably Leonid Brezhnev's declaration on 25 October 1976 that the Soviet Union was ready to normalize relations, but the Albanian leadership remained obstinate in its rejection.

Diplomatic ties between the two countries were finally restored on 31 July 1990 after a visit by Russian deputy foreign minister Kvizinsky, and a trade agreement was signed in Moscow on 28 August of that year. On 26 December 1991, Albania recognized Russia and the other successor states of the Soviet Union. Despite the normalization of diplomatic and commercial ties, relations with Russia remained cool, in particular because of Moscow's open support for **Serbia** and the regime of Slobodan Milošević during the war in **Kosova**.

RUSTEMI, AVNI (1895.09.26-1924.04.22). Political figure and revolutionary. Rustemi was born in Libohova and attended secondary school in Janina and Istanbul. In 1912-1913, he studied at a teaching college in Geneva and, in 1919, the College of Saint Adrian in San Demetrio Corone (Alb. *Shën Mitri*) in Calabria, but never graduated. He is remembered as the assassin of **Essad Pasha Toptani** in Paris on 13 June 1920, a spectacular deed which caught the attention of the European press. Rustemi was nonetheless acquitted of the crime before a French court. On his return to Albania, he was lauded as a national hero and entered the political arena. In April 1921, he took part in the founding in **Vlora** of the *Atdheu* (Fatherland) society and, when it was banned, in the founding in September 1922 of the *Bashkimi* (The Union) society, which came to constitute the political opposition. Rustemi was involved in an attempt to assassinate **Ahmet Zogu** on 23 February 1924. On 20 April, he was shot himself in **Durrës** Road in **Tirana**, allegedly by Zogu's men, and died two days later of his wounds. His widely attended funeral in Vlora on 30 April of that year gave rise to the anti-government demonstrations, which led to the **Democratic Revolution** and the rise to power of **Fan Noli**.

RYAN, ANDREW Sir (1876-1949). British diplomat and writer. Sir Andrew Ryan was the last British minister in pre-communist Albania, having served there from 1936 to 1939. He remained in **Tirana** as consul general after the **Italian** invasion of April 1939, and retired a year later. In the later war years, Ryan served as an unofficial liaison between the British Foreign Office and **King Zog**, who had sought asylum in **Britain** during **World War II**. His memoirs, *The Last of the Dragomans,* London 1951, deal with Albania in the late 1930s, in particular with politics and diplomacy at the court of King Zog.

- S -

SA'DI ORDER OF DERVISHES. Islamic Sufi sect or *tariqa*. The Albanian publicist **Eqrem bey Vlora** called the Sa'di order the fourth most important **dervish** order in Albania, after the **Bektashi**, the **Halveti** and the **Rifa'i**. This sect was founded in the fourteenth century by Sadeddin Djibawi of Djiba near Damascus, originally as a branch of the Rifa'i order. From there it spread to the Lebanon, Egypt, Libya, Iraq, Turkey and the Balkans (**Macedonia, Kosova** and Albania). Although there is little knowledge as yet of its history and development in Albania, it is apparent that the Sa'di reached southern Albania in the early seventeenth century and northern Albania in the early eighteenth century. It is known that there was a Sa'di *tekke* in Gjakova in 1600. They were both present in the country at any rate during the **Ottoman** period and thereafter.

The Albanian Sa'di were quite close to the **Bektashi**, both in their rites and customs and in their legendry. It was Sa'di dervishes who looked after the mausoleum of Demir Han in **Tepelena** and the tomb of Bektashi saint **Sari Salltëk** on the top of Mount Pashtrik near Gjakova. **Ali Pasha Tepelena**, who founded a Sa'di *tekke* near the Edirne Gate in Istanbul in 1777-1778, also appears somehow to have been connected with this order. Ottoman archives mention a Sa'di *tekke* of Ali Pasha Tepelena as well as a Sa'di *tekke* of Ibrahim Pasha in Tepelena, the presence of two Sa'di *tekkes* being documented there in the nineteenth century. Aside from Tepelena, there are also references to the presence of the Sa'di order in Leskovik, **Gjirokastra, Elbasan, Tropoja** and Peza. In the 1980s, there were still about ten Sa'di *tekkes* in Kosova.

SAKO, ZIHNI (1912.03.27-1981.02.16). Scholar, ethnologist and folklore editor. Zihni Sako was born in **Gjirokastra** and studied in Athens. He taught secondary school in Gjirokastra in 1938 and later in **Korça** and **Berat**. In 1943, he became a member of the **communist** party, to which he remained faithful for the rest of his life. After **World War II**, he was press director for the ministry of culture and a member of the people's assembly. In 1949, he was appointed director of the folklore department of the Institute of Sciences, forerunner of the University of **Tirana**, and from 1970 until his retirement in 1979, he served as director of the Institute of Folk Culture. A leading figure in folklore research, Zihni Sako edited and published many volumes of oral **literature**, including the series *Mbledhës të hershëm të folklorit shqiptar, 1635-1912* (Early Collections of Albanian Folklore, 1635-1912), Tirana 1961-1962; and the four-volume collection *Proza popullore* (Folk Prose), Tirana 1963-1966. He also collaborated in French-language editions of oral verse such as *Trésor du chansonnier populaire albanais* (Treasury of Albanian Folk

Songs), Tirana 1975; and *Chansonnier des preux albanais* (The Songs of Albanian Frontier Warriors), Paris 1967.

SALLTËK, SARI. *See* SARI SALLTËK.

SARACHI, CHATIN (1903-1974.11.27). Public figure, diplomat and painter. Chatin Pascal Sarachi (Alb. Qatin Paskal Saraçi) was born in **Shkodra** of an influential family. He attended the Theresianum secondary school in Vienna on an Austrian scholarship. It was in Vienna in 1917 that he met and befriended **Ahmet Zogu**, whom he later helped to power. Sarachi subsequently embarked upon a diplomatic career as King Zog's consul general in Vienna and, after the Anschluss, as Albanian chargé d'affaires in London.

On a trip to the United States in October 1933, where he was sent to negotiate **oil** concessions on behalf of King Zog, he met and became a close friend of oil baron John Paul Getty (1892-1976), who later visited him in London. Sarachi remained in England after **World War II**.

Chatin Sarachi was also a painter of note, who exhibited his works in London in 1948. He was a personal friend of Austrian painter Oskar Kokoschka (1886-1980), whom he assisted during the latter's years in English emigration. Sarachi traveled widely in Europe and was appreciated not only as an artist but also as a master of savoir vivre. In his unpublished memoirs entitled *King Zog of the Albanians: The Inside Story* (ca. 1940), he attacks Zog and exposes his corruption. Sarachi died in a London hospital after a short illness.

SARANDA. Town in the **District of Saranda**, of which it is the administrative center. **Population** in Dec. 1999: 31,032. Situated across from the Greek island of Corfu, Saranda is the most southerly town in Albania and, for many people, the most beautiful.

In ancient times, it was called *Onchesmos* and served as the port for the inland settlement of **Phoinike**. In the fifth century A.D., it was the seat of a bishop. Under **Ali Pasha Tepelena**, Saranda was used as a trading port for Janina. In 1878, it was razed to the ground by Greek nationalists from Corfu. It also suffered badly in the **uprising of 1997**. With its mild Mediterranean **climate** (bananas can grow here), Saranda has nonetheless revived as an important center of domestic **tourism** and for foreign tourists who come over by boat from Corfu to visit the nearby ruins of **Butrint**.

The word "Saranda" is derived from the root *sara*, common in place names in the region. It is commonly identified with the Greek word *saranda* "forty" as it was the site of a sixth century church of the forty martyrs, thus the Greek designation for the town *Hagioi Saranda* and the Italian *Santi Quaranta*. The town was renamed *Zogaj* in the 1930s and, after the Italian invasion of 1939, *Porto Edda*, after Edda Mussolini, the wife of Count Ciano and daughter of Benito Mussolini.

SARANDA, DISTRICT OF. Region of local government administration. The District of Saranda (*Rrethi i Sarandës*), with its administrative headquarters in the town of **Saranda**, borders on the Ionian Sea to the west, the districts of **Vlora** to the north, **Gjirokastra** and **Delvina** to the east and the Republic of **Greece** to the south. It has a surface area of 749 square kilometers and a present **population** of 63,267 (in 2000).

SARDA. Archeological site and medieval settlement at present-day Shurdhah on the **Drin**, eight kilometers to the southeast of **Shkodra**. The earliest remains of Sarda go back to the sixth to eighth centuries. The town grew substantially in the eleventh and twelfth centuries and came to constitute a major settlement in northern Albania, in particular from the twelfth century onwards when, as the seat of the bishop of Sapa and Sarda (Lat. Episcopus Sapatensis et Sardensis), it pledged its ecclesiastical allegiance to the metropolitan See of Bar (Antivari), set up in 1089. The settlement was ravaged by the Turks in 1491. Excavations carried out in 1967-1970 revealed not only an outer, 690-meters-long perimeter wall and eleven towers, but medieval dwellings, church remains, coins and jewelry. Sarda is now partially submerged as a result of flooding from the hydroelectric dam at Koman.

SARI SALLTËK. Bektashi holy man and legendary figure. Sari Salltëk, ~ Turk. *Sari Saltuk,* from *Sair Saltiq,* is said to have been either a **dervish** at the court of Sultan Orhan (1326-1360) or a direct disciple of Haji Bektash Veli, founder of the Bektashi order. It is more likely, however, that he was a figure of early Balkan—and not originally of Bektashi or Muslim—legendry. The Bektashi simply took advantage of his popularity as a symbol of Islamic-Christian syncretism and religious tolerance in order to promote their own doctrines. The first legends associated with Sari Salltëk were recorded by the Moroccan voyager and geographer Ibn Battuta (1304-1377). From documents dating from 1538, it is known that such legends were very popular in the Balkans. According to one tale, the sultan sent Sari Salltëk together with seventy disciples to Europe, where he traveled through Rumelia and the Crimea to Moscow and Poland. In Gdańsk (Danzig), he slew a **Catholic** holy man called Saint Nicholas and converted many people to **Islam** after putting on the saint's clothes. Sari Salltëk is, in fact, often confused with Saint Nicholas, as well as with Saint George and Saint Simeon.

In Albania, Sari Salltëk is particularly associated with the town of **Kruja**, where he is said to have appeared as a Bektashi dervish. Dutch scholar Machiel Kiel has discovered an imperial **Ottoman** register from ca. 1567-1568, which contains a note about repairs to the road leading up to the grave of Sari Salltëk in Kruja and demonstrates that Sari Salltëk was an object of widespread veneration in Albania much earlier than had been previously thought.

Sari Salltëk, to whom many miracles are attributed, died on the Greek island of Corfu and is identified in the **Orthodox** tradition with Saint Spyridon. In the nineteenth century, many Albanian Bektashi went on pilgrimage to the Church of Saint Spyridon on Corfu to worship the patron saint of the island under his Islamic name. According to other legends, Sari Salltëk lies buried in the Church of Saint Naum on the south bank of Lake **Ohrid**, or on the top of Mount Pashtrik, which forms the border between the northern Albanian district of Has and the Gjakova region of neighboring **Kosova**. Before **World War II**, thousands of Albanians from Kosova and northern Albania used to make the pilgrimage up Mount Pashtrik to the grave of Sari Salltëk on 22 August. Another important site of pilgrimage is the *tekke* in a cave at the top of Mount Kruja, Alb. *Mali i Krujës*, which had an inscription dating it from the year 1692-1693 [1104 A.H.]. The site had previously been used for a church dedicated to Saint Alexander. This *tekke* was closed and all but destroyed in 1967 during the campaign against **religion**, but it was rebuilt in 1991. The people of Kruja still go there despite the difficult climb, in particular on Sari Salltëk's feast day of 22 August, and drink holy water from the bottom of the cave. All in all, Sari Salltëk is said to have seven graves, the number seven often occurring in his legends, and each grave contains a part of his body.

SAZAN. Island off the Albanian coast near **Vlora**. Sazan is the only sizeable island on the Albanian coast. It is 5.5 square kilometers and is situated at the entrance to the Bay of Vlora, 4.8 kilometers from the peninsula of Karaburun and sixteen kilometers from the town of Vlora itself. Sazan was used by the Venetian and **Ottoman** fleets in the seventeenth and eighteenth centuries as a place of moorage in the winter, although it has no satisfactory harbor. It was occupied by English forces, with the Ionian islands, in the nineteenth century and given to **Greece** in 1864. Italian troops under General Leon Ghilardi della Ghianda occupied the island in June 1914 and it remained in Italian possession until **Italy**'s capitulation in September 1943. During the **communist** period, Sazan was the site of a military base, and numerous military families lived there under primitive conditions. Since that time, it has been virtually uninhabited. The toponym Sazan was recorded in 1303 as *Sasinum, Sasnum* and, in 1497, as *Saseno* (**Arnold von Harff**). It is known in Italian as *Saseno*.

SAZE. Musical instrument. The *saze* is a mandolin-like instrument of traditional Albanian folk **music**. It has a long neck and, as opposed to the two-stringed *çifteli*, has ten strings which are divided into three courses.

SCANDERBEG (1405-1468.01.17). Albanian prince and national hero. The real name of Scanderbeg, Alb. *Skënderbej*, def. *Skënderbeu,* was George Castriotta, Alb. *Gjergj Kastrioti.* George Castriotta stemmed from a family of landowners from the **Dibra** region in northeastern Albania who were no doubt of mixed Albanian-Slavic ancestry. His father John Castriotta (?-1440) had initially submitted to **Ottoman** rule but, after the Battle of Ankara in 1402, he declared his independence from the Turks, extending his influence from Dibra through the **Mat** valley to the Adriatic. In 1410, despite his attempts to form an alliance with the Republic of Venice, he was forced once more to give way to the supremacy of the sultan. According to legend, as a pledge of his submission, John Castriotta sent his sons, Stanisha, George and Constantine and perhaps one other, in ransom to the sultan's court at Adrianople (Edirne) in 1423. It was here that George received military training, was converted to **Islam** and took the name Alexander (Iskander). The young Iskander also participated in military campaigns against the Christians, for which his father was obliged to beg the pardon of the Venetian senate in 1428. For his military valor, Iskander was awarded the title of bey (*beg*), and thus the name Scanderbeg by which he was to be universally known.

In 1438, having gained the confidence of Sultan Murad II
(r. 1421-1451), he was appointed military commander of the
fortress of **Kruja** (Croia), where he established initial contacts
with Venice and Ragusa (Dubrovnik). In 1440, he was made
Sandjak-bey of Dibra. Scanderbeg's strength and popularity in his
native region, and the military success of the Hungarians under
John Hunyadi (ca. 1385-1456) in their battles against the Turks,
convinced him that the time was ripe to abandon Ottoman forces.
An opportunity arose during the Battle of Nish in November 1443
when Turkish troops were in disarray after a Hungarian offensive.
Scanderbeg, his nephew Hamza, and 300 horsemen abandoned
the Turkish forces and returned to Dibra, whence they carried on
to the fortress of Kruja. Within a matter of days, Scanderbeg had
assembled his own Albanian forces for a general uprising. The
fortresses of Petrela, south of **Tirana**, and Svetigrad in Dibra
were soon taken by the Albanians. To consolidate his power,
Scanderbeg formed alliances through marriage with the main
ruling families of Albania. He himself married Andronica, daughter of **George Arianiti**, and his sister Mamica was given in marriage to Charles Musachi Thopia.

On 2 March 1444, Scanderbeg convened an assembly of all
important Albanian nobles at **Lezha** (Alessio) during which it
was decided to set up a standing army to counter an impending
Turkish invasion. Scanderbeg was selected to head this force of
about 15,000 men. A huge Turkish army soon flooded into Albania but was beaten back in Dibra at the end of June 1444. In view
of the superior strength of the Turkish forces, Scanderbeg's
troops made optimal use of the terrain for guerrilla warfare. Two
further Ottoman invasions were repelled, one in October 1445 on
the Mokra Plateau near **Pogradec,** and a second in September
1446 in Dibra. The following year, Scanderbeg's relations with
the Republic of Venice deteriorated when the latter endeavored
to extend its influence into the region of Deja (Dagno). The
conflict led to two years of warfare with the Serenissima, forcing
Scanderbeg to fight on two fronts. Although his troops managed
to defeat the Turks at Oranik on 14 August 1448, he realized that
he had to reach an agreement with Venice if he wished to carry
on resistance. A peace treaty was concluded on 4 October 1448
under which Dagno and Drivast were abandoned to the Republic
of Venice in exchange for the payment of 1,400 ducats of gold
annually.

In May 1450, Sultan Murad II arrived personally at Kruja and
besieged the fortress for four and a half months. Although over-

whelmingly outnumbered, the Albanians managed to resist Turkish forces and conferred a humiliating defeat upon the sultan, who was obliged on 26 October to return to Adrianople empty-handed. Scanderbeg's victory over the Muslim hordes was widely acclaimed in the Christian world. Pope Nicholas V (r. 1447-1455), King Ladislaus V of Hungary (r. 1444-1457), and King Alfonso of Aragon-Naples (r. 1435-1458) sent messages of congratulations and offered Scanderbeg their support. On 26 March 1451, Scanderbeg concluded an alliance with King Alfonso at Gaeta under which the former pledged allegiance to the latter. Catalonian troops were subsequently stationed at Kruja under the command of the Aragonese viceroy Ramon de Ortafa.

Scanderbeg's position became somewhat more tenuous after the final Turkish conquest of Constantinople on 29 May 1453. Mehmed the Conqueror was determined to vanquish Albania in order to prepare an attack on Catholic **Italy**. Naples, the Church and Venice now came up with military and financial assistance. With Neapolitan help, Scanderbeg attempted to reconquer **Berat** in central Albania in 1455 but was forced back. The alliance of Albanian nobles which had cemented in Alessio in March 1444 also began to break up. The Dukagjini, **Arianiti** and Balsha dynasties withdrew their support and even Scanderbeg's commander Moisi Golemi and the former's nephew Hamza abandoned him. Scanderbeg nonetheless carried on and repulsed two Turkish invasions in 1456 and 1457. For his defense of Christendom against the Muslim hordes, Pope Calixtus II (r. 1455-1458) awarded the Albanian warrior the title of *Athleta Christi*.

In 1458, Scanderbeg was summoned to Italy to fulfil his obligations as vassal under the treaty of Gaeta. Ferdinand I (r. 1458-1494), successor of Alfonso who had died on 27 June 1458, required assistance to defeat the rival house of Anjou which was endeavoring to take power in Naples. Scanderbeg arranged a three-year peace treaty with the Turks and proceeded to Italy with about 2,500 troops. In Barletta and Trani, he managed to defeat Ferdinand's main rival Giovanni Antonio Orsini, Prince of Taranto. After the campaign, some Albanian forces remained in Italy and established colonies in Calabria under one Demetrio Reres, colonies which constituted the first **Arbëresh** settlements. In 1462, Scanderbeg returned to Albania to discover that the Turks had once more invaded the country despite the treaty. He defeated no less than three Turkish military expeditions in 1462 before a new six-month peace treaty could be arranged in April 1463. It was in November of that year, during the cease-fire, that

Pope Pius II (r. 1458-1464) declared a holy crusade on the infidels, absolving Scanderbeg of his obligations under the peace treaty with the Turks. The pope died, however, on 15 August 1464, bringing the crusade to a sudden and inglorious conclusion.

Scanderbeg now found himself faced with five successive Turkish invasions under the command of Balaban Pasha. All were successfully repulsed. In 1466, Sultan Mehmed II himself arrived in Albania with a large army, and laid siege to Kruja. After two months of siege, the sultan was forced to return to Turkey and left his troops under the command of Balaban Pasha. He also had a new fortress built at **Elbasan** in central Albania on the **Shkumbin** River. Scanderbeg hastened to Rome and Naples to request assistance in his struggle against Turkish forces. In April 1467, he returned to Albania just in time to repel a renewed Turkish attack during which Balaban Pasha perished at the foot of the fortress walls. In July 1467, Mehmet II returned to Albania, this time with all of his forces, determined to bring Scanderbeg to his knees. The Albanian prince once more requested assistance from Venice and called for a new assembly of nobles in Alessio in January 1468. On 17 January 1468, however, before the assembly could convene, the heroic Scanderbeg died, and resistance to the Turks soon collapsed. Albania was to return to Ottoman rule for another four and a half centuries.

Scanderbeg had gathered quite a posthumous reputation in Western Europe in the sixteenth and seventeenth centuries. With virtually all of the Balkans under Ottoman rule and with the Turks at the very gates of Vienna in 1683, nothing could have captivated readers in the West more than an action-packed tale of heroic Christian resistance to the Muslim hordes. Books on the Albanian prince began to appear in Western Europe in the early sixteenth century. One of the earliest of these histories to have circulated in Western Europe about the heroic deeds of Scanderbeg was the *Historia de vita et gestis Scanderbegi, Epirotarum Princeps* (History of the Life and Deeds of Scanderbeg: Prince of Epirus), Rome ca. 1508-1510, published a mere four decades after Scanderbeg's death by **Marinus Barletius**. The work was widely read in the sixteenth and seventeenth centuries and was translated and/or adapted into a number of foreign language versions. The English version, translated from the French of Jacques De Lavardin by one Zachary Jones, was published under the title *Historie of George Castriot, surnamed Scanderbeg, King of Albinie; containing his Famous*

Actes, his Noble Deedes of Armes and Memorable Victories against the Turkes for the Faith of Christ, London 1596.

SCHIRÒ, GIUSEPPE (1865.08.10-1927.02.17). Arbëresh poet, prose writer and scholar. Giuseppe Schirò (senior), who is known in Albanian as Zef Skiroi, was a writer whose literary works can be said to mark the transition to modern Albanian **literature** in **Italy.** He was born in the Albanian-speaking village of Piana degli Albanesi near Palermo in Sicily. During his initial studies at the Italo-Albanian seminary in Palermo, he showed great interest in his native culture. In 1887, together with Francesco Petta, he founded the periodical *Arbri i ri* (Young Albania) in Palermo and published his first verse collection. He graduated with a law degree in 1890, but the focus of his interests remained folklore and literature, in particular classical and Italian, which he taught at the Garibaldi secondary school in Palermo from 1888 to 1894. It was a period of great literary productivity for Giuseppe Schirò, the years in which his major literary works began to appear. He was a friend of Italian novelist and playwright Luigi Pirandello (1867-1936), whom he had gotten to know at school and university in Palermo, though their literary activities show few similarities.

In 1901, Schirò was appointed to the newly founded chair of Albanian studies at the Royal Oriental Institute in Naples, a post he held for the rest of his life and, in 1904, he published the short-lived fortnightly periodical *Flamuri i Shqiperîs / La Bandiera albanese* (The Albanian Flag). Also in this period appeared his work on early Arbëresh literature and folklore: *Canti popolari dell'Albania* (Folk Songs from Albania), Palermo 1901; *Canti sacri delle colonie albanesi di Sicilia* (Sacred Songs of the Albanian colonies of Sicily), Naples 1907; and *Canti tradizionali ed altri saggi delle colonie albanesi di Sicilia* (Traditional Songs and other Essays of the Albanian Colonies of Sicily), Naples 1923. Schirò worked in Albania as an inspector for Italian schools from 1912 to 1914. He later pursued his Albanological activities at home in Naples, publishing, lecturing and attending congresses. The murder of his son Mino, a victim of political intrigue in 1920, cast a heavy shadow over his final years. Giuseppe Schirò died in Naples, honored and respected as the greatest figure of contemporary Sicilian Arbëresh literature.

Among Giuseppe Schirò's major literary publications are: *Rapsodie albanesi* (Albanian Rhapsodies), Palermo 1887; *Mili e Haidhia* (Mili and Haidhia), Palermo 1891, a masterpiece of early twentieth-century Albanian verse in eighteen cantos; *Kënkat e luftës* (The Battle Songs), Palermo 1897; *Te dheu i huaj* (To the Foreign Land), Palermo 1900, a long historical idyll, which tells of the epic flight of the fifteenth-century Albanians from their homeland and of the colonization of Sicily; the eight-part elegy *Mino*, a literary digestion of the tragic death of the poet's son Milo; *Kënkat e litorit* (The Songs of the Littoral), Palermo 1926; and *Këthimi* (The Return), Florence 1965, a heroic poem of Albanian independence in forty-one cantos and 4,077 lines.

Despite his accomplishments, Schirò was less appreciated by literary historians in Stalinist Albania than earlier Arbëresh writers like **Girolamo De Rada** or **Giuseppe Serembe**. Schirò's unerring faith in Italy as a potential protector and custodian of the culture of the small Balkan state ran against the grain of subsequent aspirations of Albanian nationalism based on absolute independence from all other nations, including Italy. It was, nonetheless, Giuseppe Schirò who first succeeded in blending the romantic elements of Arbëresh folk verse with the artistic precision of Italian classical and neoclassical poetry to form a harmonious and balanced poetic corpus.

SCHIRÒ, GIUSEPPE (1905-1984). Arbëresh scholar and literary historian. Giuseppe Schirò (junior) was born in Contessa Entellina (Alb. *Kundisa*) in Sicily and pursued his education at the Corsini college in San Demetrio Corone in Calabria. He later taught in Padua and Rome. Schirò's first writings on Albanian culture appeared in the 1940s. He is remembered in particular for his *Storia della letteratura albanese* (History of Albanian Literature), Florence 1959, one of the most reliable literary history of the period.

SCHMITT, OLIVER (1973-). Swiss scholar and historian. Oliver Jens Schmitt was born in Basle and studied in Basle, Vienna, Berlin and Munich, specializing in Byzantine and Islamic studies and in the history of southeast Europe. He finished his doctorate at the University of Munich in 2000. Oliver Schmitt is the author of the most thoroughly documented study of early Albania since the works of **Alain Ducellier**: his 700-page *Das Venezianische Albanien, 1392-1479* (Venetian Albania, 1392-1479), Munich 2001. He is currently working on a biography of **Scanderbeg**.

SCHWANDNER-SIEVERS, STEPHANIE (1964.04.12-). German scholar and anthropologist. Stephanie Schwandner-Sievers was born in Munich. She finished her secondary schooling in Berlin in 1983, and from then until 1993, she studied at the Free University of Berlin, graduating with a masters degree in social anthropology on the *Funktion und Bedeutung der Besa in Vergangenheit und Gegenwart* (Function and Significance of the "**Besa**" in the Past and Present), Berlin 1993. From 1997 to 2003, she was the first Nash Fellow for Albanian Studies at the School of Slavonic and East European Studies in London, and has just finished her doctorate in Berlin with a dissertation on *Evoking a Past: Albanian Identifications and Local Power* (2003). Stephanie Schwandner-Sievers has been conducting anthropological research on the Albanians since 1992, in particular on questions of identity and social cohesion. She has recently co-edited the volumes: *Die weite Welt und das Dorf: Migration in Albanien am Ende des 20. Jahrhunderts* (The Wide World and the Village: Migration in Albania at the End of the Twentieth Century), Vienna 2001; and, with **Bernd Fischer**, *Albanian Identities: Myth and History,* London 2002.

SCIAMBRA, MATTEO (1914.01.30-1967.07.30). Arbëresh scholar. Matteo Sciambra was an Italo-Albanian priest and scholar from Sicily. He is the author of *Indagini storiche sulla comunità greco-albanese di Palermo* (Historical Research on the Greek-Albanian Community in Palermo), Grottaferrata 1963; and *Bogdanica: studi su Pietro Bogdano e l'opera sua* (Bogdanica: Studies on **Pjetër Bogdani** and His Work), Bologna 1965.

SCUTARI. *See* SHKODRA.

SELCA. Archeological site situated near the present-day village of Selca e Poshtme in the District of **Pogradec**, three kilometers south of Qukës. Selca was founded by **Illyrian** tribes in the early fourth century B.C. The hilltop site, at an elevation of 1,040 meters, revealed spectacular Illyrian tombs carved in the sandstone cliffs. These burial chambers with tunnels cut into the rock, discovered in 1948 and excavated in 1969-1972, date from the third or fourth centuries B.C. and indicate the presence of a major **Illyrian** settlement in what is now a rather remote area.

SELENICA, DAVID (eighteenth century). Painter. David Selenica was a noted fresco and icon fresco painter in the **Orthodox** tradition. He lived for some time on Mount Athos in northern Greece, but probably stemmed from the Selenica region near **Vlora**. His works, based on the style of Paleologian frescoes on Athos, can be found in particular in the Church of Saint Nicholas (1722-1726) in **Voskopoja**, as well as in Athos and Kastoria in Greece.

SEMAN. River in southern central Albania. The Seman begins at the confluence of the **Osum** and Devoll Rivers in the District of **Kuçova** northwest of **Berat** and flows past **Fier** into the Adriatic Sea, south of the Lagoon of Karavasta.

ŞEMSEDDIN SAMI. See FRASHËRI, SAMI BEY.

SERB MINORITY IN ALBANIA. See SLAVIC MINORITY IN ALBANIA.

SERBIA, ALBANIANS IN. There are about 100,000 Albanian speakers in the Presheva Valley of southern Serbia, near the borders of **Macedonia** and **Kosova.** The town of Presheva (Serb. *Preševo*) itself has an overwhelming Albanian majority, while Bujanovc (Serb. *Bujanovac*) and Medvegja (Serb. *Medvedja*) have mixed populations. A large number of Albanians, some 600 villages, from the southern Serbian regions of Prokuplje, Vranje and Nish were ethnically cleansed before the Serbian-Turkish war of 1876-1878, and many survivors resettled in Kosova and **Turkey**. Before that time, there had also been isolated Albanian settlements as far as east as Bela Palanka and Pirot. There are still Albanian speakers to be found in the Sandjak region of Novi Pazar. Aside from these traditional areas of settlement, Kosova Albanian migrants settled throughout Serbia and the rest of **Yugoslavia** in search of work in the 1970s and 1980s, in particular when economic conditions in Kosova became untenable. There are said to be some 70,000 Albanians in Belgrade alone.

SERBIA AND MONTENEGRO, RELATIONS WITH. Southern Slavic tribes invaded the Balkans in the sixth century A.D. and occupied most of Albania by the year 600. There were Slavic settlements throughout the country, in particular in the southern half, and over the coming centuries the Slavs and the non-Slav indigenous population of Albania lived in a close symbiosis. These proximal relations can be seen in the strong stratum of Slavic vocabulary in the Albanian **language**.

    Shkodra was taken over in 1180 by the Serb dynasty of Stephen Nemanja and from 1343 to 1555 virtually all of Albania came under the reign of Stephan Dushan. The Serbs also ruled **Kosova** for two centuries.

Ethnic relations with the neighboring Serbs were not always smooth over the following centuries, in particular over Kosova. With the Montenegrins, the situation was slightly different. The traditional tribal culture of northern Albania was very similar to that of neighboring Montenegro; some tribes spoke Albanian, others spoke Serbian, but they otherwise had very much in common. Even today, the northern Albanians have generally good relations with their Montenegrin neighbors, despite the vicissitudes of politics.

The nineteenth century, nonetheless, saw decades of border skirmishes between the **Catholic** and Muslim Albanian tribes and the **Orthodox** Kingdom of Montenegro under Prince Nikolla. The Serb and Montenegrin declaration of war on the **Ottoman Empire** on 2 July 1876 resulted in more warfare between the Albanians and the Montenegrins. In 1913, the **Conference of Ambassadors** in London accorded to Montenegro not only **Hoti**, **Gruda** and much of **Kelmendi** territory, but also Plava and Gucia, despite the protests of the majority Albanian populations there. Montenegro also coveted Shkodra which its troops took in April 1913, but it was obliged by the Great Powers to return the town that year. More tragically, the Serb army conquered and laid waste to Kosova in 1912, conducting what Danish correspondent Fritz Magnussen called an unspeakable war of atrocities: "The Arnaut villages were surrounded and set on fire. The inhabitants were then chased from their homes and shot like rats. The Serbian soldiers delighted in telling me of the manhunts they had conducted." The Great Powers, nonetheless, allowed Serbia to keep Kosova, which has been the main stumbling block in Serb-Albanian relations ever since.

During **World War I**, Albania proper was also invaded and occupied by Montenegrin and Serbia forces. The Montenegrins once again took Shkodra, and Serb forces occupied much of central Albanian (**Elbasan, Tirana**) until they were forced to withdraw by the advancing Austro-Hungarian troops in late 1916.

The years between the World Wars I and II were characterized by rivalry between **Yugoslavia** and **Italy** over Albania, whereby Italy gradually gained the upper hand. On 18 July 1926, the Albanian **parliament** under **Ahmet Zogu** authorized territorial concessions to Yugoslavia, giving to it the Orthodox holy site of Sveti Naum on Lake **Ohrid**.

The final years of **World War II** saw close ties between the Yugoslav and Albanian **communists**. Tito's emissaries Miladin Popović (1910-1945) and Dušan Mugoša (1914-1973) gave strong support to the Albanian communists and it is alleged that the Albanian communist party was actually founded by the Yugoslavs.

Political relations between the two countries were at their closest from 1945 to 1948. Diplomatic relations between the two countries had been restored on 1 May 1945 and **Enver Hoxha** visited Tito in Belgrade on 23 June to 2 July 1946, at which time three agreements were signed on economic cooperation, payments, and loans. On 9 July 1946, a treaty on friendship, cooperation and mutual assistance was concluded and on 27 November of that year, a customs and monetary union was created between the two countries. Serbo-Croatian was introduced as a compulsory subject in all Albanian schools and the two countries were on the verge of merging to form the cornerstone of a Balkan federation.

Policy differences between Tito and Joseph Stalin led, however, on 28 June 1948, to Yugoslavia's expulsion from the Cominform after a Warsaw conference of communist parties, and the Albanian party leadership, after some careful maneuvering by Enver Hoxha, declared its solidarity with the Soviet side. Thus, after two years of very close contacts, relations between the two neighboring countries were broken. On 30 June 1948, Albania renounced all economic agreements with Yugoslavia, although the treaty on friendship and mutual assistance remained in force until 12 November 1949. On 28 May 1950, Yugoslavia shut down its embassy in Tirana and on 11 October of that year ceased diplomatic relations with Albania.

Diplomatic ties were resumed on 22 December 1953, but relations remained cool in view of the continuing political schism between Tito and the Russians. It was not before February 1971 that relations improved somewhat, allowing for a modicum of cultural exchange with autonomous Kosova. In the 1980s, relations deteriorated once again, however, because of Belgrade's policies of discrimination and oppression of the Kosova Albanians in the wake of the 1981 uprising there. The party leadership in Albania kept its distance, however, and paid no more than occasional lip-service to the national rights and freedoms of the Kosova Albanians. A bomb was thrown at the Yugoslav embassy in Tirana on 23 May 1981, and political relations remained unstable for some time, though a long-term trade agreement was reached on 17 September 1985 and the train line between Shkodra and Titograd (Podgorica) was inaugurated for freight traffic on 26 November of that year.

In the mid-1990s, relations with Montenegro improved substantially. The border crossing was opened to the public and trade between the two countries flourished, despite the embargo on Yugoslavia. The 1998 uprising in Kosova against Serb military forces stationed there, and the subsequent **Kosova War,** resulted in the expulsion by the Serb authorities of half a million "Yugoslav citizens of Albanian ethnicity" to Albania in 1999. During the Kosova War, Yugoslav troops made several incursions into Albanian territory, notably on 13 April 1999 when they burned down houses in the village of Kamenica. Diplomatic relations between Albania and Yugoslavia were broken on 18 April 1999 and resumed only after the Kosova War and the overthrow of the regime of Slobodan Milošević on 17 January 2001. The two countries signed a trade agreement on 20 September 2002 and a travel and economic agreement on 26 November 2002.

SEREMBE, GIUSEPPE (1844.03.06-1901.12.31). Arbëresh poet. Giuseppe Serembe, known in Albanian as Zef Serembe, was born in San Cosmo Albanese (Alb. *Strigari*) in the Calabrian province of Cosenza and studied at the College of Saint Adrian. At an early age, he fell in love with a girl from his native village who emigrated to Brazil with her family and subsequently died. Obsessed by this loss and by the thought of finding at least her grave, Serembe set sail for Brazil in 1874 in search of a new life. He was received at the court of Emperor Dom Pedro II with the help of a letter of recommendation from **Dora d'Istria**, but soon returned to Europe, disappointed and dejected. On his arrival in the Old World in September 1875, his fortunes took yet another turn for the worse. Robbed of all his money, apparently in the port of Marseille, he was forced to return to Italy on foot, and is said to have lost many of his manuscripts on the way. In Leghorn (Livorno), **Demetrio Camarda** provided him with train fare for the rest of his journey back to Cosenza.

Despair, arising no doubt from chronic depression or some other form of psychiatric disorder, accompanied him wherever he went and rendered him solitary and insecure. He took refuge in the dream of the land of his forefathers, a vision marred by the reality of Turkish occupation in Albania and by the indifference of the Western powers to its sufferings. In 1886, Serembe visited Arbëresh settlements in Sicily and in 1893 traveled to the **United**

States where he lived for about two years. A volume of his Italian verse was published in New York in 1895. In 1897, he emigrated from his native Calabria to South America a second time and tried to start a new life in Buenos Aires. The following year he fell ill and died in São Paolo.

Many of Serembe's works (poetry, drama and a translation of the Psalms of David) were lost in the course of his unsettled existence. During his lifetime he published only the following: *Poesie italiane e canti originali tradotti dall'albanese* (Italian Poetry and Original Songs Translated from the Albanian), Cosenza 1883, in Italian and Albanian; *Il reduce soldato, ballata lirica* (The Returning Soldier, Lyric Ballad), New York 1895, verse in Italian only; and *Sonetti vari* (Various Sonnets), Naples 189?, an extremely rare collection of forty-two Italian sonnets with an introduction, all crammed onto four pages of tiny print. Thirty-nine of his Albanian poems were published posthumously in *Vjersha* (Verse), Milan 1926. Serembe's verse, despondent and melancholic in character, and yet often patriotic and idealistic in inspiration, is considered by many to rank among the best lyric poetry ever produced in Albanian, at least before modern times. His themes range from melodious lyrics on love to eulogies on his native land (be it Italy, land of his birth, or Albania, land of his dreams), elegant poems on friendship and the beauties of nature, and verse of religious inspiration.

SEVI, SABBETAI (1626-1676.09.17). Jewish holy man. The charismatic **Jewish** prophet Sabbetai Sevi or Zevi, the so-called Mystical Messiah, was born in Izmir. In 1648, he had a revelation which caused him to believe that he was the messiah. He was soon expelled from Izmir by the Jewish community there because of such proclivities. Sabbetai Sevi traveled throughout the Sephardic Jewish world and was joined by another Kabbalist, Nathan of Gaza (d. 1680), who supported him. With Nathan's help, the Jewish world was thrown into turmoil at the idea of a new messiah, and Sabbetai soon had thousands of followers in Jewish communities from as far as Yemen and London. Venice and Thessalonika became virtual centers of Sabbetaian kabbalistic fanaticism. In September 1666, however, the mass exaltation caused by his declamations came to an abrupt end when Sabbetai converted to **Islam** in Edirne, apparently under compulsion. Most of his followers, refusing to abandon him, converted to Islam, too, creating a Muslim sect called the Dönme or Crypto-Jews.

Despite his conversion, Sabbetai continued proselytizing until 1673, when he was sent by the **Ottoman** authorities into Albanian exile to the port of Ulqin (Ulcinj). From there, he continued to communicate with Jews elsewhere in the Balkans. In August 1676, he is known to have written a letter to the small Jewish community of **Berat** requesting a Hebrew prayer book, but died shortly afterwards. His grave was long rumored to be at the *tekke* in the courtyard of the Sultan Mosque, Alb. *Xhamia e Mbretit,* in Berat where a tomb stood until 1967. Most contemporary scholars now believe, however, that he was buried in Ulqin. Sevi's biographer Gershom Scholem states that his unmarked grave in Ulqin was visited by Dönme pilgrims from Thessalonika up to the beginning of the twentieth century.

SHALA. Northern Albanian tribe and traditional tribal region. The Shala region is situated in the **Dukagjini** area north of the **Drin** River in the District of **Shkodra,** basically the valley of the Shala River south of Theth. It borders on the traditional tribal regions of **Boga, Shkreli,** and Plani to the west, **Shoshi** to the south and **Nikaj** to the east. The name was recorded in Italian in 1634 as *Sciala* and derives from Alb. *shalë, shalësinë* "arid, infertile land." The Shalas are closely related to the Shoshi tribe and traditionally had connections with **Mirdita.** The Shala tribe, primarily **Catholic,** had a **population** of over 3,000 in the late nineteenth century.

SHANAJ, MEVLAN (1945.02.07-). Actor and **film** director. Mevlan Shanaj was born in **Fier.** He initially studied medicine in **Tirana,** but then graduated in acting from the Academy of Fine Arts (*Instituti i Lartë i Arteve*) in 1969. He worked for Albanian television for many years as a film director. Among his most successful films in this field were: *Plumba perandorit* (Bullets for the Emperor), 1980; *I Paharruari* (The Forgotten Man), 1984; and *Fletë të bardha* (White Pages), 1990. As an actor, Shanaj is remembered for his roles in *I teti në bronx* (The Bronze Bust), 1970; *Ballë per ballë* (Face to Face), 1979; and *Unë e dua Erën* (I Love Era), 1990.

SHAS. Archeological site and medieval settlement near the mouth of the Buna River, on the Montenegrin side of the present border. At its zenith during the Middle Ages, Shas was a **port** for trade with the countries of the Adriatic. It was known in Latin as *Suacium,* in Italian as *Suazzo* or *Sfazzi,* in medieval Slavic as

Svač, and in early French as *Soans.* Shas was first documented in 1067. It was plundered by the Tatars in 1242 and began to decay around the end of the fourteenth century. It was razed by **Ottoman** troops in 1406.

SHEHU, BASHKIM (1955-). Writer and intellectual figure. Born in **Tirana** as the son of **communist** political leader **Mehmet Shehu,** Bashkim Shehu enjoyed a privileged youth. He graduated from the University of Tirana with a degree in Albanian **language** and **literature** in 1979. With the death of his father, however, he was incarcerated as a political prisoner in 1982. In 1989, he was given a second sentence but was released in 1991 with the fall of the dictatorship. He subsequently emigrated to Hungary and currently lives in Barcelona, Spain. His memoirs were published in French as *L'automne de la peur* (Autumn of Fear), Paris 1993. Shehu is a writer whose works, some of which are autobiographical in spirit, have been translated into French, German, Hungarian, Spanish and Catalan. Among them are: the novels *Rrugëtimi i mbramë i Ago Ymerit* (The Last Voyage of Ago Ymeri), Prishtina 1995; and *Gostia* (The Banquet), Tirana 1996; the short story collections *Idhulli prej tymi* (The Idol Made of Smoke), Prishtina 1996; *Rrëfim ndanë një varri të zbrazët* (Tale Beside an Empty Grave), Tirana 1998; *Roman labirint me shtate hyrje* (Labyrinth Novel with Seven Introductions), Prishtina 2000; and *Mallkimi ose mbi mosqenien e autorit* (The Curse, or on the Nonexistence of the Author), Tirana 2001.

SHEHU, MEHMET (1913.01.10-1981.12.18). Political figure of the **communist** period. Mehmet Shehu was born in Çorrush in **Mallakastra** and graduated in 1932 from the **American Vocational School** of Harry Fultz in **Tirana.** After graduation, he received a scholarship to study at a military academy in Naples in 1935, but was allegedly forced to interrupt his studies there because of his procommunist activities. He attended officers' school in Tirana in 1936, and from November 1938 to 1939, took part in the Spanish Civil War as a member of the twelfth International Brigade. He also joined the Spanish communist party in 1938. In 1939, he was interned in France, where he became a member of the Italian communist party. He returned to Albania in 1942 and joined the partisan movement. It was in good part due to his military experience that the communists were able to take power and hold on to it for such a long time. In 1944, he was sent to **Shkodra** to put down an anticommunist revolt.

Following the communist takeover, Shehu trained at the Voroshilov military academy in Moscow, 1945-1946, and after the fall of **Koçi Xoxe** and the break with Tito, he took over the ministry of the interior, 1948-1954. He was known as one of the cruelest members of the communist leadership.

Mehmet Shehu was secretary of the Central Committee from 1948 to 1953 and was a member of the Politburo from 1948 to his death. He was thus the number two figure of the party and government leadership, after **Enver Hoxha**, until the end of his days. From 20 July 1954 to 1981, he served as prime minister and, after the purge of **Beqir Balluku** (August 1974), as minister of defense, 1974-1980. At the end of 1981, Shehu was purged himself. After an apparent power struggle with Enver Hoxha, he was murdered, or committed suicide, in his villa in Tirana. Hoxha subsequently accused him of having been a "polyagent" for a number of foreign secret services. Shehu's whole family clan was, thereafter, arrested and interned. His wife, Fiqrete Shehu, also a member of the Central Committee, died of a heart attack in 1988, and one of his sons committed suicide by throwing himself onto the electric wires surrounding the prison.

SHEMIMI BABA (1748-1803). Bektashi holy man and poet. Shemseddin Shemimiu was born in 1748, apparently in **Kruja**, and lived in his early years in Veles (Köprülü) in central Macedonia, where he served the Bektashi order together with his companion Hatemi Haydar Baba. In 1799, he moved back to Kruja, where the Bektashi *tekke* became one of the fundamental centers of the movement. **Ali Pasha Tepelena**, the Lion of Janina, is said to have "taken the hand" of Shemimi Baba, i.e., to have been received by him as a Bektashi follower. It was no doubt with the support of Ali Pasha that Shemimi and others were able to spread the Bektashi movement throughout southern Albania. Shemimi Baba founded the *tekke* of Melçan near **Korça**, which was subsequently run by Abdullah Baba (d. 1852) from Greece. Then followed the founding of the *tekke* of Prishta in **Skrapar**, which was taken over by Baba Tahir of Crete. Shemimi also founded the *tekkes* of Xhefaj Baba in **Elbasan** and of Sadik Baba in Koshtan near **Tepelena**, all of which served as centers for further foundations in the south. Baba Shemimi was murdered in Kruja. He was laid to rest in a *tyrbe* constructed in his honor at the *tekke* of Fushë Kruja, built itself under Asim Baba.

SHËRBIMI INFORMATIV KOMBËTAR. *See* NATIONAL INFORMATION SERVICE.

SHIMA, ALUSH (1942.10.21-). Painter. Alush Shima is widely considered to be one of the most successful contemporary Albanian painters. He was born in **Tirana** of a family from Kuç near **Vlora**. He finished school in 1955 and attended the Jordan Misja Academy under **Sadik Kaceli, Abdurrahim Buza** and **Nexhmedin Zajmi**. From 1965, he also studied at the Academy of Fine Arts (*Instituti i Lartë i Arteve*). In 1967, he began working as a painter and costume designer for the **New Albania Film Studios**. In 1973, after the arrest of his friend, painter Ali Oseku, the police came and destroyed about 150 of his works because it was felt that they contained decadent tendencies. Many other paintings only survived because they were hidden for years in the rafters of his and friends' houses.

After the fall of the dictatorship, Shima traveled abroad and was highly successful in exhibitions in England, France, Switzerland, and Greece, etc. From 1994 to 1997, he served as director of the **National Gallery** and promoted exhibitions of formerly forbidden, persecuted and imprisoned artists. He was active in political life during this period as one of the most vociferous and radically anticommunist members of the **Democratic Party**. He was a member of **parliament** from 26 May 1996 to the fall of the regime of **Sali Berisha**, when he withdrew from politics, to return to his career as a painter.

SHKODRA. Town in the **District of Shkodra**, of which it is the administrative center. **Population** in Dec. 1999: 104,667. Situated on Lake **Shkodra** and the banks of the Buna River, Shkodra is the cultural capital of northern Albania. It is known for its impressive Rozafat fortress, where a settlement of the **Illyrian** Labeates tribe was situated. In 180-168 B.C., Shkodra, Latin *Scodra,* was the residence of the Illyrian king **Genthius**. Under Diocletian (r. 284-305 A.D.) it became capital of the Roman province of Praevalitana and was the seat of a bishop by the fourth century. In 1043, it was conquered by the Slavic rulers of **Montenegrin** Zeta and served as their capital. In 1180, it was taken over by Stephen Nemanja and remained Serb until the collapse of the Nemanja dynasty. It then served as capital of the local Balsha dynasty until it was conquered by the Venetians in 1396. Finally, in January 1479, it fell to the **Ottoman** Turks after a long siege.

Shkodra was the greatest city of Albania throughout the Ottoman period. In April 1913, it was taken over by Montenegrin forces but was returned to Albania in accordance with the provision of the London **Conference of Ambassadors**. It remained the country's cultural capital until **World War II**. In 1939, it had a **population** of 30,000.

The original town of Shkodra with the old bazaar situated at the foot of the citadel was rebuilt at its present location to the northeast. It was severely damaged by the earthquake of 1979 and rebuilt in a rather rundown socialist style, which does not do it justice. Shkodra is known in Italian as *Scutari,* in Serb as *Skadar,* and in Turkish as *Iskenderiye.*

SHKODRA, DISTRICT OF. Region of local government administration. The District of Shkodra (*Rrethi i Shkodrës*), with its administrative headquarters in the town of **Shkodra**, borders on the Republic of **Montenegro** to the west, the districts of **Malësia e Madhe** to the north, **Tropoja** and **Puka** to the east and **Lezha** and the Adriatic Sea to the south. It has a surface area of 1,973 square kilometers and a present **population** of 196,431 (in 2000). It is the largest district in Albania.

SHKODRA, LAKE. Lake Shkodra, ancient *Lacus Labeatus,* is the largest lake in the Balkans, with a surface area of 368 square kilometers, of which 149 square kilometers are in Albania and the rest in **Montenegro**. It is fed primarily by the Morača River flowing in from the northern end, and is connected to the Adriatic by the Buna River flowing out of its southern end at the foot of the fortress of Shkodra. It is 44 meters above sea level and has an average depth of seven to ten meters.

SHKOLLA TEKNIKE E TIRANËS. *See* AMERICAN VOCATIONAL SCHOOL.

SHKRELI. Northern Albanian tribe and traditional tribal region. The Shkreli region is situated in the upper valley of the Përroi i Thatë River in the District of **Malësia e Madhe**. It borders on the traditional tribal regions of **Kastrati** to the northwest, and **Boga** and Plani to the east. The name was recorded in 1416 as *Shkreli,* in 1614 as *Scarglieli,* and, in 1703, as *Scrielli.* **Edith Durham** derives the term from *Shën Kerli* i.e., St. Carlo, possibly the patron saint of a church there.

SHKUMBIN. River in central Albania. The Shkumbin, which takes its source in the Mokra region of the District of **Pogradec** and, passing **Librazhd, Elbasan** and **Peqin**, flows into the Adriatic Sea north of the Lagoon of Karavasta, is traditionally regarded as the dividing line between northern and southern Albania. It has a length of 181 kilometers. The Shkumbin was known in antiquity as *Scampis* (Livy 31.39; Tab. Peut.), *Skampeis* (Ptolemy III.12.33). It was recorded in 1308 as *Scumpino* (Anonymi Descriptio Europae Orientalis) and; in 1515, as *Scombino* (John Musachi). As a toponym, it would seem to be related to Alb. *shkëmb* "rock, cliff." The Shkumbin was also known in ancient times as the *Genusus* or *Genessus* (Livy 44.30).

SHLLAKU. Northern Albanian tribe and traditional tribal region. The Shllaku region is situated in the District of **Shkodra** north of the **Drin** River and south of Mount Cukali, about halfway between Shkodra and Koman. It borders on the traditional tribal regions of **Drisht** and **Shoshi** to the north, and **Dushmani** to the east. The name was recorded in 1641 as *Scelacu*. The staunchly **Catholic** Shllaku tribe, said to be an offshoot of the **Toplanas**, had a **population** of 1,500 in 1922.

SHOQËRI E TË SHTYPURI SHKRONJA SHQIP. *See* SOCIETY FOR THE PUBLICATION OF ALBANIAN WRITING.

SHOSHI. Northern Albanian tribe and traditional tribal region. The Shoshi region is situated in the **Dukagjini** area north of the **Drin** River in the District of **Shkodra**, in the valley of the Shala River. It borders on the traditional tribal regions of **Shala** to the north, **Toplana** and **Dushmani** to the east and **Shllaku** to the south. The name was recorded in Italian in 1703 as *Sciosci*. The **Catholic** Shoshi tribe had a **population** of 1,600 in 1908.

SHPATARAKU, KOSTANDIN (eighteenth century). Painter. Kostandin Shpataraku was a painter in the **Orthodox** tradition of icons and Byzantine church frescoes who was active in the years between 1736 and 1767. He no doubt stemmed from the Shpat region, south of **Elbasan**. His works, combining Byzantine tradition and Italian Renaissance influences, can be found in the churches of **Ardenica** and Vithkuq. Some of his icons are preserved at the **museum** of medieval art in **Korça**.

SHPUZA, GAZMEND (1941.03.25-). Scholar and historian. Gazmend Shpuza was born in **Shkodra**. He finished his studies in history, **geography**, and archives in 1963 at the University of **Tirana**. In 1985, he did postgraduate training in paleography and **Ottoman** diplomacy at the University of Ankara. Shpuza has worked as a research scholar for the Institute of History of the Albanian Academy of Sciences and for the State Archives. He holds the chair of Albanian history at the University of Tirana.

Gazmend Shpuza is a specialist in nineteenth and early twentieth-century Albanian history, with particular focus on the country's **Islamic** heritage. Among his publications are: *Gjurmime në epokën e Rilindjes Kombëtare Shqiptare* (Research into the Age of the Albanian National Rebirth), Tirana 1980; *Kryengritja fshatare e Shqipërisë së Mesme, 1914-1915* (Village Uprisings in Central Albania, 1914-1915), Tirana 1986; *Bibliografi për Rilindjen kombëtare shqiptare: shkrime të botuara në RPSSh, 1945-1978* (Bibliography of the Albanian National Rebirth: Writings Published in the PSR of Albania, 1945-1978), Tirana 1988; *Aspekte të mendimit politik shoqëror shqiptar, 1913-1915* (Aspects of Albanian Social and Political Thought, 1913-1915), Tirana 1990; *Ataturku dhe shqiptarët: marrëdhëniet shqiptaro-turke dhe jehona e revolucionit qemalist në Shqipëri në vitet 20-30 të shekullit tonë* (Ataturk and the Albanians: Albanian-Turkish Relations and the Echo of the Kemalist Revolution in Albania in the 20s and 30s of This Century), Tirana 1995; *Në vazhdim e gjurmimeve për epokën e Rilindjes Kombëtare: përmbledhje shëndimesh historike dhe historiografike* (Continuing Research into the Age of the National Rebirth: A Collection of Historical and Historiographical Writings), Tirana 1997; *Në prag të pavarësise: përmbledhje studimesh* (On the Threshold of Independence: Collection of Writings), New York 1999; and *Shqipëria ndërmjet Ballkaneve e Apenineve* (Albania between the Balkans and the Apennines), Tirana 1999.

SHUPO, SOKOL (1954.02.04-). Composer and musicologist. Sokol Shupo was born in **Gjirokastra** and attended the Jordan Misja Academy from 1969 to 1972. He studied composition under **Tonin Harapi** and at the Ciprian Porumbescu Conservatory in Bucharest in Romania from 1973 to 1976. In 1978, he graduated from the Academy of Fine Arts (*Instituti i Lartë i Arteve*) in **Tirana**, where he has taught from 1982 to the present. In recent years he has attended academies and workshops in various European countries. Sokol Shupo is the chief organizer of the Autumn in Tirana (*Vjeshtë në Tiranë*) festivals for modern **music**, and is considered to be the main promoter of modern music, especially modern chamber music, in Albania. Among his publications are: *Folklori muzikor shqiptar* (Albanian Musical Folklore), Tirana 1997; *Muzika bizantine: shkrimi muzikor dhe sistemi modal* (Byzantine Music: Musical Writing and Modal System), Tirana 1997; and *Enciklopedia e muzikës shqiptare* (Encyclopedia of Albanian Music), Tirana 2002.

SHURDHAH. *See* SARDA.

SHUTERIQI, DHIMITËR (1915.07.26-2003.07.22). Scholar, literary historian and writer of the **communist** period. Dhimitër S. Shuteriqi was born in **Elbasan** and attended secondary school in **Korça**. He studied at the Universities of Grenoble and Lyon in France and taught school in Elbasan in 1942-1943. Shuteriqi began writing in the 1930s and was to become an influential literary historian during the communist dictatorship. He was a member of **parliament** for many years, president of the Albanian **Union of Writers and Artists** from 1950 to 1973, and a member of the Academy of Sciences from 1973.

Dhimitër Shuteriqi is remembered for his research in the fields of **literature**, history and folklore, in particular for his standard histories and anthologies of Albanian literature. Among his many works are: *Shkrimet shqipe në vitet 1332-1850* (Albanian Writing in the Years 1332-1850), Tirana 1976; *Autorë dhe tekste* (Authors and Texts), Tirana 1977; and *Historia e letërsisë shqiptare* (History of Albanian Literature), Tirana 1983. Shuteriqi was also author of prose and poetry. His two-volume *Çlirimtarët* (The Liberators), Tirana 1952, 1955, the first postwar Albanian novel, painted a picture not only of the squalor and sufferings of the peasants before the "liberation" but also of the rise of class consciousness among them. It helped set the rather sluggish pace for socialist realism in the 1950s.

SIGURIMI. The Sigurimi, from Alb. *sigurim* "security," also known as the *Sigurimi i Shtetit* "State Security," was the name of the notorious, ubiquitous and much-feared secret police during the **communist** dictatorship. It was set up on 19 March 1943 and was later put under the control of the ministry of the interior. Its primary purpose was to expose would-be opponents of the communist regime, but it also dealt with the investigation of normal crimes such as murder or robbery. It was so omnipresent and well-orchestrated that no organized dissent arose at all during the regime of Enver Hoxha. The Sigurimi was officially disbanded in July 1991 at the end of the communist dictatorship and was replaced in the period of **Sali Berisha** by the **National Information Service** (*Shërbimi Informativ Kombëtar* - SHIK). In accordance with the law of 30 November 1995, the extensive Sigurimi files will remain closed until the year 2025.

SIMAKU, THOMA (1958.04.18-). Composer. Thoma Simaku was born in **Kavaja** and studied composition at the Academy of Fine Arts (*Instituti i Lartë i Arteve*) in **Tirana**. From 1991 to 1996, he studied at the University of York in England, where he finished his doctorate and currently lives. Simaku has composed orchestral and chamber **music** as well as vocal pieces and the music for several Albanian **films**. His works have been performed throughout Europe and in the United States.

SKANDERBEG. *See* SCANDERBEG.

SKENDI, STAVRO (1905.08.21-1989.10.18). Scholar and cultural historian. Stavro Skendi was born in **Korça** and studied at the prestigious Robert College in Istanbul, where he obtained a B.S. in mathematics. He continued his education at the Geneva School of International Studies and in Germany and returned to Korça in 1930 to teach mathematics at the national secondary school. There he became a leading figure of the nationalist movement in the 1930s. Because of his antifascist inclinations he was interned by the **Italians**, together with many other Albanian intellectuals, for eighteen months on the island of Ventotene in the Tyrrhenian Sea. In 1941, he returned to Korça and opened a bookstore. Soon forced into hiding, he escaped to Istanbul in the summer of 1943 and remained there until 1946, when he emigrated to the **United States**. With the assistance of the American Council of Learned Societies, Skendi was able to resume his studies and, in 1951, finished his doctorate from the department of Slavic languages at Columbia University in New York. He taught for a year at the University of Toronto and then returned to Columbia, where he was active until retirement in 1970. He was a lecturer in the program on East-Central Europe and a research supervisor of the Mid-European Studies Center. In 1972-1973, he also worked for the Institute for Advanced Studies at Princeton.

Stavro Skendi, author of numerous books and articles on Albanian and Balkan history, politics and culture, was one of the leading figures of Albanian scholarship in the United States. Of his major monographs, mention may be made of: *Albanian and South Slavic Oral Epic Poetry*, Philadelphia 1954; *The Political Revolution of Albania 1912-1944*, New York 1954; *Albania*, New York 1956; *The Albanian National Awakening, 1878-1912*, Princeton 1967; and *Balkan Cultural Studies*, New York 1980.

SKENDO, LUMO. *See* FRASHËRI, MID'HAT BEY.

SKRAPAR, DISTRICT OF. Region of local government administration. The District of Skrapar (*Rrethi i Skraparit*), with its administrative headquarters in the town of Çorovoda, borders on the districts of **Berat** to the west, **Gramsh** to the north, **Korça** to the east and **Përmet** to the south. It has a surface area of 775 square kilometers and a present **population** of 44,523 (in 2000). The word "Skrapar" was recorded in **Ottoman** Turkish in 1431 as *Iskarapar*.

SLAVIC MINORITY IN ALBANIA. There are traditionally three distinct Slavic communities in Albania: Serbian-speaking Montenegrin Slavs in the **Shkodra** region; Macedonian speakers on Lake **Prespa**; and Goran-speaking settlements in northeastern Albania.

　　The Montenegrin Slavs lived in and around the village of Vraka, seven kilometers north of Shkodra. Many of them settled there after 1926 and from 1938 to 1948. A prominent member of the Montenegrin community was the Albanian poet **Migjeni**, who taught school in Vraka in 1933. Between March and December 1991, after the opening of the border, most of the Slavs of this region, about 2,000 of them, emigrated to **Montenegro** in search of jobs and a better standard of living. They found difficulties adapting in Montenegro, which was by no means prosperous itself, and some returned to Vraka in 1992 after the outbreak of the war in Bosnia. A Slav cultural association was formed in Shkodra in May 1995. Most of the Slav emigrants who stayed in Montenegro were later resettled by the Yugoslav authorities in the Deçan region of western **Kosova**, where they soon found themselves caught up in a war, fighting Albanians, with whom they had lived in peace and harmony in Albania itself.

　　The Macedonian minority, 4,697 individuals according to the census of 1989, is to be found in the villages situated along the western bank of Lake Prespa. They had Macedonian-language elementary schools and a few basic publications during the dictatorship. Many have since emigrated to **Macedonia**, or work there for extended periods of time. The Albanian writer **Sterjo Spasse** and early **communist** political leader **Koçi Xoxe** were members of the Macedonian Slav community. There are also some speakers of a peripheral Macedonian dialect around Steblleva in the southern part of the District of **Bulqiza**, They are Muslims and are known in Albanian as *gollobordcët*. Altogether, there may be about 15,000 Macedonian speakers in Albania.

The third group of Slavs in Albania, the so-called Gorans, speak a south Slavic dialect between Serbian and Macedonian, though more related to Macedonian. They live in ten villages in the districts of **Kukës** and **Dibra** in northeastern Albania, in particular in the **Luma** region along the border with Kosova. Their numbers have been estimated as high as 15,000, but there are no reliable statistics. The lofty mountain village of Shishtavec, famous for its potatoes, is Goran-speaking. Before the **Kosova War** in 1999, the Gorans had certain economic advantages because they, as opposed to ethnic Albanians, were allowed across the border into Kosova to conduct business and trade in Prizren. There are also many Gorans in the neighboring Opoja region of Kosova.

SMILEY, DAVID. British military officer and writer. Colonel David Smiley was an army officer in **World War II**, who was recruited by the **Special Operations Executive** in 1943. He was sent into Albania from Greece in April 1943 together with **Billy McLean**, as one of the first British officers to organize anti-Axis resistance. There he developed close contacts both with **Abaz Kupi** and the **Legality** movement and with **Enver Hoxha**, **Mehmet Shehu** and the **communist** partisan movement.

Smiley withdrew from Albania in September 1944 and returned to England the following year. From 1949 to 1953, he worked for M16 and was involved in the setting up of a secret camp in Malta to train anticommunist agents to overthrow the communist regime in Albania. His endeavors were, however, foiled by the British spy, **Kim Philby**, as was revealed much later. Smiley was also active in Germany in 1952-1955, Sweden in 1955-1958, Oman in 1958-1962, and Yemen in 1962-1966. He published his war memoirs in the volumes: *Albanian Assignment*, London 1984; and *Irregular Regular*, Norwich 1994.

SOCIAL DEMOCRATIC PARTY OF ALBANIA (*PARTIA SOCIALDEMOKRATE E SHQIPËRISË, PSDSH)* **(1991-).** The

Social Democratic Party arose in mid-1991 as an alternative to the new **Socialist Party**, but was only officially registered on 23 April 1992. Among its founding members were **Teodor Laço, Skënder Gjinushi**, Lisien Bashkurti and Haxhi Aliko, rector of the agricultural college in Kamza. It drew its inspiration from the admittedly not very strong social democratic traditions of the past (**Musine Kokalari** had cofounded a social democratic party in 1943, and a small group of intellectuals including **Pjetër Arbnori** had established a social democratic underground organization in 1960-1961), and from similar parties in Western Europe. It took part in the coalition government of **Ylli Bufi** in July 1991, but subsequently split into two formations: the Social Democratic Party under Skënder Gjinushi, often in coalition with the Socialist Party, and the Social Democratic Union (*Bashkimi Socialdemokrat*) under Teodor Laço, usually more allied with the **Democratic Party**. Both formations have remained small. In the **parliamentary** elections of 1992, the Social Democratic Party won 4.4 percent of the popular vote. In 1996 it won 1.5 percent, in 1997 2.5 percent, and in 2001 3.6 percent.

SOCIALIST PARTY OF ALBANIA (*PARTIA SOCIALISTE E SHQIPËRISË, PSSH*) (1991-). The Socialist Party evolved out of the **communist Party of Labor** at the tenth party congress on 13 June 1991. Since that time, it has been the major political formation in Albania, together with its rival, the **Democratic Party**. In the elections of 1991 (still as the Party of Labor) it won 56.2 percent of the popular vote. In 1992 it won 25.7 percent, in 1996 20.4 percent, in 1997 52.7 percent, and in 2001 41.5 percent. The leading political figure of the Socialist Party, **Fatos Nano**, formed a short-lived government administration in February 1991 and regained power in July 1997. The Socialist Party has been ruling the country since then, though mostly in coalition with smaller parties.

SOCIETY FOR THE PUBLICATION OF ALBANIAN WRITING (*SHOQËRI E TË SHTYPURI SHKRONJA SHQIP*) (1879). Cultural association founded in Istanbul on 12 October 1879 on the initiative of the **Central Committee for the Defense of the Rights of the Albanian People**. The Society was headed by **Sami bey Frashëri**. Among its other members were **Abdyl bey Frashëri, Pashko Vasa, Jani Vreto, Hasan Tahsini**, Koto Hoxhi (1824-1895) and Zija Prishtina. After its activities were banned, the society transferred its headquarters to Bucharest, where in 1886 it set up a printing press for the publication and distribution of Albanian-**language** books. It was there for instance that a number of Albanian-language school texts written by Sami Frashëri were published, using the so-called Istanbul alphabet: *Abetare e gjuhësë shqip* (ABCs of the Albanian Language), 1886; *Dheshkronjë* (Geography), 1888; and *Shkronjëtore e gjuhësë shqip* (Grammar of the Albanian Language), 1886, the latter being the first Albanian school grammar. It was also in the Romanian capital that the torchbearer of the nationalist movement, **Naim bey Frashëri**, first published the literary works which were to set the pace for late nineteenth-century Albanian **literature**.

SOKOLI, MIC (1839-1881). Nationalist figure and guerrilla fighter. Mic Sokoli was born in the village of Fang near Bujan in the **Tropoja** district of the north. He was a noted guerrilla leader during the years of the **League of Prizren** and took part in the fighting in Gjakova against Mehmet Ali Pasha. Mic Sokoli is remembered in particular for an act which has entered the annals of Albanian legendry as a deed of exemplary heroism. At the battle of Slivova against **Ottoman** forces in April 1881, he thrust himself against a Turkish cannon, his chest pressed against its mouth, and died in battle.

SOKOLI, RAMADAN (1920.06.19-). Composer and ethnomusicologist. Ramadan Isuf Sokoli was born in **Shkodra**, where he went to school. From 1940 to 1944, he studied at the conservatory of **music** in Florence, **Italy**. On his return to Albania he began to compose music but was soon arrested by the **communist** authorities and spent four years (1946-1950) in prison. After his release, he was appointed to teach music at the fine arts secondary school in **Tirana**. He is considered one of the founders of musicology and is his country's leading ethnologist of music. Among his publications are: *Albanskie narodnye pesni* (Albanian Folk Songs), Tirana 1965; *Folklori muzikor shqiptar: morfologjia* (Albanian Musical Folklore: Morphology); Tirana 1965; *Gjurmime folklorike* (Folklore Research), Tirana 1981; *16 shekuj* (Sixteen Centuries), Tirana 1995; *Antifonari i durrsakut Gjergj Danush Lapacaj, një përmendore muzikologjike e vitit 1532* (The Antiphonist Gjergj Danush Lapacaj of Durrës, a Musicological Monument from the Year 1532), Tirana 2000; and *Gojëdhana e përrallëza të botës shqiptare* (Legends and Short Tales of the Albanian World), Tirana 2000. He is also coauthor of *Veglat* *muzikore të artit shqiptar* (Musical Instruments of Albanian Fine Arts), Tirana 1991.

SOLANO, FRANCESCO (1914.11.14-1999.03.20). Arbëresh scholar, linguist and writer. Francesco Solano was born in the Calabrian village of Frascineto (Alb. *Frasnita*) in southern **Italy**. He studied theology in Italy and Argentina and then served for many years as a parish priest in his native village. He was active in the founding in 1975 of the chair of Albanian at the University of Cosenza and headed the department of linguistics for several years there.

Solano is the author not only of literary prose, verse and drama published in Albanian under the pseudonym Dushko Vetmo, but also of a *Manuale di lingua albanese* (Handbook of the Albanian **Language**), Corigliano Calabro 1972, and of numerous studies on Arbëresh dialects. He also played an active role in the Arbëresh literary and cultural periodical *Zjarri* (The Fire), founded in 1973.

SONGS OF THE FRONTIER WARRIORS. Cycle of epic verse. The Songs of the Frontier Warriors (*Këngë Kreshnikësh*) are the best-known cycle of northern Albanian epic verse, not dissimilar to the Bosnian and Serbo-Croatian *junačke pjesme*.

They were first recorded in the early decades of the twentieth century by **Franciscan** priests and scholars serving in the northern Albanian mountains. Preeminent among them were Shtjefën Gjeçovi, **Vinçenc Prennushi** and **Donat Kurti**.

The Songs of the Frontier Warriors, still sung by elderly men playing the one-stringed *lahuta,* are the literary reflections of legends portraying and glorifying the heroic feats of warriors of the past. The main cycle, that of "Mujo and Halil," preserves much of the flavor of other heroic cultures such as those mirrored in Homer's Iliad in Greek, Beowulf in English, in El Cid in Spanish, in the Chanson de Roland in French, in the Nibelungenlied in German and in the Russian Byliny. The leaders of this band of thirty *agas* or warriors are Gjeto Basho Mujo and his brother Halili, who inhabit a frontier region between the **Ottoman Empire** and Austria-Hungary. The Albanian songs of Mujo and Halili parallel the Bosnian versions of the cycle sung in Serbo-Croatian, or more properly, Bosnian. This heroic and epic verse occurs in both oral **literatures** and cultures since the singers in southern Bosnia, the Sandjak, and Montenegro at the time were to a good extent bilingual, i.e., reciting alternatively in Bosnian and Albanian.

Much has been written about the antiquity and origins of Albanian epic verse and about its relationship to the Bosnian epic. From the narrative and for other reasons, there is general consensus nowadays that the Songs of the Frontier Warriors crystallized in the seventeenth and eighteenth centuries in a border region of the Balkans which separated Christendom from the **Islamic** world, though many much older strata are present in the songs. We are dealing, as such, primarily with a literary reflection of the *Türkenkriege* between the Ottoman Empire and the Hapsburgs. The place names referred to in the songs, Jutbina and New Kotor etc., have been identified as being in the region of the Lika and Krbava valleys to the east of Zadar in Croatia, not far from the present Bosnian border. From this and from conspicuous Slavic terms in some of the songs, it would seem evident that this is a body of oral material which, probably after centuries of evolution, crystallized in a southern Slavic milieu and which was then transmitted by bilingual singers to (some would say back to) an Albanian milieu. It is understandable, therefore, that there are many parallels between Albanian and Bosnian epic verse. They have a common origin and, in essence, reflect a common culture. After transmission, however, the Albanian epic evolved in a solely Albanian milieu and took on many purely Albanian characteristics, values, and extra-linguistic forms of expression,

The Albanian epic is still very much alive as an oral tradition. Even as the twenty-first century marches on, one can still find a good number of *lahutars* in **Kosova**, in particular in the Rugova highlands west of Peja, and in northern Albania, as well as some rare souls in Montenegro, who are able to sing and recite the heroic deeds of Mujo and Halili and their thirty *agas*. One can safely assume that these elderly men constitute the very last traditional native singers of epic verse in Europe!

Albanian epic verse is still little known internationally, having long lived in the shadow of the Serbo-Croatian or Bosnian epic. Of works on the subject in English, mention may be made of: *Albanian and South Slavic Oral Epic Poetry,* Philadelphia 1954, by **Stavro Skendi**; *Albanian Folk Verse, Structure and Genre,* Munich 1978, by **Arshi Pipa**; *The Bilingual Singer, a Study of Albanian and Serbo-Croatian Oral Epic Traditions,* New York 1990, by **John Kolsti**; and most recently *The Songs of the Frontier Warriors: Albanian Epic Verse in a Bilingual English-Alba-*

nian Edition, Wauconda 2003, by **Robert Elsie** and Janice Mathie-Heck.

SOVIET UNION, RELATIONS WITH. *See* RUSSIA, RELATIONS WITH.

SPAHIU, BEDRI (1908.07.13-1998.01.12). Political figure of the early **communist** period. Bedri Spahiu was born in **Gjirokastra.** He attended school there and in Istanbul, returning to Albania in 1927. He continued his studies in **Shkodra,** 1928-1929, and trained at an artillery school in **Tirana,** 1931. He served thereafter as an army officer, though he was arrested for subversion and imprisoned in 1937 and again in 1938. He played a leading role in the communist resistance movement as a major-general during **World War II.** After the communist takeover, he served as minister of reconstruction, 1944-1946; minister of social assistance, 1945; public prosecutor for the special court to try "war criminals and enemies of the people"; member of the **Bektashi** council general, 1945; assistant chief of staff, 1945-1947; member of the presidium of the People's Assembly, 1948-1954; public prosecutor from May 1948 to March 1954 (including duties as investigator and chief prosecutor at the trial of **Koçi Xoxe** in 1949); chairman of the Soviet-Albanian friendship association, 1951-1955; deputy prime minister, 1951-1953; and minister of **education,** 1952, 1953 and 1954.

Bedri Spahiu was a member of the Central Committee and the Politburo from 1948 to 1955. On 17 June 1955, at the time of the de-Stalinization campaigns elsewhere in eastern Europe, he was purged with **Tuk Jakova** on charges of being pro-Yugoslav. He was first interned with his whole family and then imprisoned in the fortress of Kanina. In 1958, he was transferred to **Tirana** and sentenced to twenty-five years of prison. He was released on 6 November 1974 and interned in Selenica near **Vlora.** He was finally released from internment on 10 May 1990.

SPAHIU, XHEVAHIR (1945.03.01-). Poet. Xhevahir Spahiu was born in the village of Majlind in the Skrapar region. He is considered one of the most forceful, vociferous, and talented poets of modern Albania. Spahiu went to school in **Vlora** and finished university in **Tirana,** working thereafter, from 1961, as a journalist for *Zëri i popullit* (The People's Voice), and later for the cultural periodical *Nëntori* (November). During the 1973 Purge of the Liberals, dictator **Enver Hoxha** referred to Spahiu by name for having composed the poem *Jetë* (Life). This poem contained the lines *Jam ai se s'kam qenë, do të jem ai që nuk jam* (I am who I have not been, I shall be who I am not), which were reminiscent, though by pure coincidence, of a line by French philosopher Jean-Paul Sartre. Although the poet had never had the opportunity of enjoying the forbidden fruits of the late French philosopher (as had the Albanian dictator obviously), he was condemned as an existentialist, which was tantamount to high treason. He survived only by the skin of his teeth, by channeling his passions into appropriate revolutionary fervor. After a few years he was allowed to publish once again. After years as secretary of the Albanian **Writers' Union**, Spahiu was elected as its head on 21 February 1998, replacing **Bardhyl Londo**, a post he retained until 2002. Among his recent volumes of verse are: *Kohë e krisur* (Mad Age), Tirana 1991; *Ferrparajsa* (Hellparadise), Tirana 1994; and *Pezull* (Dangling), Tirana 1996.

SPASSE, STERJO (1914.08.14-1989.09.12). Prose writer. Sterjo Spasse is a novelist and short story writer of Macedonian Slav origin from Lake **Prespa**. It was while teaching in the little village of Derviçan south of **Gjirokastra** that the eighteen-year-old Spasse began writing his first novel, and his masterpiece, *Nga jeta në jetë—Pse!?*(From Life to Life—Why!?), Korça 1935, usually referred to for short as *Pse!?* (Why!?). The novel was written in the form of a diary and focused on the tragic dilemma of a young intellectual in a backward rural society. Its pessimistic hero Gjon Zaveri suffers from all the *Weltschmerz* of Goethe's young Werther, a hero with whom he feels great affinity. In the end, resigned to his fate, Gjon commits suicide by throwing himself into the lake.

Postwar Marxist critics were unable to deal with *Pse!?*, though it may be considered one of the most popular Albanian novels of the early twentieth century. The Schopenhauerian pessimism and the *Weltschmerz* conflicted too sharply with the positive hero demanded by socialist realism. Although *Pse?!* is the work of youthful inspiration by a writer as yet unskilled in his métier, this first novel contrasts favorably with all the "classics of socialist realism" that he produced later in life.

SPECIAL OPERATIONS EXECUTIVE, SOE (1943-1944). Set up in 1940, the Special Operations Executive was the pet project of Winston Churchill to gather intelligence, carry out acts of sabotage, and provide financial and material assistance to resistance groups fighting **Italian** and **German** occupation, in particular in the Balkans. In February 1942, Scottish anthropologist **Margaret Hasluck,** who had lived in **Elbasan** for thirteen years, was recruited in Cairo to help set up an Albanian section, which she also managed for a year. Its headquarters for Albania was in Bari in southern Italy. After an initial four-man mission, which included Lieutenant Colonel **Billy McLean** and Major **David Smiley,** had infiltrated Albania in April 1943, the SOE maintained contacts with both **communist** and anticommunist forces. Between the end of 1943 and late 1944, over 100 British officers and men had been sent into the country. Increasingly, however, the SOE was caught between the various resistance factions which were fighting more amongst one another than fighting the Germans. It ceased operations in November 1944 when German forces withdrew from Albania.

SPIRU, NAKO (1918-1947.11.20). Political figure of the early **communist** period. Spiro Naku, born in **Durrës,** was an early member of the **Korça** communist group and joined the Albanian communist party at its foundation in 1941. He was the first husband of **Liri Belishova.** Spiru was a member of the Central Committee from 1942 to 1947 and a member of the Politburo from 1943 to 1947. In 1944, he was chairman of the Albanian Union of Antifascist Youth (*Bashkimi i Rinisë Antifashiste të Shqiperisë*) and, in 1946-1947, was chairman of the state planning commission and minister of economics, in charge of trade relations with **Yugoslavia.** He was purged by **Koçi Xoxe** in 1947 for being "anti-Yugoslav," and committed suicide.

STADTMÜLLER, GEORG (1901-1985.11.01). German scholar and historian. Georg Stadtmüller was born in the village of Bürstadt in Hesse. He studied classical philology and European history at the universities of Freiburg am Breisgau and Munich, where he finished his doctorate and worked for two years for the Bavarian State Library. In 1934, he moved to Breslau (now Wrocław), where he was active at the Historical Seminar and the Library of the Eastern Europe Institute. In ca. 1935, he toured Albania on foot on his way to Constantinople, and in the following year finished the seminal habilitation thesis *Forschungen zur albanischen Frühgeschichte* (Research in Early Albanian History), Budapest 1942, for which he is best remembered. This book, republished in 1966, traces the origins of the Albanian people back to the **Mat** region and provides much thought-provoking material for the thorny issue of Albanian ethnogenesis. In December 1938, Stadtmüller was appointed professor of southeast European history at the University of Leipzig, and, in 1958, he took over the chair of southeast European history at the University of Munich, where he assisted in the establishment of the "Albania Institute" in 1963. Georg Stadtmüller is also remembered as the author of numerous articles on questions of Albanian history, religion and **literature**, and of a *Geschichte Südosteuropas* (History of Southeastern Europe), Munich 1950. He died in Passau.

STALINISM. Communist political leaders in Albania first received their political training in the 1940s, during Joseph Stalin's reign in the Soviet Union, and were deeply influenced by Stalinism and the Soviet communism of the age. After a period of strong Yugoslav influence in **communist** Albania from 1945 to late June 1948, Stalin prevailed over Tito, and Albania and the Soviet Union became close political allies, with Stalin providing Albania with much-needed economic assistance. **Enver Hoxha** met Stalin on five occasions: on 14-26 July 1947 in Moscow to negotiate a loan agreement, on 21 March-11 April 1949 in Moscow, on 26 November 1949 in Sukhumi, on 4 January 1950 in Moscow, and on 2 April 1951 in Moscow. Stalin's death was publicly commemorated on 5 March 1953 as a day of national mourning, and was genuinely felt as such by the population.

Enver Hoxha and the Albanian party leadership were first criticized openly under Nikita Khrushchev at the twentieth congress of the Soviet communist party on 14-16 April 1956 for their unwillingness to reject the heritage of Stalin and to de-Stalinize Albania. The unwillingness to follow Khrushchev's reforms in 1956 was, however, more linked to domestic power struggles among the Albanian party leaders than to any ideological whims. In his memoirs, Hoxha repeatedly stressed the gratitude of the Albanian people and the Albanian **Party of Labor** to Stalin, in particular for having saved Albania from being swallowed by **Yugoslavia.**

Stalin thus remained the fourth in the line of great Marxist-Leninist figures, after Marx, Engels and Lenin, even when his portraits had long disappeared in the rest of eastern Europe. In Albania, he remained a cult figure at least until the death of Enver Hoxha in 1985, and the Albanian Party of Labor pursued Stalinist policies, more or less, until the end of the communist dictatorship. Numerous monuments were raised to Stalin throughout the country, including one imposing statue in the center of **Tirana**. The town of Kuçova was renamed *Qyteti Stalin* (Stalin City) after Stalin on his seventy-first birthday on 19 December 1950. Stalin's works were also translated into Albanian and were made widely available. Stalin himself is said to have been quite indifferent to Albania.

STEFANI, SIMON (1929.01.03-). Political figure of the **communist** period. Simon Stefani was born in **Përmet**. He joined the communist party in 1952 and rose to power swiftly after the purges of the 1970s. He served as first secretary of the party in Përmet and **Tirana,** 1972-1979, and as chairman of the People's Assembly from 25 December 1978 to 22 November 1982. He was also head of the directorate general for petroleum research and was minister of the interior from 1989 to 1990. Stefani was a member of the Central Committee from 1976 to 1991 and a full member of the Politburo from 1981 to 1990. On 2 July 1994, after the fall of the dictatorship, he was sentenced to eight years of prison for abuse of power.

STËRMILLI, HAKI (1895-1953.01.17). Prose writer and playwright. Haki Stërmilli from **Dibra** in western Macedonia is the author of three novels, over thirty short stories, five plays, two diaries and several dozen newspaper articles. He went to elementary school in Thessalonika and attended a Turkish-language secondary school in Monastir (Bitola), the principal of which was the Albanian patriot **Bajo Topulli**. During the **Balkan War** of 1913, Stërmilli and his family were obliged to flee their native Dibra, which was occupied by the Serbian army, and to take refuge in Albania. They settled initially in **Elbasan** and later in **Durrës**. Stërmilli wished to study in western Europe but was pressured by family members instead into marrying the widow of his elder brother who had been killed in 1912. In the **Mat** district, he got a job as secretary in the vice-prefecture and by 1918 was deputy vice-prefect himself. The Mat district was the homeland of feudal landowner **Ahmet Zogu**. Stërmilli was initially on good terms with him, having tutored his numerous sisters, the future royal princesses.

In 1920, he was appointed secretary at the ministry of the interior in **Tirana**, but soon became a sworn enemy of the power-hungry Zogu. Together with **Avni Rustemi**, lionized by the youth of Albania for his assassination of landowner **Essad Pasha Toptani** in Paris on 13 June 1920, Stërmilli founded the democratic *Bashkimi* (Unity) society in 1922, which encountered wide support amidst the political turmoil of the age. When Zogu, having arranged for the assassination of Avni Rustemi, finally took power after the defeat of the **Fan Noli** government in 1924, Stërmilli was obliged to flee the country, as were many other intellectuals and democrats. After a year in Italy and France, he traveled to the Soviet Union where, during a fourteen-month stay, he met up with **Ali Kelmendi** and the first generation of Albanian **communist** revolutionaries training there. From the Soviet Union, he proceeded to Austria and collaborated in Vienna as a journalist and political activist against the Zogist regime.

On 19 March 1929, Stërmilli was arrested by the Yugoslav police and handed over to the Albanian authorities, a deed which caused an outcry in left-wing circles in Europe. The second congress of the Anti-Imperialist League, meeting in Frankfurt in the spring of 1929, sent letters and telegrams of protest to **Yugoslavia** and Albania, signed among others by French writer Henri Barbusse (1873-1935), physicist Albert Einstein (1879-1955), Bulgarian communist leader Georgi Dimitrov (1882-1949), Japanese Social-Democrat Tetsu Katajama (1887-1945), German philosopher Theodor Lessing (1872-1933) and in particular by Fan Noli (1882-1965). Stërmilli was nonetheless sentenced to an initial term of five years in prison and, in August 1935, to a second term. During **World War II**, he joined the resistance movement and headed the executive committee of the National Liberation Council in his native Dibra region. After the communist takeover, Stërmilli was elected as a member of **parliament**. In October 1946, he was also appointed director of the **National Library** and, in October 1949, director of the **museum** of the National Liberation War.

Foremost among Stërmilli's literary works is the novel *Sikur t'isha djalë* (If I Were a Boy), Tirana 1936, which recounts in diary form the struggles of a young girl named Dija Kërthiza for emancipation in an oppressive society. As one of the most popular Albanian novels of the 1930s, *Sikur t'isha djalë* was the first substantial work of Albanian **literature** to deal with the theme of **women**'s emancipation. Many Albanian girls at the time are said to have learned to read and write for the sole purpose of being able to read this book.

ŠUFFLAY, MILAN VON (1879.11.09-1931.02.18). Croatian historian. Milan von Šufflay was born in Lepoglava, southwest of Varaždin, and studied history and classical philology at the University of Zagreb. From 1904 to 1908, he worked for the national museum in Budapest and, from 1912 to 1918, was professor for medieval history in Zagreb. Šufflay was forced into early retirement for political reasons in 1918 and lived thereafter as a publisher in Zagreb. He was often in open political conflict with the new Kingdom of the Serbs, Croats and Slovenes and, in 1921, was sentenced to three and a half years in prison. In 1928, he was offered the chair of southeast European history at the University of Budapest, but the government in Belgrade refused to let him accept the position. He was murdered by two police agents in 1931.

Among Šufflay's publications of Albanian interest, mention may be made of *Povijest severnih Arbanasa* (History of the Northern Albanians), Belgrade 1924, *Städte und Burgen Albaniens hauptsächlich während des Mittelalters* (The Towns and Fortresses of Albania, Primarily during the Middle Ages), Vienna 1924; and *Srbi i Arbanasi: njihova simbioza u srednjem vjeku* (Serbs and Albanians: Their Symbiosis during the Middle Ages), Belgrade 1925; as well as numerous articles. Together with **Ludwig von Thallóczy** and **Konstantin Jireček**, he published the important two-volume collection of Albanian historical documents entitled *Acta et diplomata res Albaniae mediae aetatis illustrantia* (Acts and Diplomatic Affairs illustrating the Middle Ages in Albania), Vienna 1913, 1918, covering the years 344 to 1406 A.D. In 1929, the Austrian Academy of Sciences, in cooperation with the Albanian government, proposed that Šufflay continue the collection with a further four volumes to cover the years 1406-1536, and he was invited to Albania to continue his research. He had just completed the third volume when he was murdered. The manuscript in question was confiscated by the Yugoslav police and was long reputed lost. Rumors circulated in 2001, however, that the manuscript had been recovered and would be published.

SWITZERLAND, ALBANIANS IN. As a percentage of the general population, the Albanian community in Switzerland is one of the largest in Europe. In 1996, the Swiss Federal Office for Statistics estimated that there were about 150,000 Albanians in the country, the vast majority of whom are from **Kosova**. The Albanians thus make up the largest group of foreigners in Switzerland, after the Italians.

Albanian immigration to Switzerland began in the 1960s, almost exclusively from Kosova. It increased throughout the

1970s as more and more Kosova Albanians sought employment in the country, at least on a temporary or seasonal basis. From 1981 onwards, there was a large increase in the percentage of political refugees escaping persecution from the Serbs. In the 1990s, when Albanian immigration in Switzerland reached its zenith, most original refugees had gotten their families to safety in the country, too. According to a study carried out by Hysen Çobani in 1997, ninety percent of the Albanian community are workers with little formal education. Their only contacts with the Swiss population are at their place of work. They are all highly nationalist-oriented, and the **women**, who are substantially less educated than the men, are mostly unemployed and work at home as housewives.

SWORN VIRGIN. Popular custom. Cross-gender behavior in **women** in northern Albania was first reported by missionaries, travelers and scholars who visited the mountains in the nineteenth and early twentieth centuries. According to customary law, a woman wishing to avoid a prearranged marriage, or for some other reason, could swear an irrevocable oath before twelve village or tribal elders to remain celibate and could then take on a male gender role. Sworn Virgins, Alb. *virgjinesha* "virgin," as these individuals are known in English, assumed virtually every aspect of the male role in tribal society. They dressed as men, took on male names in most cases, carried guns, smoked, became heads of households and carried out male work. They were also accepted as men by the other males in the community and could sit and take counsel with them. The Albanian and southern Slavic Sworn Virgin is said to be the only institutionalized female-to-male, cross-gender, and cross-dressing role known in a European society. Similar institutions occur in some Indian tribes of North America. The institution of the Sworn Virgin used to be known in Dalmatia and Bosnia as well, as attested in epic folk songs, but it is presently restricted to the northern Albanian mountains and to neighboring Kosova and Montenegro.

The phenomenon has a number of possible explanations. Firstly, the categorical refusal of a girl to enter into a prearranged marriage, for which she had already been bought, in some cases as a child, would have besmirched the honor of the prospective bridegroom and thus have led to **blood feuding**. By becoming a Sworn Virgin, the girl would no longer be abrogating the marriage contract and infringing upon the honor of the bridegroom's family. Secondly, the system of patrilineal inheritance meant that a family with no male heirs would need a surrogate son. Since many of the men in northern Albanian society were (and are again) deeply involved in blood feuding, there was a constant shortage of males. The Sworn Virgin solved the problem, though for inheritance purposes, only for one generation. One can also imagine that some women simply wished to avoid the vastly inferior status and subordinate role allotted to them in traditional Albanian society, which is characterized by a high degree of sex segregation, obligatory premarital virginity and marital fidelity, heavy physical labor, abuse by men and a denial of basic human rights.

It was thought two decades ago that the Sworn Virgins had all but died out after fifty years of **communism** in Albania. Recent research, in particular by René Grémaux and **Antonia Young**, has shown, however, that there are still quite a number of them around today.

- T -

TAGLIAVINI, CARLO (1903.06.18-1982.05.31). Italian scholar and linguist. Carlo Tagliavini was born in Bologna and held the chair of linguistics at the University of Padua. His scholarly interests were focused on Balkan linguistics and he was early to make a name for himself with his research in Romanian, Hungarian, Croatian and Albanian. In the latter field, with which he is primarily associated, he is remembered for his dialect study *L'Albanese di Dalmazia: contributi alla conoscenza del dialetto ghego di Borgo Erizzo presso Zara* (The Albanian of Dalmatia: Contributions to a Knowledge of the Gheg Dialect of Borgo Erizzo near Zadar), Florence 1937; *Le parlate albanesi di tipo Ghego orientale: Dardania e Macedonia nord-occidentale* (The Eastern Gheg Dialects of Albanian: Dardania and Northwestern Macedonia), Rome 1942; and *La stratificazione del lessico albanese: elementi indoeuropei* (The Stratification of the Albanian Lexicon: Indo-European Elements), Bologna 1943, as well as numerous articles on the Albanian **language**.

TAHSINI, HASAN (ca. 1812-1881.07.04). Turkish scholar of Albanian origin. Hasan Tahsini was born in Ninat near Konispol in the district of **Saranda**. He emigrated to Istanbul, where he studied **Islamic** religion and natural sciences. At some time between 1839 and 1856, he got a government scholarship to continue his studies in Paris, where he stayed for two years. He earned his living there by working as an imam for the Ottoman Embassy. Tahsini was particularly interested in physics, chemistry, geology and astronomy. On his return to Istanbul ca. 1869, he was appointed rector of the first university in the **Ottoman Empire**, the Dar ül-Fünun in Istanbul, where he stressed the importance of the natural sciences in his lectures. He was also in contact with the growing Albanian community in Istanbul and was passionately interested in the alphabet question, i.e., finding an appropriate alphabet for the Albanian **language**.

In December 1870, he was forced to resign from his position as rector after a scandal caused by a public lecture given by the pan-Islamic writer, Jemal ed-Din al-Afghani (1839-1897), founder of Islamic modernism, whom he had invited to speak. Tahsini thereafter made his living as an imam and a science teacher. His modest home in Istanbul became a center for Albanian patriots. In 1872, he created a new alphabet for Albanian, which he endeavored to propagate on his return to Albania in the summer of that year. This resulted in his arrest in May 1874 and his expulsion to Istanbul. There, he published numerous scholarly articles and became a member of the Albanian alphabet commission in the spring of 1879. His own alphabet was, however, rejected by the commission. Hasan Tahsini would seem, at this time, to have fallen ill with tuberculosis. He died in the house of Munif Pasha in Erenköy in Istanbul. The Russian Turkologist Vasily Smirnov called him the "Turkish Lomonosov."

TASHKO-KOÇO, TEFTA (1910.11.02-1947.12.22). Singer. Daughter of the nationalist figure Athanas Tashko (1863-1915), Tefta Tashko-Koço was born in Faiyum in Egypt. She studied singing in Montpellier (1927-1931) and in Paris at the National Conservatory of Music (1931-1933), where she appeared on stage at the Comic Opera. In 1936, she returned to Albania to become a leading concert soprano. She is remembered in particular for her folk songs, many of which are now available on recordings. *See also* MUSIC.

TEATRI KOMBËTAR SHQIPTAR. *See* NATIONAL THEATER.

TEATRI I OPERAS DHE BALETIT. *See* OPERA AND BALLET THEATER.

TEPELENA. Town in the **District of Tepelena,** of which it is the administrative center. **Population** in Dec. 1999: 8,788. The little town of Tepelena is situated in southern Albania at the junction of the **Vjosa** and **Drino** Rivers. The town boasts an impressive citadel which dominates north-south traffic and the nearby gorge of Këlcyra. It is associated with **Ali Pasha Tepelena,** who was born in nearby Hormova and who reconstructed the original Byzantine citadel in 1809-1812, making it his second place of residence, after Janina. **Lord Byron** visited him here in 1809. A legend has it that Tepelena must never have more than 100 dwellings or it will be destroyed.

TEPELENA, ALI PASHA. *See* ALI PASHA TEPELENA.

TEPELENA, DISTRICT OF. Region of local government administration. The District of Tepelena (*Rrethi i Tepelenës*), with its administrative headquarters in the town of **Tepelena,** borders on the districts of **Vlora** and **Mallakastra** to the west, **Berat** to the north, **Përmet** to the east and **Gjirokastra** to the south. It has a surface area of 817 square kilometers and a present **population** of 45,538 (in 2000). The word "Tepelena" is of Turkish origin. It was recorded in 1506 as *Tepedelen.*

TERESA, MOTHER (1910.08.27-1997.09.05). Catholic religious figure. Mother Teresa, originally Agnes Gonxhe Bojaxhiu, was an ethnic Albanian from Skopje. She joined the order of the Irish Loretto Sisters when she was eighteen and set off for India in December 1928 to teach at a missionary school for girls in Calcutta, where she lived from 1936 to her death. In 1948, she left the Loretto Sisters and took a course in nursing at an American missionary hospital in Patna. On her return to Calcutta, in 1950, she founded a new order of her own, the **Missionaries of Charity.** This order is devoted in particular to orphans, leprosy patients and the terminally ill, and has over 3,370 sisters in 443 branches worldwide. On 10 December 1979, Mother Teresa was awarded the Nobel Peace Prize in Oslo. In 1990, she retired as head of the order and traveled abroad to lecture and gather funds. She visited Albania on 1-5 December 1990, and was received by **Nexhmije Hoxha.** In 1991, she established a branch of her order in Albania.

She died in Calcutta. Two Albanian presidents, **Rexhep Meidani** and **Sali Berisha**, took part in her funeral on 13 September 1997.

TEUTA. Illyrian queen who reigned from **Lezha** (ancient Lissos). Teuta was the widow of Agron, and acted from 231 B.C. onwards as regent for her stepson Pinneus. Her ships and pirates plundered Roman merchant vessels and interfered with Roman trade routes in the Adriatic and Ionian Seas. Rome sent envoys to her in **Shkodra** to demand reparations but to no avail. In 229 B.C., Rome declared war on Illyria and sent armies to the Balkans for the first time as well as a fleet of 200 ships. Teuta surrendered in 227 B.C. and, having acknowledged Rome's superiority and having paid tribute, was allowed to retain her throne in the **Shkodra**-Lezha region. Today, many Albanian **women** bear the name Teuta in her honor.

THALLÓCZY, LUDWIG VON (1854.12.08-1916.12.01). Hungarian scholar and historian. Ludwig von Thallóczy was the founder of Balkan studies in Hungary. He was born and raised in Budapest, and studied at the university there. He worked for the Hungarian State Archives and, from 1877 on, as a lecturer at the University of Budapest. He later served as director of the financial archives in Vienna and as a specialist for teaching and education in Bosnia Herzegovina. He was president of the Hungarian Historical Society and a member of the Hungarian Academy of Sciences. Thallóczy spent the early years of **World War I** in Belgrade and died in a train accident in December 1916 on his return from the funeral of Emperor Franz Josef I.

Ludwig von Thallóczy is remembered in particular as the author of two monumental collections of documents on Albania. The first is the two-volume *Acta et diplomata res Albaniae mediae aetatis illustrantia* (Acts and Diplomatic Affairs illustrating the Middle Ages in Albania), Vienna 1913, 1918, published together with **Milan von Šufflay** and **Konstantin Jireček**, which encompasses previously largely unknown documents from 344 to 1406 A.D. discovered in archives in Venice, Dubrovnik, Naples and Rome, etc. The second two-volume collection, *Illyrisch-albanische Forschungen* (Illyrian-Albanian Research), Munich 1916, contains numerous informative articles on Albanian history and ethnography by Thallóczy and others.

THEATER, ALBANIAN. Professional theater is the prerogative of an urban society. In Albania, which has always had a strong rural

population and lacked large urban centers, theater never developed to the extent that literary poetry and prose did, nor did it ever capture the attention of the Albanian public to any major extent. There is little in the way of Albanian theater to report on before the second half of the nineteenth century and, in actual fact, little professional theater at all before the second half of the twentieth century.

The earliest original Albanian dramatist was Francesco Antonio Santori (1819-1894) of the Arbëresh village of Santa Caterina Albanese (Alb. *Picilia*) in the province of Cosenza in southern **Italy**. Among his tragedies are *Jeroboam* and the **Scanderbeg** melodrama *Alessio Dukagino*, written between 1855 and 1860. **Sami bey Frashëri** was author of a play written in Turkish entitled *Besa yahud ahde vefa* (*Besa* or the Fulfilment of the Pledge). It was premiered in 1874 at the Ottoman Theater in Istanbul and published there in the following year. It was translated into English as *Pledge of Honor, an Albanian Tragedy,* New York 1945. The first Albanian-language drama to be written in Albania itself was a short nativity play entitled *Nata Këshnellavet* (Christmas Eve), Shkodra 1880, by the **Franciscan** priest and poet **Leonardo De Martino**.

One shining star in the otherwise rather vacant heaven of Albanian theater was the Albanian actor **Alexander Moissi**, who was to become one of the great European stage actors of the early twentieth century. In Albania itself, this period saw a strong increase in the number of plays being written but little actual staging. A number of amateur theater groups had formed in the country's two main cultural centers, **Shkodra** and **Korça**, and other groups arose sporadically in smaller communities: **Durrës**, **Vlora**, **Pogradec**, **Elbasan**, **Berat**, **Gjirokastra** and Boboshtica, but performances were rare and lacked any particular talent or skill.

The postwar professional theater of socialist realism was said to have its origins in the amateur theater groups of the partisan movement in Albania from 1942 to 1944, but its roots obviously go back to the amateur ensembles of the 1920s and 1930s. The amateur groups of the partisan movement provided a mixture of polemics, heroism, nationalism, sentimentality and satire.

The unprecedented wave of persecution against Albanian intellectuals in the postwar period was unnerving for all surviving and would-be writers. Albanian theater was, thus, very slow to develop after the **communist** takeover, despite its obvious utility as a means of education, propaganda and political persuasion. It was nonetheless the postwar years which saw the founding of publicly subsidized state theaters and state ensembles in most major cities. This institutionalization of Albanian theater went hand in hand with the conscious eradication of amateur groups, which might have eluded state and party control. By the 1960s, amateur theater in Albania had disappeared, one of the many cultural losses of the period.

Among the playwrights of the socialist period are Kolë Jakova (1916-2002); Spiro Çomora (1918-1973); and Loni Papa (1932-), whose play *Cuca e maleve* (The Mountain Lass), Tirana 1967, was perhaps the most obvious reflection of Chinese revolutionary theater and opera in Albania.

Some progress was made from 1982 onwards, though Albanian drama remained and continues to remain a definitely neglected genre. The quality of acting and staging improved but the subject matter remained bland throughout the communist period. In the final years of the dictatorship, there were ten well-attended professional theaters and, in addition, about fifteen variety theaters and a puppet theater. Among the best theaters in the country are: the **National Theater** of **Tirana**, the **Migjeni** Theater of Shkodra, the **A. Z. Çajupi** Theater of Korça, the **Aleksandër Moisiu** Theater of **Durrës**, the Professional Theater of the City of Vlora and the Skampa Theater of **Elbasan**.

Since the dictatorship, some attempts have been made to revive Albanian theater, but the situation remains difficult. National and municipal governments have been unable to provide the financial support necessary to keep theaters afloat, and interest in Albanian theater has declined substantially due to competition from **film** and television. *See also* OPERA AND BALLET THEATER.

THEODHOSI, KOÇO (1913-1977.05). Political figure of the **communist** period. Koço Theodosi was born in **Korça**, where he attended secondary school. He graduated with a degree in mechanical engineering from the University of Lyon in France and returned to Albania to become a member of the communist party in 1941. He took part in the partisan movement during **World War II**. After the communist takeover, he was appointed state commissar for the **Kuçova oil** fields in 1944, and headed economic delegations to Bulgaria and Romania in 1945 and the **Soviet Union** in 1949-1950. He later served as chairman of the state planning commission in 1950-1954 and 1962-1966, minister of industry in 1954-1955, deputy prime minister in 1954-1966, and minister of industry and mining in 1966-1975.

Koço Theodhosi was a member of the Central Committee from 1952 to 1975 and a full member of the Politburo from 1971 to 1975. Together with **Abdyl Këllezi**, chairman of the state planning commission, and **Kiço Ngjela**, trade minister, he fell victim to the purge at seventh Congress of the Central Committee on 26-29 May 1975, allegedly for grave "revisionist" mistakes and sabotage of the economy, and was executed.

THOPIA, CHARLES (d. 1388). Historical figure and ruler. Charles Thopia, of the noble Thopia family first mentioned in 1274, was the descendant of Tanush Thopia, who ruled the **Mat** region and was a vassal of the Angevin king of Naples. Although related to the Angevins on his mother's side, Charles Thopia, who called himself *Princeps Albaniae* (Prince of Albania), seized **Durrës** from the Angevins in 1368 after a long siege. He was thereafter in conflict not only with the Angevin dynasty, but also with Venice. When he lost Durrës to his brother-in-law Balsha II in 1385, he appealed to the Turks for assistance and defeated him at the Battle of Savra on 18 September 1385. This battle marked the first direct involvement of **Ottoman** forces in Albania. His son, George Thopia, was obliged to return Durrës to the Venetians in 1392.

TIRANA. Capital of Albania and administrative center of the **District of Tirana**. **Population** in Dec. 1999: 436,016. The centrally located city of Tirana at the foot of Mount Dajti has been the capital of Albania since 1920.

The toponym Tirana was first mentioned in 1418 by historian **Marinus Barletius** as *Plenum Tyrenae* "the field of Tirana." As a settlement it is thought to have been established around 1614 when Suleyman Pasha Bargjini of Mullet near Petrela built a mosque, a Turkish bathhouse, and a soup kitchen for the poor there. Tirana grew in size at the end of the eighteenth century when the Et'hem Bey Mosque, now the principal tourist attraction in the center of the town, was built in 1793-1822. The town was later associated with the landowning **Toptani** family. In 1916, it had a population of 1,200 and, in 1939, of 35,000.

The main thoroughfares and representative buildings of the town were built during the **Italian** occupation from 1939 to 1943. Much of the historical core of Tirana, including the old bazaar, was razed by the **communists** to provide room for the palace of culture, Hotel Tirana and **museum** of history. Tirana has almost doubled in population since the fall of the dictatorship, with huge shanty towns extending to the west towards Vora and **Durrës** and to the north through Kamza to Fushë Kruja. It suffers from all the characteristics of rapid third-world development: illegal construction, heavy air pollution and a glaring lack of adequate infrastructure. This unplanned urban conglomeration will soon include Durrës and **Kruja** to form a metropolis of over one million inhabitants. Some steps have been taken since 2001 to dismantle illegal constructions, including the myriad of kiosks, and to restore parks and green areas.

TIRANA, DISTRICT OF. Region of local government administration. The District of Tirana (*Rrethi i Tiranës*), with its administrative headquarters in the city of **Tirana,** borders on the districts of **Durrës** to the west, **Kruja** to the north, **Mat, Bulqiza** and **Librazhd** to the east and **Elbasan, Peqin** and **Kavaja** to the south. It has a surface area of 1,238 square kilometers and a present **population** of 497,961 (in 2000). It is by far the most populated district in Albania.

TIRTA, MARK (1935.05.21-). Scholar and ethnographer. Mark Tirta is an ethnographer at the Institute of Folk Culture in **Tirana** and a professor of ethnography at the University of Tirana. He has written extensively on Albanian folklore and, in particular, popular beliefs and superstitions. He is the author of many scholarly articles and of the monograph *Migrime të shqiptarëve* (Albanian Migrations), Tirana 1998.

TOCCI, TERENZIO (1880.03.09-1945.04.14). Italo-Albanian public figure and publisher. Terenzio Tocci, known in Albanian as Terenc Toçi, was born in San Cosmo Albanese (Alb. *Strigari*) in the southern Italian province of Cosenza. He studied in San Demetrio Corone (Alb. *Shën Mitri*), specializing in law. Tocci was a journalist and a prolific and formidable orator. He was also something of an adventurer, a man longing for action. In 1908-1909, he toured the western hemisphere, from Buenos Aires, Montevideo and Rio de Janeiro to New York, Chicago and Philadelphia, where he gave speeches and visited Albanian and **Arbëresh** colonies to exhort support for the liberation of Albania from the Turkish yoke,

In 1910, with the support of General Ricciotti Garibaldi and the Albanian Council of **Italy** (*Consiglio Albanese d'Italia*), Tocci set off for Albania to take part in the uprising of that year. On 26 April 1911, he gathered the chieftains of **Mirdita** near Orosh and proclaimed the independence of Albania, hoisting the Albanian **flag** for the first time since the death of **Scanderbeg**, and formed a provisional government which had the support of much of northern Albania. The Italian reinforcements promised by General Garibaldi never arrived and the rebellion was thus put down by Turkish troops within a few days. Embittered, Tocci returned to Italy in July 1912, where he founded the fortnightly journal, *La rivista dei Balcani* (The Balkan Review). In March 1913, he took part in the **Congress of Trieste** and, back in Albania, founded the daily newspaper *Taraboshi* in **Shkodra**. Tocci was deported to Italy during **World War I** and returned to Shkodra in 1920 where he was now a recognized figure of Albanian public life, working in legal affairs and as a journalist. He was appointed prefect of **Korça** in the summer of 1921, and consul general in Egypt for a short period from February to May 1922. Tocci then directed the government press office (1922-1923) in **Tirana**, where in 1923 he taught international law at the legal school. He was a member of **parliament**, 1924-1925, president of the supreme court, 1925, and secretary-general to the office of the President **Ahmet Zogu**, April 1927. In September 1928, he retired from public life, but not for long.

From December 1936 to June 1938, Terenzio Tocci served as minister of economics and supported Italian interests in Albania and, in particular, the customs union between the two countries. He also held high office during the Italian occupation in 1940, that of president of the Corporative Fascist Supreme Council, but resigned in November 1942 when it became clear to him that the policies of Benito Mussolini, whose collected speeches he had earlier translated into Albanian, were leading to disaster. During the **communist** takeover of Tirana on 17 November 1944, Tocci was warned by friends that his name was on a death list and was urged to flee the country. He nonetheless felt he had nothing to reproach himself for and could defend himself in court. He was arrested the same day and held through the winter in a window-less cell, sleeping on a bare cement floor. On the evening of 14 April 1945, he was executed with sixteen other noted figures of Albanian public life, among whom were **Fejzi bey Alizoti**, Kostandin Kotte, Zef Kadare and Bahri Omari.

Tocci is remembered as the author of *La questione albanese* (The Albanian Question), Cosenza 1901; *Albania e gli albanesi* (Albania and the Albanians), Milan 1911; *I delitti del 'Taraboshi' ovvero la civiltà europea a Scutari d'Albania* (The Crimes of Taraboshi or European Civilization in Shkodra in Albania), Shkodra 1914; *E drejta ndeshkimore: parimet e përgjithëshme* (Penal Law: General Principles), Shkodra 1926; the 400-page *Fashizmi: biseda e shkrime të B. Mussolini-t* (Fascism: Conversations and Writings of B. Mussolini), Tirana 1928; *Gramatika e italishtjes pa msues* (Italian Grammar without a Teacher), Tirana 1931; a monograph on King Zog entitled *Il re degli albanesi* (The King of the Albanians), Milan 1938; a 166-page treatise on the state of the nation called *Shqiponja arbërore* (The Albanian Eagle), Tirana 1943, and numerous articles.

TOMORR, MOUNT. Mountain, holy site and legend. Tomorr, or Tomor, Alb. *Tomorr*, ancient *Tomaros*, is a mountain range in the region of **Berat** and **Skrapar** which includes the highest peak in central Albania at an altitude of 2,417 meters Mount Tomorr is considered the home of the gods in central Albanian popular belief. The mountain is personified as a god itself: *Baba Tomorr* "Father Tomorr." The peasants of the region swear by Father Tomorr, Alb. *për Baba Tomorr*, an oath considered stronger than any sworn on the Bible or the Koran. Mount Tomorr is sacred both to the Christians, who used to climb it on August 15, Assumption Day, in honor of the Virgin Mary, and to the **Bektashi**, who honor Abbas Ali during an annual pilgrimage on August 20-25.

The legendary figure of Baba Tomorr is envisaged as an old man with a long white beard flowing down to his belt. Around him hover four long-beaked female eagles, which perch on his snowy slopes. According to **Maximilian Lambertz**, he is the remnant of some ancient **Illyrian** god. The cult of Mount Tomorr is linked in particular to the romantic nationalism of the **Rilindja** age of national revival, especially in the **literature** of the period. Albanian writers such as **Konstantin Kristoforidhi, Naim bey Frashëri, Andon Zako Çajupi, Asdreni, Hilë Mosi,** and **Ndre Mjeda** have all devoted striking poetry and prose pieces to Father Tomorr.

TOPALLI, JOZEFINA (1963.11.26-). Political figure and high-ranking member of the **Democratic Party.** Jozefina Topalli was born and raised in **Shkodra** as the daughter of banker Filip Çoba.

She studied mathematics and law at the university there and worked in 1990 for the local chamber of commerce. In 1995, she was professor and chancellor of the University of Shkodra. Topalli was elected to **parliament** in 1996 and served as head of the parliamentary committee on legislation. Since 1997, she has been deputy speaker of parliament.

TOPALLI, KOLEC (1938.12.04-). Scholar and linguist. Kolec Topalli was born in **Shkodra** and was interned at the age of ten with his family because his older brother had escaped abroad. He was persecuted for the next fifty years of his life for this reason, living and working in various isolated internment villages. It was only after the fall of the dictatorship that he was able to devote himself to scholarship and to publish a book. Topalli served as secretary-general to the president of the republic during the regime of **Sali Berisha**. Among his linguistic monographs are: *Theksi në gjuhën shqipe* (The Accent in Albanian), Tirana 1995; *Për historinë e hundorësisë së zanoreve në gjuhën shqipe* (On the History of Nasalization of Vowels in Albanian), Tirana 1996; *Zhvillimi historik i diftongjeve të shqipes* (The Historical Development of Albanian Diphthongs), Tirana 1998; *Shndërrime historike në sistemin zanor të gjuhës shqipe* (The Historical Transformation of the Vowel System in Albanian), Tirana 2000; *Sonantet e gjuhës shqipe* (Sonants in Albanian), Tirana 2001; and *Mbylltoret e gjuhës shqipe* (Occlusives in Albanian), Tirana 2002.

TOPLANA. Northern Albanian tribe and traditional tribal region. The Toplana region is situated on the right bank of the **Drin** River in the very eastern part of the District of **Shkodra**. It borders on the traditional tribal regions of **Shoshi** to the west, **Merturi** to the north, **Berisha** to the east and **Dushmani** to the south. The name was recorded in 1691 as *Toplana, Toplaia*, and is a Slavic toponym, related to Serbocr. *topao* "warm." The small Toplana tribe had a **population** of about 400 in the late nineteenth century.

TOPTANI, ESSAD PASHA (1863-1920.06.13). Political figure. Essad Pasha Toptani, also known as Esad or Esat Pasha, stemmed from a wealthy landowning family from the **Tirana** region. He was early to gain a reputation as an unscrupulous opportunist. In 1908, he joined the Young Turks and became a member of the Turkish **parliament**. He is accused, in April 1913, of having assassinated Hasan Riza Pasha, commander of **Shkodra**, and of turning the fortress of Shkodra over to **Montenegro**, in order to gain Montenegrin support for his rule in central Albania, his traditional power base. This was in contradiction to the decision of the **Conference of Ambassadors** in London which had assigned Shkodra to Albania. On 16 October 1913, to frustrate **Ismail Qemal bey Vlora**, the power-hungry Toptani set up a rival government based in **Durrës**, called the Republic of Central Albania. He reluctantly stepped down when forced to by the Great Powers on 1 February 1914, being given as a consolation the right to lead the Albanian delegation which traveled to Germany to offer the Albanian throne to **Prince Wilhelm zu Wied**. Relations between the prince and the scheming Toptani, now minister of war and minister of the interior, soon soured and he was banned from the country in May 1914 when armed nationalists under a Dutch officer arrested him for conspiracy. From exile in Rome, he maintained close links with the Serb and Montenegrin governments. In October 1914, Toptani returned to Durrës via Serbia. When Austria-Hungary occupied much of central and northern Albania, Toptani fled to France and later to London, where he presented himself as the national representative of Albania. He was assassinated in Paris in 1920 by **Avni Rustemi** as he was leaving the Hotel Continental in the rue de Castiglione and is said to be buried at a Serbian military cemetery there.

TOPTANI, IHSAN BEY (1908.08.25-2001.05.28). Historical figure. **Tirana**-born Ihsan bey Toptani was the son of Abdi bey Toptani (1864-1942), a signatory of the proclamation of independence and finance minister in the provisional government of **Ismail Qemal bey Vlora** in 1912. He was educated in Graz in Austria, where he attended secondary school from 1920 to 1928 and finished a doctorate in political science in 1940. As the scion of a leading landowning family, he led a comfortable existence on his return to Albania in 1942. He played an important role in efforts to unite the various resistance movements during the **Italian** and **German** occupation, but to no avail. It was at his family estate in Mukaj that an important conference between resistance groups was held in August 1943. He was also in close contact with the British officers on mission for the Special Operations Executive in Albania. In October 1944, he fled with **Abaz Kupi** to Italy and worked for *Newsweek* in Rome. In 1949, he joined British agent **David Smiley** in Malta and helped train anticommunist agents to infiltrate Albania. The endeavors of these Albanian agents were later betrayed by British spy, **Kim Philby**. Toptani worked in Paris before moving to England. In London, he worked for the BBC monitoring service and obtained British nationality in 1958, before retiring in 1967 to a country home in Surrey. For years, he was respected as the doyen of the Albanian community in Britain.

TOPULLI, BAJO (1868-1930). Nationalist figure and guerrilla fighter. Bajo Topulli was born in **Gjirokastra** and worked as the deputy principal of a Turkish secondary school in Monastir (Bitola). In November 1905, he founded a secret committee of Albanian nationalists called *Për lirinë e Shqipërisë* (For the Freedom of Albania), which led to the establishment of similar committees elsewhere in southern Albania (**Korça, Kolonja** and Gjirokastra). The objective of these committees was to prepare for an armed uprising against **Ottoman** rule. In March 1906, he formed the first armed guerrilla band, Alb. *çeta*, in the Korça region, with its headquarters in the **Bektashi** monastery of Melçan. This, too, served as a model for similar bands which were created in Kolonja, **Devoll, Berat** and Leskovik. These bands not only fought against Turkish forces, but also against Greek dominance in the region. On 22 September 1906, they killed Photios, the Greek bishop of Korça, who was said to be responsible for the death of Papa **Kristo Negovani**.

TOPULLI, ÇERÇIZ (1880-1915.07.15). Nationalist figure and guerrilla fighter. Çerçiz Topulli, brother of **Bajo Topulli**, was born in **Gjirokastra**. In the spring of 1907, he and **Mihal Grameno** formed a band of guerrillas in Sofia to fight for Albanian interests. In April of that year, the band landed in **Vlora**, having entered the country from Brindisi, and conducted a campaign of agitation to prepare for an armed uprising in 1908. On 25 February 1908, the band killed the commander of the Turkish gendarmerie on a street in Gjirokastra. Five of them, including Çerçiz Topulli, then fled to Mashkullora, where on 5 March they were surrounded by 150 **Ottoman** troops. Although they were vastly outnumbered, Topulli and his fighters managed to keep the Turks at bay from dawn until dusk and then fled into the mountains, an event which was later celebrated in folk ballads. In July 1908, Topulli attempted to take the town of **Korça** but his forces were pushed back by Turkish troops. When the Young Turks took power, he organized patriotic societies and assisted in the opening of Albanian-language schools. Çerçiz Topulli was active in the defense of national interests after independence, too, and was killed by **Montenegrin** forces at Fusha e Shtoit near Shkodra.

TOSK. The term Tosk refers to the southern Albanians, i.e., all Albanians living south of the **Shkumbin** River and speaking Tosk dialects. The territory of the Tosks is poetically referred to as Toskëria. The northern Albanians are called **Ghegs**.

TOURISM. Despite its tourist potential, with a beautiful Mediterranean coastline and a favorable **climate**, Albania is not yet a major tourist destination, though the tourism industry has gradually recovered after the major setbacks caused by the wars in **Yugoslavia** and the **uprising of 1997**. Though most tourists are still domestic, there is also an increasing number of visitors from **Kosova** and **Macedonia**, and a modest number of Italians and Greeks who spend their holidays in Albania, mostly on the coast. In 1999, there were 102 registered hotels with 3,575 beds, utilized by a total of 103,000 tourists and visitors (77,000 Albanian citizens and 26,000 foreigners).

TRANSPORTATION. *See* AIR TRANSPORTATION; PORTS; RAIL TRANSPORTATION.

TREBESHINA, KASËM (1926.08.08-). Writer. Kasëm Trebeshina was born in **Berat** and studied at the Normal School (*Shkolla Normale*) in **Elbasan** until joining the **communist** resistance movement in 1942. After the war he studied at the Ostrovsky Theater Institute in Leningrad. A committed communist, but by no means a conformist, Trebeshina left the party and later the **Writers' Union** in **Tirana**. Much of his work was written in the late 1940s and early 1950s but was never published. In an extremely rare act of open dissent in Albanian intellectual life, Trebeshina sent a "pro memoria" to **Enver Hoxha** on 5 October 1953, warning him that his cultural policies were leading the nation down the road to disaster. It goes without saying that the dictator was not amused. Kasëm Trebeshina, the unpublished author of eighteen volumes of verse, forty-two plays, twenty-two novels and short stories, etc., vanished from the literary scene with scarcely a trace following this voluntary act of self-destruction. After seventeen years in prison, with interruptions, a comparatively light sentence as he later noted, and twenty years of silence, Trebeshina resurfaced in the early 1990s with a handful of other writers, artists and intellectuals to find that his prediction had come true. Of Trebeshina's voluminous writing, only one collection of poetry, *Artani dhe Min'ja ose hijet e fundit të maleve* (Artani and Min'ja or the Last Mountain Shadows), Tirana 1961, and an anonymous translation of the plays of García Lorca were published at the time. Since the fall of the dictatorship, Trebeshina has published numerous volumes of prose, some of which has been translated into German and French.

TRIESTE, CONGRESS OF. *See* CONGRESS OF TRIESTE.

TRIX, FRANCES (1948-). American scholar and anthropologist. Frances Trix was born in Bellefonte, Pennsylvania. She studied Near Eastern languages and literatures at Middlebury College, 1966-1968, and at the University of Michigan 1968-1972, where, after years of teaching at home and abroad, she finished her doctorate in linguistics in 1988. She is currently associate professor of anthropology at Wayne State University in Detroit, Michigan. Trix is the foremost English-language expert on the **Bektashi** order of dervishes and was closely associated with Baba Rexhepi during his final years in Detroit. She is the author of *Spiritual Discourse: Learning with an Islamic Master,* Philadelphia 1993; *The Albanians in Michigan,* East Lansing 2001, and of numerous articles on **Islam** and the Bektashi.

TROPOJA, DISTRICT OF. Region of local government administration. The District of Tropoja (*Rrethi i Tropojës*), also known as the District of Bajram Curri, with its administrative headquarters in the town of Bajram Curri, borders on the districts of **Shkodra** to the west, **Has** and **Puka** to the south, the Republic of **Montenegro** to the north and **Kosova** to the east. It has a surface area of 1,043 square kilometers and a present **population** of 42,116 (in 2000).

TURKEY, ALBANIANS IN. Albania was an integral part of the Ottoman Empire for five centuries, during which the majority of Albanians converted to **Islam**. It is no wonder, therefore, that there were and are close connections between the two countries. Although not widely known abroad and despite the lack of reliable population statistics, the Albanian community in Turkey may, in fact, be one of the largest anywhere in the diaspora. Early Albanian emigration to Turkey resulted from forced conscription into the Ottoman army and the janissaries. Many Albanians in Istanbul subsequently attained positions of power. In the sixteenth and seventeenth centuries, no less than five grand viziers of the Empire were Albanian, of the Köprülü dynasty. Also of Albanian origin was Mehmed Ali Pasha (1769-1849), governor of Egypt from 1805; theologian and scholar **Hasan Tahsini**, the first rector of the University of Istanbul; pan-Islamic poet Mehmet Akif (1873-1936), author of the Turkish national anthem of 1921; and Riza Tevfik, one of the greatest Turkish philosophers of the period. The mother of Mustafa Kemal Ataturk (1881-1938) is also said to have been of Albanian ethnicity.

In the late nineteenth century, Istanbul became a major center for the Albanian nationalist movement. Most southern Albanian intellectuals of the period lived there for some time, in particular the Frashëri brothers. **Sami bey Frashëri**, known in Turkish as Şemseddîn Sâmî, made a name for himself primarily as a Turkish lexicographer and encyclopedist.

Aside from the intellectual community in Istanbul, there were many Albanian settlements in Thrace and on the banks of the Sea of Marmara. These **Orthodox** Albanian communities were expelled to Greece after **World War I** in the population exchange between the two countries.

Some 150,000 Albanians from **Yugoslavia** were expelled to Turkey between the two world wars, and a further 250,000 **Kosova** Albanians were expelled after **World War II**. As such, the number of ethnic Albanians in Turkey may reach one million, although many are now assimilated. There are, at any rate, still large Albanian communities in Istanbul, Bursa and elsewhere.

TURKEY, RELATIONS WITH. The Ottoman Empire conquered Albania in the early fifteenth century during its expansion northwards and westwards into Europe. Albania was to be a Turkish colony and an integral part of the Ottoman Empire for five centuries. Historical and cultural relations between the Turks and Albanians are thus very close.

The Battle of Savra, south of **Lushnja**, on 18 September 1385 marked the beginning of Turkish encroachments in Albania. On 28 June 1389, Ottoman forces overpowered a coalition of Balkan troops under Serbian leadership at the Battle of Kosovo Polje north of Prishtina to establish themselves as masters of the Balkans. The fortresses of **Vlora**, Kanina and **Berat** were conquered in 1417 and **Gjirokastra** fell in 1419.

In 1431, the Turks set up an Ottoman sandjak of Albania (*Sancak-i Arnavid*) and, despite resistance under **Scanderbeg** and others, the conquest of the country was completed by the end of the fifteenth century. **Kruja** fell to the Turks in 1478, **Shkodra** capitulated in January 1479 after a long siege and **Durrës** fell in 1501.

Albanian historians have traditionally viewed the Ottoman period in negative terms as the "long Ottoman night," i.e., as being responsible for Albania's backward state today. Despite mismanagement, in particular in the nineteenth-century period of Ottoman decay, the Turkish occupation also brought to Albania elements of a refined oriental culture. The descriptions left by Turkish traveler **Evliya Çelebi** in 1670 of flourishing Albanian cities such as Berat and **Elbasan** would surprise any visitor to those towns today. The Ottoman period also had a positive consequence for the Albanians of saving them from ethnic assimilation by the Slavs. It was only in the Ottoman period that the Albanians took full ethnic possession of their country.

During the first decades of Ottoman rule, there were few Muslims among the Albanians themselves. In 1577, it is known that northern and central Albania were still staunchly **Catholic**, but by the early decades of the seventeenth century, an estimated thirty to fifty percent of the population of northern Albania had converted to **Islam**, and by the close of that century, Muslims began to outnumber Christians throughout most of the country. The Albanians adapted to their new masters and began to look to the east, rather than west to Europe.

The Tanzimat reform of the Ottoman Empire on 3 November 1839 caused serious unrest in Albania, in particular over the issue of military conscription, and the following decades saw the rise of the Albanian national movement for more autonomy, in particular during the **League of Prizren**, 1878-1881. Albanian intellectuals, Muslims in their great majority, were not originally for independence—which for them was still inconceivable—but for one united Albanian sandjak under the suzerainty of the sultan, and for a high degree of local autonomy. They were more worried about the designs of their Christian neighbors, the Serbs, Montenegrins and Greeks, than they were about the distant Turks. Though they battled Turkish troops for decades, whenever they had to choose between the Turks and the neighboring countries, they always sided with the Empire. Curiously enough, one center of the Albanian national movement was Istanbul itself, where many noted Albanian intellectuals resided.

The Albanians initially welcomed the Young Turk Revolution in July 1908. There can be no doubt that they also played a major role in the revolution, which brought an end to an age of total stagnation and which gave the Empire a constitution and a semblance of equality among citizens, regardless of faith. But the hopes the Albanians had stored in the Young Turks were soon dashed when it became apparent that the new administration was just as centralistic as the old one, or even more so. The Albanians would have no part in the wave of pan-Turkish nationalism which spread throughout the Empire. Typical of this attitude were the remarks of publicist **Dervish Hima** at a ceremony in Shkodra in August 1909 to mark the new constitution, which was initially received with a good deal of naive enthusiasm by the northern Albanian tribes. Kazim bey, a Turkish officer speaking at the ceremony, proclaimed in the fresh spirit of Ottoman nationalism, "Now, there are no more Muslims and Christians, no different nationalities: there is only one Ottoman nation." Interrupting the officer's address, Dervish Hima countered, "The Albanians are nothing but Albanians and will not be satisfied until they are free in a free Albania as part of a confederation of independent Balkan states under the suzerainty of the sultan." While hopes for autonomy had not grown any brighter, the Albanians did take advantage of the Young Turk reforms and relative liberality in cultural affairs to set up Albanian schools and to found Albanian-language newspapers and patriotic clubs. But the tragic cycle of bloody uprisings and repression continued right until the Ottoman Empire collapsed in the **Balkan Wars**. Turkish forces withdrew and Albania declared its independence.

Though cultural relations between the Turks and Albanians remained close in the later decades of the twentieth century, the two countries had few noticeable direct political contacts. Albania looked increasingly towards Europe.

After **World War II**, Albania and Turkey reestablished diplomatic relations on 13 June 1958, and trade resumed in the 1980s after a Turkish trade delegation visited **Tirana** on 16-19 December 1980, and an Albanian delegation under Nedin Hoxha reciprocated on 22-29 December 1981.

After the fall of the dictatorship, Turkey was among the first countries to send aid to the impoverished nation, initially with a fleet of ambulances and medical assistance. Prime Minister Süleyman Demirel visited Tirana on 31 May - 1 June 1992 and signed a loan for US$50 million, and President Turgut Özal visited Albania on 18-21 February 1993.

Trade flourished early between the two countries and low-priced consumer goods from Turkey soon flooded the Albanian market, from clothes to terrible chocolate bars. In addition to furnishing the Albanian market with goods, Turkey also established a Turkish-language secondary school in **Tirana**, which in the 1990s provided select students with a better **education** than state schools could offer.

In recent years, within the framework of the North Atlantic Treaty Organization, Turkey has also supplied Albania with much military assistance. Its forces helped bring order to the country after the **uprising of 1997** and have recently assisted in the restoration of the Pasha Liman naval base in the Bay of Vlora. President **Rexhep Meidani** visited Ankara on 12-13 February 1998 to promote further economic and military cooperation, and President Süleyman Demirel reciprocated on 14-15 July 1998.

- U -

UKRAINE, ALBANIANS IN THE. There are small and now largely assimilated Albanian communities in the regions west of Odessa and north of the Crimean peninsula on the banks of the Sea of Azov. Specifically, the Ukrainian Albanians live in the village of Zhovtnevoje (Karakurt) in Bessarabia, ten kilometers from Bolgrad, and in the villages of Gamovka (Djandran), Georgievka (Tjushki) and Devnenskoje (Taz) near Melitopol' on the Sea of Azov. The Albanian colonies in the Ukraine were established after 1774, probably in the nineteenth century, from settlements in and around Varna in Bulgaria. According to statistics from the year 1959, there were 5,258 Albanians in the Ukraine and, in 1970, 4,402.

UNIATE CHURCH OF BYZANTINE RITE. Christian Church. The Uniates are sometimes known as Greek or Byzantine Catholics. Their church services follow Byzantine rite but they recognize the supremacy of the pope and are accepted as part of the **Catholic Church**. While Uniate Catholics are rare in Albania itself, they form a large part of the population of the Italo-Albanians or Arbëresh in Calabria and Sicily. In the seventeenth century, about fifty Albanian settlements were forced by the Catholic bishops of southern **Italy** to conform to Latin rite, but soon thereafter, they received support from Rome for their traditional Byzantine rite.

A decisive impetus to the intellectual and cultural advancement of the Sicilian Arbëresh was provided by the establishment of the Greek college or seminary in Palermo, subsequently known as the Greco-Albanian Seminary and then as the Italo-Albanian Seminary, founded by Giorgio Guzzetta (1682-1756). In 1732, Pope Clement XII (r. 1730-1740) founded the Collegio Italo-Greco Corsini in San Benedetto Ullano, Alb. *Shën Benedhiti*, in Calabria, which was also to serve as a seminary for the training of Byzantine rite priests. Priests trained at the seminar could go on to study at the Greek College of Saint Athanasius in Rome or at the Basilian Abbey of Grottaferrata. The **Basilian order** of Grottaferrata, with its dependencies in Mezzojuso, Alb. *Munxifsi*, in Sicily and San Basile, Alb. *Shën Vasili*, in Calabria, was indeed instrumental in preserving Byzantine rite among the Italo-Albanians. Today, there are two Italo-Albanian Uniate dioceses, one in Lungro, Alb. *Ungra,* in Calabria and the other in Piana degli Albanesi, Alb. *Hora e Arbëreshëvet*, in Sicily. In 1968, the Uniate Church, as one of the Eastern Catholic Churches, took the historic decision of replacing Greek with Albanian as the language of its liturgy.

UNION FOR HUMAN RIGHTS PARTY (*PARTIA BASHKIMI PËR TË DREJTAT E NJERIUT, PBDNJ*) (1992-). This small political party arose from the **Omonia** association, which was originally a political movement for the **Greek minority** in southern Albania and had five seats in **parliament** in 1991. Since the law on **political parties** banned parties which were formed on an ethnic basis, Omonia's supporters created the Union for Human Rights Party in February 1992, which was open to all Albanian citizens and which extended its activities throughout the country. In the **parliamentary** elections of 1992, the Union for Human Rights won 2.9 percent of the popular vote, in 1996 four percent, in 1997 2.7 percent and in 2001 2.6 percent. The party was founded by **Vasil Melo.**

UNION FOR VICTORY (*BASHKIMI PËR FITOREN*) (2001-). Political formation. The Union for Victory was a coalition of political forces established on 21 April 2001 for the June 2001 elections. It comprised the **Democratic Party** of **Sali Berisha**, the **Republican Party**, the monarchist **Movement for Legality**

Party (*Lëvizja e Legalitetit*), the National Front (*Balli Kombëtar*) and the Liberal Union Party (*Bashkimi Liberal*).

UNION OF WRITERS AND ARTISTS (*LIDHJA E SHKRIMTARËVE DHE E ARTISTËVE TË SHQIPËRISË*) (1945-). The Albanian Writers' Union was set up under the direction of **Sejfulla Malëshova** on 7 October 1945. It was initially composed of seventy members, including journalists and scholars. An Artists' Union (*Lidhja e Artistëve*) was established for painters, sculptors and composers in 1949. These two organizations were amalgamated in 1957 to form the present Union of Writers and Artists of Albania which, during the **communist** period, played a leading role in the country's literary and cultural affairs. After the fall of the dictatorship and with the privatization of the publishing industry and of cultural activities in general, it lost significance and has fallen somewhat into decay. It still exists as an institution, however.

UNITED KINGDOM, RELATIONS WITH. The first substantial ties between Britain and Albania date from **World War II** when **King Zog** and the Albanian royal family sought refuge in London following the Italian invasion of April 1939. In the course of the war, in particular between the end of 1943 and late 1944, over 100 British officers and men were sent to Albania by the headquarters of the **Special Operations Executive** in Bari to promote Albanian resistance to the German occupation, and ties with Albanian leaders were fostered. Despite the **communist** takeover in 1944, diplomatic relations between the two countries resumed on 10 November 1945. A year later, however, on 22 October 1946, the **Corfu Channel incident** occurred, in which two British destroyers hit mines and sank, resulting in the deaths of forty-four men. Britain protested sharply to Albania and took the country to the International Court of Justice in The Hague. On 15 December 1949, the court ruled that Albania must pay £843,947 in damages to Britain. At that time, the Bank of England was already in possession of the Albanian state treasury, an estimated 2.5 tons of gold. Albania's refusal to abide by the ruling of the International Court, and Britain's refusal to return the Albanian treasury until damages were paid, effectively blocked British-Albanian relations for almost half a century. Diplomatic relations were only resumed on 29 May 1991, and the Corfu Channel incident was resolved on 8 May 1993. On 29 October 1996, the two sides agreed in London that Albania would pay Britain US$2 million in reparations and would receive US$18 million in return. President **Sali Berisha** visited Britain on 27-31 March 1994 and was received by Queen Elizabeth II, as was President **Alfred Moisiu** on 11 March 2003.

UNITED STATES, ALBANIANS IN. Tangible numbers of Albanians first migrated to the United States in the early years of the twentieth century. Most of them were **Orthodox** Albanians from the southeastern **Korça** region who settled in Boston and New York. Many of them did not intend to stay in the United States, but simply wanted to make their fortune and then return to their native country. Indeed, an estimated 10,000 immigrants did return to Albania after **World War I**. This explains why most traditional areas of Albanian settlement in the United States are on the east coast. For those hoping to return to Albania, there was no reason to go any farther. Aside from Boston and New York (especially the Bronx), there were notable Albanian settlements in South Boston, Worcester, Natick, Southbridge and Framington in Massachusetts; Manchester in New Hampshire; Biddeford-Saco in Maine; Bridgeport and Waterbury in Connecticut; and Jamestown and Rochester in New York. There were later also early Albanian communities in Philadelphia, Pittsburgh, Cleveland, Detroit, Chicago and St. Louis. New waves of Albanian immigrants reached the United States in the 1920s and 1930s, this time with the intention of staying. After **World War II**, emigration from Albania fell drastically, however, because of the great difficulties involved in getting out of the isolated Stalinist country, although there was some emigration from **Montenegro** and **Kosova**. By 1980, there were an estimated 70,000 Albanians in the United States.

Since the opening of Albania in 1990-1991 and the "encouragement" given by the Belgrade authorities to Albanian emigration from Kosova in the 1980s and 1990s, there has been a very large increase in the number of Albanians living in the United States. At present, there are an estimated 400,000 Albanians (including Americans of Albanian descent) there. Of this total, about 150,000 live in the tristate area of New York, New Jersey and Connecticut; about 100,000 in Chicago and the mid-west; about 75,000 in the Detroit area; about 50,000 in Massachusetts and New England; and about 30,000 elsewhere.

UNITED STATES, RELATIONS WITH. Albanian relations with the United States developed soon after Albanian independence.

It was due in good part to the resolve and personal intervention of President Woodrow Wilson and the principle of self-determination, which he managed to uphold in Europe, in particular at the Paris Peace Conference of 1919, that Albania was not dismembered by **Greece** and **Italy** in accordance with the Tittoni-Venezelos Agreement. The large Albanian community which had settled in the United States by this time lobbied successfully on behalf of its homeland. The United States provided assistance to the Albanian government after 1920, in particular in promoting schools, such as the **American Vocational School** in **Tirana** under the direction of Harry T. Fultz, and the American-Albanian School of Agriculture and Domestic Science in **Kavaja**.

In April 1937, **King Zog** married the Hungarian-American countess **Geraldine Apponyi.** The new Queen of Albania was thus the daughter of an American, Gladys Stewart Girault, of an old family from Virginia.

After World War II, the **communist** regime resumed diplomatic relations with the United States on 10 November 1945. Soon thereafter, however, on 15 November 1946, the United States withdrew its mission from Albania because the new government refused to recognize prewar agreements. The building of the American embassy in Tirana was left to the care of the Italian government for the next forty-five years.

On 10 July 1947, in the early years of the Cold War, Albania refused an invitation to take part in the Marshall Plan, and on 7 March 1955, it rejected President Dwight Eisenhower's offer of US$850,000 worth of food to ease the chronic food shortage in the country.

There were few contacts between the two countries until the end of the communist dictatorship. After 1961, the party leadership in Albania had branded the two superpowers, the United States and the **Soviet Union**, as the enemies of the working class around the world, and only the citizens of these two countries were not allowed to visit Albania as a matter of principle. Albanian-Americans wanting to visit their original homeland had to demonstrate that their families had arrived in the United States before World War II.

American politicians Tom Lantosh and Joseph Dioguardi, both of Albanian descent, visited Tirana on 28-31 May 1990 and were received by President **Ramiz Alia**. Alia then paid a visit to the United States on 24 September - 4 October 1990 as part of an Albanian delegation to the United Nations.

Diplomatic relations between the two countries were resumed on 15 March 1991,and soon thereafter, on 22 June of that year, Secretary of State James Baker visited Tirana and was given an enthusiastic welcome by 400,000 people. On 21 December 1991, the first American ambassador, William E. Ryerson, presented his credentials. Ryerson was to become a close friend and promoter of **Sali Berisha**, who visited the United States as Albanian president on 15-20 June 1992. Prime Minister **Aleksandër Meksi** visited Washington on 21 April 1993 and held talks with President Bill Clinton. Former President George Bush visited Tirana on 12 November 1994. President Sali Berisha also visited Washington on 12 September 1995 to promote economic assistance and military cooperation, and New York on 20-24 October of that year to attend the fifthieth anniversary celebrations of the United Nations, and to meet with representatives of the Albanian-American community.

UPRISING OF 1997. *See* PYRAMID INVESTMENT SCANDAL AND THE 1997 UPRISING.

- V -

VALENTINI, GIUSEPPE (1900.07-1979.11.16). Italian scholar. Giuseppe Valentini, known in Albanian as Zef Valentini, was born in Padua. He studied theology, became a **Jesuit** priest and moved to Albania in 1922 as a missionary. There he began learning Albanian and conducting research into Albanian culture and history with the help of the Jesuit library in **Shkodra**. He was active in the publication of Jesuit cultural periodicals such as *Lajmtari i Zemers t' Jezu Krishtit* (Messenger of the Sacred Heart) and *Leka* (Leka), which he directed for several years from 1932 on. During **World War II**, he returned to **Italy** and held a post as professor of Albanian studies at the University of Palermo.

Valentini is the author of major publications on Albanian history, law, numismatics and sacred art. Among them are: *Contributi alla cronologia albanese: fonti per la storia d'Albania* (Contributions to Albanian Chronology: Sources for the History of Albania), Rome 1942; *Appunti di storia culturale albanese*

(Notes on Albanian Cultural History), Palermo 1956; *Il diritto della communità nella tradizione giuridica albanese* (Community Law in Albanian Legal Tradition). Florence 1956; *Appunti sul regime degli stabilimenti veneti in Albania nel secolo XIV e XV* (Notes on the Venetian Colonization of Albania in the Fourteenth and Fifteenth Centuries), Florence 1966; *Lo statuto personale in Albania all'epoca di Scanderbeg: appunti dagli Archivi della Repubblica Veneta* (Personal Statutes in Albania at the Time of Scanderbeg: Notes from the Archives of the Republic of Venice), Rome 1967; *Legge delle montagne albanesi nella relazioni della Missione Volante, 1880-1932* (Laws of the Albanian Highlands in Relation to the Visiting Missions, 1880-1932), Florence 1968; his two-volume *Acta Albaniae Juridica* (Legal Documents of Albania), Munich 1968, 1973; and in particular his monumental *Acta Albaniae Veneta* (Venetian Documents on Albania), Munich 1967-1979, a thirty-five-volume collection of fourteenth- and fifteenth-century documents of Albanian history.

VALONA. *See* VLORA.

VANGJELI, PANDELI. *See* EVANGJELI, PANDELI.

VARIBOBA, GIULIO (1724-1788). Arbëresh poet. Giulio Variboba, known in Albanian as *Jul Variboba*, is the first Arbëresh poet of real talent and is regarded by many Albanians as the first genuine poet in all of Albanian **literature**. Variboba was born in San Giorgio Albanese (Alb. *Mbuzati*) in the province of Cosenza to a family originally from the **Mallakastra** region of southern Albania. He studied at the Corsini seminary in San Benedetto Ullano, a center of learning and training for the Byzantine Greek priesthood. Variboba, one of its first students, was ordained as a priest in 1749 and returned to his native San Giorgio to assist his elderly father Giovanni, archpriest of the parish. Even during his studies at the Corsini seminary, Variboba had shown a definite preference for the Latin **(Catholic)** rite over the traditional Byzantine Greek rite in the Arbëresh church. In later years, his polemic support for a transition to the Latin rite made him quite unpopular with both his parish and the local church hierarchy in Rossano, in particular after his direct appeal to the pope. He was eventually forced into exile, initially to Campania and Naples, and, in 1761, he settled in Rome, where he spent the rest of his days.

Despite the turmoil of these years, Variboba must have known moments of tranquillity, too, for it was soon after his arrival in Rome that he published his long lyric poem *Ghiella e Shën Mëriis Virghiër* (The Life of the Virgin Mary), Rome 1762, the only Arbëresh book printed in the eighteenth century. This loosely structured poem of 4,717 lines, written entirely in the dialect of San Giorgio Albanese and loaded with much Calabrian Italian vocabulary, is devoted to the life of the Virgin Mary from her birth to the Assumption. Though from the poet's own life history and his uncompromising and polemic attitude to church rites, one might be led to expect verse of intense spiritual contemplation, the *Ghiella* evinces more of a light-hearted, earthy ballad tone, using Variboba's native Calabria as a background for the nativity, and transforming the devout characters of the New Testament into hearty eighteenth-century Calabrian peasants.

VASA, PASHKO (1825.09.17-1892.06.29). Political figure, poet, novelist and patriot. Pashko Vasa, also known as Wassa Effendi, Vaso Pasha or Vaso Pasha Shkodrani, was a figure from northern Albania who played a key role in the **Rilindja** culture of the nineteenth century. Born in **Shkodra**, he spent the revolutionary year 1848-1849 in Italy and published an account of his experience there in his Italian-language *La mia prigionia, episodio storico dell'assedio di Venezia* (My Imprisonment, Historical Episode from the Siege of Venice), Istanbul 1850. In Istanbul, after an initial period of poverty and hardship, he obtained a position at the ministry of foreign affairs, whence he was seconded to London for a time, to the Imperial Ottoman Embassy to the Court of St. James. He later served the Sublime Porte in various positions of authority. In 1863, thanks to his knowledge of Serbo-Croatian, as he tells us, he was appointed to serve as secretary and interpreter to Ahmed Jevdet Pasha, Ottoman statesman and historian, on a fact-finding mission to Bosnia and Hercegovina, which lasted for twenty months, from the spring of 1863 to October 1864. The events of this mission were recorded in his *La Bosnie et l'Herzégovine pendant la mission de Djevdet Efendi* (Bosnia and Hercegovina during the Mission of Jevdet Efendi), Istanbul 1865. Around 1867 he was in Aleppo. A few years later, he published another, now rare work of historical interest, *Esquisse historique sur le Monténégro d'après les traditions de l'Albanie* (Historical Sketch of Montenegro According to Albanian Traditions), Istanbul 1872.

Despite his functions on behalf of the Porte, Pashko Vasa never forgot his Albanian homeland. In the autumn of 1877, he became a founding member of the **Central Committee for the Defense of the Rights of the Albanian People** in Istanbul. Through his contacts there, he also participated in the organization of the **League of Prizren** in 1878. He was no doubt the author of the Memorandum on Albanian Autonomy submitted to the British Embassy in Istanbul. Together with other nationalist figures on the Bosporus, such as hodja **Hasan Tahsini**, **Jani Vreto** and **Sami bey Frashëri**, he played his part in the creation of an alphabet for Albanian and, in this connection, published a sixteen-page brochure entitled *L'alphabet latin appliqué à la langue albanaise* (The Latin Alphabet applied to the Albanian Language), Istanbul 1878, in support of an alphabet of purely Latin characters. He was also a member of the **Society for the Publication of Albanian Writing**. In 1879, Pashko Vasa worked in Varna on the Black Sea coast in the administration of the vilayet of Edirne with **Ismail Qemal bey Vlora**. He also acquired the title of pasha and, on 18 July 1883, became governor general of the Lebanon, a post reserved by international treaty for a **Catholic** of Ottoman nationality. He is said to have held this position in an atmosphere of Levantine corruption and family intrigue, true to the traditions of the Lebanon then and now. There he spent the last years of his life and died in Beirut after a long illness. In 1978, the centenary of the League of Prizren, his remains were transferred from the Lebanon back to a modest grave in Shkodra.

Though a loyal civil servant of the **Ottoman Empire**, Pashko Vasa devoted his energies as a polyglot writer to the Albanian national movement. Aware of the importance of Europe in Albania's struggle for recognition, he published *La vérité sur l'Albanie et les Albanais: étude historique et critique*, Paris 1879, a historical and political monograph which appeared in an English translation as *The Truth on Albania and the Albanians: Historical and Critical Study*, London 1879, as well as in Albanian, German, Turkish and Greek that year, and later in Arabic (1884) and Italian (1916). This treatise was designed primarily to inform the European reader about his people. To make the Albanian **language** better known and to give other Europeans an opportunity to learn it, he published a *Grammaire albanaise à l'usage de ceux qui désirent apprendre cette langue sans l'aide d'un maître* (Albanian Grammar for Those Wishing to Learn This Language without the Aid of a Teacher), Ludgate Hill 1887, one of the rare grammars of the period.

Pashko Vasa was also the author of a number of literary works. The first of these is a volume of Italian verse entitled *Rose e spine* (Roses and Thorns), Istanbul 1873, forty-one emotionally charged poems devoted to themes of love, suffering, solitude and death. *Bardha de Témal, scènes de la vie albanaise* (Bardha of Temal, Scenes from Albanian Life), Paris 1890, is a French-language novel which Pashko Vasa published in Paris under the pseudonym of Albanus Albano. Bardha of Temal, though not written in Albanian, is—after **Sami bey Frashëri**'s much shorter prose work Love of Tal'at and Fitnat—the oldest novel written and published by an Albanian and is certainly the oldest such novel with an Albanian theme.

Though most of Pashko Vasa's publications were in French and Italian, there is one poem, the most influential and perhaps the most popular poem ever written in Albanian, which has ensured him his deserved place in Albanian literary history, the famous *O moj Shqypni* (Oh Albania, Poor Albania). In this stirring appeal for a national awakening, thought to have been written in the period between 1878 and 1880, he calls on his country: *"Awaken, Albania, wake from your slumber, / Let us all, as brothers, swear a common oath / And not look to church or mosque, / The faith of the Albanian is Albanianism!"*

VASO PASHA SHKODRANI. *See* VASA, PASHKO.

VATRA FEDERATION (*FEDERATA PAN-SHQIPTARE VATRA*) (1912-). Vatra, the Pan-Albanian Federation of America, was founded in Boston on 28 April 1912 by **Fan Noli** and **Faik bey Konitza** to promote Albanian interests in the **United States** and, in particular, in the Balkans. It was an amalgamation of the *Besa-Besën* (Pledge for a Pledge) society and thirteen other Albanian organizations in America, and later had seventy branches throughout the country. Vatra, which in Albanian means "hearth," was initially headed by Fan Noli and then, from 1921 by Konitza. It was soon destined to become the most powerful and significant Albanian organization in America. In 1917, in view of the chaotic situation and political vacuum in Albania, it regarded itself as a sort of Albanian government in exile. The Vatra federation has gone through many ups and downs over the years. It still exists and is presently headed by Agim Karagjozi, with its headquarters in the Bronx, New York.

VELO, MAKS (1935.08.31-). Painter and writer. Maks Velo was born in Paris of Albanian parents from the **Korça** region. He graduated from the Faculty of Construction in **Tirana** in 1958 and turned to architecture and drawing. His career as a leading Albanian painter was interrupted when he was denounced by name at the party's fourth congress in 1973 for modernistic tendencies in his painting, i.e., for having created works of art allegedly inspired by Modigliani, Braque and Picasso, in contradiction to the teachings of socialist realism. He was arrested on 14 October 1978 and sentenced in 1979 to ten years in prison. Some 246 of his paintings and all of his art collections were confiscated and destroyed. Velo himself was dispatched to the infamous copper mines of Spaç and was only released on 13 January 1986, when he was allowed to work as a manual laborer until the end of the dictatorship. He has exhibited his works in Albania, France, Poland and the United States. Among his publications are the album *Kokëqethja* (Head-Shearing), Tirana 1995; memoirs, *Palltoja e burgut* (The Prison Cloak), Tirana 1995; the album, *Vizatime mbi arkitekturën shqiptare* (Drawings on Albanian Architecture), Tirana 1995; *Thesi i burgut* (The Prison Sack), Tirana 1996; *Jeta ime në figura* (My Life in Figures), Tirana 1996; *Kohë antishenjë* (Age of the Anti-Symbol), Tirana 2000; and *Zhdukja e 'Pashallarëve të kuq' të Kadaresë: anketim për një krim letrar* (The Disappearance of "The Red Pasha" by Kadare: Inquiry into a Literary Crime), Tirana 2002. His short stories have appeared in French translation under the title *Le commerce des jours* (The Commerce of Days), Paris 1998.

VENDETTA. *See* BLOOD FEUDING.

VEQILHARXHI, NAUM (1797.12.06-1846). Nationalist figure. Naum Veqilharxhi was one of the earliest figures to devote himself to the creation of a new Albanian alphabet and, at the same time, one of the first to formulate the ideals and objectives of the Albanian nationalist movement in its budding stages. He was born of a family from the village of Bredh near Vithkuq in the **Korça** region. It was no doubt after the destruction of Vithkuq in 1819 that Veqilharxhi emigrated to Romania in search of a better life. In 1821, he took part in a Wallachian uprising against the Turks and spent the rest of his life as a lawyer, as far as is known, in the port of Brăila on the Danube. He died of poisoning in Istanbul, allegedly at the hands of Greek **Orthodox** fanatics supposedly linked to the patriarch of Constantinople. Whether this is true or not will never be known. It is, however, known that the patriarchate was at odds with all expressions of non-Greek nationalism in the Balkans. In a letter in Greek, which Naum Veqilharxhi is reported to have circulated, he pointed to the backwardness and misery of the Albanians as a result of long centuries of Turkish rule, and stressed the need for a new Albanian alphabet as a means of overcoming this stagnation and of uniting the country.

In 1824 or 1825, Veqilharxhi had already begun working on the thirty-three-letter alphabet of his own invention that he had printed in an eight-page Albanian spelling book in 1844. This little spelling book was distributed throughout southern Albania, from Korça to **Berat**, and was received, as it seems, with a good deal of enthusiasm. The booklet was augmented to forty-eight pages in a now equally rare second edition of 1845 entitled *Faré i ri abétor shqip per djélm nismetore* (A Very New Albanian Spelling Book for Elementary Schoolboys). A copy of this work, long thought lost, was discovered in the Gennadius Library in Athens and was reprinted in 1983. The significance of Veqilharxhi's alphabet, which reminds one at first glance of a type of cursive Armenian, lies in the fact that it was not connected to the traditions of any particular religious community and, as a politically neutral creation, might have found acceptance among all Albanians, had it survived the test of time.

With his circular, the introduction to his spelling book, and his other letters, Veqilharxhi stands out as the first man of letters in the nineteenth century to have expressed the ideals of the growing Albanian nationalist movement.

VËRLACI, SHEFQET BEY (1877.12.15-1946.07.21). Political figure. Shefqet bey Vërlaci was born in **Elbasan** of a wealthy family who owned vast tracts of land in Albania. In 1914, he participated in the delegation of **Essad Pasha Toptani**, which traveled to Germany to offer the Albanian throne to **Prince Wilhelm zu Wied**. In 1918, he became involved in the Congress of Durrës and, in 1920, prevented his native Elbasan from taking part in the **Congress of Lushnja**. He was nonetheless elected to the senate and, as leader of the reactionary Progressive Party, commonly called the Beys' Party because it represented the interests of the landowners, he held various cabinet posts until reluctantly becoming prime minister on 3 March 1924. His government, in which he also maintained the post of minister of the interior, was supported primarily by wealthy feudal families and lasted until 27 May 1924.

Vërlaci supported **Ahmet Zogu** to whom his daughter Behije had been engaged for several years, and fled to **Italy** during the **Democratic Revolution** of **Fan Noli** to promote contacts between Zogu and the Italian government. In 1925, after Zogu had taken power, he was appointed senator. His relations with Zogu turned hostile, however, when the latter broke his engagement to Vërlaci's daughter.

Vërlaci survived an assassination attempt on 13 December 1927, no doubt instigated by Zog, and spent more time over the following years in Italy than in Albania. On 12 April 1939, after the Italian invasion, the italophile Vërlaci was appointed prime minister and minister of public works. It was his duty, on 16 April 1939 in the great hall of the Quirinal Palace in Rome, to offer the crown of **Scanderbeg** to King Victor Emmanuel III of Italy, thus making the latter King of Albania in "personal union." Vërlaci thus lost popular support in Albania. On 17 May 1941, he survived an assassination attempt made in **Tirana** on the life of Victor Emmanuel, and, supported only by conservatives and reactionaries, was forced to resign on 3 December 1941. At the end of the war he fled to Italy and died in Zürich.

VETMO, DUSHKO. *See* SOLANO, FRANCESCO.

VIA EGNATIA. Roman road built through Albania to connect Rome and Constantinople. The Via Egnatia, named after its builder, the Roman pro-consul Gnaeus Egnatius, was constructed between 146 and 120 B.C. from **Durrës** (ancient Dyrrachium) to the Evros (ancient Hebros) River, which now marks the Greek-Turkish border. It was equipped with milestones, and, being essential for Roman military expansion eastwards, was improved under the Emperor Augustine. The Via Egnatia was designed as a continuation of the Via Appia, which led from Rome to Brindisi (ancient Brundisium) in southern Italy. Travelers could then cross the Adriatic by boat to Durrës and continue their journey overland to the East. Alternatively they could cross from Otranto to **Apollonia** and begin their journey there. The two branches of the Roman road—from Durrës and from Apollonia—joined near the present town of Rrogozhina (ancient Asparagium Dyrrhachinorum) south of **Kavaja**. From there, the Albanian section of the Via Egnatia continued inland up the **Shkumbin** Valley, passing through Peqin (ancient Clodiana), Bradashesh (ancient Mutatio ad Quintum), **Elbasan** (ancient Scampa), Babja (ancient Ad Dianam), Qukës (ancient Tres Tabernae) and over the Thana Pass to the town of Ohrid (ancient Lychnidos).

The Via Egnatia remained in use throughout late antiquity and the Middle Ages as an important trade route. It was utilized by the Normans during their invasion of Albania in the eleventh century and by the Turks from the fourteenth century onwards. The present road from Durrës to Ohrid uses parts of the Via Egnatia or runs parallel and close to it. Many sections of the ancient road are still visible today.

VICKERS, MIRANDA (1959-). British scholar and historian. Born in London, Miranda Vickers acquired her B.A. in history at Thames Valley University and her masters in 1990 in Balkan history at the School of Slavonic and East European Studies in London. As a researcher and freelance journalist, she writes and broadcasts regularly on Albanian affairs. Since 1997, she has worked as a senior analyst for the Brussels-based International Crisis Group. Vickers is the author of *Albania: A Modern History,* London 1994; *Between Serbs and Albanians: A History of Kosovo,* London 1998, and is coauthor with **James Pettifer** of *Albania: From Anarchy to a Balkan Identity,* London 1996.

VIRGJINESHA. *See* SWORN VIRGIN.

VJOSA. River in southern Albania. The Vjosa takes its source in the Pindus mountains of northern Greece and flows past **Përmet**, Këlcyra and **Tepelena** into the Adriatic Sea north of **Vlora**. With a total length (in Albania) of 272 kilometers, it is the second largest river in Albania, after the **Drin**. The river was known in ancient times as Greek *Aöos* (Polybius 5.110.1; Pausanias, perieg. IV.34.3), and Latin *Aous* (Pliny III.145), which became Alb. *Vojusë, Vjosë, Vjosa* through Slavic transmission.

VLACH MINORITY IN ALBANIA. The Vlachs or Aromanians are a traditionally transhumant shepherding people found in various countries in the Balkans. Many live predominantly in the Pindus mountains around Metsovon of northern **Greece** and in the Republic of **Macedonia**. Their language, derived from Latin, is closely related to Romanian, from which it split in the ninth or tenth century. It is known in Albanian variously as *vllahçe* (Vlach language), *aromunçe* (Aromanian language) or *çobançe* (shepherd language).

In Albania there are estimated to be about 40,000 to 50,000 Vlachs, most of whom live in southeastern Albania. They are all **Orthodox**. In the District of **Korça**, the best-known Vlach, or predominantly Vlach communities are **Voskopoja**, Mborja and Boboshtica. There are also many Vlachs in the District of **Pogradec**, specifically in and around the village of Llënga in the Mokra region, to which thousands of pilgrims make their way every year on July 29 to celebrate the Orthodox feast of Saint Marina. Vlachs are also to be found in a number of villages on the coastal plain of Myzeqeja, where they arrived originally as transhumant shepherds in search of good winter pastureland. Selenica east of **Vlora** has a large Vlach population. To the south, the villages of Stjar in **Delvina** and Shkalla in **Saranda** have notable Vlach populations, and in the northern part of the District of **Gjirokastra**, a good number of Vlachs now live in the village of Andon Poçi. In addition to these rural settlements, there are now many Vlachs in the larger cities: **Tirana**, Korça, **Elbasan**, **Fier**, **Berat**, Vlora and **Lushnja**, although in this urban milieu, they are mostly assimilated and no longer speak their language.

A Vlach Association of Albania was formed in Selenica in March 1991 after the fall of the dictatorship, and a number of publications have since appeared in Vlach or about the Vlach community. There has been a certain dichotomy in the Vlach community in recent years: some Vlachs are more attached to Romania and the Romanian diaspora, and thus identify their language as a Romanian dialect, while others are allied more with the Vlach community in Greece and thus wish to underline their distinct linguistic identity.

VLORA. Town in the **District of Vlora**, of which it is the administrative center. **Population** in Dec. 1999: 103,426. Vlora is the largest town in southern Albania and the country's second largest **port**, situated in the expansive bay of Vlora. Settlement here goes back at least to the fourth century B.C. It was originally known as Aulon from the Greek word *aulôn* "ditch, channel." This word *Aulon* evolved into medieval Latin *Avlona,* Turkish *Avlonya,* Italian *Valona* and modern Albania *Vlora.*

Vlora was long part of the Byzantine Empire. In 1081 and 1107, it was conquered by the Normans, in 1204 by the Despot of Epirus, in 1272 by the Angevins, in 1343 by the Serbs, in 1378 by the Balsha dynasty and finally in 1417 by the Turks. It served throughout the **Ottoman** period as the major Turkish port in Albania and was the point of departure for the Ottoman attack on southern Italy in 1480. Sultan Suleyman the Magnificent built an octagonal fortress in Vlora following his stay there in 1531. The remains of this fortress were alas torn down in 1906 to provide construction material for the road between Vlora and the harbor. **Evliya Çelebi** who visited Vlora in 1670 wrote of it: "The open town is quite separated from the fortress. It is situated on a level grassy plain with gardens and vineyards, roses, lemons, oranges, olives, pomegranates and figs, like the fabled gardens of Irem. It has 1,000 beautiful one-and two-story stonework houses with tiled roofs.... The young men are all brigands. They are ghazis always ready for jihad. Most of these ghazis look like Kalenderi **dervishes**: shirtless, barefoot and bareheaded, with brand marks on their heads and gashes on their bare chests, and their hearts rent with anguish." Even today, the inhabitants of the Vlora region are considered excessively emotional and temperamental.

On 28 November 1912, Vlora was the venue of the declaration of Albanian independence by **Ismail Qemal bey Vlora**. It can thus be said to have been the first capital of Albania. From December 1914 to August 1920, the town and surrounding region were occupied by **Italian** troops. In 1916, it had a population of 6,500 and, in 1939, of 10,000.

Of the sites of interest in the town, mention may be made of the Murad Mosque dating from 1542 to 1557, the seventeen-meter-high monument of independence built in 1972, and the **Bektashi** *tekke* of Kusum Baba on the cliff overlooking the town.

On 14 October 1994, a new university was founded in Vlora, named after Ismail Qemal bey Vlora. In 2002, it had 1,210 students.

VLORA, DISTRICT OF. Region of local government administration. The District of Vlora (*Rrethi i Vlorës*), with its administrative headquarters in the town of **Vlora**, borders on the Ionian Sea to the west, the districts of **Fier** to the north, **Mallakastra**, Tepelena, and **Gjirokastra** to the east and **Saranda** to the south. It has a surface area of 1,609 square kilometers and a present **population** of 179,497 (in 2000).

VLORA, EQREM BEY (1885.12.01-1964.03.29). Political and public figure. Eqrem or Ekrem bey Vlora was born in **Vlora**, the son of one of the wealthiest landowning families of the south. He was educated at the Theresianum in Vienna, 1899-1903, and studied law and **religion** in Istanbul, 1904. After working for the **Ottoman** administration for a time, including a three-month tour of duty at the Ottoman embassy in St. Petersburg in 1907, and years of travel in Europe, Albania and the Orient, he joined his uncle **Ismail Qemal bey Vlora** in the movement for Albanian independence. In 1912, he was made deputy president of the senate. He was kept under arrest in **Italy** during **World War I** but subsequently became a promoter of close relations between Italy and Albania. Vlora was elected to **parliament** in 1924, representing a conservative wing and, in 1925, became a senator for a short period of time. His relations with **Ahmet Zogu** were tenuous, though he served the latter on various diplomatic missions abroad. He was a close friend of the Bavarian baroness **Marie Amelie, Freiin von Godin**, with whom he translated the *Kanun of Lekë Dukagjini* into German.

Vlora welcomed the Italian invasion of April 1939 and had close links to the Italian fascists. In 1942, **Mustaja Kruja** appointed him minister for **Kosova**, which had been reunited with Albania. His anti-Slav policies, however, gave rise to widespread resistance among the Serbs and Montenegrins. In the summer of 1944, he was made foreign minister and minister of justice before going into Italian exile during the **communist** takeover. He died in Rome. As a writer, Eqrem bey Vlora is remembered for his monograph *Aus Berat und vom Tomor: Tagebuchblätter* (From **Berat** and **Tomorr**: Pages of a Diary), Sarajevo 1911, and, in particular, for his two-volume German-language memoirs, published posthumously as *Lebenserinnerungen* (Memoirs), Munich 1968, 1973, which give fascinating insight into the world of an early twentieth-century Albanian nobleman. They have recently been translated into Albanian as *Kujtime* (Memoirs), Tirana 2002.

VLORA, ISMAIL QEMAL BEY (1844.01.16-1919.01.24). Political figure. Ismail Qemal bey Vlora, also known as Ismail Kemal bey Vlora, and in Albanian commonly as Ismail Qemali, was born in **Vlora**. He attended the Zosimeia secondary school in Janina and moved to Istanbul in May 1860. There he worked as a translator for the Ottoman ministry of foreign affairs and subsequently for district administrations in Janina (1862-1864) and Bulgaria (1866-ca.1877), carrying on business activities at the same time. As a supporter of the assassinated Turkish reform politician Midhat Pasha, he was interned in Asia Minor from 1877 to early 1884, but then became governor of Bolu. In the following years, he was governor of Gallipoli (1890), governor of Beirut (1891) and a member of the council of state in the late 1890s. He left in the summer of 1900 for Italy, France, Belgium and England and only returned to the **Ottoman Empire** after the Young Turk revolution in 1908, when he represented **Berat** as a member of the opposition in the Turkish parliament. In the spring of 1909, he took part in the counterrevolution against the Young Turks and founded the *Ahrar* (Liberal) party which sought to decentralize the empire. He hastened to Vienna at the outbreak of **World War I** to negotiate with the Austrian foreign ministry on the future of Albania. On 19 November 1912, he sailed to **Durrës** on an Austro-Hungarian naval vessel and traveled on to Vlora, where he headed the national assembly which declared Albanian independence on 28 November 1912. It was Ismail Qemal bey Vlora who read out the proclamation. He was forced to resign on 22 January 1914 and transferred government authority to the **International Control Commission**. He then went into exile to Italy, Barcelona and France, where he dictated his memoirs to the British journalist Sommerville Story in early 1917. He died of a stroke in Perugia in Italy.

VON GODIN, MARIE AMELIE. *See* GODIN, MARIE AMELIE, Freiin von.

VON HAHN, JOHAN GEORG. *See* HAHN, JOHANN GEORG VON.

VON HARFF, ARNOLD. *See* HARFF, ARNOLD VON.

VON ŠUFFLAY, MILAN. *See* ŠUFFLAY, MILAN VON.

VON THALLÓCZY, LUDWIG. *See* THALLÓCZY, LUDWIG VON.

VON XYLANDER, JOSEPH. *See* XYLANDER, JOSEPH, Ritter von.

VOSKOPOJA. Small town in the District of **Korça**. **Population** in Dec. 1999: ca. 400. Voskopoja is now a small village in the mountains twenty-four kilometers west of Korça, at an elevation of 1,115 meters. It was founded by **Vlach** shepherds in about 1300 and is known in Greek as *Moschopolis* and in Aromanian as *Moscopole*. The toponym derives from Greek *moskhos* "calf, young animal, musk" and Slav *polje* "field," thus meaning something like "musk field."

In the seventeenth century, Voskopoja increased tremendously in size to become one of the largest cities in the Balkans and a flourishing center of trade and urban culture. At its zenith, before the city was pillaged for the first time in 1768, it is said to have had a population of 40,000-50,000, greater than Athens, Sofia or Belgrade at the time, with an estimated 10,000 to 12,000 buildings, including twenty-six churches, a hospital, an orphanage, a library, the only Greek printing press in the Balkans (1720), which published at least nineteen religious works, and the so-called New Academy.

The New Academy or *Hellênikon Frontistêrion* was a center of learning founded in 1744, similar to academies known to have existed in Bucharest, Iaşi, Constantinople, Metsovon, Janina, Mt. Athos and Patmos. Many Greek scholars of note came to teach at Voskopoja among the Vlachs, who made up the majority of the population, the Albanians and the Greeks. The New Academy was not an exclusively theological institution. It enjoyed a good reputation for its teaching in ancient Greek, philosophy, mathematics and physics, and produced many a writer and scholar of repute.

Between 1769 and 1789, Voskopoja was pillaged several times and came to lose its vitality and significance as a commercial center on the trading route between Constantinople and Venice. It was finally destroyed in 1916 in fighting during **World War I** and, with the exception of four beautiful **Orthodox** churches, the historical buildings, which did survive, were razed during partisan warfare in **World War II**.

The four remaining churches, all of exceptional cultural value, are those of St. Mary, constructed with three naves in 1712; St. Nicholas, built in 1721-1726 with room for over 1,000 people and decorated with frescoes by **David Selenica**; St. Michael dating from 1722; and St. Athanasius, built in 1724.

VRETO, JANI (1820.01.14-1900.07). Nationalist figure, writer and publisher. Jani Vreto was born in the village of Postenan near Leskovik, a town situated not far from the present Greek border. He studied at a Greek school in Vurban near Konitsa and from 1843 to 1847 at the Zosimaia secondary school in Janina, which instilled in him a lasting admiration for Hellenic culture. **Faik bey Konitza** was later to call him a graecomaniac. In 1854, he moved to Istanbul, where his father owned a market garden. There he worked as secretary for a tobacco company and by the early 1870s had come into contact with the leading figures of the Albanian national movement.

Vreto's first publication was a Greek grammar translated into Albanian, *Grammatikê tês omilumenês hellênikês glôssês eis tên albanikên* (Grammar of the Spoken Greek Language in Albanian), Istanbul 1866. In autumn of 1877, he became a founding member of the **Central Committee for the Defense of the Rights of the Albanian People** and worked actively to its ends. In early 1879, he was appointed a member of the commission set up by the Central Committee to decide upon a definitive alphabet for Albanian. In 1879, the committee published an *Allfabetare e gluhësë shqip* (Alphabet of the Albanian Language), several parts of which were written by Vreto, in particular an article entitled *Udhë e të shkruarit të gluhësë shqip* (Way of Writing the Albanian Language). On 12 October of that year, he also took part in the founding of the historic **Society for the Publication of Albanian Writing**. Vreto was author of a statute (*Kanonizmë*) for the society, which had to react skillfully and diplomatically in the face of **Ottoman** opposition and, especially, of Greek intransigence to the Albanian cultural awakening. It was about this time that he was excommunicated by the **Orthodox** metropolitan of **Gjirokastra** for having committed the heresy of "creating an Albanian question."

In the summer of 1881, Vreto traveled to Bucharest to arouse interest in the nationalist movement among the many Albanians who had settled there and elsewhere in Romania, and founded a Bucharest section of the Society for the Publication of Albanian Writing. In December 1884, he cooperated in the foundation of the Bucharest *Drita* society and served as its secretary. This society set up an Albanian printing press and, in 1886, began the historic task of publishing Albanian-**language** books. Ten such books were published in the first year alone, including two of Vreto's own works: *Mirëvetija* (Ethics), Bucharest 1886, and *Numeratoreja* (Arithmetic), Bucharest 1886. It was Vreto who virtually ran the printing press. He set the texts, read the proofs and had the books bound and arranged for distribution.

As one of the most active members of the Society for the Publication of Albanian Writing in Istanbul and later in Bucharest, Jani Vreto played a key role in the realization of one major goal of Albanian intellectuals of the period—the publication of books in Albanian. The Albanian printing press in Bucharest, which he set up and operated, was as fundamental to the advancement of Albanian **literature** in the late nineteenth century as

Johann Gutenberg's invention of printing by movable type had been to European culture four and a half centuries earlier.

VRIONI, ILJAZ BEY (1882-1932.03.12). Political figure. Iljaz bey Vrioni, scion of a wealthy landowning family of southern-central Albania, was the son of Mehmet Ali Pasha who collaborated with **Abdyl bey Frashëri** at the time of the **Congress of Berlin**. Iljaz bey himself took part in the Congress of **Vlora** and was elected to the senate in 1912. In 1914, he participated in the delegation of **Essad Pasha Toptani** which traveled to Germany to offer the Albanian throne to **Prince Wilhelm zu Wied**. On 19 November 1920, after taking part in the **Congress of Lushnja**, he was chosen prime minister after the fall of **Sulejman bey Delvina**, a post he held until 19 October 1921. He was prime minister again from 27 May 1924 to 1 June 1924 when the **Democratic Revolution** under **Fan Noli** took place. From 1927 to 1929, he was foreign minister and, for a short time, minister of justice. He also served as Albanian ambassador to Paris and Rome. Like his cousin Hysen bey Vrioni, who was foreign minister in 1925-1927 and 1931-1933, he maintained close relations with **Italy**, in particular after the second Pact of **Tirana** on 22 November 1927. He was made a Grand Officer of the Légion d'Honneur in France and died in Paris after several years of drug and alcohol dependency.

VRIONI, JUSUF (1916.03.16-2001.06.01). Translator and public figure. Jusuf Vrioni was born on Corfu, the scion of an old aristocratic family of central Albania. He spent most of his early years from 1923 in Paris, where his father, **Iljaz bey Vrioni**, former prime minister, served for a time as ambassador. On 5 August 1939, he returned to Italian-occupied Albania for what he had envisaged as a short visit, but his plans were altered by the outbreak of **World War II**. Later that year he moved to Rome, where his brother had been offered a job for the Italian ministry of foreign affairs, and returned to **Tirana** in August 1943. On 13 September 1947, during the political hysteria and witch hunts under **Koçi Xoxe**, Vrioni was arrested and accused of spying for France and of playing tennis. He spent fourteen months, from February 1949 to April 1950, locked up in one of the infamous seventeen "cells of Koçi Xoxe" which were 1.20 meters by 0.90 meters in size. In July 1950, he was sentenced to fifteen years of prison and hard labor, part of which sentence he served in the notorious Burrel camp. He was released at the end of 1958 and, after a period of internal exile in **Fier**, began working as a literary translator.

Among his early translations, from Albanian into French, was "The General of the Dead Army" by **Ismail Kadare**, which was subsequently published in Paris. It was not until 1980, however, that his name ever appeared in a book as the translator. Although much of his time was taken up with translating and revising the political texts of **communist** leader **Enver Hoxha**, he found time to translate other novels by Kadare, books, which, thanks to Vrioni's elegant quill, proved to be successful abroad. By the end of the dictatorship, Jusuf Vrioni had gained a reputation in Albanian intellectual circles as the most gifted translator in the country. After the fall of the regime, he moved back to his beloved Paris in 1997, where he was appointed Albania's ambassador to UNESCO and was made a knight of the French Légion d'Honneur. His memoirs appeared in French as *Mondes éffacés, souvenirs d'un Européen* (Effaced Worlds: Memoirs of a European), Paris 1998.

- W -

WASSA EFFENDI. *See* VASA, PASHKO.

WEIGAND, GUSTAV (1860.02.01-1930.07.08). German scholar and Balkan linguist. Gustav Weigand was born in Duisburg on the Rhine and went to school in Giessen. From 1878 to 1884, he taught school in a variety of locations, but then broke off his career as a teacher to study modern languages in Leipzig. In 1887, he spent three months in northern Greece studying the Aromanian (**Vlach**) dialects of the region, research which appeared in his seminal doctoral dissertation, *Die Sprache der Olympo-Walachen nebst einer Einleitung über Land und Leute* (The Language of the Vlachs of Olympus together with an Introduction to the Country and People), Leipzig 1888. In 1890, he also visited Albania. In 1893, with the financial support of the Romanian government, Weigand founded a special Institute for the Romanian Language in Leipzig, which he headed for many years. From 1896 to 1928, he was professor of Romance Philologie at the University of Leipzig. Weigand also set up a

Bulgarian Institute (1906), supported by the Bulgarian government, and indeed an Albanian Seminar (1925), which survived
for only a few years. The library of this Albanian Seminar was
incorporated into the university library in Leipzig after Weigand's
death.

Although Weigand specialized in Romanian, Bulgarian and,
in particular, the Aromanian dialects of the Balkan peninsula, he
also made a notable contribution to research on the Albanian
language. In this field he is remembered for his *Albanesische
Grammatik im südgegischen Dialekt: Durazzo, Elbassan, Tirana*
(Albanian Grammar in the Southern Gheg Dialect: Durrës,
Elbasan, Tirana), Leipzig 1913; *Albanesisch-deutsches &
deutsch-albanesisches Wörterbuch* (Albanian-German &
German-Albanian Dictionary), Leipzig 1914; and many articles
on Albanian dialects and the origins of the Albanian people.

WIED, WILHELM, PRINZ ZU (1876.03.26-1945.04.18). German
prince and, briefly, monarch of Albania. Prince Wied was born of
a noble protestant family in Neuwied on the Rhine, situated
between Bonn and Koblenz. He was a captain in the Prussian
army and was the nephew of Queen Elizabeth of Romania. He
married Princess Sophia of Saxony. In October 1913, the Great
Powers offered him, as a compromise candidate, the throne of the
newly independent country of Albania, a land about which he
knew very little at the time. After due reflection, he accepted the
offer and arrived in **Durrës** on 7 March 1914 aboard an Austro-
Hungarian naval vessel to take the throne of his new little kingdom. The chaotic political situation both within Albania and with
respect to relations with Albania's neighbors made it virtually
impossible for the well-meaning prince to reign. In addition, he
received little or no financial or military support from abroad as
a result of the outbreak of **World War I**. On 3 September 1914,
after less than seven months of reign, the prince abandoned Albania aboard an Italian yacht, though without formally abdicating.
During World War I, he served in the German army under the
nom de guerre Count of Kruja. He had hoped to return to Albania
after the war but **Germany**'s defeat in 1918 made such expectations illusory. In 1917, he recorded an eighty-two-page
Denkschrift über Albanien (Memorandum on Albania), in which
he presented his view of his short reign. Prince Wied died in
Predeal in Romania at the end of **World War II**.

WINNIFRITH, TOM (1938.04.05-). British scholar. Tom J. Winnifrith was born in London. He completed his masters in Classics at Corpus Christi College in Oxford and his doctorate in English literature at the University of Liverpool. He taught English and Classics at Eton College, 1961-1966, and at the University of Warwick, 1970-1999, where he was chairman of the Joint School of English and Comparative Studies until retirement. Winnifrith has a particular interest in the **Vlach** minority and in southern Albania in general. Among his publications are: *The Vlachs: the History of a Balkan People,* New York 1987; *Perspectives on Albania,* Basingstoke 1992; *Shattered Eagles: Balkan Fragments,* London 1995; and *Badlands, Borderlands: a History of Southern Albania,* London 2002.

WOMEN. Women have traditionally played a very subordinate role in Albanian society, which had and still has, though to a lesser degree, a strongly patriarchal structure. It was during the **communist** dictatorship that women were first given full equality with men, but the weight of patriarchal tradition plus the fact that seventy percent of the **population** was of Muslim orientation, made their equality more theoretical than practical. The campaign initiated by **Enver Hoxha** and the **Party of Labor** to eradicate **religion** in 1967 was justified, among other things, by the need to emancipate and liberate women in real terms. Indeed, after the campaign, there were substantially more women in politics. From 1970 to 1987, women made up twenty-seven to thirty-four percent of the members of **parliament**, as opposed to seven to sixteen percent beforehand. In 1981, thirty percent of the members of the Party of Labor were women, as opposed to 12.5 percent in 1966. As such, an important step forward was taken in women's emancipation, one of the few achievements of the communist period of which Albanians are still proud. As a result of the emancipation campaign of the later 1960s and 1970s, women in Albania are today far more liberated, educated and emancipated than Albanian women in **Kosova** and **Macedonia**.

In the first decade of the post-communist period (1991-2001), women in Albania were faced with the revival of many long-forgotten traditions, and with a number of new phenomena which had not existed in Albanian society previously. With regard to social emancipation, some of the modest gains of the communist period were reversed, at least for women in the countryside. In particular, the revival of the *Kanun* in the north of the country has had a negative effect on the status of women. On the other hand, the opening up and westernization of Albanian society has given many educated middle-class women in urban centers a higher degree of social and sexual emancipation and independence than they had in the past.

When the major state enterprises closed down in the early 1990s, women were among the first to lose their jobs and thus their modicum of economic independence. Women in Albania tend to hold low-level jobs and their salaries are accordingly much lower than those of men. At the end of 1999, there was one female deputy prime minister, three ministers, three deputy ministers, one ambassador, one deputy speaker of parliament, twelve members of parliament and three mayors. In 2002, women made up only 5.7 percent of the members of parliament (as opposed to 20.4 percent in 1991), ten percent of government cabinet members, and held only twenty-four percent of management positions in public administration.

The trafficking of girls and women for prostitution has also become a serious problem of Albanian society. In 2003, there were an estimated 30,000 Albanian women working as prostitutes in Western Europe, most of whom in virtual slavery. The government and the population in general have shown themselves to be largely indifferent to the appalling situation and to women's issues in general.

WORLD WAR I (1914-1918). Albania was already in a state of anarchy before the outbreak of World War I. Reigning Prince **Wilhelm zu Wied** abandoned the country aboard an Italian yacht on 3 September 1914, and there was no central government authority of any kind for some time. As in the first **Balkan War** of 1912-1913, the Albanians were primarily concerned about preserving their country's independence and territorial integrity against the encroachments of neighboring countries. Many even favored a return of **Ottoman** rule.

The situation was chaotic in August 1914, at the time of the outbreak of World War I, in which the Albanians themselves took little part. Very soon, the country found itself invaded by at least seven foreign armies: Austrian, Italian, Greek, Serbian, Montenegrin, French and Bulgarian. The Greeks invaded southern Albania (**Gjirokastra** and **Korça**) in October and November 1914, and by April 1916, it proclaimed the incorporation of **"Northern Epirus"** into **Greece**. The Montenegrins took **Shkodra**, and Serb forces occupied much of central Albanian (**Elbasan** and **Tirana**). The Italians, ever covetous of the port of

Vlora, which is situated a mere seventy kilomteres from the southern Italian coast, occupied the island of **Sazan** on 30 October 1914 and the town of Vlora itself on 26 December. A secret Treaty of London awarded **Italy** full sovereignty over the region on 26 April 1915. In September 1915, Bulgarian forces invaded and enabled Austro-Hungarian troops in January 1916 to attack and get the upper hand in Shkodra and **Durrës** by February 1916. Greek forces were compelled to withdraw from southern Albania, only to be replaced in the summer of 1916 by the Italians in Gjirokastra and **Saranda** and down to Janina, and by French forces under General Maurice Sarrail and Colonel Descoins in Korça.

By the end of 1916, Austro-Hungarian forces were in control of northern and central Albania, and Italian forces held sway from Vlora southwards. Only the southeast was held by the French, who proclaimed an autonomous Republic of Korça on 10 December 1916.

Bulgaria surrendered in September 1918, thus forcing Austro-Hungarian troops to withdraw from Albania. By the end of the war, on 11 November 1918, Italian forces were in possession of most of the country. Albania miraculously survived as an independent nation, though only because the Italian government found it expedient to maintain a sovereign Albanian state to counter growing Yugoslav encroachments in the region.

Despite the presence of all the foreign troops, there was comparatively little actual fighting in Albania during World War I. In fact, it was a period of consolidation for the country. The Albanians themselves ceased fighting one another, and the foreign troops built roads, bridges and **railroads**, all of which had been desperately lacking in the country.

WORLD WAR II (1939-1945). The Second World War began five months early for Albania when Italian troops invaded the country on 7 April, Good Friday, 1939. The invasion had been prepared as part of fascist expansion under Benito Mussolini and had been directly and carefully planned by his son-in-law, the Italian foreign minister Count Ciano, who had been best man at **King Zog**'s wedding in April 1938. By 8 April, Italian troops had reached **Tirana** and the royal family with their newly born son **Leka** fled over the mountains to **Greece**. On 12 April, Ciano traveled to Tirana and persuaded the Albania **parliament** to offer the Albanian crown to Italian King Victor Emmanuel III. Independent Albania had ceased to exist. On 18 April, the Italian ambassador

Francesco Jacomoni di San Savino was appointed viceroy (Ital. *luogotenente generale*) of Albania, and on 23 April 1939, an Albanian Fascist Party (*Partia Fashiste Shqiptare*) was created as the only legal political formation in the country.

When **Italy** joined the Axis war with **Germany** on 10 June 1940, Albania, too, found itself at war, although there had been little fighting in the Balkans up to that time. Italian troops, including 50,000 Albanian soldiers, invaded Greece on 28 October 1940, only to be driven back by the end of the year by resolute Greek forces, which then occupied **Gjirokastra**, Leskovik, **Korça** and **Pogradeç**. Greek positions were abandoned a year later when, on 6 April 1941, German troops attacked Greece and **Yugoslavia**. On 12 August 1941, Italian forces, having occupied **Kosova** and the Albanian-speaking regions of Plava, Gucia and Ulqin (Ulcinj) in Montenegro, reunited these territories with Albania itself, thus realizing the dreams of Albanian nationalists for a unified ethnic Albania. An Albanian administration was set up in these regions, and Albanian schools, long forbidden under Ottoman and Serb rule, were opened.

After the capitulation of Italian forces on 8 September 1943, German troops swiftly occupied Albania with two divisions. The Germans were intent on setting up an autonomous administration and endeavored to persuade Albanian leaders to form a government and take over the administration of the country themselves. Many hesitated, in particular when rumors spread that British forces were preparing to invade Albania. Kosova Albanian leaders, however, realizing that a German defeat would mean a return to Yugoslav rule, were more willing to cooperate. On 14 September 1943, an Albanian government was then set up under Ibrahim Biçaku of Elbasan, and Bedri Pejani and Xhafer Deva from Kosova. The national assembly, composed of 243 members, began to function on 16 October 1943, electing a four-member High Regency Council (*Këshilli i Lartë i Regjencës*) to govern the country.

The new government, which promised to remain neutral in the war, succeeded in restoring a good deal of stability. The administration and justice systems functioned once again, and schools were reopened throughout northern and central Albania. Steps were also taken to implement a land reform. On 13 July 1944, Albania attained formal independence under German aegis.

On 2 October 1944, German troops received orders to withdraw from Albania and many Albanian politicians who had collaborated with German forces fled the country. The last German soldiers left **Shkodra** on 29 November 1944.

There had been resistance to the Italian and German occupation from the very start, though it was sporadic at first. **Myslim Peza** organized one of the first guerrilla bands in 1940 to fight openly against Italian rule and, on 7 April 1941, **Abaz Kupi**, who had resisted the Italian invasion in **Durrës**, returned to Albania with British support to found the monarchist resistance movement, **Legality**. By the end of 1941, there was also a **communist** resistance movement. In the summer of 1942, the communists invited all resistance groups to a conference in Peza, but a united front against the foreign occupiers was short-lived. Over the next two years, the three major resistance groups, the communist partisans, the **Balli Kombëtar** and the Legality movement, spent most of their time fighting one another. Indeed it is said that in World War II more Albanians fell fighting Albanians than opposing the Italians and Germans.

WRITERS' UNION. *See* UNION OF WRITERS AND ARTISTS.

- X -

XANONI, ANTON (1862.01.12-1915.02.16). Writer and educator. Anton Xanoni, also known as Ndoc Zanoni, was a leading figure of **Catholic** education in the **Rilindja** period. He exercised a far from negligible influence on the development of the **Gheg** literary language of northern Albania at the turn of the century. Xanoni was born in **Durrës** and moved to **Shkodra** as a young child, where he received a Catholic **education**. The **Jesuit** fathers, recognizing his talents, sent him on for higher education and training to their institutions abroad. These included the Carthusian monastery of Porta Coeli north of Valencia in Spain (1883), a Jesuit establishment in Kraljevica (Ital. *Porto Re*) on the Dalmatian coast (1884), Cremona in northern Italy (1886), and the Gregorian college at Kraków in Poland (1890-1892). In 1892, he was ordained as a Jesuit priest in Kraków and returned two years later to Shkodra to teach Albanian at the Saverian College, from which he had himself graduated thirteen years earlier. In 1896, he taught for a year at the Gregorian college in Chieri southeast of Turin in Italy before returning to Albania. Together with classical lyric poet **Ndre Mjeda** and his brother Lazër Mjeda, Xanoni was an active member of the *Agimi* (Dawn) literary society, founded in 1901, which aimed at stimulating the use of Albanian in **literature**, in particular by means of a new alphabet. It was Anton Xanoni at the influential Saverian College who established the norms of rhetoric and style for writing in the northern Albanian dialect, norms which he set forth in his *Prîsi në lâmë të letratyrës* (Guide to the Field of Literature), Shkodra 1911-1912. He followed a purist approach to writing Albanian, advocating the replacement of the many loanwords from Italian, Turkish and Slavic by older Albanian roots.

As the author of poetry, literary prose, drama and scholarly works in Albanian, which proved a lasting inspiration to his students and fellow writers, Xanoni was not only a linguistic innovator, but also, for the period, an excellent stylist himself. From 1908, he collaborated regularly in the Jesuit periodical *Elçija i Zemers t'Jezu Krisctit* (The Messenger of the Sacred Heart), publishing articles on history, literature, culture and politics, as well as short stories and verse of his own and much-admired translations. He is remembered for his *Gramatika shqyp* (Albanian Grammar), Shkodra 1909; a *Shkurtorja e historís së moçme* (Outline of Early History), 1910; and in particular for the Rilindja poem *Rrnoftë Shqypnia* (Long Live Albania), written on Albanian independence. Much of his work remains unedited to this day. Xanoni died in Shkodra, a veteran of Albanian education and culture.

XEGA, SPIRO (1876-1953). Painter. Spiro Xega, one of the early figures of Albanian painting, was born in Opar in the **Korça** region of southeastern Albania. He spent his early years in Turkey, where he learned to draw and paint, though without formal professional training. Back in Albania, he was a member of the guerrilla band of **Çerçiz Topulli** and later worked as a fuel and salt merchant in Korça. His earliest paintings, mostly on nationalist themes, date from before **World War I**. He is remembered in particular for his *Çeta e Shahin Matrakut* (Guerrilla Band of Shahin Matraku), 1930; and his horseback painting of *Skënderbeu* (**Scanderbeg**) 1931. Xega's style is often strangely reminiscent of Sikh paintings.

XHAFERI, BILAL (1935.05.10-1986.08.22). Writer. Bilal Xhaferi was born in the village of Ninat near Konispol in the southern

Çamëria region and was raised with his sisters in internment, where he was permitted to finish secondary school. In his early years, he published a volume of ten short stories entitled *Njerëz të rinj, tokë e lashtë* (Young People, Ancient Land), Tirana 1966, a work of artistry and ideas, but perhaps too realistic for the time. In 1968, Xhaferi spoke out at the **Writers' Union** against **Ismail Kadare**'s novel *Dasma* (The Wedding), Tirana 1968, and was severely taken to task by the then all-powerful **Fadil Paçrami**. He was expelled from his home in **Durrës** and sent to work as a farm laborer in Sukth. Xhaferi was miraculously able to escape from Albania to Greece on 30 August 1969 and emigrated subsequently to the **United States**, where he worked for the Boston periodical *Dielli* (The Sun) and organized an American-Çamërian organization. He died in Chicago. A volume of his verse, *Lirishta e kuqe* (The Red Glade), Tirana 1967, was printed shortly before his fall but never was circulated. His novel on **Scanderbeg** and another one entitled *Krasta Kraus* remained unpublished until the 1990s.

XHEPA, MARGARITA (1932.04.02-). Stage and **film** actress. Margarita Xhepa was born in **Lushnja**. She is considered to be one of the most successful actresses of the **National Theater** in **Tirana**, where she was active from 1950 and was especially noted for various Shakespearean roles. From 1965 on, she also appeared in over twenty-five Albanian films and is remembered in particular for her roles in *Dimri i fundit* (The Last Winter), 1976; *Toka e përgjakur* (The Blood-Soaked Land), 1976; *Koncert në vitin '36* (Concert in the Year 1936),1978; and *Dora e ngrohtë* (The Warm Hand), 1983.

XHEPA, NDRIÇIM (1957.01.21-). Stage and **film** actor. Ndriçim Xhepa, son of actress Margarita Xhepa, was born in **Tirana**, where he studied at the Academy of Fine Arts (*Instituti i Lartë i Arteve*) and began working for the **National Theater** in 1979. Up to 1994, he had appeared in twenty films, among which were *Hije që mbeten pas* (The Lingering Shadows), 1985; *Flutura në kabinën time* (Butterflies in my Cabin), 1988; and *Pas fasadës* (Behind the Facade), 1992.

XHUGLINI, NEXHMIJE. *See* HOXHA, NEXHMIJE.

XHUVANI, ALEKSANDËR (1888.03.14-1961.11.22). Scholar and linguist. Aleksandër Xhuvani was born in **Elbasan**. He attended

Greek-language schools in Albania and Macedonia and studied at the Faculty of Philology of the University of Athens from 1902 to 1906. In August 1906, he moved to Naples where he got to know several leading **Arbëresh** intellectuals and began teaching at the Arbëresh College of Saint Adrian in San Demetrio Corone (Cosenza). In 1909, he returned to Elbasan and taught at the Normal School (*Shkolla Normale*) until 1910, when he was forced to emigrate to **Egypt**, where he worked as a journalist. After independence, he was appointed director of the Normal School in Elbasan. In 1920-1922 and 1929-1933, he worked for the ministry of **education** in **Tirana** before returning to his native Elbasan to teach. After the **communist** takeover, Xhuvani worked for the ministry of education once again, preparing school texts. He was later a founding member of the **Writers' Union**, and from January 1947 to September 1953, served as head of the Language and Literature section of the Institute of Sciences, forerunner of the University of Tirana. Xhuvani is the author of *Për pastërtinë e gjuhës shqipe* (For the Sake of the Purity of the Albanian Language), Tirana 1956, school texts, dictionaries and countless articles on the standardization of the Albanian **language**. He was very much lauded during the communist period as a leading figure of scholarship and linguistics.

XHUVANI, GJERGJ (1963.12.20-). Film director. Xhuvani was born in Tirana, the son of prose writer Dhimitër Xhuvani (1934-), and finished his studies in directing at the Academy of Fine Arts (*Instituti i Lartë i Arteve*) in 1986. His first film *Bardhë e zi* (Black and White), 1990, was followed by the successful *E diela e fundit* (The Last Sunday), 1993; *Dashuria e fundit* (Last Love), 1995; and *Parrullat* (The Slogans), a Franco-Albanian co-production.

XOXA, JAKOV (1922.04.13-1979.11.11). Writer. Jakov Xoxa was from **Fier** on the once marshy and mosquito-infested plain of Myzeqeja. He is remembered as the author of the novel *Lumi i vdekur* (The Dead River), Tirana 1965, in which he decried the exploitation of the impoverished peasantry by ruthless beys. This novel, modeled on the Russian *Tikhiy Don* (And Quiet Flows the Don), Moscow 1928, by Mikhail Aleksandrovich Sholokhov (1905-1984), is one of the rare works of the period with any semblance of literary merit. His second novel, *Juga e bardhë* (The Fair South Wind), Tirana 1971, modeled on Sholokhov's *Podnyataya tselina* (Virgin Soil Upturned), Moscow 1932, dealt with the collectivization of **agriculture** in Myzeqeja after the war.

XOXE, KOÇI (1917-1949.06.11). Political figure of the early **communist** period. Koçi Xoxe was a tinsmith of Macedonian Slav origin and is said to have been one of the very few communist leaders of Albania with a genuine proletarian background. He was also one of the most ruthless.

Koçi Xoxe was born and raised in **Korça**, where, like **Enver Hoxha**, he came into contact with the communist movement. He became a founding member of the Albanian communist party in 1941. From 1943 to 1948, he served as organizational secretary of the Central Committee, and from 1946 to 1948, as deputy prime minister, minister of the interior and chairman of the state control commission. From December 1944 to January 1945, although he had no formal legal training, he also headed the Special People's Court of **Tirana** to try alleged collaborators and war criminals, and conducted witch hunts against many leading Albanian intellectuals of the period. During the Tito-Hoxha conflict, Koçi Xoxe had the support of **Yugoslavia** and became a real threat to the power of Enver Hoxha. This led to his purge and downfall. In May 1949, he was arrested and charged with Trotskyite and Titoist activities. Despite self-criticism, he was sentenced to death as an enemy of the people and was executed. His last words were "Long live Stalin!"

XYLANDER, JOSEPH, Ritter von (1794.02.04-1854). German scholar and linguist. Joseph von Xylander was born in Munich and, as a youth, was an intimate friend of German poet and dramatist August von Platen-Hallemünde (1796-1835). He was given a military education and worked as a teacher for the military cadet corps in Munich, and was a captain in the Bavarian engineer corps. Xylander was later a member of the Swedish Academy of Military Sciences, doctor *honoris causa* of the University of Munich, and Bavaria's representative at the national assembly in Frankfurt am Main in 1848-1849. He is remembered in general as the author of numerous standard works in the field of military science and, in Albanian studies in particular, as the author of the 320-page *Die Sprache der Albanesen oder Schkipetaren* (The Language of the Albanians or Skipetars), Frankfurt am Main 1835, which included a grammar of the **Gheg** dialect, early Bible translations and glossaries.

- Y -

YANULATOS, ANASTASIOS. *See* JANULATOS, ANASTAS.

YOUNG, ANTONIA (1936.06.03-). British scholar and anthropologist. Antonia Young was born in London. She received her B.A. in anthropology from the University of California in Berkeley and now holds research positions at the University of Bradford in England and at Colgate University in upstate New York. Ever since her first visit to Yugoslavia in 1958, she has maintained an interest in the Balkans in their changing forms. She has spent time in Albania every year since 1989, has made frequent visits to **Kosova, Macedonia** and Bosnia, and has led tour groups to the region. Young was instrumental in setting up and obtaining funding for the Peace Studies and Conflict Resolution Center in **Shkodra**. She is currently engaged in a long-term environmental cross-border mountain project for Albania, Kosova and **Montenegro**.

Antonia Young claims to have been the first outsider to have found that the tradition of **Sworn Virgins** (reported by many writers prior to **World War II**) still exists today, and she has met and interviewed several in Albania. Among her major publications are: the bibliography *Albania: World Bibliographical Series,* Oxford 1997; and *Women Who Become Men: Albanian Sworn Virgins,* Oxford 2000. She is also coauthor with John Allcock of *Black Lambs and Grey Falcons: Women Travelling in the Balkans,* New York 2000; and with **Robert Elsie** of *Berit Backer: Behind Stone Walls* (Peja 2003).

YPI, XHAFER BEY (1880-1940.11.17). Political figure. Xhafer bey Ypi was born of a wealthy landowning family in Starja in the southern **Kolonja** region. In 1920, he became prefect of **Vlora** and was soon thereafter minister of justice as well as deputy minister of the interior in the first cabinet of **Iljaz bey Vrioni**. On 24 December 1921, he was chosen as prime minister and served for a time as foreign minister, though real political power was already held by **Ahmet Zogu**. Although he was regarded as a somewhat bland bureaucrat, his centralist government managed to establish diplomatic relations with a number of European countries, introduce the *lek* as the Albanian national currency on

16 February 1922, and rid the country of Italian troops in **Shkodra** by the end of March of that year. Ypi was replaced on 16 December 1922 and fled Albania in 1924. From 1925 to 1932, he was a member of **parliament** and, from 1927 to 1929, minister of **education**. In 1931, he served as chief inspector of the court and, in 1939, gave his support to the **Italian** invasion. On 8 April 1939 he headed a short-lived provisional administration committee, i.e., provisional government, to prepare the way for the "new order" in the country, in line with the wishes of Count Ciano (1903-1944). In 1940, as minister of justice once again, he led Albanian units marching against **Greece** and was killed by a bomb.

YUGOSLAVIA, RELATIONS WITH. *See* SERBIA AND MONTENEGRO, RELATIONS WITH.

- Z -

ZADEJA, ÇESK (1927.06.08-1997.08.15). Composer. Çesk Zadeja, like most figures of early Albanian **music**, was born in **Shkodra**. In 1941-1943, he studied at the Accademia di Santa Lucia in Rome. After **World War II**, he worked for Radio Shkodra and, in 1949-1951, directed the army musical ensemble. From 1951 to 1956, he studied composition at the Tchaikovsky Conservatory in Moscow, and on his return to Albania, headed the newly founded Albanian folk music and dance ensemble from 1957 to 1962, and the **Tirana** state conservatory from 1962 to 1965. From 1973 to 1979, he headed the **Opera and Ballet Theater**. Çesk Zadeja is the author of over 100 works of concert music, including four ballets, chamber music, symphonies and songs. His work has had a substantial influence on virtually all subsequent Albanian composers. He died in a clinic in Rome.

ZADEJA, NDRE (1891.11.03-1945.03.25). Playwright. Ndre Zadeja was born in **Shkodra**. He attended the **Jesuit** college there, before being sent to Innsbruck for religious training. Upon his return to Albania, he was appointed secretary to the archbishop of Shkodra, Jak Serreqi, and later served as a parish priest in a number of northern Albanian villages, among which were

Gusht, **Boga**, Shkrel and Sheldia, and spent much of his leisure time writing. Among his literary production is verse, some of which has been published. Zadeja is, however, somewhat better remembered as the author of a number of plays of nationalist inspiration on historical and legendary themes which were performed in Shkodra in the 1920s and 1930s. Much of his work remained unpublished and was, therefore, little known, in particular during the **communist** dictatorship. Zadeja himself was arrested on 4 February 1945 and was executed after a mock trial. The priest-playwright is said to have been tortured and forced to dig his own grave before being lined up against the wall of the church courtyard with nine other people and shot.

ZADRIMA. Geographical and ethnographical region of northern Albania. Zadrima refers to the fertile plain in the District of **Lezha**, south of **Shkodra**, through which the Drin River flows before it reaches Lezha. The toponym, recorded in 1515 as *Sadrima* (John Musachi), is of Slavic origin–*za Drima* "behind or beyond the Drin."

ZAJMI, NEXHMEDIN (1916-1991.05.19). Painter. Nexhmedin Zajmi was born in Trebisht in the **Dibra** region. In 1931, he attended the **American Vocational School** in **Tirana**, where he studied agriculture and, later, art. He finished his schooling in 1938 and went on to study at the Academy of Fine Arts in Rome, where he graduated in 1943. After his return to Albania in 1944, he taught at the Jordan Misja Academy and at the Academy of Fine Arts (*Instituti i Lartë i Arteve*) until 1969. Though much of his painting falls within the category of conformist socialist realism, he is also remembered for moving portraits such as *Nëna labe* (The Laberian Mother), 1955; *Bajram Curri* (Bajram Curri), 1957; and *Malësori* (The Highlander), 1969.

ZAMPUTI, INJAC (1910.02.12-1998.03.01). Scholar, writer and historian. Zamputi was born in **Shkodra** of an Italian family. He attended the **Jesuit** Saverian college and studied law and political science in Trieste. In the 1930s, he wrote numerous articles for the **Catholic** periodicals *Hylli i Dritës* (The Day-Star) and *Leka* (Leka) and taught at the college under his mentor, the poet **Ndre Mjeda**. It was in this period that he began writing prose, though he soon returned to scholarship. His short stories appeared in the volumes *Zêmra njerzish* (The Hearts of People), Shkodra 1940, and *Atje, nën hijen e Rozafës* (There, in the Shade of Rozafa),

Tirana 1944. In subsequent decades he made a name for himself as a historian of unusual precision and reliability, although he was never allowed to leave Albania during the dictatorship. When the Academy of Sciences was founded in 1974, Zamputi was appointed to head the section on medieval history. He died in Tivoli near Rome.

Aside from countless articles on Albanian cultural history, Injac Zamputi is remembered in particular for his monumental publication of source material on Albanian history. Among his numerous volumes are: *Relacione mbi gjendjen e Shqipërisë veriore e të mesme në shekullin XVII* (Reports on the State of Northern and Central Albania in the Seventeenth Century), Tirana 1963, 1965; *Dokumenta të shekullit XV për historinë e Shqipërisë* (Fifteenth Century Documents on the History of Albania), Tirana 1967; *Regjistri i kadastrës dhe i koncesioneve për rrethin e Shkodrës, 1416-1417* (Land Registries and Concessions for the District of Shkodra, 1416-1417), Tirana 1977; *Dokumente për historinë e Shqipërisë 1479-1506* (Documents on the History of Albania, 1479-1506), Tirana 1979; *Dokumente për historinë e Shqipërisë të shek. XV, 1400-1405* (Documents on the History of Fifteenth Century Albania, 1400-1405), Tirana 1987; and his four-volume *Dokumente të shekujve XVI-XVII për historinë e Shqipërisë* (Sixteenth and Seventeenth Century Documents on the History of Albania) Tirana 1989, covering the period 1507-1699.

ZANA. Figure of northern Albanian mythology. The *zanas* are the mountain fairies of Albanian oral **literature**. They dwell near springs and torrents in the highlands of northern Albania and **Kosova**, where every mountain is said to have its own *zana*. They are envisaged as fair maidens, the muses of the mountains, who sing, gather flowers and bathe in the nude in alpine springs. *Zanas* are also exceptionally courageous and, like Pallas Athena of ancient **Greece**, they bestow their protection on warriors, thus the expression to be as "courageous as a *zana*," Alb. *trim si zana*. If the warrior is slain, it is the *zana* who begins the ritual wailing and lamenting for him, as a mother would do for her son. Originally a pre-Roman deity, the term *zana* is thought to be related etymologically to the Lat. *Diana*, Roman goddess of the hunt and the moon. The *zanas* have been a source of much inspiration in northern Albanian epic poetry, where they are wont to observe battles between the Albanian tribes and their neighbors from the distant mountain peaks, and intervene if necessary.

ZANONI, NDOC. *See* XANONI, ANTON.

ZAVALANI, TAJAR (1903.08.15-1966.08.19). Writer. Tajar Zavalani, also known as Thomas Henri Zavalani, was born in **Korça** and studied at the French secondary school in Thessalonika. In 1922, he became a civil servant and served together with **Sejfulla Malëshova** as secretary to Xhafer bey Vila (1889-1938). In June 1924, he took part in the **Vlora** uprising that brought **Fan Noli** to power. After the fall of the Noli administration at the end of 1924, he fled to **Italy**, where Soviet agents offered to let him study in Russia as a "victim of counter-revolution." After a year in Moscow, he attended the Marxist-Leninist school in Leningrad. In the summer of 1929, he returned to Moscow and worked at the Agrarian Institute, specializing in economics. In November 1930, he managed to get out of Russia, about which he now had serious misgivings because of the collectivization campaign, and settled in Berlin, from where he went to Leysin near Montreux in Switzerland for treatment of tuberculosis. In January 1933, he returned to Albania, where he was active in the translation of literary works, mostly from Russian and French. After the Italian invasion in 1939, he was interned in northern Italy, from where he escaped with his wife Selma Zavalani (1915-1995)—former lady-in-waiting to **Queen Geraldine**—via Switzerland to France and then, with **King Zog**'s party, to England in 1940. In November 1940, he was given a job in the BBC's Albanian-language service, where he worked until his death in an accident. Tajar Zavalani is the author of *How Strong Is Russia,* London 1951; and the two-volume *Histori i Shqipnis* (History of Albania), London 1957, 1963. The English-language version of the latter, *Land of Eagles: A History of Albania from Illyrian Times to the Present Day,* remains unpublished.

ZGËRDHESH. Archeological site south of the road from Fushë-Kruja to **Kruja**. Zgërdhesh is somewhat of a mystery because it is unmentioned in ancient sources. Some scholars believe, however, that it may be the site of ancient Albanopolis, referred to by Pliny. The **Illyrian** settlement here seems to have been founded in the seventh or sixth century B.C. and flourished in the fourth and third centuries, before being abandoned in the second century B.C., when the inhabitants moved to **Durrës** and **Lezha**. Among the remains at Zgërdhesh are 1,350 meters of fortification walls and heavily decayed terraces and towers spread over a hillside of 8.2 hectares. The toponym Zgërdhesh first occurs in 1431, in a

Turkish document as *Ozgurtaş* and, subsequently, in 1641, in the Italian chronicle of Marco Scura as *Sgurdessi*.

ZOG, KING. *See* ZOGU, AHMET.

ZOGOLLI, AHMED. *See* ZOGU, AHMET.

ZOGOLLI, SADIJE Hanëm (1876.08.28-1934.11.25). Mother of King Zog. Sadije Hanëm Zogolli, born Sadije Toptani, was a relative of **Essad Pasha Toptani**. In 1891, she married the tribal chieftain of **Mat**, Xhemal Pasha Zogolli. When her husband died, she took over the "regency" for her son **Ahmet Zogu**. She later had great influence over him both during his term as president of Albania and later when he was "King of the Albanians." The *nënë mbretëresha* (queen mother) died in 1934 and was buried in a pompous mausoleum, which was subsequently razed, on a hill above **Tirana**.

ZOGRAFI, KOSTANDIN AND ATHANAS (eighteenth century). Painters. Kostandin and Athanas Zografi, two brothers, were from the Mokra region near **Pogradec**. They are remembered as painters of **Orthodox** icons and church frescoes, and were active in the years between 1741 and 1783. Their works are to be seen in churches in **Korça**, **Ardenica**, **Voskopoja**, Vithkuq, **Berat** and on Mount Athos.

ZOGU, AHMET (1895.10.08-1961.04.09). Political figure and monarch of Albania. Ahmet Zogu, also Ahmet Zogolli, known abroad more commonly as King Zog, was born in Burgajet in the **Mat** district, the nephew of **Essad Pasha Toptani**. He spent his early years, from 1903 to August 1912, in Istanbul and commanded an Albanian volunteer brigade fighting on the side of Austria-Hungary during **World War I**. He took part in the **Congress of Lushnja** in 1920, and in the period 1920-1922 served as minister of the interior under **Sulejman bey Delvina** and then as minister of defense. On 2 December 1922, he formed a conservative government himself and held onto power until 23 February 1924, when an assassination attempt was made on his life. Zogu fled to **Yugoslavia** after the **Democratic Revolution**, which saw the ephemeral rise to power of **Fan Noli**. There, with Yugoslav support, he organized volunteer corps and returned to take over Albania. His forces occupied **Tirana** on 24 December 1924, bringing an end to the democratic experiment.

On 15 January 1925, he formed a new cabinet, declared Albania, which was nominally still a monarchy under the exiled **Prince Wilhelm zu Wied**, to be a republic and made himself president thereof on 31 January of that year. Despite the fact that he had come to power with Yugoslav support, he began to ally himself increasingly with Yugoslavia's rival on the Adriatic, fascist Italy. After an initial trade agreement between Albania and **Italy**, the two countries signed a first Pact of Tirana on 27 November 1926 and a second Pact of Tirana on 22 November 1927, the latter providing for mutual assistance in case of attack. These treaties gave Italy de facto control over Albania as a protectorate.

On 1 September 1928, with Italian support, Zog declared himself Zog I, King of the Albanians. In January 1931, he traveled to Vienna for health reasons, and on the evening of 20 February an attempt was made to assassinate him as he was leaving the Vienna opera house after a performance of *Pagliacci*. One member of his entourage was killed and one was wounded, but the king, who had shot back himself, survived the attack unscathed and returned to Tirana at the end of March 1931. His attackers, Aziz Çami, a southern Albanian **communist**, and Ndoc Gjeloshi, a conservative **Catholic** from **Shkodra**, were subsequently sentenced to prison by the Austrian authorities.

Over the coming decade, the authoritarian monarch endeavored to maintain a degree of independence from Mussolini's increasingly colonialist designs, but, in the end, he was forced to give in. When Italian troops invaded Albania on Good Friday, 7 April 1939, with the firm intention of staying, Zog and his family, **Queen Geraldine** and their newly born son **Leka**, fled overland to Greece and went into exile to England in 1940, holding court at the Ritz Hotel in London and then in Pangbourne in the Thames Valley. From 1946 to 1955, the royal family lived in Egypt under King Farouk (1920-1965), who was himself of Albanian origin. There, Zog reorganized the monarchist **Legality** movement and endeavored to gain the support of anticommunist Albanians in exile, but with limited success. After the deposition of King Farouk in 1952, Zog and his family moved to Cannes on the French Riviera. He died of stomach cancer in Suresnes near Paris and is buried there.

ZOGU, LEKA (1939.04.05-). Public figure and pretender to the Albanian throne. Prince Leka Zogu was born in **Tirana**, son of King Zog I (**Ahmet Zogu**) and Queen Geraldine (**Geraldine**

Apponyi). Two days after his birth, the royal family fled to Greece as a result of the Italian invasion of Albania. From there, they took refuge in England. Leka Zogu spent the subsequent years of his life in exile, initially with his parents in Egypt and France. He studied at Sandhurst military academy in England. After the death of his father in 1961, Leka moved to Pozuelo near Madrid in Spain to join his mother Geraldine. There he set up an import-export business in the arms trade. The Spanish authorities, having discovered a large cache of illegal arms at his home in 1979, objected and, as a result, under circumstances which remain unclear, he left Spain and took up residence in Rhodesia in 1979. The change of government in Rhodesia/Zimbabwe forced him to move to South Africa in 1980, where he bought a farm in Bryanston. On 10 October 1975, he married the Australian-born Susan Cullen-Ward (1941.01.28-) and has a son Leka (1982.03.26-), born in Johannesburg.

Leka Zogu made his first visit to Albania on 20 November 1993 but was refused entry into the country for passport reasons —he was traveling on a passport of the Kingdom of Albania, which he had issued himself. During his second visit on 12 April -12 July 1997, a period of political turmoil, his involvement, that of brandishing arms in a street demonstration, led once again to trouble with the Albanian government authorities. He took up permanent residence in Albania on 28 June 2002.

ZOGU, SADIJE Hanëm. *See* ZOGOLLI, SADIJE HANËM.

ZOTOS, ALEXANDRE. French scholar and translator. Alexandre Zotos, whose family is originally from Albania, graduated with a degree in classics and currently teaches French literature at the Jean Monnet University of St. Etienne in central France. He is the author of *Anthologie de la prose albanaise* (Anthology of Albanian Prose), Paris 1984; *De Scanderbeg à Ismail Kadaré: propos d'histoire et de littérature albanaises* (From Scanderbeg to Ismail Kadare: Remarks on Albanian History and Literature), St. Etienne 1997; and *Anthologie de la poésie albanaise* (Anthology of Albanian Poetry), Chambéry 1998.

Bibliography

The following bibliography presents an overview of publications on Albania and the Albanians, with concentration on works in English. Comparatively few serious works have been written about Albania in the Western world, no doubt due to the country's traditional isolation and to the glaring lack of foreign scholars who can actually speak and read Albanian. This compilation thus also includes a number of works in Albanian and other languages (principally German, French and Italian), many of which should definitely be consulted by any serious reader with specific interests.

It has really only been since 1990-1991 that Albania has received much public attention, most of which—alas—has been negative: the somber heritage of the long Stalinist period, the negative phenomena of third-world development such as destitution, illegal migration and crime, the uprising of 1997, which shook the very foundations of the Albanian state and spread weapons throughout the country and region, and the war in neighboring Kosova in 1999. Yet Albania is much more than recent newspaper headlines would have us believe. It is a European nation with a long history and a rich, though still little known, cultural heritage. There is much to learn, and much more remains to be discovered. As a scholarly discipline, Albanian studies is still very much in its infancy.

With regard to bibliographies, which are the first point of reference for any serious research, readers should initially consult Antonia Young's *Albania: Revised Edition* in the World Bibliographical Series of Clio Press (Santa Barbara 1997). For the communist period, in particular, reference may also be made to the earlier edition in the same series (Santa Barbara 1988) by William Bland of the former Marxist-oriented British Albanian Society. There are also detailed and periodized bibliographies of Albanian history in: *Albanie: une Bibliographie Historique* (Paris 1985) by Odile Daniel, and *Albania: A Bibliographic Research Survey with Location Codes* (Munich 1983) by Armin Hetzer and Roman Viorel.

For works of a general nature, readers should consult what in this writer's humble opinion is still the best and most delightful book ever written on Albania in English: Edith Durham's *High Albania* (London 1909, reprint 2000). For modern Albania, as seen and experienced by a contemporary traveler, Robert Carver's controversial *The Accursed Mountains: Journeys in Albania* (London 1998) provides much thought-provoking material.

Unfortunately, there is still no comprehensive and fully reliable history of Albania in English. The best full-length account of the country and people to date is Edwin Jacques' *The Albanians: An Ethnic History from Prehistoric Times to the Present* (Jefferson 1995). For the twentieth century, readers should also consult Miranda Vickers' *The Albanians: A Modern History* (London 1994). The following works are exceptionally informative for the first half of the century, up to the end of World War II: *King Zog and the Struggle for Stability in Albania* (New York 1984) and *Albania at War, 1939-1945* (London 1999), both by Bernd Fischer; and *Albania's National Liberation Struggle: The Bitter Victory* (London 1991) by Reginald Hibbert.

Another great lack in Albanian historiography is a full and reliable account of Albanian history during the communist period. Although not up to date, the following works can be recommended as a start: Peter Prifti's *Socialist Albania since 1944: Domestic and Foreign Developments* (Cambridge 1978); Arshi Pipa's *Albanian Stalinism: Ideo-political Aspects* (New York 1990); and Elez Biberaj's *Albania, a Socialist Maverick* (Boulder 1990). The post-communist period is better represented, in particular by *Albania: From Anarchy to a Balkan Identity* (London 1996) by Miranda Vickers and James Pettifer, which deals in depth with the years of the Berisha regime. For neighboring Kosova, readers also should consult Noel Malcolm's widely acclaimed *Kosovo, a Short History* (London 1998).

1. GENERAL
   1.1 BIBLIOGRAPHIES, DICTIONARIES AND READERS
   1.2 GENERAL INFORMATION AND INTERDISCIPLINARY STUDIES
   1.3 GUIDE BOOKS
   1.4 TRAVEL AND DESCRIPTION
   1.5 YEARBOOKS AND STATISTICAL ABSTRACTS
2. CULTURE
   2.1 LANGUAGE
   2.2 LITERATURE
   2.3 FOLK CULTURE
   2.4 ART AND ARCHITECTURE
   2.5 MUSIC
   2.6 THEATER

1. GENERAL

1.1 BIBLIOGRAPHIES, DICTIONARIES AND READERS

Bartl, Peter (ed.). *Albanica Monacensia: Verzeichnis der in München vorhandenen selbständigen Veröffentlichungen über Albanien* [Albanica Monacensia: Catalog of Book Publications on Albania in Munich]. Munich: Albanien-Institut, 1963. 83 pp.

Biçoku, Kasem, and Jup Kastrati. *Gjergj Kastrioti Skënderbeu, Bibliografi 1454-1835, I* [George Castriotta, Scanderbeg: Bibliography 1454-1835, 1]. Tirana: Biblioteka Kombëtare, 1997. 457 pp.

Bland, William B. *Albania.* World Bibliographical Series, Vol. 94. Santa Barbara, Calif.: Clio Press, 1988. 291 pp.

Buda, Aleks (ed.). *Fjalor enciklopedik shqiptar* [Albanian Encyclopedic Dictionary]. Tirana: Akademia e Shkencave, 1985. xvi + 1248 pp,

Çepani, Ilir. *Fjalor i biznesit dhe i legjislacionit ekonomik. Shqip; anglisht; frengj, gjermanisht, italisht dhe spanjisht. The Terminology of Business and Economic Laws. Albanian English, French, German, Italian and Spanish.* Tirana: Elena Gjika, 1998. 244 pp.

Çoba, A., and Z. Prela (ed.). *Albanica: vepra të botuara në shek. XVI-XVIII* [Albanica: Works Published in the XVI-XVIII Centuries]. Tirana: Biblioteka kombëtare, 1963. 109 pp.

Daniel, Odile. *Albanie: une bibliographie historique* [Albania: An Historical Bibliography]. Centre régional de publications de Meudon-Bellevue. R.C.P. Identités culturelles dans les sociétés paysannes d'Europe centrale et balkanique. Paris: Editions du CNRS, Paris s.a. [1985]. 616 pp.

Domi, Etleva, and Afërdita Sharrëxhi (ed.). *Vepra të autorëve dhe të studiuesve francezë mbi Shqipërinë dhe shqiptarët (Shek. XVI-XX): bibliografi. Oeuvres des auteurs et des chercheurs français sur l'Albanie et les Albanais (XVIe-XXe siècle): Bibliographie* [Works on Albania and the Albanians (XVI-XX centuries) by French Authors and Scholars]. Tirana: Biblioteka Kombëtare, 1997, reprint 2001. 163 pp.

Drizari, Nelo. *Albanian-English and English-Albanian Dictionary.* Second, enlarged edition with a supplement of new words. New York: Ungar, 1957. 321 pp.

Duro, Ilo, and Ramazan Hysa. *Fjalor shqip-anglisht. Albanian-English Dictionary.* Tirana: 8 Nëntori, 1981, reprint 1988. 510 pp.

Giordano, Emanuele. *Fjalor i arbëreshvet t'Italisë. Dizionario degli Albanesi d'Italia* [Dictionary of the Albanians of Italy]. Bari, Italy: Edizioni Paoline, 1963. 592 pp.

Guys, Henri. *Bibliographie albanaise: description raisonnée des ouvrages publiés en albanais ou relatifs à l'Albanie de 1900 à 1910 pars Henri Guys, Consul de France* [Albanian Bibliography: Annotated Description of Works Published in Albanian or about Albania from 1900 to 1910, by Henri Guys, French consul]. Tirana: Kristo Luarasi, 1938. 64 pp.

Hasani, Shefije. *Law Dictionary English-Albanian Albanian-English. Fjalor i terminologjisë juridike anglisht-shqip shqip-anglisht.* Prishtina, Kosova: Universiteti i Prishtinës, 1998. 386 pp.

Hetzer, Armin, and S. Roman Viorel (ed.). *Albanien: ein bibliographischer Forschungsbericht mit Titelübersetzungen und Standortnachweisen. Albania: A Bibliographic Research Survey with Location Codes.* Munich: K. G. Saur, 1983. 653 pp.

Hutchings, Raymond. *Historical Dictionary of Albania.* European historical dictionaries, No. 12. Lanham, Md.: Scarecrow Press, 1994. 277 pp.

Hysa, Ramazan. *Albanian-English Dictionary.* New York: Hippocene, 1993.

Kaceli, Luan. *Fjalor termash juridike, ekonomike dhe biznesi, anglisht-shqip. Dictionary of Law, Economy and Business, English-Albanian.* Tirana: Ada, 2002. 338 pp.

Kiçi, Gasper. *Fjalor shqip-anglisht. Albanian-English Dictionary.* Tivoli, Italy: Tipografia A. Picci, 1978. 448 pp.

———. *A Thesaurus of the Albanian Language in Dictionary Form.* Washington, D.C., 1992. 248 pp.

Kiçi, Gasper, and Hysni Aliko. *English-Albanian Dictionary. Fjalor anglisht-shqip.* Rome: Tipografica Editrice Romana, 1969. 627 pp.

Konini, Maksim, and Ilia Peçi. *Fjalor ekonomik: shqip, anglisht, gjermanisht* [Economic Dictionary: Albanian, English, German]. Puna për hartimin e këtij fjalori u koordinua nga Z. Friedrich Bremen. Botim i dytë Tirana: Civet, 1997. 318 pp.

Körner, Christine, and Peter Bartl (ed.). *Katalog der Bibliothek des Albanien-Instituts e.V. München* [Catalog of the Library of the Albania Institute, Munich]. Munich: Albanien-Institut, 1977.

Kornrumpf, Hans-Jürgen. *Osmanische Bibliographie mit besonderer Berücksichtigung der Türkei in Europa* [Ottoman Bibliography with Special Reference to Turkey in Europe]. Handbuch der Orientalistik. Erste Abteilung. Ergänzungsband VIII. Leiden, The Netherlands: E. J. Brill, 1973. 1,378 pp.

470   Bibliography

Lambertz, Maximilan. *Albanisches Lesebuch mit Einführung in die albanische Sprache. I. Teil: Grammatik und albanische Texte. II. Teil: Texte in deutscher Übersetzung* [Albanian Reader with an Introduction to the Albanian Language. Part I: Grammar and Albanian texts. Part II: Texts in German Translation]. Leipzig, Germany: Harrassowitz, 1948. 387 & 302 pp.

Legrand, Emile. *Bibliographie albanaise: description raisonnée des ouvrages publiés en albanais ou relatifs à l'Albanie du quinzième siècle à l'année 1900.* Oeuvre posthume complétée et publiée par Henri Gûys [Albanian Bibliography: Annotated Description of Works Published in Albanian or on Albania from the 15th Century to the Year 1900]. Athens: Welter, Paris and Elefthéroudakis & Barth, 1912, reprint 1973. 228 pp.

Manek, F., Georg Pekmezi, and Anton Stotz. *Bibliographija shqype. Albanesische Bibliographie* [Albanian Bibliography]. Vienna: Dija, 1909. 147 pp.

Mann, Stuart E. *An Historical Albanian and English Dictionary 1496-1938.* London: The Philological Society of London, 1937. 980 pp.

——. *An Historical Albanian-English Dictionary.* Published for the British Council. London: Longmans, Green, 1948. ix + 601 pp.

——. *English-Albanian Dictionary.* London: Cambridge University Press, 1957, reprint 1966. 433 pp.

Mele, Margarita. *Libri shqip i botuar jashtë Shqipërisë. Hyrjet në Bibliotekën Kombëtare, 1991-1995. Bibliografi* [Albanian Books Published Outside of Albania. Entries in the National Library 1991-1995. Bibliography]. Tirana: Biblioteka Kombëtare, 1996. 161 pp.

——. *Libri shqip i botuar jashtë Shqipërisë. Hyrjet në Bibliotekën Kombëtare 1996. Bibliografi* [Albanian books published outside of Albania. Entries in the National Library 1996. Bibliography]. Tirana: Biblioteka Kombëtare, 1997. 87 pp.

Mema, Shpëtim, and Lindita Bubsi (ed.). *Albanica 2: bibliografi e viteve 1800-1849* [Albanica 2: Bibliography of the Years 1800-1849]. Tirana: Biblioteka Kombëtare, 1987. 346 pp.

Mema, Shpëtim, and Afërdita Sharrëxhi (ed.). *Albanica I: Bibliography of the 15th-18th Centuries.* Tirana: National Library, 1998. 566 pp.

Newmark, Leonard. *Albanian-English Dictionary.* Oxford: Oxford University Press, 1998. 1,056 pp.

Orel, Vladimir. *Albanian Etymological Dictionary.* Leiden, The Netherlands: E. J. Brill, 1998. xxxix + 670 pp.

Orton, Lawrence D. *A Reader's Guide to Albania.* Washington, D.C., 1989. 14 pp.

Pango, Apostol. *Enciklopedia e Delvinës dhe e Sarandës* [Encyclopedia of Delvina and Saranda]. Tirana: Toena, 2002. 428 pp.

Petrovitch, Georges T. *Scanderbeg (Georges Castriota): essai de bibliographie raisonnée. Ouvrages sur Scanderbeg écrits en langues française, anglaise, allemande, latine, italienne, espagnole, portuguaise, suédoise et grecque et publiés depuis l'invention de l'imprimerie jusqu'à nos jours* [Scanderbeg (George Castriotta): Attempt at an Annotated Bibliography. Works on Scanderbeg Written in French, English, German, Latin, Italian, Spanish, Portuguese, Swedish and Greek and Published since the Invention of Printing up to Our Times]. Paris: Leroux, 1881, reprint 1967. 188 pp.

Powers, Robert. *English-Albania Dictionary for Aid Workers and Military Personnel.* Seattle, Wash.: Rodnik, 2001.

Qesku, Pavli. *Albanian-English Dictionary. Fjalor shqip-anglisht. Me 45,500 fjalë-tituj.* Tirana: Edfa, 1999. 1062 pp.

——. *English-Albanian Dictionary: 70,000 Entries, over 250,000 References. Fjalor anglisht-shqip. 70.000 fjalë bazë e mbi 250.000 referenca.* Redaktor Zef Simoni. Tirana: Edfa, 2000. 1535 pp.

Rexha, Nexhmi. *English-Albanian and Albanian-English Dictionary of Marketing Terms. Fjalor anglisht-shqip dhe shqip-anglisht i termave të marketingut.* Prishtina, Kosova: Riinvest, 1996. 114 pp.

Seewann, Gerhard (ed.). "Albanien: Bibliographie." in: *Südosteuropa, Zeitschrift für Gegenwartsforschung,* Munich, 36 (1987), pp. 759-766.

——. *Bestandskatalog der Bibliothek des Südost-Instituts München. Band 1: Druckschriften 1529-1945, unter Mitarbeit von Gerda Bartl und Wilma Kömives* [Catalog of Publications Present in the Library of the Südost-Institut, Munich. Volume 1: Publications 1529-1945, with the Assistance of Gerda Bartl and Wilma Kömives]. Südosteuropa-Bibliographie Ergänzungsband I. Munich: Oldenbourg, 1990. 840 pp.

Sharrexhi, Afërdita, and Nermin Basha. *Vepra të autorëve dhe studiuesve italianë për Shqipërinë dhe shqiptarët (shek. XV-XX). Katalog. Opere di autori e studiosi italiani sull'Albania e gli Albanesi (Sec. XV-XX). Catalogo* [Works on Albania and the Albanians by Italian Authors and Scholars (XV-XX centuries). Catalog]. Tirana: Shoqata e Italianistëve të Shqipërisë / Biblioteka Kombëtare, 1995. 312 pp.

Shema, Isak, and Ibrahim Rugova. *Bibliografi e kritikës letrare shqiptare 1944-1974* [Bibliography of Albanian Literary Criticism, 1944-1974]. Prishtina, Kosova: Instituti Albanologjik, 1976, reprint 1997. 448 pp.

Stefanllari, Ilo. *Fjalor anglisht-shqip* [English-Albanian Dictionary]. Prishtina, Kosova: Rilindja, 1988. 442 pp.

——. *Fjalor frazeologjik anglisht-shqip* [English-Albanian Phraseological Dictionary]. Tirana: Enciklopedike, 1998. 496 pp.

Susuri, Latif. *Fjalor i terminologjisë bujqësore anglisht-shqip, shqip-anglisht* [Dictionary of Agricultural Terminology English-Albanian, Albanian-English]. Prishtina, Kosova: Rilindja, 1999. viii + 412 pp.

Vaccaro, Attilio. *Italo-Albanensia: repertorio bibliografico sulla storia religiosa, sociale, economica e culturale degli Albanesi dal sec. XVI al nostri giorni* [Italo-Albanensia: Bibliographical Catalog on the Religious, Social, Economic and Cultural History of the Albanians from the Sixteenth Century to the Present Day]. Associazione culturale italo-greco-albanese. Quadreni 1. Cosenza, Italy: Bios, 1994. 314 pp.

Young, Antonia. *Albania. Revised Edition.* World Bibliographical Series, vol. 94. Santa Barbara, Calif.: Clio Press, 1997. 295 pp.

1.2 GENERAL INFORMATION AND INTERDISCIPLINARY STUDIES

Altmann, Franz-Lothar (ed.). *Albanien im Umbruch: eine Bestandaufnahme* [Albania in Transition: An Inventory]. Untersuchungen zur Gegenwartskunde Südosteuropas. Bd. 28. Herausgegeben vom Südost-Institut. Munich: Oldenbourg, 1990. 293 pp.

Baku, Pasho (ed.). *Fjalor enciklopedik.* Tirana: Bacchus, 2002. 799 pp.

Bartl, Peter, Martin Camaj, and Gerhard Grimm (ed.). *Dissertationes Albanicae in honorem Josephi Valentini et Ernesti Koliqi septuargenariorum.* Beiträge zur Kenntnis Südosteuropas und des nahen Orients. Munich: Trofenik, 1971. 206 pp.

Buda, Aleks (ed.). *The Albanians and Their Territories.* Academy of Sciences of the PSR of Albania. Tirana: 8 Nëntori, 1985. 494 pp.

Daum, Werner (ed.). *Albanien zwischen Kreuz und Halbmond* [Albania between Cross and Crescent]. Herausgegeben von Werner Daum in Zusammenarbeit mit Peter Bartl, Ferdinand Leka, Marina Marinescu, Afërdita Onuzi, Walter Raunig, Spiro Shkurti und Agron Xhagolli. Munich: Staatliches Museum für Völkerkunde, 1998. 344 pp.

Eggebrecht, Arne (ed.). *Albanien: Schätze aus dem Land der Skipetaren* [Albania: Treasures from the Land of the Albanians]. Mainz, Germany: Philipp von Zabern, 1988. 476 pp.

Ekonomi, Milva (ed.). *Vjetari statistikor i Shqiperisë. The Albanian Statistical Yearbook, 1991-1999.* Tirana: Instat, 2002. 362 pp.

Giaffo, Lou. *Albania, Eye of the Balkan Vortex.* Philadelphia: Xlibris, 1999. 365 pp.

Grothusen, Klaus-Detlev (ed.). *Albanien in Vergangenheit und Gegenwart. Internationales Symposion der Südosteuropa-Gesellschaft in Zusammenarbeit mit der Albanischen Akademie der Wissenschaften. Winterscheider Mühle bei Bonn, 12.-15. September 1989* [Albania in Past and Present. International Symposium of the Südosteuropa-Gesellschaft in Collaboration with the Albanian Academy of Sciences, Winterscheider Mühle near Bonn, 12th-15th September 1989]. Südosteuropa-Studien, Band 48. Munich: Südosteuropa-Gesellschaft, 1991. 190 pp.

——. *Albanien. Südosteuropa-Handbuch. Band VII. Albania. Handbook on South Eastern Europe. Volume VII.* Göttingen, Germany: Vandenhoeck & Ruprecht, 1993. 845 pp.

Hahn, Johann Georg von. *Albanesische Studien* [Albanian Studies]. 3 vol. Jena, Germany: Fr. Mauke, Jena 1854, reprint 1981. 347, 169, 244 pp.

Hall, Derek R. *Albania and the Albanians.* London: Pinter, 1994. 304 pp.

Keefe, Eugene, et al. *Area handbook for Albania.* Washington, D.C.: U.S. Government Printing Office, 1971. 223 pp.

Kelly, Robert C. *Country Review, Albania 2000.* Houston, Tex.: CountryWatch, 1999. 60 pp.

Kressing, Frank, and Karl Kaser (ed.). *Albania, a Country in Transition. Aspects of Changing in a Southeast European Country.* Schriften des Zentrum für Europäische Integrationsforschung, Bd. 51. Baden-Baden, Germany: Nomos Verlagsgesellschaft, 2002.

Lienau, Cay, and Günter Prinzing (ed.). *Beiträge zur Geographie und Geschichte Albaniens* [Papers on the Geography and History of Albania]. Berichte aus dem Arbeitsgebiet Entwicklungsforschung, Heft 12. Münster, Germany: Institut für Geographie, 1984. 277 pp.

Logoreci, Anton. *The Albanians: Europe's Forgotten Survivors.* London: Victor Gollancz, 1977. 230 pp.

Lubonja, Fatos, and John Hodgson. *Përpjekja / Endeavour. Writing from Albania's Critical Quarterly.* Translated by John Hodgson. Tirana: Përpjekja, 1997. 154 pp.

Marmullaku, Ramadan. *Albania and the Albanians.* Translated from the Serbo-Croatian by Margot and Boško Milosavljević. Hamden, Conn.: Archon / London: C. Hurst, 1975. 178 pp.

Ölberg, Hermann Maria (ed.). *Akten des Internationalen Albanologischen Kolloquiums. Zum Gedächtnis an Univ.-Prof. Dr. Norbert Jokl. Innsbruck, 28. September–3. Oktober 1972* [Acts of the International Albanological Colloquium. To the Memory of Prof. Norbert Jokl, Innsbruck, 28th September–3rd October 1972].Veranstaltet vom Institut für Sprachwissenschaft der Universität Innsbruck in

Verbindung mit der Innsbrucker Sprachwissenschaftlichen
Gesellschaft und der Indogermanischen Gesellschaft. Hermann
Maria Ölberg (ed.). Innsbrucker Beiträge zur Kulturwissenschaft,
Sonderheft 41. Innsbruck, Austria, 1977. 784 pp.

Olsen, Neil. *Albania: The Background, the Issues, the People.* An
Oxfam Country Profile. Oxford: Oxfam, 2000. 88 pp.

Pano, Nicholas Christopher. *People's Republic of Albania.* Baltimore:
John Hopkins Press, 1968. 183 pp.

Peacock, Wadham. *Albania: The Foundling State of Europe.* London:
Chapman & Hall / New York: D. Appleton, 1914. 256 pp.

——. *The Wild Albanian. From the Fortnightly Review, May 1913.* With
a preface by Ihsan Toptani. London: Centre for Albanian Studies,
2000. 18 pp.

Peinsipp, Walter. *Das Volk der Shkypetaren: Geschichte, Gesellschaft-
und Verhaltensordnung. Ein Beitrag zur Rechtsarchäologie und zur
soziologischen Anthropologie des Balkan* [The Albanian People:
History, Social and Behavioral Order. A Contribution to the Juridical
Archeology and to the Sociological Anthropology of the Balkans].
Vienna: Böhlau, 1985. 303 pp.

Phipps, John. *Stamps and Posts of Abania and Epirus, 1877-1945.*
Bristol, England: S. Rossiter Trust Fund, 1996. 297 pp.

Poulton, Hugh, and Suha Taji-Farouki (ed.). *Muslim Identity and the
Balkan State.* London: C. Hurst, 1997. ix + 250 pp.

Vasa, Pashko. *The Truth on Albania and the Albanians. Historical and
Critical.* By Wassa Effendi, an Albanian Christian functionary.
Translation by Edward Saint John Fairman. London: National Press
Agency, 1879. 48 pp.

——. *The Truth on Albania and the Albanians. Historical and Critical
Issues by Wassa Effendi.* Introduction by Robert Elsie. London:
Centre for Albanian Studies, 1999. 46 pp.

Selenica, Teki. *Shqipria e ilustruar. L'Albanie illustrée. Albumi i
Shqipris më 1927. Album de l'Albanie en 1927* [Illustrated Albania.
An Album of Albania in 1927]. Tirana: Tirana, 1928. xviii + 400 pp.

Skendi, Stavro. *Albania.* Published for the Mid-European Studies Center
Series of the Free Europe Committee. New York: Praeger / London:
Stevens & Sons, 1956. 389 pp.

——. *Balkan Cultural Studies.* East European Monographs, 72. New
York: Columbia University Press, 1980. 278 pp.

Snoj, Marko. *Rückläufiges Wörterbuch der albanischen Sprache* [Re-
verse Dictionary of the Albanian Language]. Lexicographia
orientalis, 3. Hamburg: Buske, 1994. xii + 482 pp.

Staatliches Museum für Völkerkunde (ed.). *Albanien: Reichtum und Vielfalt alter Kultur* [Albania: Wealth and Diversity of an Ancient Culture]. Munich: Museum für Völkerkunde, 2001. 208 pp.

Winnifrith, Tom J. (ed.). *Perspectives on Albania.* Warwick Studies in the European Humanities. Basingstoke: Macmillan, 1992. 140 pp. / New York: St. Martin's Press, 1992. 192 pp.

Zickel, Raymond E., and Walter R. Iwaskiw (ed.). *Albania: A Country Study*, 2nd edition. Federal Research Division. Library of Congress. Area Handbook Series 550-98. Washington, D.C.: Federal Research Division, 1994. 288 pp.

1.3   GUIDE BOOKS

Dawson, Peter, Andrea Dawson, and Linda White. *Albania: A Guide and Illustrated Journal,* 2nd edition. Chalfont St. Peter, England: Bradt, 1995. 216 pp.

Frashëri, Stavro. *Through Mirdita in Winter.* Translated from the Albanian by pp. R. Prifti. New York: Columbia University Press, 2001. 152 pp.

Fremuth, Wolfgang (ed.). *Albania, Guide to Its Natural Treasures.* Hatten/Sandkr.: Herwig Klemp, 2000. 144 pp.

Neza, Agim, and Miranda Hanka. *Travellers Guide to Albania.* Aylesbury, England: ACO, 1993. 170 pp.

Pettifer, James. *Blue Guide: Albania and Kosovo.* London: A&C Black, 2001. 511 pp.

Thompson, Trevor, and Dinah Thompson. *Adriatic Pilot: A Yachtsman's Guide to Albania, Yugoslavia and the Italian Coast to Santa Maria di Leuca.* St. Ives, Cambridge: Imray, Laurie, Norie and Wilson, ca. 1986. viii + 403 pp.

Ward, Philip. *Albania: A Travel Guide.* Cambridge: Oleander, 1983. 166 pp.

1.4   TRAVEL AND DESCRIPTION

Allcock, John B., and Antonia Young (ed.). *Black Lambs and Grey Falcons: Women Travellers in the Balkans.* Bradford, England: Bradford University Press, 1991. 216 pp.

——. *Black Lambs and Grey Falcons: Women Travelling in the Balkans.* New York: Berghahn Books, 2000. 274 pp.

Baçe, Apollon, Aleksandër Meksi, and Emin Riza. *Berat, son histoire et son architecture* [Berat, Its History and Architecture]. Traduit de l'Albanais par Haki Shtalbi. Tirana: Encyclopediques, 1996. 189 pp.

Baerlein, Henry Philip Bernard. *Under the Acroceraunian Mountains.* London: Leonard Parsons, 1922. 164 pp.

——. *Southern Albania: Under the Acroceraunian Mountains.* Chicago: Argonaut, 1968. 164 pp.

Barnes, James Thomas Strachey. *Half a Life Left.* New York: Coward-McCann, 1937 / London: Eyre & Spolliswoode 1938. 329 pp.

Bolognari, Mario (ed.). *La diaspora della diaspora: viaggio alla ricerca degli Arbëreshë* [The Diaspora of the Diaspora: Voyage in Search of the Arberësh]. Pisa: ETS Editrice, 1989. 224 pp.

Carver, Robert. *The Accursed Mountains: Journeys in Albania.* London: John Murray, 1998, 2nd edition 1999. 349 pp.

Courtade, Pierre. *Albania: Travel Notebook and Documentary.* With a short novel by the Albanian writer Aleks Çaçi. Translated by Charles Ashleigh. London: Fore Publications, 1956. 68 pp.

Douglas, Norman. *Old Calabria.* London: Secker & Warburg, 1915, reprint 1928, 1955, 1993. 352 pp.

Edmonds, Paul. *To the Land of the Eagle: Travels in Montenegro and Albania.* London: Routledge, 1927. 288 pp.

Heseltine, Nigel. *Scarred Background: A Journey through Albania.* London: Lovat Dickenson, 1938. 234 pp.

Hodgkinson, Harry. *The Adriatic Sea.* London: Jonathan Cape, 1955. 256 pp.

Graves, Robert Wyndham. *Storm Centres of the Near East: Personal Memories 1879-1929.* London: Hutchinson, 1933. 375 pp.

Groote, E. von (ed.). *Die Pilgerfahrt des Ritters Arnold von Harff von Cöln durch Italien, Syrien, Ägypten, Arabien, Äthiopien, Nubien, Palästina, die Türkei, Frankreich und Spanien, wie er sie in den Jahren 1496 bis 1499 vollendet, beschrieben und durch Zeichnungen erläutert hat* [The Pilgrimage of the Knight Arnold von Harff from Cologne through Italy, Syria, Egypt, Arabia, Nubia, Palestine, Turkey, France and Spain as He Conducted, Described and Illustrated It with Drawings in the Years 1496 to 1499]. Cologne, Germany: J. M. Heberle, 1860. 280 pp.

Hobhouse, John Cameron (= Broughton, Lord). *A Journey through Albania and Other Provinces of Turkey in Europe and Asia to Constantinople during the Years 1809 and 1810,* by J. C. Hobhouse. Second edition. London: James Cawthorn, 1813, reprint 1833, 1971. 518 & 1152 pp.

——. *Travels in Albania and the other Provinces of Turkey in 1809 and 1810* by the Right Hon. Lord Broughton G.C.B. In two volumes. London: John Murray, 1858. 544 & 526 pp.

——. *A Journey through Albania.* New York: Arno, 1971. 181 pp.

Holland, Henry. *Travels in the Ionian Isles, Albania, Thessaly, Macedonia, etc., during the Years 1812 and 1813.* London: Longman, Hurst, Rees, Orme & Brown, 1815, reprint 1971. 551 pp.

Holtz, William. *Travels with Zenobia. Paris to Albania in a Model T Ford. A Journal by Rose Wilder Lane and Helen Dore Boylston.* Columbia: University of Missouri Press, 1983. 117 pp.

Hughes, Thomas Stuart. *Travels in Sicily, Greece and Albania* by the Rev. Thos. Smart Hughes, late fellow of Saint John's and now fellow of Emmanuel College Cambridge. 2 vol. London: J. Mawman, 1820. 532 & 394 pp.

——. *Travels in Greece and Albania* by The Rev. T. S. Hughes, B.D. Second edition with considerable additions. 2 vol. London: H. Colburn & R. Bentley, 1830. 512 & 512 pp.

Hyman, Susan (ed.). *Edward Lear in the Levant: Travels in Albania, Greece and Turkey in Europe 1848-1849.* London: John Murray, 1988. 168 pp.

Kaplan, Robert D. *Balkan Ghosts: A Journey through History.* New York: Vintage Books, 1993. 307 pp.

Keeley, Edmond. *Albanian Journal: The Road to Elbasan.* Fredonia, N.Y.: White Pine Press, 1997. 115 pp.

Konitza, Faik bey. *Albania: The Rock Garden of Southeastern Europe and other Essays.* Edited and amplified by Gerim M. Panarity, with an introduction by Fan Noli. Boston: Vatra, 1957. 175 pp.

Kwok, Godfrey. *Rendezvous with Yesterday.* London: Merrythought, 1967. 51 pp.

Lane, Rose Wilder. *The Peaks of Shala, Being a Record of Certain Wanderings among the Hill-Tribes of Albania.* London: Chapman & Dodd, 1922, reprint 1923. 349 pp.

Leake, William Martin. *Researches in Greece.* London: J. Booth, 1814. 472 pp.

——. *Travels in northern Greece.* 4 vol. London: J. Rodwell, 1835, reprint 1967. 527, 643, 578, 588 pp.

Lear, Edward. *Journals of a Landscape Painter in Greece and Albania.* London: Richard Bentley, 1851. 428 pp.

——. *Edward Lear in Greece. Journals of a Landscape Painter in Greece and Albania.* London: Century, 1965, reprint 1988. 222 pp.

Letts, Malcolm Henry Ikin. *The Pilgrimage of Arnold von Harff, Knight, from Cologne, through Italy, Syria, Egypt, Arabia, Ethiopia, Nubia, Palestine, Turkey, France and Spain, Which He Accomplished in the*

Years 1496 to 1499. Translated from the German and edited with notes and an introduction by Malcolm Letts. Works issued by the Hakluyt Society. Second series, No. XCIV. London: Hakluyt Society 1946, reprint 1967. 325 pp.

Lyall, Archibald Laurence. *The Balkan Road.* London: Methuen, 1930. 244 pp.

Mackenzie, Georgena Muir, and A. Pauline Irby. *Travels in the Slavonic Provinces of Turkey in Europe.* Pref. Right Hon. W. E. Gladstone. 2 vol. London: Daldy, Isbister, 1877, reprint 1866, 1971. 313 + 342 pp.

Maclean, Fitzroy. *Eastern Approaches.* London: Jonathan Cape, 1949. 543 pp.

Matthews, Ronald de Couves. *Sons of the Eagle: Wanderings in Albania.* London: Methuen, 1937. 301 pp.

Mcculloch, John Irvin Beggs. *Drums in the Balkan Night.* New York: Putnam, 1936. 361 pp.

Mead, Alice. *A Journey to Kosova.* Cumberland Center, Maine: Loose Cannon Press, 1995. 197 pp.

——. *Adem's Cross.* New York: Farrar Straus Giroux, 1996. 132 pp.

Mihačević, Lovro (= Mihačević, Laurentius). *Durch Albanien: Reise-Eindrücke* [Through Albania: Travel Impressions]. Aus dem Kroatischen übersetzt durch Otto Szlavik. Prague: Bonifatius, 1913. 208 pp.

Miller, Elisabeth Cleveland. *Pran of Albania.* Illustrations by Maud and Miska Petersham. Garden City, N.J.: Doubleday, 1929. 257 pp.

——. *Children of the Mountain Eagle.* Illustrations by Maud and Miska Petersham. Garden City, N.Y.: Doubleday Doran, 1938. 328 pp.

Motes, Mary C. *Kosova Kosovo: Prelude to War 1966-1999.* Homestead, Fla.: Redland Press, 1998. 308 pp.

Newby, Eric. *On the Shores of the Mediterranean.* London: Harvill Press and Pan Books, 1984, reprint 1985. 448 pp.

Newman, Bernard. *Albanian Back-door.* London: Herbert Jenkins, 1936. 315 pp.

——. *Albanian Journey.* London: Sir Isaac Pitman, 1938. 96 pp.

——. *Balkan Background.* London: Robert Hale, 1944, reprint: 1945. 288 pp.

Noakes, Vivien. *Edward Lear: The Life of a Wanderer.* London: Collins, 1968, 1979. 359 pp.

Nopcsa, Franz Baron. *Reisen in den Balkan: die Lebenserinnerungen des Franz Baron Nopcsa* [Travels in the Balkans: The Memoirs of Baron Franz Nopcsa]. Eingeleitet, herausgegeben und mit Anhang versehen von Robert Elsie. Dukagjini Balkan Books. Peja, Kosova: Dukagjini, 2001. xii + 527 pp.

Oakley-Hill, Dayrell R. *An Englishman in Albania: Memoirs of a British Officer, 1929-1955.* Edited by B. D. Destani. Introduction by Colonel David Smiley. London: Centre for Albanian Studies, 2002. 273 pp.

O'Doneven, Captain. *A Skillet of the Balkans.* Lymington, England: Charles T. King, 1932. 210 pp.

Otten, Karl. *Eine Reise durch Albanien, 1912* [A Journey through Albánia, 1912]. Munich: H. F. S. Bachmair, 1913. 71 pp.

——. *Die Reise durch Albanien und andere Prosa* [A Journey through Albania and Other Prose]. Hrsg. von Ellen Otten und Hermann Ruch. Zürich: Arche, 1989. 195 pp.

Pandeli, James William. *Oh Albania, My Poor Albania: The History of Mother Albania from the Beginning of Time, the Beginning of the World.* s.l.: J. W. Pandeli, c.a. 1988. iv + 78 pp.

Portway, Christopher. *Double Circuit.* London: Robert Hale, 1974. 192 pp.

Pouqueville, François Charles Hugues Laurent. *Voyage en Morée, à Constantinople, en Albanie et dans plusieurs autres parties de l'Empire othoman pendant les années 1798, 1799, 1800 et 1801. Comprenant la description de ces pays, leurs productions, les moeurs, les usages, les maladies et le commerce de leurs habitants; avec des rapprochements entre l'état actuel de la Grèce, et ce qu'elle fut dans l'antiquité* [Travels through the Morea, Constantinople, Albania and to Many Other Parts of the Ottoman Empire during the Years 1798, 1799, 1800 and 1801. Including a Description of These Countries, the Produce, Customs, Habits, Illnesses and Commerce of Their Inhabitants; with a Comparison to the Present-day State of Greece and How It Was in Ancient Times]. 3 vol. Paris: Marchand, 1805. 542, 287, 344 pp.

——. *Travels through the Morea, Albania and Several Other Parts of the Ottoman Empire to Constantinople during the Years 1798, 1799, 1800 and 1801...* London: Richard Phillips, 1806, 192 pp.

——. *Travels in Greece and Turkey, Comprehending a Particular Account of the Morea, Albania, etc. A Comparison between the Ancient and Present State of Greece and an Historical and Geographical Description of the Ancient Epirus.* 2nd edition. London: H. Colburn, 1820. 482 pp.

——. *Travels in Epirus, Albania, Macedonia and Thessaly.* Classic Balkan travel series. Edited by James Pettifer. London: s.e. [Loizou Publications], 1998. viii + 122 pp.

Prévélakis, Georges. *Les Balkans: cultures et géopolitique* [The Balkans: Cultures and Geopolitics]. Paris: Nathan, 1994. 192 pp.

Quayle, Anthony. *Eight Hours from England.* London: Heinemann, 1945. iv + 224 pp.

——. *A Time to Speak.* London: Barie & Jenkins, 1990. x + 368 pp.

Reed, Fred A. *Salonica Terminus: Travels in the Balkan Nightmare.* Burnaby, B.C.: Talonbooks, 1996. 288 pp.

Robinson, [Vivian Dering] Vandeleur. *Albania's Road to Freedom.* London: George Allen & Unwin, 1941. 135 pp.

Ryan, Andrew, Sir. *The Last of the Dragomans.* London: Geoffrey Bles, 1951. 351 pp.

Shanafelt, Gary W. "An English Lady in High Albania: Edith Durham and the Balkans," in: *East European Quarterly,* Boulder, Colo., 30, 3 (1996), pp. 283-300.

Spencer, Edmund. *Travels in European Turkey through Bosnia, Servia, Bulgaria, Macedonia, Albania and Epirus with a Visit to Greece and the Ionian Ysles.* 2 vol. London: Hurst & Blackett, 1851 & 1853. 416 & 484 pp.

Strangford, Viscountess (= Smythe, Emily Anne). *The Eastern Shores of the Adriatic in 1863 with a Visit to Montenegro.* London: R. Bentley, 1864. 386 pp.

Sulzberger, Cyrus L. *A Long Row of Candles.* London: Macmillan, 1969. 877 pp.

Swire, Joseph. *Albania: The Rise of a Kingdom.* London: Williams and Norgate, 1929, reprint 1971. 560 pp.

——. *King Zog's Albania.* London: Robert Hale, 1937. 302 pp.

Thornton, Philip. *Dead Puppets Dance.* London: Collins, 1937. 331 pp.

Tilman, Harold William. *When Men and Mountains Meet.* Cambridge: Cambridge University Press, 1946. 232 pp.

Vaka, Demetra (= Brown, Mrs. Kenneth). *In the Shadow of Islam.* London: Constable, 1911. x + 315 pp.

——. *The Heart of the Balkans.* Boston: Houghton Mifflin, 1917. 248 pp.

Vlora, Eqrem bey (= Vlora, Ekrem bey). *Lebenserinnerungen 1-2* [Memoirs, 1-2]. Südosteuropäische Arbeiten, 66, 67. Munich: Oldenbourg, 1968, 1973. 275 & 301 pp.

——. *Kujtime: vëllimi i parë 1885-1912, vëllimi i dytë 1912-1925* [Memoirs: volume one 1885-1912, volume two 1912-1925]. Përktheu nga origjinali gjermanisht Afrim Koçi. Tirana: Shtëpia e Librit & Komunikimit, 2002. 320 & 360 pp.

Vrioni, Jusuf. *Mondes éffacés, souvenirs d'un Européen* [Effaced Worlds: Memoirs of a European]. Avec Eric Faye. Paris: J.C. Lattès, 1998. 318 pp.

Walker, Mary Adelaide. *Through Macedonia to the Albanian Lakes.* London: Chapman & Hall, 1864. 274 pp.

West, Rebecca. *Black Lamb and Grey Falcon: A Journey through Yugoslavia.* New York: Viking Press, 1942, reprint: 1986. 1181 pp.

Wilkins, Frances. *Let's Visit Albania.* London: Macmillan, 1988. 90 pp.

Wright, David. *Albania.* Enchantment of the World. Second series. Juv. Danbury, Conn.: Children's Books, 1997. 144 pp.

Zaimi, Nexhmie. *Daughter of the Eagle: An Autobiography of an Albanian Girl.* New York: Ives Washburn, 1937, reprint 1938. 271 pp.

1.5 YEARBOOKS AND STATISTICAL ABSTRACTS

Jaehne, Günter, and E. Schinke (ed.). *Statistikat e bujqësisë dhe ushqimit të Shqipërisë 1993 Agriculture and Food Statistics of Albania 1993. Statistisches Jahrbuch für Landwirtschaft und Ernährung Albanien 1993.* Gießener Abhandlungen zur Agrar- und Wirtschaftsforschung des Ostens. Band 202. Berlin: Dunckler & Humblot, 1994. xxii + 64 pp.

Vjetari statistikor i R.P.S. të Shqipërisë. Statistical Yearbook of the pp.S.R. of Albania. Tirana: Komisioni i planit të shtetit, 1989. 173 pp.

Vjetari statistikor i Shqipërisë 1991. Statistical Yearbook of Albania 1991. Tirana: Ministria e Ekonomisë, 1991. 373 pp.

2. CULTURE

2.1 LANGUAGE

Altimari, Francesco, and Leonardo M. Savoia. *I dialetti italo-albanese: studi linguistici e storico-culturale sulle communità arbëreshe* [Italo-Albanian Dialects: Linguistic, Historical and Cultural Studies on the Arbëresh Community]. Rome: Bulzoni, 1994. 479 pp.

Boissin, Henri. *Grammaire de l'Albanais moderne* [Grammar of Modern Albanian]. Paris: Chez l'auteur, 1975. 341 pp.

Bonnet, Guillaume. *Les mots latins de l'albanais* [The Latin Words in Albanian]. Paris: L'Harmattan, 1998. 478 pp.

Buchholz, Oda, and Wilfried Fiedler. *Albanische Grammatik* [Albanian Grammar]. Leipzig, Germany: Enzyklopädie, 1987. 582 pp.

Byron, Janet Leotha. *Selection among Alternates in Language Standardization: The Case of Albanian.* Contributions to the Sociology of Language 12. The Hague: Mouton, 1976. 158 pp.

Camaj, Martin. *Albanian Grammar with Exercises, Chrestomathy and Glossary.* Wiesbaden, Germany: Harrassowitz, 1984. 337 pp.

Çeliku, Mehmet, Mustafa Karapinjalli, and Ruzhdi Stringa. *Gramatika praktike e gjuhës shqipe* [Practical Grammar of the Albanian Language]. Tirana: Toena, 1998. 496 pp.

Demiraj, Bardhyl. *Albanische Etymologien: Untersuchungen zum albanischen Erbwortschatz* [Albanian Etymologies: Research into the Proto-Vocabulary]. Leiden Studies in Indo-European, 7. Atlanta, Ga.: Rodopi, 1997. 484 pp.

Demiraj, Shaban. *Gramatikë historike e gjuhës shqipe* [Historical Grammar of the Albanian Language]. Tirana: 8 Nëntori, 1986, reprint 1988. 1,168 pp.

———. *Historische Grammatik der albanischen Sprache* [Historical Grammar of the Albanian Language]. Österreichische Akademie der Wissenschaften. Schriften der Balkankommission. Philologische Abteilung 34. Vienna: Verlag der Österreichischen Akademie der Wissenschaften, 1993. 367 pp.

———. *Gramatikë historike e gjuhës shqipe* [Historical Grammar of the Albanian Language]. Botim i përmbledur. Tirana: Akademia e Shkencave e Shqipërisë, 2002. 512 pp.

Elsie, Robert. "The Earliest References to the Existence of the Albanian Language," in: *Zeitschrift für Balkanologie,* Munich, 27, 2 (1991), pp. 101-105.

Gut, Christian, Agnes Brunet-Gut, and Remzi Përnaska. *Parlons albanais* [Let's Speak Albanian]. Paris: L'Harmattan, 1999. 485 pp.

Haebler, Claus. *Grammatik der albanischen Mundart von Salamis* [Grammar of the Albanian Dialect of Salamis]. Albanische Forschungen 3. Wiesbaden, Germany: Harrassowitz, 1965. 178 pp.

Hamp, Eric. *Il sistema fonologico della parlata di Vaccarizzo Albanese. Edizione italiana a cura di Giovanni M. G. Belluscio. Vaccarizzo Albanese Phonology. The Sound System of a Calabro-Albanian Dialect.* [A Thesis Presented by Eric Pratt Hamp to the Department of Linguistics]. Harvard University, Cambridge Mass., June 1954. Studi e testi di albanistica 3. Rende, Italy: Centro Editoriale Librario dell'Università della Calabria, 1993. 440 pp.

Huld, Martin E. *Basic Albanian Etymologies.* Columbus, Ohio: Slavica, 1984. 213 pp.

Kurti, Çezar. *Learn Albanian. Mësoni shqip.* New York: Legas Books, 1996. 200 pp.

Lagji-Hajderi, Klara. *Practical Albanian for English-Speakers, with a Summary of Albanian Grammar.* Tirana: Violette, 2000. 235 pp.

Lambertz, Maximilan. *Lehrgang des Albanischen. Teil I: Albanisch-Deutsches Wörterbuch. Teil II: Albanische Chrestomathie. Teil III:*

Grammatik der albanischen Sprache [Course of Albanian, Part I: Albanian-German Dictionary. Part II: Albanian Chrestomathy, Part III: Grammar of the Albanian Language]. Berlin: Deutscher Verlag der Wissenschaften, 1954, 1955, Halle/Saale, 1959. 228, 251 & 268 pp.

Landi, Addolorata. *Gli elementi latini nella lingua albanese* [The Latin Elements in the Albanian Language]. Pubblicazioni dell'Università degli Studi di Salerno, Sezione di Studi Filologici, Letterari e Artistici, 14. Salerno: Edizioni Scientifiche Italiane, Univ. di Salerno, 1989. 179 pp.

——. *Studi di linguistica albanese* [Studies in Albanian Linguistics]. Pubblicazioni dell'Università degli Studi di Salerno, Sezione di Studi Filologici, Letterari e Artistici, 21. Salerno: Edizioni Scientifiche Italiane, Univ. di Salerno, 1992. 170 pp.

Losha, Mandalina. *Practical Albanian for Foreigners.* s.l., Vernon Publ., 2001. 64 pp.

Mann, Stuart E. *A Short Albanian Grammar: With Vocabularies and Selected Passages for Reading.* London: Nutt-Berry, 1932. 204 pp.

——. *An Albanian Historical Grammar.* Hamburg: Helmut Buske, 1977. 239 pp.

Massey, Victoria Walker. *Compositionality and Constituency in Albanian.* MIT occasional papers in linguistics, No. 3. Cambridge, Mass.: Massachusetts Institute of Technology, 1992. 159 pp.

Messing, Gordon M. "Politics and National Language in Albania," in: *Contributions to Historical Linguistics. Issues and Materials.* Edited by Frans von Coetsem and Linda R. Waugh. Leiden, The Netherlands: E. J. Brill, 1980. pp. 270-280.

Newmark, Leonard. *Structural Grammar of Albanian.* Indiana University Publications. Slavic and East European Series, 8. Bloomington: Indiana University, 1957. vi + 130 pp.

Newmark, Leonard, Ismail Haznedari, Philip Hubbard, and Peter Prifti. *Spoken Albanian.* Ithaca, N.Y.: Spoken Language Services, 1980. 348 pp.

——. *Spoken Albanian: New Edition.* Ithaca, N.Y.: Spoken Language Services, 1980. 522 pp.

Newmark, Leonard, Philip Hubbard, and Peter Prifti. *Standard Albanian: A Reference Grammar for Students.* Stanford, Calif.: Stanford University Press, 1982. 347 pp.

Orel, Vladimir. *A Concise Historical Grammar of the Albanian Language: Reconstruction of Proto-Albanian.* Leiden, The Netherlands: E. J. Brill, 2000. 332 pp.

Pellegrini, Giovan Battista. *Avviamento alla linguistica albanese* [Introduction to Albanian Linguistics]. Edizione rinnovata. Studi e testi di albanistica, 7. Rende, Italy: Centro Editoriale e Libraria dell'Università degli studi della Calabria, 1998. 342 pp.

Pimsleur, Paul. *Albanian: Short Course*. Pimsleur Language Learning Series. Highland Park, Ill.: SyberVision Systems, 1994.

Pipa, Arshi. *The Politics of Language in Socialist Albania*. East European Monographs, 271. New York: Columbia University Press, 1989. 283 pp.

Pipa, Fehime. *Elementary Albanian*. Boston: Vatra, Boston s.a. [ca. 1968]. 415 pp.

Prifti, Peter, and R. Kondi. "The Teaching of Albanian at Columbia University," in: *East European Quarterly*, Boulder, Colo., 34.3 (2000), pp. 381-390.

Ressuli, Namik. *Grammatica albanese* [Albanian Grammar]. Linguistica generale e storica 18. Bologna, Italy: Pàtron, 1985. xlv + 624 pp.

Sasse, Hans-Jürgen. *Arvanitika: die albanischen Sprachreste in Griechenland. Teil 1* [Arvanitika: The Remainders of the Albanian Language in Greece. Part I]. Wiesbaden, Germany: Otto Harrassowitz, 1992. 547 pp.

Schramm, Gottfried. *Anfänge des albanischen Christentums: die frühe Bekehrung der Bessen und ihre langen Folgen* [The Beginnings of Albanian Christianity: The Early Conversion of the Besoi]. Freiburg im Breisgau, Germany: Rombach, 1994. 270 pp.

Svane, Gunnar. *Slavische Lehnwörter im Albanischen* [Slavic Loanwords in Albanian]. Acta Jutlandica 68. Humanistische Reihe 67. Aarhus, Denmark: Aarhus University Press, 1992. 346 pp.

Tagliavini, Carlo. *L'Albanese di Dalmazia: contributi alla conoscenza del dialetto ghego di Borgo Erizzo presso Zara* [The Albanian of Dalmatia: Contributions to our Knowledge of the Gheg Dialect of Borgo Erizzo near Zadar]. Bibliotheca dell'Archivum Romanicum. Serie 11: Linguistica Vol. 22. Florence: Olschki, 1937. 316 pp.

——. *La stratificazione del lessico albanese: elementi indoeuropei* [The Stratification of the Albanian Lexicon: Indo-European Elements]. Bologna, Italy: Patròn, 1943, reprint 1965. 155 pp.

Toma, Ana, Zana Karapici, and Lumnije Radovicka. *Gjuha letrare shqipe: libër mësimi 1-2* [Literary Albanian: A Teaching Course 1-2]. Tirana: Libri Shkollor, 1989. 425 & 138 pp.

Tsitsipis, Lukas D. *A Linguistic Anthropology of Praxis and Language Shift. Arvanítika (Albanian) and Greek in Conflict*. Oxford Studies on Language Contacts. Oxford: Clarendon Press, 1998. 163 pp.

Voronina, Irina, Marina Domosileckaja, and Lubov Sharapova. *E folmja e shqiptarëve të Ukrainës* [The Dialect of the Albanians of the Ukraine]. Skopje, Macedonia: Shkupi, 1996. 203 pp.

Wescott, Roger Williams. *Comparative Grammar of the Albanian Language. Part 1. Phonology.* Doctoral Dissertation Series. Publ. No. 11, 858. Princeton, N.J.: Princeton University, 1948.

Ylli, Xhelal. *Das slavische Lehngut im Albanischen. 1. Teil. Lehnwörter* [Slavic Loan Material in Albanian. Part 1. Loanwords]. Slavistische Beiträge, 350. Munich: Otto Sagner, 1997. 344 pp.

———. *Das slavische Lehngut im Albanischen. 2. Teil. Ortsnamen* [Slavic Loan Material in Albanian. Part 2. Toponyms]. Slavistische Beiträge 395. Munich: Otto Sagner, 2000. 280 pp.

Zymberi, Isa. *Colloquial Albanian.* London: Routledge, 1991, third edition 1995. 359 pp.

2.2 LITERATURE

Augarde, Jacques, Simone Dreyfus, and Edmond Jouve (ed.). *Ismaïl Kadaré, gardien de mémoire* [Ismail Kadare, Guardian of Memory]. Actes du 2e colloque international francophone du Canton de Payrac organisé par l'Association des écrivains de langue française à Payrac (Lot) du 11 au 13 septembre 1992. les Colloques de l'A.D.E.L.F. Volume II. Paris: Sepeg International, 1993. 304 pp.

Autissier, Anne-Marie, Christian Montecot, and Alexandre Zotos (ed.). *Kosovo dans la nuit* [Kosova at Night]. Textes réunis, traduits, présentés par Anne-Marie Autissier, Christiane Montécot et Alexandre Zotos. Préface de Jean-Yves Potel. Paris: Editions de l'Aube, 1999. 121 pp.

Bihiku, Koço. *History of Albanian Literature.* Tirana: 8 Nëntori, 1980. 259 pp.

Brovina, Flora. *Call Me by My Name. Poetry from Kosova in a Bilingual Albanian-English Edition.* Edited, introduced and translated from the Albanian by Robert Elsie. New York: Gjonlekaj, 2001. 165 pp.

Camaj, Martin. *Selected Poetry.* Translated from the Albanian by Leonard Fox. New York University Studies in Near Eastern Civilization XIV. New York: New York University Press, 1990. 220 pp.

———. *Palimpsest.* Translated from the Albanian by Leonard Fox. Biblioteka shqipe 7. Munich: s.e., 1991. 63 pp.

Elsie, Robert. "The Albanian Lexicon of Arnold von Harff, 1497," in: *Zeitschrift für Vergleichende Sprachforschung,* Göttingen, 97, 1 (1984), pp. 113-122.

———. *Dictionary of Albanian Literature.* Westport: Greenwood, 1986. 171 pp.

———. "Modern Albanian Literature," in: *Albanien in Umbruch. Eine Bestandsaufnahme. Untersuchungen zur Gegenswartskunde Südosteuropas.* Schriftleitung Franz-Lothar Altmann, Band 28. Munich: Südost-Institut, 1990. pp. 247-292.

———. Albanian Literature in Greek Script. "The Eighteenth- and Early Nineteenth Century Orthodox Tradition in Albanian Writing," in: *Byzantine and Modern Greek Studies,* Birmingham, 15 (1991), pp. 20-34.

———. "Evolution and Revolution in Modern Albanian Literature," in: *World Literature Today,* Norman, Okla., 65.2 (Spring 1991), pp. 256-263.

———. "The Scutarine Catholic Contribution to the Development of Nineteenth-Century Albanian Literature," in: *Albanian Catholic Bulletin / Buletini Katolik Shqiptar,* San Francisco, 12 (1991), pp. 91-97.

———. "Albanian Literature in English Translation: A Short Survey," in: *The Slavonic and East European Review,* London, 70, 2 (April 1992), pp. 249-257.

———. "Albanian Literature in the Moslem Tradition. Eighteenth and Early Nineteenth Century Albanian Writing in Arabic Script," in: *Oriens, Journal of the International Society for Oriental Research,* Leiden, 33 (1992), pp. 287-306.

———. "Three Poets of the Golden Age of Scutarine Catholic Literature in Albania," in: *Albanian Catholic Bulletin / Buletini Katolik Shqiptar,* San Francisco, 13 (1992), pp. 97-101.

———. "Literature," in: *Südosteuropa-Handbuch VII. Albanien.* ed. K. D. Grothusen, Göttingen, Germany: Vandenhoeck & Ruprecht, 1993, pp. 653-680.

———. "Theatre," in: *Südosteuropa-Handbuch VII. Albanien,* ed. K. D. Grothusen, Göttingen, Germany: Vandenhoeck & Ruprecht, 1993, pp. 681-692.

———. *Anthology of Modern Albanian Poetry. An Elusive Eagle Soars. Edited and Translated with an Introduction by Robert Elsie.* UNESCO Collection of Representative Works. London: Forest Books, 1993. 213 pp.

———. "Benjamin Disraeli and Scanderbeg: The Novel 'The Rise of Iskander' (1833) as a Contribution to Britain's Literary Discovery of Albania," in: *Südost-Forschungen,* Munich, 52 (1993), pp. 25-52.

———. "Gjergj Fishta: The Voice of the Albanian Nation," in: *Albanian Catholic Bulletin / Buletini Katolik Shqiptar,* San Francisco, 14 (1993), pp. 104-113.

———. "The Currents of Moslem and Bektash Writing in Albania," in: *Albanian Catholic Bulletin / Buletini Katolik Shqiptar,* San Francisco, 15 (1994), pp. 172-177.

———. *History of Albanian Literature.* East European Monographs, 379. 2 volumes. Boulder, Colo.: Social Science Monographs. Distributed by Columbia University Press, New York, 1995. xv + 1,054 pp.

———. *Studies in Modern Albanian Literature and Culture.* East European Monographs, CDLV. Boulder, Colo.: East European Monographs. Distributed by Columbia University Press, New York, 1996. 188 pp.

———. *Histori e letërsisë shqiptare* [History of Albanian Literature]. Përktheu nga anglishtja Abdurrahim Myftiu. Tirana: Dukagjini, 1997, reprint 2001. 686 pp.

———. *Kosovo: In the Heart of the Powder Keg.* East European Monographs, CDLXXVIII. Boulder, Colo.: East European Monographs, Boulder. Distributed by Columbia University Press, New York., 1997. vi + 593 pp.

———. "Albanian Literature since the Second World War," in: *Encyclopedia of World Literature in the 20th century,* 3rd Edition, vol. 1: A-D. Steven R. Serafin, general editor. Farmington Hills, Mich.: St. James Press (1999), pp. 35-36.

———. *Who Will Slay the Wolf. Selected Poetry by Ali Podrimja.* Translated from the Albanian with an introduction by Robert Elsie. New York: Gjonlekaj, 2000. 268 pp.

———. *Flora Brovina. Call Me by My Name. Poetry from Kosova in a Bilingual Albanian-English Edition.* Edited, introduced and translated from the Albanian by Robert Elsie. New York: Gjonlekaj, 2001. 165 pp.

———. *Migjeni (Millosh Gjergj Nikolla). Free Verse.* A bilingual edition translated from the Albanian and introduced by Robert Elsie. Dukagjini Balkan Books. Peja, Kosova: Dukagjini, 2001. 143 pp.

———. *Gjergj Fishta. The Highland Lute: The Albanian National Epic. Cantos I-V. The cycle of Oso Kuka.* Translated from the Albanian by Robert Elsie. Dukagjini Balkan Books. Peja, Kosova: Dukagjini, 2003. 167 pp.

Faye, Eric. *Ismaïl Kadare: entretiens avec Eric Faye, en lisant en écrivant* [Ismail Kadare. Conversations with Eric Faye, Reading and Writing]. Paris: José Corti, 1991. 109 pp.

———. *Ismaïl Kadaré: Prométhée porte-feu* [Ismail Kadare: Prometheus, Bearer of Fire]. Paris: José Corti, 1991. 173 pp.

Fishta, Gjergj. *The Highland Lute: The Albanian National Epic. Cantos I-V. The cycle of Oso Kuka.* Translated from the Albanian by Robert Elsie. Dukagjini Balkan Books. Peja, Kosova: Dukagjini, 2003. 167 pp.

Frashëri, Naim bey. *Frasheri's Song of Albania.* Anglicized by Ali
    Cungu. Smithtown, N.Y.: Exposition Press, 1981. 32 pp.
Frashëri, Sami bey. *Pledge of Honor, an Albanian Tragedy by Sami Bey
    Frasheri.* Translated and edited by Nelo Drizari. New York: S. F.
    Vanni, 1945. 118 pp.
Ismajli, Rexhep. *Tekste të vjetra* [Ancient Texts]. Peja, Kosova:
    Dukagjini, 2000. 427 pp.
Koliqi, Ernest. *Saggi di letteratura albanese* [Essays on Albanian Liter-
    ature]. Studi albanesi. Studi i testi 5. Florence: Olschki, 1972.
    260 pp.
Laço, Teodor. *A Lyrical Tale in Winter.* Translated from the Albanian
    by Ronald Taylor. Tirana: 8 Nëntori, 1988. 201 pp.
——. "The Pain of a Distant Winter," in: *Description of a Struggle. The
    Picador Book of Contemporary East European Prose.* Edited by
    Michael March. Translated by Robert Elsie. London: Picador,
    (1994), pp. 267- 273.
Lambertz, Maximilian. *Gjergj Fishta und das albanische Heldenepos
    Lahuta e Malcís, Laute des Hochlandes. Eine Einführung in die
    albanische Sagenwelt* [Gjergj Fishta and the Albanian Heroic Epic
    'The Highland Lute': An Introduction to the World of Albanian
    Myths]. Leipzig, Germany: Harrassowitz, 1949. 76 pp.
Levy, Michele. "Brotherly Wounds. Representations of Balkan Conflict
    in Contemporary Balkan Literature," in: *World Literature Today,*
    Norman, Okla., 75. 1 (Winter 2001), pp. 66-75.
Logoreci, Anton. "Dialogue of Modern Albanian Writing," in: *Books
    Abroad,* Norman, Okla., 30.2 (Spring 1956), pp. 155-159.
Metais, Michel. *Ismail Kadaré et la nouvelle poésie albanaise* [Ismail
    Kadare and Modern Albanian Poetry]. Choix, traduction et
    présentation de Michel Métais. Avant-propos d'Alain Bosquet. Paris:
    Oswald, 1973. 186 pp.
Migjeni (= Nikolla, Millosh Gjergj). *Free Verse.* A bilingual edition
    translated from the Albanian and introduced by Robert Elsie.
    Dukagjini Balkan Books. Peja, Kosova: Dukagjini, 2001. 143 pp.
Mitchell, Anne-Marie. *Un rhapsode albanais: Ismail Kadaré* [An
    Albanian Rhapsodist: Ismail Kadare]. Marseille: Temps parallèle,
    1990. 113 pp.
Kadare, Ismail. *The Wedding.* Rendered into English by Ali Cungu.
    Tirana: Naim Frashëri., 1968, reprint 1972, 1974, 1982. 196 pp.
——. *The General of the Dead Army.* Novel translated from the French
    by Derek Coltman. London: W. H. Allen / New York: Grossman,
    1971, reprint 1983, 1986, 1991.
——. *The Castle: A Novel.* Translated by Pavli Qesku. Tirana: 8 Nëntori,
    1974. 259 pp.

——. *Chronicle in Stone.* Translated from the Albanian. London: Serpent's Tail / New York: Meredith, 1987. 277 pp.

——. *Doruntine: A Novel.* Translated by Jon Rothschild. London: Saqi, 1988. 168 pp.

——. *Broken April.* London: Saqi, 1990. 216 pp.

——. *The Palace of Dreams.* A novel written in Albanian and translated from the French of Jusuf Vrioni by Barbara Bray. New York: William Morrow / London: Harvill, 1993. 205 pp.

——. *Oeuvres, 1-11.* Paris: Fayard, 1993-2002. 575, 635, 511, 592, 645, 782, 652, 635, 668, 692, 666 pp.

——. *Vepra, 1-11.* Parathënie dhe shënime prezantuese nga Eric Faye. Paris: Fayard, 1993-2002. 519, 566, 454, 521, 582, 685, 570, 542, 570, 604, 666 pp.

——. *Albanian Spring. The Anatomy of Tyranny.* London: Saqi, 1994. 240 pp.

——. *The Concert.* A novel written in Albanian and translated from the French of Jusuf Vrioni by Barbara Bray. New York: William Morrow / London: Harvill, 1994, reprint 1998. 444 pp.

——. *The Pyramid.* Translated by David Bellos from the French version of the Albanian by Jusuf Vrioni. London: Harvill / New York: Arcade, 1996. 129 pp.

——. *The File on H.* Translated by David Bellos from the French version of the Albanian by Jusuf Vrioni. London: Harvill, 1997. 171 pp.

——. *The Three-Arched Bridge.* Translated from the Albanian by John Hodgson. London: Harvill,1997. 184 pp.

——. "The Wedding Procession Turned to Ice," in: *Kosovo: In the Heart of the Powder Keg.* Edited by Robert Elsie. Translated from the Albanian by Robert Elsie. East European Monographs, CDLXXVIII. Boulder, Colo.: East European Monographs. Distributed by Columbia University Press, New York, 1997. pp. 105-192.

——. *Three Elegies for Kosovo.* Translated from the Albanian by Peter Constantine. London: Harvill Press, 2000. 87 pp.

——. *Spring Flowers, Spring Frost.* Translated from the French by David Bellows. New York: Arcade, 2002.

Kadare, Ismail, and Noel Malcolm. "In the Palace of Nightmares, an Exchange," in: *New York Review of Books,* New York, 45, 1 (January 15, 1998), pp. 59-60.

Koliqi, Ernest. *The Symphony of Eagles.* Translated and with an introduction by Anesti Andrea. Rome: Shêjzat / Le Pleiadi, 1972. 21 pp.

Konitza, Faik bey. *Albania. The Rock Garden of Southeastern Europe and Other Essays.* Edited and amplified by Gerim M. Panarity, with an introduction by Fan Noli. Boston: Vatra, 1957. 175 pp.

——. *Selected Correspondence 1896-1942*. Edited by Bejtullah Destani. Introduction by Robert Elsie. London: Centre for Albanian Studies, 2000. 185 pp.

Lleshanaku, Luljeta. *Fresko. Selected Poetry of Luljeta Lleshanaku*. Edited with an afterword by Henry Israeli. Introduction by Peter Constantine. Translated, with Henry Israeli and Joanna Goodman, by Ukzenel Buçpapa, Noci Deda, Alban Kupi, Albana Lleshanaku, Lluka Qafoku, Shpresa Qatipi, Qazim Sheme, Daniel Weissbort and the author. New York: New Directions. 80 pp.

Mann, Stuart E. *Albanian Literature. An Outline of Prose, Poetry and Drama*. London: Quaritch, 1955. 121 pp.

March, Michael (ed.). *Description of a Struggle*. The Picador Book of Contemporary East European Prose. London: Picador, 1994. 403 pp.

Nekaj, Zef. "Remembering Gjergj Fishta, the Albanian national poet on the occasion of his 110th anniversary," in: *Albanian Catholic Bulletin,* Santa Clara, Calif. 2 (1981), pp. 73-79.

Petrotta, Gaetano. *Popolo lingua e letteratura albanese* [Albanian People, Language and Literature]. 2a tiratura con aggiunte e correzioni. Palermo, Italy: Tip. Pontificia, 1932. 528 pp.

——. *Svoglimento storico della cultura e della letteratura albanese* [Historical Development of Albanian Literature and Culture]. Palermo, Italy: Boccone del Povero, 1950. 251 pp.

Pipa, Arshi. "Milosao and Its Three Editions," in: *Südost-Forschungen,* Munich, 28 (1969), pp. 182-198.

——. "Panorama of Contemporary Albanian Literature," in: *Zeitschrift für Balkanologie,* Berlin, 7 (1969-1970), pp. 110-117.

——. "Modern and Contemporary Albanian Poetry," in: *Books Abroad,* Norman, Okla., 44.1 (Winter 1970), pp. 51-54.

——. *Albanian Folk Verse, Structure and Genre*. Albanische Forschungen 17. Trilogia Albanica 1. Munich: Dr. Dr. Rudolf Trofenik, 1978. 191 pp.

——. *Hieronymus de Rada*. Albanische Forschungen 18, Trilogia Albanica 2. Munich: Dr. Dr. Rudolf Trofenik, 1978. 319 pp.

——. *Albanian Literature, Social Perspectives*. Albanische Forschungen 19, Trilogia Albanica 3. Munich: Dr. Dr. Rudolf Trofenik, 1978. 292 pp.

——. "Fan Noli as a National and International Figure," in: *Südost-Forschungen,* Munich, 43 (1984), pp. 241-270.

——. "Subversion vs. Conformism: The Kadare Phenomenon," in: *Telos,* 73 (Fall 1987), pp. 47-77.

——. *Contemporary Albanian Literature*. East European Monographs 305. New York: Columbia University Press, 1991. 175 pp.

Podrimja, Ali. *Who will Slay the Wolf. Selected Poetry by Ali Podrimja.* Translated from the Albanian with an introduction by Robert Elsie. New York: Gjonlekaj, 2000. 268 pp.

Podrimja, Ali, and Sabri Hamiti (ed.). *Dega e pikëlluar. Poezi shqipe në Jugosllavi. The Sad Branch. The Albanian Poetry in Yugoslavia.* Edited by Ali Podrimja, Sabri Hamiti. Prishtina, Kosova: Rilindja, 1984. 96 pp.

Pogoni, Bardhyl. *Contemporary Albanian Poems.* Translations and comments by Bardhyl Pogoni. Naples: Dragotti, 1985. 117 pp.

Pynsent, Robert B., and S. I. Kanikova (ed.). *The Everyman Companion to East European Literature.* London: J.M. Dent, 1993. 605 pp.

Raifi, Mensur (ed.). *Roads Lead Only One Way: A Survey of Modern Poetry from Kosova.* Prishtina, Kosova: Kosova Association of Literary Translators, 1988. 235 pp.

——. *The Angry Cloud: An Anthology of Albanian Stories from Yugoslavia.* Translated from the Albanian by John Hodgson. Prishtina, Kosova: Kosova Association of Literary Translators, 1990. 112 pp.

Ruberto, Roberto. "An Albanian Poet from Italy: Girolamo De Rada (1814-1903)," in: *Italian Quarterly,* 10, 38 (Fall 1966), pp. 45-56.

Schirò, Giuseppe. *Storia della letteratura albanese* [History of Albanian Literature]. Florence: Nuova Accademia Editrice, 1959. 267 pp.

Schwartz, Stephen. "Ernest Koliqi: An Appreciation," in: *Albanian Catholic Bulletin,* San Francisco, 13 (1992) pp. 91-94.

——. *Intellectuals and Assassins: Writings at the End of Soviet Communism.* Preface by Roger Kimball. London: Anthem Press, 2000. 188 pp.

Shkreli, Azem: *The Call of the Owl.* Translated from the Albanian by John Hodgson. Prishtina, Kosova: Kosova Association of Literary Translators, 1989. 84 pp.

Terpan, Fabien: *Ismaïl Kadaré.* Encyclopédie Universitaire. Paris: Editions Universitaires, 1992) 176 pp.

Velo, Maks. *Zhdukja e "Pashallarëve të kuq" të Kadaresë: anketim për një krim letrar* [The Disappearance of 'The Red Pashas' by Kadare: Inquiry into a Literary Crime]. Tirana: Onufri, 2002. 156 pp.

Zotos, Alexandre. *De Scanderbeg à Ismail Kadaré: propos d'histoire et de littérature albanaises* [From Scanderbeg to Ismail Kadare: Regarding Albanian History and Literature]. Saint-Etienne, France: Université de Saint-Etienne, 1997. 205 pp.

Zotos, Alexandre (ed.). *Anthologie de la prose albanaise* [Anthology of Albanian Prose]. Présentée par Alexandre Zotos. Textes traduits par Jusuf Vrioni, Alexandre Zotos et Luan Gjergji. Paris: Fayard, 1984. 554 pp.

——. *Anthologie de la poésie albanaise* [Anthology of Albanian Poetry]. Chambéry, France: La Polygraphe, Edition Comp'Act, 1998. 388 pp.

2.3   FOLK CULTURE

Cooper, Paul Fenimore. *Tricks of Women and Other Albanian Tales.* Introduction by Burton Rascoe. New York: Morrow, 1928. 220 pp.

Elsie, Robert. *Albanian Folktales and Legends. Selected and Translated from the Albanian by Robert Elsie.* Dukagjini Balkan Books. Peja, Kosova: Dukagjini, 2001. 240 pp.

——. *A Dictionary of Albanian Religion, Mythology and Folk Culture.* London: C. Hurst, 2001. 357 pp.

——. *Handbuch zur albanischen Volkskultur. Mythologie, Religion, Volksglaube, Sitten, Gebräuche und kulturelle Besonderheiten* [Handbook of Albanian Folk Culture: Mythology, Religion, Popular Beliefs, Customs, Habits and Cultural Particularities]. Balkanologische Veröffentlichungen, Bd. 36. Fachbereich Philosophie und Geisteswissenschaften der Freien Universität Berlin. Wiesbaden, Germany: Harrassowitz, 2002. xi + 308 pp.

Haxhihasani, Qemal, Kolë Luka, Alfred Uçi, and Misto Treska (ed.). *Chansonnier epique albanais* [Albanian epic songs]. Version française Kolë Luka. Avant-propos Ismail Kadare. Tirana: Akademia e Shkencave, 1983. 456 pp.

Kolsti, John. *The Bilingual Singer: A Study of Albanian and Serbo-Croatian Oral Epic Traditions.* Harvard dissertations in folklore and oral traditions. New York: Garland, 1990. 379 pp.

Krasniqi, Mark. *Lugu i Baranit: monografi etnogjeografik* [The Dale of Barani: Ethnogeographic Monograph]. Prishtina, Kosova: Akademia e Shkencave dhe e Arteve të Kosovës, 1985. 202 pp.

——. *Rugova: monografi etnografike* [Rugova: Ethnographic Monograph]. Botime të veçanta. Libri XIV. Seksioni i shkencave shoqërore. Libri 6. Prishtina, Kosova: Akademia e Shkencave dhe e Arteve e Kosovës, 1987. 205 pp.

——. *Aspekte mitologjike: besime e bestytni. Mythological Aspects: Beliefs and Superstitions.* Prishtina, Kosova: Rilindja, 1997. 393 pp.

Lambertz, Maximilian. *Volkspoesie der Albaner, eine einführende Studie* [The Folk Poetry of the Albanians: an Introductory Study]. Zur Kunde der Balkanhalbinsel. II. Quellen und Forschungen 6, Sarajevo. 1917.

——. *Die Volksepik der Albaner* [The Folk Epic of the Albanians]. Halle, Germany: Max Niemeyer, 1958. 184 pp.

Neziri, Zymer. *Epika legjendare e Rugovës, V. Këngë kreshnike dhe balada. Lahutari Haxhi Meta-Nilaj* [The Legendary Epic of Rugova, V. Songs of the Frontier Warriors and Ballads: Singer Haxhi Meta-Nilaj]. Botime të veçanta, Libri 1. Prishtina, Kosova: Instituti Albanologjik, 1997. 400 pp.

Neziri, Zymer (ed.). *Këngë të kreshnikëve* [Songs of the Frontier Warriors]. Prishtina, Kosova: Libri shkollor, 1999. 263 pp.

Palaj, Bernardin. *Mitologji, doke e zakone shqiptare* [Albanian Mythology, Customs and Habits]. Prishtina, Kosova: Shpresa, 2000. 174 pp.

Papleka, Ndoc. *Kulte, rite, magji në traditën orale: studime* [Cults, Rites and Magic in Oral Tradition: Studies]. Tirana: Toena, 1999. 240 pp.

Ruches, Pyrrhus J. *Albanian Historical Folksongs 1716-1943: A Survey of Oral Epic Poetry from Southern Albania with Original Texts Collected and Translated by J. Ruches.* Chicago: Argonaut, 1967. 126 pp.

Sako, Zihni, Qemal Haxhihasani, and Kolë Luka (ed.). *Trésor du chansonnier populaire albanais* [Treasury of Albania Popular Songs]. Tirana: Académie des Sciences, 1975. 332 pp.

Sinani, Shaban. *Mitologji në eposin e kreshnikëve: studim monografik* [Mythology in the Epic of the Songs of the Frontier Warriors: Monographic Study]. Durrës, Albania: Star, 2000. 250 pp.

Skendi, Stavro. *Albanian and South Slavic Oral Epic Poetry.* Memoirs of the American Folklore Society, vol. 44 (1954). Philadelphia: American Folklore Society, 1954, reprint 1969. 221 pp.

Wheeler, Post. *Albanian Wonder Tales.* With illustrations by Maud and Miska Petersham. London: Lovat Dickenson, 1936. 255 pp.

Zheji, Gjergj. *Folklori shqiptar* [Albanian Folklore]. Tirana: Libri universitar, 1998. 244 pp.

2.4 ART AND ARCHITECTURE

Bužančić, V., Sh. Nimani, R. Goçi, M. Ferizi (ed.). *Arti bashkëkohor i Kosovës. Savremena umetnost Kosova. Contemporary Kosovian Art. Piktura, skulptura, grafika, arti aplikativ. Slikarstvo, skulptura, grafika, primenjena umetnost. Painting, sculpture, the graphic art, applied art.* Prishtina, Kosova: Galeria i Arteve, 1988. 231 pp.

Frashëri, Gjergj. "Realist Painting and Sculpture in Albania," in: *Münchner Zeitschrift für Balkankunde,* Munich, 9 (1993), pp.155-197.

Hudhri, Ferid. *Studime mbi artin* [Studies on Art]. Tirana: Qendra e studimit të arteve, 1996. 141 pp.

——. *Arti i Rilindjes shqiptare* [Art of the Albanian Rilindja Period]. Tirana: Onufri, 2001.

Kiel, Machiel. *Ottoman Architecture in Albania (1385-1912)*. Istanbul, Turkey: Research Centre for Islamic History, Art and Culture of the Organization of the Islamic Conference, 1990. 342 pp.

Koch, Guntram. *Albanien: Kunst und Kultur im Land der Skipetaren* [Albania: Art and Culture in the Land of the Albanians]. Cologne, Germany: DuMont, 1989. 335 pp.

Meksi, Aleksandër. *Arkitektura mesjetare në Shqipëri (shek. VII-XV)* [Medieval Architecture in Albania (VII-XV cent.)]. Tirana: 8 Nëntori, 1983. 240 pp.

Nimani, Shyqri. *Onufri dhe piktorë të tjerë mesjetarë shqiptarë* [Onufri and Other Medieval Albanian Painters]. Prishtina, Kosova: Rilindja, Prishtinë 1987. 127 pp.

Öhrig, Bruno (ed.). *Ikonen aus Albanien: Sakrale Kunst des 14. bis 19. Jahrhunderts. Katalog zu den Ikonen-Sälen der Ausstellung Albanien —Reichtum und Vielfalt alter Kultur. August 2001 bis Januar 2002* [Icons from Albania: Religious Art from the 14th to 19th Centuries. Catalog for the Icon Hall of the Exhibition 'Albania: Wealth and Diversity of an Ancient Culture']. Munich: Staatliches Museum für Völkerkunde, 2001. 97 pp.

Riza, Emin. *Qyteti dhe banesa shqiptare e mesjetës së vonë (shek. XV - mesi i shek. XIX)* [The Albanian City and Buildings of the Late Medieval Period (XV–mid-XIX centuries)]. Tirana: Akademia e Shkencave, 1991. 299 pp.

Strazimiri, Burhan, Hasan Nallbani, and Neritan Ceka (ed.). *Monumente të arkitekturës në Shqipëri* [Monuments of Architecture in Albania]. Tirana: Instituti i Monumenteve të Kultures, 1973. 162 pp.

Trésors d'art albanais: icônes byzantines et post-byzantines du XIIe au XIXe siècles [Treasures of Albanian Art: Byzantine and Post-Byzantine Icons from the 12th to 19th centuries]. (Musée National Message Biblique Marc Chagall, Nice 1993). 140 pp.

Zojzi, Rrok, Abaz Dojaka, and Hasan Qatipi (ed.). *Arti popullor në Shqipëri* [Folk Art in Albania]. Tirana: Akademia e Shkencave, 1976. 156 pp.

2.5   MUSIC

Emerson, June. *Albania: The Search for the Eagle's Song*. Studley, England: Brewin Books, 1990. 96 pp.

——. *The Music of Albania*. Ampleforth: Emerson Edition, 1994. 78 pp.

Hoerburger, Felix. *Valle Popullore: Tanz und Tanzmusik der Albaner in Kosovo und in Mazedonien* [Folk Dance: Dance and Dance Music of the Albanians of Kosova and Macedonia]. Frankfurt am Main: Peter Lang, 1994. 286 pp.

Johnson, Kirsten Renee. *A Survey of Albanian Piano Literature (1945-1996). Folk Music, Classical Music, Tonin Harapi, Feim Ibrahimi, Çesk Zadeja*. DMA thesis. Kansas City: University of Missouri, 1997. 211 pp.

Kruta, Beniamin. *Polifonia dyzërëshe e Shqipërisë jugore: tipologjia* [The Two-Voiced Polyphony of Southern Albania: Typology]. Tirana: Akademia e Shkencave, 1989. 360 pp.

Leotsakos, George, and Jane C. Sugarman. "Albania," in: *The New Grove Dictionary of Music and Musicians,* vol. 1. Edited by Stanley Sadie. London: Grove 2001. pp. 282-289.

Pettan, Svanibor Hubert. *Gypsy Music in Kosovo: Interaction and Creativity (Yugoslavia, Repertoire Development).* Dissertation. Baltimore: University of Maryland, 1992. 327 pp.

Pllana, Shevqet. "Albanian Wedding Songs of Kosovo," in: *Balcanica,* 18-19. Institut des Etudes Balkaniques. Académie Serbe des Sciences et des Arts, Belgrade (1987-1988), 337-375.

Royle, Nicholas. *Saxophone Dreams.* London: Penguin Books, 1996.

Shituni, Spiro. *Polifonia labe* [Laberian Polyphony]. Tirana: Akademia e Shkencave, 1989. 364 pp.

Shituni, Spiro, Ferial Daja, and Natasha Pano (ed.). *Këngë e melodi nga festivalet folklorike kombëtare (1968 - 1973 - 1978)* [Songs and Melodies from the National Folklore Festivals (1968 - 1973 - 1978). Tirana: Akademia e Shkencave, 1986. 432 pp.

Shituni, Spiro, and Agron Xhagolli (ed.). *Këngë polifonike labe* [Laberian Polyphonic Songs]. Tirana: Akademia e Shkencave, 1986. 636 pp.

Shupo, Sokol. *Folklori muzikor shqiptar* [Albanian Music Folklore]. Tirana: Enciklopedike, 1997. 556 pp.

——. *Enciklopedia e muzikës shqiptare.* Tirana: Asmus, 2002. 318 pp.

Sokoli, Ramadan Isuf. *Folklori muzikor shqiptar: morfologjia* [Albanian Music Folklore: Morphology]. Tirana: Instituti i Folklorit, 1965. 283 pp.

——. *Gjurmime folklorike* [Folklore Research]. Tirana: Naim Frashëri, 1981. 428 pp.

Sokoli, Ramadan, and Pirro Miso. *Veglat muzikore të artit shqiptar* [The Musical Instruments of Albanian Art]. Tirana: Akademia e Shkencave e RP e Shqipërisë, 1991. 324 pp.

Stockmann, Doris, and Erich Stockmann. "Albania," in: *The New Grove Dictionary of Music and Musicians,* vol. 1 (A to Bacilly), fifth edition. Edited by Stanley Sadie. London: Macmillan, 1980. pp. 197-202.

Stockmann, Doris, Wilfried Fiedler, and Erich Stockmann. *Albanische Volksmusik. Band 1. Gesänge der Çamen* [Albanian Folk Music. Volume 1. Songs of the Chams]. Deutsche Akademie der Wissenschaften zu Berlin. Veröffentlichungen des Instituts für Deutsche Volkskunde, Band 36. Berlin: Akademie-Verlag, 1965. 302 pp.

Sugarman, Jane C. *Engendering Song: Singing and Subjectivity at Prespa Albanian Weddings.* Chicago: University of Chicago Press, 1997. 395 pp.

Traerup, Birthe. "Albanian Singers in Kosovo: Notes on the Song Repertoire of a Mohammedan Country Wedding in Yugoslavia," in: *Studia Instrumentorum Musicae Popularis.* Edited by G. Hillestrom. Stockholm: Nordiska Musikoforlaget, 1974. pp. 244-251, 300.

Xhaçka, Gjergj. *Historia e muzikës shqiptare* [History of Albanian Music]. Ribotim. 2 vol. Tirana: Libri universitar, 1990. 270 & 162 pp.

2.6 THEATER

Böhm, Hans (ed.). *Moissi: der Mensch und der Künstler in Worten und Bildern* [Moissi: The Man and the Artist in Words and Pictures]. Zusammengestellt von Hans Böhm. Mit 40 Beiträgen von namhaften Persönlichkeiten der internationalen Kunstwelt, drei kleinen Aufsätzen von Alexander Moissi, Zeichnungen von Emil Orlik, Hendrik Lund und Kapralik, und 104 photographischen Abbildungen. Berlin: Eigenbrödler, 1927. 98 pp.

Elsie, Robert. "Theatre," in: *Südosteuropa-Handbuch VII. Albanien.* ed. K. D. Grothusen. Göttingen, Germany: Vandenhoeck & Ruprecht, 1993. pp. 681-692.

Hoxha, Ismail. *Nga jeta në teatër, nga teatri në jetë: artikuj e studime kritike* [On Life in the Theater, on Theater in Life: Articles and Critical Studies]. Tirana: Naim Frashëri, 1983. 284 pp.

Moisiu, Vangjel (=Moïssi, Vangjel). *Aleksandër Moïssi.* Published with the assistance of UNESCO. Vendôme, France: National Commission of the People's Socialist Republic of Albania for UNESCO, 1979. 141 pp.

Moisiu, Vangjel, Esat Oktrova, Todi Thanasi. *Alexander Moissi.* Tirana: Verlag 8 Nëntori, 1981.

Oktrova-Demiraj, Mirela. *Teatri si alternativë* [The Theater as an Alternative]. Peja, Kosova: Dukagjini, 2000. 262 pp.

Papagjoni, Josif. "Albania," in: *The World Encyclopedia of Contemporary Theatre. Volume 1 Europe.* Edited by Don Rubin. London: Routledge, 1994,. pp. 35-44.

Shita, Vehap. *Skena shqipe* [the Albanian Stage]. Prishtina, Kosova: Jeta e re, 1964. 125 pp.

——. *Kur ndizen dritat: vështrime e kritika të teatrit* [When the Lights go on: Observations and Criticism on Theater]. Prishtina, Kosova: Rilindja, 1977. 347 pp.

Shita, Vehap, and Hasan Mekuli (ed.). *Drama shqipe: përmbledhje pjesësh teatrale të shkrimtarëve bashkëkohore shqiptare të Jugosllavisë* [Albanian Drama: Collection of Plays by the Contemporary Albanian Writers of Yugoslavia]. Belgrade, Yugoslavia: Enti i botimeve, 1966.

Zotos, Alexandre. "Le théâtre en Albanie," in: Dictionnaire encyclopédique du théâtre. Edited by Michel Corvin. Paris: Bordas, 1991. pp. 21-22.

2.7 FILM

Hoxha, Abaz T. *Filmi artistik shqiptar 1957-1984: filmografi* [Albanian Feature Films 1957-1984. Filmography]. Tirana: 8 Nëntori, 1987. 368 pp.

——. *Enciklopedi e kinematografës shqiptare* [Encyclopedia of Albanian cinematography]. Tirana: Toena, 2002. 550 pp.

Kinostudoja. *Filmi shqiptar Kinostudioja "Shqipëria e Re"* [Albanian Film. "New Albania" Film Studio]. Tirana: 8 Nëntori, 1977. 223 pp.

Velça, Kudret, and Gjergj Zheji (ed.). *Historia e teatrit shqiptar. 1-3* [History of Albanian Theater, 1-3]. Tirana: Librit shkollor, 1984, 1984, 1985. 190, 236 & 172 pp.

3. HISTORY

3.1 GENERAL

Bartl, Peter. *Albanien: vom Mittelalter bis zur Gegenwart* [Albania: from the Middle Ages to the Present]. Südosteuropa-Gesellschaft. Regensburg, Germany: Friedrich Pustet, 1995. 304 pp.

Biagini, Antonello. *Storia dell'Albania: dalle origini ai giorni nostri* [History of Albania: From the Origins to the Present Day]. Milan: Bompiani, 1999. 174 pp.

Castellan, Georges. *Histoire des Balkans (XIVe-XXe siècle)* [History of the Balkans (XIV-XX centuries]. Paris: Fayard, 1991. 532 pp.

——. *History of the Balkans: From Mohammed the Conqueror to Stalin.* Translated from the French by Nicholas Bradley. East European Monographs, CCCXXV. Boulder, Colo.: East European Monographs, 1992. 493 pp.

——. *Histoire de l'Albanie et des Albanais* [History of Albania and the Albanians]. Crozon, France: Editions Armeline, 2002. 204 pp.

Chekrezi, Constantine Anastasi (= Çekrezi, Kostantin). *Albania Past and Present.* New York: Macmillan, 1919, reprint 1971. 255 pp.

Destani, Bejtullah D. (ed.). *Albania & Kosovo: Political and Ethnic Boundaries, 1867-1946. Documents and Maps.* Farnham Common, Slough, England: Archive Editions, 1999. 1,100 pp.

Faveyrial, Jean-Claude. *Histoire de l'Albanie* [History of Albania]. Edition établie et présentée par Robert Elsie. Dukagjini Balkan Books. Peja, Kosova: Dukagjini, 2001. xviii + 426 pp.

Jacques, Edwin E. *The Albanians. An Ethnic History from Prehistoric Times to the Present.* Jefferson, N.C.: McFarland, 1995. 768 pp.

Jelavich, Barbara. *History of the Balkans.* 2 vol. Cambridge: Cambridge University Press, 1983. 416 & 476 pp.

Kondis, Basil. *Greece and Albania 1908-1914.* Institute for Balkan Studies 167. Thessalonika, Greece: Institute for Balkan Studies, 1976. 147 pp.

Myzyri, Hysni (ed.). *Historia e popullit shqiptar për shkollat e mesme* [History of the Albanian People for Secondary Schools]. Tirana: Libri shkollor, 1994. 263 pp.

Pavlowitsch, Stevan K. *A History of the Balkans, 1804-1945.* London: Longman, 1999. 375 pp.

Pollo, Stefanaq, and Arben Puto (ed.). *Histoire de l'Albanie des origines à nos jours* [History of Albania from Its Origins to the Present Day]. Roanne, France: Horvath, 1974. 372 pp.

——. *The History of Albania from Its Origins to the Present Day.* With the collaboration of Kristo Frashëri and Skënder Anamali. Translated from the French by Carol Wiseman, Ginnie Hole. London: Routledge & Kegan Paul, 1981. 322 pp.

Ristelhueber, René. *A History of the Balkan Peoples.* New York: Twayne, 1950. xviii + 470 pp.

Schevill, Ferdinand. *A History of the Balkans: From the Earliest Times to the Present Day.* New York: Dorset Press, 1991. viii + 558 pp.

Stavrianos, Leften Stavros. *The Balkans since 1953.* New York: Rinehart, 1958, reprint 2000. 970 pp.

Sugar, Peter F. *Southeastern Europe under Ottoman Rule, 1354-1804.* History of East Central Europe 5. Seattle, Wash.: University of Washington Press, 1977. 384 pp.

Thëngjilli, Petrika. *Historia e popullit shqiptar, 395-1875* [History of the Albanian People, 395-1875]. Tirana: Shtëpia Botuese e Librit Universitar, 1999. 453 pp.

Thunmann, Johann Erich. *Über die Geschichte und Sprache der Albaner und der Wlachen* [On the History and Language of the Albanians and Vlachs]. Nachdruck der Ausgabe von 1774 herausgegeben und mit einer Einleitung versehen von Harald Haarmann. Romanistik in Geschichte und Gegenwart Bd. 4. Hamburg: Helmut Buske, 1976.

Valentini, Giuseppe. *Acta Albaniae Veneta* [Venetian Documents on Albania]. Vol. 1-24. Palermo, Milan, Munich, 1967-1977.

——. *Acta Albaniae Juridica* [Legal Documents on Albania]. *Quinto vertente saeculo a Georgii Castriotae Scanderbegii patriae christianaeque libertatis necnon antiquorum gentis suae morum propugnatoris invicti morte.* Beiträge zur Kenntnis Südosteuropas und des Nahen Orients, 6. 2 vol. Munich: Trofenik, 1968, 1973. 268, 244 pp.

Vickers, Miranda. *Albania: A Modern History.* London: I. B. Tauris, 1994. 262 pp.

Winnifrith, Tom. *Badlands—Borderlands: A History of Southern Albania / Northern Epirus.* London: Duckworth, 2002.

3.2 ARCHEOLOGY, PREHISTORY AND ANCIENT HISTORY

Boardmann, J., I. E. S. Edwards, N. G. L. Hammond, and E. Sollberger (ed.). *The Prehistory of the Balkans; and the Middle East and the Aegean World. Tenth to Eighth Centuries BC.* Cambridge Ancient History, 2nd Edition, vol. III, pt. 1. Cambridge: Cambridge University Press, 1982.

Cabanes, Pierre. *Les Illyriens de Bardylis à Genthios (IVe-IIe siècles avant J.C.)* [The Illyrians from Bardylis to Genthios [IV-II centuries B.C.]. Paris: Sedes, 1988. 342 pp.

Ceka, Hasan. *Në kërkim të historisë ilire* [In Search of Illyrian History]. Tirana: Akdemia e Shkencave, 1998. 326 pp.

Ceka, Neritan. *Ilirët* [The Illyrians]. Tirana: Shtëpia Botuese e Librit Universitar, 2000. 334 pp.

Ceka, Neritan, and Muzafer Korkuti. *Arkeologjia: Greqia, Roma, Iliria* [Archeology: Greece, Rome, Illyria]. Tirana: Soros, 1993, reprint 1998. 423 pp.

Frashëri, Mehdi bey. *Historia e lashtë e Shqipërisë dhe e Shqiptarëve* [Ancient History of Albania and the Albanians]. Tirana: Phoenix, 2000. 337 pp.

Hammond, Nichol Geoffrey Lamprière. *Epirus: The Geography, the Ancient Remains, the History and the Topography of Epirus and the Adjacent Areas.* Oxford: Clarendon, 1967. 847 pp.

Islami, Selim, Skender Anamali, Muzafer Korkuti, and Frano Prendi. *Les Illyriens: aperçu historique* [The Illyrians, an Historical Overview]. Tirana: Académie des Sciences, 1985. 272 pp.

Korkuti, Muzafer. *Shqipëria arkeologjike* [Archeological Albania]. Tirana: Instituti i historisë dhe i gjuhësisë, 1971. xi + 139 pp.

——. *Neolithikum und Chalkolithikum in Albanien* [The Neolithic and Chalcolithic Periods in Albania]. Heidelberger Akademie der Wissenschaften. Internationale Interakademische Kommission für die Erforschung der Vorgeschichte des Balkans. Monographien Bd. IV. Herausgeber Harald Hauptmann. Mainz, Germany: Philipp von Zabern, 1995. 281 pp.

Korkuti, Muzafer, Skënder Anamali, and Jorgji Gjinari (ed.). *Les Illyriens et la genèse des Albanais* [The Illyrians and the Genesis of the Albanians]. Travaux de la session du 3-4 mars 1969. Tirana: Université de Tirana, 1971. 253 pp.

Korkuti, Muzafer, and Karl M. Petruso. "Archaeology in Albania," in: *American Journal of Archaeology,* 97, 4 (1993), pp. 703-743.

Myrto, Halil. *Albania archeologica: bibliografia sistematica dei centri antichi* [Archeological Albania: Systematic Bibliography of the Ancient Centers]. Bari, Italy: Edipuglia, 1998. 144 pp.

Oost, Stewart I. *Roman policy in Epirus and Acarnania in the Age of the Roman Conquest of Greece.* New York: Ayer, 1975.

Papazoglu, Fanula (= Papazoglou, Fanoula). *Central Balkan Tribes in Pre-Roman Times. Triballi, Autariatae, Dardanians, Scordisci and Moesians.* Translated by Mary Stanfield-Popović. Amsterdam: Adolf M. Hakkert, 1978. 664 pp.

Shukriu, Edi. *Dardania paraurbane: studime arkeologjike të Kosovës* [Pre-urban Dardania: Archeological Studies of Kosova]. Peja, Kosova: Dukagjini, 1996. 242 pp.

Stipčević, Aleksandar. *The Illyrians: History and Culture.* Translated from Serbo-Croatian by S. Burton. Park Bridge, N.J.: Noyes Press, 1977. 291 pp.

Ugolini, Luigi M. *Albania antica. Vol.1* [Ancient Albania. Vol. I]. Ricerche archeologiche pubblicato sotto gli auspici della R. Societa

Geografica Italiana. Rome: Società Editrice d'Arte Illustrata, 1927. 225 pp.

——. *L'antica Albania nelle ricerche archeologiche italiane* [Ancient Albania in Italian Archeological Research]. Rome: Ente Nazionale Industria Turistiche, 1928, reprint 1931. 96 pp.

——. *Albania antica. vol. II. L'Acropoli di Fenice* [Ancient Albania, Vol. II. The Acropolis of Phoinike]. Milan: Treves-Treccani-Tuminelli, 1933. 250 pp.

——. *Butrinto. Il mito d'Enea. Gli Scavi* [Butrint. The Myth of Aeneas. The Excavations]. Rome: Istituto Grafico Tiberino, 1937 (reprint Tirana 1999). 203 pp.

——. *Albania antica. L'acropoli di Butrinto* [Ancient Albania. The Acropolis of Butrint]. Rome, 1942.

Wilkes, John. *The Illyrians.* Oxford: Blackwell, 1992. 351 pp.

3.3 PRE-TWENTIETH CENTURY

Baggally, John Wortley. *Ali Pasha and Great Britain.* Oxford: Blackwell, 1938. 95 pp.

Bartl, Peter. *Die albanischen Muslime zur Zeit des nationalen Unabhängigkeitsbewegung 1878-1912* [The Albanian Muslims at the Time of the National Independence Movement 1878-1912]. Albanische Forschungen 8. Wiesbaden, Germany: Harrassowitz, 1968. 207 pp.

——. *Der Westbalkan zwischen spanischer Monarchie und osmanischem Reich. Zur Türkenproblematik an der Wende vom 16. zum 17. Jahrhundert* [The Western Balkans between the Spanish Monarchy and the Ottoman Empire. On the Turkish Problem at the Turn of the 16th to 17th Centuries]. Albanische Forschungen 14. Wiesbaden, Germany: Harrassowitz, 1974. 258 pp.

——. *Quellen und Materialien zur albanischen Geschichte im 17. und 18. Jahrhundert* [Sources and Material on Albanian History in the 17th and 18th Centuries]. 2 Vol. Albanische Forschungen 15 & 20. Wiesbaden, Germany: Harrassowitz, 1975 / Munich: Trofenik, 1979. 135 & 257 pp.

Baxhaku, Fatos, and Karl Kaser. *Die Stammesgesellschaften Nordalbaniens. Berichte und Forschungen österreichischer Konsuln und Gelehrter (1861-1917)* [The Tribal Societies of Northern Albania. Reports and Research by Austrian Consuls and Scholars (1861-1917)]. Vienna: Böhlau, 1996. 459 pp.

Christowe, Stoyan. *The Lion of Janina: A Narrative Based on the Life of Ali Pasha, Despot of Epirus.* New York: Modern Age Books, 1941. 424 pp.

Dankoff, Robert, and Robert Elsie. *Evliya Çelebi in Albania and Adjacent Regions (Kosovo, Montenegro, Ohrid). The Relevant Sections of the Seyahatname edited with Translation, Commentary and Introduction by Robert Dankoff and Robert Elsie.* Evliya Çelebi's Book of Travels. Land and People of the Ottoman Empire in the Seventeenth Century. A Corpus of Partial Editions, vol. 5. Edited by Klaus Kreiser. Leiden, The Netherlands: E. J. Brill, 2000. 307 pp.

Drizari, Nelo. *Scanderbeg: His Life, Correspondence, Orations, Victories and Philosophy.* Palo Alto, Calif.: National Press, 1968. 102 pp.

Ducellier, Alain. *La Façade maritime de l'Albanie au moyen age: Durazzo et Valona du XIe au XVe siècle* [The Coastline of Albania in the Middle Ages: Durrës and Vlora from the 11th to the 15th Centuries]. Thessalonika, Greece: Institute for Balkan Studies, 1981. 701 pp.

——. *L'Albanie entre Byzance et Venise, Xe-XVe siècles* [Albania between Byzantium and Venice. 10th-15th Centuries]. London: Variorum reprints, 1987. xii + 334 pp.

Ducellier, Alain, Bernard Doumerc, Brunehilde Imhaus, Jean De Miceli. *Les Chemins de l'exile: bouleversements de l'est européen et migrations vers l'ouest à la fin du moyen âge* [The Paths of Exile: Upheaval in Eastern Europe and Migration to the West at the End of the Middle Ages]. Paris: Armand Colin, 1992. 461 pp.

Elsie, Robert. "Benjamin Disraeli and Scanderbeg: The Novel 'The Rise of Iskander' (1833) as a Contribution to Britain's Literary Discovery of Albania," in: *Südost-Forschungen,* Munich, 52 (1993), pp. 25-52.

Faensen, Johannes. *Die albanische Nationalbewegung* [The Albanian National Movement]. Osteuropa-Institut an der Freien Universität Berlin. Balkanologische Veröffentlichungen 4. Berlin: in Kommission Harrassowitz, Wiesbaden, 1980. 195 pp.

Fine, John Van Antwerp. *The Early Medieval Balkans: A Critical Survey from the Sixth to the Late Twelfth Century.* Ann Arbor: University of Michigan Press, 1983.

——. *The Late Medieval Balkans: A Critical Survey from the Late 12th Century up to the Ottoman Conquest.* Ann Arbor: University of Michigan Press, 1987, reprint 1990. 699 pp.

Fleming, Katherine Elizabeth. *The Muslim Bonaparte: Diplomacy and Orientalism in Ali Pasha's Greece.* Princeton, N.J.: Princeton University Press, 1999. xii + 206 pp.

Gegaj, Athanase. *L'Albanie et l'invasion turque au XVe siècle* [Albania and the Turkish Invasion of the 15th Century]. Louvain, Belgium: Geuthner, 1937. 169 pp.

Gjini, Gasper. *The Shkup-Prizren Diocese through Centuries*. Translated by Avni Spahiu. Prizren, Kosova: Drita, 1999. ca. 280 pp.

Hodgkinson, Harry. *Scanderbeg*. Edited by Bejtullah Destani and Woodrow Cooper. With an introduction by David Abulafia. London: Centré for Albanian Studies, 1999. 250 pp.

Imhaus, Brunehilde. *Le minoranze orientali a Venezia 1300-1510* [Oriental Minorities in Venice 1300-1510]. Rome: Il Veltro Editrice, 1997. 588 pp.

Miller, William. *The Ottoman Empire and Its Successors, 1801-1927, with an Appendix, 1927-1936*. Cambridge: Cambridge University Press, 1936. 644 pp.

——. *Essays on the Latin Orient*. Amsterdam: Adolf M. Hakkert, 1964, reprint 1981. 582 pp.

Nicol, Donald MacGillivray. *The Despotate of Epirus*. Oxford: Blackwell, 1957.

——. *The Despotate of Epiros, 1267-1479*. Cambridge: Cambridge University Press, 1984. 297 pp.

Noli, Fan Stilian. *George Castrioti Scanderbeg (1405-1468)*. New York: International Universities Press, 1947. 240 pp.

Peyfuss, Max Demeter. *Die Druckerei von Moschopolis 1731-1769: Buchdruck und Heiligenverehrung im Erzbistum Achrida* [The Printing House of Moschopolis 1731-1769: Book Printing and the Adoration of Saints in the Archdiocese of Ochrid]. 2. verbesserte Auflage. Wiener Archiv für Geschichte des Slawentums und Osteuropas. Veröffentlichungen des Instituts für Ost- und Südosteuropaforschung, Bd XIII. Vienna: Böhlau, 1996. 258 pp.

Plomer, William Charles Franklyn. *Ali the Lion: Ali of Tebeleni, Pasha of Janina 1741-1822*. London: Jonathan Cape, 1936. 288 pp.

——. *The Diamond of Jannina: Ali Pasha 1741-1822*. London: Jonathan Cape, 1970. 288 pp.

Rizaj, Skënder. *Dokumente angleze mbi lidhjen shqiptare të Prizrenit dhe fillimin e copëtimit të Ballkanit (1877-1885). English documents on the Albanian League of Prizren and the start of the disintegration of the Balkans (1877-1885)*. 2 vol. Prishtina, Kosova: Rilindja, 1996. 285 + 423 pp.

Roche Guilhem, Mademoiselle de la. *The Great Scanderbeg*. A Novel done out of French. London: R. Bentley, 1690. 142 pp.

Schmitt, Oliver Jens. *Das venezianische Albanien (1392-1479)* [Venetian Albania (1392-1479)]. Südosteuropäische Arbeiten, 110. Munich: Oldenbourg Verlag, 2001. 701 pp.

Shkodra, Zija. *La ville albanaise au cours de la renaissance nationale (1831-1912)* [The Albanian Town during the National Awakening (1831-1912)]. Tirana: Académie des Sciences, 1988. 202 pp.

Skendi, Stavro. *Albanian National Awakening (1878-1912)*. Princeton, N.J.: Princeton University Press, 1967. 498 pp.

Stadtmüller, Georg. *Forschungen zur albanischen Frühgeschichte* [Research into Early Albanian History]. Zweite erweiterte Auflage. Albanische Forschungen 2. Wiesbaden, Germany: Harrassowitz, 1966. 221 pp.

Šufflay, Milan von. *Städte und Burgen Albaniens hauptsächlich während des Mittelalters* [The Towns and Fortresses of Albania, Primarily during the Middle Ages]. Denkschriften der Akademie der Wissenschaften in Wien. Philos.-hist. Kl. 63,1. Vienna: Hölder Pichler Tempsky, 1924. 81 pp.

Sula, Abdul B. *Albania's Struggle for Independence*. Posthumous work by Abdul B. Sula. Former royal minister of Albania to Egypt. New York: Family Sula, 1967. xiv + 112 pp.

Sultana, Donald. *Benjamin Disraeli in Spain, Malta and Albania 1830-1832: A Monograph*. London: Tamesis, 1976. 78 pp.

Tërnava, Muhamet. *Popullsia e Kosovës gjatë shekujve XIV-XVI* [The Population of Kosova during the XIV-XVI Centuries]. Prishtina, Kosova: Instituti Albanologjik, 1995. 491 pp.

——. *Studime për mesjetën* [Studies on the Middle Ages]. Peja, Kosova: Dukagjini, 2000. 280 pp.

Thallóczy, Ludwig von (ed.). *Illyrisch-Albanische Forschungen* [Illyrian-Albanian Research]. 2 vol. Munich: Duncker & Humblot, 1916. 565 & 310 pp.

Thallóczy, Ludovicus de, Constantinus Jireček, and Emilianus de Šufflay. *Acta et diplomata res Albaniae mediae aetatis illustrantia*. *1-2*. Vienna: Adolf Holzhausen, 1913, 1918. xxxviii + 292 pp. & xxiii + 301 pp.

Treptow, Kurt William. *Of Saints and Sinners: Native Resistance to Ottoman Expansion in Southeastern Europe, 1443-1481. George Castriota Scanderbeg and Vlad III Dracula (Albania, Romania)*. Ph.D. Dissertation. University of Illinois at Urbana-Champaign, 1995, 380 pp.

Ushtelenca, Ilir. *Diplomacia e Ali Pashë Tepelenës (1786-1822)* [The Diplomacy of Ali Pasha Tepelena (1786-1822). Ribotim. Tirana: s.e., 1996. 284 pp.

Zachariadou, Elizabeth A. (ed.). *The Via Egnatia under Ottoman Rule (1380-1699)*. Halcyon Days in Greece II. A symposium held in Rethymnon 9-11 January 1994. Rethymnon, Greece: Crete University Press, 1996. 232 pp.

Zamputi, Injac (ed.). *Relacione mbi gjendjen e Shqipërisë veriore e të mesme në shekullin XVII Teksti origjinal dhe përkthimi nga Injac Zamputi. Burime dhe materiale për historinë e Shqipërisë, 3. Vëllimi I (1610-1634), Vëllimi II (1634-1650)* [Reports on the State of Northern and Central Albania in the Seventeenth Century. Original Texts and Translations by Injac Zamputi. Sources and Material on the History of Albania, 3. Volume I (1610-1634), Volume II (1634-1650)]. Tirana: Universiteti shtetëror i Tiranës, 1963, 1965. 540 & 525 pp.

———. *Dokumenta të shekullit XV për historinë e Shqipërisë Vol. 4. 1479-1506. Pjesa e parë 1479-1499* [Fifteenth-Century Documents on the History of Albania. Vol. 4, 1479-1506. Part One, 1479-1499]. Tirana: Universitetit Shtetëror i Tiranës, 1967. 311 pp.

———. *Dokumente për historinë e Shqipërisë 1479-1506. Pjesa e dytë* [Documents on the History of Albania 1479-1506. Part Two]. Tirana: Akademia e Shkencave, 1979.

———. *Dokumente për historinë e Shqipërisë të shek. XV. I (1400-1405)* [Documents on the History of Albania in the 15th Century. I (1400-1405)]. Tirana: Akademia e Shkencave, 1987. 712 pp.

———. *Dokumente të shekujve XVI-XVII për historinë e Shqipërisë. Vëllimi 1 (1507-1592)* [Sixteenth and Seventeenth-Century Documents on the History of Albania. Volume 1 (1507-1592). Tirana: Akademia e Shkencave, 1989. 492 pp.

———. *Dokumente të shekujve XVI-XVII për historinë e Shqipërisë. Vëllimi 3 (1603-1621)* [Sixteenth and Seventeenth-Century Documents on the History of Albania. Volume 3 (1603-1621)]. Tirana: Akademia e Shkencave, 1989. 465 pp.

———. *Dokumente të shekujve XVI-XVII për historinë e Shqipërisë. Vëllimi 2 (1593-1602)* [Sixteenth and Seventeenth Century Documents on the History of Albania. Volume 2 (1593-1602)]. Tirana: Akademia e Shkencave, 1990. 387 pp.

Zamputi, Injac, and Selami Pulaha. *Dokumente të shekujve XVI-XVII për historinë e Shqipërisë. Vëllimi 4 (1675-1699)* [Sixteenth and Seventeenth Century Documents on the History of Albania. Volume 4 (1675-1699)]. Tirana: Akademia e Shkencave, 1990. 569 pp.

3.4 TWENTIETH CENTURY

Amery, Julian. *Sons of the Eagle: A Study in Guerilla War*. London: Macmillan, 1948. 354 pp.

———. *Approach March, a Venture in Autobiography*. London: Hutchinson, 1973. 456 pp.

Bethell, Nicholas William. *The Great Betrayal: The Untold Story of Kim Philby's Biggest Coup.* London: Hodder & Stoughton, 1984. 214 pp.

Cabanes, Pierre, and Bruno Cabanes. *Passions albanaises: de Berisha au Kosovo [Albanian Passions: From Berisha to Kosova].* Paris: Odile Jacob, 1998. 280 pp.

Costa, Nicholas J. *Albania: A European Enigma.* East European Monographs, CDXIII. Boulder, Colo.: East European Monographs, 1995. 188 pp.

——. *Shattered Illusions: Albania, Greece and Turkey.* Boulder, Colo.: East European Monographs, 1998. 200 pp.

Davies, Edmund Frank. *Illyrian Venture: The Story of the British Military Mission to Enemy-Occupied Albania 1943-1944.* London: Bodley Head, 1952. 247 pp.

Dedet, Joséphine. *Géraldine, reine des Albanais* [Geraldine, Queen of the Albanians]. Paris: Criterion, 1997. 390 pp.

Durham, Mary Edith. *Through the Lands of the Serb.* London: Edward Arnold, 1904. 345 pp.

——. *The Burden of the Balkans.* London: Edward Arnold, 1905. 331 pp.

——. *High Albania.* London: Edward Arnold, 1909, reprints 1970, 1985, 2000. 352 pp.

——. *The Struggle for Scutari. Turk, Slav and Albanian.* London: Edward Arnold, 1914. 320 pp.

——. *Twenty Years of Balkan Tangle.* London: George Allen & Unwin, 1920. 295 pp.

——. *Albania and the Albanians: Selected Articles and Letters, 1903-1944.* Introduction by Harry Hodgkinson. Edited by Bejtullah Destani. London: Centre for Albanian Studies, 2001. 261 pp.

Fischer, Bernd Jürgen. *King Zog and the Struggle for Stability in Albania.* East European Monographs, 159. New York: Columbia University Press, 1984. 353 pp.

——. *Albania at War, 1939-1945.* Central European Studies. London: C. Hurst, 1999. 338 pp.

Grünbaum, Irene. *Escape through the Balkans: The Autobiography of Irene Grünbaum.* Translated and edited with an introduction by Katherine Morris. Lincoln: University of Nebraska, 1996. xxiii + 191 pp.

Guinard, Emile. *Inoubliable Albanie: souvenirs d'un temps difficile, 1966-1968* [Unforgettable Albania. Memories of a Difficult Age, 1966-1968]. Paris: Godefroy de Bouillon, 1996. 160 pp.

Heaton-Armstrong, D. Captain. *Albania 1914. The Six Months' Kingdom: Memories of Private Secretary of Prince William of Wied.* Tirana: Albanian Institute for International Studies, 2001. 134 pp.

Hall, Richard C. *The Balkan Wars 1912-1913: Prelude to the First World War.* London: Routledge, 2000. 176 pp.

Hibbert, Reginald. *Albania's National Liberation Struggle: The Bitter Victory.* London: Pinter / New York: St. Martin's Press, 1991. 269 pp.

Jandot, Gabriel. *L'Albanie d'Enver Hoxha (1944-1985)* [The Albania of Enver Hoxha (1944-1985)]. Paris: L'Harmattan, 1994. 383 pp.

Jensen Mangerich, Agnes, Evelyn M. Monahan, and Rosemary L. Neidel. *Albanian Escape: The True Story of the U.S. Army Nurses Behind Enemy Lines.* As told to Evelyn M. Monahan and Rosemary L. Neidel. Lexington: University Press of Kentucky, 1999. xiii + 220 pp.

Jelavich, Charles, and Barbara Jelavich. *The Establishment of the Balkan National States, 1804-1920.* Seattle: University of Washington Press, 1977, reprint 1986. 358 pp.

Kemp, Peter Mant Macintyre. *No Colours or Crest.* London: Cassell, 1958. 305 pp.

——. *The Thorns of Memory.* London: Sinclair-Stevenson, 1990. 376 pp.

Kennan, George F. (ed.). *The Other Balkan Wars. A 1913 Carnegie Foundation Inquiry in Retrospect with a New Introduction and Reflections on the Present Conflict. International Commission to Enquire into the Causes and Conduct of the Balkan Wars.* Washington, D.C.: Carnegie Endowment for International Peace, 1993. 413 pp.

Konitza, Faik Bey. *The Albanian Question.* London: Williams, Lea & Co., 1918. 27 pp.

——. *Letters and Memoranda.* London: Centre for Albanian Studies, 1999. 180 pp.

Löhr, Hanns Christian. *Die albanische Frage: Konferenzdiplomatie und Nationalstaatsbildung im Vorfeld des Ersten Weltkrieges unter besonderer Berücksichtigung der deutschen Außenpolitik* [The Albanian Question: Conference Diplomacy and the Creation of National States Prior to the First World War, in Particular German Foreign Policy]. Inauguraldissertation zur Erlangung der Doktorwürde. Vorgelegt der Philosophischen Fakultät der Rheinischen Friedrich-Wilhelms Universität zu Bonn. Bonn, 1992. 364 pp.

Malcolm, Noel. *Kosovo, a Short History.* London: Macmillan, 1998. 491 pp.

Pearson, Owen. *Albania and King Zog, a Diary of the Fight for Independence and Legality*. London: Centre for Albanian Studies, forthcoming.

Philby, Harold Adrian Russell (Kim). *My Silent War*. With an introduction my Graham Greene. London: MacGibbon & Kee, 1968, reprint 1969. 189 pp.

Pipa, Arshi. *Albanian Stalinism: Ideo-political Aspects*. East European Monographs 287. New York: Columbia University Press, 1990. 291 pp.

Prifti, Peter Rafael. *Socialist Albania since 1944: Domestic and Foreign Developments*. Studies in Communism, Revisionism and Revolution. No. 23. William E. Griffith, general editor. Cambridge, Mass.: MIT Press, 1978. xv + 312 pp.

Robyns, Gwen. *Geraldine of the Albanians, an Authorised Biography*. London: Muller, Blond & White, 1987. iv + 229 pp.

Schmidt-Neke, Michael. *Entstehung und Ausbau der Königsdiktatur in Albanien (1912-1939): Regierungsbildungen, Herrschaftsweise und Machteliten in einem jungen Balkanstaat* [The Rise and Expansion of the Royal Dictatorship in Albania (1912-1939): Government Formations, Manner of Rule and Power Elite in a new Balkan State]. Südosteuropäische Arbeiten, 84. Munich: R. Oldenbourg, 1987. 371 pp.

Schreiber, Thomas. *Enver Hodja: le Sultan rouge* [Enver Hoxha: The Red Sultan]. Paris: Jean-Claude Lattès, 1994. 269 pp.

Shala, Blerim, and Llukman Halili. *Unë, Ramiz Alia dëshmoj për historinë* [I, Ramiz Alia, Bear Witness to History]. Prishtina, Kosova: Zeri, 1992. 240 pp.

Smiley, David. *Albanian Assignment*. Foreword Patrick Fermor. London: Chatto & Windus/ Hogarth Press, 1984, reprint 1985. 176 pp.

——. *Irregular Regular*. Norwich: Michael Russell, 1994. vi + 218 pp.

Story, Sommerville (ed.). *The Memoirs of Ismail Kemal Bey*. London: Constable, 1920. 410 pp.

Szinyei-Merse, Antoinette de. *Ten Years, Ten Months, Ten Days: The Authorised Story of King Zog and Queen Geraldine*. Translated from the Hungarian by Paul Tabori. London: Hutchinson, 1940. 250 pp.

Tocci, Rita. *Terenzio Tocci mio padre: ricordi e pensieri. Mezzo secolo di vita balcanica. Albania 1911-1945* [Terenzio Tocci, My Father. Memories and Thoughts. Half a Century of Balkan Life. Albania 1911-1945]. Corigliano Calabro, Italy: Arte Grafiche Ioniche, 1977. 185 pp.

——. *Terenzio Tocci babai im: mendime e kujtime* [Terenzio Tocci, My Father: Thoughts and Memories]. Tirana: Toena, 1996. 197 pp.

Tomes, Jason. *King Zog: Self-Made Monarch of Albania.* Stroud, England: Sutton forthcoming 2003.

Tönnes, Bernhard. *Sonderfall Albanien: Enver Hoxhas 'eigener Weg' und die historischen Ursprünge seiner Ideologie* [Albania, a Case of Its Own: Enver Hoxha's 'Own Particular Road' and the Historical Origins of his Ideology]. Untersuchungen zur Gegenwartskunde Südosteuropas. Band 16. Südost-Institut. Munich: Oldenbourg, 1980. 512 pp.

Ushtelenca, Ilir. *Diplomacia e mbretit Zogu 1-rë (1912-1939)* [The Diplomacy of King Zog I (1912-1939)]. Tirana: s.e., 1996, reprint 1997. 363 pp.

Vickers, Miranda, and James Pettifer. *Albania: From Anarchy to a Balkan Identity.* London: C. Hurst, 1996. 288 pp.

Woodall, Robert Larry. *The Albanian Problem during the Peace-Making 1919-1920.* Phil. Dissertation. Memphis, Tenn.: Memphis State University. 1978. 260 pp.

4. SOCIETY

4.1 ANTHROPOLOGY AND ETHNOLOGY

Auzias, Claire. *Les poètes de grand chemin: voyage avec les Roms des Balkans* [The Poets of the Highways: Travels with the Roma of the Balkans]. Paris: Michalon, 1998. 379 pp.

Backer, Berit. *Behind Stone Walls: Changing Household Organization among the Albanians of Kosova.* Edited by Robert Elsie and Antonia Young, with an introduction and photographs by Ann Christine Eek. Dukagjini Balkan Books. Peja, Kosova: Dukagjini, 2003. 304 pp.

Bërxholi, Arqile, Seifi Protopapa, and Kristaq Prifti. *The Greek Minority in the Albanian Republic: A Demographic Study.* Tirana: Geographical Studies Institute, 1993.

Boehm, Christopher. *Blood Revenge. The Anthropology of Feuding in Montenegro and other Tribal Societies. [Blood Revenge, the Enactment and Management of Conflict in Montenegro and Other Tribal Societies].* Lawrence: University Press of Kansas, 1984, reprint 1987.

Coon, Carleton Stevens. *The Mountains of Giants: A Racial and Cultural Study of the North Albanian Mountain Ghegs.* Papers of the Peabody Museum of American Archaeology and Ethnology, Harvard

510 Bibliography

University 23.3. Cambridge, Mass.: Harvard Museum, 1950, reprint 1970. viii + 105 pp.

Demo, Constantine A. *The Albanians in America: The First Arrivals. In English and Albanian. Shqipëtarët në Amerikë: imigrantët e parë.* Boston: The Society Fatbardhësia of Katundi, 1960. 96 pp.

Dessart, Francis. "Albanian Ethnic Groups in the World. An Historical and Cultural Essay on the Albanian Colonies in Italy," in: *East European Quarterly,* Boulder, Colo., 15.4 (1984), pp. 469-489.

Dhima, Aleksandër. *Gjurmime antropologjike për shqiptarët* [Anthropological Research on the Albanians]. Tirana: Akademia e Shkencave, 1985. 267 pp.

Durham, Mary Edith. *Some Tribal Origins, Laws and Customs of the Balkans.* Illustrated by the author. London: Allen & Unwin, 1928, reprint 1979. 318 pp.

Eberhart, Helmut, and Karl Kaser (ed.). *Albanien: Stammesleben zwischen Tradition und Moderne* [Albania: Tribal Life between Tradition and Modernity]. Vienna: Böhlau, 1995. 200 pp.

Elazar, Daniel J., Harriet Pass Friedenreich, Baruch Hazzan, and Adina Weiss Liberles. *The Balkan Jewish Communities: Yugoslavia, Bulgaria, Greece and Turkey.* Center for Jewish Community Studies of the Jerusalem Center for Public Affairs. Lanham, Md.: University Press of America, 1984. 193 pp.

Gjergji, Andromaqi. *Veshet shqiptare në shekuj: origjina, tipologjia, zhvillimi* [Albanian Clothing over the Centuries: Origins, Typology, Development]. Tirana: Instituti i Kulturës Popullore, 1988. 286 pp.

———. *Ligjerata për etnologjinë shqiptare* [Lectures on Albanian Ethnology]. Tirana: Extra, 2001. 180 pp.

Kondis, Basil, and Eleftheria Manda (ed.). *The Greek Minority in Albania: A Documentary Record (1921-1993).* Thessalonika, Greece: Institute for Balkan Studies, 1994. 130 pp.

Kotani, Apostol. *Hebrejtë në Shqipëri gjatë shekujve. The Hebrews in Albania during centuries.* Tirana: Dituria, 1996. 151 pp.

———. *Albania and the Jews.* Tirana: Eureka, 1995. 159 pp.

Mosely, Philip E. *Communal Families in the Balkans: The Zadruga.* Essays by Philip E. Moseley and essays in his honor. Edited by Robert F. Byrnes with an introduction by Margaret Mead. Notre Dame, Ind.: University of Notre Dame Press, 1976. 285 pp.

Musliu, Sefer, and Daut Dauti. *Shqiptarët e Ukrainës: udhëpërshkrime dhe punime shkencore* [The Albanians of the Ukraine: Travelog and Research Work]. Skopje, Macedonia: Shkupi, 1996. 208 pp.

Nagi, Dennis Lazar. *The Albanian-American Odyssey: A Pilot Study of the Albanian Community of Boston Massachusetts.* New York: AMS Press, 1989. 152 pp.

Nasse, George Nicholas. *The Italo-Albanian Villages of Southern Italy.* U.S. National Academy of Sciences. National Research Council Publication 1149. Washington, D.C., 1964. vi + 81 pp.

Nopcsa, Franz Baron. *Haus und Hausrat im katholischen Nordalbanien* [Houses and Furnishings in Catholic Northern Albania]. Zur Kunde der Balkanhalbinsel. 1. Reisen und Beobachtungen Heft 16. Herausgegeben von Carl Patsch. Sarajevo, Bosnia: Bosnisch-Herzegowinisches Institut für Balkanforschung, 1912. 92 pp.

——. *Albanien. Bauten, Trachten und Geräte Nordalbaniens* [Albania: Buildings, Costumes and Equipment of Northern Albania]. Berlin: De Gruyter, 1925. viii + 257 pp.

Ortakovski, Vladimir. *Minorities in the Balkans.* Ardsley, N.Y.: Transnational, 2000. 384 pp.

Pettifer, James, and Hugh Poulton. *The Southern Balkans: Minority Rights Group.* Minority Rights Group International Report, London 1994, 4. 42 pp.

Pipa, Arshi, and Peter Prifti. "Albanians," in: *Harvard Encyclopedia of American Ethnic Groups.* Edited by Stephan Thernstrom. Cambridge, Mass.: Belknap, 1980, pp. 23-28.

Rotelli, Claudio (ed.). *Gli Albanesi in Calabria: Secoli XV-XVIII. 1* [The Albanians in Calabria 15th-18th Centuries. I]. Cosenza, Italy: Edizione Orizzonti Meridionali, 1988, reprint 1990. 113 pp.

Roux, Michel. *Les Albanais de Yougoslavie: minorité nationale territoire et développement* [The Albanians of Yugoslavia. Territorial National Minority and Development]. Publié avec le concours de Centre National de la Recherche Scientifique. Paris: Maison des Sciences de l'Homme, 1992. 546 pp.

Sarner, Harvey. *Rescue in Albania: One Hundred Percent of Jews in Albania Rescued from Holocaust.* Cathedral City, Calif.: Brunswick Press, 1997. 106 pp.

Sarner, Harvey, Joseph Jakoel, and Felicita Jakoel. *The Jews of Albania.* Boston: Brunswick Press, 1992. 44 pp.

Schwander-Sievers, Stephanie. "The Albanian Aromanians' Awakening: Identity, Politics and Conflicts in Post-Communist Albania." Working papers, No. 3. Flensburg, Germany: European Centre for Minority Issues. iv + 19 pp.

Schwander-Sievers, Stephanie, and Bernd J. Fischer (ed.). *Albanian Identities: Myth and History.* London: C. Hurst, 2002. xvii + 230 pp.

Seliščev, Afanasij Matveevič. *Slavjanskoe naselenie v Albanii* [The Slavic Population in Albania]. Sofia, 1931, reprint 1978, 1981) 352 pp.

512 Bibliography

Shytock, Andrew J. "Autonomy, Entanglement and the Feud. Prestige Structures and Gender Value in Highland Albania," in: *Anthropological quarterly*, 61 (1988), pp. 113-118.

Statovci, Drita. *Etnologjia flet* [Ethnology Speaks]. Prishtina, Kosova: Instituti Albanologjik, 1998. 304 pp.

Stavrou, Christodoulos. *Die griechische Minderheit in Albanien* [The Greek Minority in Albania]. Europäische Hochschulschriften. Frankfurt am Main, Germany: Peter Lang, 1993. 270 pp.

Tomić, Jovan N. *O Arnautima u Staroj Srbiji i Sandžaku* [On the Albanians in Old Serbia and the Sandjak]. Belgrade, Yugoslavia: Knjižara Gece Kona, 1913. 93 pp. reprint 1995. 82 pp.

Trix, Frances. *The Albanians in Michigan: Discovering the Peoples of Michigan*. East Lansing: Michigan State University Press, 2001. 73 pp.

Young, Antonia. *Women Who Become Men: Albanian Sworn Virgins*. Oxford: Berg Publishers, 2000. 168 pp.

Wace, A. J. B., and M. S. Thompson. *The Nomads of the Balkans: An Account of Life and Customs among the Vlach of Northern Epirus*. London 1914, reprint 1972.

Weale-Badieritaki, Jean. *A Study of the Folklore, Folkways and Social Structure of Two Arvanite Communities in Attica*. Reading University Dissertation. Reading, England, 1990. xvii + 373 pp.

Winnifrith, Tom J. *The Vlachs: The History of a Balkan People*. New York: St. Martin's Press, 1987, reprint 1995. viii + 180 pp.

4.2 SOCIOLOGY

Alderman, Harold. *Social Assistance in Albania: Decentralization and Targeted Transfers*. LSMS working paper. Washington, D.C.: World Bank, 1998. xi + 40 pp.

Bokhorst, Hermine. *Femmes dans les griffes des aigles: les filières albanaises de la prostitution*. Brussels: Labor, 2003. 126 pp.

Gjonça, Arjan. *Communism, Health and Lifestyle: The Paradox of Mortality Transition in Albania. 1950-1990*. Studies in Population and Urban Demography, 8. London: Greenwood Press, 2001. 248 pp.

Islami, Hivzi. *Demographic Reality in Kosova*. Prishtina, Kosova: Kosova Information Center, s.a.[1994]. 53 pp.

——. *Rrjedha demografike shqiptare* [Albanian Demographic Flow]. Peja, Kosova: Dukagjini, 1994. 269 pp.

Kaser, Karl, Robert Pichler, and Stephanie Schwandner-Sievers (ed.). *Die weite Welt und das Dorf: Migration in Albanien am Ende des 20.*

Jahrhunderts [The Wide World and the Village: Migration in Albania at the End of the 20th Century]. Zur Kunde Südosteuropas. Albanologische Studien, Bd. 3. Vienna: Böhlau, 2001. 296 pp.

Katro, Jeta, and Liri Shimani. *Prostitution and Trafficking of Women in Albania.* Tirana: Lilo, 2000? 80 pp.

Miria, Silvana, Valdeta Sala, and D. Fico. *Violence against Women and the Psychological Taboos Favouring Violence.* Tirana: Women Association Refleksione, 1996. 17 pp.

Misja, Vladimir and Ylli Vejsiu. *Demographic Development in the People's Socialist Republic of Albania.* Tirana: 8 Nëntori, 1985. 100 pp.

Misja, V[ladimir], Ylli Vejsiu, and Arqile Berxholi. *Popullsia e Shqipërisë* [The Population of Albania]. Tirana: Universiteti Enver Hoxha, 1987. 409 pp.

Murray, Stephen O., and Will Roscoe. *Islamic Homosexualities. Culture, History and Literature.* New York: New York University Press, 1997. 390 pp.

Post, Susan Pritchett. *Women in Modern Albania. Firsthand Accounts of Culture and Conditions from over 200 Interviews.* Jefferson, N.C.: McFarland, 1998. 320 pp.

Ramet, Sabrina Pedro. *Gender Politics in the Western Balkans: Women and Society in Yugoslavia and the Yugoslav Successor States.* University Park: Pennsylvania State University Press, 1998. 343 pp.

Raufer, Xavier, and Stéphane Quéré. *La mafia albanaise: une menace pour l'Europe. Comment est née cette superpuissance criminelle balkanique?* [The Albanian Mafia: A Threat to Europe. How Was this Criminal Superpower from the Balkans Born?]. Lausanne, Switzerland: Favre, 2000. 143 pp.

Reineck, Janet Susan. *The Past as Refuge: Gender, Migration and Ideology among the Kosova Albanians (Yugoslavia).* Ph.D. Dissertation. Berkeley: University of California, 1991. 239 pp.

Resta, Patrizia. *Un popolo in cammino: migrazioni albanese in Italia* [A People on the Move: Albanian Migration in Italy]. Verba mundi, 5. Nardò Lecce, Italy: Besa, 1996. 119 pp.

Salihu, Xhemaledin. *Kultura shqiptare në Preshevë 1945-1995* [Albanian Culture in Presheva, 1945-1995]. Presheva, Serbia: Shtëpia e kulturës Abdulla Krashnica, 1999. 407 pp.

Saltmarshe, Douglas. *Identity in a Post-communist Balkan State: An Albanian Village Study.* Aldershot-Burlington, England: Ashgate, 2001. 237 pp.

Senechal, Marjorie. *Long Life to Your Children: A Portrait of High Albania.* Photographed by Stan Sherer. Boston: University of Massachusetts Press, 1997. 240 pp.

4.3   EDUCATION

Council of Europe. *Secondary Education in Albania.* Strasbourg, France: Council of Europe, 1996.

Fultz Kontos, Joan. *Red Cross, Black Eagle: A Biography of Albania's American School.* East European Monographs, 75. New York: Columbia University Press, 1981. 216 pp.

Gogaj, Iljaz. *Shkollat amerikane në Shqipëri* [American Schools in Albania]. Tirana: Drita, 1995. 241 pp.

——. *Shkolla teknike dhe Harri Fulci* [The Technical School and Harry Fultz]. Tirana: Eurorilindja, 1999. 346 pp.

Koenig, Ann M. *An Overview of the Educational System in Albania.* Milwaukee, Wis.: Educational Credential Evaluators, 1993. 46 pp.

Mustafa, Avzi. *Edukata dhe arsimi nëpër shekuj* [Education and Learning Over the Centuries]. Skopje, Macedonia: Shkupi, 1997. 138 pp.

——. *Zhvillimi i shkollës fillore shqipe në Republikën e Maqedonisë 1945-1975* [The Development of Albanian Elementary Schooling in the Republic of Macedonia 1945-1975]. Skopje, Macedonia: Logos-A, 1998. 198 pp.

——. *Figura mësuesish shqiptarë* [Leading Figures among Albanian Teachers]. Tetovo, Macedonia: Bashkësia kulturore shqiptare, 1995. 159 pp.

Myzyri, Hysni. *Shkollat e para kombëtare shqipe (1887-1908)* [The First Albanian National Schools (1887-1908)]. Tirana: Instituti i Studimeve Pedagogjike, 1973. 294 pp.

——. *Shkollat e para kombëtare shqipe (1887-Korrik 1908)* [The First Albanian National Schools (1887-July 1908). Botim i dytë me plotësime e ndryshime. Tirana: 8 Nëntori, 1978. 250 pp.

——. *Arsimi kombëtar (1908-1912)* [National Education (1908-1912)]. Prishtina, Kosova: Enti i teksteve dhe i mjeteve mësimore të Kosovës, 1996. 441 pp.

Nikollari, Dashnnor, and Michael Schmidt-Neke. "Das Bildungswesen für die nationalen Minderheiten in Albanien [The Education System for National Minorities in Albania]," in: *Albanische Hefte,* Bochum, 4 (1999), pp. 10-18.

Pango, Ylli. *Secondary Education in Albania.* Strasbourg: Council of Europe Press, 1996. 31 pp.

Stamile, Carmine. *The Albanian Language in Primary Education in Italy. La lingua albanese nella scuola elementare in Italia.* EMU-project, 7. Ljouwert/Leeuwarden: Fryske Akademy, 1988. 23 & 51 pp.

Thomas, John I. *Education for Communism: School and State in the People's Republic of Albania.* Stanford, Calif.: Hoover Institution Press, 1969. 131 pp.

Vokrri, Abdullah R. *Shkollat dhe arsimi në Kosovë ndërmjet dy luftërave botërore (1918-1941)* [Schools and Education in Kosova between the Two World Wars (1918-1941)]. Prishtina, Kosova: Enti i teksteve, 1990. 389 pp.

4.4 RELIGION

Arnold, T. W. *The Preaching of Islam: A History of the Propagation of the Muslim Faith.* London: Luzac, 1896, reprint 1913, 1935, 1961, 1979.

Birge, John Kingsley. *The Bektashi Order of Dervishes.* London: Luzac, 1937, reprint 1965, 1982, 1994. 291 pp.

Broun, Janice (ed.). *Albania: Religion in a Fortress State.* Washington, D.C.: Puebla Institute, 1989. 47 pp.

Clayer, Nathalie. *L'Albanie. Pays des derviches: les ordres mystiques musulmans en Albanie à l'époque postottomane (1912-1967)* [Albania, Land of the Dervishes: Muslim Mystical Orders in Albania in the Post-Ottoman Period (1912-1967)]. Balkanologische Veröffentlichungen 17. Berlin: in Kommission bei Otto Harrassowitz, Wiesbaden, 1990. 505 pp.

——. "Islam and National Identity in the Albanian Space (Albania, Macedonia, Kosovo), 1989-1998," in: *Archives de Sciences Sociales des Religions,* 2001, No. 115, pp. 161-182.

Duijzings, Ger. *Religion and the Politics of Identity in Kosovo.* London: C. Hurst, 2000. 238 pp.

Elsie, Robert. "Islam and the Dervish Sects of Albania. An Introduction to Their History, Development and Current Situation," in: *The Islamic Quarterly,* London, 42. 4 (1998), pp. 266-289.

——. *A Dictionary of Albanian Religion, Mythology and Folk Culture.* London: C. Hurst, 2001. 357 pp.

——. *Handbuch zur albanischen Volkskultur. Mythologie, Religion, Volksglaube, Sitten, Gebräuche und kulturelle Besonderheiten* [Handbook of Albanian Folk Culture: Mythology, Religion, Popular Beliefs, Customs, Habits and Cultural Particularities]. Balkanologische Veröffentlichungen, Bd. 36. Fachbereich Philosophie und Geisteswissenschaften der Freien Universität Berlin. Wiesbaden, Germany: Harrassowitz, 2002. xi + 308 pp.

Gardin, Giacomo (Jak) S. J. *Banishing God in Albania: The Prison Memoir of Giacomo Gardin, S.J.* San Francisco: Ignatius Press, 1988. 165 pp.

Gjergji, Lush. *Mother Teresa: Her Life, Her Works.* Hyde Park, N.Y.: New City Press, 1991. 144 pp.

——. *Mother Teresa: To Live, to Love, to Witness. Her Spiritual Way.* Translated by Jordan Aumann, O.P. Hyde Park, N.Y.: New City Press, 1998. 139 pp.

——. *Nëna e dashurisë. Mother of Love.* Prishtina, Kosova: Akademia e Shkencave, 2000. 237 pp.

Hasluck, Frederick William. *Christianity and Islam under the Sultans.* Edited by Margaret Hasluck. 2 vol. Oxford: Clarendon, 1929, reprint 1973. 770 pp.

Hasluck, Margaret Masson Hardie. "The Nonconformist Moslems of Albania," in: *Contemporary Review,* London, 127 (1925), pp. 599-606. Reprinted in *Moslem World* 15 (1925), pp. 388-398.

Kurti, Donat, and Marin Sirdani. *Mbi kontributin e elementit katolik në Shqipëri* [On the Contribution of the Catholic Element in Albania]. Tirana: Lajmëtari, 1999. 100 pp.

Malaj, Vinçenc. "Apostolic and Educational Work of the Franciscan Order among the Albanian People," in: *Albanian Catholic Bulletin,* San Francisco, 11 (1990), pp. 23-54.

Morozzo della Rocca, Roberto. *Nazione e religione in Albania (1920-1944)* [Nation and Religion in Albania (18920-1944). Bologna, Italy: Il Mulino, 1990. 253 pp.

Noli, Fan Stilian. *Fiftieth Anniversary Book of the Albanian Orthodox Church in America (1908-1958).* Boston: Albanian Orthodox Church in America, 1960. 265 pp.

Norris, Harry Thirlwall. *Islam in the Balkans. Religion and Society between Europe and the Arab World.* London: C. Hurst, 1993. 304 pp.

Peterson, Reona. *Tomorrow You Die.* Van Nuys, Calif.: Bible Voice, 1976, reprint 1977. 132 pp.

Poghirc, Cicerone. "Albanian Religion," in: *The Encyclopedia of Religion,* vol. 1. Edited by Mircea Eliade. New York: Macmillan, 1987. pp. 178-180.

Popa, Theofan. *Mbishkrime të kishave në Shqipëri* [Church Inscriptions in Albania]. Tirana: Akademia e Shkencave, 1998. 353 pp.

Popovic, Alexandre. *L'Islam balkanique: les musulmans du sud-est européen dans la période post-ottomane* [Balkan Islam. The Muslims of Southeastern Europe in the Post-Ottoman Period]. Balkanologische Veröffentlichungen Nr 11. Berlin: in Kommission Harrassowitz, Wiesbaden, 1986. 478 pp.

Popovic, Alexandre, and Gilles Veinstein (ed.). *Bektachiyya: études sur l'ordre mystique des Bektachis et les groupes relevant de Hadji Bektach* [Bektashiyya: Studies on the Mystical Order of the Bektashi and Groups Descending from Hadji Bektash]. Revue des Etudes Islamiques 60 (1992). Numéro spécial. Paris: Paul Geuthner, 1993/Istanbul: Isis, 1995. xii + 598 pp.

Qiriazi, Gjerasim (= Kyrias, Gjerasim). *Captured by Brigands*. London: Religious Tracts Society, 1902, reprint 1994. 129 pp.

Rance, Didier. *Albanie: ils ont voulu tuer Dieu. Le persécution contre l'Eglise catholique (1944-1991). Témoignages* [Albania: They Wanted to Kill God. Persecution of the Catholic Church (1944-1991). Witness]. Mareil-Marly, France: Aide à l'Eglise en détresse, 1996. 471 pp.

Rexhebi, Baba. *The Mysticism of Islam and Bektashism*. Naples: Dragotti, 1984. 173 pp.

Schramm, Gottfried. *Anfänge des albanischen Christentums: die frühe Bekehrung der Bessen und ihre langen Folgen* [The Beginnings of Albanian Christianity: The Early Conversion of the Besoi]. Freiburg im Breisgau, Germany: Rombach, 1994. 270 pp.

Sinishta, Gjon. *The Fulfilled Promise. A Documentary Account of Religious Persecution in Albania*. Santa Clara, Calif., 1976. 247 pp.

Trix, Frances. *Spiritual Discourse. Learning with an Islamic Master*. Philadelphia: University of Pennsylvania Press, 1993. 189 pp.

——. "The Resurfacing of Islam in Albania," in: *East European Quarterly*, Boulder, Colo., 28, 4 (1994), pp. 533-549.

Ukgjini, Nikë, Willy Kamsi, and Romeo Gurakuqi (ed.). *Krishterimi ndër Shqiptarë. Simpozium ndërkombëtar, Tiranë, 16-19 nëntor 1999. Christianity among the Albanians. International symposium. Tirana, 16-19 November 1999*. Biblioteka e të Përkohshme Phoenix. Shkodra: Konferenca Ipeshkvnore e Shqipërisë/Episcopal Conference of Albania, 2000. xxvi + 588 pp.

5. POLITICS

5.1 GENERAL

Biberaj, Elez Hysen. *Albania, a Socialist Maverick*. Westview Profiles. Nations of Contemporary Eastern Europe. Boulder, Colo.: Westview Press, 1990. 157 pp.

——. *Albania in Transition: The Rocky Road to Democracy.* Nations of the Modern World. Europe. Boulder, Colo.: Westview Press, 1998. xiv + 377 pp.

Fuga, Artan. *L'Albanie entre la pensée totalitaire et la raison fragmentaire* [Albania between Totalitarian Thought and Fragmentary Reason]. Paris: L'Harmattan, 1998. 199 pp.

Lendvai, Paul. *Eagles in Cobwebs: Nationalism and Communism in the Balkans.* Garden City, N.J.: Doubleday, 1969, reprint 1970. xii + 396 pp.

——. *Das einsame Albanien: Reportage aus dem Land der Skipetaren* [Lonely Albania. Report from the Land of the Albanians]. Zürich: Edition Interfrom, 1985. 118 pp.

Merxhani, Branko. *Formula të Neo-Shqiptarismës* [The Formula of Neo-Albanianism]. Përgatitur nga Dr. Aurel Plasari. Tirana: Apollonia, 1996, reprint 1998. 391 pp.

Mustafaj, Besnik. *Entre crimes et mirages: l'Albanie* [Albania: between Crimes and Mirages]. Essai traduit de l'albanais par Christiane Montécot et Odette Marquet. Arles, France: Actes Sud, 1992. 251 pp.

O'Donnell, James Salisbury. *A Coming of Age: Albania under Enver Hoxha.* Boulder, Colo.: East European Monographs, 1998. 136 pp.

Petrie, Ruth (ed.). *The Fall of Communism and the Rise of Nationalism. The Index Reader.* Introduced by Irena Maryniak. London: Cassell, 1997. 222 pp.

Qosja, Rexhep. *Çështja shqiptare: historia dhe politika* [The Albanian Question: History and Politics]. Prishtina, Kosova: Instituti Albanologjik, 1994, reprint 1998. 363 pp.

——. *La question albanaise.* [The Albanian Question]. Traduit de l'albanais par Christian Gut. Paris: Fayard, 1995. 326 pp.

——. *Fjalor demokratik* [Democratic Dictionary]. Prishtina, Kosova: Enti i teksteve dhe i mjeteve mësimore i Kosovës / Tirana: Toena, 1997. 547 pp.

Tarifa, Fatos. *Albania's Exit from Communism in the East European Context.* Dissertation. Chapel Hill: University of North Carolina, Department of Sociology, 1998. xii + 237 pp.

5.2 DOMESTIC

Abrahams, Fred. *Human Rights in Post-Communist Albania.* London: Human Rights Watch, 1996. 156 pp.

Alia, Ramiz. *Shpresa dhe zhgënjime* [Hopes and Disappointments]. Tirana: Dituria, 1993. 224 pp.

——. *Ditari i burgut* [Prison Diary]. Athens: Papazissis, s.a. [1998]. 394 pp.

——. *Duke biseduar per Shqiperine...* [Talking about Albania]. Athens: Kurier Ekdotiki, 2000. 232 pp.

Çami, Foto, et al. (ed.). *Enver Hoxha 1908-1985*. Publication of the Institute of Marxist-Leninist Studies at the CC of the PLA. Tirana: Ndërmarrja e Përhapjes së Librit, 1986. 297 pp.

Champseix, Elizabeth, and Jean-Paul Champseix. *57 boulevard Staline: chroniques albanaises* [57 Stalin Boulevard. Albanian Chronicles]. Paris: Éditions La Découverte, 1990. 311 pp.

——. *L'Albanie ou la logique du désespoir* [Albania or the Logic of Despair]. Paris: Éditions La Découverte, 1992. 307 pp.

Halliday, Jon. *The Artful Albanian: The Memoirs of Enver Hoxha*. London: Chatto & Windus, 1986. 394 pp.

Hoxha, Ilir. *Babai im, Enver Hoxha: Kujtime, letërkëmbim, publicistikë* [My Father Enver Hoxha: Memoirs, Correspondence, Press Articles]. Tirana: Extra, 1998. 205 pp.

Hoxha, Nexhmije. *Jeta ime me Enverin: kujtime* [My Life with Enver: Memoirs]. Tirana: Lira, 1998. 400 pp.

Lubonja, Liri. *Larg dhe mes njerëzve: Kujtime internimi, 1973-1990* [Far Away and among People: Memoirs of Internment, 1973-1990]. Tirana: Dora d'Istria, 1995. 256 pp.

Lubonja, Todi. *Nën peshën e dhunës* [Under the Weight of Violence]. Tirana: Progresi, 1993, reprint 1998. 298 pp.

——. *Ankthi pa fund i lirisë: shënime* [The Infinite Anguish of Freedom: Notes]. Tirana: Albin, 1994. 270 pp.

McLain, Glenn A. *Albanian Exposé: Communism versus Liberation for Albania*. Sponsored by the Albanian American Society. Quincy, Mass.: Premier Press, 1951. 99 pp.

Milivojevic, Marko. *Wounded Eagle. Albania's Fight for Survival*. Institute for European Defence and Strategic Studies. European Security Study, No. 15. London: Alliance, 1992. 48 pp.

Morozzo della Rocca, Roberto. *Albania: le radici della crisi* [Albania: The Roots of the Crisis]. Milan: Guerini e Associati, 1997. 149 pp.

Niegellhell, Anita, and Gabriele Ponisch. *Berichte ehemaliger politischer Gefangener im kommunistischen Albanien* [Reports of Former Political Prisoners in Communist Albania]. Vienna: Böhlau, 2001. 296 pp.

Pëllumbi, Servet. *Dritëhije të tranzicionit* [The Penumbra of the Transition]. Tirana: Rinia, 2000. 401 pp.

Pipa, Arshi. *Albanian Stalinism: Ideo-political Aspects*. East European Monographs, 287. New York: Columbia University Press, 1990. 291 pp.

——. *The Politics of Language in Socialist Albania.* East European Monographs, 271. New York: Columbia University Press, 1989. 283 pp.

Puto, Arben. *Demokracia e rrethuar: qeveria e Fan Nolit në marrëdhëniet e jashtme, qershor-dhjetor 1924* [Encircled Democracy: The Government of Fan Noli in Its Foreign Relations, June-December 1924]. Tirana: 8 Nëntori, 1990. 320 pp.

Prifti, Peter Rafael. *Socialist Albania since 1944: Domestic and Foreign Developments.* Studies in Communism, Revisionism and Revolution, No. 23. William E. Griffith, general editor. Cambridge, Mass.: MIT Press, 1978. xv + 312 pp.

——. *Remote Albania: The Politics of Isolationism.* Tirana: Onufri, 1999. 251 pp.

Rama, Luan. *Le long chemin sous le tunnel de Platon: Le destin de l'artiste sous la censure en Albanie (1945-1990)* [The Long Road Under Plato's Tunnel: The Fate of Artists under Censorship in Albania (1945-1990)]. Nantes, France: Editions du Petit Véhicule, 1999. 228 pp.

Shehu, Bashkim. *L'automne de la peur: récit* [Autumn of Anguish: Narrative]. Traduit de l'albanais par Isabelle Joudrain-Musa. Préface d'Ismaïl Kadaré. Paris: Fayard, 1993. 203 pp.

Skendi, Stavro. *Albanian National Awakening (1878-1912).* Princeton, N.J.: Princeton University Press, 1967. 498 pp.

Smith, Christopher H. (ed.). *Challenges to Democracy in Albania.* Hearing before the Commission on Security and Co-operation in Europe. Collingrade, Pa.: Diane, 1998. 116 pp.

Suti, Zef. *Escape from Communist Darkness: My Life as an Emigré—An Autobiography.* New York: Vantage Press, 1996. 239 pp.

Zhiti, Visar. *Rrugët e ferrit: burgologji. Rrëfim që s'do të doja të ishte i vërtetë* [The Roads to Hell. Prisonology. A Story I Wish Were Not True]. Tirana: Onufri, 2001. 472 pp.

——. *Ferri i çarë: romani i vërtetë* [Split Hell: A True Novel]. Tirana: Omsca-1, 2002. 453 pp.

5.3   KOSOVA

Allain, Marie-Françoise, and Xavier Galmiche. *Ibrahim Rugova: la question du Kosovo. Entretiens avec Marie-Françoise Allain et Xavier Galmiche* [Ibrahim Rugova: The Kosova Question. Conversations with Marie-Françoise Allain and Xavier Galmiche]. Préfacé de Ismail Kadaré. Paris: Fayard, 1994. 263 pp.

Andryszewski, Tricia. *Kosovo, the Splintering of Yugoslavia.* Brookfield, Conn.: Millbrook Press, 2000. 64 pp.

Booth, Ken (ed.). *The Kosovo Tragedy: The Human Rights Dimensions.* Portland: Frank Cass, 2001. 386 pp.

Bouckaert, Peter. *A Week of Terror in Drenica: Humanitarian Law Violation in Kosovo.* New York: Human Rights Watch, 1999. 102 pp.

Campbell, Greg. *The Road to Kosovo: A Balkan Diary.* Boulder, Colo.: Westview Press, 1999. 256 pp.

Chiclet, Christophe, and Bernard Ravenel. *Kosovo, le piège* [Kosova, the Trap]. Paris: L'Harmattan, 2000. 287 pp.

Chomsky, Noam. *The New Military Humanism: Lessons from Kosovo.* London: Pluto Press, 1999. 200 pp.

Clark, Howard. *Civil Resistance in Kosova.* London: Pluto Press, 2000. 266 pp.

De Waele, Jean-Michel, and Kolë Gjeloshaj. *De la question albanaise au Kosovo* [On the Albanian Question in Kosova]. Brussels: Editions Complexe, 1999. 154 pp.

Elsie, Robert. "The Last Albanian Waiter," in: *The Fall of Communism and the Rise of Nationalism. The Index Reader.* Edited by Ruth Petrie. Introduced by Irena Maryniak. London: Cassell, 1997. pp. 150-153.

——. *Kosovo: In the Heart of the Powder Keg.* East European Monographs, CDLXXVIII. Boulder, Colo.: East European Monographs, 1997. vi + 593 pp.

——. *Gathering Clouds. The Roots of Ethnic Cleansing in Kosovo and Macedonia. Early Twentieth-Century Documents.* Compiled, translated and edited by Robert Elsie. Dukagjini Balkan Books. Peja, Kosova: Dukagjini, 2002. 172 pp.

Fromkin, David. *Kosovo Crossing: American Ideals meet Reality on the Balkan Battlefields.* New York: Free Press, 1999. 210 pp.

Garapon, Antoine, and Olivier Mongin (ed.). *Kosovo, un drame annoncé* [Kosova, a Pre-announced Drama]. Paris: Editions Michalon, 1999. 294 pp.

Glenny, Misha. *The Balkans: Nationalism, War and the Great Powers, 1804-1999.* New York: Viking, 2000. 726 pp.

Goff, Peter (ed.). *The Kosovo News and Propaganda War.* Vienna: International Press Institute, 1999. 582 pp.

Ignatieff, Michael. *Virtual War: Kosovo and Beyond.* New York: Metropolitan Books, 1999. 246 pp.

Independent International Commission on Kosovo (ed.). *The Kosovo Report: Conflict, International Response, Lessons Learned.* Oxford: Oxford University Press, 2000. 372 pp.

Ismajli, Rexhep. *Kosova and the Albanians in Former Yugoslavia.* Prishtina, Kosova: Kosova Information Center, 1993. 83 pp.

Judah, Tim. *Kosovo, War and Revenge.* New Haven, Conn.: Yale University Press, 2000. xx + 348 pp.

Laurent, Eric. *Guerre du Kosovo: le dossier secret* [War in Kosova: The Secret File]. Paris: Plon, 1999. 208 pp.

Maliqi, Shkëlzen. *Kosova: Separate Worlds. Reflections and Analyses.* Peja, Kosova: Dukagjini, 1998. 261 pp.

Malcolm, Noel. *Kosovo, a Short History.* London: Macmillan, 1998. 491 pp.

Mertus, Julie. *Kosovo: How Myths and Truths Started a War.* Berkeley: University of California Press, 1999. 378 pp.

Office for Democratic Institutions and Human Rights (ed.). *Kosovo / Kosova. As seen, as told. An Analysis of the Human Rights Findings of the OSCE Kosovo Verification Mission October 1998 to June 1999.* Warsaw: OSCE-ODIHR, 1999. 433 pp.

O'Neill, William G. *Kosovo, an Unfinished Peace.* Boulder, Colo., Lynne Rienner, 2002. 159 pp.

Paris, Hervé. *Carnets imaginaires d'un vrai voyage au Kosovo* [Imaginary Notebooks of a Real Journey to Kosova]. Préface de Ahmed Boubeker. Paris: L'Harmattan, 2001. 202 pp.

Petritsch, Wolfgang, Karl Kaser, and Robert Pichler (ed.). *Kosovo, Kosova: Mythen, Daten, Fakten* [Kosovo, Kosova: Myths, Data, Facts]. Klagenfurt, Austria: Wieser, 1999. 363 +xliii pp.

Pipa, Arshi, and Sami Repishti (ed.). *Studies on Kosova.* East European Monographs 155. Boulder, Colo.: East European Monographs, 1984. 279 pp.

Prifti, Peter Rafael. *Confrontation in Kosovo: The Albanian-Serb Struggle, 1969-1998.* East European Monographs, 537. Boulder, Colo.: East European Monographs, 1999. 300 pp.

Pulaha, Selami. *Popullsia shqiptare e Kosovës gjatë shek. XV-XVI: studime dhe dokumente* [The Albanian Population of Kosova during the 15th-16th Centuries. Studies and Documents]. Tirana: 8 Nëntori, 1984. 721 pp.

Qira, Zijadin. *Cell Number 31.* New York: Vantage, 1970. 269 pp.

Qosja, Rexhep. *Paqja e përgjakshme: konferencë ndërkombëtare për Kosovën. Rambuje 6-23.02.1999, Paris 14-19.03.1999* [Bloody Peace: International Conference on Kosova. Ramboullet 6-23.02.1999, Paris 14-19.03.1999]. Tirana: Toena, 1999. 438 pp.

Reuter, Jens, and Konrad Clewing (ed.). *Der Kosovo Konflikt: Ursachen, Verlauf, Perspektiven* [The Kosova Conflict: Reasons, Development, Perspectives]. Klagenfurt, Austria: Wieser, 2000. 450 pp.

Ross, Stewart, and R. G. Grant. *The War in Kosovo: New Perspective.* Austin, Tex.: Raintree/Steck Vaughn, 2000. 64 pp.

Roux, Michel. *Le Kossovo: Dix Clés pour Comprendre.* Paris: La Découverte, 1999. 127 pp.

Schnabel, Albrecht, and Ramesh Thakur (ed.). *Kosovo and the Challenge of Humanitarian Intervention: Selective Indignation, Collective Action and International Citizenship.* Tokyo: United Nations University Press, 2000. 536 pp.

Schwartz, Stephen. *Kosovo, Background to a War.* Preface by Christopher Hitchens. London: Anthem Press, 2000. 186 pp.

Thomas, Robert. *Kosovo, Serbia and the West: NATO's Balkan War.* London: C. Hurst, 2001.

Veremis, Thanos M., and Evangelos Kofos. *Kosovo, Avoiding Another Balkan War.* Hellenic Foundation for European and Foreign Policy. Athens: Eliamep, University of Athens, 1998. 443 pp.

Veremis, Thanos M., and Dimitrios Triantaphyllou. *Kosovo and the Albanian Dimension in Southeastern Europe: The Need for Regional Security and Conflict Prevention.* Athens: Eliamep, 1999. 330 pp.

Vickers, Miranda. *Between Serbs and Albanians: A History of Kosovo.* London: C. Hurst, 1998. 328 pp.

Weller, Marc. *The Crisis in Kosovo 1989-1999: From the Dissolution of Yugoslavia to Rambouillet and the Outbreak of Hostilities.* International documents and analysis, vol. 1. Cambridge: Documents and Analysis, 1999. 503 pp.

5.4 FOREIGN RELATIONS

Biberaj, Elez Hysen. *Albania and China: A Study of an Unequal Alliance.* Boulder, Colo.: Westview Press 1986. 163 pp.

Capps, Edward. *Greece, Albania and Northern Epirus.* Illustrated with an epilogue and index by Basil J. Photos. Chicago essays on world history and politics 1. Chicago: Argonauts, 1963. 82 pp.

Gardiner, Leslie. *The Eagle Spreads His Claws: A History of the Corfu Channel Dispute and of Albania's Relations with the West 1945-1965.* Edinburgh: William Blackwood, 1966. 286 pp.

Kola, Paulin. *In Search of Greater Albania.* London: C. Hurst, 2003. xxii + 416 pp.

Larrabee, F. Stephen. *The Volatile Powder Keg: Balkan Security after the Cold War.* A Rand Study. Washington, D.C.: American University Press, 1994. 346 pp.

Leggett, Eric. *The Corfu Incident.* London: Seeley, 1974; reprint, 1976. 176 pp.

Milo, Paskal. *Shqipëria dhe Jugosllavia (1918-1927)* [Albania and Yugoslavia (1918-1927)]. Tirana: Enciklopedike, 1992. 496 pp.

Pastorelli, Pietro. *Italia e Albania 1924-1927: origini diplomatiche del trattato di Tirana del 22 nov. 1927* [Italy and Albania 1924-1927: Diplomatic Origins of the Treaty of Tirana of 22 November 1927]. Florence: Sansoni, 1967. 532 pp.

——. *L'Albania nella politica estera italiana 1914-1920* [Albania in Italian Foreign Policy, 1914-1920]. Naples: Jovene, 1970. xv + 418 pp.

Plasari, Ndreçi, and Luan Malltezi (ed.). *Marrëdhëniet shqiptaro-jugosllave 1945-1948: dokumente* [Albanian-Yugoslav Relations 1945-1948. Documents]. Tirana: Drejtoria e Përgjithshme e Arkivave, 1996. 614 pp.

Puto, Arben. *From the Annals of British Diplomacy.* Tirana: 8 Nëntori, 1981.

Prifti, Peter. *Remote Albania, the Politics of Isolationism.* Tirana: Onufri, 1999. 251 pp.

Stickney, Edith Pierpont. *Southern Albania or Northern Epirus in European International Affairs: 1912-1923.* Stanford, Calif.: Stanford University Press, 1926. xi & 195 pp.

Tafaj, Sinan. *Marrëdhëniet e Shqipërisë me vendet e BE* [Albania's Relations with the Countries of the EC]. Tirana: Horizont, 1999. 200 pp.

Xhudo, Gus. *A Critique of U.S. Policy with Special Reference to Albania and the Bosnian Crisis.* Ph.D. Dissertation. University of St. Andrews, 1995.

——. *Diplomacy and Crisis Management in the Balkans: a U.S. Foreign Policy Perspective.* New York: St.Martin's Press, 1996. 219 pp.

6. ECONOMY

6.1 GENERAL

Andrews, Mary Catherine and Gulhan Ovalioglo. *Albania and the World Bank, Building the Future.* Washington, D.C.: World Bank, 1994. 88 pp.

Cluny-Ross, Anthony and Petar Sudar. *Albania's Economy in Transition and Turmoil: 1990-1997.* Aldershot, England: Ashgate, 1998. 256 pp.

Crosfield, Joseph & Sons (ed.). *An Economic Survey of Albania.* 2 vol. Warrington, England: Joseph Crosfield & Sons, 1967.

De Soto, Hermone, et al. *Poverty in Albania: A Qualitative Assessment.* World Bank Technical Paper, No. 520. Washington, D.C.: World Bank, 2002. 160 pp.

Konini, Maksim, and Ilia Peçi. *Fjalor ekonomik: shqip, anglisht, gjermanisht* [Economic Dictionary: Albanian, English, German]. Puna për hartimin e këtij fjalori u koordinua nga Z. Friedrich Bremen. Botim i dytë. Tirana: Civet, 1997. 318 pp.

La Cava, Gloria. *Albania: Filling the Vulnerability Gap.* Technical Papers Series, No. 460. Washington, D.C.: Office of the Publisher, World Bank, 2000. 88 pp.

Lemel, Harold (ed.). *Rural Property and Economy in Post-Communist Albania.* New York: Berghahn Books, 2000. xxiii + 160 pp.

Omari, Luan and Stefanaq Pollo (ed.). *The History of the Socialist Construction of Albania (1944-1975).* Tirana: Academy of Sciences of the PSR of Albania, 1988. 345 pp.

Palairet, Michael. *The Balkan Economies, ca. 1800-1914. Evolution without Development.* Cambridge Studies in Modern Economic History, No. 6. Cambridge: Cambridge University Press, 1997. xvi + 415 pp.

Pashko, Gramoz. "Obstacles to Economic Reform in Albania," in: *Europe-Asian Studies,* 45, 5 (1993), pp. 907-921.

——. "Albania: The Transition from a Command to a Free Market Economy," in: *Südost-Europa. Zeitschrift für Gegenwartsforschung,* Munich, Heft 5, 43. Jahrgang (1994), pp. 223-239.

Pernack, Hans-Joachim. *Probleme der wirtschaftlichen Entwicklung Albaniens: Untersuchung des ökonomischen und sozioökonomischen Wandlungsprozesses von 1912/13 bis in die Gegenwart* [Problems of the Economic Development of Albania: Research into the Economic and Socioeconomic Transformation Process from 1912/13 to the Present Day]. Südosteuropa-Studien Bd. 18. Munich: Südosteuropa-Gesellschaft, 1972. 196 pp.

Schnytzer, Adi. *Stalinist Economic Strategy in Practice: The Case of Albania.* Oxford: Oxford University Press, 1982. 180 pp.

Sjöberg, Örjan. *Rural Change and Development in Albania.* Oxford: Westview, 1991. 199 pp.

——. *Urbanisation under Central Planning: The Case of Albania.* Comprehensive summaries of Uppsala dissertations from the Faculty of Social Sciences, 23. Stockholm: Almqvist & Wiksell, 1991. 32 pp.

Sjöberg, Örjan, and Michael L. Wyzan (ed.). *Economic Change in the Balkan States: Albania, Bulgaria, Romania and Yugoslavia.* London: Pinter, ca. 1991. 173 pp.

Taipali, Vappu, et al. (ed.). *Albania, a Country in a Cross Swell.* Report of the Finnish Mission on Developmental Social Issues. Helsinki: National Research and Development Centre of Welfare and Health, 1999. 56 pp.

Vaughan-Whitehead, Daniel. *Albania in Crisis: The Predictable Fall of the Shining Star.* International Labour Office. Central and Eastern European Team. Cheltenham, England: Edward Elgar, 1999. xxiii + 360 pp.

Velija, Vebi. *Quo vadis, Albania? A Vision of the Economic Recovery Program of Albania. A Monograph.* Elbasan: Onufri, 1996. 123 pp.

———. *Midis ekonomisë dhe politikës* [Between Economics and Politics]. Tirana: Afërdita, 1999. 400 pp.

Wildermuth, Andreas. *Sie stützen sich auf eigenen Kräfte: die Wirtschaftspolitik Albaniens nach dem Zweiten Weltkrieg* [They Rely on Their Own Power. The Economic Policies of Albania since the Second World War]. Wirtschaft und Gesellschaft in Südosteuropa 11. Munich: LDV-Verlag, 1995. 430 pp.

6.2 FINANCE

Bundo, Sherif. *Enciklopedi: ekonomi, financë, drejtim* [Encyclopedia: Economy, Finance, Management]. Red. Bahri Musabelliu, Edmond Luçi, Ahmet Ceni, Hena Pasho. Tirana: Eurorilindja, 1998. 196 pp.

Calmès, Albert. *Report on the Financial Situation in Albania.* Geneva: League of Nations, 1922. 31 pp.

6.3 AGRICULTURE

Agolli, Shkëlqim. *Bujqësia shqiptare në vite, shifra, fakte, komente. Review of Albanian agriculture, figures, facts, comments.* Tirana: Pegi, 2000. 350 pp.

Beka, Ismail. "Agricultural Development in Albania," in: *Est-Ouest,* Trieste, 2 (1997), pp. 39-52.

Civici, A., and F. Lerin (ed.). *Albanie, une agriculture en transition* [Albania, an Agriculture in Transition]. Centre international des hautes études agronomiques méditerranéennes, série B, nr. 15, Montpellier, France, 1997. 330 pp.

Deslondes, Olivier, et al. "L'agriculture albanaise: de la coopérative à l'exploitation de survie. [Albanian Agriculture: From the Cooperative to Survival Exploitation]." in: *Revue d'études comparatives est-ouest,* Paris, 26.3 (1995), pp. 143-160.

Dethier, Jean-Jacques. *An Agricultural Strategy for Albania.* A report, prepared by a joint team from the World Bank. Washington, D.C.: World Bank, 1992. 265 pp.

Ködderitzsch, Severin. *Reforms in Albanian Agriculture: Assessing a Sector in Transition.* Washington, D.C.: World Bank, 1999. xv + 52 pp.

Neunhäuser, Peter (ed.). *Promoting Self-help Activities of Albania Farmèrs. Situation Analysis and Assessment of Potentials. Report on a Research Conducted in Co-operation with the Project 'Promotion of Self-help Organizations in Vlora District.'* Humboldt-Universität Berlin. Berlin: Margraf Verlag, 1995. 200 pp.

Pata, Kristaq, and Myslym Osmani. "Albanian Agriculture: A Painful Transition from Communism to Free Market Challenges," in: *Sociologia ruralis,* Assen NL, 34,1 (1994), pp. 84-101.

Sedlmayr, Ernst C. "Die Landwirtschaft Albaniens [Albanian Agriculture]," in: *Illyrisch-Albanische Forschungen,* Ludwig von Thallóczy (ed.), Bd. II (1916), pp. 3-44.

Segrè, Andrea. *Agricultural and Environmental Issues for Sustainable Development in Albania.* Nardò/Lecce: Besa, 1998.

Shkurti, Spiro. *Der Mythos vom Wandervolk der Albaner. Landwirtschaft in den albanischen Gebieten (13.-17. Jahrhundert)* [The Myth of the Albanians as a Nomadic People: Agriculture on Albanian Territory (13th-17th Centuries)]. Aus dem Albanischen übersetzt von Ali Dhrimo, Tirana. Redigiert und herausgegeben von Karl Kaser, Graz. Vienna: Böhlau, 1997. 302 pp.

Susuri, Latif. *Fjalor i terminologjisë bujqësore anglisht-shqip, shqip-anglisht* [Dictionary of Agricultural Terminology English-Albanian, Albanian-English]. Prishtina, Kosova: Rilindja, 1999. viii + 412 pp.

Wildermuth, Andreas. *Die Krise der albanischen Landwirtschaft. Lösungsversuche der Partei- und Staatsführung unter Ramiz Alia* [The Crisis of Albanian Agriculture. Attempts towards a Solution by the Party and State Leadership under Ramiz Alia]. Wirtschaft und Gesellschaft in Südosteuropa. Bd. 6. Werner Gumpel (ed.). Neuried, Germany: Hieronymus, 1989. xvii + 123 pp.

Zaloshnja, Eduard X. *Analysis of Agricultural Production in Albania. Prospects for Policy Improvement (Government Policy, Semi-commercial, Farm Households, Indirect Profit).* Dissertation. Virginia Polytechnic Institute and State University. 1997. 241 pp.

Zavalani, Dalib. *Die landwirtschaftlichen Verhältnisse Albaniens* [The Situation of Agriculture in Albania]. Berichte über Landwirtschaft. N.F. Sonderheft 140. Berlin: Paul Parey / Leipzig, Germany: Gustav Fock, 1938. 151 pp.

7. JURIDICAL

7.1 CUSTOMARY LAW

Elezi, Ismet. *E drejta zakonore e Labërisë në planin krahasues* [The Customary Law of Laberia at the Comparative Level]. Tirana: Libri Universitar, 1994. 206 pp.

——. *Vrasjet për hakmarrje e për gjakmarrje në Shqipëri* [Murder for Revenge and Feuding in Albania]. Tirana: Qendra shqiptare për të drejtat e njeriut, ca. 2000 122 pp.

Gjeçovi, Shtjefën. *Kanuni i Lekë Dukagjinit. The code of Lekë Dukagjini. Albanian text collected and arranged by Shtjefën Gjeçov.* Translated with an introduction by Leonard Fox. New York: Gjonlekaj, 1989. 269 pp.

——. *Der Kanun: das albanische Gewohnheitsrecht nach dem sogenannten Kanun des Lekë Dukagjini* [The Kanun: Albanian Customary Law in Accordance with the So-Called Kanun of Lekë Dukagjini]. Kodifiziert von Shtjefën Gjeçovi, ins Deutsche übersetzt von Marie Amelie Freiin von Godin und mit einer Einführung von Michael Schmidt-Neke. Herausgegeben mit Vorwort und Bibliographie von Robert Elsie. Dukagjini Balkan Books. Peja, Kosova: Dukagjini, 2001. 283 pp.

——. *Le Kanun de Lekë Dukagjini* [The Kanun of Lekë Dukagjini]. Traduit de l'Albanais par Christian Gut sur l'édition de Shjtefën Gjeçovi. Dukagjini Balkan Books. Peja, Kosova: Dukagjini, 2001. 298 pp.

Hasluck, Margaret Masson Hardie. *The Unwritten Law in Albania. A Record of the Customary Law of the Albanian Tribes. Description of Family and Village Life... & Waging of Blood-feuds.* Cambridge: Cambridge University Press, 1954, reprint 1981. 285 pp.

Illia, Dom Frano. *Kanuni i Skanderbegut* [The Kanun of Scanderbeg]. Mbledhe e kodifikue nga Dom Frano Illia. Brescia, Italy: La Rosa, 1993. 224 pp.

Meçi, Xhemal. *Kanuni i Lekë Dukagjinit: varianti i Pukës* [The Kanun of Lekë Dukagjini: Variant of Puka]. Tirana: Çabej, 1997. 267 pp.

——. *Kanuni i Lekë Dukagjinit: në variantin e Mirditës.* [The Kanun of Lekë Dukagjini: In the Variant of Mirdita]. Tirana: Geer, 2002. 390 pp.

Resta, Patrizia (ed.). *Kanun: le basi morali e giuridiche della società albanese* [The Kanun: The Moral and Legal Basis of Albanian Society]. Trad. pp. Dodaj. Nardò Lecce, Italy: Besa, 1996. 176 pp.

Talmor, Sascha. "The Kanun: The Code of Honour of Albania's High Plateau," in: *Durham University Journal,* Durham, 85, 1 (1993), pp. 121-126.

Valentini, Giuseppe. *Legge delle montagne albanesi nella relazioni della Missione Volante (1880-1932)* [The Law of the Albanian Mountains in Reports by the Seconded Missions (1880-1932)]. Studi albanesi. Studi i testi, 3. Florence: Olschki, 1968. xvi + 288 pp.

Vokopola, Aly Kemal. "The Albanian Customary Law," in: *Quarterly Journal of the Library of Congress,* Washington, D.C., 25 (Oct. 1968), pp. 306-316.

7.2 NON-CUSTOMARY LAW

Auerswald, Philip E., and David pp. (ed.). *The Kosovo Conflict: A Diplomatic History through Documents.* Cambridge, Mass.: Kluwer Law International, 2000. 1285 pp.

Elezi, Ismet. *Zhvillimi historik i legjislacionit penal në Shqipëri* [The Historical Development of Criminal Legislation in Albania]. Tirana: Albin, 1997. 234 pp.

——. *Mendimi juridik shqiptar* [Albanian Legal Thinking]. Tirana: Albin, 1999. 324 pp.

Hasani, Enver. *Dissolution of Yugoslavia and the Case of Kosova: Political and Legal Aspects.* Tirana: Albanian Institute for International Studies, 2000. 130 pp.

Nagan, W. pp., Artan Hoxha, and pp. J. Dirks. "Strengthening the Rule of Law in Albania. Impartiality, Independence and the Transformation of the Legal Profession," in: *Review of Central and East European Law,* 20 (1994), pp. 677-698.

Veleshnja, Mbaresa (ed.). *Indeksi i akteve ligjore të Shqipërisë, botuar në Fletorja Zytrare gjatë viteve 1990- korrik 2001.* Tirana: American Bar Association Central and East European Law Initiative, USAID, 2001.1034 pp.

8. SCIENCE

8.1 GEOGRAPHY AND GEOLOGY

Becker, Hans (ed.). *Jüngere Fortschritte der regionalgeographischen Kenntnis über Albanien* [Recent Progress in Regional Geographical

Knowledge of Albania]. Beiträge des Herbert-Louis-Gedächtnissymposions. Bamberger Geographische Schriften. Bamberg, Germany: Fach Geographie der Universität Bamberg, 1991. 184 pp.

Carter, Francis William (ed.). *An Historical Geography of the Balkans.* London, 1977. 599 pp.

Defense Mapping Agency (ed.). *Gazetteer of Albania.* Names approved by the United States Board on Geographic Names. 2nd Edition. Washington, D.C.: Defense Mapping Agency, August 1992.

Hall, Derek, and Darrick Danta (ed.). *Reconstructing the Balkans: A Geography of the New Southeast Europe.* Chichester, England: John Wiley & Sons, 1996. xx + 260 pp.

Lienau, Cay, and Günter Prinzing (ed.). *Beiträge zur Geographie und Geschichte Albaniens* [Contributions to the Geography and History of Albania]. Berichte aus dem Arbeitsgebiet Entwicklungsforschung, Heft 12. Münster, Germany: Institut für Geographie, 1984. 277 pp.

Magnani, Mario (ed.). *Bibliografia geologica e geografico fisica dell'Albania e delle regioni limitrofe* [Geological and Geophysical Bibliography of Albania and the Surrounding Regions]. Seconda edizione. Rome: Istituto Poligrafico dello Stato, 1941. 114 pp.

Meço, Selam, and Shyqri Aliaj. *Geology of Albania.* Stuttgart: Borntraeger, 2000.

Mžik, Hans von. "Beiträge zur Kartographie Albaniens nach orientalischen Quellen" [Contributions to the Cartography of Albania according to Oriental Sources], in: *Geologica hungarica. Fasciculi ad illustrandum notionem geologicam et palaeontologicam Regni Hungaricae.* Series geologica. Tomus III (Institutum Regni Hungariae Geologicum, Budapest 1929), pp. 625-649.

Nimani, Shyqri. *Albanian Lands in Maps and Emblems, from Strabo and Ptolemy to Our Time.* Prishtina, Kosova: Institute of Text-Books of Kosova, 1997. 126 pp.

Nopcsa, Franz Baron. "Zur Geologie Nordalbaniens" [On the Geology of Northern Albania], in: *Jahrbuch der kaiserlich-königlichen Geologischen Reichsanstalt,* Vienna, 55, 1 (1905), pp. 85-152.

——. "Geology of Northern Albania," in: *Quarterly Journal of the Geological Society of London,* London, 67 (1911), Proceedings, pp. XCIV.

——. "Zur Stratigraphie und Tektonik des Vilajets Skutari in Nordalbanien" [On the Stratigraphy and Tectonics of the Vilayet of Shkodra in Northern Albania], in: *Jahrbuch der Geologischen Reichsanstalt,* Vienna, 61 (1911), pp. 229-284.

——. "Zur Geologie der Küstenkette Nordalbaniens" [On the Geology of the Coastal Range of Northern Albania], in: *Mitteilungen aus dem*

Jahrbuch der kgl. Ungarischen Geologischen Reichsanstalt, Budapest, 24 (1925), pp. 133-164.

——. "Geologie und Geographie Nordalbaniens" [The Geology and Geography of Northern Albania], in: *Geologica hungarica. Fasciculi ad illustrandum notionem geologicam et palaeontologicam Regni Hungaricae.* Series geologica. Tomus III (Institutum Regni Hungariae Geologicum, Budapest 1929), pp. 7-620.

Nopcsa, Franz Baron, and Max Reinhard. "Zur Geologie und Petrographie des Vilajets Skutari in Nordalbanien" [On the Geology and Petrography of the Vilayet of Shkodra in Northern Albania], in: *Anuarul Institutului Geologic al României,* Bucharest, 5 (1912), pp. 1-27.

Nowack, Ernst. "A Contribution to the Geography of Albania," *in: The Geological Review,* 11, 4 (1921), pp. 503-540.

——. *Geologische Übersicht von Albanien* [Geological Overview of Albania]. Salzburg, 1929. 204 pp.

Patzelt, Gerald. *Beiträge zur Geologie des SW-Teils der Volksrepublik Albanien* [Contributions to the Geology of the Southwestern Part of the People's Republic of Albania]. Mit 33 Abbildungen und 10 Tafel. Geologie-Beihefte, Nr. 69. Berlin: Akademie-Verlag, 1971. 115 pp.

Qiriazi, Perikli, and Aleks Vranaj. *Gjeografia fizike e Shqipërisë* [Physical Geography of Albania]. Red. Marie Mato. 2 vol. Tirana: Shtëp. Bot. e Librit Universitar, 1998. 240 & 313 pp.

Roth de Telegd, Károly. *Beiträge zur Geologie von Albanien* [Contributions to the Geology of Albania]. Stuttgart: Schweizerbart, 1922-1925. 793 pp.

Rugg, Dean S., Richard E. Lonsdale, J. Clark Archer, and Jeffrey S. Peake. "Changing the Way Albanian Geographers Look at Their Land," in: *Journal of Geography* (Sept.-Oct. 1994), pp. 244-250.

8.2 PUBLIC HEALTH AND MEDICINE

Cohen, Barend A. J. *Albania: Health and Human Rights. An Inventory of Pressing Issues. Report of Five Missions in 1991-1992.* Amersfoort, The Netherlands: Johannes Wier Foundation for Health and Human Rights, 1992.

Gjonça, Arjan. *Communism, Health and Lifestyle. The Paradox of Mortality Transition in Albania. 1950-1990.* Studies in Population and Urban Demography, 8. London: Greenwood Press, 2001. 248 pp.

Schaapveld, Kees, and Rom J. M. Perenboom. *Primary Health Care in Albania: Analysis and Recommendations.* Leiden, The Netherlands: TNO Institute of Preventative Health Care, 1993. 79 pp.

Senturia, Kirsten Diana White. *The Smaller the Child, the Greater the Care: An Anthropological Approach to Pregnancy, Low Birth Weight and Perinatal Mortality in Albania.* Ph.D. dissertation. Los Angeles: University of California, 1995. 194 pp.

Tartari, Flamur. *Figura të shquara të mjekësisë shqiptare 1* [Noted Figures of Albanian Medicine, 1]. Tirana: Toena, 1998. 248 pp

8.3   FLORA AND FAUNA

Baldacci, Antonio. "Die pflanzengeographische Karte von Mittelalbanien und Epirus" [Geographical Map of the Flora of Central Albania and Epirus], in: *Dr. A. Petermanns Mitteilungen,* Gotha, 43 (1897), pp. 163-170, 179-183.

Grimmett, R. F. A., and T. A. Jones (ed.). "Albania," in: *Important Bird Areas in Europe,* Cambridge: International Council for Bird Preservation, 1989. pp. 35-41.

Hagemeijer, Ward J. M., Frans J. Schepers, and Ben Hallmann (ed.). *Wintering Waterbirds in the Coastal Wetlands of Albania, 1993.* Zeist, The Netherlands: WIWO, Foundation Working Group, 1994. 113 pp.

Markgraf, Friedrich. *An den Grenzen des Mittelmeergebietes. Pflanzengeographie von Mittelalbanien* [At the Edges of the Mediterranean Basin. Floral Geography of Central Albania]. Repertorium novarum regni vegetabilis, Beiheft 45. Dahlem bei Berlin, Repertorium, 1927. 217 pp.

——. *In Albaniens Bergen* [In Albania's Mountains]. Stuttgart: Strecker & Schröder, 1930. 244 pp.

——. *Pflanzengeographie von Albanie.* [Floral Geography of Albania]. Bibliotheca Botanica 5. Stuttgart: Schweizerbart'sche Verlagsbuchhandlung, 1930. 132 pp.

——. "Pflanzen aus Albanien, 1928" [Plants in Albania, 1928], in: Vienna: Hölder-Pichler-Tempsky, 1931. 47 pp. and in: *Denkschriften der Akademie der Wissensachften in Wien.* Mathematisch-Naturwissenschaftliche Klasse, Vienna, 102 (1931), pp. 317-360.

Mitrushi, Ilia. *Druret dhe shkurret e Shqipërisë: përhapja, kultivimi, dobia dhe përdorimi i tyre* [Trees and Shrubs of Albania: Their Range, Cultivation, Usefulness and Utilization]. Tirana: Instituti i Shkencave, 1955. 604 + vii pp.

——. *Excerpts from "Trees and Shrubs of Albania."* Washington, D.C.: U.S. Department of Commerce, 1958. 539 pp.

——. *Dendroflora e Shqipërisë* [Dendroflora of Albania]. Tirana: Universiteti Shtetëror i Tiranës, 1966. 519 pp.

Nuttonson, Michael Y. *Ecological Plant Geography of Albania, Its Agricultural Crops and Some North American Climatic Analogues.* Washington, D.C., 1947. 16 pp.

Paparisto, Kolë, Mustafa Demiri, Ilia Mitrushi, and Xhafer Qosja (ed.). *Flora e Shqipërisë, 1. Lycopodiaceae, platanaceae* [The Flora of Albania, 1: Lycopodiaceae, Platanaceae]. Tirana: Akademia e Shkencave, 1988. 460 pp.

Poljakov, G. D., Nd. Filipi, Kozma Basho, and A. Hysenaj. *Peshqit i Shqipërisë* [The Fish of Albania]. Tirana: Universiteti Shtetëror i Tiranës, 1958. 185 pp.

Polunin, Oleg. *Flowers of Greece and the Balkans: A Field Guide.* Oxford: Oxford University Press, 1988. xvi + 592, 67 pp.

Qosja, Xhafer, and Kolë Paparisto (ed.). *Flora e Shqipërisë, 2. Rosaceae, umbelliferae* [The Flora of Albania, 2: Rosaceae, Umbrelliferae]. Tirana: Akademia e Shkencave, 1992. 446 pp.

——. *Flora e Shqipërisë, 3. Pirolaceae, campanulaceae* [The Flora of Albania, 3: Pirolaceae, Campanulaceae]. Tirana. Akademia e Shkencave, 1996. 331 pp.

Rakaj, Ndoc. *Iktiofauna e Shqipërisë* [Fish of Albania]. Tirana: Libri Universitar, 1995. 700 pp.

Sejdiu, Shefki. *Fitonomia shqipe e Kosovës. Lënda, ndarja, etimologjia* [The Albanian Phytonomy of Kosova: Subjects, Divisions, Etymologies]. Prishtina, Kosova: Instituti Albanologjik, 1979. 342 pp.

——. *Fjalorth etnobotanik i shqipes* [Short Ethno-botanical Dictionary of Albania]. Prishtina, Kosova: Rilindja, 1984. 345 pp.

Turrill, W. B. *The Plant Life of the Balkan Peninsula: A Phytho-geographical Study.* Oxford: Oxford University Press, 1929. xxiii + 490 pp.

Vangeluwe, Didier, Marie-Odile Beudels, and Fotaq Lamani. "Conservation Status of Albania Coastal Wetlands and Their Colonial Waterbird Populations (Pelecaniformes and Ciconiformes)," in: *Colonial Waterbirds, Journal of the Colonial Waterbird Group,* 19, special supplement (1996), pp. 81-90.

Zekhuis, Mark J., and David Templeman. *Breeding Birds of the Albanian Wetlands.* Zeist, The Netherlands: WIWO, 1998. 146 pp.

About the Author

Robert Elsie (Vancouver, Canada, 1950) is a leading specialist in Albanian affairs. He is the author of twenty-five books on Albania and its culture, including literary translations from Albanian, and of many articles and research papers. Elsie studied at the University of British Columbia, graduating in 1972 with a degree in classical studies and linguistics. In the following years, he did postgraduate research at the Free University of Berlin, at the Ecole Pratique des Hautes Etudes and the University of Paris IV in Paris, at the Dublin Institute for Advanced Studies in Ireland and at the University of Bonn, where he finished his doctorate in 1978 at the Linguistics Institute. From 1982 to 1987, he worked for the German Ministry of Foreign Affairs in Bonn. Since that time he has worked as a freelance writer and conference interpreter, primarily for Albanian and German. He lives in the Eifel mountains of Germany, not far from the Belgian border. *See* www.elsie.de.